Counseling Adolescents
Competently

Counseling Adolescents Competently

Lee A. Underwood
Regent University

Frances L. L. Dailey
Regent University

Los Angeles | London | New Delhi
Singapore | Washington DC | Melbourne

FOR INFORMATION

SAGE Publications, Inc.
2455 Teller Road
Thousand Oaks, California 91320
E-mail: order@sagepub.com

SAGE Publications Ltd.
1 Oliver's Yard
55 City Road
London, EC1Y 1SP
United Kingdom

SAGE Publications India Pvt. Ltd.
B 1/I 1 Mohan Cooperative Industrial Area
Mathura Road, New Delhi 110 044
India

SAGE Publications Asia-Pacific Pte. Ltd.
3 Church Street
#10–04 Samsung Hub
Singapore 049483

Development Editor: Abbie Rickard
Editorial Assistant: Carrie Montoya
eLearning Editor: Lucy Berbeo
Production Editor: Kelly DeRosa
Copy Editor: QuADS Prepress (P) Ltd.
Typesetter: Hurix Systems Pvt. Ltd.
Proofreader: Susan Schon
Indexer: Mary Harper
Cover Designer: Candice Harman
Marketing Manager: Johanna Swenson

Copyright © 2017 by SAGE Publications, Inc.

Printed in the United States of America

Library of Congress Cataloging-in-Publication Data

Names: Underwood, Lee (Lee A.), author. | Dailey, Frances L. L., author.

Title: Counseling adolescents competently / Lee Underwood, Regent University; Frances Dailey, Regent University.

Description: Los Angeles : SAGE, 2016. | Includes bibliographical references and index.

Identifiers: LCCN 2015040083 | ISBN 9781483358857 (pbk. : alk. paper)

Subjects: LCSH: Teenagers—Counseling of. | Adolescent psychology. | Counseling.

Classification: LCC HV1421 .U527 2016 | DDC 362.71/6—dc23
LC record available at http://lccn.loc.gov/2015040083

This book is printed on acid-free paper.

16 17 18 19 20 10 9 8 7 6 5 4 3 2 1

BRIEF CONTENTS

Detailed Contents

PREFACE

Counseling Adolescents Competently is a unique work that moves the reader through four conceptual arenas that constitute competent counseling services in all settings. First, the book provides "Foundational Issues in Counseling Adolescents" and orients the reader to today's adolescents and how they present in counseling. It highlights how adolescents' view of the world affect them and the development of the social and cultural elements, as well as interpersonal issues that they bring to counseling. First, the textbook identifies adolescents' risk and protective factors to utilize within the counseling context. Second, the textbook provides information to help the reader gain theoretical perspectives to organize thoughts, approaches, understandings, and evidence-based processes when counseling adolescents. Using traditional theoretical approaches and integrating the newer generational evidence-based approaches will bridge the two theoretical worlds, while providing a comprehensive approach to thinking about adolescents. Evidence-based models such as multisystemic treatment, dialectical behavioral treatment, functional family therapy, and trauma-focused cognitive behavioral treatment are a few of the interventions that are highlighted. Third, the textbook provides evidence-informed interventions to help adolescents better mitigate the challenges they experience. Information on screening, assessment, and treatment planning and the uses of behavioral criteria are provided. This section provides information on a host of critical areas including family interventions; divorce challenges; school counseling; group interventions; career and relational issues; addictions; lesbian, gay, bisexual, and transgender concerns; and adolescents with sexually maladaptive behaviors. Fourth, the textbook provides legal and professional issues to include landmark ethical cases, supervision, and consultation, ending with the use of technology with adolescents.

FUNCTION OF THE BOOK

This book functions as a comprehensive textbook for adolescent counseling students and professionals compiling foundational and emerging skills in the counseling field. The book is written within the context of core competencies established by the Council for Accreditation of Counseling and Related Educational Programs (CACREP) 2016 graduate and doctoral programmatic standards where appropriate, and core competencies from other behavioral health programs are referenced. Both students in school and clinical mental health tracks, along with other behavioral health professionals, including social workers, marriage and family therapists, psychologists, and psychiatrists, will find the book useful in several ways. First, the book provides strong evidence for the role of professional providers involved in the practice of adolescent counseling. By providing an extensive review of clinical interventions ranging from assessment to diagnosis, professional providers are afforded a fresh perspective of intervention strategies.

Second, the book isolates and examines related core CACREP and other related competencies in the application of theoretical and clinical suppositions through most of the chapters. With the isolated competencies, both the clinical supervisor and the educator will be able to communicate with students those key issues in counseling adolescents that are most relevant to the provider's professional identity. Third, the book incorporates clinical case scenarios through case conceptualization models, written from a provider's standpoint, providing amplification of critical provider functions. This information assists the student in thinking about adolescent cases and forming meaningful strategies to incorporate in the actual counseling session. The clinical case studies consist of a diverse group of client issues such as school counseling needs, self-injurious behavior, addictive behaviors, disruptive behavioral disorders, substance use disorders, sexual aggression, bullying, and other commonly seen issues faced by adolescents. Fourth, the book is prepared in a way that allows instructors and professors to teach and test students, maximizing the aforementioned areas. This textbook uses "friendly" headers and subheaders throughout each chapter and highlights case conceptualization (where cases are presented), implications for counseling adolescents, clinical review of cases, ethical concerns and takeaway points (keystones), and chapter summaries, readers will have easy, accessible objectives of each chapter.

Use of Case Scenarios

Providers often lack experiential training to adequately integrate theory and clinical practice

while working with adolescents (Grisso, 2011). At times, there is a lack of scholarly informed interventions resulting in adolescents moving through the nation's counseling centers, schools, and systems of care in a manner that at times can be disconcerting to providers, clinical supervisors, and educators. These adolescents are in need of culturally specific and evidence-based intervention to remediate their behaviors, developmental challenges, immature thinking, risks, and cognitive maturation needs. This book provides information regarding the critical issues affecting today's adolescents, including their characteristics, technology issues, diagnoses and typologies, special needs, and interventions involving treatment planning.

To further highlight the information shared within this book and in efforts to move from theoretical postulates and findings to direct application, case scenarios and conceptualization models of adolescents as a means to further underscore their individual stories are discussed. The authors take advantage of qualitative research techniques in highlighting the adolescent's cognitive frame of reference by covering the themes and referral issues common to this population: trauma, grief, loss, divorce, school adjustment, emotional issues, behavioral issues, psychiatric emergencies, and sexual development.

The book explains the processes needed to successfully intervene with adolescents and addresses their multifaceted areas of need from student, provider, clinical supervisor, and educator standpoints. These needs compound any legal involvement, habilitation, developmental, social, and reintegration challenges as adolescents present in treatment. Special attention is given to the cultural nuances of this population, the adolescent's story, and the provider's understanding of the adolescent.

Grisso (2011) presented clinical learning in three stages: (1) understanding concepts, (2) practicing concepts, and (3) learning through experience and supervision. This book focuses on Stages 1 and 2 of this process. Using case scenarios, the authors have identified several adolescent profiles to move through these stages and captivate the reader. The authors offer the following benefits to utilizing case scenarios as a teaching format for adolescents:

- Provides opportunity for a slower thinking process that directs observation, didactic lecture, and role play do not allow

- Provides opportunity to safely examine provider observations treatment assumptions

- Provides new information integration and practice in each case scenario

- Brings the material to readily applicable and manageable sizes

Another benefit to the use of case scenarios is to amplify the authors' beliefs and assumptions about screening, assessing, treatment planning, and interventions that are not appropriately informed by multicultural dynamics and can be detrimental to the therapeutic alliance. The authors have learned that many adolescents will allow providers to maintain erroneous assumptions about their presenting situations without protest or clarification for the duration of referred services. In fact, the adolescent's allowing and maintaining a provider's misperceptions (erroneous assumptions) become part of the social exchange between the adolescent and the provider (Underwood & Dailey, 2016). The case scenarios shine light on adolescent resistance and ways to overcome these challenges.

PURPOSE OF THE BOOK

The purpose of this book is to provide a compendium of information on clinical areas of interest, theories, research, and key findings relating to adolescents in counseling. The text is distinguished in that it is aimed at counseling strategies utilized by (a) counseling students, (b) professional providers, (c) clinical supervisors, and (d) educators. For the student, this book provides clinical and counseling strategies and theories, research, and key findings that distinguish adolescent populations from other groups. It contains

foundational information to guide the student and the professional in establishing effective work and lasting impact in the various work modalities they find themselves. Furthermore, from the student's perspective, this book offers a unique perspective to improve counseling interventions and treatment planning activities with adolescents. While the book's primary focus is not on school counseling or counseling children, it does provide much needed insight for school providers and children's issues, including play therapy techniques, and a chapter is dedicated to school counseling needs.

For the professional provider, clinical supervisor, and educator, this book offers information from which to direct and encourage professional development of supervisees through an overview of field-specific information to establish policy and procedural best practices for counseling services. Specifically, for professional providers, this book presents the literature on adolescent counseling in a single sourcebook; guiding supervisors and educators along a much needed pathway for the students with whom they work. For all groups, this text synthesizes the past 25 to 30 years of theoretical and practical insights into work with adolescents.

This book is versatile in that it recognizes the diversity of adolescents. For example, today's adolescents are found in urban and nonurban settings; however, with the use of the Internet, social networking (e.g., Twitter, Facebook, Instagram, Tumblr, Vine, texting), and television programming (e.g., MTV, BET, VH1, and other pop-culture media), these adolescents certainly can be found in rural settings as well. Traditional interventions and ways of thinking about adolescents have left many students and providers at a loss. This book seeks to integrate critical findings from the literature. It provides information on the characteristics of adolescents and briefly provides various adolescent developmental theories. It consolidates information regarding key clinical markers, including assessment, diagnosing, treatment planning, general interventions, specialized counseling interventions, and ethical issues related to today's adolescents.

Literature related to behavioral health services for adolescents is plentiful; however, that which pertains to counseling adolescents stands in stark contrast. Many textbooks combine counseling children and adolescents at the expense of fully exploring the experience of adolescents. While there is room for books pertaining to children and adolescents, this book serves as a distinctive book for adolescents only. The authors believe that the literature and complexity of adolescent (ages 10–20) issues warrant a separate book. Today's adolescents are a potent challenge to providers-in-training, professional providers, supervisors, and educators.

RATIONALE FOR THE BOOK

As previously indicated, the literature related to behavioral health services for adolescents is vast; however, that which pertains to counseling adolescents stands in contrast. Historically, information shaping the field of adolescent behavioral health has been disseminated through the scholarly work found in psychological, social work, and marriage and family texts that are specific to those professional identities, with little attention to the counseling profession. It is through their teaching and scholarly experiences that the authors have learned that the art of counseling is often absent in popular works focusing on broad mental health issues. As such, there is an additional need to synthesize the counseling needs of adolescents as complementary to what that of other behavioral health providers.

The primary emphasis of the book is to provide a comprehensive volume of work compiling the past 25 to 30 years of research and critical findings regarding counseling adolescents. As such, the authors hope to contribute to, and encourage further research in the field of professional counseling and other behavioral health fields as it pertains to streamlining and standardizing theory and practical interventions for adolescents. One way to stimulate further research and practice is the use of case scenarios and case conceptualization models throughout this book.

TARGET AUDIENCE

This book is written for four layers of professionals: the student in behavioral health training programs, counseling and school programs, the practicing provider, and administrative/clinical supervisors and educators. As such, many counseling "engagement and people skills" processes are not presented, but assumed to be part of the readers' knowledge and skill base, focusing instead on theoretical, clinical, and ethical underpinnings that better inform the provider regarding the provider–client relationship and theories informing interventions. Competencies in the three areas are presented.

1. *The Counseling Student and Competencies:* Those attending colleges and universities in the pursuit of undergraduate and graduate degrees in counseling and related fields of study must learn not only the core competencies in counseling but also how to integrate these competencies with adolescents. Students must learn how to balance the clinical and legal issues with the ethical standards. This book equips students in critical background information, current findings on best practice interventions, theoretical models, and social, cultural, and legal underpinnings of adolescents. The authors put forth discussion topics, exercises, and case scenarios and highlight the need for an ongoing dialogue as to how foundational and core competencies affect the counseling process with adolescents.

2. *The Professional Provider and Administrative/ Clinical Supervisor and Competencies:* Those serving in clinical and leadership roles of professional provider and supervisor must keenly balance tasks associated with safety, legal issues, ethical standards, programmatic stipulations of the needs of adolescents, and those with whom they work. Supervisors must guide supervisees to better hear, recognize, and intervene effectively with this population, while adhering to ethical codes of conduct and other related competencies. This book aids professional providers and supervisors in guiding, teaching, and correcting their supervisees in a fashion that is fused with current findings and theoretical, clinical,

social, cultural, and legal underpinnings of adolescents in care. This book reviews landmark ethical cases that have improved our way of examining difficult cases.

3. *The Educator and Competencies:* A primary challenge in counseling adolescents is that they are often misunderstood and inadequately treated for their various developmental, mental health, psychiatric, academic, and social issues. Students can misattribute meaning and superimpose their own worldviews on the adolescent's story lines, and the adolescent's remediation becomes more elusive. Exacerbating the problem is that the provider's misinterpretation can move into goals and interventions that are not reflective of the adolescent's value system and aims—a second challenge to be addressed by educators. A third educational challenge that requires much attention is the fact that many of today's adolescents come from social and educational backgrounds that do not encourage introspection. Thus, a provider posing new questions about thinking processes and decision making would fare well to understand that these concepts, though understood linguistically, may require more effort and education as to their value and explicit conversation, especially how development, culture, and identity formation affect other issues within an adolescent's world.

SECTIONAL DIVISIONS OF THE BOOK

Section I: Foundational Issues

Section I defines the characteristics of adolescents and their experiences. This section reviews the characteristics and prevalence information on adolescents, adolescents' developmental considerations, and social and cultural factors including risk and protective concerns that help shape the personality and experiences of the adolescents. Furthermore, this section addresses the heterogeneity of adolescents in their various walks of life and knowledge sets required of persons seeking to competently counsel adolescents. These issues include common factors such as diversity, emotional and cultural issues, and environmental influences. These factors often exacerbated related challenges such as absent fathers, addictive behaviors, violence, self-harm, and isolation. Each chapter begins with relevant literature and closes with the relevant provider competency and implications for counseling adolescents. Regarding the core competencies, this section focuses on social and cultural diversity and integrative information pertaining to adolescents. The last part of each chapter provides implications for counseling adolescents. This section not only includes information on the application of the chapter but also includes clinical reviews of case studies, ethical applications, exercises, and "keystones" for the reader.

Section II: Theoretical Perspectives

Section II begins by articulating theoretical perspectives and associated knowledge sets. The authors present why theories are needed and how they help broaden professional understandings as professional providers are expected to pull all adolescent dynamics together in a cohesive and therapeutically useful manner. The authors assert that competent counseling of adolescents is predicated on professional providers understanding cognitive frames of reference, prioritizing their thinking, and organizing massive amounts of information. The authors talk about the following issues as they relate to theories: definition, purpose, function, counseling application, counseling implications for adolescents, and how core competencies affect effective counseling practices. The authors highlight key theories influencing the counseling field today such as cognitive behavioral, client-centered, trauma-focused, attachment, multicultural family systems, play therapy, strength-based, and juvenile-involved adolescent theories. Each chapter begins with relevant literature and closes with critical provider competencies and implications for counseling adolescents. Regarding noted provider competencies, this section focuses mostly on professional orientation and ethical practices and provides integrative information pertaining to adolescents. The last part of each chapter provides implications for counseling today's adolescents. This section not only includes information on the application of chapter information, but also includes clinical reviews of case studies, ethical applications, exercises, and "keystones" for the reader.

Section III: Evidence-Informed Interventions

Section III provides a definition of "evidence-informed interventions" and its direct link to research and findings of adolescent populations. For this section, 10 distinct areas of focus have been identified: (1) adolescent assessment, (2) diagnostic criteria, (3) treatment planning, (4) counseling interventions, (5) school counseling, (6) relational and career issues, (7) chemical and process addictions, (8) divorce implications, (9) LGBTQ considerations, and (10) sexually maladaptive behaviors. This section defines screening and assessing and its utility in competently diagnosing the needs of adolescents, distinguishing characteristics, critical factors associated with working with them, emerging trends, management strategies, information pertinent to their education and relationships, as well as addiction challenges. This section also provides case scenario information based on commonly seen diagnostic and clinical issues. Each chapter begins with relevant literature and closes with critical provider competencies and implications for counseling adolescents. Concerning the last part of each chapter, implications for counseling adolescents are provided. This section not only includes information on the application of the chapter but also includes clinical reviews of case studies, ethical applications, exercises, and "keystones" for the reader.

Section IV: Legal and Ethical Considerations

Section IV summarizes critical legal and ethical elements to consider when working with adolescents. As such, a brief highlighting of key legal decisions, the role of state and external governing agencies regarding ethics, the importance of supervision and consultation as a lifelong professional commitment, and use of technology are expressed throughout this section. The chapter provides highlights and themes identified for effective, culturally responsive, and empirically based work with adolescents. Such issues include confidentiality, identifying the client, dual relationships, consent to treatment, and supervision and consultation as key competencies. This section ends with providing information on the key summary elements of the book along with recommendations for future work. Also, the use of technology by adolescents is explored. Each chapter begins with relevant literature and closes with the critical provider competency and implications for counseling adolescents. Regarding the noted provider competency, this section focuses mostly on professional orientation and ethical practice and provides integrative information pertaining to adolescents. Let us now turn to the first chapter where the authors identify how professional providers interface with the needs of today's adolescents.

REFERENCES

Grisso, T. (2011). *Forensic evalution of juveniles.* Sarasota, FL: Publisher Resource Exchange.

Underwood, L. A. & Dailey, F. L. L. (2016). *Counseling adolescents in conflict: Understanding the backstory.* Greenville: NC: Taylor Made.

ACKNOWLEDGMENTS

We would like to thank all of the people who contributed to this work. Your contributions have been vast and meaningful. The countless hours of researching, editing, proofing, and writing have been essential to amassing the current evidenced-based research. Whether you served as a chapter contributor, providing expert level contributions for your specific specialty area or a chapter lead, providing the chapter's first cut of content, or a researcher, gathering and editing relevant data, your involvement, support, and professionalism are appreciated. A special thanks goes to Aryssa Washington and Melissa Nelson, who served as distinguished research team leads. Your fingerprints are evident throughout this work. Individuals assisting with this work can be divided into three major areas, which are provided below along with the specific persons identified with those areas.

CHAPTER CONTRIBUTORS (LISTED ACCORDING TO THEIR CHAPTER APPEARANCE)

The first grouping is that of chapter contributor, which comprises esteemed individuals who provided their expert-level insights and writings as foundational to their specific chapter.

Cheryl Smith, Regent University (Chapter 4: Multicultural Family Systems)

Cheri Meder, Adams State University (Chapter 7: Play Therapy)

Andy Orayfig, Regent University (Chapter 9: Treatment Planning Issues)

Denise Ebersole, Messiah College (Chapter 11: School Counseling Interventions)

Cyrus R. Williams III, Regent University (Chapter 13: Chemical and Behavioral Addictions)

Sally Falwell, Legacy Assessment Counseling & Consulting (Chapter 14: Divorce Impact; Chapter 19: Use of Technology With Adolescents: Telemental Health Treatment)

Travis Jordan, Hampton University (Chapter 18: Supervision and Consultation)

CHAPTER LEADS

The second grouping of individuals assisting this work is those who served as chapter leads, whose work provided foundational research and writing that spurred the authors in crafting several chapters. These individuals include (in alphabetical order):

Kourtney Crier (Chapter 17: Who is the Client? Key Ethical and Legal Issues)

Sonji Gregory (Chapter 2: Adapting Counseling Theory to Adolescents)

Paul Hoard (Chapter 5: Juvenile Justice)

Teri Hourihan (Chapter 10: Counseling Interventions)

Meagan Jones (Chapter 6: Strength-Based and Resilience Perspectives; Chapter 15: Gender Specific and LGBTQ Issues)

Carrie Merino (Chapter 8: Screening and Assessment in Adolescent Counseling; Chapter 16: Sexually Maladaptive Behaviors)

Melissa Nelson (Chapters 12: Relational and Career Issues; Chapter 17: Who is the Client? Key Ethical and Legal Issues)

Vanessa Snyder (Chapter 3: Trauma-Focused Care)

Aryssa Washington (Chapter 17: Who is the Client? Key Ethical and Legal Issues)

RESEARCHERS

The third grouping of individuals is many doctoral students from Regent University and Argosy University who spent countless hours assisting with researching, pulling articles, editing works, and adding their skills to the role of research assistants. These persons include (in alphabetical order):

Kourtney Crier, Emily Graber, Teri Hourihan, Paul Hoard, Melissa Nelson, Lisa Oddo, Andy Orayfig, LaKeitha Poole, Tricia Mikolon, Aryssa Washington, and Adam Wilcox. Of this team, two individuals served as chief team leaders: Aryssa Washington and Melissa Nelson. These two have tirelessly toiled toward fine-tuning and refinement of our directives the middle two years of this work's development and have provided much appreciated leadership to the research team.

SAGE Publications and the authors would like to thank the following reviewers for their contributions:

Adrian S. Warren, University of Texas at San Antonio

Wendy K. Killam, Stephen F. Austin State University

Laura Rauscher, Missouri Baptist University

Kristen Moran, Clemson University

Jennifer C. L. Jordan, Winthrop University

Carol J. Kaffenberger, Johns Hopkins University

Dodie Limberg, University of South Carolina

Shelly Hiatt, Northwest Missouri State University

Ivelisse Torres Fernández, New Mexico State University

Ken Sanders, Clark Atlanta University

1

INTRODUCTION

BACKGROUND

Before embarking on the journey of counseling adolescents, one must first understand what characterizes adolescents' core issues developmentally, the external and internal factors that contribute to adolescents in need of counseling services, the history of the counseling field, and the role of providers in working with adolescents. Questions to ask throughout the chapter include "What characteristics may affect counseling adolescents?" "What characterizes an adolescent?" "What adolescent factors are pertinent to counseling interventions?" "What would be the interaction between the provider and the adolescent?"

Specifically, at the end of this chapter, you will be able to do the following:

- Reason out why adolescents present in counseling services

- Provide characteristics and prevalence information on adolescents

- Know the challenges faced by adolescents

- Describe the role of providers in counseling adolescents

- Distinguish the areas in which providers may be of service to adolescents

- Identify and describe various vulnerabilities of the adolescent that would lead him or her to become involved in the counseling arena

- Use case illustrations to demonstrate one's understandings of the keystones learned in each chapter

THE ADOLESCENT

Which Adolescents Present for Counseling: Who Are They?

Throughout media, there seems to be an often repeated set of questions pertaining to adolescents today. *What are they doing? How do we interact with them to help steer them?* And if the adolescents are experiencing challenges, *whose responsibility are they? How can we best support them? In what ways can counseling be beneficial to their presenting problem?* However, before broaching these questions with credibility, insight, and guidance toward effect lasting, positive change for adolescents, the interventionist must first understand in essence—who are today's adolescents? Of course, these questions are not limited to persons within the media. They are asked within our homes, personal circles, places of worship, and community organizations, and they highlight that today's adolescents are among the most challenged generation yet. There seems to be a resounding clarion call that many of today's adolescents need help. There seems to be a nebulous cloud of challenges, concerns, and implications associated with their newfound abilities to make decisions that not only affect their present life but also their future health, careers, and relationships (Table 1.1). When the questions are asked within our offices, during case consultations, milieu meetings, school offices, program planning meetings, we answer them from a strong knowledge base, insight, and aim to be not only problem identifiers and statistic collectors but also professional providers at all levels of experience who are called to wield impactful interventions with "an attitude and philosophy (in which) excellence is a fundamental goal" (Council for Accreditation of Counseling and Related Educational Programs [CACREP], 2014b). Accordingly, for community and school counselors, burgeoning behavioral health providers, and seasoned professional providers, having a sense of mastery in working with any population takes many years (Freeman, Hayes, Kuch, & Taub, 2007).

Let us start our understanding of today's adolescents by first becoming acquainted with some alarming facts that pertain to their overall well-being. The U.S. Department of Health and Human Services (DHHS) has established a national survey to identify key indices influencing today's adolescents that lead to their death, disability, and social problems. This relevant information helps to better identify the realities facing adolescents. The Youth Risk Behavior Surveillance System is conducted every 2 years and represents data of adolescents from 9th- to 12th-grade public and private school students. Among the 2011 findings, Youth Risk Behavior Surveillance System (2012) identified key concerns facing today's adolescents. These concerns are discussed in Table 1.2.

Overall, statistics suggest that adolescents are likely experiencing some problems at home and/or at school that interfere with his or her overall functioning. Nationally, about a quarter of youth (26.1%) reported feeling sad or hopeless almost every day for 2 weeks or more in a row in 2009 (National Fact Sheet: http://www.cdc.gov/healthyyouth/data/yrbs/data.htm). Having a sense of national trends helps guide professional providers in the ethical practice of "reflecting current knowledge and projected needs concerning counseling practice in a multicultural and pluralistic society" (CACREP, 2014b, p. 9) and demonstrates our understanding of the context in which our clients live.

Specific Factors Relevant to Counseling Adolescents

Adolescents' involvement in counseling can range from those receiving services in private practice behavioral health settings, university counseling centers, guidance and school counseling programs, child welfare systems, and community-based programs. Additionally, providers across the country are encountering a significant increase in the number of adolescents who are involved in gangs, are alienated from school, are described as emotionally unstable and disproportionately rageful, have poor parental monitoring and attachments, and reside in neighborhoods where drugs and violence have become a normative feature of everyday life (Underwood, Warren, Talbott, Dailey, & Jackson, 2013).

Many of the adolescents involved in counseling are a heterogeneous group of young people between the ages of 10 and 20 (Gentry & Campbell, 2002; Ozer, Park, Paul, Brindis, & Irwin, 2003). Estimated at more than 40 million, the adolescent population in the United States is "more racially/ethnically diverse than the overall population" (National Adolescent Health Information Center, 2008; Ozer et al., 2003). According to Ozer et al. (2003), adolescents tend to live in suburban areas as opposed to rural or city areas. However, the differentiation of mental health concerns of adolescents residing in urban and rural areas appears somewhat minimal.

Table 1.1 Counseling Adolescents Competently Applicability to Students, Professional Providers, Provider Supervisors, and Educators

Counseling Students		Professional Providers	Supervisors	Educators
Community Focus	School Focus			
An orientation to foundational issues related to today's adolescents and essential background information to inform adolescent counseling services	An orientation to foundational issues related to today's adolescents and essential background information to inform adolescent counseling services	A compendium of the latest developments within the counseling adolescent's field	A useful tool for supervisee's professional development	A single education sourcebook
Attention to community practitioner settings and scholarship is provided throughout the textbook.	Attention to school practitioner settings and scholarship is provided throughout the textbook.	Attention to trends and best practices as they currently present in direct practice settings	Attention to trends in professional foundations and trends	Attention to the scholarship and trends in academia
A featuring of counseling theories and their application for adolescents	A featuring of adolescents' use of technology, sexting, social media, and career decisions		Assistance with established and reviewing policy and procedures	
Highlights best practices derived from evidence-informed interventions as outgrowths of counseling theory perspectives such as trauma-focused attachment theory	Highlights adolescent relational and vocational development			
Integration of CACREP and other competencies	Integration of CACREP and other competencies	Integration of CACREP and other competencies	Integration of CACREP and other competencies	Integration of CACREP and other competencies
Incorporation of case studies to assist with content mastery, application, and overall case conceptualization	Incorporation of case studies to content mastery, application, and overall case conceptualization			Incorporation of case studies for extended discussion, application, integration, demonstrating knowledge acquisition for students, and inform case conceptualization skills

(Continued)

Table 1.1 (Continued)

Counseling Students		Professional Providers	Supervisors	Educators
Community Focus	School Focus			
Develops and affirms burgeoning professional provider identity	Develops and affirms burgeoning professional provider identity			Supports the professional provider identity and practices, while integrating the best of other intervention fields (e.g., psychology, social work, marriage and family, risk management)
Provides foundational information and application activities to incorporate practical skills at the end of a semester and in preparation for counseling skills, practicum, and internship activities	Provides foundational information and application activities to incorporate practical skills at the end of a semester and in preparation for counseling skills, practicum, and internship activities			Provides foundational information and application activities to incorporate practical skills at the end of a semester and in preparation for counseling skills, practicum, and internship activities
Helps understand and bridge the gap between mental health providers' and school providers' respective endeavors	Helps understand and bridge the gap between mental health providers' and school providers' respective endeavors	Helps understand and bridge the gap between mental health providers' and school providers' respective endeavors		Helps understand and bridge the gap between mental health providers' and school providers' respective endeavors
Highlights critical information applicable to adolescents in crisis (e.g., trauma, attachment, LGBT, justice-related topics)	Highlights critical information applicable to adolescents in crisis (e.g., trauma, attachment, LGBT, justice-related topics)		Highlights critical information applicable to adolescents in crisis (e.g., trauma, attachment, LGBT, justice-related topics)	

Note. CACREP, Council for Accreditation of Counseling and Related Educational Programs; LGBT, lesbian, gay, bisexual, and transgender.

Table 1.2   Key Concerns

Alcohol use	70.8% had at least one alcoholic drink.
	24.1% rode in vehicles in which the driver had been drinking alcohol in the 30 days prior to the survey.
Substance use	39.9% had used marijuana.
	20.7% had taken prescription drugs without a doctor's prescription.
	25.6% had been offered, sold, or given an illegal substance on school property in the 12 months prior to the survey.
Physical fighting	32.8% were in at least one physical fight.
	16.6% had carried a weapon such as a gun, knife, or club to school in the 30 days prior to the survey.
Sexual intercourse	47.7% had sexual intercourse.
	8% were forced to engage in sexual intercourse.
	33% had sex with at least one person in the 3 months prior to the survey.
	12.9% who had sex in the 3 months prior to the survey did not use a method of birth control.
Bullying	20% were bullied at school.
	16.2% were bullied through some form of electronic communication such as e-mail, texting, or instant messaging.
Suicide	15.8% had seriously contemplated suicide in the 12 months prior to the survey.
	7.8% had attempted suicide at least one time in the 12 months prior to the survey.

Source. Statistics are from Youth Risk Behavior Surveillance System (2012, June).

Developmental Characteristics. Adolescence is a period that includes a host of physical and mental transitions. Identity and social skills formation, vocational interest, and cognitive development dominate this period (Tucker, Smith-Adcock, & Trepal, 2011). Learning to navigate these developmental tasks strengthen their intra- and interpersonal skills and cultivates both individuation and a sense of belonging within relationships (Tucker et al., 2011). This is particularly important for adolescents who are ethnic minorities who specifically benefit from developing protective traits that allow them to decrease or avoid risks of experiencing negative effects of discrimination and prejudice (Romero, Edwards, Fryberg, & Orduña, 2014). Likewise, for all adolescents, the more they feel encouraged to explore their identity and neutralize stressors, the more resilient they are to the challenges that they face during this critical life period (Romero et al., 2014). Additional information on developmental and social concerns is included in Chapter 2.

Substance Use and Mental Illness. The Substance Abuse and Mental Health Services Administration (SAMHSA, 2013) reports that in 2012, approximately 12% of adolescents aged 12 to 17 received counseling in an inpatient or outpatient setting due to emotional or behavioral problems within the past year. Half of these adolescents received services due to depressive symptoms (SAMHSA, 2013). Almost 30% received services due to problems at home (or with family), followed by 24% due to being oppositional or defiant, and 23% due to suicidal ideation or attempts (SAMHSA, 2013).

Suicide is the third leading cause of death in adolescents and young adults (SAMHSA, 2013) and is considered a crosscutting feature in many of the representative disorders of this group. Additionally, 22% of adolescents received services for anxiety, which was followed by having problems at school (19.7%) and having trouble controlling anger (18.9%). Another 12% of adolescents received mental health services in an educational setting (SAMHSA, 2013). Depressive symptoms seem to be the impetus for receiving mental health services for at least half of adolescents (ages 12–17). Interestingly, adolescents who have had a major depressive episode within a year were more likely to use illicit drugs than those who had not experienced a major depressive episode that year. This pattern persists regardless of the type of illicit drug the adolescent used (marijuana, inhalants, prescription, hallucinogen, or psychotherapeutic). One million adolescents had substance use or abuse disorders without depression and just under 2 million adolescents suffered a major depressive episode without a supplemental substance disorder (SAMHSA, 2013). Additional information on chemical addiction is included in Chapter 13.

Depression and Anxiety. Rates of depression and anxiety highly increase at the age of puberty. DHHS (1999) published information describing the rates of depression and anxiety within the adolescent population. The results showed that 10% of the adolescents reported experiencing a form of anxiety within their life and 12% of the adolescents reported experiencing depression within their lives (DHHS, 1999). In addition to these findings, it was found that 20% of the adolescents have experienced either a mental, behavioral, or emotional problem in their lives (DHHS, 1999). Dixon, Scheidegger, and McWhirter (2009) completed a study to identify the factors between the desire to matter to others in adolescents and the link between anxiety and depression. Mattering to others was defined as feeling appreciated by others, having regular contact with friends and family, and gaining recognition from others. In addition, the research showed

that during adolescent years an increase in anxiety was apparent, which was largely linked to an increase in depression (Dixon et al., 2009). When examining adolescent depression and anxiety, it is not as important to know "what comes first"; however, it does appear that anxiety is largely prevalent prior to symptoms of depression with adolescents.

Major hormonal changes occur within the adolescent's body during puberty; however, other factors tend to increase the young person's depression, albeit a combination of relationship stress, family, identity crises, or academic pressures (Berger, 2005). However standard the emotional changes are, in many cases, adolescents' changes of mood might develop beyond the routine mood shifts and their angry emotions might lead to irresponsible behavior, or their sad emotions may lead to major depression resulting in suicide (Berger, 2005). Often adolescents experience distress in their lives in which they cannot view a brighter future, thus resulting in either suicidal ideation, parasuicide, or committed suicide (Berger, 2005). As a provider, it is imperative to assess any adolescent who describes suicidal ideations by the following factors to address whether the young person's thoughts may lead to suicidal behaviors: (a) access to weapons, (b) use of any substances, and (c) lack of supervision (Berger, 2005).

In addition to the hormonal and interpersonal factors that may lead to adolescent depression, often genetic vulnerability or parental distress can lead to depression. A young person who has a parent who has experienced depression himself or herself or experienced any psychiatric disorders has a higher likeliness of developing depression during adolescence (Berger, 2005). It is clear that there is a combination of a variety of factors that lead to depression in adolescence, including interpersonal stress, identity crises, genetic factors, and relational factors (Berger, 2005).

Low or Inflated Self-Esteem. Research has shown that children and adolescents often gradually report feeling less self-assured every year

(Jacobs, Lanza, Osgood, Eccles, & Wigfield, 2002). In an examination of 7th through 12th graders, self-esteem differed as a function of peer group affiliation. Individuals who were affiliated with a group of higher peer-rated status generally showed higher self-esteem than those associated with a peer group of lower status. Among those who did not affiliate with a peer group, but considered peer group affiliation important, self-esteem suffered and was low. There was also a subset of adolescents who did not consider peer group affiliation important (Brown & Lohr, 1987). Nonetheless, for those during childhood who did not report participation in a crowd or specific peer group (i.e., those who were not popular), the literature suggests that the majority of them reported having at least one close friend (Sigelman & Rider, 2012).

Group membership in specific crowds was predictive of adolescent risk behaviors such as cigarette use, alcohol use, and sexual intercourse in an examination of eighth graders in a multiethnic school. Specifically, the individuals who focused on grades and affiliated themselves with others who were like minded were least likely to participate in alcohol use and sexual intercourse, while other groups that did not focus on education as much were most likely to participate in these behaviors (Dolcini & Adler, 1994). Moreover, group membership was related to these behaviors above and beyond the effects of self-esteem (Dolcini & Adler, 1994), and availability of alcohol and drugs appeared to mediate whether students from specific crowds participated in cigarette and alcohol use (Dolcini & Adler, 1994). In an examination of seventh-grade students using ecological momentary assessment of peer affiliations, perceptions of peer affiliates, mood, activities, and behaviors, Rusby, Westling, Crowley, and Light (2013) found that mood states were related to peer affiliations and perceptions. Specifically, happy moods tended to be associated with spending time with popular and desired peers. Sadness and anxiety were related to feeling left out of peer groups (Rusby et al., 2013). Finally, mood liability in relation

to levels of perceived social acceptance was more drastic for girls than for boys, and this may relate to a higher importance placed by girls on social acceptance (Rusby et al., 2013).

Legal Involvement and Mental Illness. Some adolescents with substance use disorders receive mental health services in specialty alcohol/drug programs; however, many also present within the juvenile justice system (Aarons, Brown, Garland, & Hough, 2004) and provide a complete spectrum of what adolescent challenges look like in their most egregious states. In 2012, a very small portion of adolescents, a mere 0.3%, received mental health services in the juvenile justice setting (SAMHSA, 2013). Unfortunately, many adolescents with mental health and substance use disorders in the juvenile justice system are not provided adequate services, or otherwise go unidentified (Aarons et al., 2004). Aarons and colleagues (2004) contend that little research exists documenting the discrepancies in receiving specialized alcohol/drug treatment in relation to adolescents involved in the juvenile justice system, which may be problematic considering that demographic factors tend to steer whether or not an adolescent receives mental health services and whether or not he or she utilizes those services.

Peer Affiliation. Adolescence is a time when the decisions that underlie peer affiliation become complex and multifaceted. Sigelman and Rider (2012) note the overall importance of being part of a peer group during the high school years. Despite misconceptions that peers generally have a negative influence on adolescent development, it seems that peer affiliation has more positive effects on behavior as a whole (Sigelman & Rider, 2012). The authors note that the extent to which peer affiliation leads to these positive outcomes depends on factors such as the type of crowd being affiliated with, the sense of dependence an adolescent has on their peers' acceptance of them, and the strength of the adolescent's relationship with their parents (Sigelman & Rider, 2012).

During childhood and adolescence, healthy friendship and peer affiliation is a crucial predictor of positive adult adjustment as well as happiness and social competence during the childhood and adolescent years (Sigelman & Rider, 2012). Moreover, it is important that friendships are with peers who are well adjusted, psychologically healthy, and supportive (Sigelman & Rider, 2012). Finally, it appears that childhood friendships prepare individuals for later cross-gender friendships and dating during adolescence and early adulthood (Sigelman & Rider, 2012).

Fear of Rejection. The fear of rejection and the quest for popularity appear to be strongly influential processes in the lives of children and adolescents. As children and adolescents begin interacting with peers, factors such as physical attractiveness and cognitive ability have some influence on one's level of popularity. However, factors such as socially competent behavior and emotional regulation abilities may be more important (Sigelman & Rider, 2012). The outcomes of childhood popularity ratings become very important later in life. Adolescents are classified as popular (liked by most), rejected (disliked by most), neglected (neither liked nor disliked), controversial (liked by many and disliked by many), and average. For those classified as rejected in childhood, outcomes may include poor later adjustment, self-esteem and social skill deficits, lowered academic performance, negative perceptions of others, and negative peer affiliate relations (Sigelman & Rider, 2012). For those classified as neglected, most attain greater acceptance later, although some suffer from social anxiety, victimization, and other negative outcomes (Sigelman & Rider, 2012).

Rejection and dislike, as well as perceived rejection and dislike, have several different associations. In a meta-analytic review of more than 23,000 children and adolescents, Card (2010) examined the outcomes of antipathetic relationships, or relationships based on mutual dislike. Overall, 35% of individuals in the studies reported antipathetic relationships, and the presence of these relationships was related to outcomes such as externalizing and internalizing concerns, lower positive regard for others, lower helpful social behavior, victimization and rejection, and lower academic achievement (Card, 2010). In another review, interpersonal sensitivity, or a dispositional concern about negative evaluation, had several negative health outcomes (Marin & Miller, 2013). These included increased risk for infectious diseases and a potentially increased risk for cardiovascular disease. Marin and Miller (2013) also provide evidence that interpersonal sensitivity precedes illness temporally and that many alternatives have been ruled out, thus suggesting a causal link. Additionally, perceived peer rejection was found to lead to cardiac slowing during the transition to adolescence (i.e., 11- to 14-year-olds), and this effect was most pronounced in adolescent girls (Moor, Bos, Crone, & van der Molen, 2014). This effect was not found as strongly among children aged 8 to 11, suggesting a higher sensitivity to peer rejection during adolescence (Moor et al., 2014).

It also appears that perceived rejection informs later responses to peer rejection and acceptance. Neurological functional magnetic resonance imaging evidence using a simulated social exclusion paradigm suggested that adolescents experiencing firsthand rejection show neural activity relating to distress when seeing another peer accepted later (Masten, Eisenberger, Pfeifer, & Dapretto, 2013). Conversely, rejected adolescents witnessing later peer rejection showed neural activity relating to perspective taking and emotion regulation (Masten et al., 2013).

Plaisier and Konijn (2013) explored the effect of peer rejection on acceptance of antisocial media content and found a relationship between peer rejection, anger, and moral judgment in adolescents. Specifically, it appears that peer rejection creates a greater state of anger among adolescents, thus leading to diminished moral judgments and acceptance of antisocial media content (Plaisier & Konijn, 2013). However, the relationship between rejection and media choice was not significant among young adults (Plaisier & Konijn, 2013). In addition to deviant behaviors, peer rejection appears to play a significant role in adolescent depression. There appears to be a reciprocal relationship between peer rejection and depressive symptoms in the teenage years that forms and preserves unhelpful cycles, although overall results also strongly indicate that peer rejection has some causal influence on negative emotional states (Platt, Kadosh, & Lau, 2013). The researchers suggested from their findings that information-processing and attentional-bias strategies may be partly responsible for differences in reactivity to peer rejection among depressed youth (Platt et al., 2013). The authors also discuss new technologies, such as neurofeedback, aimed at reducing reactivity to peer rejection by altering underlying cognitive processes (Platt et al., 2013).

Finally, it seems that estimated rejection by others, and not only actual rejection, predicts individual outcomes among adolescents (Zimmer-Gembeck et al., 2013). Specifically, in a sample of Australian adolescents, individuals who overestimated their own peer rejection from others showed higher rejection sensitivity and felt more victimized, although others did not see them as such (Zimmer-Gembeck et al., 2013). Individuals who underestimated the degree to which they were rejected were more interpersonally aggressive and their peers saw them that way; however, their interpersonal satisfaction was unaffected (Zimmer-Gembeck et al., 2013). The authors highlight the need to tailor interventions to perceived levels, as well as actual levels, of rejection (Zimmer-Gembeck et al., 2013).

Peer Pressure. The impact of peer pressure and peer influence on adolescents' thoughts, emotions, and behaviors is immense. As mentioned earlier, the drive to affiliate, the need for acceptance, and the fear of rejection characterizing this period of life is a major determinant of current and future functioning (Sigelman & Rider, 2012).

Moreover, it appears that peer influence and pressure affect individuals differently during middle and late adolescence. A longitudinal examination of antisocial adolescents in Pennsylvania and New Mexico suggests that selection (choosing to associate with antisocial peers) and socialization (the effect of deviant peer choices on personal delinquency) processes both impact development of delinquency in middle adolescence (Monahan, Steinberg, & Cauffman, 2009). However, by late adolescence (i.e., 16–20 years old), it appears that personal delinquency is primarily affected by the socialization processes (Monahan et al., 2009). The effect of peer pressure after the age of 20 appears minimal (Monahan et al., 2009).

Peer pressure influences the individuals' emotional functioning and relatedness to one another; however, the adolescent's predisposition to specific positive or negative emotions may affect their relationships. A preference of attention to positive emotional content seems to be related to avoidance, lower self-sufficiency, and more susceptibility to peer pressure. However, a preference of attention to negative emotional content was related to lower avoidance and more hostility (Buck, Kretsch, & Harden, 2013). These results were lessened for those with premorbid secure attachment styles (Buck et al., 2013). Likewise, the differential need for peer acceptance may relate to differences in individual reward pathways as it appears that peer influence is an important dynamic above and beyond some personality and family factors. This is particularly true in reference to the potential for substance use among this population. Peer use of alcohol during the teenage years predicts the use of alcohol during adolescence above and beyond the effect of self-control and parental influence. In a cohort study of more than 2,000 adolescents surveyed between 2001 and 2010, a relationship between peer use during adolescence and personal use during adolescence was discovered (Visser, de Winter, Veenstra, Verhulst, & Reijneveld, 2013). Notably, however, levels of self-control predicted which users would later become abusers (Visser et al., 2013)

Counseling Services Available to Adolescents. In a study of African American, Hispanic, and Caucasian high school students from the same high school and with the same access to school counseling services, Thomas, Temple, Perez, and Rupp (2011) found that despite similar prevalence of depressive symptoms across the ethnicities, Caucasian students were more likely to report a diagnosis and report having been treated by a school provider. Similarly, Holm-Hansen (2006) reported that adolescents raised in minority communities are less likely to receive mental health services regardless of comparable incidence of mental disorders. SAMHSA (2013) also reported that females between the ages of 12 and 17 were more likely to make use of outpatient mental health services, education services, and general medical services than males. According to Holm-Hansen (2006), Caucasian individuals are more likely to self-refer or seek out treatment based on the advice of friends/family, whereas, minority individuals tend not to unless it is to a nonmainstream agency/provider. Additional information is included in Chapter 9 on treatment planning in counseling and in Chapter 10 on counseling interventions.

The Impact of Neighborhood. High-poverty neighborhoods often have a higher representation of minorities and mentally ill clients, and unfortunately there tends to be little access to mental health care in these communities (Holm-Hansen, 2006). Differences in who is referring the adolescent to receive mental health services may also explain demographic discrepancies. Research indicates that Caucasian adolescents are likely to be referred by health care providers, while ethnic minority adolescents tend to receive referrals more so from schools, social services, or other legal agencies (Holm-Hansen, 2006). Holm-Hansen (2006) adds that these minority adolescents are, thus, more likely to receive referrals for more restrictive placements (i.e., foster care, detention, residential treatment). Thomas et al. (2011) and Holm-Hansen (2006) agree that apart from personal beliefs or attitudes about mental health, referral sources and behavioral health care providers may also interpret adolescents' symptoms and behaviors differently based on their own race/ethnicity, socioeconomic

status, and prior involvement with the legal system, which in turn may restrict the opportunities minorities have to receive mental health care. Additional information is included in Chapter 4 on multicultural family systems.

Common Challenges Adolescents Experience

Despite their heterogeneous presentations and needs in the counseling field, most adolescents in counseling share commonalities in areas of cognitive growth and development, experiencing identity development, while precariously maneuvering through the helplessness of their childhood days and striving toward the independence of adulthood. However, they differ in that they come to the attention of providers by way of various mental health needs, social skill deficits, out of home placements, educational difficulties, addictive challenges, and legal issues.

In our understanding of human growth and development, it is important to highlight that a general understanding of adolescent years (ages 10–20) reveals a myriad developments (physical, emotional, social, and vocational) and transitions that result in typically expected developmental tasks, including challenging authority, risk taking, and defiant behaviors that will be further discussed in later chapters. These adolescents are influenced by varying ability levels, stereotyping, family, socioeconomic status, gender, and sexual identity and their effects on their achievement in their education, familial interactions, social exchanges, and vocational options (Underwood & Dailey, 2014). Many adolescents are involved in systems of care ranging from juvenile justice facilities, residential group home environments, day programs, therapeutic foster care, and outpatient clinics (Coccoza & Skowyra, 2000; Underwood, Kirkwood, & Goins-Arthur, 2004). They have experienced physical and sexual abuse, come from father-absent homes, are classified as having education needs, and exploring sexual relationships (Henggeler, Melton, & Smith, 1992). If left unchecked, these youth may become chronically angry and display pervasive disproportionate patterns of aggression and that may develop into legal difficulties (Underwood et al., 2013). Nearly 50% to 75% have serious substance abuse and other unspecified co-occurring disorders (Coccoza & Skowyra, 2000). Extreme cases can present with extreme behavioral health needs, require social skills training, are placed in various forms of out-of-home placements, experience educational difficulties, and struggle with addictive behavioral challenges and legal issues.

We encounter adolescents struggling with problem internalization such as nonsuicidal self-injury and reactive sexual promiscuity problem externalization such as verbal threats, physical assaults, and misdemeanors (Underwood & Dailey, 2016). They come from families and environments that are single parented, mother-led, and fatherless (Alexander, Pugh, & Parsons, 2000; Henggeler et al., 1992), and their family of origin issues are further compounded by issues of poverty, substance use, too little or too much affection (smothering; Underwood & Dailey, 2016). Adolescents, themselves, make their distinction from other age-related demographic cohorts by shrouding their activities in secret social exchanges via Internet, colorful language, slang usage; asserting their independence (sometimes through risk-taking behaviors); and interacting with the world around them in a manner they see best fits their emerging individuality.

Adolescent behaviors may include the frequent challenging of authority figures, low self-esteem, emotional dysregulation, risk taking, and defiant behaviors. However, with some adolescents in counseling, there may be an increased concern regarding problem internalization such as self-injurious behaviors, addictive behaviors, and reactive sexual promiscuity and can include other harm involved in problem externalization including verbal threats and physical assaults. These adolescents have often experienced significant acute (onetime incidences) and chronic trauma (ongoing incidences) that can escalate a typical adolescent's angst to high risk-taking behaviors beyond expectation (Underwood & Dailey, 2016). Recent attention to trauma-informed interventions with this population has yielded a better understanding of significant change that occurs in the development of the adolescent's brain, such as prefrontal cortex development that affects executive functions included in decision making, predicting outcomes, and handling conflicting thoughts (Adolescent 4 Juvenile Justice: JJDPA Fact Book, 2012).

Behavioral health providers specializing in developmental research offer that adolescents' brains are continuing to grow well after their adolescent years and into their mid-20s (for males; Blakemore, 2012). As such, the fact that adolescents' brains are not physically developed in mature ways and do not perform at adult levels has influenced the work of some providers (see Chapter 3 on trauma-informed care). This impact is seen in mental health providers not viewing adolescents as miniature adults but as persons for whom evidence-based interventions may be used as a preventative measure to curb the influence of negative behaviors and improve prosocial skills later in life. In other words, adolescents coming to the attention of providers are recognized as works in progress and whose cognitive developmental abilities have not reached full potential; thus, these adolescents have age-appropriate decision-making difficulties that are not typical of adulthood. These difficulties are typically in the area of impulsivity, mood regulation, and reasoning abilities. In understanding these deficits, providers need to modify their treatment approaches and accommodate the needs of adolescent clients. Later chapters in this book discuss specific interventions (see Chapter 10) and considerations providers can use to best meet these needs of adolescents.

Self-Esteem and the Value of Materialism

Chaplin, Hill, and John (2014) link self-esteem with self-identity formation in adolescence. Their research indicates that adolescents seek out ways in which to enhance their self-esteem in order to build their self-identities. One way adolescents have been found to accomplish this is through materialism. Essentially, because adolescents are motivated by social stimuli (reflected in later sections), they try to enhance the way others perceive them by gaining materialistic items. However, this becomes difficult when adolescents live in poverty or are limited by a low socioeconomic status.

Chaplin et al. (2014) studied the value of materialism in both impoverished and affluent adolescents. They created two groups: (1) impoverished (guardian income $25,688—below national median income) adolescents and (2) affluent (guardian income $96,080 to $187,574) adolescents (Chaplin et al., 2014; U.S. Bureau of the Census, 2010). Out of the two groups, each person individually made his or her own collage out of a pool of 100 pictures. The results showed that impoverished adolescents had more materialistic pictures (e.g., car, house, money) and affluent adolescents had more relationship pictures (e.g., adult and child sitting closely, child playing with a dog) (Chaplin et al., 2014). The study implied materialism is more important to impoverished adolescents at a higher rate than affluent adolescents. They hypothesized that the reasons for this difference was because affluent adolescents have at their "disposal" the items they need and thus do not "fantasize" about these items; whereas impoverished adolescents are in a constant state of deprivation, so they fantasize about those things they do not have. The results of the collages from Chaplin et al. (2014) are displayed in Table 1.3. Each collage was created by two different 16-year-old males. One male represented an affluent background and the other represented an impoverished background. Each boy was presented with a stack of 100 cards to choose from to create his collage. From there, each was free to build his collage however he chose to. Represented in the two collages are the importance of materialism and the importance of relationships. The graph represented in Table 1.3 shows the cards chosen by each boy. Notice how

the impoverished boy chose more pictures representing materialism, whereas the boy from an affluent background chose more pictures representing family and relationships.

Clash of Cultures

"Clash of cultures"—or "meme competition" (Massimini & Delle Fave, 2000) defines what happens when two or more different cultures come together (Charmaraman & Grossman, 2010). A common term used to describe "clash of cultures" and "meme competition" is acculturation (i.e., a person's ability to learn the rules and customs of their new culture). Moreover, acculturation is the "non-normative" process of dealing with the challenges of life (Terzini-Hollar, 2008). A concerning issue with immigrant adolescents is that oftentimes acculturation is difficult and their adjustment to the new culture becomes stressful and can create developmental challenges (e.g., difficulty forming relationships, identity confusion; Rajiva, 2006; Terzini-Hollar, 2008). Arnett (2002) and Berman, You, Schwartz, Teo, and Mochizuki (2011) suggest that identity confusion is the result of living within two different cultures with "competing" belief systems. Berman et al. (2011) suggest that rather than trying to be independent, these adolescents are just trying to fit in—which they do by trying to become "bicultural" (i.e., integrating their traditional culture and their embedded culture). Rajiva (2006) was interested in understanding the acculturation experience of Asian adolescents. Her research specifically looked at the development of Asian adolescent girls in Western society. She found that Asian adolescents had difficulty feeling a sense of belonging from the dominant culture (e.g., white/Caucasian/American culture). In addition, Asian adolescents stated in a survey that they were frustrated with their parents not allowing them to hang out with their white peers or practice American cultural norms (e.g., dating) because their parents restricted them to only hanging out with Asian peers (Rajiva, 2006). Consequently, these adolescents felt a sense of

Table 1.3   Impoverished Versus Affluent

| *Impoverished 16-year-old male* | | *Affluent 16-year-old male* | |
Materialism	*Relationship*	*Materialism*	*Relationship*
• Money	• Friends	• Money	• Aunt
• Nike shoes	• Grandma	• Nike shoes	• Uncle
• Skateboard	• Dad	• Skateboard	• Mom
• Basketball	• Mom	• Basketball	• Sister
• Flat screen	• Grandma	• Flat screen	• Friends
• Sports car	• Snow boarding	• Football	• Grandma
• Nintendo/Wii	• Bowling	• Sports car	• Grandpa
• Bike	• Swimming	• T-shirt	• Staying up late
• Mansion			• Cousins
• Laptop			• Dad
• iPod			• Skateboarding
• Cell phone			• Getting good grades

Source. From Chaplin et al. (2014).

exclusion from their embedded culture (e.g., American culture) and their traditional culture (Asian culture). Essentially, many of them grew up feeling disconnected and confused (i.e., unable to build a secure self-identity) because they wanted to be a part of the American culture and felt a closer connection to it than to their traditional culture, as they were often first-generation Americans who had never experienced their traditional culture within its native context (Rajiva, 2006). Consequently, they felt like they were in a constant struggle between two cultures. Here is one Vietnamese girl's account of this experience:

I just dyed my hair and my mom got all upset. My friends called me white at first when I was a brunette. I notice that appearance matters to ethnicity a lot. If you have long black hair and white skin then you're fine. I cut my hair short like the little boyish look and my mom went crazy on me. She said you're not my daughter, you're like my son. I said, so! You want to do what makes you feel happy or

comfortable but they put you in this little ethnicity box. Especially here [in Westminster]. Going to church you wear ao dai [traditional Vietnamese dress]. I'm not rebelling but I don't want to be another Asian girl in an American crowd. I want to be myself. I'm not going against my parents or tradition. I want to make my own morals and traditions and it makes me happy. It's not bad. I'm not doing drugs or tattooing myself. It makes me happy to have medium hair and to dye it [italics added]. (Vo-Jutabha, 2005, p. 28)

Clearly, for some immigrant adolescents, acculturation can be a difficult process, as they have to learn the language, culture, dress, style, etiquette, rules, mannerisms, and ways of behaving of the dominant culture all while trying to fit in and make friends—a definite struggle for some (Exercise 1.1). Other dynamics that tend to cause distress for adolescents are gender and psychosocial influences (e.g., parental restrictions, academic success, and puberty).

Exercise 1.1

Fitting In: Acculturation

1. As the provider, what can you do to help minority adolescents fit into their culture?
2. How are you prepared to work with minority adolescents and their families?
3. What are the steps to take before and during treatment with minority adolescents whose parents do not speak English?
4. Please list three reasons why acculturation is helpful in reducing stress in the life of the adolescent.
5. How would you use microskills (listening skills), in assisting the adolescent in identifying the concerns related to acculturating?

Gender and Psychosocial Influences

Adolescent girls are described as "interdependent," with a propensity toward emotional and social stimuli, whereas adolescent boys are more oriented toward action and independence (Charmaraman & Grossman, 2010; Cross & Madson, 1997). Parents may be the context variable that influences girls and boys to differentiate the way they do, as research shows that parenting styles change depending on the gender of the child (Charmaraman & Grossman, 2010). For instance, parents regularly place more restrictions on girls than on boys (e.g., girls have an earlier curfew). Additionally, girls are often treated fragilely (e.g., not allowed to play sports) and encouraged to take on gender-specific roles (e.g., cleaning). As related to culture, ethnic minority (e.g., Latino) adolescent girls are expected to keep the family traditions and norms, whereas boys are given more freedom to gain autonomy (e.g., by seeking education and career status) in the world (Charmaraman & Grossman, 2010). In surveys between girls and boys of ethnic and racial minority status, girls reported more centrality than boys (i.e., family traditions, norms, race, and ethnicity more important to girls). However, only boys' centrality related to school achievement (i.e., higher centrality equaled higher achievement; Charmaraman & Grossman, 2010). Charmaraman and Grossman (2010) state the reason for the difference in

centrality rates for boys and girls are again in part because of environmental influences (e.g., parents, teachers, and society). Girls are encouraged to keep their families' traditions, while boys are encouraged to seek autonomy through education and vocation. Interestingly, this continues even through young adulthood, where girls and boys are encouraged to desire "gender"-specific careers (e.g., girl to be a nurse; boy to be an engineer; Zajko, 2007).

Girls and boys are also encouraged differently in school. Girls are encouraged to excel in language and writing, and boys are encouraged to excel in math. Furthermore, research in this area finds that when children and adolescents are encouraged to do well in certain areas and not others it is reflected in their perceived ability to succeed in those areas and in their performance (e.g., girls who were encouraged to do well in language and not math responded in a survey that they were poor performers regarding math, positive performers regarding language, and then performed accordingly). However, when the stereotype was reversed (i.e., girls believed they were good at math), performance continued to run parallel (i.e., girls outscored boys in math achievement) (Steffens & Jelenec, 2011).

Finally, in the case of expected, typical development, girls and boys alike will experience physical changes related to hormonal shifts (puberty). Adolescents in countries such as Iran and Turkey experience puberty differently than many American adolescents do (Golchin, Hamzehgardeshi, Fakhri, & Hamzehgardeshi, 2012). Golchin et al. (2012) provides an explanation for why this is so. In speaking regarding Iranian adolescent development, these researchers state that there are "cultural restrictions" in place that do not allow for sexual education. Because of this restriction, adolescent girls do not receive the education concerning what to expect (e.g., physically, emotionally, and socially) for this stage of development. As a result, Iranian and Turkish girls, for instance, who begin menstruation are at times afraid to share this occurrence with their peers or parents for fear of rejection or ridicule and may believe they are plagued with a disease or sickness (Golchin et al., 2012; Ozdemir, Nazik, & Pasinlioglu, 2010).

Ozdemir et al. (2010) studied the experience of menarche in Turkish girls. Their study consisted of a sample of 191 Turkish girls. Out of the 191 participants, a little over half, 101, thought of puberty as a natural phase, while the remaining 90 reported it being the worst experience they had ever experienced. Ekerbicer, Celik, Kiran, and Kiran (2007) confirm that the experience of menarche in the country of Turkey is regarded as "taboo," and there is lack of systems in schools (e.g., sanitary items) that support this experience.

Muslim adolescent girls are reported to experience complete separation from their communities during times of their menarche, as they are not allowed to attend mosque during these times and report feeling ashamed and inadequate as a response to physical changes brought on by puberty (Golchin et al., 2012).

UNIQUE SKILLS OF PROVIDERS WORKING WITH ADOLESCENTS

Professional Providers' Role

Professional disciplines including psychiatry, psychology, social work, and marriage and family and professional counselors are strategically positioned to meet the mental and behavioral health needs of adolescents within our modern society. Psychiatrists are poised to intervene from a medical approach to adolescent challenges and provide pharmacological interventions. Psychologists are poised to intervene and measure mental health challenges through assessment and treatment of adolescent concerns. Social workers are poised to intervene from a social activist approach for the adolescents interacting within society's various systems (e.g., family, educational, legal, and medical systems). Marriage and family therapists are positioned to respond to the individual and family needs of adolescents. The focus of this book is the contribution of providers as they work to empower diverse individuals, families, and groups to accomplish mental health, wellness, education, and career goals (www.counseling .org). Professional counselors' unique contribution is integrating the techniques and strategies from other behavioral health sciences and then contextualizing them within the relational domain. This book emphasizes the commonality of counseling, a service intervention shared by all of the behavioral health professionals. Because professional counseling's identity is most similarly related to the art of counseling, an emphasis on professional counseling and CACREP standards will lead most of the discussion through the book.

Distinctives of Professional Counseling

Behavioral health providers recognize that adolescents within the United States have a wide spectrum of presenting issues ranging from typical/expected adolescent challenges (e.g., challenging authority, differentiating from their parents, peer pressure, first-time employment, and receiving a driver's license) to remaining closely tied to traditional family values and vices (e.g., substance use, aggression, guiding younger siblings, family time, and honesty). Providers have numerous avenues by which they aim to address the multiplicity of adolescent needs in a humane, empathic, and meaningful way. Increasingly difficult generational gaps, strides in technology, and transformations of the family unit create a spinning pinwheel of trends, colors, interests, presentations, and outgrowths that can be viewed as thematic foci concerning counseling adolescents. To illustrate the texture and depth of today's adolescent challenges, let's turn to Case Scenario 1.1 of Jessica (and corresponding Table 1.4), a 17-year-old adolescent who arrives in her school guidance counselor's office (Figure 1.1). Case Scenario 1.1 tells of the challenges leading to her involvement with a school counselor.

Jessica's case is an example of one fictitious adolescent, and Table 1.4 provides how her case could be reviewed throughout this textbook.

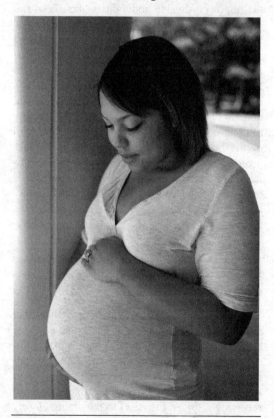

Figure 1.1   Providers Have Numerous Avenues by Which They Aim to Address the Multiplicity of Adolescent Needs in a Humane, Empathic, and Meaningful Way

Source. ©iStockphoto.com/ImagesbyBarbara

And to add rich texture and variety to the textbook's applicability to real-world counseling clients and dynamics, each chapter has a unique case study specifically tailored for that chapter's content.

CASE CONSIDERATIONS

Jessica just learned that she was pregnant and is having morning sickness during her first three classes. Jessica's story bespeaks the complication of counseling with diverse adolescent populations. Within her story, there are issues of trauma, attachment challenges, sexual abuse, human sex trafficking, poverty, homelessness, pregnancy, violence, and school challenges. Of course, our first inkling as providers is to go to the most significant areas of emotional pain for Jessica; however, her challenges are legion and require a multifaceted approach to identifying problem behavior, treatment goals, and objectives. Her ability to navigate the stressors that she faces daily can be overwhelming for the most experienced provider and potentially more so overwhelming for the new provider. Her ability to survive is a strident spark of hope for the school counselor. However, helping her in her many dilemmas is the task at hand.

To help providers conceptualize Jessica's case, we have provided a number of questions in Exercise 1.2 that should be kept in mind throughout the duration of the text. These questions seek to help develop case conceptualization skills (Exercise 1.2). This textbook helps the reader parse such difficult scenarios into meaningful component parts that are useful in safety planning, screening and assessment, treatment planning, and executing a culturally responsive service for adolescents who arrive in counseling offices, are referred by providers, join community support groups, are admitted into treatment centers, and show up at school with morning sickness. Use Jessica's case to identify possible developmental and extraneous factors that may contribute to the focal issue of counseling. Demonstrate your knowledge of your role as the acting provider.

Table 1.4   Jessica's Case by the Book

Chapter Number	Title	Application to Jessica's Case
Section I: Foundational Issues		
1	Introduction	The reader is introduced to Jessica's story of teen pregnancy, sexual abuse, childhood neglect, poverty, and exploitation. The reader learns how Jessica experiences several common counseling challenges of adolescents today such as identity formation, family of origin challenges, and struggles for independence while yet a dependent.
Section II: Theoretical Perspectives		
2	Adapting Counseling Theory to Adolescents	The reader explores aspects of Jessica's several areas of development that are common to her and other adolescents including hormonal shifts, identity formation, transitioning into adulthood, and maturing cognitive abilities all within the context of counseling theory as it pertains to adolescents.
3	Trauma-Focused Care	The reader discovers recent developments in trauma theory that have immediate application to Jessica's experience of chronic child abuse, sexual abuse, and exploitation.
4	Multicultural Family Systems	The reader explores how Jessica's family of origin, its structure, systems, and subsystems can formulate a culturally sensitive and informed counseling experience for Jessica, more healthy family members, and other family supports.
5	Juvenile Justice–Involved Adolescents	The reader learns how the legal system views and interfaces with Jessica's illegal activities. The reader quickly finds that the legal system may inadvertently criminalize her social, emotional, and behavioral needs.
6	Strengths-Based and Resilience Perspectives	The reader acquires information to better identify elements of Jessica's natural abilities, her survival mentality, and her desire for academic achievement that can help solicit her involvement with counseling, utilize her strengths and resiliencies, and provide more options for her continued growth and actualization of her goals, especially as they relate to positive psychology contributions to the field.
7	Play Therapy	The reader gains understanding of the relevance and application of therapeutic play interventions to engage Jessica in counseling, add to her self-expression, as well as help provide alternatives to traditional talk-based therapies.
Section III: Evidence-Informed Interventions		
8	Screening and Assessment in Adolescent Counseling	The reader comes to know elements that go into purposeful assessment, risk identification, and screening procedures as they might relate to Jessica's plan of services.
9	Treatment Planning Issues	The reader acquires the tools to develop theoretically informed, behaviorally specific, treatment plans that will guide Jessica's counseling focus.

(Continued)

Table 1.4 (Continued)

Chapter Number	Title	Application to Jessica's Case
10	Counseling Interventions	The reader explores the distinctions associated with professional counseling practices that inform the field's interventions and how these make a unique contribution to Jessica's counseling journey.
11	School Counseling Interventions	The reader absorbs information to best meet Jessica's academic development and daily challenges and interface with other systems to meet Jessica's academic, social, and mental health needs.
12	Relational and Career Issues	The reader acquires information to help Jessica as she grows to consider viable career options as she considers issues related to financial independence, self-sufficiency, and possibly supporting a family of her own.
13	Chemical and Behavioral Addiction	The reader gains knowledge regarding one of the most challenging aspects of healthy adolescent development and how outgrowths of addictive behaviors are a part of Jessica's familial and social exchanges.
14	Divorce Impact	The reader learns how adolescents like Jessica are affected by the dissolution of families through divorce and how divorce (and its outgrowths) affects the projected development of adolescents today.
15	Gender-Specific and LGBTQ Issues	The reader gathers information about Jessica's gender-specific needs and sexual identity formation challenges with which she may struggle.
16	Sexually Maladaptive Behaviors	The reader acquires essential information regarding adolescents whose history and experiences eventually evolve into sexually maladaptive behaviors. Jessica, for example, is not only the victim of sexual abuse and exploitation but is also challenged by her hypersexual energies, interests, and development.

Section IV: Legal and Ethical Considerations

Chapter Number	Title	Application to Jessica's Case
17	Who Is the Client? Key Ethical and Legal Issues	The reader hones an ability to distinguish between ethical indications as to who the client is when adolescent Jessica presents for counseling services, how (and when) to include caregivers/parents/legal guardians, and how including such persons affects Jessica's counseling experience and therapeutic relationship.
18	Supervision and Consultation	The reader identifies the importance of responsive, theoretical-based supervision and consultative relationships throughout one's professional career, especially as adolescent populations are increasingly complex (as indicated in Jessica's case study).
19	Use of Technology With Adolescents	The reader acquires information on how technology impacts Jessica's life via social media, for example, and how technology might be used in her counseling experience such as online support groups.
20	Conclusion and Future Direction	The reader reviews the learning acquired throughout the text, is encouraged to assimilate such learning into his or her professional identity and activities, and engages in reflective practice activities that will affect current and future caseloads.

Case Scenario 1.1

Jessica's Lives

Jessica is a 17-year-old Latina. She is a high school senior. Jessica arrives in Ms. Laymen's office after a teacher gave her a pass to see the school counselor. Ms. Laymen knew that Jessica was pregnant as this type of news travels fast in small-town, Wisconsin. Jessica looks piqued and lays her head on the provider's desk. "Oh, I just hate this feeling. You know my boyfriend hates the fact that I am pregnant, which is strange because he wants children . . . not just now though," says Jessica opening the conversation. Ms. Laymen reminds Jessica that she can consult her physician for medications to help with the morning sickness and encourages her to do so. Next, Ms. Laymen listens as Jessica shares that she really does not want to take the medication as it could possibly physically affect the baby, even though she has been assured by her health care provider that the medication has not been identified as a critical concern for the developing embryo, but would likely make her mornings more bearable. Jessica offers she'll talk to the school nurse again to review the benefits and risks of the nausea medication. To encourage further sharing, Ms. Laymen makes reference to Jessica's admirable determination to finish high school. Jessica needs little prompting on this topic and responds by giving a 3-minute diatribe of how she (Jessica) will never be poor again and education is her key to getting out of her misery. In her sharing, she asserts she and her baby will stay with her boyfriend until she finds another opportunity to live a decent life without "so many" challenges. After another 3 minutes of energetic spewing of the merits of education, a loving family, hatred of poverty, and assertions that she is a survivor, Ms. Laymen was able to gently probe about Jessica's life of challenges. What followed was Jessica sharing a life of enigmas, injustices, and perseverance of a 17-year-old girl who has lived through several lives of tragedies.

Her first tragic life she titles "Little Wife." At age 11, when her parents divorced, her mother could not pay rent, and she befriended a man who sexually abused Jessica. Jessica's dysfunctional home became worse when the boyfriend became her "husband" within their home and Jessica shared a bedroom with him. Jessica was accountable to wash his clothes and make his meals. Her abuse inadvertently secured the family's rent for 18 months because he ensured that Jessica's mother's rent was paid regularly, if the sexual encounters continued. After about a year and a half, he left home. Jessica was understandably relieved in his absence, and she was able to return to school on a consistent basis. After 4 months, however, he returned home and to their previous living arrangement. Jessica ran away from her mother's home when she was 14 years old.

Jessica's second tragic life is that of the "Nomadic Surfer." She was now a 14-year-old runaway. This life began with her living several months on the streets behind a food factory that discarded food each evening. Jessica got her meals from dumpsters and occasionally got money from patrons at a nearby karaoke bar. Eventually, she befriended a bar waitress, who took her in and cleaned her up. The waitress's home was "decked out" and the waitress had

(Continued)

Case Scenario 1.1 (Continued)

lots of extra spending money. Jessica soon learned that the waitress also worked as an escort. Though the waitress kept Jessica safe from her johns, Jessica understood her safety was not secure in the environment. However Jessica was glad to be back in school and chose to do many after-school activities to stay away from her new home. Jessica's natural academic gifting kept her academically afloat in all her courses, and when she attended school regularly, she was a model student. To make friends and keep up with the fashions, Jessica stole clothes from her waitress friend. Jessica overheard a conversation between the waitress and one of her johns. The john offered money for sex with Jessica. Jessica left that home before the waitress could assure her that this would not happen. Jessica moved back in with her mother, who had a new boyfriend with lots of friends. Her mother was extremely disappointed and initially responded harshly after finding out Jessica was pregnant. She agreed to support her during her pregnancy but asked her to be prepared to leave home on the arrival of the baby as the family could not support her financially while still having to care for her four younger siblings. On hearing this, one of the friends (Paul) offered to let Jessica live with him so that she could be away from her troubled mother. Jessica left her mother's home after a heated argument between them. She moved in with her newfound friend—Paul.

Who Is the Adolescent?

Consider answering the following questions about an adolescent whom you are currently treating or know.

1. From an ethical standpoint, who is the client?
2. What are his or her strengths and interests?
3. What is the problem as defined by Jessica? How would you define the problem?
4. Of all of Jessica's presenting problems, why focus on her pregnancy?
5. Whose responsibility is he or she?
6. What guidance does he or she need and from whom?
7. What does he or she need from me?
8. What are Jessica's strengths, needs, and resiliencies and how would you communicate these to her?
9. What evidence-based treatment approaches would be best suited to address Jessica's needs?
10. What general areas of assessment would you need to know more about in preparation of the treatment plan?
11. What are the needs of Jessica's family and how motivated are they in the treatment process?

Exercise 1.2

Conceptualizing Jessica

1. Where might you start in the counseling process?
2. What additional information might be important in conceptualizing Jessica's needs?
3. What specific concerns do you have for Jessica and her unborn baby, and how might you go about addressing and prioritizing these concerns?
4. How would you broker with Jessica's family to ensure that her emotional needs are met?
5. What cultural considerations need to be discussed as you prepare for treatment with Jessica and her family?
6. In what ways do you think Jessica's prior trauma affects her current situation?
7. How does your theoretical framework influence your conceptualization of Jessica?
8. What is the medical necessity for Jessica's treatment, and how does this affect third-party billing?

IMPLICATIONS FOR COUNSELING ADOLESCENTS

Clinical Review of Case

At the heart of the counseling practice is the desire to help, relieve, support, encourage, and journey with others. Jessica's case exemplifies the need for professionals to attend to the story of the individual and allow the individual's story to unfold. This therapeutic process is not one that happens naturally but is full of skill, insight, and a disciplined approach to listening and gathering information to complete a picture of the client's experience and meaning making regarding the client's life. Throughout this textbook, each chapter provides an example of pulling together many pieces of a client's story line and experiences that are of clinical importance. What follows is such a clinical review of Jessica's case. There are several ways that are theoretically linked (e.g., cognitive behavioral theory, solution-focused theory, existential theory), however, with this being the first case for the book and theories having not been discussed to this point, there are other approaches

that also allow a clinical understanding of Jessica's case. A key to her progress toward these foci of therapeutic work is intrinsic to the professional's ability to engage her in a manner that allows her story to unfold in an honest therapeutic dialogue. However, tailoring therapeutic interventions must be supported and crafted by the specifics of her culture, experience, understandings and explanations, possible resources and resolutions, cautions and attempts at change, as well as possible secrets and interpretations. Soliciting Jessica's story in her own words allows a professional approach that is tailored for her specific life, challenges, and strengths.

One way of approaching Jessica's multiple needs can be understood in a hierarchical manner that is within the context of her social and cultural framework. In other words, prioritizing any immediate safety and physical needs that she has, then moving toward issues related to her successfully completing the academic goals that she so highly values, and if time permits, helping her navigate a different, more promising future. First, the professional establishes a rapport that allows Jessica to share her story in her own manner, without many interruptions, few questions, and within a therapeutic relationship where Jessica is not judged, but she experiences positive regard and an attitude that she is competent to tell her story and on several levels manage her survival to this point. Second, the professional simultaneously begins to understand the circumstances that led to Jessica's appearance in her office—which seem to indicate that Jessica's ability to handle her many challenges has reached critical mass and Jessica is beginning to contemplate changes within her life, as indicated by seeking out her school's counseling services. It is important to note that Jessica specifically sought these counseling services as she already indicated that she has been seeing a medical doctor and the school nurse regarding her morning sickness. Third, attending to the details of the Jessica's story line is how Jessica organizes her own history into two distinct eras: "Little Wife" and "Nomadic Surfer." In essence, she has utilized her natural intelligence to organize what many of us would describe as a chaotic and tragic life. The professional could ascertain that Jessica has become adept at reading people and securing safety for herself in highly dangerous settings repeatedly and learned to focus her efforts on surviving and also maintaining an uncanny ability to excel academically, find refuge in school activities, and maintain hope about her life's trajectory. On the surface, Jessica's choice to move in with Paul is one that is questionable and concerning. However, after factoring in Jessica's history and her view of it, the move is one that will likely be temporary and one that she likely understands will have to protect herself and her child. Key to Jessica's life are themes of survival and forward thinking regarding her own life. She seems driven by her dreams and has learned skills to best ensure her survival, and now that she is pregnant, it seems her skills are being stretched and the realities of her lifestyles likely frighten her when she considers a newborn baby entering her life.

In summary, the provider's job is to inquire and help secure any immediate safety needs Jessica may have. At this point in their therapeutic relationship, Jessica has not revealed any immediate concerns outside of pregnancy symptoms and her growing family. Ongoing, the provider must take care to assess for any such concerns by maintaining a positive rapport in which Jessica can feel free to share the true happenings of her life. Ultimately, the provider must identify key areas of intervention and goals that will entail the work of therapy. This critical aim of therapy is then structured within the framework of counseling theory and interventions that can best encourage Jessica's optimal growth through the complexities of her life.

SUMMARY

This textbook is designed to provide critical information to those working with adolescents while simultaneously providing real-world scenarios to facilitate direct application of that knowledge. Indispensable knowledge about today's adolescents and those things that are relevant to counseling them all must be intentionally united to establish powerful and meaningful therapeutic relationships. Effective therapeutic relationships are intentional, supported by invaluable therapeutic skills, and formed by understanding adolescent developmental characteristics. Correspondingly, providers' comprehension of matters related to substance use, legal issues, and mental illness and their impact on adolescents adds to professional competency and better encourages clients' therapeutic progress. As such, it is critical that counseling services available to adolescents recognize the aforementioned topics along with a thoughtful, multiculturally informed approach to understanding and matching the client's respective neighborhoods of origin as well as the commonalities of adolescent challenges. The provider's ability to layer knowledge, therapeutic relationship building, attending to challenges (substance use, mental illness) all within a culturally informed and sensitive manner set the stage for the provider to execute the therapeutic role in a way that interfaces with adolescents throughout the counseling process in a meaningful (to the adolescent) manner.

KEYSTONES

- Today's adolescents are a diverse group that presents a vast array of counseling challenges that span several areas of their lives (e.g., personal, familial, community, education, addiction, and legal challenges); meeting their needs must be grounded in ethical practice.

- While all of the behavioral health professions are trained to intervene in the lives of clients, professional counselors are uniquely educated, ethically bound, and practically prepared to meet the needs of adolescents presenting in community mental health and school counseling settings.

- Despite their divergent needs, there are adolescent developmental commonalities that providers must attend to in their case conceptualization and interventions with this population, such as physical changes, traversing dependence and independence from childhood to adulthood status, educational expectations, for example.

- Working with adolescents in various counseling settings requires that providers master the information and the various concepts therein; readily apply those concepts in a meaningful, multiculturally sensitive, and effective manner; and are able to engage in lifelong learning and be supported by supervision and consultation in an ethically responsible manner.

- Understanding and working effectively with adolescents should be done within the context of larger cultural challenges and strengths, recognizing trends and risks, while being committed to individual and group growth for adolescents within a variety of professional counseling settings.

- Professional providers must recognize that adolescent years incorporate natural challenges (e.g., new social, physical, emotional, educational, and vocational experiences) and be able to distinguish when adolescent challenges go beyond expected developmental trajectories (e.g., gang involvement, isolation, self-harm, substance abuse).

- Professional providers working in clinical and leadership roles must keenly balance tasks associated with safety, legal issues, ethical standards, and programmatic stipulations of the needs of adolescents and those with whom they work (Exercise 1.3).

QUESTIONS TO CONSIDER

Exercise 1.3

1. What are three distinct contributions that the counseling field offers to working with adolescents?

2. How does knowledge of the Council for Accreditation of Counseling and Related Educational Programs (CACREP) curriculum standards or the standards of other behavioral health professions affect counseling services?

3. Consider an adolescent you encounter and provide a list of at least five areas of challenge, development, or concern he or she presents? Are those concerns confined to one or two central themes?

4. For that same adolescent, what are the key professional, ethical, and multicultural issues that inform your problem identification, first interventions, or future planning?

5. Reread Jessica's case study, hypothesize how you might proceed in working with her as a school counselor. Where would you start your intervention? What safety and health challenges would you consider in working with her? What other referrals or adjunct services might you refer to her?

REFERENCES

Aarons, G., Brown, S., Garland, A., & Hough, R. (2004). Race/ethnic disparity and correlates of substance abuse service utilization and juvenile justice involvement among adolescents with substance use disorders. *Journal of Ethnicity in Substance Abuse, 3*(1), 47–63.

Adolescent 4 Juvenile Justice: JJDPA Fact Book. (2012, June 15). Retrieved from Coalition for Juvenile Justice: http://www.juvjustice.org/

federal-policy/juvenile-justice-and-delinquency-prevention-act

Alexander, J. F., Pugh, C., & Parsons, B. V. (2000). *Functional family therapy* (Vol. 3). Golden, CO: Venture.

Arnett, J. J. (2002). The psychology of globalization. *American Psychologist, 57,* 774–783.

Berger, K. S. (2005). *The developing person: Through the life span* (6th ed.). New York, NY: Worth.

Berman, S. L., You, Y., Schwartz, S., Teo, G., & Mochizuki, K. (2011). Identity exploration, commitment, and distress: A cross national investigation in China, Taiwan, Japan, and the United States. *Child Youth Care Forum, 40*(1), 65–75. doi:10.1007/s10566-010-9127-1

Blakemore, S. J. (2012). Imaging brain development: The adolescent brain. *NeuroImage, 61*(2), 397–406.

Brown, B. B., & Lohr, M. J. (1987). Peer-group affiliation and adolescent self-esteem: An integration of ego-identity and symbolic-interaction theories. *Journal of Personality and Social Psychology, 52*(1), 47–55.

Buck, K. A., Kretsch, N., & Harden, K. P. (2013). Positive attentional bias, attachment style, and susceptibility to peer influence. *Journal of Research on Adolescence, 23*(4), 605–613.

Card, N. A. (2010). Antipathetic relationships in child and adolescent development: A meta-analytic review and recommendations for an emerging area of study. *Developmental Psychology, 46*(2), 516–529.

Centers for Disease Control and Prevention. *Youth Risk Behavior Surveillance System (YRBSS).* Atlanta, GA: Centers for Disease Control and Prevention; 2015. Retrieved from http://www.cdc.gov/healthyyouth/data/yrbs/index.htm

Chaplin, L. N., Hill, R. P., & John, D. R. (2014). Poverty and materialism: A look at impoverished versus affluent children. *Journal of Public Policy & Marketing, 33*(1), 78–92.

Charmaraman, L., & Grossman, J. M. (2010). Importance of race-ethnicity: An exploration of Asian, black, Latino, and multiracial adolescent identity. *Cultural Diversity and Ethnic Minority Psychology, 16*(2), 144–151. doi:http://dx.doi.org/10.1037/a0018668

Cocozza, J. J., & Skowyra, K. (2000). Youth with mental health disorders in the juvenile justice system: Trends, issues and emerging responses. *Juvenile Justice, 7*(1), 3–13.

Council for Accreditation of Counseling and Related Educational Programs. (2014b). *Draft #2 of the 2016 CACREP Standards.* Alexandria, VA: Author.

Cross, S. E., & Madson, L. (1997). Models of the self: Self-constructs and gender. *Psychological Bulletin, 122*(1), 5–37.

Dixon, A. L., Scheidegger, C., & McWhirter, J. J. (2009). The adolescent mattering experience: Gender variations in perceived mattering, anxiety, and depression. *Journal of Counseling & Development, 87,* 302–310.

Dolcini, M. M., & Adler, N. E. (1994). Perceived competencies, peer group affiliation, and risk behavior among early adolescents. *Health Psychology, 13*(6), 496–506.

Ekerbicer, H. C., Celik, M. M., Kiran, H. H., & Kiran, G. G. (2007). Age at menarche in Turkish adolescents in Kahramanmaras, Eastern Mediterranean region of Turkey. *European Journal of Contraception & Reproductive Health Care, 12*(3), 289–293.

Freeman, M. S., Hayes, B. G., Kuch, T. H., & Taub, G. (2007). Personality: A predictor of theoretical orientation of students enrolled in a counseling theories course. *Provider Education and Supervision, 46,* 254–263.

Gentry, J., & Campbell, M. (2002). *Developing adolescents: A reference for professionals.* Washington, DC: American Psychological Association. Retrieved from http://www.apa.org/pi/families/resources/develop.pdf

Golchin, N. A. H., Hamzehgardeshi, Z., Fakhri, M., & Hamzehgardeshi, L. (2012). The experience of puberty in Iranian adolescent girls: A qualitative content analysis. *BMC Public Health, 12*(698), 1–8. doi:10.1186/1471-2458-12-698

Henggeler, S. W., Melton, G. B., & Smith, L. A. (1992). Family preservation using multisystemic therapy: An effective alternative to incarcerating serious juvenile offenders. *Journal of Consulting and Clinical Psychology, 60,* 953–961.

Holm-Hansen, C. (2006). *Racial and ethnic disparities in children's mental health.* St. Paul, MN: Wilder Research.

Ipenburg, A. (2012). Indonesia. In M. Juergensmeyer & W. Roof (Eds.), *Encyclopedia of global religion* (pp. 557–561). Thousand Oaks, CA: Sage. doi:10.4135/9781412997898.n337

Jacobs, J. E., Lanza, S., Osgood, D. W., Eccles, J. S., & Wigfield, A. (2002). Changes in children's self-competence and values: Gender and domain differences across grades one through twelve. *Child Development, 73,* 509–527.

Marin, T. J., & Miller, G. E. (2013). The interpersonally sensitive disposition and health: An integrative review. *Psychological Bulletin, 139*(5), 941–984.

Massimini, F., & Delle Fave, A. (2000). Individual development in a bio-cultural perspective. *American Psychologist, 55*(1), 24–33. doi:10.1037/0003-066X.55.1.24

Masten, C. L., Eisenberger, N. I., Pfeifer, J. H., & Dapretto, M. (2013). Neural responses to witnessing peer rejection after being socially excluded: fMRI as a window into adolescents' emotional processing. *Developmental Science, 16*(5), 743–759.

Monahan, K. C., Steinberg, L., & Cauffman, E. (2009). Affiliation with antisocial peers, susceptibility to peer influence, and antisocial behavior during the transition to adulthood. *Developmental Psychology, 45*(6), 1520–1530.

Moor, B. G., Bos, M. G. N., Crone, E. A., & van der Molen, M. W. (2014). Peer rejection cues induce cardiac slowing after transition into adolescence. *Developmental Psychology, 50*(3), 947–955.

National Adolescent Health Information Center. (2008). *Fact sheet on demographics: Adolescents.* San Francisco, CA: Author.

Ozdemir, F., Nazik, E., & Pasinlioglu, T. (2010). Determination of the motherly reactions to adolescents' experience of menarche. *Journal of Pediatric and Adolescent Gynecology, 23*(3), 153–157.

Ozer, E. M., Park, M. J., Paul, T., Brindis, C. D., & Irwin, C. E., Jr. (2003). *America's adolescents: Are they healthy?* San Francisco: University of California, National Adolescent Health Information Center.

Plaisier, X. S., & Konijn, E. A. (2013). Rejected by peers—attracted to antisocial media content: Rejection-based anger impairs moral judgment among adolescents. *Developmental Psychology, 49*(6), 1165–1173.

Platt, B., Kadosh, K. C., & Lau, J. Y. F. (2013). The role of peer rejection in adolescent depression. *Depression and Anxiety, 30,* 809–821.

Rajiva, M. (2006). Brown girls, white worlds: Adolescence and the making of racialized selves. *Canadian Review of Sociology and Anthropology, 43*(2), 165–183.

Romero, A. J., Edwards, L. M., Fryberg, S. A., & Orduña, M. (2014). Resilience to discrimination stress across ethnic identity stages of development. *Journal of Applied Social Psychology, 44*(1), 1–11. doi:10.1111/jasp.12192

Rusby, J. C., Westling, E., Crowley, R., & Light, J. M. (2013). Concurrent and predictive associations between early adolescent perceptions of peer affiliates and mood states collected in real time via ecological momentary assessment methodology. *Psychological Assessment, 25*(1), 47–60.

Sigelman, C. K., & Rider, E. A. (2012). *Life-span human development* (8th ed.). Belmont, CA: Wadsworth Cengage.

Soekarjo, D. D., de Pee, S. S., Bloem, M. W., Tjiong, R. R., Yip, R. R., Schreurs, W. P., & Muhilal. (2001). Socio-economic status and puberty are the main factors determining anaemia in adolescent girls and boys in East Java, Indonesia. *European Journal of Clinical Nutrition, 55*(11), 932–939.

Steffens, M. C., & Jelenec, P. (2011). Separating implicit gender stereotypes regarding math and language: Implicit ability stereotypes are self-serving for boys and men, but not for girls and women. *Sex Roles, 64*(5–6), 324–335.

Substance Abuse and Mental Health Services Administration. (2013). *Results from the 2012 National Survey on Drug Use and Health: Mental Health Findings.* NSDUH Series H-47, HHS Publication No. (SMA) 13-4805. Rockville, MD: Author. Retrieved from http://www.samhsa.gov/data/NSDUH/2k12MH_FindingsandDetTables/2K12MHF/NSDUHmhfr2012.htm

Terzini-Hollar, M. (2008). *Daily hassles, coping, and acculturation as predictors of psychological well-being among Korean-American adolescents* (Doctoral dissertation). Fordham University, New York.

Thomas, J., Temple, J., Perez, N., & Rupp, R. (2011). Ethnic and gender disparities in needed adolescent mental health care. *Journal of Health Care for the Poor and Underserved, 22*(1), 101–110. doi:10.1353/hpu.2011.0029

Tucker, C., Smith-Adcock, S., & Trepal, H. C. (2011). Relational-cultural theory for middle school providers. *Professional School Counseling, 14*(5), 310–316.

Underwood, L. A., & Dailey, F. L. L. (2014). *Adolescents in conflict: Understanding the backstory.* Phoenix, AZ: McCord.

Underwood, L. A., Kirkwood, D., & Goins-Arthur, R. (2004). Reintegrating substance abusing offenders into the community and community corrections programs: A multi-stage approach. *Community Mental Health Report, 4*(1), 1–16.

Underwood, L. A., Warren, K. M., Talbott, L., Dailey, F., & Jackson, L. (2013). Mental health treatment in juvenile justice secure care facilities: Practice and policy recommendations. *Journal of Forensic Psychology Practice, 14,* 55–85.

U.S. Bureau of the Census. (2010). *2010 Census.* Retrieved from http://www.census.gov/2010census/

U.S. Department of Health and Human Services. (1999). *Mental health: A report of the Surgeon General.* Rockville, MD: Author.

Visser, L., de Winter, A. F., Veenstra, R., Verhulst, F. C., & Reijneveld, S. A. (2013). Alcohol use and abuse in young adulthood: Do self-control and parents' perceptions of friends during adolescence modify peer influence? The TRAILS study. *Addictive Behaviors, 38,* 2841–2846.

Vo-Jutabha, E. (2005). *The impact of historical, social, and cultural contexts on Vietnamese adolescent identity exploration* (Doctoral dissertation). Clark University, Worcester, MA.

Youth Risk Behavior Surveillance System. (2012, June). *2011 YRBS data user's guide.* Retrieved from ftp://ftp.cdc.gov/pub/data/yrbs/2011/YRBS_2011_National_User_Guide.pdf

Zajko, S. (2007). *Adolescent development and psychology.* (Unpublished manuscript)

Zimmer-Gembeck, M. J., Nesdale, D., McGregor, L., Mastro, S., Goodwin, B., & Downey, G. (2013). Comparing reports of peer rejection: Associations with rejection sensitivity, victimization, aggression, and friendship. *Journal of Adolescence, 36,* 1237–1246.

2

ADAPTING COUNSELING THEORY TO ADOLESCENTS

INTRODUCTION

Behavioral therapy, client-centered therapy, solution-focused brief therapy, and cognitive behavioral therapy (CBT) are extensively utilized counseling approaches that focus on isolating and altering detrimental thinking and subsequent behavioral patterns. Behavioral therapy and CBT have been widely recognized throughout the field of counseling and other related behavioral health fields for their consistent efficacy in the treatment of anxiety, depression, and other disorders (Butler, Chapman, Forman, & Beck, 2006; Jones & Butman, 2011) as well as for their applicability across numerous settings and populations. In fact, CBT has been shown to be successful in the treatment of adolescents across gender, age, setting, and ethnic groups (Reddy, De Thomas, Newman, & Chun, 2009; Shirk, Kaplinski, & Gudmundsen, 2009). Some of the research specific to adolescents is cited throughout this chapter; however, providers working with adolescents are encouraged to critically review journal articles and attend widely accessible theoretical-based trainings directly to glean a deeper understanding of appropriate and effective techniques as well as potential adaptations for this population.

Theoretical approaches must not only be deemed empirically sound but must also be adaptable and reflective of adolescents' developmental and cognitive functioning. As such, a full understanding of any chosen therapy must be achieved prior to its use in counseling adolescents. Given the integrative nature of behavioral therapy, client-centered approaches, solution-focused therapies, and CBT's current research base as well as its ability to be easily modified to the consumer, the following discussion offers the reader a conceptual understanding, utilizing CBT as the overarching theoretical approach. CBT serves as the underlying framework as it pertains to counseling adolescents. In doing so, the provider is more easily able to adapt and modify various techniques and approaches of CBT to the needs of the client.

It is important to note that any theoretical approach, including CBT's effectiveness, depends on the cognitive development of clients and their ability to be self-aware; however, the developmental level of the consumer does not necessarily hinder a provider's use of CBT with adolescents in that these techniques may be modified to effectively use them according to their cognitive abilities. Specific developmental considerations will be discussed in further detail below.

After reading this chapter, readers will be able to do the following:

- Recognize the adaptations of theoretical approaches for adolescents

- Provide an overview of CBT

- Demonstrate understanding of the ABC model of CBT

- Discuss the evidence-based outgrowths of behavioral therapy and CBT

- Demonstrate knowledge of research on the use of CBT with adolescents

- Identify recommendations for modification of CBT with adolescents

- Demonstrate practical applications for behavioral health providers

- Apply knowledge gained from this chapter through the case scenarios

ADAPTING THEORETICAL APPROACHES FOR ADOLESCENTS

CBT reflects the combination of behavioral and cognitive movements developed by Ulrich Neisser and behavioral movements developed by Edward Thorndike. Neisser worked within a foundation solely focusing on cognitive and information processing, resulting in his identification as the "father" of cognitive psychology. In contrast, Thorndike and John Watson, the "fathers" of behaviorism, illustrated the uses of operant and classical conditioning to modify behaviors. CBT utilizes both concepts of thought and behavior modification congruently to have a more holistic approach to address mental illness (Neisser, 1991). Aaron Beck's daughter, Judith Beck, has continued her father's development of this approach and added an integration of behavioral concepts (i.e., systems of reinforcement). As such, Judith Beck (2011) has highlighted 10 general principles for CBT and cognitive behavioral theory (Burns, 1980).

ABC MODEL OF CBT

Cognitive behavioral theory centers on the interrelationships of thoughts, emotions, and behaviors. This relationship is often described within the activating event-belief-consequence (ABC) model and is found in Figure 2.1. This model posits that the initial or activating event automatically triggers thoughts (Spiegler & Guevremont, 2010). These thoughts are rooted in internal belief systems that create patterns of either healthy cognitions resulting in positive/beneficial growth or unhealthy thought cognitions resulting in pathological or detrimental thinking. The healthy and unhealthy thoughts are often automatic and without much scrutiny in the thinking process. As a result, an emotional consequence occurs. In example, an adolescent may receive a poor grade on a test and think, *"How can I be so stupid?"* On thinking this, he or she may begin to feel a great deal of guilt or shame. These unhealthy thoughts result in negative emotional consequences; however, if the adolescent were to reframe these automatic patterns of thinking, the consequence would change. For example, the adolescent may instead think, "I did poorly on this test, so I will have to ace the next one!" resulting in increased feelings of determination. Further examples may be found in Table 2.1. The model helps adolescents and adults alike to begin to identify the beliefs and thoughts that are automatic and are often unnoticed (Exercise 2.1). By drawing attention to patterns of negative thoughts, CBT emphasizes the opportunity to change the resulting negative consequences that are typically found in mental illness (i.e., depression).

It is important to note that thoughts and emotions are conceptualized as *covert behaviors* in the CBT framework (Spiegler & Guevremont, 2010). Covert behaviors encompass activities that cannot be directly observed, such as thinking and feeling, while overt behaviors encompass observable activities, such as moving and eating. Through this lens, one can examine the learning processes that result in core beliefs by examining patterns of

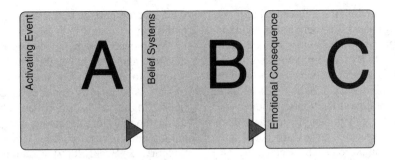

Figure 2.1   ABC Model

Table 2.1   ABC Examples

A—Activating Event	B—Belief System	C—Emotional Consequence
Parents announce divorce	*It must be my fault . . .*	Guilt
High school sweethearts break up	*I'm not as pretty as . . .*	Low self-esteem
Adolescent is bullied	*It's just not worth it . . .*	Low Confidence
Pushed out of a peer group	*Everyone is untrustworthy . . .*	Bitterness
Failing grade on test	*I am a failure . . .*	Shame
Friend is upset by something adolescent says	*I never do anything right . . .*	Depression
Adolescent doesn't make it to the sports team	*Everyone is out to get me . . .*	Hostility

Exercise 2.1

ABC Cognitive Behavioral Techniques

Take a moment and consider three more examples that could be added to Table 2.1 that are consistent with adolescents.

A – Activating Event	B – Belief System	C – Emotional Consequence
1.		
2.		
3.		

thoughts (e.g., awfulizing, all-or-nothing, and catastrophizing) as well as activating events (or triggers). Furthermore, behaviors can be modified or changed. By conceptualizing thoughts and emotions as a form of behavior, it becomes possible to modify or change the behavior using various behavioral modification techniques such as reinforcement and punishment. These techniques will be discussed in greater detail later; however, an example of such a technique may include the removal of guilt and shame (negative punishment) following modification of a negative thought.

Finally, cognitive behavioral theory conceptualizes mental illness by the automatic thoughts and core belief systems leading to negative emotional and behavioral consequences in one's life (Beck, 2011). For example, an individual diagnosed with depression may struggle with consistent thoughts of worthlessness. Following the ABC model, a friend may cancel a planned event (A). As a result, the individual may think, "No one wants to spend time with me" (B). This results in feelings of extreme sadness and loneliness (C). Changes in plans may serve as the activating event (A), resulting in a triggered belief (B), and ultimately creating an emotional consequence (C). When these negative thought patterns of worthlessness become consistent and ingrained in the individual, they become conceptualized as a core belief system. These core beliefs become an automatic part of the individual, resulting in consistently lowered mood and affect. These characteristics and thoughts are criteria for the diagnosis of depression. In this example, the interrelationship between unhealthy cognition and pathology is illustrated. The core beliefs reflecting poor self-worth result in consistently deflated affect and interpersonal withdrawal. These symptoms are consistent with criteria for diagnosis per the *Diagnostic and Statistical Manual of Mental Disorders*, fifth edition (*DSM-5*; APA, 2013) including depressed mood, decreased interest or pleasure in daily activities, and feelings of guilt or worthlessness. As such, one can see how CBT conceptualizes both symptoms as well as pathology.

When one's core belief system is consistently negative and inaccurate, these beliefs are often referred to as *cognitive distortions*. The purpose of CBT is to identify and alter cognitive distortions. Cognitive distortions are negative automatic thoughts or inaccurate interpretations an adolescent gives to life events (Wenzel, Gregory, & Beck, 2009). Continuing with the aforementioned example, an individual with depression may inaccurately attribute thoughts of worthlessness to various events. For example, a common adolescent experience is a friend cancelling an event, which is often unrelated to the worth and value of an individual; however, distorted perceptions of this event result in consistent thoughts of self-deprecation. CBT espouses that distorted thinking results in changes in emotions and behaviors. In this case, distorted thoughts of worthlessness resulted in decreased mood and affect. Oftentimes, this may also result in decreased interest or pleasure in behaviors. Next time, the individual may see the friend and become consumed by thoughts of worthlessness and be unable to enjoy the activity that was previously enjoyable. As such, the cognitive distortions result in a negative cycle that affects multiple areas of life. Various modifications to CBT such as rational emotive behavior therapy (REBT; Ellis, 1993) or dialectical behavior therapy (DBT; Linehan, 1993a) have placed more or less emphasis on the cognitions, behaviors, and emotions; however, the core conceptualization and modification of these factors remain.

Cognitive Distortions

Through identification of cognitive distortions, behavioral health providers can help adolescents learn to block negative thoughts and replace them with more positive ones. As cognitive distortions often follow patterns, numerous cognitive distortions have been identified and labeled in recent literature and research. For example, dichotomous or "black and white" thinking is a thinking behavior that fails to recognize the spectrum of possibilities and assumes only opposites, such as success or failure, happy or sad, or healthy or unhealthy. There is no moderation within these extremes. In other words, in between success and failure may be evidence of successes (even if it is miniscule to the adolescent). Further examples of these distortions are found in Table 2.2.

By accurately identifying the distortion, the provider can accurately identify potential techniques and interventions to combat negative-thinking core beliefs an adolescent may have about a subject. Returning to the example of dichotomous thinking, it may be useful for the provider to encourage the client to think on a "spectrum." For example, the provider may ask, "On a scale of 1 to 10, how do you feel?" This may help the consumer begin to understand that it is possible to have an "okay" day rather than only good or bad.

With this in mind, mental illnesses can often be categorized using cognitive thinking patterns unique to specific *DSM-5* disorders (Beck, Steer, & Epstein, 1992). Beck et al. (1992) found that individuals with clinical depression are more likely to ruminate on thoughts of hopelessness and self-deprecation, while individuals with anxiety are more likely to ruminate on thoughts of danger. Similarly, severe rumination on appearances may lead to disordered eating or body dysmorphia. Having such clearly defined characteristics allows the relationship between cognitive distortions and mental illness to be clear. The conceptual understanding of symptom reduction from a CBT lens is directly related to identification and modification of core beliefs (Beck, Rush, Shaw, & Emery, 1979).

ADAPTING TECHNIQUES FOR ADOLESCENTS

While there are numerous interventions developed in the aforementioned theoretical frameworks, there are a number of techniques that are foundational to this approach. These include thought records, cognitive restructuring (CR), behavioral activation (BA)/modification, homework, guided discovery, and assessments. As such, each will be discussed in further detail below. It is important to note that this summary is not comprehensive and serves as an introductory understanding of core techniques and interventions. For those interested in learning more about theoretical approaches, the authors recommend that students and providers become familiar with theory-specific textbooks, trainings, and a cadre of CBT scholarly journals.

Thought Records

Thought records are detailed descriptions of the events, thoughts, feelings, and behaviors of the adolescent and are frequently used strategies (Freeston et al., 1997). This technique has been shown to be effective in the treatment of obsessive and intrusive thoughts (Freeston et al., 1997). The ability for a consumer to develop self-awareness around thoughts and thought patterns is crucial to gaining control over cognitive distortions. The consumer's ability to analyze his or her own thoughts, categorize them, and change unhealthy thought processes to healthier ones is a hallmark of behavioral and cognitive behavioral therapies.

To record thoughts, providers may use a number of approaches including journaling, mapping, and charting. Most commonly, providers often use the ABC model to record thoughts. As shown in the ABC model in Figure 2.1, consumers record the activating events, thoughts or beliefs, and resulting emotions and behaviors. It is recommended that providers review this activity with adolescents during counseling sessions and assign homework where the adolescent continues recording his or her thoughts between sessions. Once recorded, the identified thoughts are analyzed and thinking patterns are identified (with special attention to cognitive distortions and harmful thinking patterns). The activity helps consumers develop skills to self-reflect and learn to identify change and change their thoughts, which then changes their lives.

Table 2.2 Cognitive Distortions

Distortion	Illustration	Therapeutic Technique Examples
All-or-nothing thinking "Dichotomous thinking" is the tendency to look at one's environment in absolutes (Burns, 1980, pp. 36–40).	Mentally healthy adolescents are notorious for "all-or-nothing" thinking. You may have heard an adolescent in your own life say, "This is the worst day ever" or "This is the best day ever" on a regular basis. But this normal tendency to move to cognitive extremes can become harmful for adolescents, particularly those with emotional problems such as depression or anxiety disorders. Adolescent propensity to focus on absolutes can exacerbate negative mental health symptoms.	*Cognitive restructuring* (CR) can be helpful in revealing *all-or-nothing thinking*. (See CR in Techniques of CBT below)
Overgeneralization Interpreting "a single negative event as a never-ending pattern of defeat" (Burns, 1980, pp. 36–40)	A failing grade on a very important test could cause an adolescent to assume that a pattern of failure will begin and dominate his or her life. Test anxiety is a phenomenon that plagues many adolescents, especially those who tend to overgeneralize. Often, the fear associated with test taking is reinforced when he or she "performs less than optimally" (Cizek & Burg, 2006). Overgeneralization may consist of thoughts such as the following: "I always do everything wrong." This type of negative self-talk can initiate a pattern of detrimental thoughts and, ultimately, self-fulfilling behaviors. Providers using cognitive behavioral theory aim to break up this negative cycle and assist the consumer in developing new patterns of positive self-affirmations.	*Guided discovery* (GD) can help consumers evaluate their own faulty beliefs by looking for evidence in their environment that refutes or confirms their assessment. (See GD in Techniques of CBT below)
Mental filter These individuals dwell on the negatives and filter out positive messages in the environment.	An adolescent who blames one parent for an impending divorce may cling to negative experiences with that same parent. This stubborn focus on the negative aspects of the environment can distort interpretations given to relationships.	*Homework assignments* (HA) can be used to help the consumer look at the totality of the relationship. (See HA in Techniques of CBT below)
Disqualifying the positive The individual discounts his or her own positive attributes.	This adolescent may have a tendency to make excuses for his or her achievements. Even when faced with obvious success like winning a drawing contest, this adolescent will insist that the winning was only due to the school's best artist being ill that day.	CR can be used to support the client in identifying instances when he or she is *disqualifying the positive* (DTP) and to teach the client how to replace those thoughts with more accurate ones. (See CR and DTP in Techniques of CBT below)

Mind reading An example of mind reading: "You assume other people are reacting negatively to you when there's no definite proof" (Burns, 1980, pp. 36–40).	Typical adolescents engage in a form of mind reading. When they enter a room, they have a propensity to assume that everyone is talking about them. This is due to a developmental stage called egocentrism. However, anxious adolescents may conclude that not only are other people talking about them but that the content is also negative. In extreme cases, this can feed into more paranoid patterns of thinking or contribute to social phobias.	*Behavioral activation* (BA) can be used to help the consumer set new social goals. Along with CR, BA could provide the consumer with positive experiences. (See BA in Techniques of CBT below)
Fortune telling For example, the person believes that future events will continue to be negative in his or her own life.	Middle school and high school can be intimidating for many adolescents. A single mistake can cause an adolescent to interpret life as a string of ongoing mishaps. For example, a high school senior committed suicide after a sexting picture that she sent to her boyfriend was circulated throughout several schools. She falsely believed that she could never recover and that her future would continue to be haunted by this photo. Most adults can see that this event, while traumatic at the moment, would eventually lose steam and would have failed to affect her life in 10 years. But for this adolescent, her crystal ball could only see a continuation of this humiliation.	Chain analysis (CA) can benefit consumers as they learn to link their thoughts, emotions, and behaviors to damaging choices. This is particularly helpful with suicidal or self-harming clients. (See CA in Evidence-Based Outgrowths Techniques below)
Magnifying/minimizing For example, "You're looking at your faults through the end of the binoculars that makes them appear gigantic and grotesque" (Burns, 1980, pp. 36–40).	An adolescent receiving feedback from a teacher on a research paper stating, "You have excellent ideas but need to firm up your writing skills" may go home and tell her parents that her teacher said that she couldn't write. This adolescent is magnifying the negative comment while minimizing the positive feedback. In another example, an adolescent with a new hair cut may receive three compliments but only remember the one person who said that it made him look like a loser.	GD can help consumers disprove their own faulty beliefs. (See GD in Techniques of CBT below)

(Continued)

Table 2.2 (Continued)

Distortion	Illustration	Therapeutic Technique Examples
Emotional reasoning		
"Reasoning from how we feel" (Burns, 1980, pp. 36–40)	As with several of the cognitive distortions, emotional reasoning may seem to fit many adolescents. Instead of reasoning through cognition, typical adolescents tend to reason through a combination of thoughts and emotions, with emotions sometimes taking the lead. However, most adolescents, with guidance, can temper their emotions and allow their cognitive thinking to prevail. Complicating this developmental stage with a mental illness like depression, anxiety, or impulse control disorders can cause decision making to become even more challenging. In fact, some of these adolescents may rely so heavily on emotions that they make life-threatening decisions. For example, a depressed adolescent may make a decision to commit suicide based on current feelings. A jealous adolescent girl may become so enraged because a boy she likes is showing attention to another girl that she decides to spread destructive rumors. This jealous adolescent is not considering the consequences of bullying another person; she is making decisions based on emotions alone. A final example would be an adolescent who insists that he wants to go to meet new people, but when it comes to participating in a social activity, he gives in to depressive symptoms and stays home watching television instead. These young people tend to make reasonable goals in the counseling session but fail to follow through when challenging emotions kick in.	BA is a strategy providers can use to help consumers change their behaviors by practicing new behaviors. (See BA in Techniques of CBT below)
Should and shouldn'ts		
This individual uses terms like *should*, *shouldn't*, and *must* to admonish himself or herself and others (Burns, 1980, pp. 36–40). For example, "I should have a perfect body and shouldn't have any fat."	Adolescents actually tend to shy away from absolutes like "should" and "shouldn't." These are the messages their parents are usually expressing to them. However, there are adolescents who struggle with obsessive/compulsive thoughts or perfectionistic propensities. Their mental messages may be riddled with shoulds and shouldn'ts.	*Homework assignments* (HA) are useful for consumers who suffer from obsessive thoughts or compulsive behaviors. The provider can ask the client to practice techniques learned in the counseling session at home in real-life situations. For example, during a session, the provider may help the consumer to learn how to identify and label obsessive thoughts and then guide the client through relaxation techniques aimed at diminishing the anxiety produced by the obsessive thoughts. The client can practice this at home and share how it went at the next counseling session (See HA in Techniques of CBT below)

34

Labeling	In the example provided in the definition, this adolescent does not see failing a test as a onetime disappointment. Instead, the adolescent has internalized the behavior and labeled himself or herself as stupid. For the typical adolescent, the reverse is also common. If an adolescent scores a touchdown on the football field, he or she will label himself or herself a star athlete. But for an adolescent suffering from mental illness, the tendency is to force negative labels on oneself: "I am ugly," "I am a loser," or "I am a failure."	GD can be used by asking the client to look for personal examples of opposite situations in his life. For example, if the young person says that he or she is a failure, the provider can help identify a time in which he or she had succeeded. (See GD in Techniques of CBT below)
Using one's behavior (e.g., failing a test) to permanently label oneself—"I am stupid."		
Personalization	An adolescent who blames himself for being raped by a neighbor when it was not his own fault is personalizing. However, this same adolescent may blame a victim he sexually offends for wearing provocative clothing. Personalization can be understood as a way of conveying blame on the wrong person to avoid a more painful reality.	Validation–clarification–redirection (VCR) can be used by the provider to clarify and even challenge the consumer's dysfunctional beliefs about himself and his victim. The provider will validate any instance where the young man takes ownership for his own choices and redirect behavior that is inappropriate. (See VCR in Evidence-Based Outgrowths Techniques below)
For example, "You blame yourself for something that did not prove entirely your fault, or you blame others, overlooking ways in which your own attitudes and behaviors contributed to the problem" (Burns, 1980, pp. 36–40).		

Source. From Burns (1980, pp. 36–40).
Note. CBT, cognitive behavioral therapy.
Note. Fictitious data, for illustration purposes only.

Cognitive Restructuring

CR focuses on identifying cognitive distortions while assisting the adolescent in making more realistic assessments by offering alternative views (Wenzel et al., 2009). While the provider directly assists the adolescent in the early sessions, the goal is for the adolescent to begin to recognize distortions and restructure cognitions independently. Successful restructuring has been shown to be related to symptom reduction associated with depressed mood and anhedonia (Shirk, Crisostomo, Jungbluth, & Gudmundsen, 2013).

Given the ability for symptom reduction to occur using CR, there is potential for CR to be used as both a treatment (e.g., depression) and a preventative technique. By teaching adolescents the skills needed to restructure cognitions, they are better equipped to recognize negative cognitions prior to the unhealthy, negative cycle of thoughts and emotions resulting in disordered thought such as that of a depressive episode.

When considering CR, it is important for providers to also recognize practical uses and applications of the technique. As in the aforementioned example of dichotomous thinking, identifying and restructuring cognitive distortions can be useful for adolescents with depression. When the adolescent makes statements such as "I never do anything right," the provider can challenge this thought by restating the comment as a question. "You *never* do anything right?" Ideally, the adolescent is able to recognize the statement's fallacy and is able to correct his or her apparent cognitive distortion. Incumbent on the adolescent's developmental level and treatment progression, this process can be a simple, direct one that becomes more complex as the cognitive distortions are more entrenched in the adolescent's thinking. Early in treatment, the provider should be prepared to guide the adolescent in answering questions related to thinking by brainstorming situations in which the consumer was right. In doing so, the provider can assist the adolescent in recognizing that it is impossible to "never" do anything, identifying instances of the "I never do anything right" statement. In this instance, the provider could intervene with "Would it be an accurate statement to say you did 'the right' thing by seeking help about your experience of hopelessness? . . . And if so, that would be at least one 'right thing' that you've done. Right?" Through the continued use of this technique, the consumer gains the ability to challenge his or her thoughts independently using Socratic questioning to identify fallacies within the distorted cognition.

Behavioral Activation/Modification

BA/modification is an effective intervention targeting behavioral cycles created by cognitive distortions (Gaynor & Harris, 2008). When an individual with depression expresses thoughts of worthlessness, a corresponding deflated mood and affect may follow. As a result of this overall mood, adolescents may withdraw from relationships. Unproductive, covert behaviors such as hopelessness, worthlessness, or lack of interest result in destructive cycles such as furthered activating events (e.g., cancelling social functions), which result in continued distortions and emotional consequences.

In BA, the provider works collaboratively with the consumer to develop "value-based activities that elicit a sense of pleasure and accomplishment" (Gawrysiak, Nicholas, & Hopko, 2009). In other words, the provider and the adolescent consumer identify specific activities and behaviors that may interrupt the negative-thinking cycle discussed earlier. Behavior goals are then established and monitored over a specified amount of time. These goals might include the establishment of a consistent exercise routine, development of consistent self-care strategies, or participation in a social function. The activation approach is idiographic and focuses on concrete or observable changes that influence functioning and give special attention to the unique contingencies within the individual's environment that maintain his or her behavior. It is important to note that BA goes beyond simply increasing pleasurable events and also examines the functions and contingencies of behavior (e.g., what behaviors reinforce vs. punish; Hopko, Lejuez, Ruggiero, & Eifert, 2003).

Given the potential damaging nature of behavioral tendencies, BA/modification is considered specifically applicable to adolescents. Not only can damaging behaviors such as avoidance or withdrawal affect the mood of the client, but it may also affect developmental skills necessary during adolescence. In other instances, unhealthy behaviors such as disordered eating may have lasting effects on the physical health and well-being of the adolescent as well. Given this, consultation with various professionals on the health of the adolescent may be necessary prior to engaging in various activities.

To increase buy-in with adolescent consumers, the collaborative determination of healthy activities and behaviors is particularly important. Insisting on a specific activity despite an adolescent's attitude can be detrimental to the therapeutic alliance; however, the provider's lack of monitoring behaviors may result in reinforcement of unhealthy behaviors such as self-injury or substance use (Exercise 2.2). The process of setting appropriate and attainable goals for adolescents needs to be a careful and collaborative process involving the adolescent, the provider, and the parent (as appropriate).

Homework

Homework includes any activities or worksheets discussed in counseling for the adolescent consumer to take home, complete, or practice in real-life situations. Homework is an essential and unique part of CBT as it allows the adolescent to practice skills and increase mastery and contributes to the effectiveness of the treatment (LeBeau, Davies, Culver, & Craske, 2013). This may in part be due to the need for adolescent participation both in counseling sessions as well as outside the sessions. Homework is especially important when a provider does not utilize psychotropic medication (Simons et al., 2012). Simons and colleagues (2012) found that homework completion significantly predicted clinical improvement, decreased self-reported hopelessness, suicidality, and self-reported depression of adolescents with depression who received CBT intervention.

Adolescents may have cognitive distortions regarding parental separation and divorce. As an example, a provider may assign homework to an adolescent whose parents are divorcing in order to decrease feelings of blame surrounding the divorce. The provider may ask the adolescent to make a list of positive interactions experienced with each parent. In doing so, the provider helps the adolescent to remove the "mental filter" (one that neglects positive ways of thinking about the separation) affecting the client's ability to focus on positive aspects about the relationship. Other examples of homework may include journaling, thought tracking, records of BA, or making lists. Homework can be easily adapted to the situation and needs of the consumer, and a wide variety of resources are available.

Exercise 2.2

Mind Reading

Table 2.2 provides several examples of cognitive distortions along with a corresponding illustration and technique. Read the definition of *mind reading* and the corresponding illustration. Provide three clinically appropriate goals related to *behavior activation* that may be appropriate for the adolescent in this illustration.

When considering specific applications with adolescents in the use of homework, providers must recognize that an adolescent may be less motivated to do homework when mandated to counseling versus being self-referred. Furthermore, normal developmental desires for autonomy as well as typical lack of motivation toward homework may affect efficacy of this technique. Engaging in a power struggle with a young person over therapeutic homework can be counterproductive and can damage the therapeutic relationship, diminishing the value of in-session interventions. Monitoring the client's reaction to homework and its perceived effectiveness is crucial. It is recommended that providers attempt to avoid power struggles over homework compliance with an adolescent consumer (Exercise 2.3). To increase efficacy, homework may be assigned in collaboration with parents when appropriate.

Guided Discovery

Guided discovery is a process of Socratic questioning to challenge maladaptive beliefs (Jones & Butman, 2011). This can include asking consumers to gather information that proves or disproves their assumptions. In working with a consumer who insists that he or she always does everything wrong, the provider may ask the adolescent for information about his or her academic grades, interpersonal relationships, and overall strengths. If the adolescent is able to identify any positive strength, the provider is able to disprove

the adolescent's rationale of failure. Furthermore, the provider can also teach both the parents and the adolescent to begin to use Socratic questioning to dispel distorted thinking.

Assessments

Assessments can be helpful in diagnosing mental health disorders and useful measures for conceptualization of treatment. Many measures are adapted for use with children and adolescents. For example, the Beck Depression Inventory-II (Beck, Steer, & Brown, 1996) developed by The Beck Institute is normed for those 13 years of age and older. The Child Depression Inventory 2 (Kovacs, 2010) developed by Dr. Maria Kovacs is a comprehensive assessment that can be used for children and adolescents of ages 7 to 17 years. Other assessments including intelligence tests, personality inventories, and psychiatric measures are also valuable in counseling adolescents; however, considerations for the normed age of any assessment must be made prior to use with children and adolescents.

DEVELOPMENTAL CONSIDERATIONS IN ADAPTING TO ADOLESCENTS

Given that many of the theoretical approaches were originally identified as a treatment intervention for adult clients, it is important for providers to consider the developmental implications with adolescents. In general, adolescence is often

Exercise 2.3

Mental Filter

Table 2.2 provides several examples of cognitive distortions along with a corresponding illustration and technique. Read the definition of *mental filter* and the corresponding illustration. Provide two clinically appropriate homework assignments that you could assign to the adolescent described in the illustration.

marked by periods of "storm and stress" and normal developmental distress that are typically resolved without intervention (Sigelman & Rider, 2012, p. 533). Adolescent development may include crises of self-esteem, identity confusion and formation, relational distress, and transitional stress (Sigelman & Rider, 2012). Unfortunately, this period is often marked with transitions and stresses that can go awry and result in anomalous conditions such as substance abuse, anxiety, depression, eating disorders, or suicidal ideation. Providers have the task to differentiate between thought patterns and ruminations that are typical to normal adolescent development and those that are atypical.

An integral part of behavioral and cognitive behavioral approaches is the cognitive development and abilities of the consumer. Given the need for adolescents to reflect on their thoughts and recognize interrelationships between cognitions, emotions, and behaviors, the provider's assessment of these developmental aspects is critical. For this reason, counselors of adolescents understand development as it pertains to thought. In his model of cognitive development, Jean Piaget described adolescence as the beginning of a formal operational thought stage. Formal operational thought is characterized by the following: abstract thinking, scientific analysis, and hypothetical–deductive reasoning (Piaget, 1972; Piaget & Inhelder, 1969). In other words, individuals begin to manipulate not tangible items but ideas, concepts, and beliefs during adolescence (Sigelman & Rider, 2012). This ability forms the basis of identifying, challenging, and responding to one's thoughts or beliefs; however, adolescents vary drastically in development speed. Many will not formally acquire abstract thinking abilities until later adolescence or early adulthood, and the acquisition of these abilities is somewhat dependent on experiences and culture (Sigelman & Rider, 2012).

As such, it is imperative that providers conduct an initial assessment, whether formal or informal, of the adolescent's level of cognitive functioning as well as continue to monitor appropriateness of interventions throughout the process.

Providers must be flexible in psycho-education, intervention, and relational approaches and quickly adapt to adolescents' cognitive capacities and mental development level. Furthermore, understanding the potential modifications of treatment is crucial for providers.

MODIFICATIONS OF THEORETICAL APPROACHES

As adolescents are still maturing and developing intellectually, there may be occasions when modifications need to be made to theoretical-based techniques that reflect the needs of younger adolescents. Simple modifications can be easily made while maintaining the foundations of the approach (i.e., thoughts are helpful or harmful, behaviors are outgrowths of thoughts, changed thoughts generate changed behaviors).

When therapeutic modifications are made to reflect the developmental needs of the consumers, outcomes have been shown to be positive. For example, providers who made modifications to the structure of CBT, such as providing less structure in the first session, found that adolescents were more motivated to participate in the therapeutic process in later sessions (Jungbluth & Shirk, 2009). Furthermore, providers who were less focused on rigid adherence to the structure of CBT were perceived as more flexible (in areas of session structure, ordering of content addressed, time spent on relationship development, or specific goals identified), attentive, and supportive of their young clients (Jungbluth & Shirk, 2009). For example, providers who made modifications to the structure of CBT found that adolescents were more motivated to participate in the therapeutic process in later sessions than in earlier counseling sessions (Jungbluth & Shirk, 2009).

Flexibility within the counseling session is crucial in working with consumers; however, it is of particular importance in working with adolescents. Providers must use best judgment as well as consultation when necessary to adjust structure to best meet the needs of adolescents as well as keep them interested and involved in the therapeutic process.

In addition to structural adjustments, modifications can also be made in techniques and interventions used while maintaining the efficacy of treatment (Weersing, Rozenman, & Gonzalez, 2009). For this reason, it is important for providers to develop a wide array of techniques and interventions to use depending on the adolescent, the setting, and treatment goals. In example, providers may choose to utilize board games, books, or toys in various stages of counseling to help gain information, develop the therapeutic alliance, or achieve goals. Modifications to techniques and interventions should reflect careful consideration of the stage of development. A provider may be able to utilize Socratic questioning to challenge an older adolescent's cognitive distortions but may need to gain material evidence to challenge a younger adolescent's cognitive distortions. This simple modification may better match the cognitive development of the adolescent consumer.

In addition to considerations for development and personal differences, it is also important to study the multicultural aspects as well. For example, given CBT's efficacy, brevity, cost-effectiveness, and ability to be paired with medication (Weersing et al., 2009; Weisz et al., 2009), it has a great deal of appeal; however, the structured, directive approach may potentially be incongruent with some cultural values. Cultural values that are crucial to assess prior to the establishment of goals and direction of treatment include collectivist versus individualist values, the level of direction provided by the provider, and meaning given to authority figures. While this is not all-inclusive, each of these factors influences culturally sensitive goals, conversation, and treatment approaches. Furthermore, special considerations regarding cultural differences between the parent and the adolescent may also need to be addressed given the potential for values and goals to conflict (e.g., dating behaviors). For this reason, providers must take precautions and make considerations to the appropriateness of various exercises and interventions given the culture of the consumer; however, it is important to note that CBT with adolescents has been shown to be effective in numerous international settings (Abela et al., 2011; Naeem, Gobbi, Ayub, & Kingdon, 2010; Weersing et al., 2009; Weisz et al., 2009). This efficacy illustrates the ability for culturally appropriate modifications to be made.

Overall, general trends in research have shown that minor modifications to CBT do not appear to change the effectiveness of the approach, enhancing its generalizability. Providers working with adolescents should be cognizant of the cognitive ability of their adolescent consumers during the assessment stage, utilize this information to guide the modifications that are made, and maintain a collaborative relationship with the adolescents throughout their change processes.

EVIDENCE-BASED OUTGROWTHS

Evidence-based treatments are techniques that are modified versions of the original therapy but have in themselves been researched and shown to be statistically useful in therapeutic treatment. Given the efficacy and popularity of behavioral and cognitive behavioral approaches, several theoretical outgrowths of the approach have been developed. These approaches maintain the conceptual framework of its original theoretical framework while modifying the emphasis on treatment, structural approach, and techniques and interventions used. Oftentimes, these outgrowths are developed to reflect specific population needs. While there are numerous outgrowths, the summary below includes DBT, REBT, trauma-focused cognitive behavioral therapy (TF-CBT), mode deactivation therapy (MDT), and acceptance and commitment therapy. As these are among the most commonly used and recognized branches of CBT (Dobson, 2010). Furthermore, each of these approaches has been used with adolescents with proven success in the areas of symptom reduction including decreasing high-risk behaviors (Gonzalez et al., 2004; Kinch & Kress, 2012),

Figure 2.2   Chain Analysis

pathological symptomatology (Cohen, Deblinger, Mannarino, & Steer, 2004; Gonzalez et al., 2004; Kinch & Kress, 2012), and use of medication (McDonell et al., 2010) as well as increasing overall functioning (McDonell et al., 2010) and academic performance (Gonzalez et al., 2004).

Dialectical Behavior Therapy

DBT was originally conceived by Marsha Linehan (1993a) as a means of treating borderline personality disorder. The comprehensive, collaborative treatment approach emphasizes the importance of emotional regulation using CBT techniques as well as concepts adapted from Eastern meditation such as meditation and mindfulness (Kinch & Kress, 2012). The goal of DBT is to decrease self-injury, noncompliance with counseling, and other high-risk behaviors (Kinch & Kress, 2012). Common DBT principles include mindfulness (attending to one's thoughts and emotions), acceptance (accepting one's emotions, thoughts, and life events), and control (gaining control over one's own choices; Linehan, 1993b).

There are four hierarchical phases of DBT (Nickelson, 2013). The first phase focuses on gaining control of life-threatening and harmful behaviors. The second phase focuses on emotional processing and experience to reduce traumatic stress. The third stage focuses on everyday behaviors and life skills, and the fourth stage focuses on transcendence and capacity for joy (Nickelson, 2013). During each of these stages, the provider utilizes four basic modules: (1) core mindfulness, (2) emotional regulation, (3) interpersonal effectiveness, and (4) distress tolerance (Chapman, 2006). Various interventions may be used throughout treatment including chain analysis, a widely used intervention detailing the chain of events (thoughts, emotions, and behaviors) leading to a given behavior such as self-injury (Kinch & Kress, 2012). An illustration of the chain of events is found in Figure 2.2. As with the ABC model, it is recommended that providers help consumers process through each of these events to increase self-awareness (Exercise 2.4).

DBT has been shown to have promising effects in the treatment of borderline personality disorder when compared with other modalities of treatment (Neacsiu, Lungu, Harned, Rizvi, & Linehan, 2014). In a study of adolescents, improvements in overall functioning as measured by the Global Assessment of Functioning Scale and decreases in psychotropic medications

Exercise 2.4

Fortune Telling

Table 2.2 provides several examples of cognitive distortions along with a corresponding illustration and technique. Read the definition of *fortune telling* and the corresponding illustration. Create one or more *chain analysis* that would represent the adolescent in this illustration.

given for conditions related to long-term psychiatric inpatient settings such as suicidal self-injurious behavior were shown (McDonell et al., 2010). It was also found that the adolescents receiving DBT showed significantly fewer self-injurious behaviors (McDonell et al., 2010). Given the historic difficulty in treating borderline personality disorder, the demonstrated efficacy of DBT despite therapeutically incongruent behaviors such as anger, avoidance, and noncompliance has made this approach increasingly popular among practitioners.

Rational Emotive Behavior Therapy

REBT was founded by Dr. Albert Ellis in 1955 and is analogous to CBT, engaging the interrelationship between cognition, emotion, and behavior (Neenan & Dryden, 2006); REBT, however, is unique in that the approach emphasizes a greater level of introspection. REBT emphasizes the emotional consequence as a result of irrational belief systems as well as the importance of rational belief in mental health and wellness (Aggarwal, 2014). Similar to CBT, REBT also uses a model in understanding this relationship but includes additional steps in the process. Specifically, REBT espouses to the ABCDE model in which A is critical A (activating event), B is irrational beliefs, C is emotional and behavioral consequences, D is disputing, and E is effective outlook (Neenan & Dryden, 2006). In essence, the model encompasses both thought identification and also CR. Throughout this model, REBT emphasizes the maintenance of emotional health rather than the formation of unhealthy patterns of cognition and emotion (Neenan & Dryden, 2006).

Most important, REBT has shown promising effects in the treatment of children and adolescents in a meta-analysis examining 19 applicable studies (Gonzalez et al., 2004). REBT was shown to reduce symptoms such as anxiety, disruptive behaviors, irrationality, self-concept, and grade point average across settings; however, children tended to have higher effect sizes than adolescents (Gonzalez et al., 2004). It is, however, considered a generally acceptable treatment in work with adolescents.

Trauma-Focused Cognitive Behavioral Therapy

TF-CBT is a branch of CBT developed specifically for the treatment of traumatized children and adolescents by Drs. Judy Cohen, Esther Deblinger, and Anthony Mannarino (National Crime Victims Research and Treatment Center [NCVC], 2005). TF-CBT utilizes the conceptual framework of CBT in combination with current understanding of trauma to help alleviate traumatic stress in children and adolescents, and it has also been adapted for adult, family, and marriage counseling settings (NCVC, 2005). TF-CBT offers a manual for providers utilizing the concept as the content and approach are rather structured, but the approach stresses the importance of creative adaptations to best meet the needs of consumers (NCVC, 2005).

TF-CBT espouses nine sequential topics for providers to address across sessions: (1) psychoeducation, (2) stress management, (3) affect expression and modulation, (4) cognitive coping, (5) creating the trauma narrative, (6) cognitive processing, (7) behavior management training, (8) parent–child sessions, and (9) evaluation (NCVC, 2005). The purpose of this sequential structure is to provide adolescents and parents with the necessary coping and processing skills to better equip them to handle the intense emotions and overwhelming cognitions associated with the trauma. By doing so, the provider is able to process the trauma with the consumer in an emotionally controlled environment in conjunction with using already taught techniques such as progressive muscle relaxation and deep breathing (NCVC, 2005).

TF-CBT has consistently shown strong, positive effects in the treatment of trauma-related stress and disorders (Cohen et al., 2004), resulting in its recommendations as a best practice by the U.S. Department of Justice, National Child Traumatic Stress Network, and Substance Abuse and Mental Health Services Administration (NCVC, 2005). Numerous training opportunities are available for providers both in-person and online. CBT providers working with traumatized youth are strongly encouraged to seek out these opportunities prior to beginning counseling.

Mode Deactivation Therapy

MDT was developed explicitly to treat young, male, conduct-disordered clients, including sexual offenders (Apsche, Bass, & Backlund, 2012). The purpose of MDT is to help adolescents to modify their behaviors, regulate their emotions, and overall become more self-aware. Early intervention is a key aspect to MDT.

MDT is a structured outgrowth of CBT, embracing the importance of changing negative thinking and destructive behavior while additionally providing emphasis on motivation (Thoder & Cautilli, 2011). These factors contribute to the individual's beliefs and schemas also referred to as "modes." The primary goal of MDT is to reduce destructive behaviors that stem from dysfunctional modes and to keep the young men in their homes and out of correctional institutions or residential treatment by providing individualized treatment.

Validation–clarification–redirection (VCR) is a key treatment technique used in MDT. The goal of VCR is to redirect offensive behaviors and clarify dysfunctional beliefs about the environment that were learned at an early age, while validating positive thinking patterns and behaviors (Apsche et al., 2012).

MDT has demonstrated effectiveness in the treatment of aggressive adolescent males ranging in age from 14 to 18 years (Apsche, Bass, & DiMeo, 2011; Apsche et al., 2012; Thoder & Cautilli, 2011). There was a reduction in a variety of behaviors including violent behaviors, sexual offenses, and/or antisocial traits. MDT has proved to be successful in the treatment of conduct-disordered youth demonstrated by decreases in the recidivism rates, antisocial traits, anger, aggression, and overall reduction of internal and external symptomatology. In addition, the use of VCR showed promise in the treatment of aggression (Apsche et al., 2012).

Acceptance and Commitment Therapy

Acceptance and commitment therapy (ACT) utilizes mindfulness as a way to help adolescents become cognizant of their own thoughts and emotions (Bass, van Nevel, & Swart, 2014). Similar to CBT, the provider encourages the adolescent to be aware of negative thoughts and emotions, but ACT does not focus on rejecting these cognitions; instead, the focus is on helping adolescents to accept them. ACT encourages the adolescent to detach from the emotional feelings that these cognitions provoke and approach them with objectivity (Bass et al., 2014). Once the adolescents accept their own cognitions, they are able to use mindfulness techniques to change their thoughts and beliefs into more positive ones. Systematically, the adolescent is asked to decide whether a thought or feeling is functional or dysfunctional. Then the adolescent commits to changing dysfunctional cognitions into more useful ones (Bass et al., 2014). In a review of CBT, DBT, MDT, and ACT, Bass et al. (2014) found that there were more similarities than differences; however, there were a few notable variations. One variation is that MDT, DBT, and ACT are less judgmental than CBT and focus on allowing the adolescent to have more control over decision making. This can be particularly helpful for adolescents who have not sought out treatment on their own. Another difference is that DBT and ACT use mindfulness as a core component. Finally, each of the outgrowths described previously makes modifications to CBT, which can increase their efficacy with specific populations. For example, MDT has proved to be more effective than CBT with adolescents displaying aggressive behaviors, and DBT has been more effective when treating personality disordered clients (Bass et al., 2014). In general, the combination of these outgrowths with CBT seems to be consistently effective (Apsche et al., 2012). Competent providers will be aware of their specific adolescent's diagnostic presentation and select modifications to CBT that best address the needs of their consumers.

CASE CONSIDERATIONS

To apply knowledge learned, a case scenario and exercise have been included. While reading this case scenario (Case Scenario 2.1), it is important for providers to use CBT as a framework to both conceptualize the consumer as well as guide the treatment progress. Consider the suggested structure of CBT as well as any adaptations that may be needed for the client's multicultural identity and development needs.

IMPLICATIONS FOR COUNSELING ADOLESCENTS

Clinical Review of Case

When making a clinical assessment, it is important to consider the adolescent's previous constitution as compared with his or her current demeanor. Previously, James was active in sports and social activities with his peers. However, after the announcement of his parents' divorce, James has become withdrawn and shows little interest in athletics or social activities. When an adolescent shows drastic changes in interests, this could be indicative of either an adjustment disorder or depression. The provider would want to conduct a thorough assessment to determine which diagnosis is more appropriate. The Beck Depression Inventory-II or Children's Depression Inventory (1996) is a widely researched assessment in the diagnosis of depression for consumers 13 years of age and older. The provider could administer the assessment if he or she is appropriately trained or refer to a competent provider for testing. A diagnostic interview consistent with CBT would include identifying cognitive distortions that James has had using the *ABC model* to determine the corresponding emotional consequences. Since James's distortions

---

Case Scenario 2.1

James

James is a 16-year-old high school junior. He has been actively involved in athletics, including football and track. Unfortunately, James has struggled with his school work and has been placed on academic probation. James has always had difficulty with reading and writing, but his previously acceptable grades have dropped considerably. This may be due to his difficulty in understanding abstract concepts addressed in class. James has also recently gotten into trouble for drinking alcohol with his friends at a party. Over the past weekend, James's parents have announced that they will be divorcing after 13 years of marriage.

James has not taken this news very well and has experienced extreme feelings of guilt and sadness about the divorce. While he wants the best for his parents, he feels as though his recent lack of academic success and trouble with alcohol have contributed to his parents' conflict. This has caused James to withdraw from normal activities. He appears to have little interest in playing ball outside or going out with friends. He has made promises to improve academically and spends considerably more time doing his homework. However, his grades have not improved much. James appears to get frustrated when doing his homework and makes comments like "I am so stupid" and "I never do anything right." Given his change in mood, his parents brought him in for counseling (Exercise 2.5).

Exercise 2.5

Case Exercise

1. Consider the ABC model. What events, beliefs, and emotional consequences might James be experiencing?
2. What goals specific to CBT might be appropriate for James?
3. What interventions might you want to use in your work with James?
4. Given James's developmental stage, consider the factors related to adaptations and techniques for treatment.

are more directed toward himself—"I am so stupid" and "I never do anything right"—the emotional consequence may in fact be sadness or depression. Asking James to conduct *thought records* could help the provider to isolate negative patterns of thinking that could be influencing James's acceptance of his parents' divorce in a more positive way.

In addition, James was caught drinking alcohol with his friends. At the surface level, this appears to be experimental in nature. There was no mention of alcohol or drug paraphernalia being found in James home, which would be indicative of James having moved from experimental drinking to dependence. However, the provider should ensure that a substance abuse screening is conducted.

Finally, James has had academic issues both prior to and after the announcement of his parents' divorce. Therefore, James could benefit from an educational evaluation to determine if he needs academic intervention. This could be

requested by the parents in writing through the school district (Exercise 2.6). The outcome of this evaluation may affect the type of modifications to CBT that are selected for James.

Application of Ethics

Counseling adolescents creates unique ethical issues. These issues include deciding who can sign for treatment (i.e., parents, adolescents, social workers, foster parents), what information is shared with guardians, and who is entitled to the records. Providers should also be acquainted with ethical issues surrounding therapeutic treatment decisions. Most therapeutic techniques are researched with adults first. Therefore, selection of therapeutic interventions and settings for adolescent counseling can be riddled with ethical landmines.

Deciding the setting for CBT with adolescents is an important consideration. Take, for example, providing CBT in a school setting, home setting,

Exercise 2.6

Therapeutic Goals

After reading Case Scenario 2.1 and reading the clinical review, develop three therapeutic goals for James. Discuss three CBT techniques that would be helpful in achieving the stated goals. Would you specifically use these techniques to achieve the stated goals? Be specific.

or through cyber-counseling. These settings require that additional safeguards be instituted to reduce risk to the adolescent. In addition, the confidentiality agreement may need to be individualized to reflect unique environmental threats to privacy for each of these settings.

Although developmental modifications of therapeutic techniques may be necessary in the treatment of adolescents, the modification of CBT techniques may reduce its effectiveness. Major modifications to CBT may require additional research and disclosure. According to Affordable Care Act guidelines, consumers should be informed and permitted to refuse any experimental treatment (Patient Protection and Affordable Care Act, 2010).

Selecting culturally appropriate interventions is another ethical consideration. The selection of therapeutic techniques for minority adolescents should be deliberative as not all therapeutic approaches are effective with diverse populations. CBT has been effective with youth of different cultural backgrounds. In a study that used a modified version of CBT with Mexican adolescents, the outcomes of treatment were deemed successful (Wood, Chiu, Hwang, Jacobs, & Ifekwunigwe, 2008). In another study, Weisz et al. (2009) found CBT to be successful with ethnically diverse youth. Seventy-five percent of the youth (white and nonwhite) no longer showed signs of depression after treatment using CBT. CBT also improved parent alliance and reduced the need for psychotropic medication, while also being briefer and more cost-effective (Weisz et al., 2009).

Although CBT and its corresponding interventions are among the most widely researched, using CBT with adolescents, changing the setting, modifying techniques, or utilizing experimental outgrowth methods could require additional research and disclosure. Providers should weigh the risk of making any modifications with the benefits that it affords.

SUMMARY

Given its proven efficacy and adaptability, CBT and other behavioral approaches have proved useful within a variety of settings and populations. There are several characteristics of behavioral and cognitive behavioral approaches that make it conducive to the treatment of adolescents, including its ability to be modified to reflect developmental concerns, its efficacy in the treatment of a wide variety of issues, and its structure. By addressing cognitions, emotions, and behaviors, the adapted approaches offer a more holistic approach to problems than do modalities limited to behavior or cognition, perhaps contributing to its efficacy with numerous disorders and problems. Furthermore, CBT has become one of the most popular treatment modalities used today, with increased pressure from health care to shorten the length of treatment and demonstrate efficacy in order to improve affordability and accessibility. The popularity of behavioral and cognitive behavioral approaches has also resulted in the development of several theoretical branches and approaches, including DBT, REBT, TF-CBT, and ACT among others. Given this, it is imperative that counselors-in-training as well as other providers have a thorough understanding of the theoretical frameworks most commonly used with adolescents.

KEYSTONES

- Behavioral and cognitive behavioral approaches emphasize the interrelationship of cognitions, emotions, and behaviors and focus on the identification and modification of maladaptive core beliefs and cognitive distortions.

- CBT has been shown to be effective in the treatment of adolescents with a wide variety of concerns and can be adapted to a variety of settings, including inpatient, community agencies, schools, home-based, and e-counseling.

- Outgrowths of behavioral and cognitive behavioral approaches such as DBT, REBT, TF-CBT, and ACT have developed with proven efficacy in response to the varying needs of populations.

- CBT is among the most commonly utilized theoretical approaches, given its efficacy, adaptability, and affordability, and thus, providers should have a working knowledge and understanding of the approach.

- The ABC model posits that the initial or activating event automatically triggers thoughts and that the thoughts are rooted in internal belief systems that create patterns of either healthy cognitions resulting in positive/beneficial growth or unhealthy thought cognitions resulting in pathological or detrimental thinking.

- Cognitive distortions are utilized to create a false pretense of circumstances, allowing the adolescent "permission" to act out his or her negative behavior.

- Behavioral and cognitive behavioral techniques such as thought records, CR, BA/modification, guided discovery, homework, and assessments are common techniques in decreasing irrational thoughts and fears.

REFERENCES

Abela, J. R., Stolow, D., Mineka, S., Yao, S., Zhu, X. Z., & Hankin, B. L. (2011). Cognitive vulnerability to depressive symptoms in adolescents in urban and rural Hunan, China: A multiwave longitudinal study. *Journal of Abnormal Psychology, 120*(4), 765–778. doi:10.1037/a0025295

Aggarwal, I. (2014). Albert Ellis' theory of personality and its influence on youth smoking: A critical review. *Canadian Young Scientist Journal, 7*(1), 43–48. doi:10.13034/cysj-2014-001

American Psychiatric Association. (2013). *Diagnostic and statistical manual of mental disorders* (5th ed.). Washington, DC: Author.

Apsche, J. A., Bass, C. K., & Backlund, B. (2012). Mediation analysis of mode deactivation therapy (MDT). *The Behavior Analyst Today, 13*(2), 1–10.

Apsche, J. A., Bass, C. K., & DiMeo, L. (2011). Mode deactivation therapy (MDT) comprehensive meta-analysis. *International Journal of Behavioral Consultation and Therapy, 7*(1), 47–54.

Bass, C., van Nevel, J., & Swart, J. (2014). A comparison between dialectical behavior therapy, mode deactivation therapy, cognitive behavioral therapy, and acceptance and commitment therapy in the treatment of adolescents. *International Journal of Behavioral Consultation and Therapy, 9*(2), 4–8.

Beck, A. T., Rush, A. J., Shaw, B., & Emery, G. (1979). *Cognitive therapy of depression.* New York, NY: Guilford Press.

Beck, A. T., Steer, R. A., & Brown, G. K. (1996). *Beck Depression Inventory-II (BDI-II).* Upper Saddle River, NJ: Pearson.

Beck, A. T., Steer, R. A., & Epstein, N. (1992). Self-concept dimensions of clinically depressed and anxious outpatients. *Journal of Clinical Psychology, 48*(4), 423–432.

Beck, J. S. (2011). *Cognitive behavior therapy: Basics and beyond* (2nd ed.). New York, NY: Guilford Press.

Burns, D. D. (1980). *Feeling good: The new mood therapy.* New York, NY: William Morrow.

Butler, A. C., Chapman, J. E., Forman, E. M., & Beck, A. T. (2006). The empirical status of cognitive-behavioral therapy: A review of meta-analyses. *Clinical Psychology Review, 26*(1), 17–31. doi:10.1016/j.cpr.2005.07.003

Chapman, A. L. (2006). Acceptance and mindfulness in behavior therapy: A comparison of dialectical behavior therapy and acceptance and commitment therapy. *International Journal of Behavioral Consultation and Therapy, 2*(3), 308–313.

Cizek, G., & Burg, S. (2006). *Addressing test anxiety in a high stakes environment.* Thousand Oaks, CA: Corwin.

Cohen, J. A., Deblinger, E., Mannarino, A. P., & Steer, R. A. (2004). A multi-site, randomized controlled trial for sexually abused children with PTSD symptoms: *Journal of the American Academy of Child & Adolescent Psychiatry, 43,* 393–402.

Dobson, K. S. (2010). *Handbook of cognitive-behavioral therapies* (3rd ed.). New York, NY: Guilford Press.

Ellis, A. (1993). Reflections on RET. *Journal of Counseling and Clinical Psychology, 61*(2), 199–201.

Freeston, M. H., Ladouceur, R., Gagnon, F., Thibodeau, N., Rhéaume, J., Letarte, H., & Bujold, A. (1997). Cognitive-behavioral treatment of obsessive thoughts: A controlled study. *Journal of Consulting and Clinical Psychology, 65*(3), 405–413.

Gawrysiak, M., Nicholas, C., & Hopko, D. R. (2009). Behavioral activation for moderately depressed university students: Randomized controlled trial. *Journal of Counseling Psychology, 56*(3), 468–475. doi:10.1037/a0016383

Gaynor, S. T., & Harris, A. (2008). Single-participant assessment of treatment mediators strategy description and examples from a behavioral activation intervention for depressed adolescents. *Behavior Modification, 32*(3), 372–402.

Gonzalez, J. E., Nelson, J. R., Gutkin, T. B., Saunders, A., Galloway, A., & Shwery, C. S. (2004). Rational emotive therapy with children and adolescents: A meta-analysis. *Journal of Emotional and Behavioral Disorders, 12*(4), 222–235.

Hopko, D. R., Lejuez, C. W., Ruggiero, K. J., & Eifert, G. H. (2003). Contemporary behavioral activation treatments for depression: Procedures, principles, and progress. *Clinical Psychology Review, 23*(5), 699–717.

Jones, S., & Butman, R. (2011). *Modern psychotherapies* (2nd ed.). Downers Grove, IL: InterVarsity Press.

Jungbluth, N. J., & Shirk, S. R. (2009). Therapist strategies for building involvement in cognitive-behavioral therapy for adolescent depression. *Journal of Consulting and Clinical Psychology, 77*(6), 1179–1184. doi:10.1037/a0017325

Kinch, S., & Kress, V. E. (2012). The creative use of chain analysis techniques in counseling clients who engage in non-suicidal self-injury. *Journal of Creativity in Mental Health, 7*(4), 343–354. doi:10.1080/15401383.2012.739960

Kovacs, M. (2010). *Children's Depression Inventory* (2nd ed.). Tonwanda, NY: Multi-Health Systems.

LeBeau, R. T., Davies, C. D., Culver, N. C., & Craske, M. G. (2013). Homework compliance counts in cognitive-behavioral therapy. *Cognitive Behaviour Therapy, 42*(3), 171–179. doi:10.1080/16506073.2013.763286

Linehan, M. M. (1993a). *Cognitive-behavioural treatment of borderline personality disorder.* New York, NY: Guilford Press.

Linehan, M. M. (1993b). *Skills training manual for treating borderline personality disorder.* New York, NY: Guilford Press.

McDonell, M. G., Tarantino, J., Dubose, A. P., Matestic, P., Steinmetz, K., Galbreath, H., & McClellan, J. M. (2010). A pilot evaluation of dialectical behavioural therapy in adolescent long-term inpatient care. *Child & Adolescent Mental Health, 15*(4), 193–196. doi:10.1111/j.1475-3588.2010.00569.x

Naeem, F., Gobbi, M., Ayub, M., & Kingdon, D. (2010). Psychologists experience of cognitive behaviour therapy in a developing country: A qualitative study from Pakistan. *International Journal of Mental Health Systems, 4*(2). doi:10.1186/1752-4458-4-2

National Crime Victims Research and Treatment Center. (2005). *TF-CBTWeb: A web based learning course for trauma-focused cognitive behavioral therapy.* Charleston, SC: Author.

Neacsiu, A. D., Lungu, A., Harned, M. S., Rizvi, S. L., & Linehan, M. M. (2014). Impact of dialectical behavior therapy versus community treatment by experts on emotional experience, expression, and acceptance in borderline personality disorder. *Behaviour Research and Therapy, 53,* 47–54. doi:10.1016/j.brat.2013.12.004

Neenan, M., & Dryden, W. (2006). *Rational emotive behavior therapy: In a nut shell.* London, England: Sage.

Neisser, U. (1991). Two perceptually given aspects of the self and their development. *Developmental Review, 11*(3), 197–209.

Nickelson, C. A. (2013). *Key elements of dialectical behavior therapy* (Master of Social Work Clinical Research Papers, Paper No. 241). Retrieved from http://sophia.stkate.edu/msw_papers/241

Patient Protection and Affordable Care Act, 42 U.S.C. § 18001 (2010).

Piaget, J. (1972). Intellectual evolution from adolescence to adulthood. *Human development, 15*(1), 1–12.

Piaget, J., & Inhelder, B. (1969). *The psychology of the child.* New York, NY: Basic Books.

Reddy, L. A., De Thomas, C. A., Newman, E., & Chun, V. (2009). School-based prevention and intervention programs for children with emotional disturbance: A review of treatment components and methodology. *Psychology in the Schools, 46*(2), 132–153.

Shirk, S. R., Crisostomo, P. S., Jungbluth, N., & Gudmundsen, G. R. (2013). Cognitive mechanisms of change in CBT for adolescent depression: Associations among client involvement, cognitive distortions, and treatment outcome. *International Journal of Cognitive Therapy, 6*(4), 311–324. doi:10.1521/ijct.2013.6.4.311

Shirk, S. R., Kaplinski, H., & Gudmundsen, G. (2009). School-based cognitive-behavioral therapy for adolescent depression. *Journal of Emotional and Behavioral Disorders, 17*(2), 106–117.

Sigelman, C. K., & Rider, E. A. (2012). *Life-span human development* (7th ed.). Belmont, CA: Wadsworth Cengage Learning.

Simons, A. D., Marti, C., Rohde, P., Lewis, C. C., Curry, J., & March, J. (2012). Does homework "matter" in cognitive behavioral therapy for adolescent depression? *Journal of Cognitive Psychotherapy, 26*(4), 390–404. doi:10.1891/0889-8391.26.4.390

Spiegler, M. D., & Guevremont, D. C. (2010). *Contemporary behavior therapy* (5th ed.). Belmont, CA: Wadsworth Cengage Learning.

Thoder, V. J., & Cautilli, J. D. (2011). An independent evaluation of mode deactivation therapy for juvenile offenders. *International Journal of Behavioral Consultation and Therapy, 7*(1), 41–46.

Weersing, V., Rozenman, M., & Gonzalez, A. (2009). Core components of therapy in youth: Do we know what to disseminate? *Behavior Modification, 33*(1), 24–47.

Weisz, J. R., Southam-Gerow, M. A., Gordis, E. B., Connor-Smith, J. K., Chu, B. C., Langer, D. A., . . . Weiss, B. (2009). Cognitive-behavioral therapy versus usual clinical care for youth depression: An initial test of transportability to community clinics and clinicians. *Journal of Consulting and Clinical Psychology, 77*(3), 383–396. doi: 10.1037/a0013877

Wenzel, A. B., Gregory, K., & Beck, A. T. (2009). *Cognitive therapy for suicidal patients: Scientific and clinical applications.* Washington, DC: American Psychological Association.

Wood, J. J., Chiu, A. W., Hwang, W., Jacobs, J., & Ifekwunigwe, M. (2008). Adapting cognitive-behavioral therapy for Mexican American students with anxiety disorders: Recommendations for school psychologists. *School Psychology Quarterly, 23,* 515–532. doi:10.1037/1045-3830. 23.4.515

3

Trauma-Focused Care

Failure to acknowledge the reality of trauma and abuse in the lives of children, and the long-term impact this can have in the lives of adults, is one of the most significant clinical and moral deficits of current mental health approaches. Trauma in the early years shapes brain and psychological development, sets up vulnerability to stress and to the range of mental health problems.

—Louise Newman

Introduction

A traumatic event is defined by the *Diagnostic and Statistical Manual of Mental Disorders*, fifth edition (*DSM-5*; American Psychiatric Association, 2013) as an "exposure to actual or threatened death, serious injury, or sexual violence" (p. 271) through direct experience, witnessing the event, learning it occurred to a family member or friend, or being repeatedly exposed to the details of a traumatic event. Experiences such as death or threat of death, physical and sexual violence, major accidents, natural disasters, violent crime, and combat are often events that challenge an individual's sense of safety and control, often leading to physical and psychological experiences of traumatic stress. Traumatic stress symptoms are complex, engaging both mind and body in the immediate experience of fear, shock, and pain as well as physical, emotional, and social disconnection. Individual trauma results

from an event, a series of events, or a set of circumstances that is experienced by an individual as physically or emotionally harmful or threatening and that has lasting adverse effects on the individual's functioning and physical, social, emotional, or spiritual well-being (Substance Abuse and Mental Health Services Administration [SAMHSA], 2012).

As many studies suggest, the typical adolescent who has experienced a traumatic event or repeated traumatization might not fulfill the official *DSM-5* diagnostic criteria for posttraumatic stress disorder (PTSD) but will present with a number of other symptoms such as affect and behavior dysregulation; conduct problems, irritability/anger, impulsive, aggressive, and/or self-harming behaviors; difficulty with identity and self-perception; low social and academic functioning; somatic complaints; anxiety; depression; and dissociative symptoms (Habib & Labruna, 2011; Schmid, Petermann, & Fegert, 2013).

Individual reactions vary considerably between people, circumstances, and events. Trauma, by nature, changes the way in which people see and experience the world. Imagine a single traumatic event or chronic victimization in the life of an individual when he or she is most vulnerable—during early childhood into adolescence (Blaustein & Kinniburgh, 2010; Perry, Pollard, Blakely, Baker, & Vigilante, 1995). The rate of exposure to a traumatic event in the life of an adolescent is alarmingly high, with many adolescents experiencing multiple traumatic incidences. Children and adolescents in most nations worldwide have access to immediate information and are exposed on a daily basis to individual and mass devastation and violence (Nader, 2008). In a large longitudinal study of more than 2,000 participants, more than two thirds of children and adolescents have experienced at least one traumatic event such as maltreatment, domestic violence, medical trauma, a traffic accident, loss of significant other, or sexual assault before the age of 16 (Copeland, Keeler, Angold, & Costello, 2007; Costello, Erkanli, Fairbank, & Angold, 2002). Added to these challenges, economic and social deprivation, sexism, homophobia, and racism or cultural bias produce severe negative effects that contribute to and intensify victimization or create polyvictimization (Briere & Lanktree, 2013).

Other research examining the prevalence of traumatic stress in adolescents reflect more than half of American males and females reporting exposure to at least one or more traumatic experience, while the percentage of trauma exposure for urban youth increases to more than 80% by the time they have reached 23 years of age (Breslau, Wilcox, Storr, Lucia, & Anthony, 2004; Kessler, Sonnega, Bromet, Hughes, & Nelson, 1995). The adolescent's reaction to trauma is determined by many factors such as the pattern, nature, and duration of the trauma; characteristics of the child (gender, personality, cognitive development); and contextual facets of the child's life such as family of origin, support systems, attachment, socioeconomic status, and culture (Perry &

Azad, 1999). There are many adolescents with enough resiliency (personality, psychobiological development, family system, and/or community support) and for them facing a traumatic event is simply that—one traumatic event (Black, Woodworth, Tremblay, & Carpenter, 2012). Other adolescents experience the traumatic event and its impact in ways that have a pervasive impact in many areas of their lives (e.g., school, family, interactions, and extracurricular interests) and can continue over a life span.

Experiencing a trauma early in life can have adverse effects on current functioning as well as on personality and psychobiological development resulting in an array of traumatic stress symptoms and comorbid diagnoses into adolescence. Unlike adults whose trauma experience might alter their behavior, trauma in younger persons literally becomes a part of the organizational framework of neurodevelopment. Stated simply, the body's biology develops from infancy well into adolescence. According to the National Child Traumatic Stress Network (NCTSN, 2008), one's biology is partially responsible for the environments to which that person is exposed. So if a child grows up in a traumatic or stressful environment, it can impair his or her physical, emotional, behavioral, or cognitive development.

Being trauma informed is an essential part of creating a therapeutic alliance with this population, particularly when practitioners first start out in the field. As with any individual who has experienced trauma, Stage 1 counseling work starts with safety and stabilization. This includes feelings of safety and connection in the counseling relationship, psycho-education on what trauma is and its effect on brain development, consistent boundary development and experiences, and self-regulation. It is imperative for the provider working with an adolescent who has experienced trauma to help create safety as well as self-regulation before beginning any kind of traumatic memory processing.

Counseling then focuses on attending to symptoms of trauma-related stress, such as anxiety, depression, anger, aggression, and self-harming behaviors. Interventions such as cognitive behavioral therapy, trauma-focused CBT, and dialectic behavioral therapy are useful in handling such stress. For other symptoms such as hyperarousal (e.g., reduced pain tolerance, anxiety, insomnia, and fatigue), hypervigilance (e.g., a high responsiveness to stimuli), and intrusive thoughts (e.g., unwelcome involuntary thoughts) and nightmares, more trauma-focused treatments are utilized and discussed later in the chapter. For an adolescent who has experienced trauma with his or her primary caregiver relationships (e.g., parents), developing a safe and trusting therapeutic relationship becomes complex and challenging as the adolescent's attachment style has likely become distorted by the unhealthy relationship/interactions either by acts of commission (e.g., deliberate) or concerns.

After reading this chapter, readers will be able to do the following:

- Better understand that trauma is pervasive and affects the cognitive, emotional, and social development of adolescents

- Understand that trauma forms and deforms the emerging personality in adolescents

- Better comprehend that more than half of adolescents have experienced a traumatic event

- Understand that trauma causes developmental disruptions that are felt through one's life

- Articulate the signs and symptoms of trauma and differentiate these symptoms from those in adults

- Discuss how attachment relationships are critical to healthy brain development as well as contribute to trauma responses in adolescents

- Understand the importance of trauma-informed therapy and its relationship to evidence-based treatment interventions

- Understand the impact of vicarious trauma when working with adolescent trauma survivors and ways to minimize burnout

- Apply knowledge gained from this chapter to a case scenario

Attachment, Brain Development, and Trauma

Attachment theory was developed through the combined work of the British psychiatrist John Bowlby and the American psychologist Mary Ainsworth. Bowlby revolutionized developmental thinking on the relationship between parent and child and the disruption of this relationship due to deprivation, separation, or loss (Bowlby, 1958, 1960; Bretherton, 1992), while Ainsworth expanded the theory utilizing innovative research methods to study the differences and outcomes of mother–infant interactions (Ainsworth, 1963, 1967, 1969, Ainsworth & Bell, 1970; Bretherton, 1992). According to Bowlby (1980),

> Intimate attachments to other human beings are the hub around which a person's life revolves, not only when he is an infant or a toddler or a schoolchild but throughout his adolescence and his years of maturity as well, and on to old age. From these intimate attachments a person draws his strength and enjoyment of life and, through what he contributes, he gives strength and enjoyment to others. (p. 442)

In its most simplified state, attachment theory posits that the earliest primary relationship shapes psychobiological functions (e.g., the use of biological methods to study normal and abnormal emotional and cognitive processes), organizes brain structure, and ultimately is critical for optimal development. Attachment itself is described as the emotional bond between child and primary caregivers who are responsible for the child's nurture, care, support, and protection (Breidenstine, Bailey, Zeanah, & Larrieu, 2011). According to Pearce and Pezzot-Pearce (2001), there is considerable research indicating a significant association between attachment organization and children's functioning across multiple domains. Infants become attached to individuals who are sensitive and responsive in social interactions with them and who remain as consistent caregivers for some months during the period from 6 months to 2 years of age; this is called sensitive responsiveness. Caregivers' responses lead to the development of patterns of attachment; these, consequently, lead to internal models that will guide the perceptions, emotions, thoughts, and expectations in later relationships. Although the relationship is not causal, there seems to be a correlation between early insecure attachments to later issues, particularly when parental behaviors continue throughout childhood. "It is clear that traumatic experiences can compromise attachment relationships, and occur within attachment relationships or can influence the attachment patterns of infants/children when the parent has been previously traumatized" (p. 275).

When early attachment to the primary caregiver is "good enough," the child is able to formulate a secure attachment style. Young children with a secure attachment "demonstrate a balance between proximity-seeking and exploration" that indicates comfort with their primary caregiver (Breidenstine et al., 2011, p. 276). Much like Erikson's (1950, 1963) initial trust versus mistrust psychosocial stage, this confidence in the attachment object helps form a framework for security, exploration, and future relationships. These children become adolescents who are able to successfully modulate affect, especially strong

emotions; self-sooth; and relate to others in their social environment (James, 1994). Children in attachment relationships where needs are not met, experience what Ainsworth (1969, 1985) classified as one of three insecure attachments: (1) *avoidant*, (2) *ambivalent*, and (3) *disorganized* (see Table 3.1). An *avoidant* attachment style is one in which the child ignores the caregiver and shows little emotion when the caregiver leaves or returns. An *ambivalent* attachment style develops when the caregiver is inconsistent in his or her emotional and physical availability; this causes the child to actively seek the caregiver's attention by being fussy or clingy. The *disorganized* attachment style is one in which children with a disorganized-insecure attachment style show a lack of clear attachment behavior, including avoidance or resistance. The parents of these children range from unresponsive, insensitive, and intrusive to neglecting, rejecting, and abusive. This maladaptive behavior becomes a schema with which the adolescent bases all other interpersonal relationships (Ainsworth, Blehar, Waters, & Wall, 1978; Bowlby, 1969, 1973). Children who do not get their needs met from their caregivers will alter their behavior to preserve the attachment relationship.

Table 3.1　　Attachment Style, Parenting Style, and Adolescent Response to Them

Attachment Style	Parenting Style	Adolescent Response
Secure	In tune with the child's needs and emotions	Affect and emotion regulation; ability to build and maintain interpersonal relationships; appropriate sense of self
Avoidant	Rejecting, unresponsive, or otherwise inaccessible caregivers	Disconnected or unresponsive to others' needs; condescending and/or hostile; minimizing or denying distress while externalizing negative behavior
Ambivalent	Intrusive or inconsistent caregivers	Dependency ("clingy" or "needy") in relationships; immature or incompetent in relationship with parents
Disorganized	Frightening behavior; inability to respond to fear or distress	Emotions dysregulation, fragmented information processing, and impulsive/avoidant behavior; distrust and alienation in relationships

Source. Patterns of attachment: A psychological study of the strange situation. Mary D. Salter Ainsworth, Mary C. Blehar, Everett Waters, and Sally Wall. Hillsdale, N.J., Erlbaum, 1978. Wiley.

Rejecting, unresponsive, or otherwise inaccessible caregivers create an avoidant attachment style evident in young children who show very little distress when they are separated from their parent/caregivers and instead focus on other objects. Such children get lost in an inner world and avoid emotional connection (Barker, 2010). In adolescence, this can present as an adolescent who has difficulty in relationships as he or she appears to be self-centered, disconnected from the needs of others, and at times can seem hostile or condescending to peers (Brown & Wright, 2003). It can also lead to anxiety, anger, and hostility over the rejection experienced by one's primary caregiver even as the adolescent denies or minimizes the symptoms and distress (Rosenstein & Horowitz, 1996). Research suggests adolescent pathologies such as conduct disorder or other externalizing symptoms (e.g., oppositional defiant disorder [ODD] and attention-deficit/hyperactivity disorder symptoms). Substance abuse and eating disorders in adolescent girls are associated with the avoidant attachment pattern of relationship as their attachment strategy is to deny distressing thoughts and feelings while behavior acts them out (Brown & Wright, 2003; Cole-Detke & Kobak, 1996; Rosenstein & Horowitz, 1996).

The ambivalent attachment pattern, also known as preoccupied, develops when the parent is intrusive or inconsistent causing the child to become fearful or anxious, not knowing what to expect next (Barker, 2010). This child develops into an adolescent who experiences extreme dependency in relationships, appearing immature or incompetent in the presence of parents or attachment figures, and might be classified by peers as "clingy" or "needy." Unlike the avoidant strategy in which the adolescent dismisses the attachment system, the ambivalent system becomes inflated or maximized to catch the attention of the inconsistent caregiver or relational object (Cassidy & Berlin, 1994; Rosenstein & Horowitz, 1996). Simply stated, the avoidant strategy is one in which the adolescent avoids and/or does not seek contact or comfort from the parent, whereas the ambivalent strategy is one in which the adolescent actively seeks the parent's

attention but does not seem to be comforted by the parent. Brown and Wright (2003) label these opposite strategies as "deactivating strategy" versus "hyperactivating strategy." Anxiety and mood disorders are most associated with the ambivalent attachment style (Brown & Wright, 2003; Rosenstein & Horowitz, 1996).

The least secure form of attachment is considered to be disorganized attachment (Main & Solomon, 1986; Weinfield, Whaley, & Egeland, 2004). The disorganized attachment pattern in childhood is created through exposure to a parent's or caregiver's frightened or frightening behavior or the caregiver's inability to respond to distress or fear caused by something else (Bureau, Easterbrooks, & Lyons-Ruth, 2009; Hesse & Main, 2006). This disorganized attachment pattern can be seen in adolescents who have been traumatized by a loss, abused, and/or maltreated. As the child moves into adolescence, the disorganized attachment evolves into

> a constellation of forms of relational dysregulation, including generalized expectancies based on profound distrust, alienation, devaluation, and patterns of interpersonal interaction characterized by all of the hallmarks of complex traumatic stress disorders: emotion dysregulation, fragmented information processing, impulsive/avoidant behavioral self-management, dissociation, and somatization. (Courtois & Ford, 2009, p. 62; see also Ford, 2005; van der Kolk, 2005)

Limited research on the link between disorganized attachment and adolescent psychopathology "underscore the association between disorganized attachment and symptoms of depression, social reticence, inattention and thought problems, and suggest that the link between disorganized attachment and these symptoms may have clinical significance" (Borelli, David, Crowley, & Mayes, 2010, p. 253).

Adolescence in and of itself is a stage of development that is characterized by profound change when schemas and structures are shifted, updated, and reworked as a result (Kobak & Cole, 1994). Although it is evident that the early attachment relationship between parent and child is critical to healthy development, research suggests that this attachment offers adolescents an opportunity to restructure or reorganize attachment strategies as they have more accessibility to memories, thoughts, and feelings as well as the ability to mentalize the self and others (Brown & Wright, 2003; Reimer, Overton, Steidl, Rosenstein, & Horowitz, 1996). The implications of this window of opportunity is critical to mental health care providers as it suggests that brain development during adolescence offers us an opportunity through intervention to revise and restructure attachment information processing (Brown & Wright, 2003).

> Trauma is an experience. How it is that this experience can transform a child's world into a terror-filled, confusing miasma that so dramatically alters the child's (or adolescent's) trajectory into and throughout adult life? Ultimately, it is the human brain that processes and internalizes traumatic (and therapeutic) experiences. It is the brain that mediates all emotional, cognitive, behavioral, social, and physiological functioning. It is the human brain from which the human mind arises and within that mind resides our humanity. Understanding the organization, function, and development of the human brain, and brain-mediated responses to threat, provides the keys to understanding the traumatized child. (Perry et al., 1995)

Brain Development

Understanding an adolescent's development starts with understanding his or her brain functioning. When considering trauma's impact on the brain itself, counselors must first understand "typical" or expected brain development, at least in a broad sense.

In the hierarchical sequence of brain development, the three primary interdependent brain systems that develop over time depend on the health and development of previous systems. This psychobiological developmental system begins with the primitive brain stem and evolves into the more complex limbic and cortical systems (Perry et al., 1995). "Early patterns of adaption provide a framework for, and are transformed by, later experiences to yield increasing complexity, flexibility, and organization" (Yates, Egeland, & Sroufe, 2003, pp. 246–247). A single

trauma occurring on the neurodevelopmental continuum may interrupt normal development of the essential building blocks of intrapersonal, interpersonal, regulatory, and neurocognitive competencies (Blaustein & Kinniburgh, 2010). This impact has the capacity to "induce biochemical changes that impede maturation of the brain's coping mechanisms" (Nader, 2008, p. 25). According to Nader (2008), traumatized youth live in a state of hypervigilance, anxiety, and fear of reexperiencing the trauma. Deprivation of critical attachment experiences as well as traumatizing experiences in childhood can shift a "learning brain" into a "survival brain" (Courtois & Ford, 2009). The primary self-regulatory functions in healthy brain development are learning and experiencing emotional awareness, problem solving, and distress tolerance. When an adolescent has experienced traumatic stress during his or her developmental years, the brain shifts into survival mode.

> The survival brain seeks to anticipate, prevent, or protect against the damage caused by potential or actual dangers, driven and reinforced by a search to identify threats, and an attempt to mobilize and conserve bodily resources in the service of this vigilance and defensive adjustments to maintain bodily functioning. (Courtois & Ford, 2009, p. 32)

Ultimately, the two biological defense systems, the sympathetic nervous system and the parasympathetic nervous system, are activated, triggering fight, flight, or freeze responses that lead to an interference of the already immature prefrontal cortex functioning (Tyler, 2012). In an attempt to reduce this trauma-related stress response of the autonomic nervous system, teens often participate in numbing coping activities such as substance abuse or "acting out" behaviors such as self-injury, anorexia/bulimia, problematic sexual behavior, compulsive or excessive risk taking, or defiance and aggression (Briere & Lanktree, 2013). In 2011, the Child Welfare Information Gateway (childwelfare.gov) offered a general guidance provided in Table 3.2 to help professionals identify adolescent and parent symptomology that shows a potential risk for developmental delay caused by traumatic stress.

Table 3.2   Child Development, Parenting Strategies, and Causes for Concern, 11 to 18 Years

Age	Developmentally Appropriate Behavior	Causes for Concern	Parenting Strategies	Causes for Concern
11–14 years	May have frequent mood swings or changes in feelings	Eats or sleeps less (or more) than before	Establish fair and consistent rules	Worries that the child is maturing very early or very late
	Gradually develops own taste, sense of style, and identity	Has strong negative thoughts or opinions about himself or herself	Provide opportunities for new and challenging experiences	Doesn't set reasonable limits for the child's behavior
	Has a hobby, sport, or activity	Has an extreme need for approval and social support	Address the potential consequences of risky behaviors	Is uninterested in helping the child address overwhelming emotions or situations
	Learns to accept disappointments and overcome failures	Has highly conflicted relationships or regularly causes family conflicts	Help teens resolve conflicts, solve problems, and understand changing emotions	Expects the child to adhere to strict rules and severely punishes mistakes
	Has one or more "best" friends and positive relationships with others of the same age	Is alone most of the time and seems happier alone than with others	Encourage goals for the future and help create systems for time and task managements	Often has conflicts and loses temper with the child
			Discuss the physical changes in puberty that affect height, weight, and body shape	Frequently criticizes, nags, or judges the child
15–18 years	Begins to develop an identity and self-worth beyond body image and physical appearance	Feels hopeless and unable to make things better	Available for help and advice when needed	Doesn't provide the child any privacy and finds it overly difficult to "let go" as he or she becomes more independent
	Is able to calm down and handle anger	Withdraws from family or friends	Tolerate (within reason) teens developing likes and dislikes in clothes, hairstyles, and music	
	Sets goals and works toward achieving them	Often gives in to negative peer pressure		
	Accepts family rules and completes chores and other responsibilities	Becomes violent or abusive		
	Needs time for emotions and reasoning skills to catch up with the rapid physical changes	Drives aggressively, speeds, and drinks and drives		
		Has a favorable attitude toward drug use		
		Diets excessively, even when not overweight		

Source. From Child Welfare Information Gateway (2011).

Other Environmental Contributors to Trauma

The majority of adolescents who are referred to mental health services are often survivors of adverse life experiences. Based on the statistics of adolescent trauma experiences and our knowledge of trauma and brain development, it is evident that there is more to trauma than a standard PTSD diagnosis (Shapiro, 2010). Trauma can also be manifested as dissociative identity disorder, acute stress disorder, and depression. According to Greeson et al. (2011), untreated adolescent traumatic stress leads to an increased use of mental health and health services as well as an increased involvement of the juvenile justice system. Untreated stress also contributes to a large portion of the problems families and communities face on a daily basis. For example, low academic functioning, poverty, crime, poor health, addiction, and poor mental health. Fang, Brown, Florence, and Mercy (2012) highlight that the human impact on individuals is vast, that nationally more than $124 billion per year is spent as a result of child maltreatment, and that more than 772,000 victims were identified in 2008.

Through the lens of attachment, trauma, and its effect on brain development, counselors create a more accurate case conceptualization and ultimately a better treatment plans for their consumers. Counselors are trained not only to recognize problematic behaviors but also to look behind the behaviors to identify their impetus. A provider's best approach to identifying and offering treatment for adolescent trauma and resultant complex symptomology begins with becoming educated and knowledgeable about trauma-informed theory. Under the premise that "people make sense" and "individuals function in the way that they function for a reason," treatment plan formulation must also include the multifaceted and complex reasons for why adolescent clients are reacting and responding the way they are (Blaustein & Kinniburgh, 2010). The biopsychosocial model is a general model or approach positing that biological, psychological, and social factors all play a significant role in human functioning in the context of disease or illness. This involves taking a systemic and contextual look at the biopsychosocial development, attachment style, roles and patterns in relationships, beliefs, strengths, triggers, stressors, caregivers, community, and culture.

What Is Trauma-Informed Theory?

Trauma-informed theory is an integrated system involving a comprehensive understanding of trauma's definition, characteristics, various categories, and effect on childhood psychobiological brain development; the symptomology of traumatic experiences over a life span; the constitution of *trauma-informed care*, a perspective where healing is led by the client and supported by the provider; and *trauma-informed approach*, an approach designed to avoid retraumatizing those who seek assistance, to focus on "safety first" and a commitment to "do no harm," and to facilitate participation and meaningful involvement of consumers and families and trauma survivors in the planning of services and programs, as well as the subsequent implementation of or referral toward *trauma-specific assessment, therapies, interventions,* and *services*. A trauma-informed service provider does not necessarily have to be a trained trauma provider capable of trauma-specific treatment. However, the service provider should be aware of and welcome the complex needs of a trauma survivor (Harris & Fallot, 2001). The term *trauma-informed approach* is similar in definition to *trauma-informed care*, but it is often utilized by systems and organizations, such as juvenile justice, that are not necessarily identified as "caregiving" but have the capacity to incorporate trauma-informed theory. Although a trauma-informed approach is relatively new in youth detention centers and developmental camps, evidence suggests that identifying trauma and related symptoms, reducing retraumatization, and maintaining a "do no harm" approach have reduced criminal risk factors and increased responsivity to cognitive behavioral treatments (Miller & Najavits, 2012). Table 3.3 shows the difference between tradition and trauma-informed systems.

Table 3.3   Traditional Versus Trauma Informed

	Traditional	*Trauma Informed*
What is trauma?	Trauma is a single event the response to which is defined/diagnosed as posttraumatic stress disorder. Impact is predictable.	Trauma makes the survivor question even the most fundamental assumptions about the world—in the wake of trauma, the survivor constructs a new theory of how the world works and how people behave. Trauma is viewed not as a single discrete event but rather as a defining and organizing experience that forms the core of an individual's identity. Practitioners assume that trauma changes the rules of the game.
Who is this consumer/ survivor?	The consumer and her or his problems are synonymous. The problem has a life of its own, independent of context. There is a blurring of the distinction between a problem and a symptom. Allocation of responsibility on the consumer is either too great or too little.	Emphasis is on understanding the whole individual and appreciating the context in which he or she lives her or his life—i.e., "How do I understand this person?" rather than "How do I understand this problem?" Trauma-related symptoms arise as attempts to cope with intolerable circumstances, and those symptoms emerge as a context of abuse. The consumer-survivor evaluates his or her responsibility for change—is not a passive victim.
What services are available?	In many cases, the only viable goal is stabilization (in most efficient manner possible)—once the symptoms have been managed, treatment ends. Services are crisis driven. The system strives to minimize risk to itself. Services are content specific, time limited, and outcome focused.	The goal is to return a sense of control and autonomy to the consumer-survivor. Emphasis is on skill building and only secondarily on symptom management. Service time limits are set in collaboration with the consumer-survivor. Services are strengths based. There is a focus on the prevention of further trauma within the client's system. Weigh risks to consumers along with risks to the organization.
What is a service relationship?	The consumer is a passive recipient of services. The provider is accorded more status and power within the relationship. Consumers often find themselves frightened and cautious. Trust is assumed.	The core of the service relationship is a genuine collaboration. Trust must be earned. Provider and consumer both bring strengths to the relationship.

Source. From Harris and Fallot (2001, pp. 11–12).

Presuppositions of trauma-informed theory include the following (Fallot & Harris, 2009):

- Trauma is pervasive.

- Trauma's impact is considerably broad, deep, and contextual, touching and shaping all life domains.

- Violent trauma perpetuates violent trauma.

- Those who are most vulnerable, the young, the poor, the diseased, and the addicted are at greater risk for victimization.

- Trauma corrupts the fabric of all relationships.

- Trauma often occurs in the context of the helping relationship.

- Trauma affects not only the victim but also those in the position of offering human services.

Adolescence is a time of accelerated change; cognitive functioning develops as social skills and perspective/self-reflection abilities mature (Blaustein & Kinniburgh, 2010). This is also the time when separation from the primary caregiving system begins as teens discover and develop their own identities. Due to this developmental position of adolescence, specifically with regard to Erikson's stage identity versus role confusion, trauma-informed theory recognizes that adolescence is a high-risk time to be exposed to trauma (Blaustein & Kinniburgh, 2010).

Trauma-informed care is defined by the SAMHSA's National Center for Trauma-Informed Care as an approach to engaging individuals with a history of trauma. This approach recognizes trauma symptoms and understands the role trauma has played across an adolescent's life. A trauma-informed care system has an understanding of the global impact of trauma and the potential avenues for healing. This understanding involves recognizing signs and symptoms of trauma in adolescent clients as mentioned earlier (e.g., insecure attachment styles; affect and behavior dysregulation; conduct problems; irritability/anger; impulsive, aggressive, and/or self-harming behaviors; difficulty with identity and self-perception; low social and academic functioning; somatic complaints; anxiety; depression; and dissociative symptoms (Schmid et al., 2013). Trauma-informed care also recognizes that symptoms of trauma exist in the familial system of the adolescent as well as in the providers and health caregivers working with trauma survivors. A system, program, or organization that is trauma informed has an understanding of the pervasive impact of trauma as well as all the potential paths to healing. It recognizes and builds resilient characteristics in individuals and families. Trauma-informed care also contributes to the reduction of secondary or vicarious trauma and implements self-care in those in a position to care for traumatized individuals.

According to the current literature, the following are the foundational principles of trauma-informed care in systems (Guarino, Soares, Konnath, Clervil, & Bassuk, 2009):

- Understanding trauma and its impact

- Promoting safety

- Ensuring cultural competence

- Supporting consumer control, choice, and autonomy

- Sharing power and governance

- Integrating care

- Healing happens in relationships

- Recovery is possible

Promoting safety is paramount in creating a good therapeutic alliance as well as best practice when treating trauma survivors who need respectful and consistent responses from counseling providers. Cultural competence, supporting autonomy and agency, and sharing power are not only ethical standards but also core principles in the treatment of adolescents. Helping teens develop autonomy, regain a sense of control, and build skills in their daily lives allow both the adolescents and the system in which they function to create and maintain hope that in spite of all the challenges they have faced, recovery is a possibility as strength and resiliency are developed.

There are a number of treatment interventions that are symptom specific; however, there are significantly fewer treatment interventions that are trauma informed and evidence based. Although the following list of trauma-specific therapies is not exhaustive, it does encompass some of the most widely used therapies for counselors working with individuals, groups, or in school settings.

EVIDENCE-BASED OUTGROWTHS

The remainder of this chapter provides information on several outgrowths of trauma-informed and evidence-based treatment methodologies. Evidence-based treatment modalities and methodologies are based on quantitative research studies. It is important to note that the majority of these treatment modalities require advanced training of the provider.

Trauma-Focused Cognitive Behavioral Therapy

As briefly discussed in Chapter 2, trauma-focused cognitive behavioral therapy (TF-CBT) is a cognitive behavioral and stress inoculation approach to treating trauma that includes the adolescent discussing the traumatic event or events directly (exposure) while utilizing anxiety management techniques to regulate the emotional and biological responses to the memory of the trauma. This evidence-based treatment was originally developed by Wolpe (1969) and Beck (1976) in the treatment of adults experiencing fear and anxiety. Positive results with adults experiencing PTSD was established and followed up with the application of TF-CBT with children and adolescents (Beidel & Turner, 1998; Foa, Rothbaum, Riggs, & Murdock, 1991) It has been identified as an efficacious treatment for adolescents and well supported in many major studies (Chorpita et al., 2002; Cohen, Mannarino, Berliner, & Deblinger, 2000).

Identifying and challenging the distorted beliefs and thoughts surrounding the traumatic event contribute to alleviating traumatic stress and other posttraumatic symptoms. Cognitive distortions may arise in an attempt for the adolescent to understand why a traumatic event occurred. Beck (1976) stated that these distorted cognitions can lead to negative emotional states and behaviors like anxiety, depression, PTSD symptomology, and self-destructive behavior. The goal of TF-CBT is to prevent the negative emotional states and behaviors by correcting cognition errors and enhancing their coping mechanisms. TF-CBT is the strongest research evidence approach to treating adolescents who have experienced trauma, multiple traumas, or complex trauma. It has been modified to fit a socially and culturally diverse population of adolescents across a spectrum of settings, including inpatient and outpatient care, foster homes, residential homes, and schools. It is used on an individual basis or with the adolescent and the parent/primary caregiver. Parents and/or primary caregivers are usually included in TF-CBT with their children. The aforementioned is done for a number of reasons. According to Cohen et al. (2000), the inclusion of the parents or primary caregiver assists in (a) obtaining collateral information on the child's functioning, (b) addressing family dysfunction to resolve the child's symptoms, and (c) providing therapeutic interventions at home in the form of parental support to help the child's recovery from emotional and behavioral problems. Parental inclusion is essential to treatment, because often parents and/or primary caregivers are directly or vicariously traumatized themselves. Research shows that parental distress is correlated to higher levels of symptoms found in the child. TF-CBT assists in resolving not only the child's but also the parent's emotional upset and negative cognitive distortions.

Eye Movement Desensitization Reprocessing

Eye movement desensitization reprocessing (EMDR) is an evidence-based treatment modality designed specifically for the treatment of PTSD and traumatic stress created by Shapiro (1996). In 2010, it was declared to be well supported by quantitative research through The California Evidence-Based Clearinghouse for Child Welfare. According to the World Health Organization's 2013 guidelines for stress management, EMDR and TF-CBT are the only psychotherapies recommended for adolescents with PTSD. The American Psychiatric Association (2004) and the Department of Veterans Affairs and Department of Defense (2008) both recommend EMDR as effective treatment for trauma. In EMDR, the client is directed to focus on a negative image and the cognitions associated with it. Seidler and Wagner (2006) stated, "Once the client has established contact with the disturbing material, the therapist induces a bilateral stimulation" (p. 1515). This may include moving his fingers in front of the clients face after telling the client to follow the movement with his or her eyes. EMDR can be effective in exploring the thoughts and emotions of adolescents as it relates to trauma. By identifying an adolescent's cognitions and feelings to a trauma and distinguishing whether they are positive or negative, the clinician can help the client adapt better coping mechanisms. This is because the adolescent will be able to identify positive alternatives to the negative cognitions and emotions in relation to the trauma. EMDR facilitates adaptive information process and incorporates an eight-phase treatment approach used to identify and address traumatic memories that originally overwhelmed the brain's natural coping capacity and resiliency. In the information processing, new and more adaptive associations are made to reduce symptomology (Shapiro, 2001).

Attachment, Self-Regulation, and Competency Treatment Framework

Attachment, self-regulation, and competency treatment framework (ARC) is a components-based model utilizing three core domains of interventions for adolescent trauma survivors: (1) attachment, (2) self-regulation, and (3) competency. ARC is a comprehensive framework for intervention with adolescents and caregivers and is designed to be adaptable to real-life needs and circumstances of adolescents and caregivers. ARC is designed for chronic developmental trauma and targets the client's treatment, the caregiver, and the community system. It is grounded in childhood development and attachment theories and has multiple modalities and interventions (Blaustein & Kinniburgh, 2010). According to Kinniburgh, Blaustein, Spinazzola, and van der Kolk (2005), "the goal of ARC is to address vulnerabilities created by exposure to overwhelming life circumstance that interfere with healthy development" (p. 426). The ARC method is based on a phase-oriented approach. It is theorized that by developing abilities, alleviating stress, and strengthening the security of the caregiving system, resiliency can be enhanced. The aforementioned key areas allow the therapist to customize interventions and activities to meet the needs of each adolescent in his or her own context based on assessment.

Trauma Affect Regulation: A Guide for Education and Therapy of Adolescents

Trauma Affect Regulation: A Guide for Education and Therapy of Adolescents (TARGET-A) is an evidence-based, trauma-informed treatment that has been used and tested specifically on juvenile offender samples and can be executed effectively in individual and groups settings. TARGET has been used with adolescents and adults to treat both PTSD and substance use disorders. TARGET is composed of three main factors: (1) education, (2) guided implementation, and (3) development/incorporation. Therapy emphasizes the client's core values, resilience, and strengths. Or said more simply, the therapist helps the client see the symptoms as an indication that the individual has survived a trauma. Ford and Russo (2006) stated that clients learn that they have the ability to reset their "biological alarm," which has caused them to suffer in life. It is based largely on CBT strategies with goals of emotion regulation and trauma processing.

TARGET utilizes the FREEDOM treatment model (*F*ocus, *R*ecognize triggers, *E*motion self-check, *E*valuate thoughts, *D*efine goals, *O*ptions, and *M*ake contributions) and can be accommodated to work with parents or with adolescents alone (Ford, Courtois, van der Hart, Nijenhuis, & Steele, 2005).

Multimodality Trauma Treatment or Trauma-Focused Coping in Schools

Multimodality trauma treatment or trauma-focused coping (TFC) is a components-based, skills-oriented, CBT-driven approach to individual or group work in school settings. Significant here is that TFC can actually work conveniently in the places where adolescents spend most of their time, such as school, while being offered in a format adolescents are comfortable with (e.g., a peer group setting). It is designed for adolescents experiencing PTSD symptoms following a single-incident trauma. However, TFC also works for those adolescents who have experienced more than one single-incident trauma. In addition, it has been found to be successful with adolescents who are experiencing "psychosocial stressors" because of TFC's flexibility to work within other models of therapy (e.g., family therapy and/or pharmaceutical interventions) (Sullivan et al., 2011). Components of TFC include psycho-education, anxiety management, cognitive restructuring, anger and grief management, and trauma memory processing (Amaya-Jackson et al., 2003). The FREEDOM treatment model assists clients in both processing and managing trauma-related behaviors in current distressful situations. These steps are defined as follows: (1) *F*ocus helps decrease anxiety and improve attentiveness, (2) *R*ecognize specific stressful triggers, (3) *E*motions assist in identifying primary emotions, (4) *E*valuate primary thoughts, (5) *D*efine the client's primary personal goals, (6) *O*ption helps the client discover one choice that signifies a successful step toward a goal accomplished during a current stressful experience, and (7) *M*ake aids in distinguishing

how that option is reflected in the client's core values and has made a contribution in others' lives. Although the treatment can last anywhere from 6 months to several years, typical treatment lasts over 12 weekly sessions.

TFC consists of one individual assessment followed by weekly sessions lasting for 14 weeks. Each session teaches adolescents specific skills on how to cope with their trauma (e.g., "anxiety management, cognitive training, and grief coping") (Sullivan et al., 2011, p. 5). TFC is a "graded-exposure" therapy, which begins with psycho-education and cognitive therapy before moving on to an individual's trauma (March & Amaya-Jackson, 1999). It is designed to be implemented with adolescents between the ages of 8 and 18 and should be adjusted accordingly based on age. The reason for the adjustment based on age is because younger adolescents learn differently than their older peers (e.g., younger adolescents oftentimes will use role playing, while older adolescents are often open to cognitive discourse; March & Amaya-Jackson, 1999). The two primary goals of TFC are (1) to guide adolescents in the development of their own trauma narrative, with cognitive errors being absent and the trauma placed in the past, and (2) for adolescents to believe that the world is safe (March & Amaya-Jackson, 1999). To meet these goals, adolescents have to write a "narrative chapter book," narrating in the book their experience with the trauma, their ability to move through the trauma, and their life today as a result of coming through it (March & Amaya-Jackson, 1999). In this way, adolescents come to think of their trauma as no longer present and thus no longer a part of their lives. Finally, the aim of TFC is to reduce the symptoms of trauma (e.g., anxiety, grief, or anger) that oftentimes work to disable adolescents from being productive in school and in society (Sullivan et al., 2011). However, those who tend not to benefit from TFC are those adolescents who have had long-stemming trauma (e.g., sexual molestation) or who have significant "behavior problems," grief concerns, suicide ideation, psychosis, or substance abuse problems. For these adolescents, interventions should first aim to reduce the prior-mentioned concerns before beginning TFC (Sullivan et al., 2011).

Structured Psychotherapy for Adolescents Responding to Chronic Stress

Structured psychotherapy for adolescents responding to chronic stress (SPARCS) is an empirically supported, culturally driven, manu-alized group treatment plan to improve social, emotional, behavioral, and academic functioning in children and adolescents exposed to individ-ual or chronic traumatic events. SPARCS is a present-centered intervention approach to treat-ing trauma in adolescents who are experiencing problems with emotional regulation and impul-sivity along with dissociation, self-perception, relationships, somatization; and systems of meaning (Habib, 2006). It was specifically designed to meet the needs and address the symptoms of adolescents still living in situations of ongoing stress. In addition, it enhances an adolescent's current strengths and resiliency through skill building, which is delivered through a cognitive behavioral approach (Habib, 2006). Goals for treatment include mindfulness and awareness of the moment (derived from dialectic behavioral therapy), increase of self-efficacy, developing supportive relationships, and creat-ing meaning making. It has been incorporated successfully in various at-risk service systems and addresses the comorbidity that is symptom-atic of trauma in adolescence (Courtois & Ford, 2009; Weiner, Schneider, & Lyons, 2009).

Generally speaking, SPARCS is most effec-tive over a 16-week session course, consisting of one 50- to 60-minute therapy session each week. Again, it is designed for those adolescents dealing with trauma related to PTSD; however, it can also be implemented with adolescents who present with high-risk behavior problems (e.g., substance abuse, school absences, and/or pregnancy; Habib, 2006).

Trauma and Grief Component Therapy for Adolescents

Trauma and grief component therapy for ado-lescents (TGCT) is a modularized, manual-designed treatment for adolescents that can be implemented in community mental health, school, or other service-oriented settings. It is designed to address traumatic grief and loss in adolescents affected by school or community violence, natu-ral disasters, accidents, war, domestic/gang/inter-personal violence, and terrorism. Interventions include psycho-education, skill building, emo-tion regulation, cognitive restructuring, and relapse prevention. It is designed to incorporate families into sessions and includes assessments for outcome measurements (Layne, Saltzman, Pynoos, & Steinberg, 2002).

In addition, TGCT encompasses four mod-ules: (1) adolescents are taught emotional regula-tion skills and are educated about trauma, (2) adolescents process through their trauma, (3) adolescents learn how to endure the feelings of grief, and (4) adolescents learn how to reframe their grief and address their negative choices and are taught how to be more socially acceptable (Ritschel, 2011).

Cox et al. (2007) used TGCT to treat postwar adolescents in Bosnia who had experienced trauma as a result of the war and found that at the end of treatment these adolescents showed greater coping skills (e.g., problem-solving abil-ity), had changed attitudes (e.g., greater self-esteem), were better communicators, began to advocate the program to others (i.e., stood up for the rights of other war victims), and showed more interest and skill in interpersonal relation-ships (Cox et al., 2007). In fact, adolescents who underwent TGCT reported that after the treat-ment they oftentimes had better relationships with peers and with family members (Cox et al., 2007). The downfall of the TGCT, as reported by the study from Cox et al. (2007), was the quanti-tative scoring for evaluation due to its length of questioning and the inability of the program used within this study to affect all adolescents who would benefit from it. However, overall, the positive benefits of the program were found to far surpass the limitations of it (Cox et al., 2007).

Again, there are a number of evidence-based trauma treatment modalities not outlined that are included as best practice or considered promising in the treatment for trauma and complex trauma in adolescence. The majority require advanced training to become competent to treat these young survivors of trauma. Organizations such as NCTSN and SAMHSA are resources that offer a wealth of current and effective evidence-based treatment and training options.

Psychological First Aid

According to Ruzek et al. (2007), the purpose of Psychological First Aid for adolescents is to reduce the immediate distressing response to trauma as it fosters short- and long-term coping skills and adaptive functioning. To adhere to best practice, it is necessary to fulfill the following four standards:

1. It should be consistent with research evidence on risk and resilience following trauma.

2. It should be applicable and practical in field settings.

3. It should be appropriate for developmental levels across the life span.

4. It should be culturally informed and delivered in a flexible manner.

In working with adolescents, Psychological First Aid begins with listening and helping adolescents verbalize their experience, including their questions, concerns, and their emotions. The developmental position of the adolescent must be taken into consideration, as regression in language and behavior is common under traumatic stress. Based on the development stage of the brain during the traumatic event, the following core actions have been developed in 2000 by the NCTSN (Ruzek et al., 2007) to perform psychological first aid in the field:

1. Contact and Engagement

2. Safety and Comfort

3. Stabilization

4. Information Gathering: Current Needs and Concerns

5. Practical Assistance

6. Connection with Social Supports

7. Information on Coping

8. Linkage with Collaborative Services (p. 19)

CASE CONSIDERATIONS

James and Lisa provide two very different but excellent examples of traditional versus trauma-informed treatment (Case Scenarios 3.1 and 3.2).

Case Scenario 3.1

James

James presented as a troubled 16-year-old adolescent who was recently suspended from school for smoking marijuana on campus and caught by his parents for texting sexually explicit pictures of himself to his 15-year-old girlfriend. A recent psychological evaluation reported a diagnosis of ODD as exhibited by *DSM-5* (American Psychiatric Association, 2013):

(Continued)

Case Scenario 3.1   (Continued)

A. A pattern of angry/irritable mood, argumentative/defiant behavior, or vindictiveness lasting at least 6 months as evidenced by at least four symptoms and exhibited during interaction with at least one individual who is not a sibling:

   1. Is often touchy or easily annoyed

   2. Is often angry and resentful

   3. Often argues with authority figures or adults

   4. Often deliberately annoys others

   5. Often blames others for his or her mistakes or misbehavior

B. The disturbance in behavior is associated with distress in the individual or others in his immediate social context or its negative impacts on social, educational, occupational, or other important areas of functioning.

C. The behaviors do not occur exclusively during the course of a psychotic, substance use, depressive, or bipolar disorder.

Through the interview process, it was revealed that James was adopted at 18 months of age from a single mother who was in and out of jail for cocaine possession. Although he does not remember his life with his mother, Child Protective Services report finding James living in filth, unattended to, and with no food or suitable clothing to keep him warm. During early childhood, he appeared to feel at home and comfortable with his three older siblings but would often purposely irritate them. He would at times hoard food or take from his siblings when they weren't around. When James began middle school, his parents noticed a withdrawal from family time and an increased irritable mood, misbehavior, and a lack of responsibility for negative behavior. At 15, James was caught with beer, which he blamed on his 19-year-old brother. Since then, through the recent expulsion, James has demonstrated consistent symptoms of ODD (Exercise 3.1).

Exercise 3.1

Discussion Questions

1. How would a trauma-informed approach differ from a traditional approach with regard to case conceptualization?

2. What information would a trauma-informed provider gather to better understand and treat James?

3. Having discovered that James's symptoms of opposition defiance stem from an insecure attachment to his biological mother before his adoption at 18 months, how does treatment shift from traditional to trauma informed?

4. What would be the difference for James if his school adopted a trauma-informed approach in working with their students?

Case Scenario 3.2

Lisa

Lisa presented as a 14-year-old high school freshman with anxiety and insomnia. She complained of stress due to the inability to retain information when she studied and a lack of sleep for the previous several weeks due to intense nightmares. She was a successful student and a gifted tennis player. Through the interview process, it was revealed that Lisa had struggled in the recent past with an eating disorder as well as current chronic pain due to long-standing back issues. Lisa was born as the second daughter to an alcoholic mother and a financially successful but disconnected father. As a very small child, Lisa became her mother's security in the alcohol-fueled, late-night arguments between her and her husband. Because of this parentification and enmeshed relationship, Lisa believed that she could not tell her mother when the father of her childhood friend began to sexually abuse her from 7 through 9 years of age. This preceded a shift from Lisa's role as caretaker to scapegoat for her mother. At the age of 13, Lisa chose to tell her mother about her sexual abuse during one of her mother's many alcohol-fueled arguments. She was subsequently blamed by her mother for sexual abuse. Over the past year, Lisa has been chronically verbally abused by her mother and has experienced two incidents of rape by an older neighbor (Exercise 3.2).

Exercise 3.2

Discussion Questions

1. As a trauma-informed provider, what are your primary principles in working with Lisa?
2. What types of interventions might benefit Lisa on her journey of healing?
3. Where will you find information concerning best-practice treatment protocols for adolescent trauma survivors?
4. What are some ethical considerations in dealing with Lisa as a client?
5. What precautions would a provider take to prevent burnout while working with Lisa?

IMPLICATIONS FOR COUNSELING ADOLESCENTS

Providers, educators, supervisors, and other professionals in the field need to be well versed in all aspects of trauma-informed theory, including trauma-informed care, trauma-specific assessments, therapies, and interventions in order to incorporate these standards to practice,

program objectives, and syllabi (Webber & Mascari, 2009).

Strategies and Interventions

Trauma-specific strategies and interventions for adolescents are an integral part of trauma-informed theory, as they have been developed specifically to deal with trauma and the related symptoms experienced by the individual, the family, and the surrounding community. The dilemma of treatment for this age-group is determining whether they should be kept in the care of people or systems that are sources of fear and pain or to take them away from people they have an attachment to and from their familiar environments all the while playing into separation and abandonment stress (van der Kolk, 2005). Although many organizations see the reunification of families as the end goal for treatment, abusive or neglectful homes will only continue the trauma cycle. Maintenance of the foundational principle of safety promotion is primary and will be a consideration in choosing the appropriate trauma treatment modality as well as the incorporation of core components of trauma-informed interventions such as the National Center for Trauma-Informed Care (Black et al., 2012; Cloitre, Courtois, Charuvastra, Carapezza, Stolbach, & Green, 2011):

- *Screening and triage:* The process of sorting a group of clients to determine the immediacy of an individual's need for treatment. Although many adolescents who experience traumatic events exhibit traumatic symptoms, there are others who exhibit resiliency and growth from traumatic events. Screening for trauma symptoms and the severity of such symptoms have significant importance as immediate psychological first aid might be needed.

- *Assessment, case conceptualization, and treatment planning:* Postscreening, evidence-based measures must be implemented to obtain an accurate scope of the problem. From this point, case conceptualization and treatment planning is based on client specificity.

- *Psycho-education:* The process of educating adolescents, families, and counselors on what trauma is, how it affects their overall development, and how it can be treated. Psycho-education is one of the most common standard practices in trauma-informed care. It is often one of the first steps in treatment and helps the adolescent understand what trauma is, how and why it affects him or her as an individual, and how trauma symptoms can continue to affect

him or her long after the traumatic event has taken place.

- *Coping skills:* The process of (a) identifying and exploring triggers and stressors that lead to trauma responses and (b) identifying coping resources that highlight the adolescent's strengths and useful strategies to manage trauma responses. Coping skills can include but are not limited to becoming educated on identifying triggers, grounding exercises, relaxation techniques, and emotional expression methods. Techniques in relaxation include meditation and yoga, controlled breathing, and muscle relaxation.

- *Emotional regulation, anxiety management, and adaptive routines:* The utilization of learned coping skills will in turn help the adolescent navigate the process of regulating his or her emotional and affective responses to trauma. Reducing anxiety and affect regulation is imperative to emotional health and functioning. Other techniques include cognitive restructuring and the creation of adaptive routines that help alleviate the affective response to trauma.

- *Parent skill building and behavior management:* Educating parents on the adolescent's emotional and physical responses to trauma can be life giving to parents who are overwhelmed by the experience of their child. Skill building includes improving communication, boundary building, and developing a system of behavior management to build a positive relationship with their teens and making room for healing to take place.

- *Trauma narrative and organization:* The process of re-creating and/or retracing the traumatic experiences as to make meaning. Retelling of the traumatic event is not necessary to obtain healing. Often, providers make the mistake of pushing the adolescent into a discussion of what happened in a way that can retraumatize the individual and increase traumatic stress symptoms. Other trauma survivors utilize the retelling of their trauma narrative to put a voice to and make meaning out of the experience. Trauma narratives can be told through talk therapy, EMDR, prolonged exposure, writing or journaling, art, dance, music, as well as other therapeutic modalities.

- *Cognitive restructuring and developmental progress:* The process of identifying and rewiring maladaptive and/or irrational thoughts and beliefs. Cognitive restructuring is a CBT technique used to control and change negative beliefs and thinking patterns in order to rewire maladaptive cognitive styles due to trauma during brain development. It serves to increase developmental progress and reconstruct more accurate thoughts about self and others in the context of relationships.

- *Addressing grief and loss:* Due to the nature of trauma, grief and loss can often partner along with other traumatic symptoms experienced by the adolescent. Utilizing effective coping skills, building a supportive family and community, and psycho-education are necessary. For trauma-informed providers, having a working understanding of grief and loss will benefit those who have experienced a traumatic event.

- *Future planning:* Being able to work with adolescents to build hope for a future will allow for empowerment and motivation. Providers help create a plan to maintain what was accomplished in treatment.

- *Psychological First Aid:* The process of intervention of choice by disaster mental health professionals when responding to adolescents affected by terrorism or disaster (Brymer et al., 2006).

The Traumatized Care Provider

Having an understanding of the impact of trauma on clinicians is equally important in trauma-informed theory. Caregivers working with individuals who have experienced trauma and complex trauma are vulnerable to trauma-related stress as well as professional burnout (Figley, 1995; Newell & MacNeil, 2010). Much like their traumatized clients, clinicians are susceptible to distortions in worldviews. Threats or perceived threats to safety and security, burnout, secondary trauma, and compassion fatigue are common fallouts for counselors who work in this field. Although vicarious trauma is the norm for counselors working with this population, burnout is the result of a traumatized provider. Burnout is defined "as a state of physical, emotional,

psychological, and spiritual exhaustion resulting from chronic exposure to (or practice with) populations that are vulnerable or suffering" (Newell & MacNeil, 2010, p. 58; see also Pines & Aronson, 1988). More than any other factor, a lack of trauma-informed care education heightens the negative impact of trauma work (Harris & Fallot, 2001). Provider self-care is imperative while working with adolescent trauma survivors. Education on trauma and its impact, speaking openly about negative feelings concerning counseling work, personal therapy, as well as restoring connection to community, spirituality, and other areas of life to avoid isolation are beneficial in the welfare of a provider working with traumatized clients.

Application of Ethics

Working with adolescent trauma survivors is a delicate dance when considering the ethical components attached to treatment. Alongside client identification, consent, confidentiality, and clinical competence, it is imperative to have a working understanding of the laws in the provider's state on mandated, reported, and other pertinent issues surrounding the legislation of the state. Specifically, the trauma of physical and sexual abuse in the life of an adolescent generally falls under the laws of immediate and mandated reporting of any health care provider. According to an article written for the American Psychological Association (Behnke & Warner, 2002) thinking through three perspectives—the law, clinical practice, and ethics—are necessary in working with this population over any other. The law is clear with regard to reporting and who has the right to know the content of the adolescent's treatment. However, good clinical treatment is encapsulated with a "zone of privacy" (p. 44) that helps develop the individual's sense of autonomy. It is the judgment of the provider to ethically determine whether or not information such as a nonreportable traumatic event is beneficial to discuss with anyone outside of that zone of privacy. Advanced training, expert supervision, and consultation are the appropriate ethical steps in determining what information should be shared and what should be kept between the provider and the adolescent.

CLINICAL REVIEW OF CASES

The cases of James and Lisa presented earlier in the chapter provide examples of the need for providers to become trauma informed. Having a working understanding of attachment, trauma, and brain development is imperative for accurate assessment, diagnosis, and treatment of adolescents who have experienced a single traumatic event or chronic trauma over their lifetimes. While working with James, working beyond his psychological evaluation and examining his relational history in relationship to understanding trauma and attachment, assessing James's attachment style would reveal his strong avoidant attachment style connected to his clinical diagnosis of ODD. By taking a "what happened to you" versus a "what is wrong with you" approach to treatment, helping James understand why he does what he does through psycho-education helps begin his own self-assessment process and builds the therapeutic alliance. Through the use of coping skills, emotion regulation, cognitive restricting, and behavior management, along with parent skills building, James can begin working on healthy empowerment that does not infringe on others in the context of relationships.

Lisa's case becomes complicated due to the legal and ethical requirements for the provider based on her claim of early child sexual abuse and rape. Once these aspects are worked through adequately, the clinical work of alleviating and eradicating the traumatic stress symptoms Lisa experiences begins. Being aware of the attachment style of Lisa and the familial dynamic of addiction is necessary for future health in the context of her current relationships.

SUMMARY

Trauma affects the body, brain, beliefs, judgments, and interpersonal relationships of adolescents in a unique and complex way. The chronic trauma many adolescents experience forces them to question basic core assumptions about the world (Harris & Fallot, 2001). It is imperative that mental health professionals and the organizational systems in which they work understand and implement trauma-informed care and trauma-specific services that address the needs and vulnerabilities of adolescent trauma survivors. As awareness of the impact of trauma increases, trauma-informed theory should be incorporated in all mental health service systems. Providers working with this population must commit to working in tandem with the core principles of safety, trustworthiness, choice, collaboration, and empowerment as they navigate and promote resiliency and healing. To become competent in working with adolescent survivors of trauma, the need for advanced training is a necessity. Implementing trauma-informed theory may seem daunting but is richly rewarding as a provider.

KEYSTONES

- Trauma is pervasive and affects the cognitive, emotional, and social development of adolescents.

- More than half of all adolescents have experienced a traumatic event.

- Trauma symptoms look different in adolescents than in adults.

- Attachment relationships are critical to healthy brain development as well as contribute to trauma responses in adolescents.

- Trauma-informed theory encompasses defining trauma and understanding trauma and attachment on brain development, traumatic symptoms over a life span, trauma-informed care, trauma-informed approaches, and trauma-specific assessment, therapies, interventions, and services.

- Vicarious trauma is expected in working with adolescent trauma survivors; however, provider self-care is required to prevent burnout.

REFERENCES

Ainsworth, M. D. (1963). The development of infant–mother interaction among the Ganda. *Determinants of infant behavior, 2,* 67–112.

Ainsworth, M. D. S. (1967). *Infancy in Uganda: Infant care and the growth of love.* Baltimore, MD: Johns Hopkins University Press.

Ainsworth, M. D. S. (1969). Object relations, dependency, and attachment: A theoretical review of the infant–mother relationship. *Child development, 40*(4), 969–1025.

Ainsworth, M. D. (1985). Attachments across the life span. *Bulletin of the New York Academy of medicine, 61*(9), 792.

Ainsworth, M. D. S., & Bell, S. M. (1970). Attachment, exploration, and separation: Illustrated by the behavior of one-year-olds in a strange situation. *Child Development, 41,* 49–67.

Ainsworth, M. D. S., Blehar, M. C., Waters, E., & Wall, S. (1978). *Patterns of attachment: A psychological study of the strange situation.* Hillsdale, NJ: Lawrence Erlbaum.

Amaya-Jackson, L., Reynolds, V., Murray, M. C., McCarthy, G., Nelson, A., Cherney, M. S., . . . March, J. (2003). Cognitive-behavioral treatment for pediatric posttraumatic stress disorder: Protocol and application in school and community settings. *Cognitive and Behavioral Practice, 10*(3), 204–213.

American Psychiatric Association. (2004). *Practice guideline for the treatment of patients with acute stress disorder and posttraumatic stress disorder.* Arlington, Virginia: Author.

American Psychiatric Association. (2013). *Diagnostic and statistical manual of mental disorders* (5th ed.). Arlington, VA: Author.

Barker, G. (2010). *The effects of trauma on attachment.* Retrieved from http://www.ccaa.net.au/documents/TheEffectsOfTraumaOnAttachment.pdf

Beck, A. (1976). *Cognitive therapy and the emotional disorders.* New York, NY: International Universities Press.

Behnke, S. H., & Warner, E. (2002). Confidentiality in the treatment of adolescents. *Monitor on Psychology, 33*(3), 44.

Beidel, D. C., & Turner, S. M. (1998). *Shy children, phobic adults: The nature and treatment of social phobia.* Washington, DC: APA Books.

Black, P. J., Woodworth, M., Tremblay, M., & Carpenter, T. (2012). A review of trauma-informed treatment for adolescents. *Canadian Psychology, 53*(3), 192–203.

Blaustein, M. E., & Kinniburgh, K. M. (2010). *Treating traumatic stress in children and adolescents: How to foster resilience through attachment, self-regulation, and competency.* New York, NY: Guilford Press.

Borelli, J., David, D., Crowley, M., & Mayes, L. (2010). Links between disorganized attachment classification and clinical symptoms in school-aged children. *Journal of Child and Family Studies, 19*(3), 243–256.

Bowlby, J. (1958). The nature of the child's tie to his mother. *International Journal of Psycho-Analysis, 39,* 350–373.

Bowlby, J. (1960). Grief and mourning in infancy and early childhood. *Psychoanalytic Study of the Child, 15,* 9–52.

Bowlby, J. (1969). *Attachment and loss: Vol. 1. Attachment.* New York, NY: Basic Books.

Bowlby, J. (1973). *Attachment and loss: Vol. 2. Separation: Anxiety and anger.* New York, NY: Basic Books.

Bowlby, J. (1980). *Attachment and loss: Vol. 3. Loss: sadness and depression* (International Psycho-Analytical Library No. 109). London, England: Hogarth Press.

Breidenstine, A. S., Bailey, L. O., Zeanah, C. H., & Larrieu, J. A. (2011). Attachment and trauma in early childhood: A review. *Journal of Child & Adolescent Trauma, 4*(4), 274–290.

Breslau, N., Wilcox, H. C., Storr, C. L., Lucia, V. C., & Anthony, J. C. (2004). Trauma exposure and posttraumatic stress disorder: A study of youths in urban America. *Journal of Urban Health: Bulletin of the New York Academy of Medicine, 81,* 530–544.

Bretherton, I. (1992). The origins of attachment theory: John Bowlby and Mary Ainsworth. *Developmental Psychology, 28,* 759–775.

Briere, J., & Lanktree, C. (2013). *Integrative treatment of complex trauma for adolescents (ITCT-A) treatment guide* (2nd ed.). Los Angeles: University of Southern California, Adolescent Trauma Training Center.

Brown, L. S., & Wright, J. (2003). The relationship between attachment strategies and psychopathology in adolescence. *Psychology and Psychotherapy: Theory, Research and Practice, 76,* 351–367.

Brymer, M., Jacobs, A., Layne, C., Pynoos, R., Ruzek, J., Steinberg, A., . . . Watson, P. (2006). *Psychological first aid: Field operations guide* (2nd ed.). Washington, DC: National Child Traumatic Stress Network and National Center for PTSD. Retrieved from http://www.nctsn.org/sites/default/files/pfa/english/1-psyfirstaid_final_complete_manual.pdf

Bureau, J. F., Easterbrooks, M. A., & Lyons-Ruth, K. (2009). Attachment disorganization and controlling behavior in middle childhood: Maternal and child precursors and correlations. *Attachment & Human Development, 11*(3), 265–284.

Cassidy, J., & Berlin, L. J. (1994). The insecure/ ambivalent pattern of attachment: Theory and research. *Child Development, 65,* 971–991.

Child Welfare Information Gateway. (2011). *Supporting brain development in traumatized children and youth.* U.S. Department of Health and Human Services, Administration for Children and Families, Administration on Children, Youth, and Families, and Children's Bureau. Retrieved from http://www.childwelfare.gov/pubPDFs/braindevtrauma.pdf

Chorpita, B. F., Yim, L. M., Donkervoet, J. C., Arensdorf, A., Amundsen, M. J., McGee, C., . . . & Morelli, P. (2002). Toward large-scale implementation of empirically supported treatments for children: A review and observations by the Hawaii empirical basis to services task force. *Clinical Psychology: Science and Practice, 9*(2), 165–190.

Cloitre, M., Courtois, C. A., Charuvastra, A., Carapezza, R., Stolbach, B. C., & Green, B. L. (2011). Treatment of complex PTSD: Results of the ISTSS expert clinician survey on best practices. *Journal of Traumatic Stress, 24*(6), 615–627.

Cohen, J., Mannarino, A., Berliner, L., & Deblinger, E. (2000). Trauma-focused cognitive behavioral therapy for children and adolescents. *Journal of Interpersonal Violence, 15*(11), 1202–1223.

Cole-Detke, H., & Kobak, R. (1996). Attachment processes in eating disorder and depression. *Journal of Consulting and Clinical Psychology, 64,* 282–290.

Copeland, W. E., Keeler, G., Angold, A., & Costello, E. J. (2007). Traumatic events and posttraumatic stress in childhood. *Archives of General Psychiatry, 64,* 577–584.

Costello, E. J., Erkanli, A., Fairbank, J. A., & Angold, A. (2002). The prevalence of potentially traumatic events in childhood and adolescence. *Journal of Traumatic Stress, 15,* 99–112.

Courtois, C. A., & Ford, J. D. (2009). *Treating complex traumatic stress disorders: An evidence-based guide.* New York, NY: Guilford Press.

Cox, J., Davies, D. R., Burlingame, G. M., Campbell, J. E., Layne, C. M., & Katzenbach, R. J. (2007). Effectiveness of a trauma/grief-focused group intervention: A qualitative study with war-exposed Bosnian adolescents. *International Journal of Group Psychotherapy, 57*(3), 319–345.

Retrieved from http://www.ncbi.nlm.nih.gov/pubmed/17661546

Department of Veterans Affairs and Department of Defense. (2008). *Analysis of VA health care utilization among US Global War on Terrorism (GWOT) veterans: Operation Enduring Freedom, Operation Iraqi Freedom, January 2008.* Washington, DC: Department of Veterans Affairs and Department of Defense, VHA Office of Public Health and Environmental Hazards.

Erikson, E. H. (1950). *Childhood and society.* New York, NY: W. W. Norton.

Erikson, E. H. (Ed.). (1963). *Youth: Change and challenge.* New York, NY: Basic Books.

Fallot, R., & Harris, M. (2009). *Creating cultures of trauma-informed care (CCTIC): A self-assessment and planning protocol.* Washington, DC: Community Connections.

Fang, X., Brown, D. S., Florence, C. S., & Mercy, J. A. (2012). The economic burden of child maltreatment in the United States and implications for prevention. *Child Abuse & Neglect, 36*(2), 156–165.

Figley, C. (Ed.). (1995). *Compassion fatigue: Coping with secondary traumatic stress disorder in those who treat the traumatized.* New York, NY: Routledge.

Foa, E. B., Rothbaum, B. O., Riggs, D. S., & Murdock, T. B. (1991). Treatment of posttraumatic stress disorder in rape victims: A comparison between cognitive-behavioral procedures and counseling. *Journal of Consulting and Clinical Psychology, 59*(5), 715.

Ford, J. D. (2005). Treatment implications of altered neurobiology, affect regulation and information processing following child maltreatment. *Psychiatric Annals, 35,* 410–419.

Ford, J. D., Courtois, C., van der Hart, O., Nijenhuis, E., & Steele, K. (2005). Treatment of complex posttraumatic self-dysregulation. *Journal of Traumatic Stress, 18,* 467–477.

Ford, J. D., & Russo, E. (2006). Trauma-focused, present-centered, emotional self-regulation approach to integrated treatment for posttraumatic stress and addiction: Trauma adaptive recovery group education and therapy (TARGET). *American Journal of Psychotherapy, 60*(4), 335–355.

Greeson, J. K., Briggs, E. C., Kisiel, C. L., Layne, C. M., Ake, G. S., 3rd, Ko, S. J., . . . Fairbank, J. A. (2011). Complex trauma and mental health in children and adolescents placed in foster care: Findings from the National Child Traumatic Stress Network. *Child Welfare, 90*(6), 91–108.

Guarino, K., Soares, P., Konnath, K., Clervil, R., & Bassuk, E. (2009). *Trauma-informed organizational toolkit.* Rockville, MD: Center for Mental Health Services, Substance Abuse and Mental Health Services Administration, and the Daniels Fund, the National Child Traumatic Stress Network, and the W. K. Kellogg Foundation 17.

Habib, M. (2006). Structured psychotherapy for adolescents responding to chronic stress (SPARCS). Retrieved from http://www.cebc4cw.org/program/structured-psychotherapy-for-adolescents-responding-to-chronic-stress/detailed

Habib, M., & Labruna, V. (2011). Clinical considerations in assessing trauma and PTSD in adolescents. *Journal of Child & Adolescent Trauma, 4,* 198–216.

Harris, M., & Fallot, R. (Eds.). (2001). *Using trauma theory to design service systems: New directions for mental health services.* San Francisco, CA: Jossey-Bass.

Hesse, E., & Main, M. (2006). Frightened, threatening, and dissociative parental behavior in low-risk samples: Description, discussion, and interpretations. *Development and Psychopathology, 18,* 309–343.

James, B. (1994). *Handbook for treating attachment problems in children.* New York, NY: Simon & Schuster.

Kessler, R. C., Sonnega, A., Bromet, E., Hughes, M., & Nelson, C. B. (1995). Posttraumatic stress disorder in the National Comorbidity Survey. *Archives of General Psychiatry, 52,* 1048–1060.

Kinniburgh, K. J., Blaustein, M., Spinazzola, J., & van der Kolk, B. A. (2005). Attachment, self-regulation, and competency. *Psychiatric Annals, 35*(5), 424–430.

Kobak, R., & Cole, C. (1994). Attachment and meta-monitoring: Implications for adolescent autonomy and psychopathology. In D. Cicchetti (Ed.), *Rochester symposium on development and psychopathology: Vol. 5. Disorders of the self* (267–297). Rochester, NY: Rochester University Press.

Layne, C. M., Saltzman, W. R., Pynoos, R. S., & Steinberg, A. M. (2002). *Trauma and grief component therapy.* New York: New York State Office of Mental Health.

Main, M., & Solomon, J. (1986). Discovery of an insecure-disorganized/disoriented attachment pattern: Procedures, findings and implications for the classification of behavior. In T. B. Brazelton & M. Yogman (Eds.), *Affective development in infancy* (pp. 95–124). Norwood, NJ: Ablex.

March, J., & Amaya-Jackson, L. (1999). Trauma focused coping manual: Treatment of pediatric post traumatic stress disorder after single-incident trauma. Retrieved from http://epic.psychiatry.duke.edu/sites/epic.psychiatry.duke.edu/files/documents/TRauma%20Focused%20Coping%20Manual%2012.19.08-1.pdf

Miller, N. L., & Najavits, L. M. (2012). Creating trauma-informed correctional care: A balance of goals and environment. *European Journal of Psychotraumatology, 3,* 1–8.

Nader, K. (2008). *Understanding and assessing trauma in children and adolescents: Measures, methods, and youth in context.* New York, NY: Routledge.

National Child Traumatic Stress Network. (2008). *Effects of complex trauma.* Retrieved from http://nctsnet.org/trauma-types/complex-trauma/effects-of-complex-trauma

Newell, J. M., & MacNeil, G. A. (2010). Professional burnout, secondary traumatic stress, and compassion fatigue: A review of theoretical terms, risk factors, and preventive methods for clinicians. *Best Practices in Mental Health: An International Journal, 6*(2), 57–68.

Pearce J. W., & Pezzot-Pearce T. D. (2001). Psychotherapeutic approaches to children in foster care: Guidance from attachment theory. *Child Psychiatry and Human Development, 32,* 19–44.

Perry, B. D., & Azad, I. (1999). Post-traumatic stress disorders in children and adolescents. *Current Opinion in Pediatrics, 11,* 121–132.

Perry, B. D., Pollard, R., Blakely, T., Baker, W., & Vigilante, D. (1995). Childhood trauma, the neurobiology of adaptation and "use-dependent" development of the brain: How "states" become "traits." *Infant Mental Health Journal, 16*(4), 271–291.

Pines, A., & Aronson, E. (1988). *Career burnout: Causes and cures.* New York, NY: Free Press.

Reimer, M. S., Overton, W. F., Steidl, J. H., Rosenstein, D. S., & Horowitz, H. (1996). Family responsiveness and behavioral control: Influences on adolescent psychopathology, attachment and cognition. *Journal of Research on Adolescence, 6,* 87–112.

Ritschel, L. A. (2011). School-based group psycho-therapy for at-risk adolescents. *International Journal of Group Psychotherapy, 61*(2), 311–317. doi:10.1521/ijgp.2011.61.2.311

Rosenstein, D. S., & Horowitz, H. A. (1996). Adolescent attachment and psychopathology. *Journal of Consulting and Clinical Psychology, 64*(2), 244–253.

Ruzek, J. I., Brymer, M. J., Jacobs, A. K., Layne, C. M., Vernberg, E. M., & Watson, P. J. (2007). Psychological first aid. *Journal of Mental Health Counseling, 29*(1), 17–49.

Schmid, M., Petermann, F., & Fegert, J. M. (2013). Developmental trauma disorder: Pros and cons of including formal criteria in the psychiatric diagnostic systems. *BMC Psychiatry, 13*(1), 1–12.

Seidler, G., & Wagner, F. (2006). Comparing the efficacy of EMDR and trauma-focused cognitive-behavioral therapy in the treatment of PTSD: A meta-analytic study. *Psychological Medicine, 36*(1), 1515–1522.

Shapiro, F. (1996). Eye movement desensitization and reprocessing (EMDR): Evaluation of controlled PTSD research. *Journal of Behavior Therapy and Experimental Psychiatry, 27*(3), 209–218.

Shapiro, F. (2001). *Eye movement desensitization and reprocessing (EMDR): Basic principles, protocols, and procedures* (2nd ed.). New York, NY: Guilford Press.

Shapiro, R. (2010). *The trauma treatment handbook: Protocols across the spectrum.* New York, NY: W. W. Norton.

Substance Abuse and Mental Health Services Administration. (2012). *Trauma and violence.* Retrieved from http://www.samhsa.gov/trauma-violence

Sullivan, K., Amaya-Jackson, L., Briggs-King, E., Murphy, R., Burroughs, J., Vreeland, E., & Houston, F. (2011). How to implement trauma focused coping: A trauma focused cognitive behavior treatment for youth. Retrieved from http://epic.psychiatry.duke.edu/sites/epic.psychiatry.duke.edu/files/documents/TFC_Implementation_Manual.pdf

Tyler, T. A. (2012). The limbic model of systemic trauma. *Journal of Social Work Practice, 26*(1), 125–138.

van der Kolk, B. (2005). Child abuse and victimization. *Psychiatric Annals, 35,* 374–378.

Webber, J. M., & Mascari, J. B. (2009). Critical issues in implementing the new CACREP standards for disaster, trauma, and crisis counseling. In G. R. Walz, J. C. Bleuer, & R. K. Yep (Eds.), *Compelling counseling interventions: VISTAS 2009* (pp. 125–138). Alexandria, VA: American Counseling Association.

Weiner, D. A., Schneider, A., & Lyons, J. S. (2009). Evidence-based treatments for trauma among culturally diverse foster care youth: Treatment retention and outcomes. *Children and Youth Services Review, 31*(11), 1199–1205.

Weinfield, N. S., Whaley, G. L., & Egeland, B. (2004). Continuity, discontinuity, and coherence in attachment from infancy to late adolescence: Sequelae of organization and disorganization. *Attachment & Human Development, 6*(1), 73–97.

Wolpe, J. (1969). *The practice of behavior therapy.* New York, NY: Pergamon Press.

Yates, T. M., Egeland, B., & Sroufe, L. A. (2003). Rethinking resilience: A developmental process perspective. In S. Luthar (Ed.), *Resilience and vulnerability: Adaptation in the context of childhood adversities* (pp. 243–266). Cambridge, England: Cambridge University Press.

4

MULTICULTURAL FAMILY SYSTEMS

In every conceivable manner, the family is linked to our past, bridge to our future.

—Alex Haley

INTRODUCTION

It is estimated that nearly 60% of the U.S. population will consist of minorities by 2100 (U.S. Census Bureau, as cited in Hays, 2008). The increase in minority status creates a need for cultural diversity–informed providers. Providers should have knowledge of historical issues related to a group's historical experiences, cultural traditions, interaction and communication styles, and overall general approaches to life and its challenges. In fact, when a provider is uninformed about the types of historical and current-day challenges of adolescents, the provider has the potential of causing harm to the client and unknowingly offend, misinterpret, minimize, misattribute, or misdiagnose culturally diverse groups, especially minority, protected class, educationally disadvantaged, economically challenged, or physically disabled consumers in unintended ways (Hays, 2008). This harm may take the form of poor therapeutic alliance, misdiagnosis, and disproportionate

representation of minority groups in various systems of care because of mental health issues and uninformed, noncustomized treatment plans and interventions.

McAuliffe (2012) offers that indeed whenever two people meet it is a multicultural interaction, and the provider should maintain a "culturally alert" stance in all professional interactions. This alertness is a "consistent readiness to identify the cultural dimension of consumers' lives and a subsequent integration of culture into counseling work" (McAuliffe, 2012, p. 6). Such an approach allows for providers to respond to the inevitable cross-cultural contact they will encounter in their various work settings and allow for equity in access to services and inclusiveness that matters to individuals and society at large (McAuliffe, 2012).

The starting point of multicultural competence is to increase the provider's own self-awareness (i.e., understand their own beliefs and attitudes about their own cultural and ethnic makeup as well as those of others) and understanding of how oppression can affect the counseling dynamic (e.g., Caucasian young female provider counseling a Latino family) and teach providers how to use affective assessment tools designed for specific cultures (Hays, 2008). When working with adolescents and families, multicultural providers "understand their client's worldview and can intervene in a culturally appropriate manner" (Hays, 2008, p. 95). Hays (2008) offers that when providers provide services to diverse consumer groups, the provider should openly and directly discuss cultural diversity, and how the consumer views differences and similarities between himself or herself and how the provider may influence the counseling relationship. Not doing so could potentially harm the counseling relationship and increase minority consumer dropout rates (Hays, 2008).

Multiculturalism, according to Bingham, Porche-Burke, James, Sue, and Vasquez (2002), is defined by race and ethnicity and topics related to gender, sexual orientation, and disability (physical and intellectual). To meet a consumer's need for positive regard within the counseling relationship requires providers to extend positive regard (Rogers, 1961), possess a self-understanding of one's own culture and reactions to that of others, gain knowledge of the consumer populations being served, and wield all that information in a manner that a best-fitting, customized, and effective treatment plan can be utilized throughout the counseling service delivery process.

Consider Case Scenario 4.1 and refer back to this case to apply the knowledge you gain from this chapter.

Identifying and valuing the differences of an individual's gender, culture, disability, and/or sexual orientation is inherent to the therapy process. According to Bartol and Bartol (2008), each individual has a unique view of the world through the lens of one's unique cultural experiences, and culture impacts all of us in different ways. These experiences, in addition to affecting the individual, can greatly influence family structure and societal structures (e.g., government, religious). To ignore multiculturalism, particularly within the family system, is to not only overlook our ethical standards as providers but also possibly intensify the issue that brought

Case Scenario 4.1

Dr. Clark

Dr. Michael Clark is a Caucasian, licensed professional provider who is looking to build his private practice after moving to a midsized, metropolitan city in Louisiana. After getting accepted by a number of insurance panels and receiving referrals from some of his former clients, Dr. Clark feels confident that he is ready to operate a successful and profitable practice. Within the first month, Dr. Clark sees a surprisingly overwhelming number of clients, particularly families, which he considers to be his specialty. In the second month, he receives two new clients: (1) a middle-class African American family that consists of a father, mother, two children, and an aging grandparent and (2) a Spanish-speaking Latino mother and her 15-year-old son. On reviewing their initial paperwork from their appointment requests, Dr. Clark realizes that he has never worked with members of diverse populations before. Although he recalls taking multicultural counseling courses during his master's and doctoral programs, these courses were a while ago and he worries that he may not be competent enough to handle the unique needs of each of these families.

them to therapy. This chapter focuses on the multicultural aspects of families and the adolescents within them.

This chapter focuses on multicultural counseling and family systems theory as the underpinning for treating families and adolescents.

After reading this chapter, readers will be able to do the following:

- Understand the history of integrated family and multicultural counseling

- Understand integrated multicultural family systems and demonstrate how it may be useful with adolescent clients

- Be able to identify family therapy techniques and therapeutic modalities

- Be able to describe the operational definitions in multi-cultural practice

- Be able to describe the multi-cultural presuppositions for providers

- Understand the multi-cultural counseling competencies

- Be able to describe characteristics of culturally competent counselors, including racial/ethnic identity models, issues of discrimination, marginalization, and oppression

- Identify cultural factors in assessment and treatment of adolescents and families

- Apply knowledge gleaned from case studies.

A History of the Integration of Family and Multicultural Counseling

Origins of Family Systems

The transition from individual psychotherapy to family therapy originated with a shift in perception about how individuals were being treated and what helped them recover. Group therapy was the first attempt to work with families, mainly because a family is a type of group. Using concepts from group dynamics, Kurt Lewin (1951) hypothesized that groups were coherent wholes rather than a collection of individuals. The concepts of process (being aware of how people talk and interact) and content (what they talk about) became a cornerstone to the development of family systems therapy.

Family therapists encounter a multitude of issues within therapy; however, family composition, communication and interaction styles, as well as traditions, holidays, and other customs play critical roles within the family. According to Patterson, Williams, Grauf-Grounds, and Chamow (1998) these issues include (a) learning core theories of family therapy, (b) developing basic counseling skills (e.g., intake, joining, problem identification, empathy), (c) mastering intervention skills, and (d) establishing competencies for managing aspects of therapy that occur outside the therapy room (e.g., consultation, referral, and record keeping).

An additional key concept presented by Patterson et al. (1998) within family therapy includes respect and empathy. Respect, in this sense, is defined as attention and reverence to the therapeutic relationship. It also extends to respecting the consumer's preferences within the counseling process, their mores, cultures, preferences, religion, and traditions. It has been shown that respect can be difficult to develop and maintain in family therapy, particularly when the client(s) is seen as distressed, inappropriate, or dangerous and is essential to the therapeutic process (Corey, Corey, Corey, & Callanan, 2014). Family therapists should respect both—the client's individuality and the client's need to maintain that individuality to reach outcome goals. Respect for the individual, the family, and culturally informed therapeutic goals set by the client must be established. A lack of respect in all these areas could lead the client to feel disregarded or disrespected by the therapist; thus ending the therapeutic relationship.

A Family Therapy and Cultural Sensitivity

Family therapy, from its origin, has been viewed as a culturally sensitive theory (Gladding, 2011). The development of family therapy and its groundwork philosophy was situated within a broad system where the health of a family's functioning is based on universal principles centered on dynamic (ever changing) and reciprocal (affecting, as well as, being affected on) processes, interpersonal transactions, boundaries, and hierarchies. Indeed, the very premise of family systems is centered on understanding the individual and the problem within the context of a larger system (e.g., the family) and implies an openness to culture, especially as it relates to a particular family's framework, interactions, constellation, and experiences.

Classic family therapy models, such as structural family therapy (Minuchin, 1974; Minuchin & Fishman, 1981), strategic family therapy (Haley, 1987), and Bowen's family systems therapy (Bowen, 1966; Kerr & Bowen, 1988), have been criticized for failing to meet the needs of multicultural families (Gushue, Sciarra, & Mejía, 2010; Nichols, 2013). There are a number of reasons for these criticisms. One particular reason is that many of these theories assumed that the theoretical and methodological frameworks that were already established would be applicable and appropriate for individuals from diverse races and ethnicities without consideration of their backgrounds. This, at the time, may have also been related to the fact that the percentage of individuals who identified themselves as a race other than "Caucasian" was relatively small (Gladding, 2011). While this was a stark shift from their ethnocentric and individual focus, much was left to be desired in the family systems' applicability across diverse people groups. As a result, newer models were developed that rejected the premise that all families operated from a universal worldview. This brought about an understanding that families are unique and separate with varying characteristics and needs. This second wave of family therapy models are sometimes referred to as postmodern, or contemporary, and include social construction models, solution-focused therapy (Berg & de Shazer, 1993; Miller & de Shazer, 1998, 2000), feminist (critique and feminist family) therapy, and narrative therapy (e.g., postconstructionism and deconstructionism; White & Epston, 1990).

Notwithstanding the traditional and more recent theories, overall, family theories have developed either without explicit attention to cultural contexts or by presuming that theories developed in one context are applicable to other contexts. These perspectives have been described as emic (culturally localized) and etic (culturally generalized) and will be discussed in more detail. The goal of this chapter is to elaborate on the multicultural knowledge base as applied to diverse families. It aims to provide a more comprehensive and practical understanding for counseling students and professionals on how to work with adolescents and families that present with an increasingly diverse and rich cultural history and present-day interactions with the outside world and within the inner world of their family units (i.e., nuclear units with parents and children and extended family members, including grandparents and honorary family members such as non-blood-related "aunts," "uncles," and "cousins"). The first section of the chapter will provide a brief overview of the general principles of family systems followed by a brief overview of therapeutic approaches. The next section will be devoted to discussing multicultural counseling theory literature and exploring and delineating the guiding principles in treating adolescents and families using a multicultural family systems framework. In the third section, we will highlight ecological and systemic techniques for treating adolescents and review the two major evidence-based therapies: (1) functional family therapy (FFT) and (2) multisystemic family therapy.

History and Development

The child guidance movement greatly contributed to understanding family dynamics (Ruberman, 2009). In working with children, their families, and teachers, therapists realized that the real sources of children's problems were not internal, but came from tensions (e.g., stress, interaction styles) in the family creating negative symptoms (e.g., anxiety, aggression) within the individual. Freida Fromm-Reichmann (1948) identified that a caregiver's parenting style can have ill effects (e.g., the schizophrenic mother). As a means of explaining children's (and adult's) challenges, parents were intrinsically blamed for ills and shortcomings of the individual child. Negative stigma emerged toward parents and identified them as the source of blame for their children's challenges. This stigma was present in mental health professions and seeped into the larger society. In fact, the parental blame continues to be present in popular culture's understandings of society ills and individual challenges (Nichols, 2013). As family theory continued to develop, social workers and other behavioral health providers took the helm and made practical application of the theory within their fieldwork and treated the family as a system within a larger societal system. The etiology of schizophrenia also influenced family systems as therapists realized the impact of the family environment. Developers of family therapy within the United States were typically psychoanalysts who viewed pathology as a function of family dynamics (i.e., Evelyn Millis Duvall, 1956) and treatment as having to do with seeing the whole family rather than the individual and the individual's internalized family experiences (Ackerman, 1958; Bowen, 1966; Whitaker, 1975). In 1950, a group of therapists who would later form the Mental Research Institute, met in Palo Alto, California. They included prominent figures like Gregory Bateson, Jay Haley, and Don Jackson. They would go on to recruit others, such as John Weakland and Paul Watzlawick. Together, the group produced numerous seminal papers (see Bateson, Jackson, Haley, & Weakland, 1956; Weakland & Jackson, 1958) and are credited with being the pioneers of family therapy.

Currently, there is general consensus that cultural competence involves therapists' use of relevant knowledge, dynamic sizing, diversity skills, and awareness (e.g., Sue, 2006). Until the early 1980s, theory and methodology in the field of family therapy had not been rigorously tested or challenged. As a result, in each of the family therapy

schools, methods of interventions were directly or indirectly derived from a Eurocentric worldview, lacked cultural awareness, and excluded attention to structures of injustice. Ho (1987) has suggested, "Some of these therapeutic approaches diametrically oppose indigenous cultural values and structure of ethnic minority families" (p. 1). Culturally insensitive family therapy can lead to errors of judgment and negatively affect treatment resulting in misdiagnosis, ineffective or harmful interventions, reduced outcomes, and/or dropout.

Family System Theory Concepts

Family system theory is an organized way of thinking about and assessing family functioning. The client's symptoms and issues are understood in the context of interpersonal relations with the goal of most family approaches being to enhance the social functioning of all family members. General systems theory in most family approaches is the attempt to alleviate family difficulties by focusing on one family member's behavior toward another. Generally, family-centered interventions are recommended when the family is unable to perform its basic functions (Greene, Kropf, & Frankel, 2009); this is also the time they tend to seek counseling intervention as the system is not working as they have grown accustomed to and come to expect.

In family systems, a problem is usually identified by an individual presenting with a specific concern and desiring resolution of the dysfunctional interactions. In family therapy, the child or adolescent is usually brought in by the parent(s) or the caregiver with the goal of "fixing" the child. This process is referred to as *scapegoating*, where the scapegoat is understood to merely be a messenger signaling a need for change as opposed to the problem.

General systems theory asserts that individuals can be viewed within the context of a group of elements all interacting with one another as a single entity.

Let's consider the case of Lupe, a 6-year-old Latino male, whose family is seeing the therapist for therapy due to "consistent unrest" in the home. During the initial consultation, each family member is asked to describe his or her view of the problem. At the end of each individual's statement, they close with some variation of, "If Lupe would just . . ." or "When Lupe realizes that's not how to behave . . ." It is clear to the therapist that Lupe is being viewed as the cause of the family's issues. Because the therapist understands that no single individual can be blamed for the dysfunction of the entire family (Gladding, 2011), the therapist transitions the conversation to how other members might be contributing to the tension they feel among one another.

The concepts of *wholeness* and *nonsummativity* (the whole is greater than the sum of its parts) are key principles. As such, a family is viewed as more than a collection of individuals. Systems can be understood by looking at process and structure. As stated earlier, attention is not only on the "what" (content) but the "how" (process); thus, family structure can be understood by assessing the boundaries between and within subsystems.

Gregory Bateson (1972) introduced the concept of cybernetics as the backdrop of a systems framework. Cybernetics describes the process of family rules that govern the family's homeostatic range. Negative feedback/mechanisms are used to enforce these rules. Homeostasis is a level or threshold created by the system. A feedback loop is related to the reciprocal nature of the family's interactions and is incorporated to maintain the system or homeostasis. In examining family processes, a systems approach uses circular causality rather than linear causality.

General family systems theory provides a multicausal context for understanding human behavior. Thus, symptoms can be understood in the context of interpersonal relations (Greene et al., 2009). Over time, this interaction becomes stable, thus, creating boundaries within and between itself and the environment, resulting in the development of its own character. Triangles are a subsystem within the family that form when two people cannot solve a problem between themselves and, thus, pulls in a third party to

minimize and stabilize the interaction. These shifts and changes are called the family life cycle, which is a key construct in family therapy as it recognizes specific developmental and situational stages through which families navigate.

Family Therapy Approaches

There are a number of family therapy approaches available to meet the needs of any type of family structure. Constructivism is a family systems epistemological paradigm that posits that knowledge is created or constructed by the observer. Constructivist approaches moved away from traditional theories of family therapy and focused on individual approaches, emphasizing cognition and the individual's subjective experience rather than the structure or process of the interaction. These include solution-focused, collaborative language, and feminist therapy.

Similarly, social constructivism expands constructivism and examines the way we perceive and relate to the world. Narrative therapy believes that adolescents and their problems are a result of social and political influences, resulting in narratives that are destructive and oppressive. The goal of narrative therapy is to help individuals create more positive, empowering narratives and solutions.

The degree of emphasis on the general principles varies within major schools of family therapy (Skynner, 1981, as cited in Greene et al., 2009). Family treatment methods form a treatment continuum where at one end the emphasis is emotional and interpersonal relationships and at the other end the therapist intervenes in the structure and communication patterns to improve functioning (Greene et al., 2009). Selection of family therapy techniques is influenced by the provider's style and theoretical beliefs; characteristics of the family system; personalities of family members; developmental stage of the family; nature and severity of the presenting problem, particularly of the family members present; and desired therapeutic goals (McLeod, 1986, as cited in Greene et al., 2009). In the remaining section of the chapter, we will turn our attention to an important development in the field of counseling and family therapy—recognizing and understanding how to address diverse family types, known as multicultural family systems.

MULTICULTURAL FAMILY SYSTEMS: CULTURALLY SENSITIVE STRATEGIES FOR ADOLESCENTS

The overarching objective when treating adolescents from a multicultural perspective is gaining a thorough understanding of the adolescent, culture, and environmental settings of family, neighborhoods, schools, and communities. Using a systemic and ecological approach, a comprehensive and thorough assessment of each system lays the foundation for culturally relevant treatment and interventions. While there are myriad models and programs designed to treat a wide variety of family issues, it can be difficult to know which theory and approach works best for which issues? This section provides a review of culturally sensitive techniques for adolescents.

Relevant Adolescent Developmental Considerations

According to Erikson (1963, pp. 5–56), the primary psychological issue of adolescence is *identity versus role confusion*. Adolescents struggle to define who they are and attempt to achieve an identity that is uniquely their own.

Situational conditions that face adolescents:

- Changes in family structure and diminished parental nurturance and guidance
- Overexposure of media and influence in adolescents' lives
- Dominance of media in music and violence in video games—(e.g., media influence often implicated when teens commit desperate acts of violence.)

Life Stages

According to Havighurst (1972), these include the following:

- Preparing for a career
- Developing more mature relationships with peers
- Achieving socially responsible behavior
- Gaining greater independence

Risk Facto)rs

Thompson (1998) reviews risk factors and categorizes them as follows:

- A disruptive home environment
- Low self-esteem
- Learning disabilities
- Developmental delays
- Emotional difficulties
- Interpersonal problems
- Lack of social support

Success for Adolescents

Keys to success for adolescents include the following:

- The extent to which they are able to be empathic
- The ability to form and maintain lasting and meaningful relationships with both genders
- The ability to tolerate diversity of opinion and values
- A system of ethics and moral guidelines for behavior
- The capacity to be both independent and work collaboratively
- Success in academic endeavors
- The ability to be assertive and to resist peer pressure

- Relationships with important adults
- Social and emotional skills appropriate to the age-group
- The ability to express a wide range of emotions
- Understanding how to reach out to others in meaningful ways
- Creativity and a sense of humor
- Beginning acceptance of personal responsibility
- Planning for the future

In a meta-analysis study Kazak et al. (2010), which examined evidence-based practices for children and adolescents, it was found that evidence-based practice for assessments were those that identified problems and symptoms to appropriately diagnose and clarify treatment focus and matched the condition with the intervention. Characteristics of best practice assessments are provided below:

1. Recognition of strengths
2. Problems
3. Personal, family, and community resources
4. Attention to environmental, cultural, and system resources

Techniques and Interventions

Several techniques and interventions relevant to culturally sensitive therapy with adolescents and families are provided below:

- Diagnostic clinical interview: Initial
- Cultural formulation interview (CFI): Throughout treatment
- Complete psychosocial: Initial
- Genogram: Initial and throughout (see Figure 4.1 for an example)
- Ecological assessment: Examines the ecological aspects of individual characteristics and developmental tasks associated with adolescent (situational conditions, high-risk behaviors, resiliency factors, and resources.)—initial and throughout
- Family and environmental measures: Family Adaptability Cohesion Scale (FACES)/Family Evaluation Scale (FES)—initial and may be used as a baseline to monitor progress and for research outcome studies (see Figure 4.2 for an example).
- Mental health assessment: World Health Organization Disability Assessment Schedule (DSM-5) comprehensive assessment to examine global mental health function and levels of impairment. Also measures geared for specific symptoms and level of impairment.
- Ethnic identity development assessment
- Functional family therapy
- Parent peer support groups
- Psycho-education: Provide prospective guidance to parents on adolescent transitions
- Deconstructive listening
- Deconstructive questions
- Externalizing the problem
- Preference
- Letters and certificates
- Audience/witnesses
- Genogram
- Ecomap (see Figure 4.3 for an example)
- Eliciting strengths and resources
- Inspiring solutions and solution building
- "On track"
- Miracle question
- Psycho-education—Parenting, communication, and topics relative to adolescent developmental stages/tasks

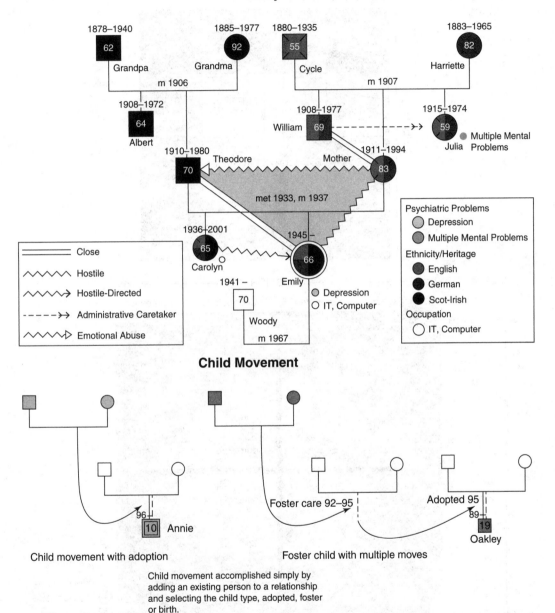

Emily

Child Movement

Child movement with adoption

Foster child with multiple moves

Child movement accomplished simply by adding an existing person to a relationship and selecting the child type, adopted, foster or birth.

Figure 4.1   Genograms

Sources. Genogram Analytics, LLC (2002–2014). Genograms: Child Movement, Retrieved from, http://www.genogram analytics.com/examples_genograms.html

Genogram Analytics, LLC (2002–2014). Genograms: Emily, Retrieved from, http://www.genogramanalytics.com/examples_genograms.html

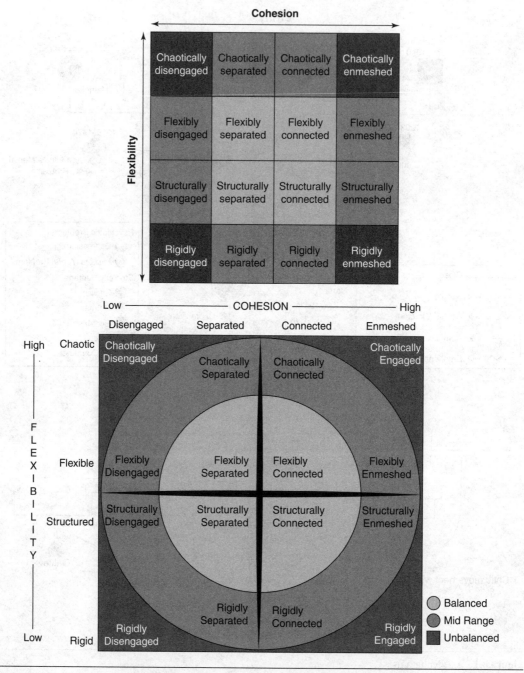

Figure 4.2   Family Adaptability and Cohesion Scales—FACES IV

Note. FACES (Kouneski, E., 2000) include six scales, derived from a 42-item self-report questionnaire from the Circumplex model. The six scales are (1) Balanced, (2) Rigidly Cohesive, (3) Midrange, (4) Flexibly Unbalanced, (5) Chaotically Disengaged, and (6) Unbalanced. It measures cohesion and flexibility by examining communication styles and family interactions.

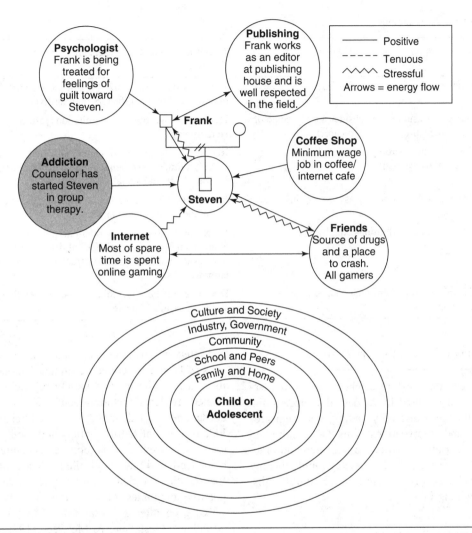

Figure 4.3 Ecomap

Source. Genogram Analytics, LLC (2002-2014). Ecomaps: Steven Ecomap, Retrieved from, http://www.genogramanalytics .com/examples_ecomaps.html

Table 4.1 Characteristics of Multicultural-Sensitive Therapy

Nondiscriminatory/Nonracist Counseling	*Empowerment/Multiculturalist/Social Justice Aware Counseling*
Avoids initiating discussion of race, ethnicity, or identity (e.g., marginalized status) unless central to presenting problem	Proactive in exploring counselor's/and consumer's ethnic and cultural identities and their impact on consumer, perception of problem, treatment, and the counseling relationship

(Continued)

Table 4.1   (Continued)

Nondiscriminatory/Nonracist Counseling	Empowerment/Multiculturalist/Social Justice Aware Counseling
Does not reinforce stereotyped roles	Helps consumer recognize the impact of social, cultural, and political factors on their lives
Encourages consumers to consider a wide range of choices, especially in regard to careers	Helps consumer transcend limitations resulting from stereotyping
Avoids allowing micro-aggressions, biases to affect diagnoses and treatment	Recognizes the degree to which individual identities, values, attitudes, and behaviors may reflect internalization of harmful social standards
Avoids use of discriminatory assessment instruments	Includes multicultural analysis and competencies as a component of assessment
Treats individuals and groups equally	Helps consumers examine their cultural statuses, ethnic identity, and experiences of discrimination/oppression and help them construct and integrate empowered stories
Avoids misuse of power in the counseling relationship	Develops collaborative counselor–client relationships and issues of power.

EVIDENCE-BASED OUTGROWTHS

In recent decades, researchers and providers have been required to validate the success and overall benefit of family therapy treatment programs and interventions. This has resulted in more rigor and specificity in research and practice. This section will discuss key family therapy and adolescent evidence-based outgrowths, highlighting FFT.

Functional Family Therapy

FFT, initially developed by Alexander and Parsons in the late 1960s, was the first of its kind to be applied to youth in juvenile justice contexts and focused on engagement in the treatment process and in client motivation. It is found to be an effective, clinical-specific treatment model and one of the emerging evidence-based intervention programs for at-risk adolescent youth and their families (Sexton, 2009; Sexton, Chamberlin, Landsverk, Ortiz, & Schoenwald (2010). FFT is delivered both in the office and in the client's home and is spread over a 3- to 6-month period,

and interventions target populations between the ages of 11 and 18. Outcome studies demonstrate its efficacy with a wide variety of adolescent-related problems, including youth violence, drug abuse, and other delinquency-related behaviors. FFT is a mix of family therapy and family psychology, meaning it is both a systemic and evidence-based practice, while being a clinically focused therapy that is highly interactive. The positive outcomes of FFT remain relatively stable even after a 5-year follow-up (Gordon, Arbuthnot, Gustafson, & McGreen, 1988), and the positive impact also affects siblings of the identified adolescent (Klein, Alexander, & Parsons, 1977). The great benefit of this model is that it can improve client care in community settings. However, a significant gap exists in understanding many of the issues involved in the successful implementation of effective programs in community settings. FFT clinical staff have extensive training. The focus of therapy examines strengths and influential factors (Sexton, 2009). FFT is known to be able to attend to a wide variety of cultures and has been used in agencies that serve Chinese Americans, African

Americans, Dutch, Moroccan, Russian Turkish, Caucasians, Cubans, and Jamaicans, among others, and is provided in eight different countries. The most recent evolution of FFT focused on two major developments with an expansion of a clinical model with three phases. The model was based on the concept that the clinical process was guided by both the system and treatment and with assessment goals representing successful change (with this population) drawing on the "constant relational process that was played out in the room" (Sexton, 2009, p. 329).

Multisystemic Therapy

Multisystemic Therapy (MST) is an evidence-based treatment approach used to meet mental health needs in an intensive, multi-modal, family-based approach. This approach fits treatment with identified causal factors and correlating factors of delinquency and substance use (National Mental Health Association [NMHA], 2004). Extant literature lends support for the effectiveness of MST with adolescents who have emotional and behavioral problems (NMHA, 2004) with demonstrated reductions has high as 70 percent in rates of negative behaviors and improvements in familial functioning, and decreases in mental health concerns (NMHA, 2004). Timmons-Mitchell et al. (2006), highlight that MST produced significant reductions with juvenile justice involved adolescents. Specifically, there was a reduction in the number of rearrests and improvements in four areas of functioning measured by the Child and Adolescent Functional Assessment scale at 18 months and 6 months' post treatment (Curtis, Ronan, Borduin, 2004). A meta-analysis of MST outcome studies (Curtis et al., 2004), effect sizes of MST efficacy studies tend to be quite larger than MST effectiveness studies (Borduin, Mann, Cone, Henggeler, Fucci, Blaske, & Williams, 1995; Henggleler, Melton, Smith, 1992; Henggeler, Melton, Brondino, Scherer, Hanley, 1997).

Traditional Counseling and Negative Impacts for Diverse Consumers

Behavioral health professionals are becoming more aware of multicultural issues and of the need to improve the accessibility and quality of mental health services for individuals from historically oppressed racial/ethnic groups (Griner & Smith, 2006; Sue, 2001). Overall, traditional counseling theories and family therapy approaches have not modified counseling interventions to be appropriate for the specific culture of the client. Evidence has demonstrated the need to integrate culture, ethnicity, and race among other variables into counseling interventions (Constantine, 2002; Griner & Smith, 2006; Sue, 2003). To address these challenges, many researchers have identified a variety of treatment problems that minority populations experience: (a) mistrust of mental health services (Sue, 2001; Sue & Sue, 2003), (b) underutilization of mental health services, (c) seeking therapy only when problems have become severe, and (d) dropping out of therapy prematurely (Griner & Smith, 2006).

Specifically, in addressing the quality of services provided, research has urged that behavioral health interventions be adapted to consumers' cultural contexts and values. Another area that has received attention and debate is the similarity between the therapist and the client and the cultural traits or differences that should be studied. Consistent with this perspective, evidence suggests that client–therapist ethnic dissimilarity is associated with clinicians' overpathologizing or misdiagnosing consumers (Sue, 2001), lower provider judgments of client functioning (Russell, Fujino, Sue, Cheung, & Snowden, 1996), and less positive client–clinician communication (Cooper et al., 2003). Moreover, empirically based treatments are not examined in these studies. Other studies in the area include analog studies that demonstrated significant associations between cultural values and client ratings of providers. Research in this area is inconclusive, and more needs to be examined to determine the exact nature or quality of the similarity responsible for the change. Cultural values are indeed a broad condition and aspect of an individual, but a more specific analysis of which values in particular affect certain aspects of the treatment process or counseling relationship is needed.

INTEGRATED MULTICULTURAL FAMILY SYSTEMS

It was not until the 1980s that researchers and practitioners began to address the needs of diverse families. The study of integrated multicultural family systems is a result of a response by the mental health community to provide treatment that is adapted to the particular culture of its consumers. As such, multicultural competencies were established addressing the specific skills and knowledge necessary for the provider and the consumer (American Counseling Association [ACA], 2014). This section explains the development of multicultural family systems beginning with theoretical presuppositions that lay the foundation for addressing diverse family forms followed by a delineation of the purposes for multicultural family systems. Finally, this section concludes with guidelines and a general theoretical framework for integrating multicultural competencies and family systems.

OPERATIONALIZATION OF THE MULTICULTURAL COUNSELING COMPETENCIES

Multicultural providers are equipped with "culture-specific awareness, knowledge, and skills" (Arredondo et al., 1996, p. 42) to guide their counseling services. *Culture-specific awareness* implies that providers are informed of the different cultures and ethnicities (e.g., African American, Asian, Hispanics/Latino, Native American or Indigenous, and Caucasians; Arredondo et al., 1996). Multicultural providers understand that there are distinctions between what cultures contribute to a person's sense of well-being, resilience, resources, cultures, identity,

and sustainability. Common experiences such as historical migration, slavery, war, famine, and other natural and human-made disasters all serve as means in which group identities are further solidified and persons within the group have more intense opportunities to bond within the overall goal to survive. These experiences can result in marked group distinctions and serve as identity markers/clarion calls in which a group's similarities to other groups might be minimized or even disdained. As such, it is important to recognize that people have many similarities that bring us together or attest to the commonness of humanity. For example, within the U.S. culture, many groups are experiencing interethnic marriages and multiethnic children, have shared religious beliefs and practices required for basic needs for survival, and are concerned with the success of their offspring. Arredondo et al. (1996) offers that even when the provider perceives more similarities, such as both the provider and the consumer sharing similar phenotypic characteristics (those expected of a Caucasian/Western European decent), the provider must be mindful to recognize that individuality and its expression can be markedly unique to each of them. In other words, culture and diversity are present despite the perception of physical similarities. As such, culturally competent providers possess a knowledge of individual differences, their own beliefs, attitudes, and biases and how these interact with providing services to consumers (Arredondo et al., 1996). Furthermore, staying informed of the latest scientific research—regarding different cultural populations—can be done through attending seminars and advocating for the rights of diverse populations while simultaneously increasing their skill level (ACA, 2014; Arredondo et al., 1996).

This knowledge not only includes understanding that ethnic phenotypes, customs, and ways of living are not comprehensive in describing consumers but also includes issues related to racism, poverty, and alternative lifestyle choices (i.e., lesbian, gay, bisexual, transgender, and queer, open marriages, multiple life partners; McAuliffe, 2012). Utilizing their cultural awareness, knowledge, and skills, Arredondo and Glauner (1992) suggest that providers follow a dimensional approach when serving consumers to offer a holistic approach to counseling through using a multicultural lens (as cited in Arredondo et al., 1996). These dimensions include aspects of provider interaction and conceptualizations such as misattributions like the misinterpretation of body language (e.g., lack of eye contact, volume of speech), historical contexts that include political, sociocultural, and economic issues (e.g., experiencing Depression Era, wars, earthquakes), and consequences from the other two dimensions. More practically, other consequences might include the provider viewing the consumer, an African American adolescent student struggling with math performance based on larger majority test score norms, as one who then will always struggle in the area of mathematical testing and performance. Within this thorough process, as highlighted by Arredondo and Glauner's (1992) model, multicultural providers should be able to observe and adjust their own thought patterns, worldviews, and thus better serve consumers (Arredondo et al., 1996).

Operational Definitions in Multicultural Practice

Much of the terminology used in multicultural practice is socially constructed through casual, nonacademic, nonscientific exchanges and is fluid in nature. Terms such as *culture, race,* and *ethnicity* have multiple meanings and complex histories. For example, race has traditionally been defined as a scientific and biological system of classifying individuals by physical traits such as skin color, hair texture, and other physical attributes. Psychological and personal characteristics have subsequently been applied to groups and to identify individuals by race, such as a mild-tempered and intelligent people or a boisterous and fun-loving group. This perspective, especially when those attributes are negative (e.g., hot-tempered, unintelligent), has led, in part, to the propagation of personal prejudice, personal racism, and institutional racism.

However, there is a lack of empirical support for strict groups and personal classifications, the term *race* currently being recognized as pseudo-scientific at best and discriminatory at worst (Okun, 1996). As a result, current definitions tend to emphasize the historically and socially constructed nature of a people group, as well as influencing factors that have major economic, social, educational, and political overtones (Okun, 1996).

Therefore, it is important to provide tentative operational definitions for these terms in order to establish a common understanding for researchers and practitioners. Thus, the present section includes a brief exploration of a few of the terms that are commonly represented in the multicultural literature. Some diversity will ultimately be lost in such a narrowing of definitions, but serves as a useful framework to discuss commonalities among groups that can later be expanded on through further study of specific topics.

The next case example describes definition of multicultural terms becomes a key factor for the multiculturally sensitive family therapist. While reading the vignette, be sure to consider some of the key definitional issues in a multicultural family counseling scenario with these individuals. Okun (1996) put forth the case of Cynthia found in Case Scenario 4.2. Review the case of Cynthia and complete Exercises 4.1 and 4.2 to practice specific interventions and techniques using the case example.

Several professional-oriented topics and areas of inquiry emerge from this scenario regarding the provider's operational definitions of multicultural issues. For example, how does this provider define race, and is this similar to how the client views his or her own racial background? How does ethnicity interact with race in the provider's perspective? How does the provider define the development of culture within this family's racial, ethnic, and social context? Does the provider examine this family's concerns from a broad macroculture paradigm or from an idiosyncratic, case-specific cultural conceptualization? Finally, how will the

Case Scenario 4.2

Cynthia

The Wilson family, consisting of mom, an African American nurse; dad, a Caucasian writer; Cynthia, age 17 (light skinned); and Tony, age 14 (darker skinned), was referred to family therapy by the high school guidance provider. The family was shocked and polarized in response to Cynthia's experiences applying for college. Cynthia's behavior changed drastically, as she turned from being a bubbly, high-achieving, popular high school senior to an avoiding, nonproductive, withdrawing isolate. When she visited the campuses of her two top choices, she was shown around by students. She asked to meet with black students and was quite open about her racial identity. When one of the black student guides took her to the black Students' Association, she was told in no uncertain terms by the group that she was not "black" enough for these universities, that she had sold out to the Caucasians by virtue of having a Caucasian father, and that these students were only interested in recruiting black activists. When Cynthia returned home and reported these experiences, the family members began to argue and blame each other for this unexpected happening. Mom, light skinned enough to "pass" (for Caucasian), was furious at Cynthia for acknowledging her racial heritage in the first place, dad was sympathetic, and Tony was derisive at "Miss Perfect" finally having her "comeuppance." The parents began to argue in front of the children, which had never happened before. Cynthia felt as if the rug had been pulled out from under her—her parents had encouraged her to consider herself bicultural, but now her mother was abandoning that, and she was beginning to see her family as not being the secure harbor she had always thought. Her grades began to slip, she skipped school, and she displayed many symptoms of clinical depression (Okun, 1996, pp. 291–292).

Exercise 4.1

Genogram Activity

Based on Case Scenario 4.2, use the Genogram(s) and identify what the factors and stressors are on each level.

Exercise 4.2

A Storytelling Intervention: Examining Family and Cultural Stories

1. Using the Case Scenario 4.2, what are some cultural stories that may have been influential?

2. What are the two possible negative and oppressive stories being played out with the adolescent, and the family? In your work with this family, how might you begin to deconstruct (disassemble and examine taken-for-granted assumptions) a dominant problem-saturated story?

provider propose to help this family from a stance that acknowledges its unique understanding of and experiences with culture, diversity, and mental health? Each of these concerns requires the provider to have an adequate understanding of his or her own, as well as his or her consumer's, multicultural worldview. In short, defining the terms between parties becomes essential to the therapeutic process.

Ethical guidelines set forth by the ACA (2014) speak unequivocally about the importance of multicultural competence in working with consumers, and this extends to family systems as well as individuals. The ethical values espoused by the counseling profession provide guidance in this regard. Values such as honoring diversity, embracing multicultural strategies to support dignity and uniqueness, practicing competently, and practicing ethically all support a multicultural approach. The ethical principles of fostering autonomy, avoiding harm, and justice and equality support this goal as well (ACA, 2014).

Finally, the mandate to counsel from a culturally sensitive manner is found throughout the specific ethical standards. This includes considerations in areas such as informed consent (ACA, 2014, A.2.c), confidentiality (ACA, 2014, B.1.a), diagnosis (ACA, 2014, E.5.b), assessment (ACA, 2014, E.8), supervision (ACA, 2014, F.2.b), education (ACA, 2014, F.2.b), and training (ACA, 2014, F.11).

Definitions of multicultural terms here include those related to acculturation, multiculturalism, culture, emic (culturally specific) and etic (culturally universal) perspectives (King & McInerney, 2014), ethnicity, and race. The topics are necessarily limited but provide a useful initial framework for discussion.

Acculturation is a major topic of discussion in reference to multicultural counseling and interventions. Acculturation has been defined as

> a [dynamic] process used to describe the experiences of immigrants from an array of places (e.g., Europe, China, Japan, and Mexico) . . . where one leaves their country of origin and involves the process of assimilation to another culture.

Acculturation can occur on both the group level and the individual levels thus including more of the consequent psychological adaptation and adjustment. Four acculturative stages have been described: contact, conflict, crisis, and adaptation. Furthermore, adaptation can include several strategies: (1) assimilation—the individual or group gives up (or is forced to give up) the cultural identity of origin and desires a positive relationship with the host culture; (2) separation—the individual or group retains the original culture (or is restricted from adopting the new culture through segregation) and desires no positive relationship with the host culture; (3) integration—the individual or group desires to retain the culture of origin as well as maintain a positive relationship with the host culture; and (4) marginalization—the individual or group no longer retains the original culture and has no desire (or is not allowed) to have a positive relationship with the host culture. (Jackson, 2006, p. 6)

Multiculturalism is another term that requires an operational definition. *Multicultural*, as defined by the Council for Accreditation of Counseling and Related Educational Programs (CACREP, 2009), is a term denoting the diversity of identities that individuals may use to describe themselves. These include, but are not limited to, racial, ethnic, and cultural heritage, socioeconomic status, age, gender, sexual orientation, religious and spiritual beliefs, and physical, emotional, and mental abilities.

Another definition that is important to the counseling process is culture. *Culture* is a rich term encompassing all elements of society, including values, attitudes, and spiritual beliefs. It is continuously evolving and produces its own meaning in relation to specific contexts within it (Jackson, 2006).

Within the study of multiculturalism, two opposing perspectives on analyzing and describing cultural phenomena have been described. These perspectives have been described as emic (culturally localized) and etic (culturally generalized). These terms refer to the two contrasting perspectives used when one is analyzing and describing observations. The emic–etic dichotomy describes a way of looking at a culture either from the outside or from the inside. Looking at the culture as represented by individuals could be described as taking an idioemic perspective (i.e., examining a particular manifestation of the emic). Thus, emic, etic, and idioemic are categorically related, because they are all classes of contextualization and how one views experiences, understandings, and differing perspectives (Johnson, 1990).

Another loaded term in multicultural practice is the concept of ethnicity. Ethnicity can be defined as the national, regional, or tribal origins of one's oldest recorded ancestors and the customs and traditions that have transcended through generations. Ethnic, including cultural and racial, variability exists among members of the same racial or ethnic groups. For example, Native American and African American people may speak Spanish, French, or English, and many Latinos self-identify as "black," whereas others see themselves as "Caucasian" (Jackson, 2006, p. 190).

Race is a term that originally was used to refer to a category or class of persons without reference to anything biological. In the 18th century, the word was ascribed a physical connotation which eventually resulted in racial types and pseudoscientific theories that are now discredited. W. E. B. DuBois, the most noted in the United States for conceptualizing race, argued that race was not scientific or biological but a sociohistorical concept. Race, racial difference, and the many forms of racism experienced by African Americans and other ethnic minority groups are neither fixed categories nor merely illusionary. It is the outcome of practices of (de)racialization, which position groups and individuals in advantageous and discriminatory ways. Although the construct of race has no scientific basis, today clinicians and researchers use the conceptualization of race to get to the truth regarding difference, meaning, genetics, and culture (Jackson, 2006).

Clearly, there are several definitional considerations that help frame multicultural-related questions that providers ask and the answers they find in their work with consumers. The importance of personal knowledge, reflection, knowledge application regarding various cultures, and differentiating between terms may be considered a presupposition for culturally competent family counseling. In addition to general terminological agreements, other specific assumptions are also important to establish as a starting point for providers working with culturally diverse families. These multicultural presuppositions are described below.

Multicultural Presuppositions for Providers

The adoption of a multicultural professional identity is founded on a set of presuppositions that providers are encouraged to adopt in their professional and personal stance. The ACA Code of Ethics (ACA, 2014) highlights standards in a few different areas that are especially relevant to culturally sensitive work with families. These can be considered in four broad areas that concern provider's knowledge about one's multicultural characteristics, associated values and beliefs, and other cultures, racial development and acculturation models (Cross, 1991; Sue & Sue, 1991). These include (1) the need to adapt confidentiality practices to the preferences and needs of families and couples (ACA, 2014, B.4.b); (2) the mandate to become aware of and to avoid imposing personal values onto consumers, especially when those values discriminate against clients or are inconsistent with client goals (ACA, 2014, A.4.b); (3) the mandate to advocate for client when appropriate in order to address barriers and obstacles at various levels that limit client wellness (ACA, 2014, A.7.a); and (4) the mandate to practice within one's boundaries of competence as a provider and to gain general cultural competence with a variety of consumers (ACA, 2014, C.2.a).

In addition, culturally skilled providers are constantly seeking to understand themselves as racial and cultural beings and are actively seeking a nonracist identity (AMCD [Association for Multicultural Counseling and Development] C2; Arredondo et al., 1996). Please refer to Table 4.2.

Table 4.2   Helping Responses and Intervention Skills

Verbal and nonverbal helping responses (AMCD III, C1; Arredondo et al., 1996)	• Send and receive messages accurately and appropriately
	• Not tied down to one method or approach
	• Recognize that helping styles may be culturally bound
	• When sensing personal helping style is limited, appropriately anticipate and modify it
Institutional intervention skills (AMCD III, C2; Arredondo et al., 1996)	• Help consumers determine whether a "problem" stems from racism or bias in others (the concept of health paranoia)
	• Assist consumers to not inappropriately personalize problems

Culturally skilled providers should be aware of relevant discriminatory practices at the social and community level that may be affecting the psychological welfare of the population being served (AMCD III, B.5; Arredondo et al., 1996). Similarly, providers have a responsibility to address institutional and social barriers that impede access, equity, and success for consumers (CACREP, 2009, G.1.i.).

Historically, mental health–related scholarship and literature have highlighted the essential need for providers to adapt their approaches and orientations to better serve individuals of differing cultural backgrounds (Collins & Arthur, 2010). Previous suggestions specific to working with interracial and interethnic families include the following: (a) self-awareness of one's attitudes toward others from different races and ethnicities, (b) self-awareness of one's position on mixed marriages and families, (c) sociocultural contextual knowledge of client culture, (d) ability to develop therapy goals consistent with cultural and individual differences, (e) familiarity with relevant community supports, (f) understanding of racial identity development, and (g) ability to create a culturally sensitive therapy climate (Okun, 1996).

The historically ingrained racism and prejudice that has marked the history of Western culture, as well as corresponding Eurocentric values that have emerged within professional and academic realms, such as mental health, have been highlighted (Okun, 1996). When this history is coupled with contemporary trends in managed health care necessitating that clinicians accept work with more increasingly diverse populations, it becomes apparent that a set of clearly defined assumptions is necessary for clinicians to intentionally embrace a multicultural identity.

Although somewhat dated, the following brief testimonials exemplify the dangers of failing to adopt a culturally sensitive perspective as a provider. The testimonials also show the ways in which otherwise well-meaning professionals may easily pathologize behavior that is incongruent with their perspectives, thus missing the opportunity to promote healthy consumer autonomy. One can imagine the ways in which these perspectives and attitudes would likely cause harm to consumers and society in general, as well as the ways in which a more culturally sensitive approach might better facilitate clearer and more accurate presuppositions (Okun, 1996):

• A Caucasian provider at a university counseling center referring to a client's decision to be involved in an interracial relationship as "rebellious."

• An African American male being told by his sister that he is a "sell out" after proposing to his Caucasian girlfriend.

• A Caucasian adoption worker warning a Caucasian couple that Blacks are more likely to grow up with a learning or psychological disability even when adopted in infancy. (p. 277)

What are the perspectives that providers need to adopt in this changing multicultural society?

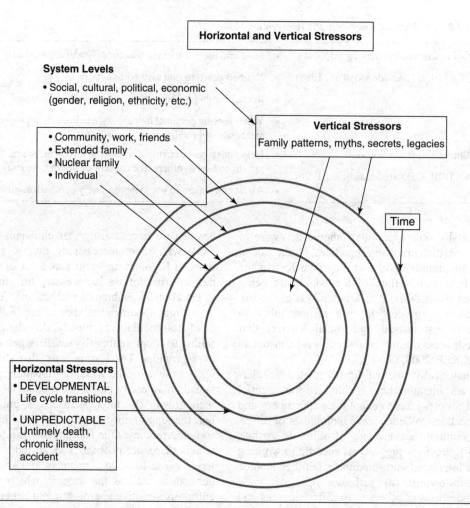

Figure 4.4   Understanding Stressors

How can providers adopt general principles that enable them to do the best and avoid doing harm across a diverse array of consumers and families? How can a provider discern when he or she has committed a lapse in multicultural sensitivity to seek remediation? All these questions require an appropriate set of presuppositions.

Providers should possess knowledge of multicultural and pluralistic trends, including characteristics and concerns within and among diverse groups nationally and internationally (CACREP, 2009, G.2.a). Acculturative experiences of culturally diverse consumers are significant and

create myriad stressors (Figure 4.4). Providers can gain knowledge and understanding regarding this phenomenon and its impact on such consumers and become aware of their attitudes and beliefs in this area (CACREP, 2009, G.2.b). Furthermore, multicultural competence includes an awareness of context and culture and the interactive process. The individual shares the group in a unique way, but the individual context is never the same as the context of the group.

Clearly, fostering these skills, abilities, and attitudes takes intentional effort on the part of the provider. However, this effort is well spent in the service of their diverse family consumers and the adolescents with whom they will work.

Purpose of Integrated Multicultural Family Systems

There are myriad factors warranting a multicultural framework and model for treating diverse families. For the purposes of this chapter, we have identified three key rationales for integrated multicultural family systems. First, the mental health field (CACREP, American Psychological Association, and AMCD) has recognized the importance of providing culturally competent counseling that is modified toward the client's culture and values. Second, addressing culturally competent counseling manifests across many domains (individual, social, cultural, vocational, political, and financial) and levels (intrapersonal, interpersonal, familial, social, and global). Over the past 30 years in the United States, the social and cultural landscape has drastically changed (Landale, Oropesa, & Bradatan, 2006). It is logical, then, that families have also changed in form, purpose, process, goals, and function. Family demographics provide a picture or context for the family members and reveal potential strengths, resources, and risk factors. Understanding the family context has counseling implications for addressing diverse family needs. Some of the family changes reflect the choices and values (intentional, unintentional, or subconscious) of the members in the family. Conversely, some family changes or conditions were the result of choices or changes within the family that were not desired, and/or the result of something outside of their control (e.g., death of a spouse, unemployment, serious illness).

Defining Family: Stable and Adaptable Systems

Family definitions and classifications have changed in a variety of ways. For example family structure in the United States over the past

half-century has included increased divorce rates, nonmarital cohabitation, single-parent family, and stepfamilies (Fomby & Cherlin, 2007).

In light of these changes, it is important to examine its impact and implications for diverse families. To begin with, we will explore the recent demographic trends related to family systems from a local level and then macrolevel.

The 21st century has ushered in social and cultural advances, thus creating both opportunities and challenges. In 1950, only 4% of all children were born outside of marriage; by 2007, in comparison, 39.7% of all children were born outside of marriage (U.S. Bureau of the Census, 2005; U.S. National Center for Health Statistics, 2009)

The drastic statistics on births is only one example of the major demographic changes that have occurred over the past 30 to 40 years. While the United States has experienced strides socially and culturally, the changes have created gaps and social concerns that must be addressed.

While progress within a social (or family) system can infuse energy and strengthen the system on one level, it also has ecological effect on other levels, for example, individual, social, and environmental levels. Any addition to the system on one level will affect the entire system, thus eliciting reactions within and on other levels. Using a cybernetics paradigm, we can attempt to understand the United States as a social and cultural system. Given this context, the changes and growth occurring over the past 50 years had an impact on and within the society (e.g., system). Consequently, this change in the system produces instability, which triggers mechanisms or feedback loops to enforce the rules. Negative feedback loops are used to enforce the system. If the society does not respond to the rules or negative feedback, then positive feedback will be generated. Positive feedback loops can destroy a system or can help it to adjust to changed circumstances. So in reference to the advancements, evolution, and cultural changes within the U.S. system, the system's mechanisms or social rules will be commissioned to provide feedback to the system. This feedback could be any condition, policy, and/or social problem elicited. If society does not respond to the negative feedback, then positive feedback loops are used to destroy the system or help it adjust to the new conditions.

Changes in Traditional Family Life Cycle

The definition and composition of family life has changed and expanded to include new family forms. They include lesbian, gay, transgender, and bisexual families, cohabitating partners, noncohabitating partners, grandparents, and extended family. Most recently, a new family classification and term has emerged, multiple partner fertility, referring to adults who have children with more than one partner. Women who had children with multiple partners were less likely, according to one study, to say that they had family or friends they could count on for social support, such as a small loan or a place to stay—although whether the lack of support is a cause or an effect of multiple partner fertility is unclear (Harknett & Knab, 2007).

Since the 2000s, the family has increasingly evolved away from the conventional, uniform family life cycle. A significant change in the family life cycle is the continuing separation of family and household resulting from delaying of marriage, nonmarital childbearing, fragile cohabiting unions, and because of new phenomena, such as the growth of transnational immigrant families (Elliot & Umberson, 2007). An important distinction for families is related to education and household status. About half a century ago, most Americans, rich or poor, lived in two-parent families that resembled one another. Today, there exists a stratum of education levels that tends to send individuals on differing paths through family formation and dissolution (Fomby & Cherlin, 2007). Similarly, the divorce rate lowered for spouses with a college degree, while roughly staying the same or increased for the less educated (Gushue & Constantine, 2007).

As has been the case since cohabitation became common several decades ago, individuals with less education are more likely to cohabit. However, cohabitation has become common among all educational groups. With these caveats, the 2000 Census found that children were commonly present in same-sex cohabiting unions: 33% of women in same-sex partnerships and 22% of men in same-sex partnerships had children living with them. Women were postponing marriage but not postponing having children as much. By the mid-2000s, the birth rates for unmarried women in their 20s far exceeded the birth rates for unmarried teens (U.S. National Center for Health Statistics, 2009). Less-educated and low-income women and men are increasingly having children prior to marrying. Cohabitation increases the risk that children will experience the breakup of their parents' cohabiting relationship by their fifth birthday.

The inclusion of same-sex relationships is another family issue to consider. The effects of discrimination, and being legally unable to marry in most states, have included an inability to inherit property, be recognized as a socially acceptable family unit, and adopt children and share health insurance benefits afforded heterosexual unions. The lesbian, gay, bisexual, transgender, and queer community experiences widespread discrimination across many areas. For lesbians and gay men, cohabitation remains the only form of partnership available except in states where same-sex marriage is legal, which at the time of this writing includes Connecticut, Iowa, Maine, Massachusetts, New Hampshire, and Vermont.

Children and Caregiving

Since the 1980s, the propensity of children to live with both parents has fallen due to a massive increase in incarceration, particularly of African Americans (Pettit & Western, 2004). One in four African American children born in 1990 had a parent imprisoned by the time they were age 14 compared with one in 25 for Caucasian children (Wildeman, 2009). The correspondence between family and household had weakened by the end of the century. A study by

Wu and Martinson (1993), and other researchers, found that the number of transitions that children experience is associated with undesirable outcomes such as behavior problems (Fomby & Cherlin, 2007; Osborne & McLanahan, 2007) and less competency in interacting with peers at school (Cavanagh & Huston, 2006), although it is unclear if the association was causal or descriptive (as cited by Patterson & Sexton, 2013).

Grandparents' caregiving role has increased, causing more children to be raised by their grandparents. Of the one third of the families with grandparent caregivers, the middle-parent generation was absent from the household—perhaps due to incarceration, illness, or substance abuse. More broadly, the percentage of grandparents who have partial or full responsibility for caring for grandchildren is substantial (Table 4.3). This group has often been referred to as the so-called skipped generation. Figure 4.3 gives more details about this unique, yet essential group.

Immigration

The ethnic composition of the immigrant population continues to be heavily Latino and Asian. Among Latinos, Mexican Americans continue to constitute the largest national immigrating group. During the first decade of the 2000s, Latinos surpassed African Americans as the largest minority group in the United States. (U.S. Bureau of the Census, 2008b)

As the number of diverse populations increase, it becomes more and more difficult to sort out descriptive information and to find common patterns and overarching principles for how families actually work. This provides challenges to developing treatment programs that fit each of these groups (Patterson & Sexton, 2013).

WHY AN INTEGRATED MULTICULTURAL FAMILY SYSTEMS APPROACH?

Research on the necessities of designing mental health treatment to include culture has been extensively researched over the past 30 years. Understanding how to match effective evidence-based treatments to multicultural families is one of the major barriers to moving effective family treatments into community settings (Sexton et al., 2012). Furthermore, multicultural theory and family therapy have the potential to develop the knowledge of family diversity and clinical practice (Patterson & Sexton, 2013). However, presently a comprehensive multicultural integrative family theory has not been developed. A presentation of proposed principle-based integrated multicultural family system is presented and includes principles based on multicultural counseling competencies.

The U.S. culture and counseling profession has sent a message that not only are racism and openly expressed intolerance unacceptable and viewed as politically and socially unacceptable,

Table 4.3   Grandparents as Caregivers

Grandparents as Caregivers
U.S. Bureau of the Census, 2008a

Working mothers	In 2005, grandparents were the primary care providers for 20.5% of preschool-aged children whose mothers were employed
Financial support	Of the 5.8 million grandparents in the 2000 Census who lived with their grandchildren, 42% responded that they were "currently responsible for most of the basic needs of one or more of these grandchildren."
Cultural responsibility	The percentage rose to 52% among African American grandparents and 56% among American Indians and Alaska natives.

but specific competencies have been compromised in this regard. As a result, there is significant research delineating the most salient aspects of multicultural development and counseling. Sue, Arredondo, and McDavis (1992) constructed a list of multicultural counseling competencies to ensure a provider's ability to attend to the breadth and complexities of culture in consumers' lives in a respectful and productive way. They can be divided into three main areas: (1) provider awareness of own cultural values and biases, (2) provider awareness of client's worldview, and (3) culturally appropriate intervention strategies. This section will cover the main components for integrated multicultural family systems adapted from Kelly, Maynigo, Wesley, and Durham (2013).

The proposed model uses the historical and present-day ecological systems and status identities to explore impacts of racism and social class that may be relevant for multicultural individuals and families. This review will address the relevance of principle-based integrative family systems models of treatment and how it can be tailored to diverse groups using core diversity principles. There are four key systems-related diversity principles that address differences that often arise when treating diverse cases: (1) differences in worldview and values between the therapist and the members of the family, (2) differences in their experiences and contexts, (3) differences in the power that they wield in and out of the therapy session, and (4) the felt distance experienced by the therapist and/or the couple or family owing to one or more of the foregoing differences. This work uses a comprehensive perspective that takes systemic, developmental, and other common factors into account relevant to the particular family.

The relevance of applying an integrated multicultural and systems model for diverse groups is considered. An important consideration is the necessity of applying evidence-based treatments, with considerable flexibility, by application of core principles to keep therapists attuned to the intricacies of diversity and how to be mindful of such principles (Kelly et al., 2013). The position of flexibility and openness are important

distinctions in guiding this work. The inherent complexity of coming to know a client and the client's cultural values and identities is an important focus of counseling on which the effective, culturally appropriate treatment and interventions are built. We fill a gap in the field by providing a comprehensive and explicit framework to assist therapists to identify, understand, and address core diversity principles that can be manifest across all groups and to hone their ability to tailor treatments using cultural competence in a flexible, principle-based manner.

To illustrate the ignorance of this topic, the most recently released *Diagnostic and Statistical Manual of Mental Disorders,* fifth edition (*DSM-5*) contains additional resources for clinicians such as dimensional assessments, rather than categorical, that provide a more holistic approach to diagnosis as well as a section that contains a listing of disorders that are specifically associated with cultural issues and concerns. Last, an assessment measure offered is the Cultural Formulation Interview (CFI). The CFI is a set of 16 questions that clinicians may use to obtain information during a mental health assessment about the impact of culture on key aspects of an individual's clinical presentation and care. It may be accessed online and can be found in the *DSM-5*, Section III—Emerging Issues and Measures. The Cultural Formulation Interview—Informant Version collects collateral information on the CFI domains from family members or caregivers. Supplementary modules to the CFI can help clinicians conduct a more comprehensive cultural assessment. This interview covers specific questions pertaining to their cultural beliefs/feelings about their condition; general understanding about their condition; illness prototype; course of illness; level of functioning; social network; spiritual, religious, and moral traditions; cultural identity; language, migration, coping, and help seeking; immigrants and refugees; patient–clinician relationship; and age-related issues. The first eight supplementary modules explore the domains of the core CFI in greater depth. The next three modules focus on populations with specific needs, such as children and adolescents, older adults, and immigrants and refugees. The last module explores the experiences and views of individuals who perform caregiving functions.

The scant data on tailoring treatment support the need to address the following four diversity principles. First, across ethnic groups, meta-analysis reveals that treatment adapted to consumers' *cultural beliefs and worldview* concerning their mental health problems and how to treat them is a moderator that accounts for superior outcomes of culturally adapted treatments (Benish, Quintana, & Wampold, 2011, as cited in Kelly et al., 2013). To apply your knowledge on how cultural and ethnic identity influence counseling with adolescents and families, complete Exercises 4.3 and 4.4.

IMPLICATIONS FOR COUNSELING ADOLESCENTS

There has been much debate about multicultural application and significance within the counseling field, including within family therapy. Traditional family therapy approaches and models were revolutionary for the time in suggesting that individuals can be viewed as such and instead situate the problem and solutions within the system. This shift from an individual focus to a family and systemic focus has been pivotal and laid the groundwork for richer discussions and conceptualizations paving the way for development and integration with contextual, proximal, and distal influences such as social, developmental, and ecological considerations.

Exercise 4.3

Achievements and Disappointments

Materials: Six 5 inches × 8 inches cards, crayons or felt markers, paper, and a writing instrument

Directions: Sit in silence with your eyes closed. Reflect on your adolescent years from ages 13 to 17. Allow images and memories to emerge in no particular order or sequence. Sit for as long as you wish. When you are ready, open your eyes and draw a symbol or symbols on separate cards to represent your greatest disappointments. Use one card per disappointment. Do the same for your greatest achievements during your adolescent years. When you are finished, spread all the cards out on a table and look at what you drew. Give each card a title. Then, consider the following questions:

1. Did you have more achievements than disappointments? Or was it more disappointments than achievements? An equal number of each?

2. As you remember the achievements and disappointments, write the feelings you remember for each on the back of the card. Make a list of feelings aroused as you review the cards today.

3. Write a brief description of how the events portrayed on the cards shaped you as you are today.

4. How did your culture and values (ethnic, family, spiritual, etc.) affect the above events and the way in which you responded? As an adolescent, how aware where you of the people and your surroundings that influenced you?

Exercise 4.4

Cultural and Ethnic Identity Activity

Reflection

Phinney's (1992) ethnic identity model consists of three statuses. In what way does her model resonate with your personal experience of ethnic identity development?

1. Unexamined or diffused identity

2. Search moratorium

3. Identity achievement

Activity

In small groups, reflect on your ethnic identity, cultural heredity, and experiences with privilege, discrimination, and oppression? List three ways your cultural heritage is shaping your emerging professional identity. How might the manifestations of your cultural heritage have an impact on your work with individuals and families similar to yours and different from yours?

While general systems theories have been applied in a variety of contexts, family therapy approaches overall have fallen short in their ability to address the multicultural needs of diverse populations in a systemic, efficacious, and reliable way. Researchers have criticized family therapy approaches as being ethnocentric with many of its traditional models and premises being in direct opposition to many non-Western cultural values.

While recent research and clinical advances have created two specific models, FFT and MST, that are culturally relevant, overall the field has yet to develop a comprehensive theory or framework for addressing the needs of diverse family groups. The challenge from a subset of those within the field is pushing for a dialogue to broaden and deepen the foundational structures and premises. Critics have argued that the principles are both flexible and culturally sensitive. Using systems concepts, the mental health field and family systems in particular is no longer a one-size-fits-all approach.

Traditional family systems theory originated within a time period embedded in a tacit, homogeneous, and cultural paradigm. Although the principles were thought to have been "universal," they could not help but be influenced by the larger ecological system characterized by ethnocentrism. The family therapy movement, which began in the era of the civil rights movement in the United States, failed to address or accommodate alternative realities that in that time included significant social and political upheaval. There are no major family theories/approaches and/or modifications for addressing diverse families. Failing to account for cultural and ethnic families is akin to the concept of color blindness (Gushue & Constantine, 2007) where color, and other socially constructed identities are overlooked. As such, the tenets of family systems, while not overtly excluding or discriminating against minority groups did so by default. Simply put, family systems theory was based on a tacit understanding of normative family development that grew out of a homogeneous cultural identity (e.g., Caucasian, middle class, and nuclear family system). Theorists were oblivious to experiences and needs of diverse families. Thus, today this affects and compromises our ability to competently provide culturally relevant treatment to diverse populations. As the Chinese sage Chang-Tsu often asserted, "How we view the world is not only about what we see, but about what we do not see" (Sue, 2004, p. 761).

Summary

This chapter emphasized multicultural counseling and family systems theory relative to treating families and adolescents. As such, integrated multicultural family systems and its usefulness with adolescent clients were discussed. Characteristics vital to the culturally competent counselor were identified and described to include racial ethnic identity models and issues related to discrimination, marginalization, and oppression. Also inferred from this chapter is clarification regarding the difference between conducting nonracist counseling versus culturally sensitive counseling. For those interested in counseling adolescents, the chapter also describes cultural factors relevant in assessment and treatment of adolescent families. Additionally, several family therapy techniques and therapeutic models are reviewed. Finally, the chapter offers several learning activities to help students apply new knowledge.

Keystones

- By 2100, nearly 60% of the U.S. population will consist of minorities, increasing the need for culturally competent and diversity-informed providers.

- Providers should consistently be culturally alert and maintain a readiness in identifying the various dimensions of consumers' lives. This allows providers to respond and assist consumers in a way that is equitable and maintains access to services and inclusiveness that matter to individuals and society at large.

- Working with adolescents inevitability constitutes working with their families. There are a number of family therapy approaches available to meet the needs of any type of family structure.

- In combining family and multicultural therapy, special care should be taken in both choosing the right approach (i.e., FFT vs. general systems theory) and tailoring it to meet the unique structural and cultural needs of the family system.

- Providers should possess knowledge of multicultural and pluralistic trends, including characteristics and concerns within and among diverse groups nationally and internationally (CACREP, 2009, G2a).

- Grandparents' caregiving role has increased, causing more children to be raised by their grandparents. Of the one third of the families with grandparent caregivers, the middle-parent generation was absent from the household – perhaps due to incarceration, illness, or substance abuse. More broadly, the percentage of grandparents who have partial or full responsibility for grandchildren is substantial.

- The U.S. culture and counseling profession has sent a message that not only are racism and openly expressed intolerance unacceptable and viewed as politically and socially inappropriate, but specific competencies have been compromised in this regard.

References

Ackerman, N. W. (1958). *The psychodynamics of family life*. Oxford, England: Basic Books.

American Counseling Association. (2014). *2014 ACA code of ethics: As approved by the ACA governing council*. Retrieved from http://www.counseling.org/docs/ethics/2014-aca-code-of-ethics.pdf?sfvrsn=4

American Psychiatric Association. (2013). *Diagnostic and statistical manual of mental disorders* (5th ed.). Washington, DC: Author.

Arredondo, P., & Glauner, T. (1992). *Personal dimensions of identity model*. Boston, MA: Empowerment Workshops.

Arredondo, P., Toporek, M. S., Brown, S., Jones, J., Locke, D. C., Sanchez, J., & Stadler, H. (1996). Operationalization of the multicultural counseling competencies. Alexandria, VA: Association for Multicultural Counseling and Development.

Bartol, C. R., & Bartol, A. M. (2008). *Introduction to forensic psychology: Research and application* (2nd ed.). Thousand Oaks, CA: Sage.

Bateson, G. (1972). From Versailles to cybernetics. In *Steps to an ecology of mind* (pp. 475–483). New York, NY: Bantam Books.

Bateson, G., Jackson, D. D., Haley, J., & Weakland, J. (1956). Toward a theory of schizophrenia. *Behavioral Science, 1*(4), 251–254.

Berg, I. K., & de Shazer, S. (1993). Making numbers talk: Language in therapy. *The new language of change: Constructive collaboration in psychotherapy, 1,* 5–24.

Bingham, R. P., Porche-Burke, L., James, S., Sue, D. W., & Vasquez, M. J. (2002). Introduction: A report on the national multicultural conference and summit II. *Cultural Diversity and Ethnic Minority Report, 8*(2), 75–87.

Borduin, C.; Mann, B.; Cone, L.; Henggeler, S.; Fucci, B.R.; Blaske, D.M.; Williams, R.A. (1995). Multisystemictreatment of serious juvenile offenders: Long-term prevention of criminality and violence. *Journal of Consulting and Clinical Psychology, 63,* 569–578.

Bowen, M. (1966). The use of family theory in clinical practice. *Comprehensive psychiatry, 7*(5), 345–374.

Cavanagh, S. E., & Huston, A. C. (2006). Family instability and children's early problem behavior. *Social Forces, 85*(1), 551–581.

Collins, S., & Arthur, N. (2010). Culture-infused counselling: A model for developing multicultural competence. *Counselling Psychology Quarterly, 23*(2), 217–233.

Constantine, M. G. (2002). Racism attitudes, white racial identity attitudes, and multicultural counseling competence in school counselor trainees. *Counselor Education and Supervision, 41*(3), 162–174.

Cooper, L.A., Roter, D. L., Johnson, R. L., Ford, D. E., Steinwachs, D. M., & Powe, N. R. (2003). Patient-centered communication, ratings of care, and concordance of patient and physician race. *Annals of Internal Medicine, 139,* 907–915.

Corey, G., Corey, M., Corey, C., & Callanan, P. (2014). *Issues and ethics in the helping professions with 2014 ACA Codes.* Stamford, CT: Cengage Learning.

Council for Accreditation of Counseling and Related Educational Programs. (2009). *2009 Standards.* Retrieved from http://www.cacrep.org/doc/2009%20Standards.pdf

Cross, W. (1991). *Shades of Black: Diversity in African American identity.* Philadelphia, PA: Temple University Press.

Curtis, N.; Ronan, K.; Borduin, C. (2004). Multisystemic treatment: A meta-analysis of outcome studies. *Journal of Family Psychology 18,* 411–419.

Duvall, E. M. (1956). *Facts of life and love for teenagers.* New York, NY: Association Press.

Elliott, S., & Umberson, D. (2007). Recent demographic trends in the US and implications for well-being. In J. Scott, J. Treas, & M. Richards (Eds.), *The Blackwell companion to the sociology of families* (pp. 34–53). Malden, MA: Blackwell.

Erikson, E. H. (1963). *Childhood and society* (Rev. ed.). New York, NY: W. W. Norton.

Fomby, P., & Cherlin, A. J. (2007). Family instability and child well-being. *American Sociological Review, 72*(2), 181–204.

Fromm-Reichmann, F. (1948). Notes on the development of treatment of schizophrenics by psychoanalytic psychotherapy. *Psychiatry, 11*(3), 263–273.

Gladding, S. T. (2011). *Family therapy: History, theory, and practice.* Upper Saddle River, NJ: Pearson Education.

Gordon, D. A., Arbuthnot, J., Gustafson, K. E., & McGreen, P. (1988). Home-based behavioral-systems family therapy with disadvantaged juvenile delinquents. *American Journal of Family Therapy, 16*(3), 243–255.

Greene, R. R., Kropf, N., & Frankel, K. (2009). A systems approach: Addressing diverse family forms. In R. R. Greene & N. Kropf (Eds.), *Human behavior theory: A diversity framework* (2nd rev. ed., pp. 167–200). New Brunswick, NJ: Aldine.

Griner, D., & Smith, T. B. (2006). Culturally adapted mental health intervention: A meta-analytic review. *Psychotherapy: Theory, Research, Practice, Training, 43*(4), 531–548.

Gushue, G. V., & Constantine, M. G. (2007). Color-blind racial attitudes and white racial identity attitudes in psychology trainees. *Professional Psychology: Research and Practice, 38*(3), 321–328.

Gushue, G. V., Sciarra, D. T., & Mejía, B. X. (2010). Family counseling: Systems, postmodern, and multicultural perspectives. In J. G. Ponterotto, J. Casas, L. A. Suzuki, & C. M. Alexander (Eds.), *Handbook of multicultural counseling* (3rd ed., pp. 677–688). Thousand Oaks, CA: Sage.

Haley, J. (1987). *Problem solving therapy.* San Francisco, CA: Jossey-Bass.

Harknett, K., & Knab, J. (2007). More kin, less support: Multipartnered fertility and perceived support among mothers. *Journal of Marriage and Family, 69*(1), 237–253.

Havighurst, R. J. (1972). *Developmental tasks and education.* New York, NY: David McKay.

Hays, D. G. (2008). Assessing multicultural competence in provider trainees: A review of instrumentation and future directions. *Journal of Counseling & Development, 86,* 95–101.

Henggeler, S.; Melton, G.; Smith, L. (1992). Family Preservation using multisystemic therapy: an effective alternative to incarcerating serious juvenile offenders. *Journal of Consulting and Clinical Psychology 60,* 953–961.

Henggeler, S.; Melton, G.; Brondino, M.; Scherer, D.; Hanley, J. (1997). Multisystemic Therapy with Violent and Chronic Juvenile Offenders and Their Families: The role of treatment fidelity in successful dissemination. *Journal of Consulting and Clinical Psychology, 65,* 821–833.

Ho, D. Y. F. (1987). Fatherhood in Chinese culture. In M. E. Lamb (Ed.), The father's role: *Crosscultural perspectives* (pp. 227–245). Hillsdale, NJ: Erlbaum.

Jackson, Y. (Ed.). (2006). *Encyclopedia of multicultural psychology.* Thousand Oaks, CA: Sage.

Johnson, S. D., Jr. (1990). Toward clarifying culture, race, and ethnicity in the context of multicultural counseling. *Journal of Multicultural Counseling & Development, 18*(1), 41–50.

Kazak, A. E., Hoagwood, K., Weisz, J. R., Hood, K., Kratochwill, T. R., Vargas, L. A., & Banez, G. A. (2010). A meta-systems approach to evidence-based practice for children and adolescents. *American Psychologist, 65*(2), 85-97.

Kelly, S., Maynigo, P., Wesley, K., & Durham, J. (2013). African American communities and family systems: Relevance and challenges. *Couple and Family Psychology: Research and Practice, 2,* 264–277.

Kerr, M. E., & Bowen, M. (1988). *Family evaluation.* New York, NY: W. W. Norton.

King, R. B., & McInerney, D. M. (2014). Culture's consequences on student motivation: Capturing cross-cultural universality and variability through personal investment theory. *Educational Psychologist, 49*(3), 175–198.

Klein, N. C., Alexander, J. F., & Parsons, B. V. (1977). Impact of family systems intervention on recidivism and sibling delinquency: A model of primary prevention and program evaluation. *Journal of Consulting and Clinical Psychology, 45*(3), 469.

Kouneski, E. (2000). Circumplex model and FACES: Review of literature. Retrieved from http://www.facesIV.com

Landale, N. S., Oropesa, R. S., & Bradatan, C. (2006). Hispanic families in the United States: Family structure and process in an era of family change. In M. Tienda & F. Mitchell (Eds.), *Hispanics and the future of America.* Washington, DC: National Academies Press.

Lewin, K. (1947/1951). Frontiers in group dynamics. In D. Cartwright (Ed.), *Field theory in social science: Selected theoretical papers by Kurt Lewin* (pp. 188–237). New York, NY: Harper & Row.

McAuliffe, G. J. (Ed.). (2012). *Culturally alert counseling: A comprehensive introduction.* Thousand Oaks, CA: Sage.

Miller, G., & de Shazer, S. (1998). Have you heard the latest rumor about . . .? Solution-focused therapy as a rumor. *Family Process, 37*(3), 363–377.

Miller, G., & de Shazer, S. (2000). Emotions in solution-focused therapy: A re-examination. *Family process, 39*(1), 5–23.

Minuchin, S. (1974). *Families and family therapy.* Cambridge, MA: Harvard University Press.

Minuchin, S., & Fishman, H. C. (1981). Family therapy techniques. Cambridge, MA: Harvard University Press.

National Mental Health Association (2004). Mental Health Treatment for Youth in The Juvenile Justice System: A Compendium of Promising Practices; John D. and Catherine T. MacArthur Foundation: Chicago, IL.

Nichols, M. P. (2013). *Family therapy: Concepts and methods* (10th ed.). Upper Saddle River, NJ: Pearson Education.

Okun, B. F. (1996). *Understanding diverse families: What practitioners need to know.* New York, NY: Guilford Press.

Osborne, C., & McLanahan, S. (2007). Partnership instability and child well-being. *Journal of Marriage and Family, 69*(4), 1065–1083.

Patterson, J., Williams, L., Grauf-Grounds, C., & Chamow, L. (1998). *Essential skills in family therapy: From the first interview to termination.* New York, NY: Guilford Press.

Patterson, T., & Sexton, T. (2013). Bridging conceptual frameworks: A systemic heuristic for understanding family diversity. *Couple and Family Psychology: Research and Practice, 2*(4), 237–245.

Pettit, B., & Western, B. (2004). Mass imprisonment and the life course: Race and class inequality in US incarceration. *American Sociological Review, 69*(2), 151–169.

Phinney, J. (1992). The multigroup ethnic identity measure: A new scale for use with adolescents and young adults from diverse groups. *Journal of Adolescent Research, 7,* 156–176.

Rogers, C. R. (1961). *On becoming a person.* Boston, MA: Houghton-Mifflin.

Ruberman, L. (2009). Working with parents: Implications for individual psychotherapeutic work with children and adolescents. *American Journal of Psychotherapy, 63*(4), 345–362.

Russell, G. L., Fujino, D. C., Sue, S., Cheung, M. K., & Snowden, L. R. (1996). The effects of therapist–client ethnic match in the assessment of mental health functioning. *Journal of Cross-Cultural Psychology, 27*(5), 598–615.

Sexton, T. L. (2009). Functional family therapy: Traditional theory to evidence-based practice. In J. H. Bray & M. S. Stanton (Eds.), *The Wiley-Blackwell handbook of family psychology* (pp. 327–340). New York, NY: Wiley.

Sexton, T. L., Chamberlin, P., Landsverk, J., Ortiz, A., & Schoenwald, S. K. (2010). Action brief: Future directions in the implementation of evidence based treatment and practices in child and adolescent mental health. *Administration and Policy in Mental Health and Mental Health Services Research, 37*(1–2), 132–134.

Sexton, T., Yaffe, E., Kenigsberg, E., Bantignies, F., Leblanc, B., Hoichman, M., . . . Cavalli, G. (2012). Three-dimensional folding and functional organization principles of the Drosophila genome. *Cell, 148*(3), 458–472.

Sue, D., & Sue, D. W. (1991). *Counseling the culturally different: Theory and practice.* New York, NY: Wiley.

Sue, D. W. (2001). Multidimensional facets of cultural competence. *The Counseling Psychologist, 29*(6), 790–821.

Sue, D. W. (2003). *Overcoming our racism: The journey to liberation.* San Francisco, CA: Jossey-Bass.

Sue, D. W. (2004). Whiteness and ethnocentric monoculturalism: Making the "invisible" visible. *American Psychologist, 59*(8), 761.

Sue, D. W., Arredondo, P., & McDavis, R. J. (1992). Multicultural counseling competencies and standards: A call to the profession. *Journal of Counseling and Development, 70*(4), 477–486.

Sue, D. W., & Sue, D. (2003). *Counseling the culturally diverse: Theory and practice* (4th ed.). New York, NY: Wiley.

Sue, S. (2006). Cultural competency: From philosophy to research and practice. *Journal of Community Psychology, 34*(2), 237–245.

Thompson, R. A. (1998). Early sociopersonality development. In W. Damon & N. Eisenberg (Eds.), *Handbook of child psychology: Vol. 3. Social, emotional and personality development* (5th ed., pp. 25–104). New York, NY: Wiley.

Timmons-Mitchell, J.; Bender, M.; Kishna, M.; Mitchell, C. (2006). An Independent Effectiveness Trial off Multisystemic Therapy with Juvenile Justice Youth. *Journal of Clinical Child and Adolescent Psychology, 35*, 227–236.

U.S. Bureau of the Census. (2005). *Number, timing, and duration of marriages and divorces, 2001.* Retrieved from http://www.census.gov/prod/2005 pubs/p70-97.pdf

U.S. Bureau of the Census. (2008a). *Primary child care arrangements of preschoolers under 5 years old living with employed mothers by selected characteristics: Spring 2005* (Table 2B). Retrieved from http://www.census.gov/population/socdemo/ child/ppl-2005/tab02B.xls

U.S. Bureau of the Census. (2008b). *Statistical abstract of the United States: 2008.* Retrieved from http://www.census.gov/compendia/statab/

U.S. National Center for Health Statistics. (2009). *Changing patterns of nonmarital childbearing in the United States* (NCHS Data Brief No. 18). Retrieved from http://www.cdc.gov/nchs/data/ databriefs/db18.pdf

Weakland, J. H., & Jackson, D. D. (1958). Patient and therapist observations on the circumstances of a schizophrenic episode. *AMA Archives of Neurology & Psychiatry, 79*(5), 554–574.

Whitaker, C. A. (1975). Psychotherapy of the absurd: With a special emphasis on the psychotherapy of aggression. *Family Process, 14*(1), 1–16.

White, M., & Epston, D. (1990). *Narrative means to therapeutic ends.* New York, NY: W. W. Norton.

Wildeman, C. (2009). Parental imprisonment, the prison boom, and the concentration of childhood disadvantage. *Demography, 46*(2), 265–280.

Wu, L. L., & Martinson, B. C. (1993). Family structure and the risk of a premarital birth. *American Sociological Review, 58*(2), 210–232.

5

JUVENILE JUSTICE–INVOLVED ADOLESCENTS

Treatment rests on the basic strategy of making the adolescent so clearly aware of his/her pattern of irresponsible thinking that he cannot continue except by a full, conscious, and deliberate choice.

—Jon Bush

INTRODUCTION

Many providers have never been involved or worked in the legal system and have little idea what it is like to be arrested, adjudicated, and sentenced. Yet at younger than 18 years of age, thousands of adolescents are brought before a judge annually and become, in some way, involved in the juvenile justice system (Ryan, Williams, & Courtney, 2013). Some are arrested for substance abuse, domestic violence, trespassing, or running away, while others are arrested for defiant or antisocial behaviors.

Providers working with adolescents involved in the juvenile justice system are faced with a unique set of challenges. While other populations seek treatment for a variety of disorders and symptoms that have caused them distress, most adolescents in the juvenile justice system have engaged in a behavior that has demanded at least some level of legal involvement. Counseling this population requires additional knowledge relating to engagement skills and an extra dose of

patience and willingness to work with the complications in the adolescents' lives and those associated with governmental agencies. By the time an adolescent gets involved in the juvenile justice system, he or she may be involved in multiple other organizations and systems.

"Who is the client?" becomes a convoluted question when many diverse organizations and systems are involved in the care of these adolescents. Beyond the obvious answer to the question, "The adolescent" is the client. Providers, however, must also consider other key persons and systems along with their associated concerns such as the needs of the family, the desires of the court system, and the wishes of child services as well as community safety. Competent providers must manage all of these factors to work toward the greatest outcome of improving the lives of adolescents. Additionally, providers working with the juvenile justice system are, at times, called on to offer expert opinions about placement, custody, and treatment for delinquent adolescents. Providers must often balance the desires of the court, family, volunteer advocates, treatment goals, and the adolescent, although these desires (and associated goals) do not always align. Consider the following case example of Ken (Case Scenario 5.1).

This chapter provides a brief overview of critical issues in addressing the needs of adolescents involved in the juvenile justice system. The reader will learn about theories, techniques, and presuppositions to paint a full picture of what working with this population can entail. More specifically, this chapter will provide a brief history of the juvenile justice system and discuss the different viewpoints that have influenced policy as it relates

to delinquent adolescents. Furthermore, this chapter explores the presuppositions of the juvenile justice system and how these system providers continue to influence decisions regarding the placement and sentencing of adolescents. Readers will learn the various types of adolescents who are commonly found in the juvenile justice system and, after reading the chapter's content, should be competent to discuss important treatment considerations for counseling adolescents with various externalizing (e.g., behaviors toward others, such as fighting and arguing) and internalizing (e.g., behaviors toward self, such as self-harm) behavior disorders. Additionally, the chapter will identify

Case Scenario 5.1

Ken

Ken is a 17-year-old boy who 2 years ago was arrested for drug use and sexually offending his younger sister. He has spent the past 2 years in therapeutic foster care receiving weekly, home-based, individual, and family counseling. He has been meeting with a juvenile probation officer on a weekly basis as well. He tested positive for marijuana on a recent drug test, and his probation officer has stated a desire to send Ken to a residential treatment program to work on his sexually maladaptive behaviors and drug use.

Ken has a number of individuals involved in his case. Apart from his probation officer and home-based counselor, a judge, a court-appointed special advocate, a lawyer, and foster and biological parents are all involved in Ken's case. His probation officer is most concerned with the safety of the public and Ken's violation of his probation. His advocate and mother want professional efforts to be aimed at reunifying Ken with his family. His foster mother is concerned that his biological family is an unhealthy stress on Ken's life. She states that his family has been creating problems and encouraging Ken to violate his probation and the rules at the foster home by contacting them outside of the stated limits of his probation. His judge is concerned with Ken's age and ensuring Ken learns the skills essential to thriving as an adult. Ken's lawyer continues to argue that the probation officer has placed too many barriers on Ken and his family, thereby hindering his rehabilitation.

Ken's counselor, Tom, works for a private organization that is contracted by the probation department to provide services to at-risk youth and families. As such, Tom's services are provided free of charge to Ken and his family, but the probation officer receives monthly reports on the status and progress of the case. Tom has been trying to fulfill this role as a service provider to the family for the state but struggling with what that looks like in this situation.

At Ken's next court hearing with all parties present, the judge calls for Tom's recommendation on how to proceed with Ken's case (Exercise 5.1).

Exercise 5.1

Who Is the Client?

1. Who is the client in this case? Who is Tom most responsible to in this case?

2. What are some of the ethical considerations that Tom must weigh in this case as he deals with all the members of Ken's team?

3. How would you try to handle Ken's case if you were in Tom's position?

4. How should Tom balance Ken's emotional and delinquent needs related to ongoing work with Ken?

---

and analyze the different theories surrounding the development of delinquent behavior. It will then analyze the different placement options to which adolescents are referred and the benefits and concerns of each. Readers will be introduced to the basics of various evidence-based treatments for antisocial and delinquent adolescents.

After reading this chapter, readers will be able to do the following:

- Understand that the juvenile justice system creates a unique set of issues for providers working with delinquent adolescents based on multiple treatment and ethical areas

- Comprehend that the juvenile justice system wrestles with how best to treat the mental health and substance abuse needs of adolescents while maintaining the safety of the community

- Articulate that many adolescents involved in the juvenile justice system have a history of maltreatment and abuse and are considered crossover youth

- Discuss that crossover youth create extra issues for counseling due to dealing with multiple agencies and systems

- Discuss that sexual offenders require more specific treatment and special supervisory and ethical considerations

- Articulate that aggressive, antisocial adolescents often have a wide variety of diagnoses and have a risk of developing mood and anxiety disorders

- Understand that the different pathways to delinquency are important in case of conceptualization and treatment planning

- Appreciate that adolescents can be placed in a number of treatment settings based on their needs and the risk they pose to society (residential and lockdown facilities can be useful for more high-risk adolescents but must be properly supervised and structured)

- Discuss that research has validated a number of home-based treatments that can be effective with adolescents who are allowed to stay in their communities

- Apply knowledge gained from this chapter to a case scenario

HISTORICAL OVERVIEW OF THE JUVENILE JUSTICE SYSTEM

The juvenile justice system dates back to 1899 when the first juvenile court was established in Chicago, Illinois. Before this time, common law stated that children under 7 years were incapable of having criminal intent and were considered "legally incompetent." Anyone older than 7 years was tried and punished as an adult offender, though these adolescents lacked many of the rights of adults, including due process (McMillin, 2014; Silva, 2014). At times, courts referred to schools or families to intervene with some younger children, but many older adolescents were sentenced to adult facilities.

As a result of the Industrial Revolution, there was a shift of parents working on family farms and spending time in rural home environments to a time where parents' days were spent in factories and cities. This shift left children and adolescents with times of self-supervision and supervision from extended family members or friends and even resulted in increased times at their schools. This urbanization greatly affected the American family and, ultimately, led to the states being forced to address the problem of increasingly delinquent adolescents in lieu of the once stronger family unit that took care of these concerns. Around the turn of the 20th century, with the formation of the first juvenile courts, delinquency was believed to be an "outgrowth of immorality and poverty" (Silva, 2014). Care and treatment for such adolescents aligned with a belief in protecting the community and harshly punishing adolescents' misbehaviors and legal infringements. Furthermore, the very makeup of the juvenile court was purposefully informal to better "facilitate a more efficient, personalized resolution of the case" (McMillin, 2014, p. 1493). This meant that the courts were given free rein to make decisions regarding adolescents without having to follow any of the rules or checks that are required by adult courts such as legal representation, notice of charges, and protection against self-incrimination (McMillin, 2014).

The court's concern focused on the malleability of children and adolescents and the importance of environment on shaping behavior. As a result, early juvenile court philosophy concentrated less on the guilt or innocence of the adolescent and more on the adolescents' rehabilitation. This was known as the "Best Interest" standard (Silva, 2014). In other words, from the earlier vignette regarding Ken, it would have been considered the best interest of the adolescent to remain in a treatment or correctional facility where he would be safe from the negative environment of his home, and society would be safe from him. Moreover, a judge could order this without needing any of the formalities of a regular hearing.

Public thought has developed and fluctuated over the past century with regard to dealing with delinquent adolescents. Society has continued to wrestle with identifying the most effective way to respond to the problems incited by adolescent misbehaviors while keeping in mind both the adolescent's best interests as well as the safety of the community. Early juvenile court approaches began with an individualized treatment philosophy for the adolescent, but over the years, it shifted to resembling adult punitive penal sentencing as the number of cases increased and the very structure of juvenile court changed to accommodate more delinquent adolescents. Practical concerns of handling the heightened number of adolescents flooding the courts continued to affect trends in dealing with adolescents. In the 1970s, with the generation called "baby boomers" (born between 1946 and 1964) first reaching adolescence, there was a perceived increase in adolescent crime in American society, and the public called for more punitive measures as payment for adolescent delinquency—viewing the adolescents as heinous, purposeful, and willful offenders. As a result, stricter punishments were adopted like incarceration in detention facilities instead of treatment facilities that target erroneous thinking, teach new behaviors, and reward prosocial behaviors and minimum (rather than maximum) detention requirements (McMillin, 2014). Juvenile courts began to resemble adult criminal courts with more official guidelines and rules implemented to standardize adult-like procedures (McMillin, 2014). Concomitantly, state legislatures passed statutes allowing adolescents to be waived to adult courts. Public opinion shifted away from protecting adolescents to more "tough on crime," punishment-type approaches. The next couple of decades continued to see an increase in juvenile cases with little increase in resources (Silva, 2014).

Today, the juvenile justice system continues to wrestle with the practical concerns of addressing the number of violent crimes committed by adolescents. Society still wavers between wanting to punish offenders in order to "scare them straight" and wanting to treat them by using mental health services that eradicate unlawful behaviors. Today, judges are often faced with having to choose between what is the best treatment for the adolescent and what is the safest choice for society (Herz, Ryan, & Bilchik, 2010). Providers can be invited in to these decisions to offer expert opinions that have the potential to greatly affect the future of an adolescent.

PRESUPPOSITIONS OF THE JUVENILE JUSTICE SYSTEM

The juvenile justice system has developed a unique culture and set of beliefs. The system began, as we saw earlier, as an answer to the problem of juvenile delinquency and was created around the standard of "Best Interest of the Child" (Silva, 2014). Through the years, the interpretation of that standard, and its application across different scenarios, has changed. However, some basic presuppositions have remained that continue to influence the juvenile justice system.

The primary presupposition from which the system developed is that children and adolescents are different from adults, and therefore, they cannot be treated in the same way in the eyes of the law. Legally, children and adolescents are viewed differently than adults in that they are not of "full legal capacity" (Office of Juvenile Justice and Delinquency Prevention [OJJDP], 1999, p. 2), meaning that they are not fully responsible for their actions. This is most obviously shown in the laws prohibiting children from activities such as voting, using alcohol, entering into contracts, and so on. When considering the detention facilities housing adolescents, state agencies must protect these minors from their adult counterparts in adult facilities. In light of the protection need, the juvenile justice system exists separately from the adult justice system (McMillin, 2014).

Based on this premise of the difference between adults and adolescents, two further presuppositions have developed that have shaped the way in which the juvenile justice system operates and makes decisions. These presuppositions are that adolescents have a diminished capacity and that juveniles (adolescents involved in the juvenile justice system) are malleable.

Juveniles and Diminished Capacity

Diminished capacity (or responsibility) is a legal defense that is used to argue that one cannot be held criminally responsible for his or her actions, as his or her mental functions were impaired. Legally, minors are prohibited from voting, entering into contracts, drinking alcohol, smoking, and participating in a variety of other activities because they are seen as not having the capacity to fully understand the impact of their decisions and behaviors. This same principle applies to infractions of the law in that adolescents are not viewed as fully responsible for their actions due to their lesser capacity to make decisions. This lesser capacity can be attributed to adolescents' ongoing cognitive, neurological (the decision-making center in the brain [the prefrontal cortex], especially), and moral development.

Depending on many factors (e.g., adolescent's delinquency history, type and intensity of delinquent act, state laws, and precedent), exceptions exist allowing for adolescents to be waived to adult court under certain circumstances. Some examples include when previous rehabilitation efforts were unsuccessful, the charge is particularly serious, or if the minor is older. In the United States, "Approximately 200,000 juveniles are transferred to adult court each year" (Silva, 2014, p. 415). In theory, this waiver is only for extreme cases.

Juveniles Are Malleable

One of the primary differences between adults and adolescents is the potential for change. Juveniles are developmentally in a period of transition. Legally, physically, emotionally, and mentally, they are in a state of adjustment, moving from dependence to independence. Decisions made about adolescents in the juvenile justice system under the "best interest" principle take into consideration that, to a much greater degree than for adults, there remains the hope of change (McMillin, 2014; Underwood, & Washington, 2015).

This "best interest" goal plays itself out in a number of ways, but one of its primary outpourings is that "Juvenile courts are to decide the needs of a child as opposed to criminally prosecute" (Silva, 2014, p. 432). In this best interest approach, treatment is preferred over containment or punitive measures. It is important to note that this approach and its outgrowths can be waived at times, and adolescents have been treated harsher or lighter over the years as cultural shifts and practical concerns are weighed. However, the principle still remains that the adolescent's needs are to be taken as paramount to the need to punish misbehaviors (Exercise 5.2).

OVERVIEW OF THE JUVENILE JUSTICE SYSTEM–INVOLVED ADOLESCENTS

So who are these delinquent adolescents, and what are they like? Adolescents involved in the juvenile justice system are anything but homogeneous. While the term *delinquent youth* is often used as a catchall, it can be a very misleading overgeneralization. Being involved with the juvenile justice system may mean that an adolescent has been adjudicated for at least one offense. Adjudication is defined as being sentenced by the court. This simply means that the adolescent has been arrested and brought before a judge who has found him or her guilty of a delinquent act.

When working with these adolescents, the impact of this sentencing on the counseling process can be rather significant. Adjudicated adolescents can often see all adults in their lives as part of the system that has sentenced them. Counseling is not something the adolescent usually request or desire; it is something in which they are mandated participants.

Demographics

In the United States, the adolescent arrest rate has been seeing a decline (see Figure 5.1) since hitting a peak in 1996 (OJJDP, 2013). However, adolescent offenders continue to make up 15% of all violent crimes and 24% of all property crimes (OJJDP, 2011, 2013).

Looking at the demographics of adolescent delinquents, some general trends are evident. The population disproportionately involves minorities. For example, in 2009, the general U.S. population aged 10 to 17 years was

76% white, 17% black, 5% Asian/Pacific Islander, and 2% American Indian. . . . More than half (51%) of all adolescent arrests for violent crimes in 2011 involved black adolescents, 47% involved white adolescents, 1% involved Asian adolescents, and 1% involved American Indian adolescents. (OJJDP, 2013, p. 5)

Also, more males than females constitute the delinquent adolescent population with females making up only 29% of all adolescent arrests in 2011 (OJJDP, 2013).

Research has shown the high prevalence of mental health disorders among adolescents involved in the juvenile justice system. Studies between 2002 and 2006 found the prevalence of

Exercise 5.2

Changes in the Juvenile Justice System

The juvenile justice system in the United States has gone through a number of changes as discussed in this chapter. What are your thoughts on how the system was originally formed, and what it is like today? How do you think society should deal with adolescent offenders?

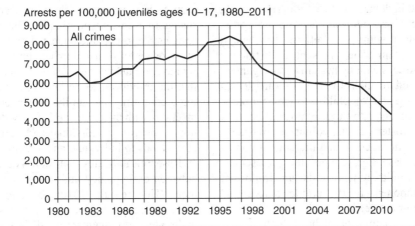

Figure 5.1 Arrests per 100,000 juveniles

Source. Office of Juvenile Justice and Delinquency Prevention (2013).

at least one mental health disorder to be between 67.2% and 70.4% (Shufelt & Cocozza, 2006). A study by the National Center for Mental Health and Juvenile Justice that examined national population sample identified disruptive disorders to be the most common with a rate of 46.5%, followed by substance abuse disorders at 46.2%, anxiety disorders at 34.4%, and mood disorders at 18.3% (Shufelt & Cocozza, 2006). This study further noted that 79% of the adolescents who met a criteria or at least one diagnosis also met the criteria for multiple disorders. The most common co-occurring disorder was found to be substance abuse. Additionally, 60.8% of the adolescents with a disorder also met the criteria for a substance abuse disorder.

While it is a recognized fact that there is a high prevalence of mental health disorders among delinquent adolescents, effectively diagnosing this population is extremely difficult and creates a problem in placing them into appropriate categories (Kinscherff, 2012). Symptoms of mental health disorders in adolescents are non-specific and can be found in several different diagnoses. For example, "Functionally significant impairments in attention and concentration may be found in Attention Deficit Disorder (with or without Hyperactivity), PTSD, Major Depressive Episode, Bipolar Disorder, or persisting effects of concussion after a blow to the head" (Kinscherff, 2012, p. 6). Moreover, a diagnosis is not necessarily sufficient to connect the link between the mental health disorder and the delinquent behavior. In other words, the diagnosis may not be the entire reason for the juvenile's behavior.

Common diagnoses that are seen in delinquent adolescents can be insufficient in understanding the whole person. For purposes of considering the different needs of various types of delinquent adolescents, this section examines adolescents in three different categories: (1) crossover youth, (2) sexual offenders, and (3) antisocial/aggressive adolescents. It is important to remember that these categories are not exclusive of each other, in that adolescents may be able to fall into multiple categories. However, this chapter presents the categories separately in the next three sections.

Crossover Youth

The first category, crossover youth, refers to adolescents who have experienced maltreatment and engaged in delinquent behaviors (Herz et al., 2010). These are adolescents who are often dually involved with child welfare services and the court system. They present a distinctive problem due to the many systems and organizations involved in their lives. For example, an adolescent may have child services workers, probation officers, attorneys, biological parents, stepparents, foster parents, volunteer advocates, judges, case managers, and a therapist involved in his or her case. Furthermore, the adolescents' history of maltreatment adds an important trauma component to the circumstances and ensuing treatment needs.

Crossover youth usually have both dependency concerns (e.g., needing adult supervision, financial support, guidance, etc.) and delinquency involvement (e.g., legal concerns, detainment, treatment compliance, etc.) and are often caught between them. This means that an adolescent may be simultaneously involved with both probation and child welfare services as a result of parental acts of abuse and/or neglect. In these cases, one agency will usually take the "lead" and have primary jurisdiction over the adolescent's care (Herz et al., 2010). All of this can be very confusing for the adolescent, the family, and the service providers involved with the family. As Cashmore (2011) writes, "Children in need of care or in care who move into the juvenile justice system are arguably neglected by both the child protection and juvenile justice systems" (p. 36). In other words, adolescents involved with multiple organizations often fall between the cracks of the different systems, and important needs can be missed in the confusion. Providers working with families in these situations are particularly obliged to act as advocates for their clients, a very difficult and confusing process that requires much collaboration and negotiation between various professions, systems of care, and family.

The earlier example of Ken and the multiple systems of care in his life illustrates this well. The provider working with Ken and his family should remember that, as confusing as the situation may seem to him or her, it is far more scary and confusing to Ken and his family. The provider is responsible to become educated on the best way to advocate for Ken and to help him and the family navigate the various systems. This may mean that the provider will be involved in court hearings, educating the family, and attending team meetings with the other service providers in addition to providing individual and family therapy that attends to individual and system concerns.

Research indicates that there is a connection between delinquency and histories of maltreatment (Herz et al., 2010; Ryan et al., 2013; Ryan & Testa, 2005). One study shows that maltreated adolescents have 47% higher delinquency rates as compared with their peers from the general population (Ryan & Testa, 2005). More specific statistics are difficult to find due to factors such as the intervention of various agencies, managing ethical compliance to confidentiality, information sharing between them all, and working with the same individual client.

Not surprisingly, crossover youth are also at a greater risk for substance abuse and mental health problems than adolescents without a history of maltreatment (Herz et al., 2010). As such, crossover youth often present with a wide variety of disorders and diagnoses. Treating and accurately diagnosing them can be extremely difficult because the same behaviors can be attributed to a number of different diagnoses. Furthermore, on studying adults who were emancipated from the foster care system on their 18th birthday, 25% were incarcerated within the first few years of their 18th birthday (Krinsky, 2010). Ryan et al. (2013) noted from a study of charged minors in the state of Washington with an ongoing case or history of neglect that "adolescents with an ongoing case of neglect were significantly more likely to continue offending as compared to adolescents with no official history of neglect" (p. 454).

Juvenile Sexual Offenders

When considering community safety, the category of juvenile sex offenders comes to mind because of the heinous and sexual nature of their acts provides a more comprehensive review of juveniles with sexually maladaptive behavior). These adolescents are a population with very specific needs. While treatment for this population can, at times, be similar to working with other delinquent adolescents, there are enough important distinctions that this category will be addressed in much greater detail in a separate chapter. The provider is responsible for considering the safety of the adolescent, family, and all others in that adolescent's environment (e.g., school, neighborhood, etc.) in addition to the normal considerations of competent treatment. For more information on juvenile sex offenders, see Chapter 16, which has been dedicated to the assessment and treatment of this specialized population.

Ethical conditions about confidentiality can become more complicated when working with juvenile sexual offenders. Ethics must be considered when making decisions about maintaining confidentiality over warning schools and families. Providers working with sexual offenders often learn about their clients' previously unreported sexual offenses, thus further expanding the counseling role from one that is solely concerned with the individual to one that interacts with multiple systems (e.g., family, child welfare, mental health, juvenile justice, educational, etc.). In this expanded role, effective and ethical providers must balance the needs of the client with their duty to report abuse in such situations. Therefore, competent supervision and consultation throughout one's professional career and from experienced providers is extremely important for all of these reasons and more.

Antisocial Adolescents

Another group that present as challenges to community safety is that of the antisocial adolescent. Antisocial adolescents generally present with disruptive behavior disorders (conduct disorder [CD], oppositional defiant disorder, intermittent explosive disorder, etc.) and a greater association with violent street gangs (Sanders, 2012). They often present more aggressive and angry nature in their counseling sessions. Additionally, they have been shown to have a greater prevalence of suicidal ideation (Ruchkin, Schwab-Stone, Koposov, Vermeiren, & King, 2003; Thompson, Kingree, & Ho, 2006). Interpersonal callousness and antisocial traits are also frequently associated with this category of adolescents.

Research has shown a frequent occurrence of comorbidity with attention-deficit/hyperactivity disorder, conduct disorder, and oppositional defiant disorder (ODD; Chen et al., 2013). Because several of the symptoms of these disorders can appear very similar to one another, and many of these adolescents have been diagnosed with a wide range of behavioral health disorders, diagnostic confusion can further reign when the symptoms are interpreted as being the result of mood disorders and not simply disruptive behavior. Consequently, these types of adolescents have been strongly associated with a greater prevalence for mood disorders (Chen et al., 2013).

When examining the risk of delinquency persisting into adulthood, researchers have noted specific symptoms that seem to pose a greater risk of ongoing delinquency. For example, adolescents who demonstrate CD and particularly interpersonal callousness symptoms are more likely to develop antisocial personality disorder and continued criminal activity as adults (Byrd, Loeber, & Pardini, 2012). However, adolescents who demonstrate primarily attention-deficit/hyperactivity disorder and/or ODD symptoms are more likely to discontinue their antisocial behavior as they age.

While these categories are presented here as distinct, it is important to remember that they are not exclusive and adolescents rarely fall neatly into the categories that adults set for them. Understanding these differences is important when developing a thorough case conceptualization and treatment plan (Exercise 5.3).

Exercise 5.3

Categories of Juvenile Justice Adolescents

Consider the different categories of juvenile justice–involved adolescents in this chapter. What are your thoughts on providing services to these populations? Is there a category that interests or concerns you more than others? Why do you think that is?

JUVENILE JUSTICE AND DELINQUENCY THEORIES

Several different theories have emerged over the years regarding the development of antisocial and delinquent behaviors. Much of the debate can be boiled down to two sides: (1) theorists who focus more on developmental factors and (2) those who focus more on environmental factors (Tremblay, 2000). As theorists continue studying the causes of human behavior and the direct impact of nature and nurture, these findings affect the general understanding of and beliefs about delinquent adolescents and their problematic behaviors. Though the two theories make up two categories, and this division assists in the ease of understanding and learning, caution should be taken by the reader to remember that, but it does not mean that they are mutually exclusive in practice (Exercise 5.4).

Developmental Theories

Developmental theorists place greater importance on the makeup of the individual than on the environmental factors that influence the adolescent. Environmental theorists, alternatively, look more at the social context surrounding the adolescent. Much of the debate stems from a philosophical disagreement on the starting nature of a human being. "Are children born with an aggressive instinct or do they have to learn to aggress?" (Tremblay, 2000, p. 129). The answer to this question has significant implications on the delivery of interventions. Should interventions be more geared toward protecting adolescents from learning aggression or toward teaching them to control their aggressive reactions? Is it more effective to treat the individual or the system or both?

Developmental theorists answer these questions by focusing on the individual adolescent's attributes and less on the system or environment in which that adolescent is found. With regard to delinquency, developmental theorists point to studies that show a great increase in delinquent and aggressive behavior in children when they reach adolescence. The rapid increase in delinquent behavior, which begins at adolescence and then sees an equally rapid decrease, is called the age–crime curve. Studies have found that as

Exercise 5.4

Factors in Development

As you reflect on your own upbringing, what factors played a bigger role in your development? What was the accepted narrative that explained adolescent behavior in your home culture? Where do you think that narrative originated? How has it shaped your view of delinquent adolescents?

children age, they become more physically aggressive (Tremblay, 2000). Therefore, age is seen as a major factor in the development of aggressive behavior. Researchers, however, have also found connections with other specific factors that can further complicate the development of delinquent and aggressive behavior. Beauchaine, Hinshaw, and Pang (2010) studied disruptive behavior disorders and state that

> delinquent boys usually traverse a developmental pathway that begins with severe hyperactive/impulsive behaviors as early as toddlerhood, followed by ODD (oppositional defiant disorder) in preschool, early-onset CD (conduct disorder) in elementary school, substance use disorders (SUDs) in adolescence, and antisocial personality in adulthood. (p. 328)

Byrd et al. (2012) took this research a step further and found that interpersonal callousness, in particular, was the primary indicator of disruptive behavior disorders that would persist into adulthood antisocial behavior. Additionally, the comorbidity of CD and mood disorders have also been connected to an increase in delinquent behavior (Chen et al., 2013). Gender differences have been examined in relation to the development of delinquency as well (Walters, 2014). In this way, developmental theories focus more specifically on the qualities that make up the individual.

Environmental Theories

Unlike developmental theorists, environmental theorists look to the context and systems that interact with the adolescent. These theorists point to the powerful impact that families, peers, and neighborhoods can have on development (Tremblay, 2000) as evidence that the environment plays the primary role in shaping behavior. Deviant behavior, in particular, has been linked to social contexts in several studies (Jennings, Maldonado-Molina, Reingle, & Komro, 2011).

An example of one environmental theory is called social disorganization theory. This theory "emphasizes the importance of the ability of a community's residents to realize shared goals and values and regulate the conduct of its citizens" (Jennings et al., 2011, p. 393). Adolescents residing in communities that are characterized by higher crime rates and greater residential instability are at a far greater risk of developing delinquent behavior than their peers in other areas of town. Moreover, the impact of deviant peers on other adolescents has long been studied and shown to have negative effects on treatment outcomes and future offending behavior (Dodge, Dishion, Lansford, & Society for Research in Child Development, 2006; Sanders, 2012). Parenting techniques and familial disruption have also been shown to have a great impact on a child's propensity to develop aggressive and delinquent behaviors (Cashmore, 2011; Krinsky, 2010; Piquero, Farrington, Welsh, Tremblay, & Jennings, 2009; Walters, 2014). Research has shown how aggression in parents directly affects the development of externalizing, disruptive behaviors in their children (Hops, Davis, Leve, & Sheeber, 2003).

Differing Pathways

Taking a different route, some theorists have begun concentrating on what they consider differing pathways to developing offending and delinquent behavior. These theorists place less emphasis on finding the cause and more on identifying the paths and factors that can play important roles in promoting such behavior (Walters, 2014). One of the dangers of looking at these pathways, however, is to begin following a one-size-fits-all approach to every adolescent. Every adolescent is unique with his or her own story that deserves attention. Notwithstanding, these pathways can help create a framework that allows providers to better conceptualize the problems and life events with which the adolescent presents in counseling sessions.

One pathway to delinquent behavior that has been extensively examined is the trauma pathway. We have already discussed crossover youths in this chapter. Studies have shown the connection between child maltreatment and neglect and aggressive/disruptive behavior (Krinsky, 2010; Ryan et al., 2013; Ryan & Testa, 2005). This pathway views adolescent aggressive behavior as primarily reactions to previous maltreatment. In a study that examined externalizing behaviors across generational lines, researchers found that "adolescents who were exposed to greater levels of parental hostility were more likely to display aggressive behavioral styles as adolescents, with this behavioral style predicting the nature of their interactions with their own children" (Hops et al., 2003, p. 167). In short, adolescents who have developed delinquent behaviors through the trauma pathway are victims of direct (to the adolescents specifically) or indirect (observed, anticipated, or threatened) abuse or neglect. These adolescents have unresolved histories of trauma that are fueling their delinquent behaviors. From this perspective, helping an adolescent alter his or her aggressive behavior must, in some way, address the earlier trauma.

Another pathway to delinquent behavior focuses predominantly on the familial and environmental factors. Adolescents from this pathway have been powerfully influenced by the context around them. Researchers have identified that parental behavior and deviant peer association have been closely linked to antisocial adolescent behavior (Deutsch, Crockett, Wolff, & Russell, 2012). Parenting styles that have less parental control (or influence that results in the adolescent restraining their behaviors, following directives, or heeding parental guidance) over the adolescent are directly correlated with an increase in delinquency rates and affiliations with delinquent peers. One study from 2012 showed that "maternal support was related to less association with deviant peers for African American and European American adolescents, which in turn predicted lower involvement in delinquent behaviors" (Deutsch et al., 2012, p. 1089). This means that the adolescents whose mothers were more involved in their lives were less likely to engage in delinquent behavior than their peers with more distant mothers. Furthermore, neighborhood factors such as crime rates, socioeconomic status, and neighborhood cohesion have

also been shown to greatly affect delinquency rates (Jennings et al., 2011).

In other words, adolescent delinquency is closely related to contextual, environmental, and familial factors. Adolescents are influenced by the world around them. For the provider working with adolescents who have developed delinquent behaviors through this pathway, it is paramount to be able to identify and address the external factors that influence the adolescent toward delinquency.

The resiliency theory is a specific derivation of the impact that trauma studies have had on working with juvenile populations. This theory combines the family pathways toward delinquency with environmental pathways to understand and treat delinquent adolescents. It uses a positive psychology outlook and, as such, is more concerned with adolescent strengths rather than deficits. This resiliency theory looks at what makes it possible for adolescents to overcome the difficult settings in which they are raised by addressing the adolescents' assets (internal positive factors such as intelligence, temperament, impulse control) and resources (external positive factors, e.g., effective schools, family supports, activities, and hobbies). From this perspective, it is important to focus on the strengths of the adolescent and the protective factors (e.g., family involvement, social skills, competency, and community involvement) from which to build more individualized treatment plans and interventions (Fergus & Zimmerman, 2005) and life in general.

In summary, theories on the development of aggressive and delinquent behavior have followed the same nature–nurture debate as in other aspects of psychology and continue to change as studies further shape our understanding of human behavior. Through the past 30 years, longitudinal studies and research have shown us some of the important factors and pathways to delinquency. From these, it is evident that factors associated with the adolescent's development (physical), experience (daily life), biology (disease or mental health challenges), environment (neighborhood safety), social (peer associations), and familial (support, supervision) all play a part and must be assessed and addressed to effectively treat delinquent adolescents.

TECHNIQUES FOR TREATING DELINQUENT ADOLESCENTS

Counseling adolescents involved in the juvenile justice system presents a unique set of challenges for providers. Families are often much more resistant to treatment and may view the provider as another member of a system that is against them. Providers' opinions, assessments, and treatment outcomes can have a great impact on the placement of the adolescent as well as the role of the family in the adolescent's life. As alluded to throughout this chapter, family services and legal/ probation also give input into the adolescents' treatment at times.

Adolescents in the justice system are often mandated to receive mental health treatment (Kinscherff, 2012). These services can range from outpatient counseling to home-based family therapy, group therapy, placement in residential treatment facilities, or lockup in a detention or secure care facility. Each of these modalities carries with it its own merits, drawbacks, and peculiarities that affect treatment, like family involvement and risks of delinquency. Despite inherent challenges, they all share some traits that are important for providers to understand.

Issues of motivation for change are common issues for all persons entering therapeutic relationships. Juvenile clients often present as unmotivated and resistant to therapy (Apsche & Bailey, 2003). Unlike therapy with adolescents who may be seen at the request of a parent (generally indicating some level of parental motivation and support), therapy for court-order adolescents often includes heavy resistance from the family as well. When the court or state is paying for mental health services provided and request notes and reports from the provider on treatment progress, the family may perceive the provider as another arm of law enforcement. This perception may increase the family's resistance and defensiveness to treatment overall and set-up a defensive stance for family members trying to prove that they are good parents, have strong caring families, and rear children appropriately.

Addressing these barriers through the therapeutic vehicle of motivational interviewing (MI) techniques and criminal thinking errors approach has proved beneficial to families, their adolescents, and the aims of professional providers. MI takes a directive, person-centered approach to addressing client resistance and views motivation as the responsibility of the provider. In other words, providers are to understand clients to the point of identifying and understanding the client's underlying motivations to their overt behaviors. This identification and understanding is then used to message and encourage an increase in the client's motivation toward said goals. The provider bares that task of being able to help craft therapeutic goals that are cocreated by clients while simultaneously meeting the mandates established by the various systems involved in the juvenile's life. For example, a provider highlighting that a juvenile's goal is to have "the courts out of my (the juvenile's) life" can be used as a vehicle to articulate what is required for such to happen (e.g., attend counseling sessions, show progress and learning, comply with other services such as substance use services). From there, the provider can wield much creativity in smaller treatment goals to make progressive approximations of the overarching goal of eliminating court involvement in the juvenile's life. Studies have shown the effectiveness of MI in supplementing other treatment techniques and increasing motivation to change. Stein et al. (2006) offer that

> MI (Motivational Interviewing) is ideally suited for correctional settings in that it is brief, can be used as a prelude to other treatments and has also been found effective as a stand-alone treatment for substance abuse. MI is well suited for settings with few resources and for persons who may be high in anger or hostility. As many as 40% of juveniles show significant anger when initially detained. (p. 51)

Treatment Environments

Providers treating delinquent adolescents continue to wrestle with questions of safety and mental health as they pertain to the adolescent. These questions include the following: (a) What is the safest environment for the adolescent and society? (b) What level of danger does the adolescent pose for the community? (c) What is the best treatment modality for the adolescent? Delinquent adolescents find themselves along a continuum of services ranging from extremely restrictive, lockdown facilities to outpatient mental health counseling where they reside at their homes and are overseen by probation officers or community-based clinics. A general expectation is that the greater the risk that the adolescent poses, the more restrictive the placement and services they should receive. For example, an adolescent may be mandated to meet with a probation officer regularly and attend group therapy. He or she may also be placed on house arrest for a period of time. However, if the delinquent behaviors persist, the adolescent may then require increased supervision and restraint, thereby warranting his or her

move to a residential treatment facility or secure care correctional facility, depending on the nature of his or her case, the severity of the offending behavior, and the risk of future delinquent acts.

Juvenile justice–related treatment settings all have a significant impact on how treatment is conducted with adolescents. See Table 5.1 for various juvenile justice treatment environments, which will contain various programs within to manage their populations served. Home-based services, for instance, allow providers with access to their family members, community, school, and other social systems but have fewer controls on the adolescent. Residential or lockdown facilities, on the other hand, allow for more intense behavioral controls and modification therapy. They also provide opportunity for therapeutic group work and social learning. Family involvement in residential programs can be difficult to encourage, however, due to the increased number of external barriers such as the necessity for the family to travel to and from the program. Furthermore, the adolescent is seen in a clinical setting, outside of his or her natural environment. In summary, it is important to be conscious of the setting in which the adolescent

Table 5.1   Treatment Environments

Treatment Environment	Strengths	Drawbacks
Home-based	Access to client's family and environment	Fewer controls over implementation of treatment interventions
Outpatient	Less pressure on the client and more control over the treatment environment leads to a greater feeling of safety and fewer interruptions	Less access to the community and the client's environment; more clinical feel, less interaction with the client's real world
Residential	Greater control over the client's environment and opportunity for more intense interventions	Less access to family and environment; treatment happens in a sterile environment completely separate from the real world; more chance of delinquency training from negative peers
Lockdown/detention	Extreme control over client's environment allows for very intense behavioral interventions; greater safety for the community and "real-world" consequences for misbehavior	More focus on punishment than treatment or rehabilitation; strong risk of delinquency training; limited family involvement; complete separation from home environment and supports

is placed and work to maximize the opportunities available.

Another option for juveniles are out-of-home placements. These placements vary from institution to institution with some focusing on specific issues like sexually maladaptive behaviors or substance abuse and others having a more general, behavioral focus. Residential placements can also vary in their degree of clinical attention. Some are primarily facilities meant to contain adolescents, while others have very intense clinical and specialized programs. These highly supervised placements can be categorized into either lockdown detention centers (tend to have a punitive, containment focus) or treatment facilities (tend to be designed for rehabilitation).

The year 2000 saw the greatest number of adolescent offenders in residential placement with a total of 108,802, but that number has since steadily diminished (OJJDP, 2010; Sickmund, 2010). Between 2000 and 2008, adolescents in residential placements decreased 26% to fewer than 81,000 (OJJDP, 2010). Since 2009, public policy regarding the handling of juveniles have pushed for more home-based treatments for delinquent adolescents in place of residential programs. Residential placements are expensive, and research has shown the dangers of delinquency training and the iatrogenic effects (complications resulting from treatment) of grouping delinquent adolescents together in a facility (Dodge et al., 2006). In other words, adolescents who are involved in deviant behaviors who were sent to residential placements, at times, regressed due to their affiliation with other high-risk peers. Furthermore, home-based services, like multisystemic therapy, have been shown to be effective in treating conduct and other disruptive

behavior disorders (Henggeler & Sheidow, 2012; Schaub et al., 2014). Home-based services also cause less disruption for the family. As such, out-of-home placements are now one of the last options considered for delinquent adolescents.

Residential programs, however, are still important. Studies have found that steps can be taken to help alleviate some of the negative effects of residential treatment for adolescents. For example, Dodge et al. (2006) identified two factors that can lessen the severity of such effects. Their study showed that well-trained adult leaders who are effectively supervised on site as well as programs with a highly structured environment where free, unsupervised times are minimized were important factors in dampening the contagion effect of all-deviant peer settings (Exercise 5.5).

EVIDENCE-BASED OUTGROWTHS

Providers working with juveniles do well to understand the different treatment options that are evidence based, promising within the counseling field, and indicated for this population. Within the juvenile justice system, evidence-based treatments are defined as "a body of knowledge, also obtained through the scientific method, on the impact of specific practices on targeted outcomes for youth and their families" (Underwood, von Dresner, & Phillips, 2006, p. 287). According to the National Institute of Mental Health, evidence-based practices include the following:

1. A minimum of two control group studies or a large series of single-case studies

2. At least two researchers

Exercise 5.5

Treatment Settings

After reading about the different settings in which delinquent adolescents are treated, consider the case of Ken. From which setting do you think he would most benefit? Why?

3. Treatment manual utilization

4. Training for therapists with written protocols

5. Adequate clinical samples

6. Significant results from outcome tests

7. Clinical reviews of program functioning and symptom outcomes

8. Reports on long-term outcomes following treatment completion

9. Two or more studies that demonstrate treatment superiority over medication, placebo, or other established treatment protocols (Underwood, Robinson, Mosholder, & Warren, 2008)

With previous discussions on the profiles of delinquent adolescents and effective overarching techniques for working with adolescents involved in the juvenile justice system in mind, a few effective treatments will be examined.

Work with adolescents involved in the juvenile justice system has spawned a number of positive treatment additions to adolescent literature. While cognitive behavioral therapy (CBT) continues to be a dominant therapy, several new juvenile justice–indicated approaches have emerged that build on its foundation. The specialized treatments have more attention to trauma-focused understanding and interventions that have recently been shown to effectively treat juvenile populations. Additionally, many of these treatments can be utilized in conjunction with one another in the appropriate situation. Providers working with adolescents in the juvenile justice system should be aware of the plethora of effective treatments and should take into consideration which approaches are best fitting for their populations served. This chapter does not attempt to provide a comprehensive review of all evidence-based treatments, but a few of the more prominent treatments that continue to show positive outcomes. See Table 5.2 for four juvenile treatment approaches, their primary foci, and delivery methods.

Thinking for a Change

Thinking for a Change (TFC) is one recent example of a CBT-based treatment that is commonly used with adolescents in the juvenile justice system (Bush, Glick, Taymans, & Guevara, 2011; Figure 5.2). It was developed under the guidance of the National Institute of Corrections and is uniquely suited for delinquent populations. The core of the TFC program is founded on problem solving and is augmented with cognitive restructuring and social skills interventions (Table 5.3). The program strives to effectively combine tools from cognitive restructuring programs with cognitive skills paradigms. The delivery of the treatment is systematic in nature and the lessons build on one another as the program unfolds. This treatment can be delivered in a group or individual setting.

TFC is arranged into 25 lessons that are ideally suited for small groups (Bush et al., 2011). These lessons are broken down into three types of interventions with an introductory lesson and

Table 5.2 Evidence-Based Outgrowths

Treatment	Primary Focus	Delivery Method
Thinking for a change	Problem solving	Group
Trauma-focused cognitive behavioral therapy	Trauma	Parent–child and individual sessions
Mode deactivation therapy	Cognitive behavioral therapy with added emotional component	Individual, group, or family
Multisystemic therapy	Environmental and family systems	Home-based and family

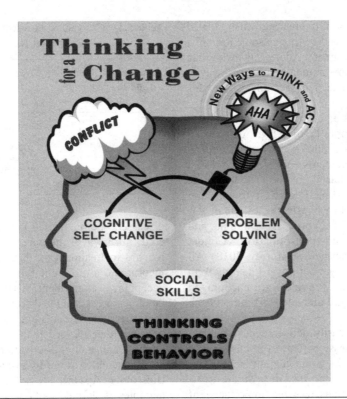

Figure 5.2   Thinking for a Change Illustration

Source. Bush, Glick, Taymans, and Guevara (2011).

Table 5.3   Thinking for a Change Key Focuses

Thinking for a Change	*Key Focuses*
	Social skills
	Cognitive self-change process
	Problem-solving skills

a wrap-up lesson at the beginning and the end, respectively. Lessons 2 to 5 and 11 to 15 focus on teaching social skills. Lessons 6 to 10 then teach cognitive self-change process, and lessons 16 to 24 address problem-solving skills.

Special credentialing for becoming a group facilitator of TFC exists for those interested in leading groups. Other information is available online through the National Institute of Corrections (2012).

Trauma-Focused Cognitive Behavioral Therapy

Trauma-focused cognitive behavioral therapy (TF-CBT) is another treatment option that is commonly used with delinquent adolescents (Kerig, Ward, Vanderzee, & Arnzen Moeddel, 2009). While this treatment was not created with offenders in mind, it has been shown to be effective in helping bring about effective change, in part due to the high number of delinquent adolescents with histories of abuse, neglect, or some other trauma in their background (Amatya & Barzman, 2012). Providers working with adolescent offenders who present with complex trauma and other related concerns should consider utilizing some form of a trauma-focused treatment. Adolescents who may have followed a more trauma-focused pathway to delinquency are excellent candidates for this treatment.

TF-CBT, as its name suggests, falls primarily under the umbrella of CBT. As such, it focuses a great deal on cognitive restructuring with behavioral elements and is delivered in a systematic, skills-based method. The treatment is centered on healing from past trauma and breaks down into three basic phases: (1) developing coping skills, (2) processing trauma, and (3) integration and consolidation (Cohen, Mannarino, Kliethermes, & Murray, 2012). All of these phases are geared toward dealing with the trauma element. Providers are encouraged to try to spend equal amounts of time on each of the phases.

TF-CBT is primarily delivered in individual and parent–child sessions; however, elements of it can be utilized in group therapy settings as well. Regardless of the modality of the treatment, TF-CBT emphasizes the importance of building a strong rapport with the client since "youth with complex trauma view most relationships as dangerous" (Cohen et al., 2012).

Because TF-CBT was not developed exclusively with delinquents in mind, when it is utilized with adolescents in the juvenile justice system, it is often coupled with additional, more offense-specific treatment, like the ones mentioned here. Furthermore, using a trauma-focused approach in treating delinquency can help increase the effectiveness of the other therapies (Table 5.4). Trauma-focused treatments are also recommended in residential treatment to help mitigate the traumatizing effect of the detention process (Kerig et al., 2009).

Third-Wave Therapies: Mode Deactivation Therapy

Another evidence-based treatment, which is further removed from CBT than the previously

Table 5.4   Trauma-Focused Cognitive Behavioral Therapy Phases

Trauma-Focused Cognitive Behavioral Therapy	Treatment Phases
	Developing coping skills
	Processing trauma
	Integration and consolidation

discussed one, is aligned with what are considered third-wave therapies. Third-wave approaches to treatment are branches of CBT that incorporate a more emotional mindfulness and acceptance component. Classical behavioral therapies are considered first wave and cognitive therapies are second wave. Dialectical behavior therapy, acceptance and commitment therapy, and mode deactivation therapy (MDT) are all examples of third-wave therapies (Bayles, Blossom, & Apsche, 2014). Mindfulness in these therapies is defined as "one being fully aware and accepting oneself as you are in the moment without judgment" (Bass, van Nevel, & Swart, 2014, p. 5).

MDT is the most recent of these therapies and has been shown to be effective in treating delinquent adolescents. It was developed in an effort to address the deficiencies found in CBT (Bass et al., 2014) for treating this population. MDT utilizes mindfulness in helping the clients become aware of and accept their strong emotions in a nonjudgmental manner. MDT can be delivered in group, individual, and family settings. It is considered a positive therapy and views CBT as too judgmental of the client's emotions. Unlike CBT, MDT relies on a technique of "validation, clarification and redirection (VCR)" (Bass et al., 2014, p. 5) to address the dissonance between what the client has believed to be true and what is real. This validation, clarification, and redirection technique allows the adolescent to identify the reason behind the client's distortions and from there correct them.

"MDT systematically assesses and restructures dysfunctional *compound core beliefs* (schemas) into *functional alternative beliefs* in the adolescents" (Apsche & DiMeo, 2012, p. 17). In this way, the adolescent's core beliefs are acknowledged as truth for the adolescent. The care providers understand that these core beliefs were developed as a result of past experiences. Treatment involves working collaboratively with the adolescent to deactivate these maladaptive responses and transform them into more functional beliefs (Apsche & DiMeo, 2012). This is accomplished through the process of an initial, exhaustive case conceptualization, followed by "acceptance, mindfulness and diffusion techniques" (Apsche & DiMeo, 2012, p. 17). The validation, clarification, and redirection technique is also an integral part of MDT treatment in helping the adolescent balance beliefs and regulate emotions (Table 5.5).

Table 5.5   Mode Deactivation Therapy Process

Mode Deactivation Therapy	*Treatment Process*
	Case conceptualization
	Mindfulness
	Acceptance
	Diffusion
	Validation, clarification, and redirection

Family-Integrated Treatments

The last example of an evidence-based outgrowth for treating adolescents in the juvenile justice system focuses specifically on the family. While TF-CBT may be appropriate for adolescents who have experienced a more trauma-focused pathway to offend, family-based treatments focus not only on the individual but also on the family and social contexts of the individual.

A growing body of research has confirmed the effectiveness of family-integrated treatments (FITs) in treating a wide range of adolescent behaviors (Henggeler & Sheidow, 2012; Schaub et al., 2014; Swart & Apsche, 2014). FITs are any treatments that focus on the family system as well as on the individual adolescent. While many different treatment modalities can be adapted to be incorporated in a family therapy context, FITs concentrate explicitly on the family. "Adolescents are invariably part of a family system, which is often where the origins of distress and dysfunction can be found" (Swart & Apsche, 2014). As such, it is effective to treat the family system as a whole, not merely the adolescent. Several studies have found that FIT is more effective than standard individual psychotherapy (Schaub et al., 2014). Multisystemic therapy (MST), multidimensional treatment foster care, functional family therapy, and brief strategic family therapy are examples of family-based, evidence-supported treatments.

MST, in particular, "is one of the most extensively validated and widely transported evidence-based psychosocial treatments" (Henggeler & Sheidow, 2012, p. 34). MST is based on Bronfenbrenner's theory of social ecology and views antisocial behavior as multidetermined. In other words, pertinent factors of antisocial behavior are found at the individual, family, peer, school, and community levels. MST is conducted by a supervised team of two to four therapists who deliver the services in a variety of settings depending on the convenience and needs of the family, which has been shown to greatly effect family dropout rates (Henggeler & Sheidow, 2012). As such, therapy at times is delivered in home or community settings. The treatment is intensive for the family and lasts approximately 3 to 5 months.

MST utilizes an extensive assessment process from which specific interventions are chosen to address targeted behaviors. The most commonly observed contributing factors to adolescent antisocial behavior are "ineffective parenting practices, association with deviant peers, and poor school performance" (Henggeler & Sheidow,

2012, p. 35). Providers also pay particular attention to caregiver barriers to treatment success (Table 5.6). Interventions are always evidence based and closely adhere to MST principles. Results are closely monitored, and based on their success or failure, plans are made to implement lasting change (Exercise 5.6).

IMPLICATIONS FOR COUNSELING ADOLESCENTS

Clinical Review of Case

The case of Ken, presented at the beginning of this chapter, provides a number of issues regarding the care of adolescents and the role of treatment providers. First, Tom must have established his role clearly with all parties involved in the case. The limits of confidentiality should have been very clearly discussed with Ken and his family at the very start of providing services. It is important in this case that Tom particularly highlights the desires of the probation officer to receive monthly reports on Ken's progress. Furthermore, Tom should have communicated the expectation that Ken's involvement in therapy and progress could have a direct effect on his status in the justice system. It is also paramount that Tom discusses with the probation officer the duties of his role as a service provider. It is important that Tom is not simply a mouthpiece for the probation or the "good cop." Tom must be able to build trust and rapport with the family if any progress is to be made.

Concerning what recommendation Tom makes to the court, there are several important notes to make. Before Tom talks in open court about a client, it is extremely important that he has a good grasp of what the limits of his

Table 5.6   Multisystemic Therapy Aspects

Multisystemic Therapy	Key Aspects
	Rigorous assessment process
	Short-term, intensive treatment
	Family involved in treatment decisions
	Treatment delivered at home and in the community
	Treatment delivered by a team of providers
	Special attention to caregiver barriers

Exercise 5.6

Thoughts on Evidence-Based Treatments

Describe your thoughts on two of the evidence-based treatments discussed in this chapter. Is there one that you are more drawn toward? Which do you think would be the most difficult for you as a provider? Consider the case of Ken again. Which evidence-based treatment would you choose to use with him?

confidentiality with Ken and Ken's family are. Tom should always keep the family's best interest in mind while fulfilling his duty to the state. Additionally, situations like this are often accompanied by the dynamics of an "us versus them" between the client and the justice system. Providers can be pulled into this dynamic and feel as though they must "choose sides" but it is important that they remain aware of any such dynamics and not fall into them. Unlike the public defender whose role it is to defend and argue for the client, the provider must remain impartial. Tom should be able to make a fair recommendation of what the best interest of the youth and society are, void of any personal bias.

Application of Ethics

As the case of Ken shows, ethical competency is extremely important when working with adolescents in the juvenile justice system. Providers must be keenly aware of their duty to the legal system as well as to the families.

Providers working with other populations of adolescents will more than likely run into the legal system in one way or another at some point in their career. However, service providers for adolescents in the juvenile justice system will routinely run across it. These providers must know what is expected of them and how they can best serve hurting families and adolescents inside the system (see Chapter 17 for a more detailed analysis). When judgment calls by providers can have direct impacts on the length of detention sentences, contact between family members, and continuation of parental rights, providers do not have the luxury of good guesses. They must be fully competent to judge situations, clients, and risks fairly. Mistakes and carelessness can cost their clients dearly. As such, providers should ensure that they are competent to make the recommendations that are being asked of them. Providers should ensure that they are properly supervised and consult whenever necessary. Furthermore, providers are encouraged to become experts in the legal intricacies of the limits of

confidentiality of the state or country in which they practice.

Summary

The juvenile justice system has been in place since 1899 and continues to struggle with the best way to treat delinquent adolescents. Are they criminals or victims? Can they be kept in their homes, or should they be sent to correctional facilities? Are they a danger to the rest of society? Can they be scared straight? Does it help to lock them up, or are we making the situation worse? Should they be waived to adult court?

Working with delinquent adolescents can be extremely tiring and difficult. Clients tend to be unmotivated if not outright antagonistic to treatment, and families are often resistant, disinterested, or absent. The many systems involved can complicate the treatment process, and the legal implications of treatment outcomes can add a much heavier weight onto the shoulders of providers. At the same time, though, the population is one that is in desperate need of help, advocacy, and treatment. Adolescents in the justice system have often lost their voice and any sense of control over their lives. The juvenile justice system is confusing and complicated for adults, but it is even more so for adolescents.

While this population is unique in many ways, the clients are still adolescents with all of the complications, questions, and troubles of their peers and families. Providers working with them must wade through the same theoretical questions and treatment decisions, as with any other group of adolescents, yet these adolescents also require extra consideration for the safety of themselves and society. Working with delinquent adolescents is a challenge that involves a good deal of patience and a healthy sense of humor. However, this population has greatly enriched our understanding of externalizing behavior and the value of effective treatment in changing lives for the better.

KEYSTONES

- The juvenile justice system creates a unique set of issues for providers working with delinquent adolescents based on concerns regarding confidentiality, client resistance, and community safety.

- The juvenile justice system was born out of a need to help delinquent adolescents and is based on the idea of treating, not punishing, adolescents. Presently, it wrestles with how best to accomplish this while maintaining the safety of the community.

- The juvenile justice system has gone through a number of philosophical changes under social and practical pressures leading to a currently more punitive form.

- The juvenile justice system operates under the base assumption that adults and children are different. This has been played out in different ways but remains an important tenet in decision making.

- Many adolescents involved in the juvenile justice system have a history of maltreatment and abuse and are considered crossover youth.

- Crossover youth create extra issues for counseling due to dealing with multiple agencies and systems. The situation can be even more confusing and difficult for the families who are involved in both.

- Sexual offenders require more specific treatment and special supervisory and ethical considerations.

- Aggressive, antisocial adolescents often have a wide variety of diagnoses and have a risk of developing mood disorders.

- Understanding the different pathways to delinquency is important in case conceptualization and treatment planning. It is important to identify what factors were more influential in developing the delinquent behavior and which protective, resilient factors can be built on.

- Adolescents can be placed in a number of settings based on their needs and the risk they pose to society. Residential and lockdown facilities can be useful for more high-risk adolescents but must be properly supervised and structured.

- Research has validated a number of home-based treatments that can be highly effective with adolescents who are allowed to stay in their communities.

- While CBT is still a standard for treating adolescents, recent research has developed it by adding a trauma focus for this population.

- Other third-wave therapies have further added to the CBT base and include a more emotional component.

REFERENCES

Amatya, P. L., & Barzman, D. H. (2012). The missing link between juvenile delinquency and pediatric posttraumatic stress disorder: An attachment theory lens. *ISRN Pediatrics, 2012*(2012), 1–6. doi:10.5402/2012/134541

Apsche, J. A., & Bailey, S. (2003). Mode deactivation therapy: A theoretical case analysis (Part 1). *Behavior Analyst Today, 4*, 68–77.

Apsche, J. A., & DiMeo, L. (2012). *Mode deactivation therapy for aggression and oppositional behavior in adolescents: An integrative methodology using ACT, DBT, and CBT*. Oakland, CA: New Harbinger.

Bass, C., van Nevel, J., & Swart, J. (2014). A comparison between dialectical behavior therapy, mode deactivation therapy, cognitive behavioral therapy, and acceptance and commitment therapy in the treatment of adolescents. *International Journal of Behavioral Consultation & Therapy, 9*, 4–8.

Bayles, C., Blossom, P., & Apsche, J. (2014). A brief review and update of mode deactivation therapy. *International Journal of Behavioral Consultation and Therapy, 9*, 46–48.

Beauchaine, T. P., Hinshaw, S. P., & Pang, K. L. (2010). Comorbidity of attention-deficit/hyperactivity disorder and early-onset conduct disorder: Biological, environmental, and developmental mechanisms. *Clinical Psychology: Science & Practice, 17*, 327–336.

Bush, J., Glick, B., Taymans, J., & Guevara, M. (2011). *Thinking for a change: Integrated cognitive behavior change program*. Washington, DC: U.S. Department of Justice, National Institute of Corrections. Retrieved from http://static.nicic .gov/Library/025057/default.html

Byrd, A. L., Loeber, R., & Pardini, D. A. (2012). Understanding desisting and persisting forms of delinquency: The unique contributions of disruptive behavior disorders and interpersonal callousness. *Journal of Child Psychology and Psychiatry, 53,* 371–380. doi:10.1111/j.1469-7610.2011.02504.x

Cashmore, J. (2011). The link between child maltreatment and adolescent offending: Systems neglect of adolescents. *Family Matters, 89,* 31–41.

Chen, M., Su, T., Chen, Y., Hsu, J., Huang, K., Chang, W., . . . Bai, Y. (2013). Higher risk of developing mood disorders among adolescents with comorbidity of attention deficit hyperactivity disorder and disruptive behavior disorder: A nationwide prospective study. *Journal of Psychiatric Research, 47,* 1019–1023. doi:10.1016/j.jpsychires.2013.04.005

Cohen, J. A., Mannarino, A. P., Kliethermes, M., & Murray, L. A. (2012). Trauma-focused CBT for youth with complex trauma. *Child Abuse & Neglect: The International Journal, 36,* 528–541.

Deutsch, A., Crockett, L., Wolff, J., & Russell, S. (2012). Parent and peer pathways to adolescent delinquency: Variations by ethnicity and neighborhood context. *Journal of Youth & Adolescence, 41,* 1078–1094. doi:10.1007/s10964-012-9754-y

Dodge, K. A., Dishion, T. J., Lansford, J. E., & Society for Research in Child Development. (2006). Deviant peer influences in intervention and public policy for youth. *Society for Research in Child Development, 20,* 1.

Fergus, S., & Zimmerman, M. A. (2005). Adolescent resilience: A framework for understanding healthy development in the face of risk. *Annual Review of Public Health, 26,* 399–419. doi:10.1146/annurev.publhealth.26.021304.144357

Henggeler, S., & Sheidow, A. (2012). Empirically supported family-based treatments for conduct disorder and delinquency in adolescents. *Journal of Marital & Family Therapy, 38,* 30–58. doi:10.1111/j.1752-0606.2011.00244.x

Herz, D. C., Ryan, J. P., & Bilchik, S. (2010). Challenges facing crossover youth: An examination of juvenile-justice decision making and recidivism. *Family Court Review, 48,* 305.

Hops, H., Davis, B., Leve, C., & Sheeber, L. (2003). Cross-generational transmission of aggressive parent behavior: A prospective, mediational examination. *Journal of Abnormal Child Psychology, 31,* 161–169.

Jennings, W., Maldonado-Molina, M., Reingle, J., & Komro, K. (2011). A multi-level approach to investigating neighborhood effects on physical aggression among urban Chicago Youth. *American Journal of Criminal Justice, 36,* 392–407. doi:10.1007/s12103-011-9118-2

Kerig, P. K., Ward, R., Vanderzee, K. L., & Arnzen Moeddel, M. (2009). Posttraumatic stress as a mediator of the relationship between trauma and mental health problems among juvenile delinquents. *Journal of Youth & Adolescence, 38,* 1214–1225. doi:10.1007/s10964-008-9332-5

Kinscherff, R. (2012). *A primer for mental health practitioners working with youth involved in the juvenile justice system.* Washington, DC: Technical Assistance Partnership for Child and Family Mental Health. Retrieved from http://www.tapartnership.org/docs/jjResource_mentalHealthPrimer.pdf

Krinsky, M. (2010). Disrupting the pathway from foster care to the justice system: A former prosecutor's perspective on reform. *Family Court Review, 48,* 322. doi:10.1111/j.1744-1617.2010.01313.x

McMillin, P. N. (2014). From pioneer to punisher: America's quest to find its juvenile justice identity. *Houston Law Review, 51,* 1485–1517.

National Institute of Corrections. (2012). *Thinking for a change 3.1.* Retrieved from http://static.nicic.gov/Library/025057/default.html

Office of Juvenile Justice and Delinquency Prevention. (1999). *1999 National report series—Juvenile justice: A century of change.* Washington, DC: U.S. Department of Justice. Retrieved from https://www.ncjrs.gov/pdffiles1/ojjdp/178995.pdf

Office of Juvenile Justice and Delinquency Prevention. (2010). *OJJDP fact sheet: Juveniles in residential placement 1997–2008.* Washington, DC: U.S. Department of Justice. Retrieved from https://www.ncjrs.gov/pdffiles1/ojjdp/229379.pdf

Office of Juvenile Justice and Delinquency Prevention. (2011). *Highlights from pathways to desistance: A longitudinal study of serious adolescent offenders.* Washington, DC: U.S. Department of Justice. Retrieved from https://www.ncjrs.gov/pdffiles1/ojjdp/230971.pdf

Office of Juvenile Justice and Delinquency Prevention. (2013). *Juvenile arrests 2011.* Washington, DC: U.S. Department of Justice. Retrieved from http://www.ojjdp.gov/pubs/244476.pdf

Piquero, A. R., Farrington, D. P., Welsh, B. C., Tremblay, R., & Jennings, W. G. (2009). Effects of early family/parent training programs on antisocial behavior and delinquency. *Journal of Experimental Criminology, 5,* 83–120. doi:10.1007/s11292-009-9072-x

Ruchkin, V., Schwab-Stone, M., Koposov, R., Vermeiren, R., & King, R. (2003). Suicidal ideations and attempts in juvenile delinquents. *Journal of Child Psychology and Psychiatry and Allied Disciplines, 44,* 1058–1066.

Ryan, J. P., & Testa, M. F. (2005). Child maltreatment and juvenile delinquency: Investigating the role of placement and placement instability. *Children & Youth Services Review, 27,* 227–249. doi:10.1016/j.childyouth.2004.05.007

Ryan, J. P., Williams, A., & Courtney, M. (2013). Adolescent neglect, juvenile delinquency and the risk of recidivism. *Journal of Youth & Adolescence, 42,* 454–465. doi:10.1007/s10964-013-9906-8

Sanders, B. (2012). Gang youth, substance use patterns, and drug normalization. *Journal of Youth Studies, 15,* 978–994. doi:10.1080/13676261.2012.685707

Schaub, M. P., Henderson, C. E., Pelc, I., Tossmann, P., Phan, O., Hendriks, V., . . . Rigter, H. (2014). Multidimensional family therapy decreases the rate of externalizing behavioral disorder symptoms in cannabis abusing adolescents: Outcomes of the INCANT trial. *BMC Psychiatry, 14,* 1–16. doi:10.1186/1471-244X-14-26

Shufelt, J., & Cocozza, J. (2006). *Youth with mental health disorders in the juvenile justice system: Results from a multi-state prevalence study.* Delmar, NY: National Center for Mental Health and Juvenile Justice. Retrieved from http://www.unicef.org/tdad/usmentalhealthprevalence06(3).pdf

Sickmund, M. (2010). *OJJDP fact sheet: Juveniles in residential placement, 1997–2008.* Washington, DC: U.S. Department of Justice, Office of Justice Programs.

Silva, L. R. (2014). The best interest is the child: A historical philosophy for modern issues. *BYU Journal of Public Law, 28,* 415–470.

Stein, L. R., Colby, S. M., Barnett, N. P., Monti, P. M., Golembeske, C., & Lebeau-Craven, R. (2006). Effects of motivational interviewing for incarcerated adolescents on driving under the influence after release. *American Journal on Addictions, 15,* 50–57. doi:10.1080/10550490601003680

Swart, J., & Apsche, J. (2014). Mindfulness, mode deactivation, and family therapy: A winning combination for treating adolescents with complex trauma and behavioral problems. *International Journal of Behavioral Consultation & Therapy, 9,* 9–14.

Thompson, M. P., Kingree, J. B., & Ho, C. (2006). Associations between delinquency and suicidal behaviors in a nationally representative sample of adolescents. *Suicide and Life-Threatening Behavior, 36,* 57–64.

Tremblay, R. E. (2000). The development of aggressive behavior during childhood: What have we learned in the past century? *International Journal of Behavioral Development, 24,* 129–141. doi:10.1080/016502500383232

Underwood, L. A., Robinson, S. B., Mosholder, E., & Warren, K. M. (2008). Sex offender care for adolescents in secure care: Critical factors and counseling strategies. *Clinical Psychology Review, 28,* 917–932. doi:10.1016/j.cpr.2008.01.004

Underwood, L. A., von Dresner, K. S., & Phillips, A. L. (2006). Community treatment programs for juveniles: A best-evidence summary. *International Journal of Behavioral and Consultation Therapy, 2*(2), 286–304.

Underwood, L.A., & Washington, A. (2016). Mental illness and juvenile offenders. International Journal of Environmental Research and Public Health. Edited by Dr. Deborah Shelton.

Walters, G. D. (2014). Pathways to early delinquency: Exploring the individual and collective contributions of difficult temperament, low maternal involvement, and externalizing behavior. *Journal of Criminal Justice, 42,* 321–326. doi:10.1016/j.jcrimjus.2014.04.003

6

STRENGTHS-BASED AND RESILIENCE PERSPECTIVES

Perhaps I am stronger than I think.

—Thomas Merton

Life should be more about holding questions than finding answers. The act of seeking an answer comes from a wish to make life, which is basically fluid, into something more certain and fixed. This often leads to rigidity, closed-mindedness, and intolerance. On the other hand, holding a question—exploring its many facets over time—puts us in touch with the mystery of life. Holding questions accustoms us to the ungraspable nature of life and enables us to understand things from a range of perspectives.

—Thubten Chodron (on Buddhism)

INTRODUCTION

In today's world of psychopathology, diagnosis, symptoms, expectations from clients or from parents, and guidelines set by managed care, it is easy for providers to focus on the negative things going on in the client's life. The provider may get reports from parents and teachers about physical violence, acting out in school, self-injurious behavior, emotional mismanagement, or substance abuse, and these symptoms and behaviors demand immediate attention. Often, there is pressure on the provider to diagnose the client in order to be reimbursed by managed care

entities. In this world, the strengths that the client possesses or the client's natural abilities and inclinations can easily and understandably be missed, leaving out valuable information that can help the client function better using his or her own resources. Adolescents, especially those who have been acting out at school or at home, may feel that everyone is only telling them what is wrong with them while neglecting to tell them what they are doing right. When adolescents are simply diagnosed and told to change their behavior, they may get the message that they are *broken or bad* when they may actually have strengths or resilience—factors they could be tapping into in order to find solutions to their problems. In the strengths-based and resilience perspectives, the focus shifts from the psychopathology or what is "wrong" with the client to the resources that they already possess or what they are doing "right." Recent policies in mental health have promoted the idea of providing services that focus on strengths rather than deficits (Cox, 2006), including the Children's System of Care initiative (Stroul & Friedman, 1994).

Strengths-based and resilience perspectives begin with a philosophy that stems from a social constructivist point of view (Gergen, 1999; Gergen & McNamee, 1992; Hoyt, 1998). Social constructivist theory basically states that people construct their realities rather than uncovering them. Kant laid the groundwork for postmodern, constructivist thinking in his claim that human assumptions about reality cannot be separated from the knower who experiences, sorts out, and labels the reality using his or her own internal methods and processes (Hamilton, 1994; Sciarra, 1999). Constructivist thought builds on this idea by saying that there are multiple equally valid and attainable realities that are constructed in the mind of each individual (Hansen, 2004; Ponterotto, 2005). Following this mind-set, constructivist theory states that human knowledge and meaning is not universal or absolute, but it evolves within different contexts or communities. In strengths-based philosophy, the provider seeks to understand the realities of the client's life and then comes alongside the client in order to help the client construct a more suitable reality based on the strengths and resources that the client already possesses.

The strengths-based movement began in the late 1970s and early 1980s with the advent of solution-focused therapy in which the focus of therapy shifts from the problems clients are having to finding the solutions to the problems (O'Hanlon & Weiner-Davis, 1989; de Shazer, 1988, 1991, 1994). A central theme of solution-focused therapy is the idea that there were exceptions to problems or times when they were diminished in their intensity or were absent altogether, so whatever resources the client used during these times might be applied to other contexts. Another tenet of solution-focused therapy is that there are things that are already working in people's lives that should be encouraged. The way to effect change was not solely by correcting deficits but by building on the client's strengths. The strengths-based perspective was initially proposed by Weick, Rapp, Sullivan, and Kisthardt (1989) as a model that was founded on the assumption that all individuals, including children, possess strengths in one form or another. The idea of focusing on a client's strengths was not a new one, and other disciplines such as family therapy and social work were also employing those principles (Bertolino & O'Hanlon, 2002; Madsen, 2007; Rapp, 1998; Saleeby, 2006). A distinction between solution-focused therapy and the strengths-based model is that the original solution-based approaches were developed as therapy models, whereas strengths-based ideas were more of a philosophical point of view that fueled these models (Bertolino, Kiener, & Patterson, 2010). The strengths-based ideology is now used in conjunction with many other models of therapy and is becoming an increasing part of assessment and therapy.

The idea of resilience came about in the 1970s when a group of pioneering psychiatrists and psychologists began to draw attention to the concept of resilience in children who were at risk of psychopathology or developmental problems due to genetic or environmental factors (Masten, 2001). These practitioners stated that research on children who thrived in this context of risk or adversity might hold the potential to inform theories of etiology in psychopathology and to learn what affects adolescents at risk that could guide intervention and policy (Anthony, 1974; Garmezy, 1971, 1974; Murphy, 1974; Murphy & Moriarty, 1976; Rutter, 1979; Werner & Smith, 1982). These ideas have sparked much investigation, and since then, many models and theories have been formed on the concept of resilience. In the early days of resilience research, the phenomenon got a little out of hand, and the following headlines spurred unrealistic ideas about resilience in children: "The Invulnerables" in the *APA Monitor* (Pines, 1975) and "Trouble's a Bubble to Some Kids" in the *Washington Post* on March 7, 1976, and "Superkids of the Ghetto" appeared as the title for a book review on resilience in inner-city children published in a 1995 edition of *Contemporary Psychology* (Buggie, 1995). More recent literature has shown that resilience is more of an ordinary phenomenon that stems from basic human adaptational systems, such as the ability to cope with stress or finding positives in negative situations rather than superhuman strength (Masten, 2001).

The objective of this chapter is to provide a review of the strengths-based and resilience perspectives, as well has how these perspectives might be used competently in counseling adolescents. After reading this chapter, readers will be able to do the following:

- Define and describe the strengths-based and resilience perspectives

- Discuss the purpose and presuppositions of these perspectives

- Identify specific strengths-based and resilience techniques and demonstrate applicability

- Discuss the evidence-based model that has grown out of this perspective

- Understand the techniques of strengths-based perspective

- Understand the implications for counseling adolescents, including the ethical implications regarding these perspectives

- Apply knowledge gained in the case scenarios

What Are Strengths-Based and Resilience Perspectives?

At their core, the strengths-based and resilience perspectives focus on the positives or the strengths that the client possesses. Epstein and Sharma (1998) define strengths as

> emotional and behavioral skills, competencies, and characteristics that create a sense of personal accomplishment; contribute to satisfying relationships with family members, peers and adults; enhance one's ability to deal with adversity and stress; and promote one's personal, social, and academic development. (p. 3)

Rawana and Brownlee (2009) similarly define strengths as "developed competencies and characteristics that [are] valued both by the individual and society and [are] embedded in culture" (p. 256). From these definitions, we can see that strengths are competencies and characteristics of an individual that are important for their overall development and well-being. Strengths-based perspectives use a client's strengths as the basis for change in the client's life using the client's own resources to help the client construct a new reality that is customized to his or her needs.

Resilience is grouped with strengths-based perspectives here and in other literature because of their similarity, and the way they complement one another through resilience is a somewhat different concept. Masten (2001) describes resilience as "a class of phenomena characterized by good outcomes in spite of serious threats to adaptation or development" (p. 228). Put another way, Luthar and Cicchetti (2000) define resilience as when individuals or groups react positively in the face of adversity or risk. Implicit in the notion of resilience are two conditions: (1) that the individual or group is exposed to a significant threat or adversity and (2) that the individual or group has achieved positive adaptation despite these threats or other major assaults on the developmental process (Masten, Best, & Garmezy, 1990; Werner & Smith, 1982). One key difference between strengths-based and resilience perspectives is that fundamental to resilience is the assumption of the presence of adversity, whereas strengths-based perspectives are not limited by this assumption and can be applied more universally (Brownlee et al., 2013). Figure 6.1 sums up

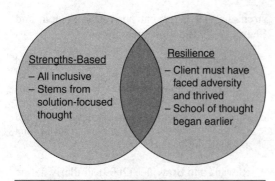

Figure 6.1   Strengths-Based Versus Resilience Perspectives

the differences and similarities of the strengths-based and resilience perspectives.

EQUAL PARTNERS IN HELPING PROCESS

A Lion was awakened from sleep by a Mouse running over his face. Rising up angrily, he caught him with his paw and was about to kill him, when the Mouse cried "Forgive me this time and I shall never forget it." The Lion took pity on the Mouse and let him go. As he was leaving the Mouse said "Who knows but I may be able to do you a good turn one of these days?" The Lion laughed at this idea saying "How could you a little Mouse help me the King of the jungle?" Some time later the Lion was caught in a trap by hunters who wanted to take him alive to a zoo. The Lion roared out in fear and he was heard by the little Mouse who came to his aid. The little Mouse quickly gnawed through the ropes that bound the King of the jungle and freed him.

—Aesop (The Lion and the Mouse)

Fundamental to the strengths-based and resilience perspectives is the idea that the adolescent client is an equal partner in the helping process. This is contradictory to the psychopathology model where the provider is the expert and the client does what the expert says to get better.

When you read the story of the lion and the mouse, you can see an important principle of the strengths-based and resilience perspectives illustrated. The mouse can be likened to the client, and he or she appears to have very little to offer in the way of knowledge and experience; however, in the end, the mouse held the key to the best solution to the lion's quandary. This story shows us that even the person who seems to have the least to offer can bring forward the most useful ideas, and if you are working with families, the youngest and least powerful person in the room may hold the key to the best solution for the whole family. In the strengths-based perspective, the provider should always keep in mind that though the provider may have suggestions for his or her clients, the client is the one who possesses the resources and it is the client who is the largest stakeholder in the therapy process. The role of the provider is to encourage and bring out those resources that the client may not recognize or be applying to the situation. The recognition of the strengths and capabilities is thought to convey a sense of respect for the client, which then results in the motivation toward lasting change (Weick, 1992; Weick & Chamberlain, 2002).

Positive Approaches

Implicit in the strengths-based and resilience approaches is the tendency to focus on the positive things in the adolescent's life as opposed to focusing on the negatives or pathologies. The guiding idea behind this is that every person has something positive going for him or her, and being able to capitalize on those good things can be very powerful in the therapy process. This focus on the positive may lead some providers to not use diagnosis because it is seen as focusing on the negative or the pathology, which is viewed as unhelpful to the client; however, this is not true of all clinicians who ascribe to the strengths-based or resilience perspectives (Cox, 2006; Ungar, 2006).

Asset Based

Underlying the strengths-based and resilience perspectives is the assumption that all clients have strengths or assets that can be built on or used to help them improve their lives. Ungar (2006) says,

> In our haste to change our adolescent's behavior, we overlook how those behaviors make sense to the children themselves. Try as we might as adults to guide children, they will not heed our words of advice until they are confident we understand they are already doing the best they can with what they have. (p. 3)

When faced with difficulties in life, we can sometimes use whatever strategies or assets we have to get through them the best way that we know how. In hindsight, we might realize that we could have used a different strategy or a better way to get through it, but while in the situation, we did the best we could with what we had at the time. Adolescents face many different challenges associated with physical development, emotional and intellectual development, as well as their environment. They face these challenges with the assets that they possess and do the best they can with what they have. In the strengths-based counseling, the provider focuses on helping the client to discover the assets that the client possesses and then helps the client to build on these assets in order to face present and future challenges more effectively.

Researchers from the Search Institute, an organization that is linking research and practice to address critical issues in education and youth development, developed a list of 40 developmental assets that are important to adolescent development (Benson, 2003; Lerner & Benson, 2003). This list includes things such as social relationships, experiences, environments, and interaction patterns that promote successful development. They list two types of assets: (1) internal assets and (2) external assets (Edwards, Muniford, & Serra-Roldan, 2007). Internal assets are thought

to be more of the emotional or psychological traits that come from inside the person. Some internal assets may be passion for learning, positive values, social competencies, determination, positive work ethic, creativity, and positive identity (Edwards et al., 2007). External assets are considered to be positive experiences coming from outside people or entities. Some external assets may be support, empowerment, boundaries, and expectations (Edwards et al., 2007). Each client will possess unique internal and external assets, and finding these assets and encouraging them or building them up is a key piece to strengths-based and resilience perspectives (see Table 6.1 for examples).

Problem Solving

Though strengths-based and resilience perspectives are different from solution-focused therapy, there are many basic commonalities that they share. One of these is the focus on problem solving. In these perspectives, clients are viewed as equal partners in the helping process, and the provider collaborates with the clients to help build on their strengths in order to help them discover the most effective solution to their problem. The reason for the problem or the background is not always discussed unless it is relevant and helpful for solving the problem. This keeps the focus on the purpose of the clients seeking help in the first place and prevents the clients from getting caught up in other details that may not be relevant to solving their problem. Adolescents often have an instant gratification or a get-to-the-point attitude when it comes to counseling (or when it comes to most things), making the problem-solving aspect particularly appealing to them. The strengths-based and resilience perspectives operate from the presupposition that everyone has the resources to solve one's problems; one just may need some help in pointing this out and building on the resources (see Figure 6.2).

Table 6.1 Internal and External Assets

Internal Assets	External Assets
• Passion for learning	• Social support
• Passion for positive interests	• Positive family relationships
• Positive values	• Positive school relationships
• Social skills or competencies	• Positive peer relationships
• Determination	• Empowerment
• Drive	• Positive boundaries (set by others)
• Positive work ethic	• Involvement in prosocial activities
• Positive boundaries (set by self)	• Positive expectations from others
• Areas of intelligence	• Involvement in church or religious activities
• Creativity	• Church support
• Positive identity	• Involvement in the community
• Self-esteem	• Community support
• Spirituality	
• Positive concept of religion	

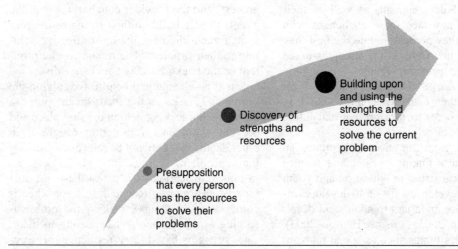

Figure 6.2 Strengths-Based and Resilience Perspective

PURPOSE OF STRENGTHS-BASED AND RESILIENCE PERSPECTIVES

Counseling is a complicated endeavor that is never the same from client to client. A sense of purpose can guide the therapeutic relationship and can even be the difference between helping the client and not helping the client. A provider who ascribes to the strengths-based and resilience perspectives should always have a goal or purpose in mind, which is to build up the existing strengths of the client in order to solve the problem for which counseling was sought and helping the client to develop the skills that will help improve his or her life overall for the future. The present and future orientations of strengths-based and resilience perspectives are what makes them unique.

Client as Expert

In strengths-based and resilience perspectives, the client and even the family are the sources of information on the client's strengths. Merriam-Webster (n.d.) defines the word *expert* as "a person having or showing special skill or knowledge because of what you have been taught or what you have experienced." Clients are the experts in their own experiences, and they have a special knowledge of their situation that no one else in the world has, so they are a specialist or authority on their own lives. They are the experts in the area of their own lives, so it follows that the provider is a collaborator or an equal partner in the helping process and not an expert to be consulted. The source of the client's solution to his or her problem is believed to be within the client rather than in a textbook or the opinion of someone else. It seems to make sense that the person who would have the most insight into his or her own strengths and life would be the client.

Future Orientation

If you give a man a fish he eats for a day, but if you teach a man to fish he eats for a lifetime.

—Chinese Proverb

Strengths-based and resilience perspectives are highly oriented toward the present and future goals. These perspectives are not geared toward primarily reliving past traumas or digging deep into past hurts. You will not see clients being hypnotized to recover deep memories or long sessions about the past in these perspectives. Though the past may have some influence in determining what the client's strengths are, the strengths-based provider is focused on coming up with solutions to the current problems so that the client can have a better future. In resilience perspectives, the past adversity will determine in what areas the client has experienced resilience, but again, the goal is to use that experience to solve the present problems thereby equipping the client for a better future. The goal of the provider in these perspectives is to help the client solve the present problem so that the future will be better. One way that the provider might help the client determine what the future goals should be is to ask the client what he or she wants the future to look like or what does the client see in the future after the problem is solved. This gives direction to the goal setting and helps the provider to suggest the best steps to getting there.

In both perspectives, there is an emphasis on equipping clients with the skills to solve their problems in the future. Essentially, with the future orientation, the provider is teaching the clients to fish so that they can feed themselves in the future rather than just handing them a quick fix solution. Clients often do not even realize that their situations can change or get better and that they have the resources to make it that way. A large part of the provider's job is to empower the clients and show them that they are capable of having the future they hope for.

Motivation Enhanced

Motivation is a key factor in strengths-based and resilience perspectives. The client must be motivated to participate in the counseling process and to enact the strategies that the client and the provider devise together. From a strengths-based perspective, there really is no such thing as an "unmotivated client." The reason for this is that most adolescents are motivated to achieve *something* or desires things to be a certain way. These goals may differ from the implicit goals of therapy and may not necessarily be healthy goals, but the motivation is still there. In working with adolescents, providers may find that they want things to go their way, which is not always the most positive way, but the motivation can be used and shaped into something positive. Also, motivation is not a fixed concept; it is open to change over time. It may take a long time for someone to generate a goal and then to develop the willingness to work toward it. If you experience a "motivated" client in a first therapeutic session, this is probably due to the work he or she has already done prior to coming to counseling in the form of developing an awareness of a problem, clarifying a goal for the self, and deciding on a method to achieve it like coming to therapy (Sharry, 2004).

In the solution-focused therapy model, there are three levels of client motivation: customer, complainant, and visitor (Berg & Miller, 1992; Sharry, 2004; de Shazer, 1988), and the client may move between these levels depending on his or her motivation. At the customer level, the client may be aware that there is a problem, and the client is motivated and willing to make the changes necessary to improve his or her life (Berg & Miller, 1992; Sharry, 2004; de Shazer, 1988). On this level, the therapeutic relationship is more collaborative, and the provider is able to work with the client to help the client improve his or her situation. The complainant is less motivated to change and more focused on the fact that there is a problem, and in this level, the client would rather vent than do something about the problem (Berg & Miller, 1992; Sharry, 2004; de Shazer, 1988). The complainant might see the problem as beyond his or her control or as a result of the actions of others. At this stage, the therapeutic relationship could be challenging because the client may want the provider to do something on his or her behalf or persuade someone else to change. The visitor tends to not think that there is a problem and is not interested in changing things (Berg & Miller, 1992; Sharry, 2004; de Shazer, 1988). The visitor level can oftentimes be where the adolescent client starts out because the visitor is often made to go to counseling by an outside entity. It is important to remember that these levels of motivation are not fixed, and just because a client may enter counseling at one level does not mean that he or she will stay there. For example, an adolescent girl who is forced to come to counseling by her mother because they are constantly arguing may begin at the visitor level, but once counseling begins, she may decide that there is a problem and it's all her mother's fault so she is now on the complainant level. After some time in counseling, she may realize that she too plays a role in the conflicts and she will progress to the customer level. Other clients may begin as a customer and then become a complainant or visitor at times so it is not a progression but more of a cycle (see Figures 6.3 and 6.4 for a representation of this process).

In counseling adolescents, this can be very useful because often adolescents are forced to go to counseling by their parents or other entities rather than by their own motivation. Adolescents may say that they think everything is fine and they don't see why they need to be in counseling; however, there is usually some problem they will want to find a solution to such as fighting with their parents, getting more privileges, or getting in trouble at school. Once the provider finds the issue that the adolescent is willing and motivated to solve, the adolescent will most likely become more engaged in the process.

Motivational interviewing is a way to elicit the information needed and boost the motivation of the client. Motivational interviewing uses the following five steps: (1) counselors help clients

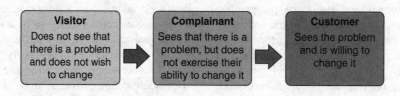

Figure 6.3   Levels of Motivation as a Progression

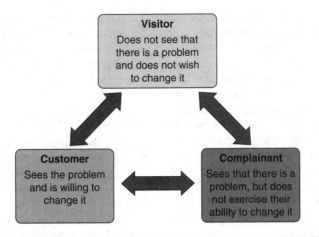

Figure 6.4   Levels of Motivation as a Cycle

understand and believe in their own ability to create change; (2) working together, the provider and the client set goals and objectives for treatment; (3) the provider asks the client's permission to speak on certain topics (e.g., a provider may ask if it is okay to discuss a certain memory or topic); (4) in a step-by-step fashion, the provider asks a question, gives feedback, and then asks for the client's opinion (e.g., What do you think?); and (5) once rapport is established, counselors ask clients open-ended questions (Naar-King, Templin, Wright, Frey, Parsons, & Lam, 2006).

PRESUPPOSITION OF STRENGTHS-BASED AND RESILIENCE PERSPECTIVES

Truth is not what we discover, but what we create.

—Saint Exupery

Any model or perspective will involve some assumptions or presuppositions in one form or another. Table 6.2 describes the presuppositions of strengths-based and resilience perspectives. The most basic assumption in a strengths-based perspective is that every person has some kind

Table 6.2   Presuppositions of Strengths-Based and Resilience Perspectives

Strengths Based	*Resilience*
Every person has strengths in one form or another	The client has gone through some type of adversity and has prospered or adjusted positively
Strengths can be built on	The same strengths that helped the client through the previous problem will help him or her again or can be built on to help again
Current problems can be solved or improved	Current problems can be solved or improved
The client's strengths can be used to solve or improve the current problem	
Strengths are unique and are different from pathology	

of strengths to build on. This means that even adolescents with behavioral, emotional, and psychological problems have some kind of strengths that can be used in therapy. In addition to this, Epstein and Sharma (1998) say that strengths are unique and are different from pathology. The most basic assumption in resilience perspectives is that the client has gone through some type of adversity and has prospered or adjusted positively. The resilience perspective assumes that there is the presence of adversity and thriving in some way whereas the strengths-based perspective does not. These assumptions drive the strengths-based and resilience perspectives.

Clients Want to Change

Inherent in the practice of strengths-based and resilience perspectives is the assumption that the adolescent wants to change. This does not mean that the client wants to change in the first session, but eventually, there should be some desire for things to be different. It is important to note that the fact that a client wants to change does not implicate that the client is motivated to change or does what is necessary for the change. Clients may want something different in their lives, but they may not be willing to make the sacrifices that it takes to make that desire happen. In strengths-based and resilience perspectives, an important assumption is that clients actually desire to make a difference in their lives. In this perspective, if the client did not want something different, there would not be much of a reason to go to counseling since it focuses on solutions to problems rather than deep-seated memories.

Clients Can Change

Another key assumption in strengths-based and resilience perspectives is that the client is actually able to change or make changes in his or her life. Focusing on a client's strengths would not get the provider very far if the client was not even able to change. There is some debate as to what "able to change" means and whether people really change or not. Looking at it from a

strengths-based perspective means being less concerned with the provider's perceptions of whether the client can change and more focused on what works for the client or what the client wants for his or her life.

Power in Therapeutic Relationship

As with most perspectives and theories in the behavioral health field, the actual relationship that the client has with the provider is assumed to play a key role in helping the client. The therapeutic relationship between the client and the provider can make or break counseling and plays a key role in the client's motivation. If you have ever had an experience with someone whom you didn't necessarily *click with*, you will understand why this is important. Often, we are more motivated to accept advice or examine ourselves when we feel known, safe, and accepted, so if the person who is offering the advice is not someone you feel this way with, you might be less inclined to take it. In the context of a good therapeutic relationship, the client can be very motivated to make great strides, but if the client does not feel safe and respected, therapy can be next to useless for him or her. In the strengths-based and resilience perspectives, the therapeutic relationship is key because the provider will need to be able to understand and articulate the client's strengths and also help motivate the client to build on those strengths. For adolescents, having many adults involved in their lives telling them what to do can be confusing and frustrating. This can often lead to them having a more difficult time trusting adults or can make them less willing to engage in the therapy process. The therapeutic relationship with an adolescent may take more time and effort to build, but it can be so powerful once it is established.

Clients Can't Fail

In the strengths-based and resilience perspective, the client does not fail. This is because therapy is client focused, and if the therapy does not "work," there is a better solution to devise or a different strength to use. For example, the provider is working with an adolescent who wants to get better grades and the client chooses to focus on studying more, but then continues to receive low grades. The client does not fail at his or her goal; the client might need to focus more on the quality of the study time rather than the quantity. When the therapy is focused on the client's strengths, the possibility of the client failing is taken away. Clients may feel as though they have failed or the therapy has failed them if they do not see immediate results; however, we must all remember that change is a process. Bertolino et al. (2010) discuss three key points in focusing on change as a process in a strengths-based and resilience perspective: (1) instead of searching for explanations about the nature of the problem, the focus is on enhancing change; (2) change is a constant thing, so people and their problems are not static; and (3) change is predictable. These are the key points when working with clients from a strengths-based and resilience perspective because they show that clients can't fail.

Change Occurs in All Contexts

Think back to the beginning of this section where it said that a basic assumption of a strengths-based perspective is that everyone, no matter what state they are in, has strengths. The client may be facing challenges from within or from his or her environment, but in either case, the client is still capable of change. In a resilience perspective, a basic assumption is that no matter how bad one's environment is one can still adapt and prosper. The client thrives in spite of difficult things going on around him or her. In the strengths-based and resilience perspectives, it is assumed that even the most inhospitable environments or contexts cannot completely inhibit the change process.

TECHNIQUES OF STRENGTHS-BASED AND RESILIENCE PERSPECTIVES

In preparing for battle I have always found that plans are useless, but planning is indispensable.

—Dwight Eisenhower

Now that we have discussed the background of strengths-based and resilience perspectives, we will start to look at the actual techniques the provider would use when counseling adolescents. Strengths-based and resilience perspectives can be likened to "a lens of capacity in which people are seen as having capabilities and resources within themselves and their social systems" (Bertolino et al., 2010, pp. 274–275). Due to the fact that this is a perspective or philosophy and not necessarily a treatment modality, there is room for personal interpretation and style in the implementation of it. When using a strengths-based or resilience perspective with adolescents, there are special considerations to take into account such as parental and family influence, peer influences, developmental stage, and identity formation. These factors can affect the client's views of change but can also be used as strengths when relevant. See Table 6.3 for some specific strengths-based techniques.

One of the most important parts of the session for a strengths-based provider is information gathering because becoming familiar with the client's strengths and situations is the first step in the process. Before the information gathering can truly begin, the provider must create a space in which the client feels comfortable sharing his or her stories and problems (Bertolino et al., 2010). According to Bertolino et al. (2010), "the primary doorways into clients' lives are their stories" (p. 1504). Sharry (2004) puts it in different words when he says the following:

A strengths-based approach to listening contributes greatly to overcoming blame, to the creation of trust and to establishing a working alliance. The provider listens carefully and sensitively within the clients' narrative for strengths, skills and resources, for what they are doing right rather than what they are doing wrong. Every provider statement to the client should reflect and imply these potentials and strengths. (pp. 1214–1215)

Flexibility in information gathering can help clients reveal their stories in a way that is comfortable and relevant to them. Often, just the act of telling their story is therapeutic to the

Table 6.3   Strengths-Based Techniques

Technique Name	Definition	Example
Scaling	Asking clients to rate various concepts on a scale of 1 to 10 in order to ascertain where they are or what they are feeling about the concept. This can also be a way of checking in to see what is working and what isn't.	On a scale of 1 to 10 with 1 being horrible and 10 being perfect, how committed/motivated are you to fixing this problem? How confident/hopeful are you that this problem can be fixed? How much progress have you made?
Miracle question	This is a line of questioning that invites the client to imagine and describe in detail how the future will be different when the problem is no longer present.	Suppose one night, while you are asleep, a miracle happened and fixed this problem. Only you are asleep, so you don't know it happened. What would be different? How would you know a miracle happened?
Presuppositional language	Careful attention to the use of language is an integral part of SFBT. The use of presuppositional language can convey possibilities or expectations of a positive outcome.	How did you do that?" rather than "How did that happen?"

"What will be different when you are feeling in control of your gambling?" rather than "What would be different if you are feeling in control of your gambling?" |

Note. SFBT, solution-focused brief therapy.

clients and can build their rapport with the provider. Consider beginning the information-gathering process with very open-ended questions such as "Where would you like to start?" or "What would you like to talk about?" to allow space for the clients to talk about what is important to them without leading them. As the clients are telling the story, it is important for the provider to note their potential strengths and resilience factors always checking with the clients and allowing them to be a part of the information-gathering process. Exercise 6.1 is adapted from an exercise written by Bertolino et al. (2010), and it is a good example of questions to ask in order to understand clients' strengths.

Once the information is gathered and rapport has been established, it is important to set treatment goals and objectives for therapy. In the strengths-based and resilience perspectives, goal setting is an essential piece of the process because this is the part where the client gets to set the stage for the whole purpose of the client being

there: to improve his or her life. The provider will work with the client to establish two types of goals: (1) goals for therapy and (2) goals for the client's life (Sharry, 2004). The goals for therapy will help direct the counseling relationship and make the most efficient use of the time together. The goals for life will give the client achievable steps to improving his or her situations. A preliminary part of establishing goals is to understand and establish the client's hopes and expectations for life and for seeking professional help. These will be the building blocks for the goals to be established and will guide the provider in forming goals that are client centered based on the strengths or resiliencies that the client has. Sometimes, the goals will be big and will need to be broken down into small achievable steps in order to keep from overwhelming the client. The provider should work with the client to help him or her figure out what is doable in the agreed-on amount of time. Exercise 6.2 includes questions designed to help a client come up with goals for the future.

Exercise 6.1

Understanding Client Strengths

You can begin this exercise during your first meeting when you are in the gathering background information stage. You will want to become as familiar as possible with the client resources because that will direct the conversation toward assets and strengths and away from negativity or deficits. The following questions focus on the strengths and can shift the client into that mind-set.

1. What is the number-one quality or trait that you like most about yourself? _____

   _____

   _____

   _____

2. How could you use that quality or trait to improve your situation just a little bit? _____

   _____

   _____

   _____

3. What area in your life or what quality do you have that you would like to develop further?

   _____

   _____

   _____

4. How would you or someone else know that you are developing that quality? _____

   _____

   _____

   _____

5. What needs to happen for you to increase the qualities you like most about yourself?

   _____

   _____

   _____

6. If you had to name or label your "new" self, what would it be? _____

   _____

   _____

   _____

7. Describe how you value your strengths differently, now that you have made these changes. Or would you value them differently? _____

   _____

   _____

Exercise 6.2

Goal Setting

Part I

The Crystal Ball

Imagine that you have a crystal ball and you can peer into the past, the present, and the future.

1. Focus on the present, what do you see? Now focus on the future, what do you see?

    _____

    _____

    _____

2. With your crystal ball you can look a few days, months, or years, whatever makes sense for you, into the future. When you are ready, go to a time in the future when things are going better for you. What are you seeing?

3. Notice that the problem you had in the past that brought you to therapy has gone away. What happened? _____

    _____

    _____

    _____

Miracles

Suppose that tonight, while you were sleeping, a miracle happened. The miracle is that the problem that brought you to therapy has vanished completely.

1. What would be the first thing you noticed when you woke up that would tell you that the miracle happened? How do you know that things are different? _____

    _____

    _____

    _____

2. What would be different about your life as you went through that day? _____

    _____

    _____

    _____

The Dreamer

Let us say that last night or a few nights ago, you had a wonderful dream about the future. In this dream, you had a major change in your life where the problem that brought you here has disappeared and gone away. Take a moment to think about that and then tell me about it.

1. What happened? _____

   _____

   _____

   _____

2. What changed? _____

   _____

   _____

   _____

The Time Machine

Pretend that there is a time machine sitting here right now, and you climb in. It takes you into the future, to a time when things are going the way you want them to go. After arriving at your future destination, the first thing you notice is that the problems that brought you to therapy have disappeared.

1. What happened? _____

   _____

   _____

   _____

2. What changed? _____

   _____

   _____

   _____

Part II

For this second part, please refer back to the method you chose in Part I. Next, complete the questions in this section to further develop the vision of the future without the problem.

1. What happened to the problem? Was it resolved? _____

   _____

   _____

   _____

2. How do you think the problem was resolved? _____

   _____

   _____

   _____

(Continued)

Exercise 6.2 (Continued)

3. What did you do to resolve the problem? _____

_____

_____

_____

4. What would it take to begin resolving the problem in the way you described right now?

_____

_____

_____

Source. Adapted from Bertolino et al. (2010).

The next step in the therapeutic process is to evaluate the progress on the goals. In the initial assessment, the provider may ask the client what he or she has tried so far to reach the goals. Looking at exceptions to the problem in detail will also provide valuable information that can guide the solutions. For example, if an adolescent speaks disrespectfully to all of his or her family members except for his or her father, you would want to know what is different about his or her interactions with the father that cause him or her to be more respectful. After the initial information gathering, the evaluation of progress becomes focused on the progress the client has made toward the goals set in the previous session. The provider's job is to explore and elaborate on the progress made, and this can be done using the EARS technique (Berg, 1994). EARS stands for *Eliciting* examples of progress, *Amplifying* the progress, *Reinforcing* the progress, and then *Starting over* with another example (Berg, 1994). See Table 6.4 for an example of how the EARS technique (Berg, 1994) can be used in practice. Keep in mind that this perspective is client centered, and therefore, if the client does not feel satisfied with the outcome, it needs to be reexamined and possibly reworked. Formulating an understanding of the goals and the conceptualization of progress toward those goals is essential for the provider as well as the client.

Table 6.4 The EARS Technique

E	Elicit	What has been better?
		What has changed?
A	Amplify	How did you do it?
		How did you get the idea to do this?
R	Reinforce	Great job!
		What an achievement!
S	Start over	What else is better?
		What else is different?

Source. From Berg (1994) and Sharry (2004).

Once the client and the provider have an understanding of the goals and the progress toward them, it is time to summarize and formulate the next steps. Often, the client will have new steps in mind at this point, but if he or she does not, then the provider can work with the client to help the client devise a plan. If the client does have some next steps in mind, then the provider can work with the client to clarify those and help take action steps. The provider could also give the client a small break to think about what has been discussed in the session and to formulate new goals. After the break, the provider should first focus on the client's understanding and opinions about the next step. Then, if the provider needs to give feedback, the provider can join with the client and provide feedback that is positive and empowering. The main goal of the strengths-based and resilience perspectives is to help the client move forward toward the goals that he or she has devised through empowerment and positive feedback.

Strengths-Based Assessment

For counselors who conduct assessments, there is another way to look at them that is different from the traditional deficit-based model. Strengths-based assessment, which is referred to as the "cornerstone of a strengths-focused practice" (Cox, 2006, p. 288), moves away from focusing on an individual's problems or symptoms and puts more of an emphasis on the client's strengths. Epstein and Sharma (1998) define strengths-based assessment as

> the measurement of those emotional and behavioral skills, competencies and characteristics that create a sense of personal accomplishment; contribute to satisfying relationships with family members, peers and adults; enhance one's ability to deal with adversity and stress; and promote one's personal, social, and academic development. (p. 3)

Strengths-based assessment recognizes that even the most stressed families or individuals have positive talents, abilities, or resources that can be built on in the therapy process (Epstein, 1999). This practice allows practitioners to assess for the client or family's strengths from the beginning of therapy, and continue to build on those strengths throughout the therapy.

EVIDENCE-BASED OUTGROWTHS

There are several elements that appear to be core aspects of strengths-based and resilience perspectives. The most common modalities for treatment include mostly individual interventions though it is very possible to incorporate the principles into group and family work as well. These perspectives are rather flexible and tend to be a guiding philosophy rather than hard-and-fast techniques.

FRIENDS Curriculum

The FRIENDS curriculum is an evidence-based, well-validated curriculum that has primarily been used with children and adolescents in Australia for stress relief and anxiety prevention (Barrett, Sonderegger, & Xenos, 2003). This curriculum draws from the cognitive behavioral tradition and works with families and youths to teach social and emotional learning and build strengths by developing or building on existing protective factors. FRIENDS is an acronym for the strategies taught; the letters stand for the following: *F—Feeling* worried?; *R—Relax* and feel good; *I—Inner* thoughts; *E—Explore* plans; *N—Nice* work so reward yourself; *D—Don't forget to practice*; and *S—Stay* calm, you know how to cope now (Shortt, Barrett, & Fox, 2001). The FRIENDS curriculum is usually delivered in a family-based group context and has been shown to be effective in reducing anxiety and depression symptoms, increasing self-esteem, and improving outlook on the future (Brownlee et al., 2013). This curriculum uses the strengths and resilience factors that the clients possess to help them manage their anxiety while empowering them to live more fulfilled lives in the future.

The FRIENDS program has a number of unique features while still maintaining the core components of CBT for childhood anxiety (exposure, relaxation, cognitive strategies, and contingency management). First, FRIENDS has two parallel forms to accommodate the developmental needs of children in different stages: one for children (ages 6–11 years) and the other for adolescents (ages 12–16 years). Second, it incorporates a family skills component. The family skills component includes cognitive restructuring for parents, partner-support training, and parent training in the use of appropriate reinforcement strategies and encourages families to build social support networks. Parents and children are also encouraged to practice the skills learned in FRIENDS as a family, on a daily basis. Third, the FRIENDS program emphasizes peer support and peer learning through making friends and building their social networks while the parents are encouraged to facilitate their children's friendships. Adolescents are also encouraged to learn from one another's experiences. Finally, the program includes attention training for anxiety and encourages children to make internal attributions about their accomplishments.

Implications for Counseling Adolescents

As the strengths-based and resilience perspectives are growing in popularity, they are being incorporated more and more into the standards of practice. For example, the Council for the Accreditation of Counseling and Related Educational Programs (CACREP, 2009) has included strengths-based and resilience perspectives in their standards. In the eight common core curricular areas under the Human Growth and Development area, it says that a provider should have knowledge of "theories and models of individual, cultural, couple, family, and community resilience" (CACREP, 2009, p. 11). Strengths-based and resilience perspectives are also included in several other areas in the CACREP (2009) standards as a background philosophy. As CACREP (2009) demonstrates, it is important for

counselors to be aware of their clients' strengths and resilience factors and include them in treatment and treatment planning.

Application of Ethics

Counseling adolescents adds several more layers of ethical concerns onto an already complicated relationship. It is important to remember the ethical principle of beneficence or "doing good" for the client. This pairs nicely with strengths-based and resilience perspectives because they are so focused on doing good for the client. When counseling adolescents, it is important for providers to respect the privacy of the minor while also respecting the responsibilities of the parent or guardian (American Counseling Association, 2014). It is important for the provider to be aware of state and federal laws that pertain to the confidentiality of minors and their parents.

In this chapter, you have learned about the history of the strengths-based and resilience perspectives and why we should focus on clients' strengths rather than their deficits. We have discussed the basic assumptions of these perspectives and some basic techniques for using them with adolescents. We began by defining and explaining the perspectives and then discussed the purpose of these perspectives followed by the presuppositions or assumptions of these perspectives. We then moved into a discussion of the techniques of strengths-based and resilience perspectives and provided practical applications for counseling and an evidence-based model that uses the strengths-based and resilience perspectives.

When counseling adolescents, it can be tempting to focus solely on their deficits because the deficits are often loud and demanding. For example, the adolescent who is becoming physically violent with peers and teachers demands swift attention to the deficit behavior because it is a risk to the safety of others and the adolescent. When looking at this child, it would be easy to focus only on the acting out behavior, but the adolescent may have the ability to cope with his or her anger through music or other coping mechanisms when at home. If the provider was not aware of this strength, the provider would miss valuable information that could really help this child and save the child from labeling and costly treatment centers in the future. Incorporating a client's strengths and resilience factors into the treatment gives the client the message that he or she is not broken and gives the hope that one can have a better life using one's own resources (Case Scenario 6.1).

Case Scenario 6.1

Tina

Tina is a 14-year-old Caucasian female living in a middle-class suburban neighborhood. She and her two younger brothers are being raised by their biological mother and rarely see their biological father who lives in another state. After Tina's father left, she took on major roles in helping with her brothers and keeping the house while her mom worked. Tina's mother reports that Tina has done very well in school as far as her grades go, and her grades have never dropped despite all of the stress from the divorce.

When it was reported by one of Tina's friends at school that Tina had been cutting, a meeting was called with her mother, her teachers, and the school provider. It was decided at this meeting that Tina would need to receive weekly counseling from a private practice nearby. Tina has been in trouble at school a few times for disrespectful and disruptive behavior in the classroom, but these incidents are isolated to one teacher and one class. When asked why just this one class, Tina shrugs and says, "I don't know, I think that the teacher doesn't like me or something."

At home, Tina's mother reports that they have loud arguments almost every day. Tina's mother works long hours to support her family and is not home much of the time. When she is home, she says that it is very unenjoyable because she is constantly arguing with Tina over chores, friends, and boys. Tina's mother says that they used to be very close, but since the divorce, Tina has become increasingly disrespectful and irritable. Tina's mother is too stressed and does not know what to do to make things right with her daughter.

Tina says that her strengths are her singing voice, guitar-playing ability, her ability to make friends, and her loyalty. Tina's teachers say that Tina is a good student who gets above-average grades and is usually very pleasant to be around. Tina's mother says that Tina is very likeable and has a great personality. She says that Tina can accomplish anything that she puts her mind to, and she is very intelligent (Exercise 6.3).

Exercise 6.3

Case Review—Tina

Review Case Scenario 6.1, then answer the following questions:

1. From a strengths-based perspective how would you conceptualize Tina's situation? What additional information would you want to know? Why?

(Continued)

Exercise 6.2 (Continued)

2. From a resilience perspective, how would you conceptualize Tina's situation? What additional information would you want to know? Why?

3. What level of motivation do you see Tina in right now? Is she a visitor, a complainant, or a customer?

4. What are some internal and external assets that you notice right away that could be built on?

5. What are some resilience factors that could be built on in treatment? How would you go about this?

6. Devise a treatment plan for Tina. How would you go about forming goals? What would you want to know in order to form short-term goals? What about long-term goals?

SUMMARY

The objective of this chapter is to provide a review of the strengths-based and resilience perspectives. Additionally, the usefulness of these perspectives in counseling adolescents competently is provided. Specific strengths-based and resilience techniques are identified and described for their particular use with specific clients. The underlying assumptions of these perspectives are described. There are various implications for counseling adolescents, including the ethical implications regarding the use of a strengths-based or resilience approach. The implications and proper clinical attention to them assist in providing an ethically responsible and culturally-specific intervention for adolescent clients.

KEYSTONES

- Strengths-based and resilience perspectives are increasing in popularity because they focus less on psychopathology or what is "wrong" with the client and more on strengths or what the client is doing "right."

- Though strengths-based and resilience perspectives are grouped together, they are two distinct perspectives. One key difference between strengths-based and resilience perspectives is that fundamental to resilience is the assumption of the presence of adversity, whereas strengths-based perspectives are not limited by this assumption and can be applied more universally.

- Underlying the strengths-based and resilience perspectives is the assumption that all clients have strengths or assets that can be built on or used to help them improve their lives.

- Problem solving plays a key role in these perspectives, and the client's natural abilities and strengths are built on to help devise solutions to the client's problems.

- In the strengths-based perspective, there is no such thing as an unmotivated client because everyone is motivated to achieve or get something. The responsibility of the provider is to find and capitalize on that goal.

- The most basic assumption in a strengths-based perspective is that every person has some kind of strengths to build on. This means that even youths with behavioral, emotional, and psychological problems have some kind of strengths that can be used in therapy.

- The therapeutic relationship between the client and the provider is very important in strengths-based and resilience perspectives because the client's strengths and motivations are best understood within the context of a strong relationship.

- Information gathering is the first step in the strengths-based counseling process, and it is an indispensable part of the process. Good information gathering is then followed by goal setting in the counseling process.

- After the goals are set and strategies are tried, the provider evaluates the progress toward the goal with the client and then either tries new strategies or sets new goals.

- Strengths-based assessment recognizes that even the most stressed families or individuals have positive talents, abilities, or resources that can be built on in the therapy process and assesses for those strengths rather than for a diagnosis. This practice allows practitioners to assess the client's or the family's strengths from the beginning of the therapy and continue to build on those strengths throughout the therapy.

REFERENCES

American Counseling Association. (2014). *2014 ACA code of ethics: As approved by the ACA governing council*. Retrieved from http://www.counseling .org/docs/ethics/2014-aca-code-of-ethics.pdf? sfvrsn=4

Anthony, E. J. (1974). The syndrome of the psychologically invulnerable child. In E. J. Anthony & C. Koupernik (Eds.), *The child in his family: Children at psychiatric risk* (pp. 529–545). New York, NY: Wiley.

Barrett, P. M., Sonderegger, R., & Xenos, S. (2003). Using FRIENDS to combat anxiety and adjustment problems among young migrants to Australia: A national trial. *Clinical Child Psychology and Psychiatry, 8,* 241–260.

Benson, P. L. (2003). Developmental assets and asset-building community: Conceptual and empirical foundations. In R. Lerner & P. L. Benson (Eds.), *Developmental assets and asset-building communities: Implications for research, policy, and practice* (pp. 19–43). New York, NY: Kluwer Academic.

Berg, I. K. (1994). *Family-based services: A solution-focused approach*. New York, NY: W. W. Norton.

Berg, I. K., & Miller, S. D. (1992). *Working with the problem drinker: A solution-focused approach*. New York, NY: W. W. Norton.

Bertolino, B., Kiener, M., & Patterson, R. (2010). *The therapist's notebook on strengths and solution-based therapies: Homework, handouts,* *and activities* (Kindle ed.). New York, NY: Taylor & Francis.

Bertolino, B., & O'Hanlon, B. (2002). *Collaborative, competency-based counseling and therapy*. Boston, MA: Allyn & Bacon.

Brownlee, K., Rowana, J., Franks, J., Harper, J., Bajwa, J., O'Brien, E., & Clarkson, A. (2013). A systematic review of strengths and resilience outcome literature relevant to children and adolescents. *Child Adolescent Social Work Journal, 30,* 435–459. doi:10.1007/s10560-013-0301-9

Buggie, S. E. (1995). Superkids of the ghetto. *Contemporary Psychology, 40,* 1164–1165.

Council for Accreditation of Counseling and Related Educational Programs. (2009). *2009 Standards*. Alexandria, VA: Author.

Cox, K. F. (2006). Investigating the impact of strength-based assessment on youth with emotional or behavioral disorders. *Journal of Child and Family Studies, 15,* 287–301.

de Shazer, S. (1988). *Clues: Investigating solutions in brief therapy*. New York, NY: W. W. Norton.

de Shazer, S. (1991). *Putting difference to work* (1st ed.). New York, NY: W. W. Norton.

de Shazer, S. (1994). *Words were originally magic* (1st ed.). New York, NY: W. W. Norton.

Edwards, O. W., Muniford, V. E., & Serra-Roldan, R. (2007). A positive youth development model for students considered at-risk. *School Psychology International, 28,* 29–45.

Epstein, M. H. (1999). The development and validation of a scale to assess the emotional and behavioral strengths of children and adolescents. *Remedial and Special Education, 20,* 258–262.

Epstein, M. H., & Sharma, J. (1998). *Behavioral and Emotional Rating Scale: A strengths-based approach to assessment*. Austin, TX: PRO-ED.

Garmezy, N. (1971). Vulnerability research and the issue of primary prevention. *American Journal of Orthopsychiatry, 41,* 101–116.

Garmezy, N. (1974). The study of competence in children at risk for severe psychopathology. In E. J. Anthony & C. Koupernik (Eds.), *The child in his family: Children at psychiatric risk* (Vol. 3, pp. 77–97). New York, NY: Wiley.

Gergen, K. J. (1999). *An invitation to social construction*. London, England: Sage.

Gergen, K. J., & McNamee, S. (Eds.). (1992). *Therapy as social construction*. London, England: Sage.

Hamilton, D. (1994). Traditions, preferences, and postures in applied qualitative research. In N. K. Denzin & Y. S. Lincoln (Eds.), *Handbook of qualitative research* (pp. 60–69). Thousand Oaks, CA: Sage.

Hansen, J. T. (2004). Thoughts on knowing: Epistemic implications of counseling practice. *Journal of Counseling & Development, 52,* 146–155.

Hoyt, M. F. (1998). *The handbook of constructive therapies: Innovative approaches from leading practitioners* (1st ed.). San Francisco, CA: Jossey-Bass.

Lerner, R., & Benson, L. P. (2003). *Developmental assets and asset-building communities: Implications for research, policy, and practice.* New York, NY: Kluwer Academic.

Luthar, S. S., & Cicchetti, D. (2000). The construct of resilience: Implications for interventions and social policies. *Development and Psychopathology, 12,* 857–885.

Madsen, W. C. (2007). *Collaborative therapy with multi-stressed families* (2nd ed.). New York, NY: Guilford Press.

Masten, A. S. (2001). Ordinary magic: Resilience processes in development. *American Psychologist, 56,* 227–238.

Masten, A. S., Best, K. M., & Garmezy, N. (1990). Resilience and development: Contributions from the study of children who overcome adversity. *Development and Psychopathology, 2,* 425–444.

Merriam-Webster (n.d.) In *Merriam-Webster's online dictionary.* Retrieved from http://www.merriam-webster.com/dictionary/expert

Murphy, L. B. (1974). Coping, vulnerability, and resilience in childhood. In G. V. Coelho, D. A. Hamburg, & J. E. Adams (Eds.), *Coping and adaptation* (pp. 69–100). New York, NY: Basic Books.

Murphy, L. B., & Moriarty, A. E. (1976). *Vulnerability, coping, and growth: From infancy to adolescence.* New Haven, CT: Yale University Press.

Naar-King, S., Templin, T., Wright, K., Frey, M., Parsons, J., & Lam, P. (2006). Psychosocial factors and medication adherence in HIV-positive youth. *AIDS Patient Care & STDs, 20,* 44–47.

O'Hanlon, W. H., & Weiner-Davis, M. (1989). *In search of solutions: A new direction in psychotherapy.* New York, NY: W. W. Norton.

Pines, M. (1975, December). In praise of "invulnerables." *APA Monitor,* p. 7.

Ponterotto, J. G. (2005). Qualitative research in counseling psychology: A primer on research paradigms and philosophies of science. *Journal of Counseling Psychology, 52,* 126–136.

Rapp, C. A. (1998). *The strengths model: Case management with people suffering from severe and persistent mental illness.* New York, NY: Oxford University Press.

Rawana, E., & Brownlee, K. (2009). Making the possible probable: A strength-based assessment and intervention framework for clinical work with parents, children, and adolescents. *Families in Society, 90,* 255–260.

Rutter, M. (1979). Protective factors in children's responses to stress and disadvantage. In M. W. Kent & J. E. Rolf (Eds.), *Primary prevention of psychopathology: Social competence in children* (Vol. 3., pp. 49–74). Hanover, NH: University Press of New England.

Saleeby, D. (2006). *The strengths perspective in social work practice* (4th ed.). Boston, MA: Allyn & Bacon.

Sciarra, D. (1999). The role of the qualitative researcher. In M. Kopala & L. A. Suzuki (Eds.), *Using qualitative methods in psychology* (pp. 37–48). Thousand Oaks, CA: Sage.

Sharry, J. (2004). *Counselling children, adolescents and families: A strengths-based approach* (Kindle ed.). Thousand Oaks, CA: Sage.

Shortt, A. L., Barrett, P. M., & Fox, T. L. (2001). Evaluating the FRIENDS program: A cognitive-behavioral group treatment for anxious children and their parents. *Journal of Clinical Child Psychology, 30*(4), 525–535.

Stroul, B. A., & Friedman, R. M. (1994). *A system of care for children and youth with severe emotional disturbance.* Washington, DC: Georgetown University, Child and Adolescent Service System Program (CASSP) Technical Assistance Center.

Ungar, M. (2006). *Strengths-based counseling with at-risk youth.* Thousand Oaks, CA: Corwin.

Weick, A. (1992). Building a strengths perspective for social work. In D. Saleebey (Ed.), *The strengths perspective in social work practice* (pp. 18–26). White Plains, NY: Longman.

Weick, A., & Chamberlain, R. (2002). Putting problems in their place: Further explorations in the strengths perspective. In D. Saleebey (Ed.), *The strengths perspective in social work practice* (3rd ed., pp. 95–105). Boston: Allyn & Bacon.

Weick, A., Rapp, C., Sullivan, W. P., & Kisthardt, S. (1989). A strengths perspective for social work practice. *Social Work, 34,* 350–354.

Werner, E. E., & Smith, R. S. (1982). *Vulnerable but invincible: A study of resilient children.* New York, NY: McGraw-Hill.

7

PLAY THERAPY

INTRODUCTION

Play is viewed as a universal language in which toys become one's words during play therapy, thus making the modality of play therapy applicable to a wide variety of individuals (Landreth, 2012). Play therapy focuses on the child's ability to express himself or herself through play. Historically, play therapy has been utilized with children between the ages of 2 and 12. However, due to the nature and various theoretical approaches of play therapy, it has been found beneficial with children, adolescents, adults, and those with various developmental delays (Knell, 1993). The period of adolescence is characterized by cognitive development, individuation, separation from parental figures, and preparation for adulthood. During this period, adolescents struggle for autonomy and often desire verbal expression of their inner feelings. Adolescents between the ages of 10 and 18 may be reserved in counseling. Their reticence may benefit from the provider utilizing play therapy techniques that can elicit responses that are not limited to verbal expression alone and can extend to nonverbal communication. The use of play therapy can help adolescents appropriately express interpersonal conflicts and feelings that they may not otherwise be able to articulate. Play therapy can often be viewed as similar to creative approaches in counseling, but it is marked by specific techniques and assumptions that set it apart from creative interventions.

Play therapy as discussed in this chapter focuses on utilizing play with adolescents as a means of expression for the adolescents instead of focusing solely on verbal communication. After reading this chapter, readers will be able to do the following:

- Understand what play therapy is and demonstrate how it may be useful with adolescent clients

- Be able to describe the basic presuppositions of play therapy

- Be able to identify various play therapy techniques and therapeutic modalities

- Understand the differences between nondirective and directive play therapies

- Apply knowledge from case scenarios

WHAT IS PLAY THERAPY?

To best understand the context of play therapy, one must first understand the role of play in an adolescent's life. Play is considered to be the natural and universal language of children (Landreth, 2012). By using play, children are able to express their life experiences through their natural medium of communication. According to Garry Landreth (2012), play does not need to be taught and is the one activity that can occur at all times in all places, making it a great tool to reach diverse populations. Historically, play has been viewed as a valuable communication therapeutic tool that allows the child to express his or her individuality and utilize his or her inner resources. Early psychoanalytic work conducted by Anna Freud (1928) and Melanie Klien (1932) recognized the importance of play for children and emphasized play to replace verbal free association. Freud and Klien's observations suggested that children were able to communicate using play instead of verbal communication. The 1930s saw other providers utilizing the early psychoanalytic work that integrated and began to formalize the burgeoning play therapy works into more formalized techniques. However, it was not until the 1940s when Virginia Axline (1947) extended the work of Carl Rogers's (1951) nondirective/person-centered therapy and applied these principles to children that play therapy gained momentum in the profession.

Axline (1947) proposed that through play therapy a child could work on his or her problems as the child moves toward self-actualization. Applying Rogers's (1951) principles of person-centered therapy in which the individual strives for growth and has the capacity for self-direction, she applied these principles to the therapeutic work with children. Axline found that the play experience was therapeutic for children as they had the freedom to engage in play on their own terms while experiencing a secure relationship with the adult/therapist and in a manner that is not directed by the therapist but by the child or the adolescent—by extension. As a result, the objectives of nondirective play therapy centered on the child's self-awareness and self-direction (Axline, 1947; Landreth, 2012). After Axline's (1947) groundbreaking work, many others continued to develop play therapy approaches. Among them was Landreth (2002, 2012), who expanded on the child-centered play therapy (CCPT) by promoting awareness of play therapy and creating centers focused on training play therapists and meeting the client's needs.

Landreth views play as the natural and universal language of children that does not need to be taught, allowing play therapy to occur naturally for the child. Landreth described play therapy as the opportunity to respond to the total behavior of the client, rather than to just the verbal behavior. His nondirective approach gives the client the opportunity to play out his or her expressions similar to adults who engage in counseling sessions that rely on verbal communication. Landreth promotes that children and adolescents are not miniature adults and that they experience life through their own filter. As a result, play therapy strives to honor the client's world and his or her ability to make meaning from the play he or she engages in or chooses not to engage in.

In addition to the founders and contributors to play therapy, the national Association for Play Therapy (APT, 2013) defines play therapy as "the systematic use of a theoretical model to establish an interpersonal process wherein trained play therapists use the therapeutic powers of play to help clients prevent or resolve psychosocial difficulties and achieve optimal growth and development." As broadly defined by the APT, play therapy includes a variety of theoretical approaches, including ecosystemic, Gestalt, Jungian, Psychodynamic, Theraplay, child-centered, and cognitive behavioral play therapy (Drewes, 2009; Kottman, 2011). Regardless of the therapeutic approach utilized, play therapy allows children and adolescents to use toys, art, games, and other creative play items to freely communicate. In the therapeutic relationship, therapists are then allowed to enter the child's/adolescent's world as he or she experiences it through play.

Play therapy, as described above, allows the child/adolescent to engage in play that assists him or her in making meaning of his or her experiences. While play therapy can appear simplistic and is relatively easy to use, providers choosing to implement individual techniques of play with adolescents should minimally have a foundational knowledge of play therapy application. Play therapy will be discussed in a very general manner in this chapter with attention to nondirective play therapy and CBPT as important evidence-based outgrowths among play therapy. It is important to note there are many theoretical approaches to play therapy.

Purpose of Play Therapy

Play therapy serves many purposes for children and adolescents. Possibly one of the most important is to bridge the gap between a child's and an adolescent's concrete experience and abstract thought (Piaget, 1962). Bratton, Ray, Rhine, and Jones (2005) describe the purpose of play therapy as "a developmentally responsive modality uniquely suited for children/adolescents to help prevent or resolve psychosocial difficulties and achieve optimal growth and development" (p. 376). Therapeutic play therapy approaches allow the adolescent to freely express his or her interpersonal experiences, feelings, and thoughts. According to Landreth (2012), "play involves the child's physical, mental, and emotional self in creative expression and can involve social interaction. Thus when the child/adolescent plays, one can say that the *total child is present*" (p. 11). Due to the various developmental tasks an adolescent undertakes in his or her development, there is a possibility that his or her feelings are inaccessible at a verbal level, making play therapy intentional and purposeful.

Adolescents are able to engage in play therapy to meet their cognitive and emotional developmental needs. According to Jean Piaget's (1962) theory of cognitive development, play therapy can be seen as beneficial for adolescents. Piaget presented four stages of cognitive development that correspond with an individual's respective ages. Piaget identified adolescents aged 11 years and older to be within the concrete operational stage and formal operational stage. The concrete operational stage begins at age 7 and continues till the child is 11 or 12 years old. This stage is marked by the client's ability to think more rapidly and efficiently than at prior ages. Likewise, adolescents are gaining the ability during this time to organize their thoughts and reason logically about concrete events. The formal operational stage begins around age 12 and lasts through adulthood. Adolescents in this stage are able to process hypothetical scenarios and begin to process abstract thoughts. Young adolescents during this stage are able to think logically about hypothetical situations. For adolescents who are not cognitively able to engage in abstract reasoning or thinking, play can be the concrete expression and their way of understanding the world (Landreth, 2012).

In addition to the cognitive development, adolescence also involves transitioning from childhood to adulthood. This transition is marked by rapid physical changes, including gains in height and weight, hormonal shifts, and development of sexual functions. Adolescents intensely pursue independence while struggling for individuation and separation from their caregivers. These changes begin around the ages of 10 to 12 and continue until 18 to 22 years of age. Therapy can allow adolescents the opportunity to learn, develop, and demonstrate a sense of mastery over their environments. As they experience this mastery, they have the opportunity to increase self-management of their behaviors and practice better management of the impulsivity characteristic of earlier childhood. Adolescents often struggle with emotional regulation and experience difficulty when verbalizing or expressing their emotions (Trice-Black, Bailey, & Riechel, 2013), especially regarding emotionally charged experiences, reactions, or interactions. Adolescent play permits concrete objects to be used as tools to express their emotions, concerns, and other abstract (nonconcrete) issues in a nonthreatening and nonjudgmental manner through thoughtful play therapy interventions.

When determining the adolescent's play therapy interventions, his or her cognitive and emotional development should be considered. Clinically, being able to match the adolescent's development level with the play therapy interventions chosen is of utmost importance. The goal with adolescents in play therapy should be to encourage development that fosters healthy choices and allows them the ability to move through Piaget's (1962) developmental stages working toward a more self-actualized stage (Table 7.1). Adolescents will present at different stages of development, so not all techniques of play therapy used with an adolescent should be assumed effective with another. Individuation of play therapy and the accompanying techniques should be utilized. For example, one adolescent can benefit from a nondirective approach in that it allows him or her to seek his or her own meaning, while another may need more of a directive or cognitive behavioral play therapy approach that allows the adolescent to integrate techniques as he or she negotiates his or her inner world and solidifies his or her worldview. It is important to note that play therapists must determine the appropriateness of engaging adolescents in play therapy, as developmentally this is not the appropriate intervention for all adolescents. In fact, some adolescents may disengage from participating in play therapy due to what they perceive as childish. However, when adjusted to the development and therapeutic processes, play therapy is able to appropriately meet the adolescent's individual cognitive and emotional development through the natural language of play. This will be discussed further in the Techniques of Play Therapy section of this chapter.

Presupposition of Play Therapy

Play therapy is based on the assumptions that play holds therapeutic value for a child/adolescent (Axline, 1947; Gallo-Lopez & Schaefer, 2005; Landreth, 2012). In traditional talk therapy, verbal communication is necessary for therapy to progress and for clients to express their thoughts and feelings. This traditional school of thought is contrary to play therapy as play therapists do not deem talk or verbal communication necessary (Cochran, Fauth, Cochran, Spuregeon, & Pierce, 2010). In play therapy, *play* is the therapeutic modality. Various theoretical approaches, such as CCPT, narrative play therapy, Adlerian play therapy, CBPT, Gestalt play therapy, and Theraplay, have common underlying assumptions. Three further assumptions are (1) play is spontaneous, (2) play does not need to be taught, and (3) the focus of therapy is on the therapeutic relationship with the child (Kottman, 2011), and by extension, the adolescent. Depending on the play therapy theoretical approach, there will be additional and changing assumptions. VanFleet, Sywulak, and Sniscak (2010), however, suggest that many play therapists follow nine basic assumptions when engaging in play therapy:

1. Play is a drive or strong motivation that is a part of a person's biological makeup. Although

Table 7.1 Goals of Play Therapy in Piaget's Cognitive Development Stages

Piaget's Developmental Stage	Age	Developmental Markers	Goal of Play Therapy
Concrete operational stage	7 to 11/12	✓ Ability to think rapidly	Match adolescent's developmental stage/level with play therapy intervention to foster healthy choices, allowing him or her to move through Piaget's stages toward self-actualization
		✓ Efficiently organize thoughts	
		✓ Reason logically about concrete events	
Formal operational stage	12 to adulthood	✓ Process hypothetical scenarios	
		✓ Begin to process abstract thoughts	
		✓ Ability to think logically about hypothetical situations	

humans play throughout the life span, children/adolescents do so more frequently and pervasively.

2. Play is a powerful developmental feature of childhood that contributes to child/adolescent development on many dimensions. Through play, children develop motor, cognitive, affective, social, and moral capacities and competencies. Many adolescent development theorists have derived their ideas from observations of play.

3. Play expresses children's/adolescent's inner world, including their feelings, struggles, perceptions, and wishes.

4. Play is a form of communication. Through play, children/adolescents communicate ideas, intentions, feelings, and perceptions to their playmates, parents, and therapists.

5. Play builds social bonds. Children and adolescents seek play with others (especially other children), enact social themes, and learn social behaviors and customs through play. Transgenerational play, such as when parents play with their children, builds attachment in adult–child relationships.

6. Play has a freeing effect. Play unleashes joy and excitement. It discharges distress and reduces or eliminates inhibitions.

7. With play, clients can resolve and overcome emotional, relational, and other problems. The freedom of play allows them to try alternative solutions without penalty and provides emotional safety that explores their inner and outer worlds and applies their creativity and innovation to the resolution of their difficulties.

8. Play offers clients an experience of power and control rarely afforded them in other situations. Children and adolescents typically learn to modify their behavior in accordance with "socially accepted" norms, through the guidance of adults. In most settings, including home and school, they are expected to conform to adult rules and expectations. In their play, however, children and adolescents assume charge, practice possible solutions, explore social exchanges, and role play in a manner that entails less risk of failure, harm, or other unexpected or negative consequences with less risk

and harmful outcomes. In other words, they can experience a sense of control while learning to manage or regulate their feelings and impulses.

9. Play occurs within many contexts. Social play in all its forms takes place in the context of relationships—with siblings, peers, parents, or therapists. Furthermore, play typically arises only when clients feel safe both physically and emotionally. Play also occurs within extended social contexts, such as neighborhoods, communities, and cultures. Children and adolescents play within the constructs and characteristics of their own culture and simultaneously reflect that culture and their perceptions of their world. Even the broader sociopolitical context, such as the influence of poverty, can have an impact on children's play (VanFleet et al., 2010).

All in all, these and other play therapy assumptions are geared to meet the developmental needs of children and adolescents.

Techniques of Play Therapy

Determining the developmental level of adolescent clients is the first priority of play therapists. With this understanding, these therapists realize that some adolescents respond negatively to engaging in therapies they view as childlike, or they view that the interventions do not take into consideration their abilities to effectively use verbal language to express emotions, do not recognize any cognitive strength, and do not have any understanding of their life issues. As such, assessment of the adolescent's abilities, strengths, and needs is essential to the successful use of play therapy with adolescents. Kottman (2011) suggests that play therapists working with adolescents should ask the adolescents if they would find more comfort in talking with the therapist or use their therapeutic time to engage in some therapeutic activities that utilize toys, art materials, and other mediums of expression. Additionally, for some adolescent clients, it may be beneficial to explicitly discuss the benefits of such activities, in very general, developmentally appropriate, and engaging language.

The engaging language is critical to this stage of the therapeutic process as it continues work on the therapeutic relationship, can normalize what might seem awkward and embarrassing activities, solicits the adolescent's compliance, and expresses the therapist's confidence in the methodology and possible benefits of the technique. As such, it is essential that play therapists hold attitudes and qualities that are conducive to executing successful play therapy services with adolescents. These personal qualities include basic things such as having a positive regard for the adolescents; valuing them; extending kindness, respect, and hope to them; possessing a sense of humor (especially about oneself); having a flexible, playful, and fun-loving nature; maintaining self-confidence; not being externally dependent on others; and interacting with clients in an open and honest manner (Kottman, 2011). Among these attributes is the importance of the therapist conveying unconditional acceptance to the adolescent while simultaneously setting limits that engender the adolescents' emotional and physical safety (Kottman, 2011). Landreth (2012) offers that play therapists who engage in play authentically are best suited to make a strong therapeutic connection with that adolescent. In contrast, providers who fail to be inviting and enthusiastic with play techniques can expect adolescents' resistance to such modalities.

After creating an inviting environment for the adolescent, providers can then focus on the play therapy setting, adjusting and tailoring specific techniques and making the necessary toys available. Therapists who have access to play therapy rooms are encouraged to use them, especially if they deem that such a room is beneficial to the adolescent client. Again, consideration of appropriate action should entail the consideration that some adolescents may find the playroom to be too childlike or may not relate to the toys (and activities) provided. It is of utmost importance when utilizing a playroom that the therapist allows play to be the choice of the adolescent and not refer to therapy as "play therapy" but find other words to describe and identify the techniques and processes. As a matter of form,

adolescents should be allowed to engage in the therapeutic process as they deem beneficial. Other options that may be extended to the adolescent are choice of sitting and talking, exploring toys, engaging in the play process, or all three at various times (Gallo-Lopez & Schaefer, 2005).

General supplies for play therapists include items within a play therapy kit such as sand tray supplies, art supplies, board and/or card games, dolls, animals, and sports balls, and so on. A traveling play therapy kit might also include some of these items and is easily transported for sessions that happen outside of a predetermined location. Despite the setting, all play therapy should have toys that allow the adolescent to engage in tactile activities such as Play-Doh, Silly Putty, or simple drawing. These tactile activities allow the adolescent the opportunity to manage anxiety or feelings of being overwhelmed during therapy. Table 7.2 provides a list of suggested toys and materials for play therapy. Likewise, Knell (1993) provides cognitive behavioral play therapy (CBPT) interventions directed specifically for younger children but that can be adapted to working with adolescents; these are presented in Table 7.3.

EVIDENCE-BASED OUTGROWTHS

The current movement in the behavioral health professions is the recognition of research studies providing empirical support to guide clinical practice. As a result of this movement, therapeutic modalities, interventions, and theories are expected to include empirical evidence that supports the therapeutic efficacy. As this movement continues to grow and propel the profession, so does the need for evidence-based assessments that are practice friendly, easily implemented, and evaluated by the literature to be effective (Steele, Elkin, & Roberts, 2008). Similarly, play therapy and its postulates are expected to follow professional trends and insights.

Historically, play therapy has been criticized for lacking empirical support of the modality itself (Cohen, Mannarino, & Rogal, 2001; Knell,

Table 7.2   Suggested Toys and Materials for Play Therapy

Play Activity	*Suggested Toys/Materials*
Arts and crafts	Paper, pencils, markers, paints, glitter, glue, clay, popsicle sticks, felt, foam sheets, Styrofoam, thread, beads, and stickers
General play	Barbie dolls
	Easy-bake oven
	Dollhouse
	Stuffed animals
	Puppets
	Baby dolls with supplies
Sports	Baseball
	Football
	Jump rope
	Frisbee
	Tennis ball
	Nerf balls
Sand tray	Sand, colored Crayola sand, and figurines that include female, male, adults, babies, children, families, siblings, soldiers, religious figures; wild and domestic animals; insects; fences; gates; bridges; buildings; transportation; cars; trucks; trains; and planes. Figurines should come in all shapes and sizes and should include various cultural heritages.
Music technology	CD player, camera, and music player
Games	Board games, cards, UNO, LIFE, Battleship, SORRY, JENGA, etc.

Source. Knell, 2011, pp. 318–319; Knell, S. M. (2011). Cognitive-Behavioral Play Therapy. In C. Schaefer (Ed.), *Foundations of Play Therapy* (pp. 313–328). Hoboken, N.J: John Wiley & Sons.

1993; Lin & Bratton, 2015). Despite this criticism, play therapists continue to discuss and highlight the benefits of engaging in play therapy—as anecdotal and professional experiences have attested to its value within the therapeutic relationship of adolescents (and children). Perhaps the most notable play therapy studies were conducted by Bratton et al. (2005). In their meta-analysis, they combined the results of 93 individual play therapy and filial therapy studies conducted between 1953 and 2000 to determine rates of clients' positive change as they participated in treatment groups versus those in control groups. The researchers then averaged the measured change across studies. Bratton et al.'s work showed large treatment effect sizes for all 93 studies, thereby indicating that the treatment was effective across all studies. Of specific interest in their findings is that nondirective, person-centered play therapy approaches have larger positive impacts on clients than do directive approaches.

Continuing this work, Lin and Bratton (2015) conducted a meta-analysis reviewing 52 controlled studies covering CCPT outcome studies spanning between 1995 and 2010. Using a hierarchical linear model, Lin and Bratton sought to examine CCPT and the effectiveness of this modality compared with children not receiving CCPT interventions. Results yielded from the hierarchical linear

Table 7.3   Cognitive Behavioral Play Therapy (CBPT) Interventions

CBPT Intervention	Play Example
Positive reinforcement	A puppet fearful of talking that is used by the child in therapy is rewarded with a sticker each time the puppet talks.
Shaping/positive reinforcement	A puppet fearful of talking begins to make sounds, and talk (shaping) is encouraged and given positive feedback (positive reinforcement).
Systematic desensitization	Puppet with a fear is able to systematically process situations that are least feared to most feared while engaging in relaxation.
Stimulus fading	Puppet that is clingy is able to remove itself from this behavior and begins a new pattern, therefore not relying on the old attachment of the behavior.
Extinction/differential reinforcement of other behavior	Doll acting negatively does not receive positive attention (extinction), and adaptive behaviors are rewarded with differential reinforcement of other behavior.
Time-out	Toy is placed in time-out when engaging in play that is not within the rules of the playroom.
Self-monitoring	Child uses a scale measure to visually represent his or her feelings.
Activity scheduling	For children who withdraw, events and activities are scheduled.
Recording dysfunctional thoughts	Using a method appropriate to the child's developmental level (i.e., writing, talking into a tape recorder, drawing, etc.), he or she is able to capture thoughts about a particular situation.
Countering irrational beliefs	The therapist then has the puppet examine this by talking to its friend, exploring alternatives to events that have taken place.
Coping self-statements	Puppet that is afraid of putting its head in the water uses statements indicating that it can in fact put its head in the water—"I can put my head in the water."

Source. From Knell (2011, pp. 318–319).

model "estimated a statistically significant moderate treatment effect size (.47) for CCPT" (p. 45). With the current professional movement for evidence-based interventions and past criticism of play therapy lacking empirical research, Lin and Bratton provide much-needed empirical evidence for providers to implement CCPT interventions when working with children in a play therapy setting. In addition to results regarding CCPT, results indicate significant relationships between effect size and the child's age, ethnicity, caregiver involvement, study quality, and presenting issue (Lin & Bratton, 2015). It is important to note that Lin and Bratton highlight and support CCPT as a beneficial treatment while suggesting that results indicate that children who are 8 years and younger showed greater benefit from CCPT. Lin and Bratton do not refute the benefit for older children; rather, they find this significant result to be of particular importance for young children considered at risk who may have low parental involvement.

Directive and Nondirective Play Therapy. Studies in the past decade have emerged supporting nondirective play therapy when used with children and adolescents who have a variety of interpersonal issues (Danger & Landreth, 2005; Drewes, 2009; Fall, Navelski, & Welch, 2002; Garza & Bratton, 2005; Jones & Landreth, 2002; Lin & Bratton, 2015; Packman & Bratton, 2003; Ray, 2007; Ray, Schottelkorb, & Tsai, 2007; Shen, 2002). CBPT has gained acceptance in the field for the integration of cognitive behavioral therapy (CBT) as supported intervention used with adults, yet to date, CBPT has one noteworthy quasi-experimental published study by Hansen, Meissler, and Ovens (2000). Susan Knell (2011) who is credited for the development of CBPT has recognized the lack of empirical support yet remains committed to the efficacy of the approach. With the empirical support of CBT in adult populations, this chapter includes the discussion of CBPT and the implications with adolescents as well as nondirective play therapy as evidence-based outgrowths. Nondirective play therapy and CBPT will be highlighted for their specific interventions and implementation with adolescents.

As previously mentioned, there are a variety of theoretical approaches for the use of play in counseling. Play therapy that is directive in nature operates under the assumption that the therapist is responsible for the direction and interpretation of the client's play. Nondirective play therapy on the other hand operates under the assumption that with well-established boundaries, the adolescent chooses the issues and focus of play during therapy (Gallo-Lopez & Schaefer, 2005; Kottman, 2011; Landreth, 2012). Directive play therapies are sometimes referred to as prescriptive play therapy and include release play therapy, CBPT, developmental play therapy, structured play therapy, Gestalt play therapy, and Theraplay to name a few (Kottman, 2011; Schaefer, 2011). There are several well-established approaches to play therapy, but nondirective CCPT has the longest history of use, the strongest research support, and, according to recent surveys of practicing play therapists, is most used by play therapy practitioners (Landreth, 2012). For the purposes of this chapter, nondirective CCPT and CBPT directive play therapy and the implication for using these modalities with adolescents as developmentally appropriate interventions will be discussed.

NONDIRECTIVE PLAY THERAPY

Theoretical Constructs and Features of Nondirective/Child-Centered Play Therapy

The most common and widely supported approach to nondirective play therapy is CCPT. Axline (1947) was the first to take client-centered concepts put forth by Rogers (1951) and apply them to work done with children and developed nondirective CCPT. Through the years, Guerney, Landreth, Sweeney, VanFleet, and Wilson and Ryan have refined and contributed their ideas to CCPT (Kottman, 2011). Perhaps the most important theoretical constructs surrounding CCPT begins with the fundamental constructs of personality developed by Rogers, which include (a) the person, (b) the phenomenal field, and (c) the self (Rogers, 1951; Sweeney & Landreth, 2011). The person includes the thoughts, feelings, and behaviors of an individual, and these are continually developing and changing (Kottman, 2011; Sweeney & Landreth, 2011). As this change occurs for the child (and by extension the adolescent), it leads to change across all dimensions of moving the client toward actualizing the self (Sweeney & Landreth, 2011). The phenomenal field refers to the experiences of the child. These experiences can be conscious or unconscious or internal and external, and they include perceptions, thoughts, feelings, and behaviors (Sweeney & Landreth, 2011). Of these experiences, the client's perception of his or her world is foundational for the play therapist to be able to understand the client and his or her behavior (Sweeney & Landreth, 2011). The self refers to how the child/adolescent takes his or her perceptions and develops the concept of "me." Based on these theoretical concepts of CCPT, the focus is on the inner dynamics of the client's processing related to discovering the self and what the client is capable of (Sweeney & Landreth, 2009). Of special note is that the CCPT does not rely on theoretical constructs related to a client's age, development, or issue at hand, making it applicable to adolescents experiencing a range of issues.

CCPT rests on the belief that clients are able to work through their own issues with minimal intervention from the play therapist and that they have the capacity for self-direction. The adolescent's self-direction and awareness are important in the developmental process of gaining a sense of self and personal identity. The CCPT focus and creation of an environment centering on the adolescent allows the adolescent the opportunity to express himself or herself as he or she deems appropriate while promoting self-identity and self-control. This approach encourages autonomy, independence, and self-exploration needed for the adolescent to engage in meaningful personal growth. This requires the understanding and willingness of the therapist to allow the adolescent to "lead" the session and make decisions on where the discussion/play goes. Adolescents will find value in what they tell a therapist, and the therapist should equally value and trust the adolescent's process in doing so. Landreth (2012) discussed that when relating to children/

adolescents, 10 basic tenets needed to be present and are applicable to working with adolescents as well (see Table 7.4). Counselors will find that remembering these basic tenets while working with adolescents will enhance the client–therapist relationship.

Perhaps the most notable text to date regarding integrating play therapy approaches with adolescents is Gallo-Lopez and Schaefer's (2005) work titled *Play Therapy With Adolescents*. The authors quite frankly state in their work, "Nondirective play therapy is a theoretically justifiable approach to working with adolescents" (p. 96). The key here is that nondirective play therapy considers the developmental needs of adolescents, and the techniques are adapted appropriately. Nondirective play therapy can help adolescents during a time they are beginning to discover who they are and developing a sense of self. Because the approach encompasses both play and verbal communication, adolescents are encouraged to participate in a manner that is most beneficial to their personal development. According to Wilson and Ryan (2005),

Table 7.4   10 Basic Tenets

10 Basic Tenets of Therapist–Child/Adolescent Relationship

1. Children are not miniature adults.

2. Children are people.

3. Children are unique and worthy of respect.

4. Children are resilient.

5. Children have an inherent tendency toward growth and maturity.

6. Children are capable of positive self-direction.

7. Children's natural language is play.

8. Children have the right to remain silent.

9. Children will take the therapeutic experience where they need to be.

10. Children's growth cannot be speeded up.

Source. Landreth, G. (2012). *Play therapy: The art of the relationship.* (3rd ed.). New York; London: Routledge, Taylor & Francis Group.

Nondirective play therapy is a flexible and adaptable method that can take into account the varying responses and needs of adolescents and allows exploration of emotional difficulties in a creative, individually directed way on all levels of mental functioning. Behavioral, perceptual and motor levels, as well as cognitive and emotional levels, are active and reworked simultaneously during nondirective play therapy. (p. 97)

Not only has nondirective CCPT been used with adolescents, it has also been utilized with adolescent boys identified as highly aggressive (Cochran et al., 2010). In the Cochran et al. (2010) article, the authors discuss the rationale for using CCPT with these adolescents who were thought to be reluctant to therapy and were struggling to relate to a counselor about their personal concerns and feelings. The authors found that by using CCPT they were able to reach what they described as a high-need population by providing an "alternative means for them to experience counselor empathy, unconditional positive regard and genuineness, without pressure to talk" (p. 290). When implementing the techniques of CCPT, the authors found that the adolescent boys were able to communicate and connect with the provider through self-expressive, self-generated play or artistic activity as opposed to relying on verbal language. The adolescents were allowed to engage in silent or verbal activities inclusive of molding clay, drawing models, or constructing models; the choice of silence or verbal communication during these activities was solely the adolescents'. As the session progressed and the adolescents began to find comfort with the counselor, they began to verbally communicate more frequently. Overall, it appeared to the authors that the option of engaging in talk with the counselor or not engaging in talk was important to the adolescent, and some utilized silence regularly. The developmental considerations to using CCPT have made implementing the techniques a great resource for adolescents at varying stages of development with a wide variety of presenting issues.

Role of the Provider in Child-Centered Play Therapy

In CCPT, the role of the therapist is to actively reflect the client's thoughts and feelings (Landreth, 2012). CCPT assumes that when play therapists are able to identify the client's expressed feelings, accept them, and assist the client in doing the same, the adolescent client's expression, identification, and acceptance lead the adolescent toward being better able to acknowledge, work with, experience, and resolve feelings that may arise within the session and eventually within their relative "real worlds." Gallo-Lopez and Schaefer (2005) clarify that play therapists must develop a close, trusting therapeutic relationship and reflect and respond to the client's thoughts, feelings, and play activities in such a way as to facilitate the resolution of the client's emotional difficulties at the client's own pace and chosen manner. A core therapeutic skill is being able to reflect feelings in an accurate and nonthreatening manner. In addition to reflecting back to the adolescent and accepting his or her emotions, the provider is responsible for setting behavioral limits aimed at keeping the adolescent physically and emotionally safe during counseling. These limits can include not only physical safety but also keeping the playroom materials safe and establishing time limits for play therapy (Gallo-Lopez & Schaefer, 2005; Landreth, 2012). Key characteristics of the therapist's role in CCPT play therapy include developing a trusting relationship with the adolescent that creates a relaxed environment, enabling the adolescent to choose the focus and direction of the activities he or she engages in, applying therapeutic limits meant to keep the adolescent safe, and recognizing and reflecting the adolescent's thoughts, feelings, and actions as they present them in the play therapy session in a nonjudgmental manner. Play therapists who practice CCPT are essentially facilitators of therapy with the adolescent and accompany the adolescent on his or her self-determined journey. Axline (1989) put forth eight basic principles that need to be present in CCPT and illustrate the play therapist's role:

1. The provider must develop a warm, friendly relationship with the child/adolescent, in which good rapport is established as soon as possible.

2. The provider accepts the child/adolescent exactly as he is.

3. The provider establishes a feeling of permissiveness in the relationship so that the child/adolescent feels free to express his feelings completely.

4. The provider is alert to recognize the feelings the child/adolescent is expressing and reflects those feelings back to him in such a manner that he gains insight into his behavior.

5. The provider maintains a deep respect for the child's/adolescent's ability to solve his own problems if given an opportunity to do so. The responsibility to make choices and to institute change is the child's/adolescent's.

6. The provider does not attempt to direct the child's/adolescent's actions or conversation in any manner. The child/adolescent leads the way; the provider follows.

7. The provider does not attempt to hurry the counseling along. It is a gradual process and is recognized as such by the provider.

8. The provider establishes only those limitations that are necessary to anchor the counseling and make the child/adolescent aware of his/her responsibility in the relationship. (pp. 69–70)

Goals of Child-Centered Play Therapy

The therapeutic term *goal* in CCPT is somewhat counterintuitive to the theoretical philosophy, as goals are viewed as evaluative and require external recognition of the client's work in therapy (Sweeney & Landreth, 2011). Since the focus of CCPT is on the adolescent and not the problem, the emphasis is on facilitating the adolescent's growth as a person and allowing him or her the ability to deal with current and future problems.

Despite the lack of "goals," Landreth (2012) proposes 10 objectives to be used when engaging in CCPT:

1. Develop a more positive self-concept.

2. Assume greater self-responsibility.

3. Become more self-directing.

4. Become more self-accepting.

5. Become more self-reliant.

6. Engage in self-determined decision making.

7. Experience a feeling of control.

8. Become sensitive to the process of coping.

9. Develop an internal source of evaluation.

10. Become more trusting of himself. (p. 88)

DIRECTIVE/COGNITIVE BEHAVIORAL PLAY THERAPY

Theoretical Constructs and Features of Directive/Cognitive Behavioral Play Therapy

CBT has been blended with play therapy to address a variety of issues that children/adolescents present with. These issues include obsessive-compulsive disorder, depression, anxiety, sexual abuse, trauma, and attention-deficit/hyperactivity disorder among many others (Kaduson & Finnerty, 1995; Myrick & Green, 2012; Schottelkorb, Doumas, & Garcia, 2012). Knell (2011) first developed CBPT in 1993. She emphasized the importance of the child/adolescent as an active participant in the process of change and believed that the most critical issues related to clients in therapy are that of their cognitive functioning. By failing to not focus on the verbal language in therapy, the therapist may ultimately fail to focus on the client's cognitive limitations. Knell contends that if increased understanding or insight is the goal of therapy, then one must include cognitive activities, and in this manner, CBPT incorporates cognitive and behavioral interventions within its paradigm.

CBPT as presented by Knell (1993, 2011) promotes a strong emphasis on the client's involvement in the therapeutic process, similar to nondirective play therapy. CBPT incorporates cognitive and behavioral interventions within a play therapy paradigm. Play therapy as well as verbal and nonverbal forms of communication are used in resolving problems. The focus of cognitive therapy or CBT is on psychopathology and the factors that lead to difficulties in emotional development (Kottman, 2011). CBPT does not include a theory of personality development (Knell, 1993). The focus of CBPT is on what leads to difficulties in one's emotional development and psychopathology. Just like in CCPT, CBPT rests on three major ideas that originated from Aaron Beck's (1976) cognitive therapy theory (Knell, 2009). These key ideas in cognitive therapy are (1) thoughts influence emotions and behavior (2) beliefs and assumptions influence perceptions and interpretations of events, and (3) most individuals who are having psychological problems have errors in logic, irrational thinking or cognitive distortions (Kottman, 2011).

Knell (1993) took from behavior therapy that all behavior is learned. A key factor in behavior therapy is to discover what reinforces and maintains behavior that is viewed as inappropriate. By changing these factors, the therapist can alter the child's behavior. A cognitive behavioral play therapist might use behavioral techniques directly with the child/adolescent client or teach parents to do so (Kottman, 2011). According to Knell (1993), behavior interventions prepare the child to benefit from treatment and possibly influence the child/adolescent directly. An example of this is the use of modeling in which the child/adolescent has access to direct information that may not have been accessible when relying on verbal cues. Cognitive interventions allow the client's involvement by addressing issues of control, mastery, and responsibility for one's own behavior change.

Knell puts forth six properties important to understanding CBPT:

1. The child/adolescent is involved in treatment through the play.

2. Provider deals with the thoughts, feelings, fantasies, and environment of the child/adolescent.

3. Emphasis is on developing new more adaptive thoughts and behaviors and developing more helpful coping strategies for dealing with problems.

4. CBPT is structured, directive, and goal-oriented.

5. The provider uses behavioral and cognitive techniques that have empirical evidence that supports their efficacy.

6. The therapist has many opportunities to empirically examine the effectiveness of specific treatments for specific problems. (p. 43)

Role of the Therapist in Cognitive Behavioral Play Therapy

CBPT is done in four stages (1) assessment, (2) introduction, (3) middle, and (4) termination, which require the therapist to be extremely active and directive. Within the first stage, the play therapist uses formal and informal measures to assess the current functioning of the client and his or her relationship with the parents. The play therapist then engages the child and/or parents in creating a treatment plan that is concrete with measureable goals for changes in behavior, feelings, attitudes, and beliefs. The provider implements the plan, which consists of cognitive and behavioral techniques aimed at the child's specific therapeutic concerns. As the provider works with the child, the provider usually uses techniques such as modeling, role-playing, or empirically supported CBT techniques as they are adapted to the child's developmental level (Knell, 2011; Kottman, 2011). Modeling is the most critical component as it is used in CBPT to help demonstrate adapting coping skills to the child (Knell, 2011). Overall, the provider uses the CBPT techniques to create developmentally appropriate strategies for children to develop more adaptive thoughts and behaviors. The CBPT provider uses toys to model such skills and to meet the child's developmental needs. The CBPT therapist's role is very delineated and prescriptive in nature, making it relatively easy to follow during therapy and on reflection.

Goals of Cognitive Behavioral Play Therapy

Goals and direction are the fundamental basis for CBPT (Knell, 1993). The CBP therapist works collaboratively with the parents and child/adolescent to establish goals for the client to work toward. As part of the therapeutic process, goals are constantly assessed and reevaluated. In CBPT, the therapist is providing the direction and introduction of counseling themes, but they may not be based on the feedback received from the client directly. CBP therapists in general work toward increasing the client's ability to cope with problematic situations and stressors; help the client master tasks that have been difficult; decrease the client's irrational, faulty thinking patterns; and/or assist the client in meeting developmental milestones that have been stalled for some reason (Kottman, 2011). All specific goals for children/adolescents are based on their particular problem or current situation. These goals can range from helping the child/adolescent express his or her feelings to utilizing appropriate problem-solving skills. The ultimate development of goals in CBPT is that they do not originate from the client himself or herself, rather they are established by the play therapist and/or parents.

Implementing CCPT or CBPT should depend on the adolescent's developmental ability, presenting problems, and the play therapists' beliefs about play therapy. Play therapists who do not ascribe to the fundamental beliefs of either approach should avoid integrating them into practice with adolescents. However, therapists should recognize the benefits and be flexible in understanding that not every approach will meet the needs of the adolescent they are working with, therefore calling for flexibility

and understanding of potential play therapy approaches that will be suitable at meeting the needs of the adolescent.

IMPLICATIONS FOR COUNSELING ADOLESCENTS

Clinical Application

When counseling adolescents, it is important for therapists to take their developmental needs into consideration. This calls for the provider to understand adolescent developmental theory and the appropriate interventions based on the developmental stage of the individual adolescents. One of eight Council for Accreditation of Counseling and Related Educational Programs (CACREP, 2009) core curricula areas emphasizes the need for providers in training to understand people, their nature and needs across the life span, developmental levels, and the influence of multicultural contexts on them. With this in mind, providers working with adolescents should consider the benefits of utilizing play therapy with adolescents who are developmentally working toward stages of self-actualization and Piaget's (1953) formal operational stage. Play has been identified as the universal language of children and is able to transcend different ethnicities, languages, and cultures (Drewes, 2009; Landreth, 2012), thus meeting part of the human growth and development CACREP core curricula standard. The developmental tasks and implications of using play therapy address the CACREP human growth and development standard. Focusing on play therapy in the developmental stage an adolescent is in and integrating appropriate therapeutic interventions aimed at healthy development embody the human growth and development standard. Play therapy continues to gain recognition for its developmentally appropriate techniques, which are appropriate throughout the life span (Gallo-Lopez & Schaefer, 2005). The use of nondirective play therapy approaches respect adolescents' emerging adult identities and interpersonal conflicts when appropriately implemented. When play therapy is implemented in an "individualized, flexible and integrated" manner, adolescents develop "complex, individual and hopefully manageable relationships with significant adults and peers at crucial developmental periods in their lives" (Gallo-Lopez & Schaefer, 2005, p. 117–118).

For adults, play can be viewed as part of developing relationships with others. Attending recreational events or participating in sports or games with other adults can often lead to more intimate relationships (Gallo-Lopez & Schaefer, 2005). With adolescents, the role of play can be very similar. As play is typically viewed as fun, adolescents who enter counseling may view meeting with a provider and engaging in fun activities less intimidating and therefore more apt to build more meaningful relationships with the provider. Adolescents might present with a defensive attitude toward participating in play therapy as their primary developmental task at their age includes individuation, separation, and preparation for adulthood (Gallo-Lopez & Schaefer, 2005). This is important for providers to consider as they work with adolescents. Play therapists want to engage adolescents in play therapy focusing and taking into consideration the developmental task adolescents are engaged in.

> Rather than being contraindicated for the use with adolescents, incorporating play into therapy allows adolescents to use the therapeutic relationship to move back and forth along the developmental continuum while striving for healthy individuation and separation from a non-abusive and non-punitive adult. (Gallo-Lopez & Schaefer, 2005, p. 4)

Application of Ethics

As previous chapters have highlighted, when working with adolescents, appropriate ethical codes and legal statutes should be adhered to. When determining whether to engage the adolescent using play therapy techniques, providers should consider their professional discipline and training (i.e., psychologists, social workers, school counselors, clinical mental health counselors, etc.) and practice within the discipline's ethical and legal boundaries. Exercise 7.1 provides questions requiring the application of knowledge gained in this chapter with regard to a clinical case using play therapy interventions.

Exercise 7.1

Advanced Ethical Scenario

This activity is intended as an advanced ethical scenario for working with adolescents and fosters discussion surrounding ethical and legal issues, multicultural issues, cognitive and emotional development, and play therapy techniques and goals.

A 15-year-old Hispanic female is referred to you because she refuses to speak with her school counselor, parents, or teachers at her school. On entering your office, she sits on the couch and crosses her arms, stating she has "nothing to say." You cover your informed consent document and the boundaries and limits of counseling, to which she verbally agrees to understanding and says she is willing to stay if she can play with some of the "things" in your office or draw. The adolescent begins to draw at her leisure. While doing so, she explains that her parents are "making" her come to counseling to "talk" to someone but that talking is difficult for her as she does not always have the words to describe what she is feeling. She continues to draw,

(Continued)

Exercise 7.1 (Continued)

talking when she chooses and interacting with the provider by choice. Her images depict three individuals engaging in what appears to be an intimate relationship. She explains that her parents support her current relationship with her male partner and even condone sexual activity so long as she discontinues her additional intimate relationship with her female partner, of which her parents do not approve. She continues to draw and cry while talking with the provider and states that she struggles to verbalize her "feelings" with others.

Question 1

Based on the scenario above, what if any are your ethical and/or legal concerns/obligations to report or break confidentiality of the adolescent based on her reported sexual activity with both partners? Please outline your response using a chosen ethical decision-making model?

Question 2

Using a nondirective play therapy approach, outline your role as the play therapist and the following: role of the play therapist, cognitive and emotional development considerations, play therapy techniques, goals of play therapy, and ethical considerations using this approach.

Question 3

Using a directive play therapy approach, outline your role as the play therapist and the following: role of the play therapist, cognitive and emotional development considerations, play therapy techniques, goals of play therapy, and ethical considerations using this approach.

Question 4

Compare and contrast your nondirective and directive approaches outlined in Questions 2 and 3.

Currently, the APT (2012) provides *Play Therapy Best Practices*, a document serving as a guideline for instruction, supervision, and practice of play therapy. Professionals considered Approved Providers of Play Therapy, Registered Play Therapists, and Registered Play Therapist-Supervisors through APT must attest familiarity with the *Play Therapy Best Practices* document. A second document, *Paper on Touch: Clinical, Professional and Ethical Issues*, addresses appropriate use of touch in the clinical setting, outlining clinical, professional, and ethical issues of touch in play therapy. This document while not part of the best practices guidelines is of equal importance for those implementing play therapy.

Touch is a complex therapeutic tool and should be utilized intentionally and appropriately

by the play therapist after consideration for the adolescent's individual needs and prior consent (adolescent and parent). Neither of the documents put forth by APT is intended to replace or substitute any professional code of ethics or legal statutes professionals adhere to; rather, they are intended to provide additional information specific to play therapy practices (APT, 2013). While Gallo-Lopez & Schaefer (2005) do not address ethical issues specific to working with adolescents in play therapy, they identify special issues to be considered. These special issues include recommendations aligning with standard professional code of ethics. Table 7.5 highlights special considerations and issues as presented by Gallo-Lopez and Schaefer when working with adolescents using play therapy.

Table 7.5   Special Issues Beyond Ethics

Special Issue	*Considerations When Working With Adolescents in Play Therapy*
Confidentiality	• Adolescents are keenly sensitive to the potential of being ridiculed or of others being insensitive to them engaging in play therapy, thus potentially wanting more confidentiality.
	• Adolescents need verbal and direct observation to reassure them that the therapist when with others, including parent and/or guardian, will not openly discuss their play activities without their permission.
	• If the adolescent is nervous or uncertain about someone entering the room while engaging in play therapy, he or she should be given permission to lock the door, cover a two-way mirror, and ensure the video recording equipment is turned off.
Caregiver (parent) response	• Caregivers should be given information on how to respond to the needs of their adolescent.
	• Caregivers should be encouraged not to tease or make sarcastic comments regarding adolescents' play or regressive behaviors in the play room.
	• The caregiver should be told that the adolescent may need to take on different roles within the play therapy room as part of the therapeutic process in order to meet a previously unmet need of the past that may affect current functioning.
Interpretation	• When interpreting play, the goal is to assist in the client's development of insight; this requires a level of abstraction that may not be available to the child.
	• Interpretation by the therapists is not always necessary for adolescent clients to have successful treatment outcomes.
	• If left unsaid, the adolescent will choose to interpret his or her own metaphors during play.
	• Highly defended adolescents may become overwhelmed or vulnerable if interpreting play themes occurs too early.
Developmental issues	• Adolescents choosing to play can be the result of unmet needs related to an earlier stage of development.
	• Playing with a nonjudgmental, nurturing adult can repair and become a cathartic experience for adolescents experiencing trauma or neglect and allows them to share painful experiences from their past and process them therapeutically.
	• If the activities have the potential to be sexually stimulating or to arouse sexual fantasies in an adolescent, using cotherapists who are of the same gender should be considered; in addition, alternative methods of playing out particular themes may need to be suggested when therapist–client boundaries seem as if they may be violated.
	• The therapist must set clear limits regarding the client's and the therapist's comfort and safety during sessions.

(Continued)

Table 7.5   (Continued)

Special Issue	*Considerations When Working With Adolescents in Play Therapy*
Adolescent culture	• Knowing what is important to the adolescent is a great way to establish and maintain relationship.
	• Showing an interest in the culture and likes and dislikes of adolescents is validating for them.
	• Adolescents are more likely to openly share when they experience their media idols to be similar to them.

Source. Adapted from Gallo-Lopez and Schaefer (2005).

SUMMARY

Play is often thought of as an approach with children; however, play can be used with adolescents as a means of expression for the adolescent. Play therapy can help adolescents appropriately express interpersonal conflicts or affective experiences that they may not otherwise be able to articulate. To use play effectively in treating adolescents, the basic presuppositions of play therapy must be understood. While play therapy can be viewed as a creative approach, it is specifically marked by various therapeutic techniques and modalities described in this chapter. This chapter also highlights the differences between nondirective and directive play therapy.

KEYSTONES

• Despite the misconceptions that play therapy is only useful with children, providers should remember that play therapy can be just as effective and useful with adolescents.

• Play therapy does not need to be interpreted, analyzed, or directed for the adolescent to find developmental benefits from engaging in play therapy.

• When working with adolescents, it is important that the provider considers the developmental needs of the adolescent and plans play therapy interventions appropriately.

• The key is that some adolescents will find it beneficial to have tactile objects available to them while they engage with the provider, while others may use the chosen medium (e.g., painting, games, puppets, dartboards, puzzles, clay, etc.) to express themselves and their internal processes.

• For providers who utilize nondirective play therapy, the adolescent should choose how they interact versus the directive, which would be more structured by the therapist. Both can be beneficial for the adolescent, but both the goals of counseling and the time frame for working with the adolescent should be considered.

• "Play therapy is an effective method of intervention with adolescents, provided that the approach is adapted to address some of the particular age-related issues which arise in working with adolescents" (Gallo-Lopez & Schaefer, 2005, p. 117).

REFERENCES

Association for Play Therapy. (2013). *Definition of play therapy.* Retrieved from http://www.a4pt .org//?page=AboutAPT

Axline, V. (1947). *Play therapy: The inner dynamics of childhood.* Boston, MA: Houghton Mifflin.

Axline, V. (1989). *Play therapy.* Edinburgh, Scotland: Churchill Livingstone.

Beck, A. T. (1976). *Cognitive therapy and the emotional disorders.* New York, NY: International Universities Press.

Bratton, S., Ray, D., Rhine, T., & Jones, L. (2005). The efficacy of play therapy with children: A meta-analytic review of the outcome research. *Professional Psychology: Research and Practice, 36*(4), 376–390.

Cochran, J., Fauth, D., Cochran, N., Spuregeon, S., & Pierce, L. (2010). Growing play therapy up: Extending child-centered play therapy to highly aggressive teenage boys. *Person-Centered & Experiential Psychotherapies, 9*(4), 290–301. doi: 10.1080/14779757.2010.9689073

Cohen, J., Mannarino, A., & Rogal, S. (2001). Treatment practices for childhood posttraumatic stress disorder. *Child Abuse & Neglect, 25,* 123–135.

Council for Accreditation of Counseling and Related Educational Programs. (2009). *2009 standards for accreditation.* Alexandria, VA: Author.

Danger, S., & Landreth, G. (2005). Child-centered group play therapy with children with or speech difficulties. *International Journal of Play Therapy, 14*(1), 81–102.

Drewes, A. (2009). *Blending play therapy with cognitive behavioral therapy: Evidence-based and other effective treatments and techniques.* Hoboken, NJ: Wiley.

Fall, M., Navelski, L. F., & Welch, K. K. (2002). Outcomes of a play therapy intervention for children identified for special education services. *International Journal of Play Therapy, 11*(2), 91–106.

Freud, A. (1928). *Introduction to the technique of child analysis* (L. P. Clark, Trans.). New York, NY: Nervous and Mental Disease.

Gallo-Lopez, L., & Schaefer, C. E. (2005). *Play therapy with adolescents.* Lanham, MD: Jason Aronson.

Garza, Y., & Bratton, S. (2005). School-based child-centered play therapy with Hispanic children: Outcomes and cultural consideration. *International Journal of Play Therapy, 14*(1), 51–80. doi:10.1037/h0088896

Hansen, S., Meissler, K., & Ovens, R. (2000). Kids together: A group play therapy model for children with ADHD symptomalogy. *Journal of Child and Adolescent Group Therapy, 10*(4), 191–211.

Jones, E., & Landreth, G. (2002). The efficacy of intensive individual play therapy for chronically ill children. *International Journal of Play Therapy, 11*(1), 117–140.

Kaduson, H., & Finnerty, K. (1995). Self-control game interventions for attention-deficit-hyperactivity disorder. *International Journal of Play Therapy, 4,* 15–29.

Klien, M. (1932). *The psycho-analysis of children.* London, England: Hogarth Press.

Knell, S. M. (1993). *Cognitive-behavioral play therapy.* Northvale, NJ: Jason Aronson.

Knell, S. M. (2009). Cognitive behavioral play therapy: Theory and applications. In A. A. Drewes (Ed.), *Blending play therapy with cognitive behavioral therapy: Evidence-based and other effective treatments and techniques* (pp. 117–134). Hoboken, NJ: Wiley.

Knell, S. M. (2011). Cognitive-behavioral play therapy. In C. Schaefer (Ed.), *Foundations of play therapy* (pp. 313–328). Hoboken, NJ: Wiley.

Kottman, T. (2011). *Play therapy: Basics and beyond.* Alexandria, VA: American Counseling Association.

Landreth, G. (2002). *Play therapy: The art of the relationship.* New York, NY: Brunner-Routledge.

Landreth, G. (2012). *Play therapy: The art of the relationship* (3rd ed.). New York, NY: Routledge, Taylor & Francis.

Lin, Y.-W., & Bratton, S. C. (2015). A meta-analytic review of child-centered play therapy approaches. *Journal of Counseling & Development, 93,* 45–58. doi:10.1002/j.1556-6676.2015.00180.x

Myrick, A. C., & Green, E. J. (2012). Incorporating play therapy into evidence-based treatment with children affected by obsessive compulsive disorder. *International Journal of Play Therapy, 21*(2), 74–86. doi:10.1037/a0027603

Packman, J., & Bratton, S. (2003). A school based group play/activity therapy intervention with learning disabled preadolescents exhibiting behavior problems. *International Journal of Play Therapy, 12*(2), 7–29.

Piaget, J. (1953). *The origin of intelligence in the child.* London, England: Routledge & Paul.

Piaget, J. (1962). *Play, dreams and imitation in childhood.* New York, NY: Routledge.

Ray, D. (2007). Two counseling interventions to reduce teacher–child relationship stress. *Professional School Counseling, 10*(4), 428–440.

Ray, D., Schottelkorb, A., & Tsai, M. (2007). Play therapy with children exhibiting symptoms of attention deficit hyperactivity disorder. *International Journal of Play Therapy, 16*(2), 95–111.

Rogers, C. (1951). *Client-centered therapy.* Boston, MA: Houghton Mifflin.

Schaefer, C. E. (Ed.). (2011). *Foundations of play therapy.* Hoboken, NJ: Wiley.

Schottelkorb, A., Doumas, D., & Garcia, R. (2012). Treatment for childhood refugee trauma: A randomized, controlled trial. *International Journal of Play Therapy, 21*(2), 57–73. doi:10.1037/a0027430

Shen, Y. J. (2002). Short-term group play therapy with Chinese earthquake victims: Effects on anxiety, depression and adjustment. *International Journal of Play Therapy, 11*(1), 43–64.

Steele, R. G., Elkin, D. T., & Roberts, M. C. (Eds.). (2008). *Handbook of evidence-based therapies for children and adolescents.* New York, NY: Springer.

Sweeney, D., & Landreth, G. (2009). *Child-centered play therapy.* In K. O'Connor & L. Braveman (Eds.), *Play therapy theory and practice: Comparing theories and techniques* (pp. 123–162). Hoboken, NJ: Wiley.

Sweeney, D., & Landreth, G. (2011). *Child-centered play therapy.* In C. Schaefer (Ed.), *Foundations of play therapy* (pp. 129–152). Hoboken, NJ: Wiley.

Trice-Black, S., Bailey, C. L., & Riechel, M. E. K. (2013). Play therapy in school counseling. *Professional School Counseling, 16*(5), 303–312.

VanFleet, R., Sywulak, A. E., & Sniscak, C. C. (2010). *Child-centered play therapy.* New York, NY: Guilford Press.

Wilson, K., & Ryan, V. (2005). *Play therapy: A nondirective approach for children and adolescents* (2nd ed.). Philadelphia, PA: Elsevier.

8

SCREENING AND ASSESSMENT IN ADOLESCENT COUNSELING

INTRODUCTION

When working with adolescents, a provider has an ethical obligation to ensure that treatment is efficacious and meets the needs of adolescents, their families, and communities. Often the provider, the adolescent, and the family must identify what problems are present before a treatment plan is designed and implemented. This is frequently accomplished through screening and assessment (Merrell, 2003). The process of screening and assessment cannot only identify clinical concerns but it can also help providers focus on solutions (Grisso & Underwood, 2004). There are numerous modalities that can be utilized for assessment, and those most useful for adolescents will be discussed in this chapter. To be intentional about the screening and assessment process, providers are encouraged to seek education, consultation, and supervision around various techniques and instruments. While reading this chapter, the following questions can help guide direct application of the material presented in this chapter: What is screening? What is assessment? How can screening and assessment

help answer questions or solve problems? What needs to be understood about the instruments identified as useful with this population? How does one go about ensuring that issues concerning culture and diversity are appropriately attended to in choosing the best-fitting tool for an organization?

By the end of this chapter, the reader will be able to do the following:

- Identify how screening and assessment can be used with adolescents as part of a problem-solving process

- Explain issues related to test use, including reliability, validity, normalization, and multicultural uses

- Describe how the clinical interview can be used as part of the assessment process

- Explain how confidentiality and informed consent with adolescents is different from other clients

- Identify several screening instruments used with adolescents for various presenting problems or concerns

- Identify several assessment instruments used with adolescents as part of a comprehensive evaluation

- Apply knowledge gained from this chapter to a case scenario

CASE SCENARIO

The following case of Stefania is intended to help students apply assessment and screening knowledge (see Case Scenario 8.1). Pretend you are a provider and read through the case scenario. Now, with a partner try to apply the knowledge you've gained in this chapter to the case. You may wish to write out the applicable assessment and screening tools or jot down a few notes about the case. Afterward, complete the questions provided in Exercise 8.1 to put your knowledge into practice; then, continue reading the subsequent sections in this chapter.

STAGES OF SCREENING AND ASSESSMENT

There are numerous ways by which screening and assessment may be undertaken. This depends on the clinical setting, the population, and any immediate crisis needs. Providers typically work from a specific theoretical orientation, which often includes guidelines for assessment and screening. For example, humanistic approaches

---

Case Scenario 8.1

Stefania

Stefania and her family come to Scott's office asking for assistance. They were referred to Scott, a mental health provider, by a neighbor. Stefania's mother, Maria, is of Mexican descent and speaks little English. Her father David is African American and speaks for her, translating into Spanish when necessary. Stefania is currently 14 years old and is the eldest of four children. She has two younger brothers and a younger sister. Maria reports that Stefania has been sullen, moody, and has been lashing out verbally at her family members. They also are concerned about the amount of time that Stefania has been spending on the Internet, either on her phone or while using the family computer. Her grades have also fallen into the D and F range, when they were previously in the B and C range. David expresses concerns about Stefania suddenly refusing to go anywhere other than school and home. He also describes how she has recently pushed many of her friends away, refusing to do things that she previously enjoyed, such as shopping or spending time at friends' homes. The family is Roman Catholic and state that Stefania has also refused to attend weekly mass with the family as well as other church-related activities, which is particularly upsetting to Maria. David also reports that they found marijuana in Stefania's backpack, which was the factor that brought them to therapy.

    Stefania had little to say while her parents were talking. Once alone, Stefania is still reluctant to talk about herself. She states that she is feeling tired most of the time and that she "wants to sleep." She also states that her mind is always "full of thoughts," and she has a hard time "shutting it off." When asked about marijuana and other substance use, she shrugs her shoulders and states, "everyone is doing it." She then states that she is "done" with talking and walks out of the room to join her parents in the waiting area.

Exercise 8.1

Identification—Stefania

From the information garnered very briefly with the family and Stefania, answer the following questions:

1. What are the problems being identified by Maria, David, and Stefania?

2. What additional information do you feel is needed?

3. What would you specifically do to build a therapeutic relationship with Stefania? With her parents?

4. What multicultural aspects do you feel might be important in this case?

---

may favor allowing the client to take the lead and present problems as he or she desires, with the provider asking few questions. Other traditions, such as the cognitive behavioral approach, have very specific and sometimes even manualized assessment questions. Some traditions rely more on psychological testing (Ingram, 2006). There are, however, generic models for the assessment process that compliment most therapeutic orientations and that can be helpful in organizing this first step of working with a client. One such example is a model proposed by K. W. Merrell (2003). Based on data-oriented problem-solving techniques, this model provides a useful guide in arriving at the problem as well as in generating solutions. These steps are at the heart of the assessment process. The model has four phases and is summarized in Table 8.1. This model will be utilized as an organizational framework for the remainder of the chapter.

PHASE 1: IDENTIFICATION AND CLARIFICATION

The first phase, identification and clarification, is where problems are first identified and guides the rest of the assessment process. One of the first questions that must be answered involves identifying the client and how he or she was referred. There are numerous pathways of referrals for a provider working with adolescents. Depending on the setting, referral sources could include parents, schools, physicians, the adolescent, juvenile justice systems, hospitals, or colleagues. Typically, adolescents are referred by someone else, although self-referrals are becoming more commonplace in mental health settings (Merrell, 2003). Additional questions include how others may be involved in the client's life. While the adolescent may be presenting for counseling, could this be more of a family issue? Perhaps it is rooted more in the community than requiring social action? The provider has the difficult job of determining where intervention is most needed (Grisso & Underwood, 2004). This is also the phase where the clients express their views of the problems that brought them in, in their own words. In fact, before administering screening and assessment instruments and formulating a treatment plan, some form of a clinical interview will be necessary not only to clarify referral information but also to begin building rapport (Underwood & Rawles, 2002). Table 8.2 includes a suggested checklist for an assessment interview with an adolescent.

For adolescents, the process of going to a provider can be anxiety provoking, and the adolescent may have numerous presumptions and fears

Table 8.1   Assessment as a Problem-Solving Process

Phase 1: Identification and clarification of the problem

   Identify the client or clients

   From the client's perspective, what is the problem?

   From the perspective of family or others, what is the problem?

   What questions do screening and assessment instruments need to answer?

Phase 2: Data collection

   What information is needed to clarify the problem?

   Which assessment methods or tests would provide this information?

   What are the best ways of obtaining information for this client? For the problem?

Phase 3: Analysis

   Does the information gathered through assessment and screening answer the questions?

   What additional information was provided through the assessment?

   What contributing factors were identified through the assessment?

   Is there still missing information that needs to be gathered?

Phase 4: Solution and evaluation

   Based on the assessment information, what should be the target(s) for intervention?

   What types of intervention will be most appropriate?

   What resources are available?

   What types of assessment can be used for ongoing treatment evaluation?

Source. Merrell (2003).

about the process. Through empathic listening, the provider can help place the adolescent and his or her family at ease, improving the likelihood that the process will be beneficial. One approach could be beginning the interview in a nondirective manner, which can help the adolescent feel more at ease. Once the client has provided enough background information, the provider can switch to focused questioning, eliciting information that is more specific to the presenting problems at hand (Merrell, 2003).

When looking at a specific problem, Linden (1998) proposed four "frames" of reference to help with exploration. The first is to clarify basic information about the problem, such as onset, course, history, and attempts at solving already utilized. The next frame looks at the outcome or what the adolescent and his or her family would like to have happen. The third frame focuses on the barriers to the outcome from multiple perspectives, including cultural, environmental, personal, and familial. Finally, resources to help solve the problem are identified. Adolescents may also benefit from active and more creative elements as part of the clinical interview. For example, creating a time line of the adolescent's life or a specific time frame can be helpful for visual processing. Role-playing can also be used

Table 8.2   Adolescent Assessment Interview Domains

Problem History	
Description	Duration
Previous treatment	Attempts to solve
Antecedents	Consequences

Family Background	
Family constellation	Cultural background
Parents' relationship status	Parents' occupations
Socioeconomic status	

Personal History	
Infancy	
Pregnancy/delivery	Developmental milestones
Early medical history	Family atmosphere
Childhood	
Academic achievement	Peer relationships
Relationship with parents/siblings	Hobbies/activities/interests
Significant events/experiences	
Adolescence	
All areas above	Reaction to puberty
Acting out	Changes in relationships

Source. Groth-Marnat (2009).

as an assessment technique, as well as various art techniques like drawing, sculpture, or collage (Ingram, 2006).

When working with adolescents, an important part of the clinical interview will also involve obtaining a developmental history (Underwood, Phillips, von Dresner, & Knight, 2006). Have there been difficulties in meeting physical or psychological developmental milestones? In terms of psychological development, where is the adolescent? For example, an adolescent who does not effectively complete the basic trust versus mistrust stage may have the belief that people in their world are not to be trusted. This may be contributing to presenting problems or ways of functioning and may need to be addressed in treatment (Berger, 2011).

Another important dimension of a clinical assessment interview with adolescents includes obtaining information about culture. Some important aspects of culture to inquire about include cultural identity, cultural explanations of mental illness, cultural factors related to the psychosocial environment, and how culture might influence the relationship with the therapist (Underwood et al., 2006). Cohort factors may also be important to note. A cohort refers to a group of people who are born at the same time. This can help organize information about the social, political, and economic factors that influence life experience. The cohort factor may be important not only for the adolescent but also for other important individuals in their life, as cohort effects may influence parenting practices as well as community functioning (Ingram, 2006).

ETHICAL/LEGAL CONSIDERATIONS OF SCREENING AND ASSESSMENT

The clinical interview is also an opportunity to address legal and ethical obligations. When working with adolescents, providers will often speak with parents or other caregivers who may have an interest in the outcome or affect the client in some way. Multiple perspectives on problems can help clarify needs and build a stronger treatment plan. When working with an adolescent, the provider is also working with the family and may need to consider broader interventions that focus on systems and not necessarily on the individual alone. This, however, can complicate the therapeutic relationship and requires additional ethical consideration. For example, most laws state that the adolescent's parent or guardian has legal access to all treatment records, limiting confidentiality. Issues related to informed consent are also pertinent while working with adolescents and various other entities, including schools. There are several recommendations for providers working with adolescents during the assessment process to navigate some of these difficulties.

Informed Consent

Informed consent is the process of describing the nature and the purpose of the evaluation, limits to confidentiality, and, if applicable, the involvement of third parties. Clients are given the opportunity to ask questions about the process and then sign their consent on a legal document that becomes part of the clinical record (Urbina, 2004). Research has suggested that when clients are able to give their informed consent, they are more likely to engage in treatment

and to be vested in the outcome (Groth-Marnat, 2009). With adolescent clients, the provider must obtain informed consent from the legal guardian. However, the provider may wish to gain assent, feeling that the adolescent should understand the process, especially when formal testing may be utilized. Assent allows the adolescent to verbally agree after a developmentally appropriate explanation has been provided. Although assent does not give the adolescent permission to refuse treatment, it does open up the opportunity for further conversation with parents or other legal guardians about the proposed assessment or treatment procedures if the adolescent has concerns (Merrell, 2003). For youth in state's custody, the state will often give consent and require assessment, regardless of the adolescent's thoughts or concerns. In working with court-ordered adolescents, the provider will need to pay special attention to building rapport and encouraging participation from the adolescent (Underwood et al., 2006).

Confidentiality

Confidentiality refers to the right to privacy and is regulated by legal systems and documented in the American Counseling Association Code of Ethics. If cognitive testing is being provided, the Family Educational Rights and Privacy Act of 1974 also guarantees confidentiality of results (Merrell, 2003). The legal guardian is informed about the rights to confidentiality as well as the limitations as part of the informed consent process. However, providers must also be careful in how they present confidentiality to their adolescent clients. Adolescents should know that their parents or legal guardian may have access to their records or be verbally informed of anything that is discussed in session. They should also understand the limits to confidentiality that will require discussion not only with parents but also with authorities. Issues related specifically to assessment are also important to discuss. For example, how test scores are going to be safely stored is an important part of confidentiality. Additionally, if any third parties are to have access to the scores, conditions related to disclosure should also be discussed (Groth-Marnat, 2009).

THE CONTINUING CASE OF STEFANIA

As the provider, Scott needed more information to understand what is needed to help Stefania and her family. Before conducting a more concentrated clinical interview, he made the following list of problems that he had identified:

- Symptoms identified by Stefania's parents might indicate a mood disorder and possible concerns with substance abuse

- Symptoms identified by Stefania may also indicate a mood disorder as well as an anxiety disorder

- Stefania's parents are concerned with her school performance, self-isolation, time on the Internet, and refusal to participate in religious activities

- Symptoms identified by Stefania may also indicate an idiosyncratic learning disability or information-processing problem

Now, read the continuation of the Stefania case (see Case Scenario 8.2) and complete the following exercise (see Exercise 8.2) to further apply the knowledge you have gained thus far in this chapter. Afterward, continue reading the subsequent sections of this chapter.

Case Scenario 8.2

Stefania—Continued

Scott spoke with Stefania, Maria, and David to obtain informed consent and describe the limits of confidentiality. Maria stated that she wanted to know everything that Stefania had discussed. David indicated that he wanted to know only if Stefania was having suicidal thoughts or if there were other behaviors that put her in danger. Stefani did not outwardly react to this part of the conversation. When asked if she would like to provide assent, she stated that she would do "whatever to get them off my back."

In a clinical interview with David and Maria, they describe their family as "unique." They stated that they speak both Spanish and English at home. David works as a journalist for a local TV station and newspaper, while Maria remains at home to take care of the children. They deny any concerns about their marriage, stating that they "fight" verbally on occasion, but they deny any physical violence. They have been married for 16 years and met at a restaurant they both worked at when Maria was a new immigrant to the country and David was in college. David states that his family is close and states that he was raised primarily by his grandmother, as both of his parents spent time in prison. He states that he was able to go to college because of several mentors from his high school, and he is grateful to them for their influence. He expresses concerns that Stefania might end up in a similar situation to his parents and other family members who have struggled with substance abuse and other addictive behaviors. Maria reports that she came to the United States from Mexico at the age of 18 to "build a better life." She states that her mother and several siblings still live in Mexico, but her father

(Continued)

Case Scenario 8.2 (Continued)

and several brothers are here in the United States. She states that her faith is very important to her and she wants to pass along that tradition to her children. She states that she enjoys cooking for the family and that family meals each night are important to her. Maria denies a family history of mental health problems. David states that his family "has some depression" but that he is unaware of other problems other than the substance abuse. David states that he and Maria differ in their approach to parenting. He states that Maria is more authoritarian but that he expects this as part of her culture. He states that he tries to be "more open and flexible" with the children.

Maria states that Stefania was born full term and has not had any medical concerns. She states that Stefania has always struggled academically but usually is able to "pass her classes." She states that Stefania has not been in any special education classes and that they have never pursued any academic testing for her. Both parents report that Stefania has never had trouble making friends and typically enjoyed being social and going places. Stefania was more open during her clinical interview and stated that she has been feeling sad. She denies suicidal ideation or previous attempts. She states that, since beginning the ninth grade, she has had to work harder at school and this makes her "tired." When asked about her Internet use, she states that she is spending her time on social media sites. She states that she prefers to talk to "people I will never meet in person, because then I am not worried what they think about me." Scott asked Stefania what she believes others might think about her. She states that "they see my crazy hair, my big nose, my dark skin, and they know I speak Spanish, so I must not belong."

Exercise 8.2

Clinical Interview—Stefania

With the new information gained in the clinical interview, answer the following questions:

1. What additional problems or concerns were identified from the narrative?
2. What family factors might be important in this case?
3. What cultural factors were identified that are important in this case?
4. As you begin to think about screening and assessment, what areas do you think you might want to find out more about?
5. How do multicultural factors influence the case of Stefania?

PHASE 2: ACTIVE DATA COLLECTION

Following the clinical interview and discussion of informed consent and confidentiality, the provider begins Phase 2 of the assessment process. This is when the question of what information is needed and what means will be used to gather that information is answered (Merrell, 2003). Many providers utilize psychological assessment instruments during this phase of the problem-solving process.

However, instead of administering a "standard" battery of assessments or screenings, it is recommended that the provider handpick instruments to aid in the problem-solving process specific to the characteristics of the client and the problem (Urbina, 2004). Providers who are purposeful in selecting assessments are more able to utilize information in effective treatment planning. Within a multimodal assessment, there are several distinct advantages to utilizing assessment instruments as part of the process. Usually, a test is a highly efficient way to gather information. For example, when considering behaviors, the cost in terms of time and resources for a provider to make observations renders this form of assessment impractical for most providers. Test instruments are often more effective in compiling information and presenting summaries in a useful way. Additionally, test instruments add a dimension of objectivity to the assessment process, with the clients providing information about themselves, as well as others, including parents or teachers, doing so as well. Of course, there are also reasons to not use assessment instruments. Some of these are summarized in Table 8.3. Providers who wish to use formal assessment measures face the task of selecting the most applicable measures and understanding psychometric properties as well as how

best to utilize them with diverse populations (Merrell, 2003).

Instrument Selection

When selecting screening and assessment instruments, the most important factor is the extent to which the measure is useful in answering questions related to the adolescent's problems and concerns (Merrell, 2003). Additionally, the provider has the ethical obligation to ensure that they are properly trained in using the particular instrument in question, as well as have access to the appropriate testing manual and instruments. Through training, the provider is made aware of the strengths and weaknesses of the measure, issues related to reliability and validity of the test, as well as interpretation with diverse populations. Providers are ultimately responsible for accurate test use and interpretation. While most psychological instruments are prepared and published according to established psychometric processes, providers must keep in mind that they are products that are marketed for specific clinical uses (Urbina, 2004). In considering different assessment instruments, the provider should consider if the test in question will help identify problems or provide additional

Table 8.3   Reasons Why Providers Should Not Use Tests

1. The purpose of testing is unknown or unclear.

2. The provider is not completely familiar with all the necessary test documentation or is not trained.

3. The provider is not clear what the results will be used for or how to safeguard them.

4. The information sought through testing is already available or can be gathered more efficiently.

5. The client is not willing or able to cooperate.

6. The client may experience harm due to the testing process itself.

7. The environment or setting for the test is not adequate.

8. The test materials or format is inappropriate for the client in some way, such as age, gender, linguistic background, culture, or disability status.

9. The test norms are outdated, inadequate, or inapplicable.

10. The documentation on reliability and validity is not adequate.

information for a particular clinical issue. If the disadvantages of using a particular instrument outweigh the advantages, utilizing the measure is not advisable (Groth-Marnat, 2009).

Understanding the psychometric properties of the instruments is also necessary in determining if the test will be useful. The value derived from using screening and assessment instruments depends largely on several factors, including the context in which the scores were originally obtained and the frame of reference used to interpret them (Grisso & Underwood, 2004). For example, a test that utilizes norm-referenced interpretations provides results based on administration of the instrument to specific groups of people. This can be useful in the assessment process with adolescents when their score is compared with the scores of other adolescents, giving a sense of what might be considered "normal" or "abnormal." However, before making any clinical judgment based on a score, the provider must be aware of the characteristics of the reference group. If the reference group is upper-middle-class Caucasian adolescents, the test norms may not reflect the performance of an African American lower socioeconomic status adolescent. Other factors to consider include the size of the norm group, how long ago the group was sampled, and where the sample was gathered. While cutoff scores from normative samples can provide important information, keeping in mind unique variables of each client is important for meaning making throughout the assessment process (Urbina, 2004).

Reliability and Validity

Another important feature of psychological tests is their reliability and validity. In selecting measures, the provider should have a thorough understanding of these terms and how they relate to the specific test in question. Reliability refers to the extent to which the results of a test are trustworthy. According to Urbina (2004), "reliability is a quality of the test scores that

suggests they are consistent and free from measurement error to be useful" (p. 117). Measurement error is any change in scores that results from factors not associated with the content of the test. When an instrument is termed *reliable*, in the fullest sense this would mean that the measure is reliable in all settings, for all uses, and for all users. Since this is rarely the case, instruments should be used as one piece of a comprehensive evaluation and interpreted with caution (Groth-Marnat, 2009). Often, reliability coefficients can be a useful guide in determining the reliability of an instrument and are reported both in the literature as well as in testing manuals. Although a simplistic definition, the coefficient is essentially the correlation of the test with itself. They are based on data derived from different sources, including several administrations of the same test or administrations of two versions of the test. Most providers rely on instruments with reported coefficients above .80 (Urbina, 2004).

Reliability is a precursor to validity, yet an instrument that is reliable is not always valid. Validity refers to the extent to which scores are accurate for their intended purpose and context (Boyle et al., 2009). Validity is a property of the instrument in question. For a test to be valid, the provider utilizing the instrument must understand how the construct is operationally defined to best interpret the score. How scores are interpreted and used is an essential part of a test's validity. For example, some scores can be used to determine a person's current status on a criterion or their current level of functioning. Scores can also be used to predict future performance or behaviors. If the scores on the instruments allow the provider to clearly conceptualize status or predict future behavior, then the test is likely to be valid. Test scores can also be used for placement or classification and again the degree of validity of the test scores is correctly sorting individuals into different groups (Urbina, 2004). Attention to various types of validity as well as reliability as reported in test manuals and the literature is an important step in the selection, administration, and interpretation process.

Use of Instruments With Multicultural Populations

The utilization of assessment instruments with minority populations continues to fuel much research in the literature. In the United States, the minority population comprises one third of the total population and continues to grow exponentially (Underwood & Rawles, 2002). When considering what tests to utilize as part of the assessment process, multicultural issues should be at the forefront of the provider's decision-making process. Cultural identity can influence thoughts, feelings, and behaviors in unique ways, and cultural influence can vary based on how strongly the individual identifies with his or her culture or ethnic group of origin. Culture can be explored as part of the clinical interview. There are also several formal assessment instruments that examine the degree to which an individual may identify with the features of his or her culture. Although there is often variation within cultural or ethnic groups, these instruments attempt to highlight commonalities and could supplement conversation about the topic (Groth-Marnat, 2009). For African Americans, the African American Acculturation Scale (Landrine & Klonoff, 1994) is a culturally sensitive tool deemed useful in the literature. The Asian Values Scale (Kim, Atkinson, & Yang, 1999) has been utilized for Asian American cultural groups. For Hispanic or Latinos from Mexico, the Acculturation Rating Scale for Mexican Americans (Cuellar, Arnold, & Maldonado, 1995) can be utilized. Finally, Native Americans and Alaska Natives can complete the Northern Plains Bicultural Immersion Scale (Allen, 1998) to examine acculturation. Although these types of instruments are not always necessary, they can provide a baseline for further conversation and help determine if specific assessment instruments will be useful within the cultural context of the client.

In addition to level of identity with culture, there are other factors to consider when selecting instruments for clients different from the reference group. If English is not their native language, the provider may need to look for an instrument available in their native tongue or assess language skills to determine if they are at an appropriate level to make the results meaningful. Additionally, the provider may need to determine if the construct being measured is conceptualized in a similar manner within the culture. An example of this might be the concept of family, which can vary from blood relatives to neighbors or close friends based on cultural norms (Groth-Marnat, 2009). Furthermore, the provider will need to conduct his or her own research to determine if there is research with the instrument and the particular cultural group of the client. Score interpretation can vary greatly based on cultural norms. For example, some groups have higher or lower cutoff scores for somatic complaints on clinical scales within the Minnesota Multiphasic Personality Inventory (MMPI), as it is more common to present with physical symptoms in response to psychological distress in some cultures. Ultimately, it is the provider who is responsible for ensuring that test scores are not unduly biased by limitations related to a cultural or ethnic group. If there are no alternatives, any interpretation made from a test that is not culturally sensitive should be done cautiously (Urbina, 2004).

Test Administration

When administering psychological screening and assessment instruments, providers need to be adequately prepared. For example, the testing environment needs to be carefully attended to. Any possible distractions should be eliminated, and there should be adequate light and proper ventilation. There should be adequate space within the test environment for the test taker to feel comfortable. Additionally, the provider should follow the guidelines set forth in the testing manuals with regard to required supplies (pencil, computer) and time. Depending on the measure, it may also be important for the provider to be aware of any scripted directions or limitations in providing additional explanations. It becomes particularly important to mimic testing conditions when using instruments that are norm referenced, as this can introduce a degree of error into the analysis and could affect the results. While these details can seem minute, they can have a large impact on the test taker's performance and, if neglected, can introduce a degree of error that can affect outcomes of not only assessment but also treatment (Urbina, 2004).

PHASE 3: ANALYSIS

Once all tests and procedures have been completed, the provider must begin to analyze the information that has been gathered (Merrell, 2003). First, all instruments need to be scored based on each individual test's procedures. When available, computerized scoring programs are often provided by publishers and help make this process easier. Sometimes, reports with results are also available that can be used as part of interpretation. When scoring by hand, providers should be vigilant and avoid unnecessary error. This may require double checking any hand-scored forms to ensure accuracy (Urbina, 2004). This is also the phase where results are compiled together into a meaningful profile that can be explained to the client as well as used in treatment planning. Here, the original problems are compared with the data and any additions or deletions are made. For example, contributing factors such as personality variables may have been identified, which were not fully conceptualized during the clinical interview. The provider has the opportunity to also consider any data that are still missing and if additional testing or methods need to be utilized to complete the clinical picture. If needed, a clinical report is constructed at this stage for inclusion in the client's file (Grisso & Underwood, 2004). Although there is no single, agreed-on way of writing a clinical report, there are important elements to include (Groth-Marnat, 2009). Table 8.4 presents one

format for writing a psychological report for an adolescent client.

To provide analyses of tests, often the provider will need additional training. Such training could come from graduate-level courses in assessment and appraisal and professional training activities. Additionally, some providers might develop a consultative relationship with an expert psychometrician to receive supervision and consultation on test administration, analyses, interpretation, and report writing (Grisso & Underwood, 2004).

PHASE 4: SOLUTION AND EVALUATION

Now, the provider must use the information gathered throughout the assessment process to complete a treatment plan and begin therapeutic work (Merrell, 2003). Depending on the setting, the provider may be the clinician who will conduct the counseling or the client may be referred to someone else. Regardless, in this phase, the provider has two main objectives. The first is to inform the adolescent and his or her family about the results of the assessment process and make treatment recommendations. Then, together with the client and his or her family a treatment plan will be constructed. The provider must also decide how progress will be assessed and include ongoing assessment as part of the treatment plan. Because testing provides only one source of data, providers should include data gathered from the clinical interview as well as any other sources when presenting findings. Although testing provides a wealth of information, the provider should always keep in mind that assessment is a means to an end and that the clear purpose is identifying problems in an adolescent's life that leads to solutions (Groth-Marnat, 2009).

EVIDENCE-BASED SCREENING AND ASSESSMENT INSTRUMENTS FOR ADOLESCENTS

In the remaining part of the chapter, various assessment instruments used with adolescents are

Table 8.4   General Format for a Psychological Report

Organization Name

Psychological Report

Name:

Age (date of birth):

Sex:

Ethnicity:

Date of report:

Name of provider:

Referred by:

Referral question:

Evaluation procedures:

Behavioral observations:

Background or relevant history:

Medical:

Developmental:

Family:

Educational:

Test Results:

Impressions and interpretations:

Summary and recommendations:

Thank you and contact information:

Signature line with credential

Source. Groth-Marnat (2009).

summarized. While there are numerous tests that could be utilized, those that demonstrate sound psychometric properties and clinical utility within the current literature are emphasized (Grisso & Underwood, 2004). Providers are urged to seek additional training on any instruments that they wish to utilize with adolescent populations. Whether utilizing screening, assessment, or both with adolescents, the provider should be aware of and utilize evidence-based instruments. According to the National Institutes of Mental Health,

evidence-based instruments have met rigorous research criteria. For example, an instrument should have been utilized in a minimum of two control group studies by two different researchers. A manual for administration and scoring must be provided, as well as training for clinicians utilizing the instrument. Validity and reliability data must also be adequate. Results from any studies utilizing the instruments must also show significance and clinical utility ((Underwood, Warren, Talbott, Jackson, & Dailey, 2014).

Screening

Before or after the clinical interview, screening may be conducted to identify problems or concerns across several different domains. With adolescents, there are several "gold standard" screening instruments that have good reliability and validity. When selecting a screening instrument, providers are encouraged to consider factors such as culture, gender, referral source, developmental level, and prior diagnoses. Screening is not used for diagnosis but is a useful process to highlight possible concerns in functioning. Results from screening should be utilized to determine further assessment procedures (Grisso & Underwood, 2004).

Screening for Mental Health Disorders

While there are numerous screening instruments available to detect risk of mental health concerns in adolescence, a good screening tool has several characteristics. For instance, the instrument should be brief and easy to administer and score. Typically, they should take less than 15 minutes to complete (Grisso & Underwood, 2004). Screening instruments must also have high sensitivity as well as high specificity, as these tools are utilized to identify those in high-risk categories (Pietsch, Allgaier, Frühe, Hoyler, Rohde, & Schulte-Körne, 2013). Typically, mental health screening instruments in adolescence seek to identify youth who have risk factors for psychopathology, such as depression, anxiety, substance abuse, and suicidal ideation (Husky, McGuire, Flynn, Chrostowski, & Olfson, 2009). Some tools also include other psychosocial factors, such as concerns about home environment, education/employment, and sexual behaviors (Hopper, Woo, Sharwood, Babl, & Long, 2012). Most screening instruments are meant to be self-reports, with the adolescents providing their input, as opposed to many assessment instruments that rely on feedback from other sources (Patalay, Deighton, Fonagy, Vostanis, & Wolpert, 2014).

Screening instruments can be utilized to identify specific mental health concerns, such as depression, or a wide array of symptoms. For general risk of psychopathology across many categories of diagnoses, several instruments have demonstrated high utility in the literature. One is the Diagnostic Predictive Scales-8 (DPS-8; National Institutes of Mental Health, Lucas et al., 2001) an 84-item computerized self-report specifically for adolescents between the ages of 9 and 18. The scale is modeled after the National Institutes of Mental Health's Diagnostic Interview Schedule for Children-IV. Administration takes approximately 10 minutes, and adolescents can hear the questions through earphones and also read them on screen. Questions examine suicidal ideation, depression, substance use, anxiety disorders, social phobia, and obsessive-compulsive disorder. The DPS-8 also measures the magnitude of impairment the adolescents feel as a result of their symptoms (Husky, Miller, McGuire, Flynn, & Olfson, 2011). In several studies, the DPS-8 has demonstrated sensitivity ranging from 72% to 100% and specificity ranging from 60% to 100% (Roberts, Stuart, & Lam, 2008). The DPS-8 can be utilized in many diverse settings where a computer and Internet are available.

The Columbia Health Screen (Brown & Grumet, 2009) is another assessment tool that can be utilized to identify mental health symptoms in adolescents. This 14-item paper-and-pencil test is designed to identify the presence of suicidal ideation, suicide attempts, health problems, and emotional problems, including depression, anxiety, irritability, social withdrawal, and substance abuse. A 5-point Likert-type scale is utilized to rate the severity of each symptom, and the questions generally refer to the last 3 months in the adolescent's life (Husky et al., 2009). Additionally, there are several mental health screenings for adolescents that are utilized primarily in pediatric or primary care settings. One such instrument is the Pediatric Symptom Checklist-Youth Report (Jellinek et al., 1988), which is a 35-question self-report tool for identifying behavioral and psychosocial problems. There is also a parent version that can be completed in addition to the adolescent version (Jackson Allen & McGuire, 2011).

Screening for Depression

Due to the prevalence of several disorders in the general population, screening instruments for specific disorders have also been developed. Depressive disorders are one example with up to 25% of adolescents endorsing symptoms of depression by age 18. Depression is associated with poor social functioning, academic problems, and higher risk of suicidal ideation and attempts among youth (Allgaier, Pietsch, Frühe, Sigl-Glöckner, & Schulte-Körne, 2012). There are several specific instruments used to screen for depression among adolescents. The Children's Depression Inventory (CDI; Kovacs, 1984) was adapted from items on the Beck Depression Inventory, specifically for children and adolescents. The CDI can be administered in 15 minutes or less and contains five subscales that address (1) negative mood, (2) interpersonal problems, (3) ineffectiveness, (4) anhedonia, and (5) negative self-esteem. The age range for the CDI is 7 to 17 years and is based on the functioning during the last 2 weeks (Timbremont, Braet, & Dreessen, 2004). The CDI has been translated into 23 languages and has shown high reliability and validity with diverse ethnic and cultural groups (Huang & Dong, 2014).

The Reynolds Adolescent Depression Scale-2 (RADS-2; Reynolds, 2002) is another self-report instrument consisting of 30 items that focuses on four domains of depressive disorders: (1) dysphoric mood, (2) anhedonia/negative affect, (3) negative self-evaluation, and (4) somatic symptoms. A total score is computed with higher scores indicating higher levels of depressive symptoms. The range of possible scores is 30 to 120 with a clinical cutoff score of 76 (Gutierrez & Osman, 2009). In the primary care settings, several specific instruments for depression are also utilized. The Patient Health Questionnaire for Adolescents (Spitzer, Kroenke, Williams, & Patient Health Questionnaire Primary Care Study Group, 1999) is one such tool. A sensitivity of approximately 73% and a specificity of around 94% have been demonstrated for diagnoses of major depression (Allgaier et al., 2012). The Center for Epidemiologic Studies Depression Scale is also frequently utilized in primary care settings with adolescents and has high sensitivity (90%) as well as high specificity (75%). This is a self-report measure that takes less than 20 minutes to complete and can be scored relatively quickly (Pietsch et al., 2013).

Screening for Suicide Risk

Suicide risk is another specific screening area of particular importance in adolescence. Suicide is the fourth leading cause of death among adolescents of ages 10 to 24, with 13.8% of adolescents reporting serious suicidal ideation, 10.9% making a detailed plan, and 6.3% attempting suicide in the previous 12 months (Erickson & Abel, 2013). Additionally, approximately half of the adolescents with suicidal ideation do not receive mental health services because they are not identified as "at risk" (Husky et al., 2009). There are several valid and reliable screenings for suicide risk that can be utilized with adolescents. The Suicidal Ideation Questionnaire (Reynolds, 1988) is a 30-item self-report measure that measures the frequency of suicidal thoughts. A severity of suicidal ideation score is calculated with higher scores indicating greater frequency (Gutierrez & Osman, 2009). The Risk of Suicide Questionnaire-Revised (Osman et al., 2001) is a verbally administered four-question derivative of the Suicidal Ideation Questionnaire that can also be used for rapid screening of suicidal ideation, especially in primary care settings (Hopper et al., 2012).

Screening for Anxiety

Anxiety symptoms are extremely prevalent in childhood and adolescence, although at times it is difficult to differentiate it from other disorders, such as depression or attention-deficit/hyperactivity disorder. Therefore, screening instruments for anxiety in adolescence must have a high degree of sensitivity as well as specificity. The Revised Children's Manifest Anxiety Scale (RCMAS;

Reynolds & Richmond, 1985) has been in use for several decades and has demonstrated good utility in the literature. The RCMAS consists of 37 items that measure three dimensions of anxiety: (1) physiological anxiety, (2) worry/oversensitivity, and (3) social concerns. A total anxiety score is calculated, with higher scores indicating greater anxiety. There is also a lie scale that measures possible attempts at denial of negative characteristics (Seligman, Ollendick, Langley, & Baldacci, 2004). The RCMAS has shown good reliability and validity with European American, African American, and Mexican American adolescents (Varela & Biggs, 2006).

Screening for Substance Abuse

Co-occurring substance abuse disorders have also been identified as problematic in adolescence. Youth who abuse substances are at greater risk of academic problems, are frequently involved with the juvenile justice system, and are at increased risk of depressive disorders in adulthood (Perera-Diltz & Perry, 2011). Adolescence is an ideal point for intervention. The Adolescent Substance Abuse Subtle Screening Inventory-A2 (SASSI-A2; Miller & Lazowski, 2001) is one brief instrument that can be used to screen for substance-related problems. The SASSI-A2 is a self-report, paper-and-pencil measure that takes less than 20 minutes to complete. One strength of the SASSI-A2 is that it can still yield clinically relevant information, even if the adolescent is not willing to be open and honest about his or her use of substances. The SASSI-A2 also recognizes the multifaceted nature of substance abuse, including questions regarding family dysfunction, exposure to abuse or violence, and affiliation with substance-using peers with questions addressing these issues (Perera-Diltz & Perry, 2011). The SASSI-A2 is a highly useful screening tool for substance abuse problems in adolescence.

Screening for Cognitive Functioning

Cognitive abilities may also need to be part of a screening to identify concerns with functioning in this domain. There are several measures that can be administered quickly and provide information regarding cognitive functioning. One example is the Peabody Picture Vocabulary Test-III (Dunn & Dunn, 1997), which can be utilized beginning at 2 years of age through adulthood. The test is often used for two purposes: (1) to determine achievement on receptive vocabulary as well as (2) to serve as a screening test for verbal ability. Typically, an adolescent will need approximately 11 to 12 minutes to complete it, and raw scores are converted to standard scores with an average of 100 and a standard deviation of 15 (Bell, Lassiter, Matthews, & Hutchinson, 2001). The Wechsler Abbreviated Scale of Intelligence-II (Wechsler, 2011) is used on adolescents to obtain an estimate of verbal comprehension abilities as well as perceptual reasoning abilities. The Wechsler Abbreviated Scale of Intelligence-II can also be used to obtain estimates of IQ (intelligence quotient) scores rapidly and efficiently when administration of a full battery is not feasible (Grisso & Underwood, 2004). Although cognitive screenings will vary based on setting and needs, having several readily available tools can be useful for determining any needs for further assessment.

Screening Special Populations: Juvenile Justice

For adolescents involved in the juvenile justice system, co-occurring mental health disorders are extremely common and may be overlooked (Grisso & Underwood, 2004). For providers working with this population of adolescents, screening for mental health disorders becomes imperative, given the risk of problems in functioning in adulthood as well as recidivism. Common disorders in the juvenile sex offender population include anxiety disorders, depressive disorders, psychosis, attention-deficit/hyperactivity disorder, behavior disorders such as conduct disorder, and substance abuse disorders (Hempel, Buck, Cima, & van Marle, 2013; Underwood et al., 2014). The Massachusetts Youth Screening Instrument-Version 2

(MAYSI-2; Grisso & Barnum, 2006) was designed specifically for use with juvenile justice populations to identify those in need of immediate mental health treatment (i.e., suicidality) as well as to identify underlying mental health concerns. The MAYSI-2 has seven subscales: (1) Alcohol/Drug Use, (2) Angry-Irritable, (3) Depressed-Anxious, (4) Somatic Complaints, (5) Suicidal Ideation, (6) Thought Disturbance, and (7) Traumatic Experiences (Ford, Chapman, Pearson, Borum, & Wolpaw, 2008). The MAYSI-2 has shown good reliability and validity and can be quickly administered and scored, making it an ideal instrument when working with adolescents in the juvenile justice system (Gilbert, Grande, Hallman, & Underwood, 2014).

Assessment

Assessment, as previously discussed, requires greater time, is more expensive, and often requires specialized training as opposed to screening. Assessment instruments have the advantage of providing a greater quantity of information that can be used in identifying clinical concerns (Grisso & Underwood, 2004). The following are assessment instruments that can be used on adolescents.

Assessing for Mental Health Disorders

Symptoms of mental health disorders are often a primary reason that adolescents are brought to a provider for treatment. Issues related to specific diagnoses as well as personality factors can have a profound effect on treatment outcome and can be useful to understand for the provider. One assessment instrument utilized to assist with diagnosis is the Adolescent Diagnostic Interview (Winters & Henley, 1993). This instrument provides diagnostic information related directly to the *Diagnostic and Statistical Manual of Mental Disorders*, fifth edition (*DSM-5*; American Psychiatric Association, 2013) and is a semistructured interview lasting approximately 45 to 60 minutes for youth between the ages of 12

and 18 years. The Adolescent Diagnostic Interview assesses the effect of psychosocial stressors, school and interpersonal functioning, and cognitive impairment. It also assists with identifying, referring, and treating adolescents with substance abuse problems (Grisso & Underwood, 2004). The Adolescent Psychopathology Scale (APS; Reynolds, 1998) is a 346-item (long-form) self-report instrument, which examines psychopathology, personality, and social–emotional problems. The APS is used to assess psychological problems and behaviors that may interfere with an adolescent's psychological adaptation and personal competence. Some specific disorders that the APS highlights include conduct disorder, adjustment disorder, sleep disorders, posttraumatic stress disorder, major depression, and substance abuse disorders (Merrell, 2003).

The Brief Psychiatric Rating Scale for Children (Overall & Pfefferbaum, 1982) can also be utilized with juveniles to identify mental health disorders. The Brief Psychiatric Rating Scale for Children yields ratings of severity for a variety of psychiatric symptoms and a total symptom severity score (Timmons-Mitchell et al., 1997). Administration takes 20 to 30 minutes and provides information related to somatic concerns, anxiety, depressive mood, hostility, feelings of inferiority, peculiar fantasies, and delusions (Grisso & Underwood, 2004). The Child and Adolescent Needs and Strengths-Mental Health (Lyons, Sokol, Khalsa, Lee, & Lewis, 2000) is another instrument useful in classifying psychopathology. This assesses children and adolescents prospectively and retrospectively for systems related to the needs and strengths of child and family. The Child and Adolescent Needs and Strengths-Mental Health provides a structured assessment of mental health challenges along dimensions relevant to case service decision making. It identifies service gaps and is helpful in developing community-based treatment plans (Lyons et al., 2000).

The Child Behavioral Checklist (Achenbach, 1991) has three separate forms that are completed by (1) the adolescent, (2) a parent, and (3) a teacher. The youth self-report examines overall mental, emotional, and adaptational functioning. The parent and teacher forms ask similar questions from a different point of view, which is a strength of this measure (Achenbach, 1991). Another measure that utilizes other sources of information is the Connor's Rating Scale-Revised (CRS-R), an interviewer- and a caretaker-rated questionnaire designed to measure a wide range of problem behaviors. The CRS-R measures dimensions rather than categories of symptoms and includes school/employment, medical, psychosomatic problems, social relations, and family and relationships. The CRS-R can be utilized through age 17 (Connors, 1997). The Diagnostic Interview Schedule for Children-Version-IV is an individually administered, structured interview that is designed to supply information needed to make diagnoses according to the *DSM-5* diagnostic categories (Shaffer, Fisher, Lucas, Dulcan, & Schwab-Stone, 2000). The interview is organized into six diagnostic sections: (1) anxiety disorders, (2) mood disorders, (3) disruptive disorders, (4) substance use disorders, (5) schizophrenia, and (6) miscellaneous disorders (Grisso & Underwood, 2004).

The Problem-Oriented Screening Instrument for Teenagers is also a useful instrument in assessing adolescents—a 139-item, yes–no, self-administered instrument that measures 10 problem areas, including mental health and substance abuse. The Problem-Oriented Screening Instrument for Teenagers includes information on the history of juvenile justice and mental health contacts, health care utilization, and current stressors. It is designed to quickly identify problems in areas requiring further assessment (McLellan & Dembo, 1993). The Symptom Checklist-90-Revised is a frequently used assessment instrument for adults that can also be used for adolescents aged 13 to 18 years (Grisso & Underwood, 2004). A 90-item, self-report measure, the Symptom Checklist-90-Revised can identify current psychological symptom patterns and levels of symptomatology. Each item is rated on a 5-point scale of distress, and the measure covers nine primary symptom dimensions: (1) somatization, (2) obsessive-compulsive, (3) interpersonal sensitivity, (4) depression, (5) anxiety, (6) hostility,

(7) phobic anxiety, (8) paranoid ideation, and (9) psychoticism (Derogatis, 1994).

Assessing Personality

Personality constructs can be an important factor from both a needs- and a strengths-based perspective in working with adolescents. Personality is pervasive and difficult to change, and can positively or negatively affect treatment outcome (Groth-Marnat, 2009). There are several instruments designed to assess personality in adolescence. The MMPI-Adolescent (MMPI-A; Butcher et al., 1994) is an extensive self-report, true-and-false inventory that is used to broadly assess clinical symptomatology and personality characteristics. The MMPI-A uses familiar categories in describing personality and behavioral characteristics that are most associated with degrees of psychopathology. The MMPI-A is appropriate for adolescents aged 14 and up and can take from 60 to 90 minutes to complete. Clinical scales include hypochondriasis, depression, hysteria, psychopathic deviate, masculinity–femininity, paranoia, psychasthenia, schizophrenia, hypomania, and social introversion. Additional subscales are also available (Butcher et al., 1994).

The Millon Adolescent Clinical Inventory (MACI; Millon, 1993) is another frequently used personality instrument. The test includes 160 true-and-false items in 31 subscales and is appropriate for adolescents between the ages of 13 and older. The MACI measures clinical syndromes and is useful in identifying personality dysfunctions. Personality patterns identified include introversive, inhibited, doleful, submissive, dramatizing, egotistic, unruly, forceful, conforming, oppositional, self-demeaning, and borderline tendency. The clinical syndromes measured include eating dysfunctions, substance abuse proneness, delinquent predisposition, impulsive propensity, anxious feelings, depressive affect, and suicidal tendency. The MACI also includes a reliability scale to determine patterns of disclosure, desirability, and debasement. Additionally, concerns such as identity diffusion, self-devaluation, body disapproval, sexual discomfort, peer insecurity, social insensitivity, family discord, and childhood abuse can also be identified (Millon, 1993).

The Sixteen Personality Factor-Fifth Edition Quest
releva
based
inclu(

-
-
-
-
-
-
-
-
-
-
-
-
- Self-discipline (undisciplined vs. self-disciplined)
- Tension (relaxed vs. tense) (Grisso & Underwood, 2004)

Cognitive Assessment

When cognitive testing is needed or concerns with functioning are suspected, there are several instruments that can be used with adolescents that have shown good utility. Intelligence testing can be time-consuming and often requires special training. The Stanford-Binet Intelligence Scale-Fifth Edition (Roid, 2003) is the most well-known of intelligence tests and is a standardized test that assesses intelligence and cognitive abilities in children and young

adults. The age range for the Stanford-Binet is 2 to 23 years. A downside to this test is the need for doctoral-level preparation, which is recommended by the test publisher. The Wechsler Intelligence Scale for Children-Fourth Edition (WISC-IV; Wechsler, 2003) can be administered by a master's-level clinician after additional training. The WISC-III provides a scale IQ score and has been updated to include cultural and societal norms. The Vineland Adaptive Behavior Scales-Second Edition (Sparrow, Cicchetti, & Balla, 2005) are designed to assess social and personal sufficiency in daily situations. The Vineland's comprehensive content makes it useful in determining intellectual disability. This instrument comes in an interview edition survey (297 items), an interview edition expanded form (577 items), and a classroom edition (244 items). Constructs measured include communication, daily living, socialization, motor skills, adaptive behavior, and maladaptive behavior (Grisso & Underwood, 2004).

Other Assessments

There is a wide range of other assessment measures that can be utilized with adolescents. For adolescents up to the age of 16 who may have been exposed to a traumatic event, the Trauma Symptom Checklist for Children (Briere, 1996) can be useful in differentiating between posttraumatic stress disorder and other disorders with similar symptoms. A 54-item, self-report instrument, the Trauma Symptom Checklist for Children is designed to evaluate acute and chronic posttraumatic symptoms. When assessing relationships with family of origin, the Relationship with Family of Origin Scale (REFAMOS) can be a useful tool. As a standardized interview, the REFAMOS provides assessment information on relationships between young people (i.e., ages 15–35 years) and their parents (Hill, Mackie, Banner, Kondryn, & Blair, 1999). While most assessment is deficit based, measuring resiliency can be beneficial for adolescents as well. The Resiliency Attitude

Scale is one option. The scale provides a brief self-report of resiliencies and measures persistence in working through difficulties. Constructs examined include insight, independence, relationships, initiative, creativity, humor, and morality (Biscoe & Harris, 1994). Complete the tasks in Exercise 8.3 to explore other assessments of interests.

IMPLICATIONS FOR COUNSELING ADOLESCENTS

Clinical Review of Case

As an ethical provider, Scott is aware of which instruments he is trained to administer and which he has appropriate access to. Scott, taking into consideration information gleaned from the clinical interview, selected the following screening and assessment instruments for Stefania:

Diagnostic Predictive Scales-8 (DPS-8)

Reynolds Adolescent Depression Scale-2 (RADS-2)

The Revised Children's Manifest Anxiety Scale (RCMAS)

The Adolescent Substance Abuse Subtle Screening Inventory-A2 (SASSI-A2)

The Wechsler Intelligence Scale for Children-Third Edition (WISC-III, Wechsler, 1991)

Relationship with Family of Origin Scale (REFAMOS)

Once Stefania had completed these instruments, Scott began to analyze the data available, putting it into a report format that could be shared with others involved in the case. For Stefania, the following information became important to note:

- Stefania scored in the clinical range for depression, demonstrating a wide range of symptoms. Scott noted that relieving symptoms of depression could be one clinical focus.

- Stefania also scored in the clinical range for anxiety. Scott noted that Stefania's anxiety was not situation specific but appeared to be more generalized. Coping with anxiety was also noted as a possible treatment focus.

- Stefania's use of substances included not just marijuana but also alcohol. Although her use did not appear to be extremely problematic to her, she reported that others, including friends, saw her use as a concern, indicating the need for possible intervention.

Exercise 8.3

Assessment Search

1. After looking over the list of screening and assessment instruments are there several instruments you would like to learn more about? List them here.

2. Based on a quick Internet search, answer the following for each instrument you identified:

    a. Is it a privately published instrument or in the public domain?

    b. What is the level of training needed?

    c. Where can you get the needed training?

    d. Are there any studies with a reliability coefficient or other data on reliability or validity?

    e. Are there any other details about the instrument worth noting?

- Stefania's IQ score according to the WISC-III was slightly below average but still within normal range. Scott concludes that academic difficulties at present may be due more to psychological dysfunction.

- Stefania reported a problematic relationship with her mother Maria and with her younger siblings. As part of a comprehensive treatment plan, building healthier relationships may be warranted.

Once Scott had completed a report, he spoke to Stefania and her parents regarding treatment. Both Maria and David agreed that depression and substance abuse were concerns for them as well. They were unaware of her anxiety but state that they would also like this to be part of treatment. Scott discussed family interventions in addition to individual sessions with Stefania, and both Maria and David agreed. Stefania also agreed that she would like to feel happier and less worried. She continued to state that she did not feel that her substance abuse was problematic. However, this was included as part of her treatment plan given her elevated scores on several of the assessment measures as well as concerns from her parents.

Once the treatment plan was completed, Scott decided that he would utilize the RADS-2, the RCMAS, and the SASSI-A2 to help monitor treatment progress. Now that you have read the entire case of Stefania, complete Exercise 8.4 to discuss case implications before proceeding to the next section in this chapter (see Exercise 8.4).

Clinical Implications

Screening and assessment are the first steps in the evaluation and treatment of adolescent populations and their families seeking mental health services, and therefore, competent providers will be aware of the many nuances of this process (Grisso & Underwood, 2004). The Council for Accreditation of Counseling and Related Educational Programs standards have been met across several different areas when providers develop competence in screening and assessment of

---

Exercise 8.4

Implications—Stefania

1. Scott selected several instruments to use with Stefania for further assessment. As you study the list, write several reasons why he may have selected each particular instrument.
    a. Diagnostic Predictive Scales-8 (DPS-8)
    b. Reynolds Adolescent Depression Scale-2 (RADS-2)
    c. The Revised Children's Manifest Anxiety Scale (RCMAS)
    d. The Adolescent Substance Abuse Subtle Screening Inventory-A2 (SASSI-A2)
    e. The Millon Adolescent Clinical Inventory (MACI)
    f. The Wechsler Intelligence Scale for Children-Third Edition (WISC-III)
    g. Relationship with Family of Origin Scale (REFAMOS)
2. Would you have selected different instruments? Which ones would you have utilized and why?
3. Do you feel like Stefania's treatment plan adequately addresses her presenting issues?
4. How might you evaluate treatment progress in the case of Stefania?

adolescents. Specifically, basic concepts of standardized and nonstandardized testing, including norm-referenced and criterion-referenced instruments have been explored. Additionally, reliability and validity of assessment instruments have been explained, along with principles of test interpretation with diverse groups of adolescents. Ethical strategies for selecting, administering, and interpreting results have also been discussed. Finally, the importance of research and the use of evidence-based measures were specifically considered as part of the multimodal assessment process.

Assessment and screening of adolescents is an important beginning step in treatment. It provides valuable knowledge and information for the therapeutic team as well as others who may be invested in the outcome. As there are many instruments that can be utilized, the providers are encouraged to familiarize themselves with various tests and determine which are most valuable for the clients they serve. At clinical sites, the provider should ask a supervising provider which instruments are used and obtain the necessary training on those that are available. Providers can also seek supervision and training opportunities for specific instruments that they would like to learn more about. Through continuing education, extra coursework, and clinical placements, providers can learn more about assessment with adolescents and obtain the training needed to enhance the treatment process.

Application of Ethics

There are several important ethical considerations related to screening and assessment with adolescents. Mental health professionals are guided by ethical codes maintained through professional organizations, such as the American Counseling Association (2014), the American Psychological Association (2010), the National Association of Social Workers (2008), and the American Association for Marriage and Family Therapy (2011), among others. As previously noted, anytime a provider is working with a minor client, his or her parents must give consent for treatment. Parents also have access to all records or session content, which limits confidentiality. In considering screening and assessment instruments, providers must pay special attention to required training and levels of preparation. For example, some instruments require doctoral-level preparation, while others can be utilized by master's level or even by paraprofessionals. It is the responsibility of the provider to ensure that they have the qualifications and necessary training before administering and interpreting any tests. Additionally, providers must obtain tests through the appropriate channels, purchasing those that are copyrighted (Grisso & Underwood, 2004).

When considering psychological testing, results can reveal characteristics, traits, or diagnoses that can affect the adolescent in diverse ways. In choosing a particular instrument, the provider must be certain that the information will be used for the intended purpose and that any additional information about the client can be safeguarded. Because there are limits to confidentiality with adolescents, it is important that the provider include a discussion related to possible testing outcomes with the parent or guardian during the informed consent process (Urbina, 2004). For example, testing which provides an IQ score may have positive benefits, such as helping an adolescent qualify for special education services. However, a personality instrument could indicate undesirable patterns of personality, which, when known, could influence negative attitudes about the adolescent from parents, teachers, or others in the community. These are important aspects of the assessment process with adolescents to consider.

Summary

The screening and assessment of adolescents as part of a comprehensive evaluation is necessary for treatment planning and positive outcomes. No matter how providers receive referrals, the assessment process allows the provider to hone in on specific problems and concerns. Based on these, the provider then selects assessment modalities to obtain needed information. Often, this includes utilizing formal screening or assessment instruments. In selecting tests to be administered, the provider must be aware of the psychometric properties of the instrument, including reliability and validity, the population with which the test was normalized, and clinical utility. Above all, the provider should select screening and assessment instruments needs based on the adolescent's presenting problems. While there are numerous screening and assessment instruments that can be utilized with adolescents, those presented are most frequently used with adolescents. Once screening and assessment have been completed, the provider can use the data to help formulate a treatment plan and can continue to use assessment to gauge treatment success. To provide adequate screening and assessment of mental health and other related needs of adolescents, providers must have access to relevant instruments and procedures designed for these purposes. Screening and assessment methods must not only meet various psychometric standards but they must also be adaptable to the needs and circumstances of the adolescent and his or her family.

Keystones

- Screening and assessment constitute a problem-solving process through which the adolescent's needs and concerns are identified so solutions can be generated.

- Screening and assessment are two separate processes.

- Screening involves identifying areas of concern, including depression, anxiety, trauma, thought disorder, suicide, substance use, and other mental health disorders.

- Assessment is an in-depth process that takes more time and more training on the part of the provider. Often, longer psychological tests are administered for additional information.

- As part of the problem-solving process, a clinical interview is conducted with the adolescent, family, and others.

- When screening or assessing adolescents, issues of confidentiality and informed consent require additional attention.

- When selecting instruments, providers should be aware of the purpose of the instrument, the psychometric properties, and usefulness.

- Reliability refers to the trustworthiness of the instrument and is measured by a reliability coefficient. A coefficient above .80 indicates high reliability.

- Validity refers to the extent to which scores are accurate for their intended purpose.

- Providers need to understand how the tests were normalized in order to ensure that they are using the tests and interpreting the scores properly.

- When working with multicultural populations, instruments need to be carefully monitored for applicability or interpreted with caution.

- Once data have been gathered from screening and assessment, the provider must take the information and develop working hypotheses to present to the adolescents and their families.

- Together, the adolescent, his or her family, and the provider will use screening and assessment information to formulate a treatment plan.

- The provider will continue to utilize screening or assessment instruments to measure treatment progress.

References

Achenbach, T. M. (1991). *Manual for the child behavior checklist.* Burlington: University of Vermont, Department of Psychiatry.

Allen, J. J. (1998). Personality assessment with American Indians and Alaskan Natives: Instrument considerations and service delivery style. *Journal of Personality Assessment, 70,* 16–42.

Allgaier, A.-K., Pietsch, K., Frühe, B., Sigl-Glöckner, J., & Schulte-Körne, G. (2012). Screening for depression in adolescents: Validity of the Patient Health Questionnaire in pediatric care. *Depression and Anxiety, 29,* 906–913.

American Association for Marriage and Family Therapy. (2011). *AAMFT code of ethics.* Alexandria, VA: Author.

American Counseling Association. (2014). *2014 ACA code of ethics (as approved by the ACA governing council)*. Alexandria, VA: Author.

American Psychiatric Association. (2013). *Diagnostic and statistical manual of mental disorders* (5th ed.). Arlington, VA: Author.

American Psychological Association. (2010). *Ethical principles of psychologists and code of conduct*. Washington, DC: Author.

Bell, N. L., Lassiter, K. S., Matthews, T. D., & Hutchinson, M. B. (2001). Comparison of the Peabody Vocabulary Test-Third Edition and Wechsler Adult Intelligence Scale-Third Edition with university students. *Journal of Clinical Psychology, 57*(3), 417–422.

Berger, K. S. (2011). *The developing person through the life span* (8th ed.). New York, NY: Worth.

Biscoe, B., & Harris, B. (1994). *Resiliency Attitude Scale*. Oklahoma City, OK: Eagle Ridge Institute.

Boyle, M. H., Cunningham, C. E., Georgiades, K., Cullen, J., Racine, Y., & Pettingill, P. (2009). The Brief Child and Family Phone Interview (BCFPI): 2. Usefulness in screening for child and adolescent psychopathology. *Journal of Child Psychology and Psychiatry, 50*(4), 424–431. doi:10.1111/j.1469-7610.2008.01971.x

Briere, J. (1996). *Trauma Symptom Checklist for Children*. Odessa, FL: Psychological Assessment Resources.

Brown, M. M., & Grumet, J. G. (2009). School-based suicide prevention with African American youth in an urban setting. *Professional Psychology: Research and Practice, 40*(2), 111.

Butcher, J., William, C., Graham, J., Archer, R., Tellegen, A., Ben-Porath, V., & Kaemmer, B. (1994). *Manual for administration, scoring and interpretation: MMPI-A*. Minneapolis: University of Minnesota Press.

Cattell, R. B. (1990). Advances in Cattellian personality theory. In L. A. Pervin (Ed.), *Handbook of personality: Theory and research* (pp. 101–110). New York, NY: Guilford Press.

Connors, C. K. (1997). *The Connors Rating Scale-Revised user's guide*. North Tonawanda, NY: Multi-Health Systems.

Cuellar, I., Arnold, B., & Maldonado, R. (1995). Acculturation Rating Scale for Mexican Americans-III: A revision of the original ARSMA scale. *Hispanic Journal of Behavioral Science, 17*, 275–304.

Derogatis, L. R. (1994). *SCL-90-R: Administration, scoring and procedures manual* (3rd ed.). Minneapolis, MN: National Computer Systems.

Dunn, L. M., & Dunn, L. M. (1997). *Peabody Picture Vocabulary Test* (3rd ed.). Circle Pines, MN: American Guidance Services.

Erickson, A., & Abel, N. R. (2013). A high school provider's leadership in providing school-wide screenings for depression and enhancing suicide awareness. *Professional School Counseling, 16*(5), 283–289.

Ford, J. D., Chapman, J. F., Pearson, G., Borum, R., & Wolpaw, J. M. (2008). Psychometric status and clinical utility of the MAYSI-2 with girls and boys in juvenile detention. *Journal of Psychopathology and Behavioral Assessment, 30,* 87–99. doi:10.1007/s10862-007-9058-9

Gilbert, A., Grande, T., Hallman, J., & Underwood, L. (2014). Screening incarcerated juveniles using the MAYSI-2. *Journal of Correctional Health Care, 21*(1), 35–44. doi:10.1177/1078345814557788

Grisso, T., & Barnum, R. (2006). *Massachusetts Youth Screening Instrument, Version 2: MAYSI-2: User's Manual and Technical Report*. Worcester: University of Massachusetts Medical School.

Grisso, T., & Underwood, L. A. (2004). *Screening and assessing mental health and substance use disorders: A resource guide for juvenile justice practitioners*. Delmar, New York: National Center for Mental Health and Juvenile Justice Policy Research Associates.

Groth-Marnat, G. (2009). *Handbook of psychological assessment* (5th ed.). Hoboken, NJ: Wiley.

Gutierrez, P. M., & Osman, A. (2009). Getting the best return on your screening investment: An analysis of the Suicidal Ideation Questionnaire and Reynolds Adolescent Depression Scale. *School Psychology Review, 38*(2), 200–217.

Hempel, I., Buck, N., Cima, M., & van Marle, H. (2013). Review of risk assessment instruments for juvenile sex offenders: What is next? *International Journal of Offender Therapy and Comparative Criminology, 57*(2), 208–228. doi:10.1177/0306624X11428315

Hill, J., Mackie, E., Banner, L., Kondryn, H., & Blair, V. (1999). Relationship with Family of Origin Scale (REFAMOS): Interrater reliability and associations with childhood experiences. *Journal of Psychiatry, 175,* 565–578.

Hopper, S., Woo, J., Sharwood, L., Babl, F., & Long, E. (2012). Prevalence of suicidality in asymptomatic adolescents in the paediatric emergency department and utility of a screening tool. *Paediatric Emergency Medicine, 24,* 540–546. doi:10.1111/j.1742.6723.2012.01576.x

Huang, C., & Dong, N. (2014). Dimensionality of the Children's Depression Inventory: Meta-analysis of pattern matrices. *Journal of Child and Family Studies, 23,* 1182–1192. doi:10.1007/s10826-013-9779-1

Husky, M. M., McGuire, L., Flynn, L., Chrostowski, C., & Olfson, M. (2009). Correlates of help-seeking behavior among at-risk adolescents. *Child Psychiatry & Human Development, 40,* 15–24. doi: 10.1007/s10578-008-0107-d

Husky, M. M., Miller, K., McGuire, L., Flynn, L., & Olfson, M. (2011). Mental health screening of adolescents in pediatric practice. *Mental Health Screening, 38*(2), 159–169.

Ingram, B. (2006). *Clinical case formulations: Matching the integrative treatment plan to the client.* Hoboken, NJ: Wiley.

Jackson Allen, P., & McGuire, L. (2011). Incorporating mental health checkups into adolescent primary care visits. *Pediatric Nursing, 37*(3), 137–140.

Jellinek, M. S., Murphy, J. M., Robinson, J., Feins, A., Lamb, S., & Fenton, T. (1988). Pediatric Symptom Checklist: Screening school-age children for psychosocial dysfunction. *Journal of Pediatrics, 112*(2), 201–209.

Kim, B. S., Atkinson, D. R., & Yang, P. H. (1999). The Asian Values Scale: Development, factor analysis, validation, and reliability. *Journal of Counseling Psychology, 46,* 342–352.

Kovacs, M. (1984). The Children's Depression Inventory (CDI). *Psychopharmacology Bulletin, 21*(4), 995–998.

Landrine, H., & Klonoff, E. A. (1994). The African American Acculturation Scale: Development, reliability, and validity. *Journal of Black Psychology, 20,* 104–127.

Linden, A. (1998). *Mindworks: Unlock the promise within: NLP tools for building a better life.* New York, NY: Berkeley.

Lucas, C. P., Zhang, H., Fisher, P. W., Shaffer, D., Regier, D. A., Narrow, W. E., . . . Lahey, B. B. (2001). The DISC Predictive Scales (DPS): Efficiently screening for diagnoses. *Journal of the American Academy of Child & Adolescent Psychiatry, 40*(4), 443–449.

Lyons, J. S., Sokol, P. T., Khalsa, A., Lee, M., & Lewis, M. (2000). *Child and adolescent needs and strengths (CANS) manual.* Chicago, IL: Northwestern University, Institute for Health Services Research and Policy Studies.

McLellan, T., & Dembo, R. (1993). *Screening and assessment of alcohol and other drug abusing adolescents.* Rockville, MD: U.S. Department of Health and Human Services, Substance Abuse and Mental Health Services Administration, Center for Substance Abuse Treatment.

Merrell, K. (2003). *Behavioral, social, and emotional assessment of children and adolescents.* New York, NY: Lawrence Erlbaum.

Miller, F. G., & Lazowski, L. E. (2001). *The adolescent SASSI-A2 manual: Identifying substance use disorders.* Springville, IN: SASSI Institute.

Millon, T. M. (1993). *Millon Adolescent Clinical Inventory (MACI) manual.* Minneapolis, MN: National Computer Systems.

National Association of Social Workers. (2008). *NASW code of ethics* (Guide to the Everyday Professional Conduct of Social Workers). Washington, DC: Author.

Osman, A., Bagge, C. L., Gutierrez, P. M., Konick, L. C., Kopper, B. A., & Barrios, F. X. (2001). The Suicidal Behaviors Questionnaire-Revised (SBQ-R): Validation with clinical and nonclinical samples. *Assessment, 8*(4), 443–454.

Overall, J. E., & Pfefferbaum, B. (1982). The Brief Psychiatric Rating Scale for Children. *Psychopharmacology Bulletin, 18*(2), 10–16.

Patalay, P., Deighton, J., Fonagy, P., Vostanis, P., & Wolpert, M. (2014). Clinical validity of the Me and My School Questionnaire: A self-report mental health measure for children and adolescents. *Child and Adolescent Psychiatry and Mental Health, 8*(1), 17.

Perera-Diltz, D., & Perry, J. C. (2011). Screening for adolescent substance-related disorders using the SASSI-A2: Implications for non-reporting youth. *Journal of Addictions & Offender Counseling, 31,* 66–79.

Pietsch, K., Allgaier, A.-K., Frühe, B., Hoyler, A., Rohde, S., & Schulte-Körne, G. (2013). Screening for adolescent depression in paediatric care: Validity of a new brief version of the Center of Epidemiological Studies Depression

Scale. *Child and Adolescent Mental Health, 18*(2), 76–81. doi:10.1111/j.1475-3588.2012. 00650.x

Reynolds, C. R., & Richmond, B. O. (1985). *Revised Children's Manifest Anxiety Scale (RCMAS): Manual.* Los Angeles, CA: Western Psychological Services.

Reynolds, W. M. (1988). *Suicidal Ideation Questionnaire: Professional manual.* Odessa, FL: Psychological Assessment Resources.

Reynolds, W. M. (1998). *Adolescent Psychopathology Scale.* Melbourne, Victoria, Australia: Australian Council for Educational Research.

Reynolds, W. M. (2002). *Reynold's Adolescent Depression Scale: Professional manual* (2nd ed.). Lutz, FL: Psychological Assessment Resources.

Roberts, N., Stuart, H., & Lam, M. (2008). High School Mental Health Survey: Assessment of a mental health screen. *Canadian Journal of Psychiatry, 53*(5), 314–322.

Roid, G. H. (2003). *Stanford-Binet intelligence scales* (5th ed.). Rolling Meadows, IL: Riverside.

Seligman, L., Ollendick, T., Langley, A., & Baldacci, H. (2004). The utility of measures of child and adolescent anxiety: A meta-analytic review of the Revised Children's Manifest Anxiety Scale, the State-Trait Anxiety Inventory for Children, and the Child Behavior Checklist. *Journal of Clinical Child & Adolescent Psychology, 33*(3), 557–565.

Shaffer, D., Fisher, P., Lucas, C. P., Dulcan, M. K., & Schwab-Stone, M. E. (2000). NIMH Diagnostic Interview Schedule for Children Version IV (NIMH DISC-IV): Description, differences from previous versions, and reliability of some common diagnoses. *Journal of the American Academy of Child & Adolescent Psychiatry, 39*(1), 28–38.

Sparrow, S. S., Cicchetti, D. V., & Balla, D. A. (2005). *Vineland adaptive behavior scales* (2nd ed.). Circle Pines, MN: America Guidance Service.

Spitzer, R. L., Kroenke, K., Williams, J. B., & Patient Health Questionnaire Primary Care Study Group. (1999). Validation and utility of a self-report version of PRIME-MD: The PHQ primary care study. *Journal of the American Medical Association, 282*(18), 1737–1744.

Timbremont, B., Braet, C., & Dreessen, L. (2004). Assessing depression in youth: Relation between the Children's Depression Inventory and a structured interview. *Journal of Clinical Child & Adolescent Psychology, 33*(1), 149–157.

Timmons-Mitchell, J., Brown, C., Schultz, S. C., Webster, S. E., Underwood, L. A., & Semple, W. (1997). *Final report: Results of a three-year collaborative effort to assess the mental health needs of youth in the juvenile justice system in Ohio.* Columbus: Ohio Department of Youth Services.

Underwood, L. A., Phillips, A., von Dresner, K., & Knight, P. D. (2006). Critical factors in mental health programming for juveniles in corrections facilities. *International Journal of Behavioral and Consultation Therapy, 2*(1), 108–141.

Underwood, L. A., & Rawles, P. (2002). Screening and assessing the mental health and substance use needs of African-American youth involved in the juvenile justice system: Practical considerations. *Juvenile Correctional Mental Health Report, 2,* 49–64.

Underwood, L. A., Warren, K. M., Talbott, L., Jackson, L., & Dailey, F. L. (2014). Mental health treatment in juvenile justice secure care facilities: Practice and policy recommendations. *Journal of Forensic Psychology Practice, 14,* 55–85. doi: 10.1080/15228932.2014.865398

Urbina, S. (2004). *Essentials of psychological testing.* Hoboken, NJ: Wiley.

Varela, R., & Biggs, B. (2006). Reliability and validity of the Revised Children's Manifest Anxiety Scale (RCMAS) across samples of Mexican, Mexican American, and European American children: A preliminary investigation. *Anxiety, Stress, & Coping, 19*(1), 67–80.

Wechsler, D. (1991). *Manual for the Wechsler Intelligence Scale for Children-Third Edition.* San Antonio, TX: Psychological Corporation.

Wechsler, D. (2003). *Wechsler Intelligence Scale for Children-WISC-IV.* New York, NY: Psychological Corporation.

Wechsler, D. (2011). *The Wechsler Abbreviated Scale of Intelligence-Second Edition (WASI-II).* San Antonio, TX: Pearson.

Winters, K. C., & Henley, G. A. (1993). *Adolescent diagnostic interview schedule and manual.* Los Angeles, CA: Western Psychological Services.

9

TREATMENT PLANNING ISSUES

INTRODUCTION

Treatment planning is an important and often underutilized component of the counseling process. It has been defined as "a complex process involving sequential decisions, with weighting of information concerning client characteristics . . . treatment context, relational variables, and treatment strategies and techniques" (Clarkin & Kendall, 1992, p. 906, as cited in Maruish, 2002). Planning a client's treatment is a dynamic process involving several different factors, and this may be especially true during the tumultuous adolescent years. From the moment a client enters the counseling room until the last session, the provider should continuously monitor the treatment planning process. Despite the common dichotomy of assessment and treatment, the assessment process itself can be considered therapeutic and may be understood as the beginning of treatment. In fact, treatment begins from the first interview as the provider begins establishing rapport and building a relationship with the client (Morrison, 2008). It is from the assessment that the treatment plan emerges.

Diagnostic considerations have been highlighted in the earlier chapters, and several treatment modalities have also been highlighted. However, the process of choosing an effective treatment approach based on individual needs and scientific evidence, planning a course of treatment, tailoring treatment for individual and cultural concerns, and documenting services is worth its own discussion. It behooves providers to adopt a specific approach to treatment planning that suits their clinical training, modalities, and client needs. This chapter, although not exhaustive, will review some important considerations regarding utility, approaches, modifications, and implications regarding treatment planning. Hopefully, the provider can leave with an increased skill set in designing and modifying his or her treatment approach with each client he or she sees. After reading this chapter, the reader will be able to do the following:

- Understand the purpose and function of the treatment planning process
- Be able to identify the advantages and limitations of treatment planning
- Understand the importance of documentation and demonstrate knowledge of the differing levels of documentation
- Demonstrate his or her ability to develop a treatment plan (initial assessment, goal setting, monitoring outcomes, etc.) using a step-by-step process described in this chapter
- Be able to respond to ethically challenging cases unique to adolescents
- Be able to understand the relationship between documenting professional services and ethical practice

- Be able to apply treatment planning skills gained from review of this chapter to a practice case scenario

UTILITY OF TREATMENT PLANNING

Purpose and Function of Treatment Planning

The provider may believe that the dynamic and evolving relationship involved in counseling adolescents may preclude a strict and predefined plan. Despite the fluid aspects intrinsic in the counseling relationship, the development of a specific plan for treatment near the beginning of the provider's work with an adolescent has several purposes and advantages. In a guide to essential treatment planning strategies, Maruish (2002) has highlighted several of the aims and benefits of treatment planning. Broadly, purposes for treatment plans include developing a preliminary strategy for counseling, making adjustments or increases in service provision, or meeting any governing or certification requirements. More specific aims include defining the emphasis of counseling, defining common beliefs about counseling between the client and the provider, determining a means to define treatment success, and assisting in continuity of care with other professionals (Maruish, 2002). In addition, treatment plans complement applications to managed health care organizations (MHOs) and other funding sources for eligibility determination, quality assurance, and review and standardization purposes (Maruish, 2002).

When working with adolescents and their families, the related issues of defining and planning the initial counseling relationship, defining common beliefs about the work being done, defining the role of the provider and scope of services, and defining what constitutes successful treatment are important to consider. Adolescents and their families may enter treatment with unrealistic ideas of what can be expected from treatment by its conclusion, their required level of involvement and investment in treatment, or

the degree to which multiple parties will need to be included in counseling (Maruish, 2002).

With adolescents, it is especially important to involve parents and families in treatment, and there is a need to address positive and negative emotions of parents, address faulty expectations about their child's needs, and show respect for parenting skills (Sattler & Hoge, 2006). With parents and adolescents, addressing in a developmentally appropriate manner what treatment might look like is an important part of engagement in treatment (Sattler & Hoge, 2006). This may involve including families or school systems as an active component of treatment, as socialization through parenting and school systems have been identified to play an important development role for adolescents in several domains such as self-esteem and achievement (Carlson, Funk, & Nguyen, 2013).

In addition to defining the context of counseling, defining both the content and the goals of the counseling relationship has benefits for the adolescent and his or her family, as well as the provider. These benefits include keeping both parties on course as the counseling relationship is initiated. A treatment plan serves as a roadmap to compare against the current course of counseling and as a point of discussion for the adolescent and his or her family during counseling. Once a primary objective has been identified based on the provider's understanding of the client's concerns, goals can be developed, and progress can be identified jointly (Maruish, 2002). The provider's understanding of the client's concerns should be shared with the client before beginning the process of treatment planning (Maruish, 2002). This process of joint conceptualizing and treatment planning may be considered a component of the informed consent process for providers and their adolescent clients.

As mentioned, another important goal of treatment planning with adolescents is monitoring outcome and making adjustments as necessary. Although the process of monitoring outcome will be explored further in the following sections, it is worth briefly noting that treatment planning and goal setting serve the important function of providing the provider with an objective measure of whether the client's problems have been resolved or whether continued treatment, change in approach, or referral for further services is necessary (Maruish, 2002).

Potential measures suggesting the possibility of termination from the counseling process include symptom management or reduction, effective medication use, relapse prevention, effective harm reduction, increased level of employment or otherwise improved psychosocial circumstances, involvement in appropriate organizational settings, and improved relationships (Maruish, 2002). Setting appropriate goals and measuring pretreatment indicators of distress as a component of treatment planning allows a degree of objectivity in this process. For example, several objective measures exist that may serve as pretreatment symptom indicators, such as the Brief Symptom Inventory, the Trauma Symptom Checklist for Children, the Beck Youth Inventory, the Behavioral Assessment System for Children-Second Edition, the Minnesota Multiphasic Personality Inventory for Adolescents, the Millon Adolescent Clinical Inventory, and the Child Behavior Checklist (Maruish, 2002; Sattler & Hoge, 2006), and other specific outcome measures described in Chapter 8). The use of behavioral self-reports, provider-rated reports, and other less objective measures are also helpful (Maruish, 2002) and include syndrome-specific instruments such as instruments measuring depression, anxiety, trauma, resiliency, substance use, suicidality, cognitive issues, and academic issues. If assessment is the compass and counseling is the terrain, then the treatment plan serves as the provider's roadmap against which to judge whether expected changes are being made. If this is not the case, then termination, a change in service modality, or referral to another professional may be necessary (Duncan, 2010; Maruish, 2002).

In addition to treatment planning, another component of treatment planning that serves an important purpose is case formulation. Case formulation refers to "a hypothesis about the underlying psychological mechanisms that drive or maintain a client's problems" (Tompkins, 1990, as cited in Maruish, 2002). The process of case formulation will be discussed later in more detail. In short, the case formulation arises from the assessment made by the provider based on the results of screening and assessment tools, their clinical interview, and other sources of collateral information including, but not limited to, provider reports, parental observations, teacher observations, and information from the courts if applicable. Case formulation constitutes a lens from which the provider views his or her client. Case formulation has several functions, including directing choice and approach of treatment, directing initial counseling goals and objectives, and troubleshooting the relationship and the treatment course (Maruish, 2002). Case formulation is clearly an important part of the treatment planning process, and its purpose requires careful consideration. As with the rest of the treatment plan, using a collaborative approach that informs the client of any conclusions and recommendations borne from the formulation is often the best approach (Duncan, 2010; Maruish, 2002; Morrison, 2008). In the case of working with adolescents, this may include sharing insights with the adolescents and their families, challenging discrepancies, explaining the use and rationale of microskills, and asking for their participation in a specific course of counseling.

In addition to the benefits gained by the adolescent, his or her family, and the provider, a final purpose of treatment planning involves its use by MHOs and other governmental or behavioral health authorities. Third parties may briefly review treatment plans for documentation and organizational purposes, or they may closely scrutinize them to ensure that outlined plans are appropriate for the presenting condition, medical necessity, and are feasible in terms of resource allocation. Third parties may require revision of a treatment plan in order for providers to successfully request additional services for a client. Finally, third parties may use treatment plans to conduct quality assurance audits to meet regulatory guidelines, to conduct internal reviews for quality assurance, or to provide a uniform method of documentation for treatment services (Maruish, 2002). In an age of increasing health care availability, it is important for providers to understand the purpose of treatment planning for various parties.

DOCUMENTATION OF SERVICES

As mentioned, documentation of intended services is often completed by submission of a written treatment plan to the client, parent, and third party (Maruish, 2002). This written treatment plan then serves as a reference for both the provider and the client throughout the process. A full, written treatment plan may not be lengthy, but it has several important components that should be addressed. These include the referral source; the adolescent's (or family's) statement of the presenting concerns; a list of additional problems generated by the history, interview, or any testing; strengths and resiliencies of the client and family; treatment goals and objectives; and ways to measure progress. From presenting concerns, any diagnostic impressions generated are important to include in the treatment plan. Then, goals and objectives for treatment, interventions to be used, choice of treatment approach, and stipulations for ending treatment are specified (Maruish, 2002). Strengths and limitations of the client as well as other possible roadblocks to treatment are often specified. These may include environmental factors, individual factors, or relational factors, as mentioned earlier (Duncan, 2010; Maruish, 2002; Sue & Sue, 2008). Finally, responsible treatment providers, any referrals for further services, and a review date are often included (Maruish, 2002).

Despite the help rendered by all parties in generating a formal treatment plan outlining counseling approach, goals, and objectives, not all settings will require a formal written treatment plan and system to determine treatment progress. However, the standardized and ubiquitously utilized method for documenting mental health services is the *s*ubjective, *o*bjective, *a*ssessment, and *p*lan (SOAP) note (Cameron &

Turtle-Song, 2002). While there are other systems available to document treatment progress, the SOAP note is worth looking at as a representation of the other systems. During cases in which formal treatment plans are not required, providers are encouraged to utilize their successive progress notes as an emergent treatment plan by outlining initial goals, choice of treatment, and emergent issues in their monthly and quarterly reports and their progress notes.

The SOAP note first outlines the client's narrative in a given session in the subjective portion of the note. This may include changes after treatment response, current interpersonal functioning, and any remaining symptoms noted by the adolescents or their families (Cameron & Turtle-Song, 2002). For example, a depressed adolescent may report experiencing suicidal thoughts during parental arguments but attempting to proactively participate in social outings with friends to counter such thoughts. Then, any objective data derived through the provider's observations, as well as through other sources such as formal assessment, are included. This often includes a quick assessment of the mental status as well as findings from an objective measure (Cameron & Turtle-Song, 2002). For example, the provider may note that the adolescent appears tearful while discussing his relationship with his mother but appears angry while discussing his relationship with his father. The treatment plan will need to be modified accordingly to ensure that these changes in treatment are addressed.

The last two portions of the SOAP note may be utilized similarly to a treatment plan's case formulation and treatment specification. The assessment section integrates the current information known about the client into a clinical formulation (Cameron & Turtle-Song, 2002). This consists of the provider's opinions about what is happening, and no new information about the client is included in this session. For example, the provider may postulate that the adolescent's depression continues to be maintained by poor family functioning. Then, the final section of the note outlines a plan for continued services. This section may serve as an informal, emergent treatment plan (Cameron & Turtle-Song, 2002). For example, the provider may recommend two sessions of parent training or a referral for couples counseling to assist in the adolescent's treatment. The initial SOAP notes created during the first few sessions of counseling may be especially helpful for the provider in understanding the adolescent's presenting concerns as well as in specifying initial treatment goals and specific objectives. Clearly, then, the assessment and plan in a SOAP note can serve as an important means of documenting the provider's clinical thinking and working treatment plan. Nonetheless, the helpfulness of a formalized treatment plan has been outlined above, and it would behoove the professional provider to consider writing a formalized treatment plan whenever possible.

TREATMENT PLANNING: A STEP-BY-STEP TRANSTHEORETICAL APPROACH

Initial Assessment and Case Formulation

Several theoretical orientations have been discussed in the present text, and each of them has its merits in terms of treatment planning. However, it is possible to discuss a transtheoretical approach to treatment planning that may serve as a template from which to include theoretical considerations in one's work with adolescents or as a stand alone treatment planning approach for the provider. Maruish (2002) has outlined such an approach, which will be briefly discussed here.

First, it is important to give adequate attention to the initial interview (see Morrison, 2008, for an in-depth look at the initial interview). The provider's initial interview with the adolescent may serve as the beginning of a relationship and should thus be treated with care. The provider should be prepared by knowing what questions he or she wants to ask and having a strategy in mind for asking them (Sattler & Hoge, 2006).

The goal of the first session (and perhaps subsequent assessment sessions) is to gather enough information to learn about the reason for seeking counseling, presenting issues, as well as the psychosocial circumstances. Sattler and Hoge (2006) presented several guidelines to assist providers in the initial interview, including deciding on a structure and preparing questions beforehand, speaking with an empathic and kind tone, integrating an awareness of the adolescent's developmental level, using good listening skills such as summaries and reflections, and using adjustments and follow-up questions when necessary (Sattler & Hoge, 2006). Additionally, it is important to remain attentive to emotions, to handle sensitive and challenging subjects skillfully, to manage client resistance tactfully, and to balance control and flexibility in order to maintain rapport and answer important questions (Morrison, 2008).

After conducting an initial session as well as any follow-up sessions, a provider is ready to provide diagnostic impressions as well as a prognosis and a case formulation. The use of diagnostic impressions among professional providers has been discussed throughout this text, and helpful volumes exist to assist the provider in the successful use of diagnostic criteria (e.g., Morrison, 2014). Prognosis involves a prediction of the outcomes for one's clients in several different domains, including symptomology, course and consequences of illness, and likelihood and degree of treatment response (Morrison, 2008). This prediction of outcome may depend on several different factors, including, for example, primary diagnosis, availability of effective treatment, past course of illness and previous treatment effectiveness for the individual, and available supports and strengths for the individual (Morrison, 2008). The current edition of the *Diagnostic and Statistical Manual of Mental Disorders*, fifth edition (*DSM-5*) provides prognostic information for most diagnoses (American Psychiatric Association, 2013).

Finally, the case formulation, as discussed earlier, is a working model of the client that is usually based on a particular theoretical approach

(Maruish, 2002). However, a nontheoretical approach to developing this hypothesis is also possible. This bottom-up approach involves developing a comprehensive list of concerns and problems, including client- and provider-identified problems. These problems ought to be described in terms of their origins, precipitants, nature, and consequences. Finally, common patterns should be sought among problems that have been listed, and a working model should be proposed based on conclusions that emerge. Hypotheses evolve from patterns derived from theoretical factors, nontheoretical considerations, or analysis of content (Maruish, 2002). For example, an adolescent's conduct problems may all lead to a date of origin around the time of the adolescent's parents' divorce, which assists a provider in diagnosing an adjustment disorder and prescribing an interpersonal treatment.

Once case formulations have been made, they should be tested and modified if necessary based on the degree to which available information fits into the model and the degree to which the explanation makes sense to the client. Finally, during counseling, the hypothesis may be further revised as treatment progresses (Maruish, 2002).

Goal Setting and Intervention Planning

Once a case formulation has been developed and refined, the next step of treatment planning is setting goals and objectives for counseling. While goals are broadly defined benchmarks specifying the overall desired outcome for a client, objectives are narrowly and behaviorally defined outcomes that constitute the components of a larger goal. Objectives are also usually specified within a given time frame with measurable outputs. Goals can be considered the "what" of the problem, and objectives can be considered "how" the goal will be met. Goals and objectives ought to be achievable and reasonable, indicating that the client is able to reach the goal, given his or her current resources and strengths. The objectives should also be realistic, indicating that

motivational, external, and other factors do not hinder the client's ability to reach an otherwise achievable goal. Additionally, specific objectives should be measurable, suggesting that desired outcomes ought to be quantified and easily comprehensible. Both goals and objectives should be mutually discussed and agreed on by the client, his or her family, the provider, and any other involved collateral sources. This has implications for monitoring treatment outcome and justifying treatment to third parties and clients. Finally, goals should be stated positively rather than negatively whenever possible (Maruish, 2002). Questions to ask to assist clients in setting goals include the following: "What do you see as your biggest problem? Do you think there is an immediate crisis that needs to be addressed?" "How will you know if you have achieved your goal?" "How will you be different after reaching that goal?" (Maruish, 2002, p. 141). Additional questions include "How do you plan to sustain your goal?" and "What resources do you need to support ongoing goal attainment?"

Goals with individual adolescents may be based on a specific theoretical framework. For example, increasing cognitive reframing, increasing proactive social behaviors, and increasing emotional regulation skills are all borne from a cognitive behavioral tradition (Spiegler & Guevremont, 2010). The treatment planning process is often guided by theoretical frameworks in this manner. A chosen theoretical framework such as cognitive behavioral theory is utilized to conceptualize the initiation and maintenance of the client's presenting concerns, and interventions are created that reflect the proposed theoretical change processes, such as those described above.

However, goals and objectives, and treatment plans by extension, may also be based on transtheoretical factors. Prochaska and DiClemente (1982) noted five processes of change through which clients may progress, as well as several processes necessary within each stage. These five stages each represent a different level of readiness to consider and make changes in one's life and are termed (1) *precontemplation*, (2) *contemplation*, (3) *preparation*, (4) *action*, and (5) *maintenance*. The processes used within each stage are varied but include processes such as consciousness raising, stimulus control, and self-reevaluation (Prochaska & DiClemente, 1982). These broad goals are applicable to several different theories. Although mentioned elsewhere, the use of basic motivational interviewing and motivational enhancement techniques (Miller & Rollnick, 2013) can also serve as transtheoretical treatment interventions. Table 9.1 provides a review of the basic stages of change.

Table 9.1   Basic Stages of Change

Stages of Change	
Precontemplation	Many clients are in this stage. It is identified by the person's inability to see or accept that a problem exists. They have no intention of changing the problem and deny what others are so concerned about. They will place the responsibility for their problem outside of themselves. In this stage, a young person needs to have strong relationships with adult caregivers, needs to be allowed to see why they like the behavior in question, and what they don't like about the behavior in question.
Contemplation	Here, the client wants to stop feeling "stuck," is fearful of failure, and is ambivalent about change, in general. They will see good reasons to change and good reasons not to change. They will also seek out information to help them decide. Helping clients resolve ambivalence through supportive relationships and education relating to the problem is a worthy goal.
Preparation	At this stage, the client will make public the intention to change. More planning will be needed as obstacles will have to be overcome. The client is also likely to do self-examination and question his or her own capability of actually changing the behavior. Professionals in this stage will utilize the relationships they have developed to support and build self-efficacy within the client. Providers will also help identify and solve problems inherent in changing habitual behavioral problems.
Action	The action stage is where a client outwardly demonstrates what has been happening within him or her during the first three stages. Here, lifestyle changes will be made, and the behavior itself is modified. A client will need support and encouragement as the reality of change and the problems inherent will come to the surface. Pointing out the benefits of healthy choices and its positive impact in this adolescent's life will serve to assist that client in moving forward.
Maintenance	Here, the client will work to consolidate gains made in behavior change up to this point. The person is learning how to guard against dangerous situations and triggers. This stage can last for several months to a life time. Having already developed a strong relationship with this client, the provider is now in a place to process through the change process and how it can be applied to other aspects of the client's life.
Termination/relapse	In this stage, the client has either mastered enough new skills so that the old behavior is no longer a threat or a problem or he or she relapses into earlier stages of change. It is important to understand that termination and relapse are both normal, and a client may experience either after a significant behavior change. Whether termination or relapse, all the skills learned in treatment can now be utilized to either move on to a new behavior challenge or assess what can be done to get the juvenile back on track.

Source. Adapted from Prochaska and DiClemente (1982).

Finally, specific interventions can be chosen based on desired goals, objectives, and outcomes. The interventions recommended by the providers may not all be psychotherapeutic in nature. The provider may also recommend that the adolescent and his or her family participate in psychophar-macological, medical, psycho-educational, supportive group, bibliotherapy, technologically based, or other interventions (Maruish, 2002). Within psychotherapeutic intervention choices, decisions must be made such as the frequency of treatment, specific tools to be utilized, and the modalities best suited to the presenting issues of the adolescent. Broadly, a few questions that may assist in choosing appropriate interventions include "Will the planned intervention enable the [client] to meet all or most of the selected goals?" "Is what the [client] is expected to do realistic? Is what the [provider] is expected to do realistic?" "Will the [provider] be able to know within a reasonable amount of time if the intervention is working?" (Maruish, 2002, p. 157). Although formulations and subsequent interventions will vary considerably based on several factors mentioned here such as diagnosis, cultural dynamics, and prognosis, some general resources may be helpful in planning treatment. For example, the Adolescent Psychotherapy Treatment Planner (Jongsma, Peterson, McInnis, & Bruce, 2014) as well as the Child and Adolescent Psychotherapy Treatment Planner (Jongsma, Peterson, & McInnis, 1996) offer a variety of empirically supported and practically applicable treatment plans for several different presenting concerns.

Monitoring Outcomes

The importance of monitoring client response to treatment cannot be overstated. Several methods are available to do so, including standardized testing, self-report, other report, and behavioral monitoring. Criteria for termination from counseling could include reduction in symptomology, statistically significant change in behavior as measured by objective measures, clinically significant change as measured by clinical impression and objective measures, or advancement

toward an agreed on goal or standard (Maruish, 2002). Enlistment of help from the family may be important in this process when working with an adolescent. Enlistment of the adolescent's cooperation is important in both initial and subsequent assessments. It may help explain to the adolescent why the assessment is important and build his or her confidence in the process first (Maruish, 2002; Sattler & Hoge, 2006). Regardless of how it is achieved, monitoring outcomes remains an important part of the treatment relationship.

Integrating the Helping Relationship

One last consideration is the importance of collaborating with the client in every step of this process. The quality of the counseling relationship accounts for a significant amount of the variance in the outcome of treatment (Duncan, 2010). Therefore, the adolescent's active participation with the provider is of paramount importance. With any client, however, this process is not done in isolation. It is instead accomplished by checking in regularly with the client about assumptions and plans concerning the direction of treatment. Although scores on a standardized assessment may reflect improvement, it matters most that the adolescent and the family believe that they are doing good work with the provider and that they are making progress (Duncan, 2010). The provider will need to interpret the findings from objective testing and make it relevant to the client and his or her family.

An important component of integrating the helping relationship is attending to broad and proximal cultural factors. Individuals' cultural and subcultural backgrounds affect the way in which they interpret and report clinical and growth-related phenomena (e.g., Calhoun, Cann, & Tedeschi, 2010; Calhoun & Tedeschi, 2013), and attending to these differences plays an important role in showing respect to adolescents and families from different backgrounds and families. For example, adolescents from an Asian American background may place a higher emphasis on parental authority than differentiation, or adolescents from an Arab American background may place a comparatively high emphasis on hard work and education (Sue & Sue, 2008). The *DSM-5* provides a cultural formulation section with assessment questions meant to assist the provider in formulating a culturally sensitive model of the client during the assessment process (American Psychiatric Association, 2013).

CASE SCENARIO

Now, let's put your knowledge and skills to the test. The following case of Thomas is intended to help students apply diagnostic and treatment planning skills (see Case Scenario 9.1). Pretend you are a provider and read through the case scenario. Now, with a partner try to apply the treatment planning knowledge you've gained in this chapter to the case. You may wish to write out a treatment plan or jot down a few notes for later discussion. Afterward, read the following sections on diagnostic issues, key clinical concerns, and appropriate counseling responses. Finally, with a partner or in a small group, discuss your treatment plan in relation to the counseling concerns and responses delineated in this section of the chapter.

IMPLICATIONS FOR COUNSELING ADOLESCENTS

Clinical Review of Case

Let's review the case of Thomas and identify some important components that assist in the treatment planning process. First, some diagnostic considerations are important here. It is important to assess the degree to which Thomas's reactions may be related to the trauma of his

---

Case Scenario 9.1

Thomas

Thomas is a 13-year-old adolescent presenting for counseling with his mother after a recent family divorce. His parents were married for 15 years but have recently divorced after his father began consuming alcohol excessively and displaying verbal and physical abuse toward his mother. Thomas now lives with his elder brother Benjamin, his younger brother Steven, and his mother, Ashley, while the father, Ron, has left and moved to an adjacent town. Thomas and his brothers do not currently have visits with their father, and Thomas would like, however, to have a positive relationship with his father. During the divorce process and the height of his parents' marital conflict 1 ½ years ago, Thomas displayed significant withdrawal and appeared depressed. This was indicated by significantly decreased mood, loss of interests and significant relationships, significantly increased sleep, poor concentration, and a verbalized sense of hopelessness about his family and future.

After the divorce, Thomas showed a period of improvement in which his mood improved, he regained old friendships, and he returned to some of his regular interests and hobbies. However, shortly thereafter, Thomas began to display oppositional behavior at home and at school. He displayed significant anger and irritability at home toward both his mother and

(Continued)

Case Scenario 9.1   (Continued)

his brothers, which include, for example, losing his temper and getting easily annoyed. He also displayed defiant behavior, such as arguing with his mother and swearing at her, annoying his brothers and mother at inappropriate times, and defying commands and rules at home. Reports from his school have begun to arrive at home, indicating that he has begun having physical fights and verbal altercations with other students, has begun forming a "gang" with other students who have been labeled as bullies, and was found carrying a pocket knife during class. Although his behavior has not escalated to the level of criminal activity, his concerns led the school provider to recommend that the family seek therapeutic support services in the community.

Thomas and his mother deny significant childhood physical, sexual, or emotional trauma. His only significant medical history is a history of allergies. He and his family live in a safe environment and school district in which aggressive behavior is not a common response to environmental stressors. In terms of family history, his mother reported a positive history for depression in her family and a positive history for alcohol and substance abuse in Thomas's father's family. He and his mother did not endorse any manic or psychotic symptoms.

parents' divorce in order to rule out a posttraumatic stress reaction. Assessing how Thomas perceived the divorce, as well as symptoms such as hypervigilance, trauma-related reenactments, and changes in beliefs or mood, may be important here (American Psychiatric Association, 2013). The use of a short, standardized symptom assessment may be helpful in this regard. Also, the use of motivational engagement strategies might assist in determining Thomas's perception of the divorce (Miller & Rollnick, 2013).

In a related vein, an adjustment disorder may be considered if the provider believes that these reactions are temporal and situational in nature. It will also be important to consider the temporal onset and exact nature of the symptoms to differentiate between a few different likely diagnoses. Gaining additional information about the extent of the conduct-related issues as compared with oppositional behaviors will help the provider differentiate between oppositional defiant disorder, conduct disorder, and underlying mood disorder, as Thomas

appears to display symptoms of all (American Psychiatric Association, 2013). Finally, comorbidity of behavior disorders with attention-deficit/hyperactivity disorder is usually a concern, so an additional developmental history and the use of specific symptom-related standardized assessments may be helpful to clarify differential diagnoses (American Psychiatric Association, 2013; Barkley, Edwards, & Robin, 1999).

The process of thorough case formulation and treatment plan will likely require gathering additional information to form a complete picture of what is occurring. Key concerns that the provider might consider in this case involve the family dynamics that evolve from the current conflict as well as the results that the current conflict may have on subsequent family functioning. In many cases, parents of defiant adolescents use ineffective parenting strategies to encourage compliance with adult commands. Requests are met with defiance due to the negative reinforcement an adolescent receives from delaying and procrastinating. Parents continue to utilize the same strategies to ask for compliance and, eventually, become overwhelmed (Barkley et al., 1999). They may resort to physical aggression or simply verbal outbursts to gain compliance, or they may acquiesce and do the task themselves. A cycle of negative reinforcement and parent–teen conflict ensues (Barkley et al., 1999).

In combination with a premorbid level of impaired family management, this conflict may cause increases in hostility in the family system with the adolescent identified as the problem child despite the clear systemic concerns present. Increases in hostility will often lead to several other consequences, such as decreased positive social interactions, reduced adolescent reactivity to positive modeling and reinforcement skills, loss of parental sense of efficacy, increasing hostility or blaming of other family members, and family isolation (Barkley et al., 1999). Parents may even begin to punish positive behavior due to this hostility by using phrases such as "Oh, so you finally cleaned your room? Well, why didn't you clean it yesterday?" (Barkley et al., 1999). In addition to these conceptual and formulation-related issues, common concerns that should be explored include the presence of suicidal ideation, any use of physical force, as well as verbal abuse. Clearly, there are several key concerns that should be explored to formulate a strong idea of what is occurring in the conflict cycle. However, preliminarily, it appears that a behavioral and family-based strategy may be helpful to resolve initial symptoms, increase compliance, and improve family relationships (Barkley et al., 1999).

Based on a validated model originally designed for use with defiant children (Barkley, 1997), a model of behavioral parent training and family counseling targeting increased compliance and improved family relations has been designed for use with adolescents (Barkley et al., 1999). If an assessment and case formulation reveals some of the issues shown above, and if diagnostic considerations accurately suggest the primary presence of nondefiance (as opposed to nondefiance secondary to traumatic stress), a behavioral model

may be indicated. Briefly, this model involves several components, beginning with psycho-education about the causes of defiance and behaviorally based appropriate parental responses. Then, development of positive attending skills, effective use of response cost, effective grounding, school-related intervention, problem-solving skills, communication skills, and cognitive components are discussed and practiced in turn (Barkley et al., 1999). Additionally, a positive reinforcement-oriented behavioral management system could be implemented to decrease negative behaviors and to improve desired behaviors. Such a model will likely be effective in meeting the family's goals. As mentioned earlier, the case formulation and treatment can be modified based on the adolescent and the family's response to the treatment approach described here.

Application of Ethics

The treatment planning process can be facilitated by an understanding of current ethical requirements. The American Counseling Association's (2014) ethical code necessitates that providers fulfill certain ethical mandates with regard to counseling plans. In treatment planning, providers should first "respect the dignity and promote the welfare of clients" (p. 4), "respecting clients' freedom of choice" (p. 4), and "avoid imposing their own values, attitudes, beliefs, and behaviors" (p. 5). As a component of this, "counselors and their clients work jointly in devising counseling plans that offer reasonable promise of success and are consistent with the . . . circumstances of clients" (p. 4). Finally, "counselors and clients regularly review and revise counseling plans to assess their continued . . . effectiveness" (p. 4).

In the vignette provided above, an awareness of these requirements may help the treatment provider keep Thomas's family involved in the decision-making process for appropriate treatment recommendation and serves as a reminder to keep the family involved in monitoring the effectiveness of treatment. Broadly, these requirements set helpful boundaries around the relationship between providers and clients in terms of the treatment planning process (Table 9.2).

SUMMARY

This chapter has highlighted several aspects of competent treatment planning with the adolescent client. Both theoretically informed and transtheoretical components have been discussed. Moreover, the overall importance of the helping relationship has been highlighted as a key factor. Steps in formulation, goal creation, and treatment outcome monitoring have all been described. Several functions and components of a treatment plan have been outlined. The knowledge and utilization of active listening skills is a central and foundational component of the treatment process and should be an implicit intervention in each treatment plan. Table 9.2 lists some of the key

skills relevant to active listening in the provider's relationship with each client.

Clearly, several issues are important when considering the case formulation and treatment planning process. Regardless of the expectations of those entities with which professional providers will work, the goal of the present review is to suggest the importance to all providers of giving the treatment planning process the time and attention it deserves to better serve the clients with whom professional providers will work (see Exercise 9.1).

KEYSTONES

- Treatment planning is a dynamic and multifaceted process that can be broken down into several different components, including initial assessment, case formulation, goal and objective creation, intervention choice, discussion of

Table 9.2   Foundational Listening Skills in the Helping Profession

Nonverbal encouragers	Using cues such as good eye contact, effective use of silence, open and relaxed posture, and learning to encourage the client to continue, facilitate rapport, and indicate listening
Verbal encouragers/prompts	Short words or vocalizations such as *ah, right, okay,* and *hmm* that encourage the client to continue, facilitate rapport, and indicate listening
Reflection of content	Speaking the client's stated experiences, behaviors, and cognitions to indicate listening as part of an empathic formula
Reflection of emotion	Speaking the client's stated or expressed emotions back using the same or similar words to indicate listening as part of an empathic formula
Empathy	"Understanding each client from his or her own point of view together with the feelings surrounding that point of view and . . . communicat[ing] this understanding whenever it is deemed helpful . . . understand[ing] individuals in and through the context of their lives" (e.g., You feel scared because you don't know what the future holds with this new move; Egan, 2010, p. 45).
Probing statement or question	Using statements, requests, questions, and single words to further explore, understand, direct, or augment the client's previous statements (e.g., "Tell me more about how things changed when you got the diagnosis.")
Immediacy	Observations and statements intended to address problems arising in the overall helping relationship as well as in the here-and-now of the client–provider interaction

Source. From Egan. *The Skilled Helper*, 9E. © 2010 South-Western, a part of Cengage Learning, Inc. Reproduced by permission. www.cengage.com/permissions.

assets and limitations, and means of monitoring outcome, among other things.

- Treatment planning serves several purposes, some of which include developing an initial strategy for counseling, providing a benchmark for later adjustments, providing documentation to third parties such as managed care organizations, and providing a contract between the client and the provider. There are several steps to the completion of a treatment plan, and a written treatment plan has several components.

- Case formulation is a specific aspect of treatment planning that involves developing a working model of the client, and it serves the purpose of guiding treatment decisions. Case formulation and treatment planning can be accomplished through both theoretical lenses as well as through a bottom-up, nontheoretical approach that integrates various problem areas through common themes.

- Treatment planning and case formulation should integrate cultural considerations as well as the therapeutic relationship itself. It is not a process that the provider does in isolation, but it is accomplished by checking in with clients about the provider's plans and ideas and receiving feedback, goals, and suggestions from the clients.

- In some instances, formal treatment plans may not be required, but providers can still adopt the principles and guidelines discussed here in their working progress notes.

QUESTIONS TO CONSIDER

Exercise 9.1

1. Consider the case of Thomas described earlier.
   a. In addition to the considerations presented here, what are some additional considerations that would assist you in planning Thomas's treatment goals and interventions?
   b. In addition to the general ethical guidelines discussed above, what are some ethical considerations specific to the case presented here that would assist in planning treatment?

2. How comfortable do you feel with the treatment planning process from beginning to end?

In which component of treatment planning would you still like to gain more experience or knowledge, and what is your plan for doing so?

3. How will the principles and guidelines discussed here change the way you work with clients or understand the process of counseling? How have you understood treatment planning in the past, and how will you approach it differently?

4. What function does treatment planning have for the professional counselor as compared with treatment providers in other professions?

5. How does your particular theoretical viewpoint influence the ways in which you will plan treatment with clients?

REFERENCES

American Counseling Association. (2014). *2014 ACA code of ethics: As approved by the ACA governing council.* Retrieved from http://www.counseling.org/docs/ethics/2014-aca-code-of-ethics.pdf?sfvrsn=4

American Psychiatric Association. (2013). *Diagnostic and statistical manual of mental disorders* (5th ed.). Washington, DC: Author.

Barkley, R. A. (1997). *Defiant children: A provider's manual for assessment and parent training* (2nd ed.). New York, NY: Guilford Press.

Barkley, R. A., Edwards, G. H., & Robin, A. L. (1999). *Defiant teens: A provider's manual for assessment and family intervention.* New York, NY: Guilford Press.

Calhoun, L. G., Cann, A., & Tedeschi, R. G. (2010). The posttraumatic growth model: Sociocultural considerations. In T. Weiss & R. Berger (Eds.), *Posttraumatic growth and culturally competent practice: Lessons learned from around the globe* (pp. 1–14). Hoboken, NJ: Wiley.

Calhoun, L. G., & Tedeschi, R. G. (2013). *Posttraumatic growth in clinical practice.* New York, NY: Routledge.

Cameron, S., & Turtle-Song, I. (2002). Learning to write case notes using the SOAP format. *Journal of Counseling & Development, 80,* 286–292.

Carlson, C., Funk, C. L., & Nguyen, K. T. (2013). Families and schools. In J. H. Bray & M. Stanton (Eds.), *The Wiley-Blackwell handbook of family psychology* (pp. 515–526). Malden, MA: Wiley-Blackwell.

Duncan, B. L. (2010). *On becoming a better therapist.* Washington, DC: American Psychological Association.

Egan, G. (2010). *The skilled helper* (9th ed.). Belmont, CA: Brooks/Cole.

Jongsma, A. E., Jr., Peterson, L. M., & McInnis, W. P. (1996). *The child and adolescent psychotherapy treatment planner.* Hoboken, NJ: Wiley.

Jongsma, A. E., Jr., Peterson, L. M., McInnis, W. P., & Bruce, T. J. (2014). *The adolescent psychotherapy treatment planner: Includes DSM-5 updates.* Hoboken, NJ: Wiley.

Maruish, M. E. (2002). *Essentials of treatment planning.* New York, NY: Wiley.

Miller, W. R., & Rollnick, S. (2013). *Motivational interviewing: Helping people change* (3rd ed.). New York, NY: Guilford Press.

Morrison, J. (2008). *The first interview* (3rd ed.). New York, NY: Guilford Press.

Morrison, J. (2014). *Diagnosis made easier: Principles and techniques for mental health clinicians* (2nd ed.). New York, NY: Guilford Press.

Prochaska, J. O., & DiClemente, C. C. (1982). Transtheoretical therapy: Toward a more integrative model of change. *Psychotherapy: Theory, Research, and Practice, 19*(3), 276–288.

Sattler, J. M., & Hoge, R. D. (2006). *Assessment of children* (5th ed.). San Diego, CA: Jerome M. Sattler.

Spiegler, M. D., & Guevremont, D. (2010). *Contemporary behavior therapy* (5th ed.). Belmont, CA: Wadsworth Press.

Sue, D. W., & Sue, D. W. (2008). *Counseling the culturally diverse: Theory and practice* (5th ed.). Hoboken, NJ: Wiley.

10

COUNSELING INTERVENTIONS

INTRODUCTION

Adolescents attending counseling for the first time may feel apprehensive in the beginning. Naturally, providers should expect their adolescent clients to experience feelings of anxiety, difficulty trusting the therapeutic relationship, and a restriction of emotional expression within the first session. Many times, these clients are reluctant to participate in counseling but were referred by their parents/caretakers and other authority figures to do so (Higham, Friedlander, Escudero, & Diamond, 2012). More than likely, it was their parents who suggested counseling because of some untoward symptom manifestation (e.g., isolation, depressed mood, irritability, or self-harm) that was presenting itself. At a loss of what to do, parents/caretakers bring their adolescents into counseling, with an expectation that the provider will somehow "fix" them to match what their (the parents') outlook on life should be. However, many times, it is the family system where the issue resides rather than just one person within the family (Lander, Howsare, & Byrne, 2013). When to address the family as a whole is up to the expertise of the provider (more on family counseling later in the chapter).

When adolescents enter into counseling, providers should begin assessing them the moment they enter into the room. Asking specific questions during the assessment process that uncover clients' concerns and needs is crucial to know the direction the counseling should take. Part of this direction includes what interventions to use in order to undermine their client's issues and to help them to stabilize and get better.

This chapter focuses on what counseling interventions to use with adolescent clients who present with various emotional and behavioral symptoms; a few of these symptoms include depression, anxiety, trauma, school problems, suicidal thoughts, self-harm, and substance abuse. Also highlighted in this chapter are suggestions for future research and practice.

The purpose of counseling interventions is quite simple; they are used to change behavior through self-awareness and skill development. When a person employs an intervention, he or she often does so with intentional purposes (Hazelden Betty Ford Foundation, 2014). Therefore, each section in this chapter is dedicated to educating readers on current and applicable counseling interventions to use with adolescent clients who present to treatment with various mental health concerns. Several areas are considered:

- Individual counseling
- Coaching and mentoring
- Group counseling
- Crisis counseling
- Family counseling

After reading this chapter, readers will be able to do the following:

- Understand select counseling interventions available to use with adolescents

- Differentiate individual, crisis group, and family interventions with adolescents

- Implement interventions in times of crisis, disaster, and suicide

- Understand the difference between counseling, coaching, and mentoring

- Understand the stages of change

- Gain discernment concerning normal adolescent behavior versus abnormal behavior

- Improve understanding of the legal and ethical concerns in counseling

- Apply knowledge gained in this chapter through case scenarios

INDIVIDUAL COUNSELING AND RELATED INTERVENTIONS

Individual counseling refers to the therapeutic relationship between one client and a provider. People are attracted to individual counseling because it resembles other two-person relationships they are already comfortable in (e.g., mother–daughter relationship, husband–wife relationship, peer-to-peer relationship; Skovholt, Trotter, & Kao, 2008). Providers facilitating one-on-one counseling should be supportive, attentive, able to accurately reflect on their client's issues, and empathetic (Skovholt et al., 2008). Here, it is important for providers to consider their client's needs and goals by including them in the treatment process. One of the best models representing individual counseling is client-centered therapy.

As clients learn skills to more effectively manage target behaviors, they require individual sessions to learn how and when to apply these skills to different persons, places, and situations. Individual counseling is utilized to address crises, develop plans to be used in crisis situations, reinforce the use of skills, and address other needs that are not appropriate for the skills-training groups. It may target treatment concerns such as personal trauma, victimization issues, and anger management issues, particularly those clients classified as seriously mentally ill. In addition, individual counseling may occur weekly, bimonthly, or otherwise indicated by the provider. The frequency and duration of individual counseling services will be driven by the treatment plan (see Exercise 10.1).

Exercise 10.1

Individual Therapy With Adolescents

1. What are your ideas about the individual counseling dynamic? What are some concerns you have about a one-on-one therapeutic focus?

2. Considering the often criticalness of adolescents and their attitudes toward difference, what areas of personal appearance and levels of expertise do you think are important to consider before entering into the counseling room with adolescents for the first time?

3. Certainly, nonverbal behavior has a way of at times speaking louder than words; evaluating your own nonverbal behavior becomes critical to your adolescent clients' readiness to change. How do you personally change your nonverbal behavior to meet the environmental contexts or personal needs of others? How can this change of behavior promote positive counseling outcome?

4. Oftentimes, adolescents are resistant to the counseling process. What stage of change would you say a resistance client is operating? How would you go about encouraging a client to move beyond initial resistance?

Stewart (2014) cautions providers that their adolescent clients may have expectations of counseling and of the provider that are based only on perception rather than fact or experience. Because of this, providers will need to properly discuss the purpose and function of the counseling process with their clients during the first session.

First Impressions

Research shows interesting findings in the area of first impressions. Regardless of whether or not people meet someone through a literal encounter or through the glimpse of a picture, first impressions are still at work (Kirby, 2008). Gillath, Bahns, Ge, and Crandall (2012) had the idea to study first impressions through the pictures of shoes. Gillath et al. (2012) devised a research study seeking to discover whether participants, based only on a picture of a person's shoes, could identify a person's personality characteristics, gender, age, socioeconomic status (SES), and political affiliation. When holding age, gender, and income stable, it was realized that raters of the pictures were actually picking up on a person's SES, and then based on that person's SES, people were assigned into subcategories. For example, raters assumed that clean shoes meant that people who wear clean shoes are conscientious, but this was not the case. Therefore, Gillath et al. (2012) discovered that people make judgments based on stereotypes.

Gillath et al. (2012) conducted a study utilizing only an adult sample. Their research, nonetheless, is still applicable to adolescent populations. Consider, for instance, how drawn adolescents seem to be to materialism, fashion, and the latest trends. Bing and Hongling (2013) state that adolescents are more influenced by their affluent, high-income peers. Their research shows that boys and girls are influenced by

wealth and high status: Low-status girls are more influenced by high-status girls and high-status boys by high-status boys. Also, Bing and Hongling (2013) found that black adolescents are more influenced by high status and income than Hispanics are, but Hispanics are more influenced by these areas than white adolescents are. Interestingly, low-status white adolescent boys were the only group that was not significantly influenced by peers' status and income.

On these grounds, providers should consider their appearance prior to entering into the counseling room with a new adolescent client. At every moment, their adolescent client may be observing their (providers') dirty shoes, uncombed hair, or colorful tattoo, creating images and messages in their minds that what they believe about their provider must be true. Unfortunately, the research by Gillath et al. (2012) suggests that clients' thoughts and images about their providers' personality are not guided by truth but rather by stereotypes and error. To address the issues concerning appearance and nonverbal behavior, providers may find it helpful to openly talk about any possible stigmas that may present themselves. For instance, if the provider and the client do not share the same racial background (the client is Asian American and the provider is Caucasian), then the provider can ask the client to tell about his or her culture, stating the obvious "we are two different colors, does that make a difference to you?" Zhang and Burkard (2008) state that when providers (in their study, Caucasian providers were studied) talk to their racially different clients, they were viewed by their clients as having a greater working alliance with them.

Providers should care not only about the messages their clothing, demeanor, and appearance send but also about the messages sent through their nonverbal behavior. Grace, Kivlighan, and

Kunce (1995) believe that nonverbal behavior is a silent conversation between the client and the provider; this conversation leads the way for the development of a therapeutic alliance. They theorized, and found, that when providers receive formal training on understanding nonverbal behavior and on how to adjust their own nonverbal behavior, providers and clients have more therapeutic alliance. Alliance, then, leads to a greater therapeutic outcome (Falkenström, Granström, & Holmqvist, 2014; Ferreira et al., 2013; Ormhaug, Jensen, Wentzel-Larsen, & Shirk, 2014). Reading, accurately, a client's nonverbal behavior, therefore, may itself act as an intervention, as it can give a provider a hint into the client's stage of change and a chance to intervene appropriately.

Stages of Change

When providing counseling to adolescents, it is important to realize the various stages of counseling. For example, the stages of change model (Table 10.1) postulates that change happens through a six-stage sequence (Mander et al., 2014). The six stages of change are (1) precontemplation (client feels that there is no need for change), (2) contemplation (client is beginning to believe that there is a need for change), (3) preparation (client is beginning to plan for change), (4) action (client has begun to act out his or her plan), (5) maintenance (long-term changes are evident), and (6) termination (Guo,

Aveyard, Fielding, & Sutton, 2009; Kirby, 2008). During the initial assessment or first session, providers should be listening to their clients as they speak to discover what stage of change they are in. Formulating an intervention for someone who is in the precontemplative stage is going to be much different than the intervention designed for a person who is in the maintenance stage. Adolescent clients who often begin counseling on account of their parents are likely to be within the precontemplative stage, as most adolescents do not receive mental health treatment let alone ask for it (Culp, 1995).

A counseling intervention for adolescents in the precontemplative stage may consist of simple techniques such as listening, establishing rapport, and attending to the clients' concerns, whereas, interventions employed with adolescents in the maintenance stage may include homework assignments, out of session agendas (social interaction), and journaling, and so on. The overall purpose in the stages of change model is to understand what stage a client is in so that providers know what interventions to use. Providers can begin by asking questions concerning clients' desire for treatment. As cited already, many times, adolescents are not willing participants in their own treatment and are only there on the referral and wishing of their parents. In this case, it is easy to see why at times counseling adolescents may prove more difficult than counseling the adult client who is self-referred. Providers in this position should remain patient and extend their adolescent clients

Table 10.1 Stages of Change Model

Precontemplation	"I do not have a problem."
Contemplation	"I think I might have a problem."
Preparation	"I feel like I want to begin to change my life."
Action	"Today I am going to follow through."
Maintenance/relapse	"I go to recovery meetings every day (habit)."
Termination	"I am no longer tempted to use and I am (appropriately) sure that I will not return to this unhealthy coping behavior."

Source. Mander, J., Wittorf, A., Klingberg, S., Teufel, M., Zipfel, S., & Sammet, I. (2014). The patient perspective on therapeutic change: The investigation of associations between stages of change and general mechanisms of change in psychotherapy research. *Journal of Psychotherapy integration, 24*(2), 122–137. doi:10.1037/a0036976

the opportunity to tell their story without interruption. Just as important to discerning what stage a client is in before employing interventions is discerning whether or not a client is displaying a behavior that is common or uncommon for his or her developmental age.

Discerning a Client's Behavior

The *Diagnostic and Statistical Manual of Mental Disorders*, fifth edition (*DSM-5*), is clear on the issue of what constitutes a mental health disorder and what does not. A mental health disorder is generally diagnosed when the person's symptoms are elevated to a point of dysfunction and unmanageability (American Psychiatric Association [APA], 2013). Therefore, providers need to understand that not all adolescents brought in for counseling to address their symptoms may have only those issues to address; additional concerns may emerge during the counseling process. For example, some adolescents come to counseling for substance use–related concerns. Some are simply experimenting with a behavior that is more common than uncommon among their age-group, and others may have co-occurring mental health issues that drive their substance use. For instance, a high percentage of adolescents have already experimented with alcohol (70%), marijuana (22.7% of 12th graders in 2013 were frequent smokers), unprotected sex, and cigarettes by the time they reach their 18th birthday (Falck, 2012; Gogel, Cavaleri, Gardin, & Wisdom, 2011; King & Vidourek, 2011; Livingston, Bay-Cheng, Hequembourg, Testa, & Downs, 2013; National Institute on Alcohol Abuse and Alcoholism, 2014; U.S. Department of Health and Human Services, 2011). Though risk factors do exist for adolescents who use alcohol and drugs, the high percentage of adolescents engaging in these behaviors may require additional investigation in other areas of their lives.

Since this is the case, providers should ask themselves whether they believe that their adolescent clients, who, for instance, came to counseling on referral by their parents for their drug use,

are displaying a behavior that is normal (experimenting with marijuana) or abnormal (using marijuana every day). Several researchers call this process "Screening and Brief Intervention" (Zgierska, Amaza, Brown, Mundt, & Fleming, 2014). Screening and Brief Intervention is effective at ferreting out those who are abusing alcohol versus those who are only experimenting. Using the material gained through assessment, providers are in line to implement interventions and assessments accordingly (Zgierska et al., 2014).

COACHING AND MENTORING

Coaching and mentoring are two areas of recent research focus, as each represents a way to intervene in the lives of young people through less extreme measures (Qing & Millward, 2014). Coaching gives [adolescents] real-life solutions for their everyday issues (Grant, 2013). Counseling and family interventions can represent extreme measures; sometimes, these forms of counseling can be intimidating for young people to encounter. In addition, therapy is a more formal way of addressing adolescents' concerns, whereas coaching and mentoring often take place in the adolescent's own environment (at school or at home). Counseling is more centered on the emotional experiences and issues of a person; coaching and mentoring, on the other hand, are primarily focused on academic concerns and learning agendas. Subsequently, counseling is focused on "healing" the person's inner turmoil and staying within the comfort zone of the client, whereas coaching and mentoring are focused on challenging the person to venture outside his or her comfort zone and grow academically and personally, for instance (Qing & Millward, 2014).

Coaches tend to be optimistic regarding the "changeability" of their clients. They encourage their clients to see the exceptions to their issues (e.g., nobody is sad forever), point out positive aspects, use language of possibility (e.g., "If one person made it that far you can make it too"), and to help a person make small goals leading up to big goals so success is experienced along the way (Grant, 2013). Building adolescents' level of achievement can have positive effects on their mental health; nonetheless, when adolescents experience failure, even just the perception of failure or low status, they are at risk of depression (Quiroga, Janosz, Bisset, & Morin, 2013), suicidal thoughts (Lee, Wong, Chow, & McBride-Chang, 2006), and dropping out of school (Werblow, Urick, & Duesbery, 2013), among other risk factors. Hence, the usefulness of coaching is implied. There are several areas of coaching, including cognitive coaching, solution-focused coaching, and narrative coaching (NC).

Cognitive Coaching

A cognitive coach is someone trained to address adolescents' cognitive thinking, decision making, and relationship building (Qing & Millward, 2014). Essentially, a cognitive coach helps adolescents address their cognitions that are presenting them with barriers to their own learning. It is an educational tool for teachers to use to address students' learning with more precision, and it facilitates the learning experience of students by promoting their ability to self-learn through "independent learning" (Sirmaci & Ceylan, 2014). Furthermore, cognitive coaching provides adolescents with insight about their thoughts, emotions, and choices of action, arming them with strategies to use once their coach is absent. The aim, therefore, is for adolescents to eventually be able to function without the coach present (Gyllensten, Palmer, Nilsson, Regnér, & Frodi, 2010; Sirmaci & Ceylan, 2014).

Applied in a mathematical setting, cognitive coaching was deemed more effective than traditional teaching. Students in the experimental group showed more academic achievement in their mathematical skills, their outlook on mathematics changed (students stated in surveys that they looked forward to learning mathematics and appreciated their teacher's way of providing instruction), and they became more aware of avenues of learning (students were taught how to formulate their own style of learning through

self-directed learning agendas). This research shows the degree to which cognitive coaching places the learning experience on the student. This study has implications for researchers.

Providers can use this information to inform their own direction in counseling with adolescents. Knowing that adolescents perform better when they are taught how to take their own initiative, providers should feel more comfortable giving their adolescent clients room to develop their own strategies for change and progress. According to Eunsook, Milgram, and Rowell (2004), adolescents are more likely to complete homework assignments when school providers create opportunities for them to learn their homework based on their own personal style of learning. When, for instance, providers form groups based on the areas of adolescent difficulty (e.g., motivation to do homework), adolescents show more progress and motivation. It is recommended that providers take cultural and personal characteristics of adolescents into consideration and then create opportunities for them to learn within these contexts (Eunsook et al., 2004).

Solution-Focused Coaching

Grant (2013) gives specific step-by-step directions for how to implement solution-focused coaching. He addresses, at the start of his article, the lack of research in this area of coaching, but nonetheless, he underlines the value of solution-focused coaching for professionals. Solution-focused coaching begins with helping people change their thinking from negative to positive. It helps them see solutions rather than problems. It has an effect on the people's perception of experience; it changes their outlook and helps them define their experience as less concerning and, instead, more promising. Providing a person with hope, solution-focused coaches encourage people to focus on their future. They, for instance, will not try to inquire into a person's past; rather, they may ask a person, "What do you want out of life?" "What does your future hold?" Or "What is important to you at this very moment in life?"

Adams (2012) agrees that solution-focused coaching is done in a step-by-step process. He suggests a seven-step process. *Step 1:* It is important to identify the problem. The coach ascertains from the client(s) what the issue is and what they hope the outcome to be. *Step 2:* Both the coach and the client set specific and realistic goals. Setting goals helps them keep similar perspectives and ideas concerning the reason for the process. *Step 3:* The coach and the client search for solutions. They begin by going over different ideas for how to arrive at a particular outcome (i.e., what works and what does not work). *Step 4:* The consequences are considered; considering their solutions in Step 3, the coach and the client try to ascertain the likely consequences that will occur as a result of each solution. For instance, if a school wanted to end school 30 minutes earlier every day and the school had to figure out what to take out of the children's schedule to do so, one of their solutions may be to take out physical education (PE). In the fourth step, then, they are considering what consequences this may bring and whether the consequences are lesser or greater than their outcome (since taking PE out of the schedule, are students acting out more behaviorally?). Suggested as an intervention piece, providers in this step may create a pros and cons chart, containing the solutions and consequences of their decision. *Step 5:* Choose the most "feasible" solution. *Step 6:* Implement the chosen solution. *Step 7:* In this last step, the coach and the client evaluate their decision. Continuing with the already used example, observing the children's behavior during classroom hours could inform their decision to take PE out of the school's schedule.

These steps are a general approach to this model, and the aforementioned samples are from research concerning adult populations. A link can be made from the adult studies to adolescent populations, as solutions-focused *coaching* is similar to solution-focused *therapy*—a highly substantiated therapeutic modality used with adolescents (Bond, Woods, Humphrey, Symes, & Green, 2013; Cepukiene & Pakrosnis, 2011; Hopson & Kim, 2004; Kramer, Conijn, Oijevaar, & Riper, 2014). Research showing solution-focused

coaching's applicability for adolescents still needs to be undertaken.

Narrative Coaching

Naturally, humans try to create meaning out of their experiences (Vogel, 2012). Unfortunately, many of the stories people create are marked with negative events and outcomes (Hannen & Woods, 2012; Vogel, 2012). Their stories can be detrimental to their well-being, and they can begin to see life as punishing and burdensome. The role of the narrative coach, here, is to teach a person how to retell one's stories based on one's own desires. They encourage people to create their own ending and to stop viewing their stories as truths. Moreover, narrative coaches educate people on how their stories, not their actual lives, are the issue (Vogel, 2012). Vogel (2012) interviewed six narrative coaches; each coach adhered to a narrative style throughout his or her work with the adult clients and found it to be a productive way of addressing client concerns.

Interestingly enough, when NC is used within a counseling dynamic (two people), it can have a tremendous effect on an adolescent's ability to think about his or her life under a positive light (Qing & Millward, 2014). Highlighted in current research is the finding that adolescents are well adapted to speaking in narrative form. Nippold et al. (2014), for example, states that adolescents who speak in narrative form (storytelling) have improved language skills. It was noticed by Nippold et al. (2014) that when adolescents spoke in stories, their use of complex syntax increased (their spoken sentences contained 5.43 more words than when they spoke in day-to-day conversation).

Research in the area of narrative *therapy* (NT) is consistent, showing that this type of counseling is effective with adolescent clients (Cashin, 2008; Hannen & Woods, 2012; Nippold et al., 2014). NC, however, is nonexistent (as for our search) with adolescents, revealing yet another research need. NT, on the other hand, is not limited to only adult populations. On examining the differences between NC (as it is used with adults) and NT (as it is used with adolescents), it was discovered that both resemble each other in style and manner (the same thing took place with solution-focused coaching and therapy). Narrative interventions, then, will be looked at from the perspective of NT.

NT is similar to NC, as it stands. NC purports that adolescents experience distress in their lives as a result of their life stories and negative thoughts and cognitions (Cashin, Browne, Bradbury, & Mulder, 2013). The focus of one study was to use NT with adolescents diagnosed with autism (Autism currently falls under the subheading "Autism Spectrum Disorder (ASD)" in the *DSM-5* (APA, 2013; Cashin et al., 2013). Autism, referred to in Cashin et al. (2013), creates difficulty in thinking, emotional displays (laughing when everybody else is laughing), relationship building (difficulty understanding how to be social), processing and storing information into memory, and being flexible (wanting to play with yellow trucks only). Unfortunately, those who struggle with autism have bouts of depression and anxiety that can be detrimental to their emotional and psychological well-being; in fact, depression and anxiety are the two greatest risk factors for adolescents with autism (Cashin et al., 2013; Matson & Williams, 2014; Mayes, Calhoun, Murray, & Zahid, 2011; McCoy, 2012).

Rather than editing out parts of an adolescent's life, NT is used with adolescents who have autism by helping them build a new story (Cashin et al., 2013). Following five, 1-hour counseling sessions over a duration of 10 weeks, adolescents who received NT displayed less emotional disturbance (depression, anxiety), as accounted for through parent surveys (Cashin et al., 2013). Providers working with adolescents with developmental disorders should be encouraged by these findings. This is a brief therapeutic approach that can be fun and engaging for both the provider and the adolescent client. NT can also help build provider–client rapport, relationship, and trust, well needed during counseling with young people (Bennett, 2012).

NT is also effective with adolescents struggling with language-literacy deficits (Wolter, DiLollo, &

Apel, 2006), Aspergers Disorder (this disorder has since been removed from the *DSM-5*—APA, 2013; Cashin, 2008), and self-harm (cutting; Hannen & Woods, 2012). Hannen and Woods (2012), for instance, discovered that when NT was employed with one 12-year-old adolescent girl who self-harmed, her mood increased (she became happier), she stopped cutting, and her anger decreased.

Mentoring and Related Interventions

Mentorship programs employ men and women, often volunteers, to be role models for young people. They offer adolescents support, encouragement, and motivation to succeed in life and to make positive life choices. Research shows that mentors increase adolescents' self-esteem and ambition for school (Meyer & Bouchey, 2010). Boys are motivated to achieve in school, have higher school expectations, have increased self-esteem, and desire to match their mentors' hobbies (traveling) when their mentor is of the same race, gender, and SES. Girls, on the other hand, are more inspired, interestingly enough, to achieve academically when they are paired with a male mentor. In fact, Meyer and Bouchey (2010) discovered that when girls are paired with female mentors, their academic expectations (desire to succeed in school, future-oriented thinking) went down. This finding suggests that female mentees and mentors may carry in their relationship stereotypes about women's role in society and in work (Meyer & Bouchey, 2010). Together, female mentors and mentees, therefore, may be upholding stereotypes. For example, if the mentee tells the mentor she wants to be a doctor the mentor may say, "Girls don't become doctors; be a stewardess instead."

Bartle-Haring, Slesnick, Collins, Erdem, and Buettner (2012) were interested in testing out a mentorship program for homeless adolescents addicted to drugs. Ninety young people (ages 14–22) constituted their sample; two groups were formed (Group 1: standard treatment; Group 2: mentorship program). Mentors and mentees were paired based on their similar gender, race, and sexual orientation. Compared with substance abuse treatment, mentoring was found to decrease adolescents' high-risk behavior related to their substance abuse. However, mentoring was found to be no more effective, or even less effective, than the substance abuse treatment alone (e.g., externalizing behaviors decreased as substance abuse treatment sessions increased—with or without mentorship; Bartle-Haring et al., 2012). Obviously, further research is needed in these areas. However, despite the lack of substantiated research in this area, research underlines mentors' potential benefit (Frels et al., 2013; Hurd & Zimmerman, 2010; Mitchell, 2013), and the desire of youth to have positive adult relationships is realized (Dang & Miller, 2013; Thompson, Corsello, McReynolds, & Conklin-Powers, 2013).

What can providers' roles be in providing mentorship to adolescents? For one, they can use the evidence that the quality of the provider–client relationship is crucial to counseling outcome to give credence to the mentorship model agenda. In effect, providers can align themselves to be a role model, while still adhering to their position of authority, in order to promote the well-being of their clients. Providers can also design into their model of therapy an emphasis on encouraging their clients to create bonds and relationships in their families, communities, and schools. Consistently, research gives evidence that relationships and bonds with peers or adults have significant effects on adolescents' self-esteem, outlook on life, and academic success (Farruggia, Bullen, & Davidson, 2013; Hughes & Chen, 2011; Liem & Martin, 2011; Lynch, Lerner, & Leventhal, 2013; Vitaro, Boivin, Brendgen, Girard, & Dionne, 2012).

GROUP COUNSELING

An integral part of treatment for adolescents is group counseling. Based on the symptom presentation, different groups may be more appropriate for clients struggling with mental health concerns. Groups are designed to target specific knowledge and skills believed to be critical to functional behavior (e.g., cue recognition,

cognitive restructuring, and affect modulation). Specialized groups can also target broader social–ecological factors that research suggests contribute to aggressive and disruptive behaviors (e.g., peer and family influences, distorted concepts of masculinity). The key components of group counseling are skill acquisition, skill generalization, and fostering an understanding of how the imparted skills/knowledge can assist in managing problematic behaviors. While the format of groups varies, each group tends to adhere to a very specific format as follows:

- Introduction of the specific concept (e.g., impulse control)
- Understanding the linkage between the skill and the problematic behavior
- Provider modeling of the skill and resident practicing of the skill through role-play exercises
- Clinical homework assignments designed to reinforce acquisition and understanding of the skill/concept
- Measurement of concept/skill acquisition and generalization.

Consistent with a social–ecological model, clients are expected to demonstrate each skill within the therapeutic environment and also in the broader social environment in which they live and function (i.e., school). While all skills will be linked to increasing the clients' awareness and understanding of how it can assist them in managing their problematic behavior, there should also be discussion of how clients can apply the skill in their everyday life.

It is important to understand how group counseling grew out of the work of a few people and now is exploding as a well-established therapeutic tool to use with just about any population. It works exceptionally well because it normalizes people's experience and helps them to know that they are not alone in their suffering. For providers, group counseling is convenient and provides an incentive financially. Two populations will be highlighted in the next two sections: (1) shy adolescents and (2) depressed adolescents. The idea was to show how group counseling can be used with extremely isolated individuals to bring out in them a sense of peace, comfort, and hope.

Shy Adolescents and Group Counseling

Shyness has a way of isolating young people who are uncomfortable with the inability to participate in group interaction away from their peers (Umeh, 2013). Shyness is both an emotional experience and a psychological one (Umeh, 2013). Shyness deters adolescents from taking opportunities, risks, and pursuing their dreams; it can have a crippling effect over time (Umeh, 2013). Walker, Degnan, Fox, and Henderson (2013) state that shyness is equitable to being fearful. These researchers believe that shy adolescents are controlled by an approach–avoidance stance (they want to participate [approach] but choose not to out of fear and anxiety [avoidance]). Shy adolescents are also more likely to react more negatively, compared with nonshy peers, to facial expressions that represent fear, sadness, or anger (Ozono, Watabe, & Yoshikawa, 2012).

On account of this evidence, Umeh (2013) designed a group intervention based on cognitive behavioral therapy (CBT; challenging cognitions to change behavior—thinking precedes reaction; changed thinking changes behavior). After only 10 sessions of CBT, adolescents prone to shyness were less anxious, they had less cognitive distortions related to social situations, their beliefs were more rational, and they were less focused on their need to be perfect. Though medication alone was able to reduce anxiety, it was not able to reduce cognitive distortions, irrational beliefs, or perfectionism (Umeh, 2013).

Depressed Adolescents and Group Counseling

Similar to shyness, depression influences a person's decision to withdraw from social stimuli (APA, 2013). In fact, the experience of depression can make a person who was once named a "social butterfly" to want nothing to do with people, places, and things based solely on their state of mind (APA, 2013). The outcome is reduced social competence, social problem solving, and total functioning within a social context (Ozdemir, Kuzucu, & Koruklu, 2013; Uhrlass, Schofield, Coles, & Gibb, 2009). Different, however, from the shy individuals studied, depressed people tend to avoid both happy and mean faces. For example, the happy face says, "Come talk to me," yet depressed people do not want to engage; consequently, they turn away from people altogether. So there is not only an emotional and psychological fear for these individuals to participate in social situations but there is also a loss of sensitivity (because of the depression) to want to be a part of the group formation (Radke, Güths, André, Müller, & de Bruijn, 2014).

Depression in adolescence or in emerging adulthood (17–19 years old) has long-term adult consequences: reduced income (Fletcher, 2013), suicide attempts (Goldston et al., 2009), anxiety disorders (Costello, Copeland, & Angold, 2011), poverty (Frederick & Goddard, 2007), dropping out of college (Wintre & Bowers, 2007), poor relational ties (Salmela-Aro, Aunola, & Nurmi, 2008), obesity (Goosby, Bellatorre, Walsemann, & Cheadle, 2013), to name a few. Subsequently, the period of adolescence is the perfect time to intervene to change the trajectory of young peoples' lives and adult outcomes.

Providers, and parents for that matter, should consider a group therapeutic intervention approach for adolescents experiencing depression. One such approach that has been substantiated in the literature as successful with this population is the Penn Resiliency Program (PRP; Gillham et al., 2012). PRP is an intervention designed to be implemented in a school atmosphere by teachers and school providers. It is a cognitive behavioral (CB) approach to group therapeutic treatment. Since 2012, PRP has shown to be effective in at least 17 empirical research designs (Gillham et al., 2012).

Providers should note the design of the PRP intervention program. Addressed in the study by Gillham et al. (2012) was PRP's effectiveness at decreasing both anxiety and depression in adolescents in sixth, seventh, and eighth grades. These researchers employed a group intervention facilitated by school providers and teachers. Teachers and providers received specialized training in CB therapy prior to the group intervention. This was a 3-year longitudinal research study that assessed adolescents throughout the duration of the study to find out whether the treatment was valid over time. Indeed, PRP reduced adolescents' depression and anxiety by raising their level of hope; the level of hopelessness was linked to PRP's impact (the greater the amount of hopelessness, the greater the impact of PRP).

PRP is structured, giving facilitators specific directions for how to run groups. Again, based on CB techniques (Beck's model of therapy), facilitators teach adolescents about the connection between thoughts and behaviors. Learning the difference between what a maladaptive thought is versus a productive thought is a highlight of the PRP intervention. Providing insight into the link between thoughts, hopelessness, and depression is also a key. Then, facilitators teach adolescents not only how to recognize and challenge their maladaptive thoughts but also how to cope under the distress of the thoughts themselves. The result is that adolescents are more assertive, solve problems more efficiently, are able to experience relaxation, and show greater competence and skill in decision making (Gillham et al., 2012).

Compelling evidence also exists for the usefulness of group counseling with adolescents who are suicidal (Bannan, 2010), aggressive (Currie & Startup, 2012), diagnosed with attention-deficit/hyperactive disorder (Cantor, 2000), victimized (Habib, Labruna, & Newman, 2013), self-harming (Moran, Pathak, & Sharma, 2009), addicted to the Internet (Du, Jiang, & Vance, 2010), developmentally delayed (Siu, 2014), and grieving (Granados, Winslade, De Witt, & Hedtke, 2009). All of the aforementioned studies support providers' being the main facilitators for these interventions.

Though CBT and CB were especially advertised as being therapies of choice for group counseling with adolescents, other therapeutic orientations also show promising results. For instance, solution-focused therapy combined with Ericksonian counseling theory (e.g., belief in the influence of a person's unconscious and the usefulness of using metaphors and language of change to instigate change in the lives of people) increased sexually abused adolescent girls' self-esteem, social comfort, connection with others, and their outlook on life (Kress & Hoffman, 2008); group counseling techniques derived from Gestalt therapy was successful at reducing adolescent girls' high-risk behavior (e.g., unhealthy relationships, lack of boundaries, substance abuse) through a change in attitude (Zinck & Littrell, 2000); adolescent boys' aggressiveness is reduced when they learn how to control their impulses through mindfulness-based group counseling (Waltman, Hetrick, & Tasker, 2012); and structure therapy for adolescents responding to chronic stress implemented through a group format is able to reduce symptoms of posttraumatic stress disorder (PTSD), anxiety, and depression and improve social skills, physical comfort, and self-control delivered to adolescents who experienced a personal crisis (e.g., physical abuse; Habib et al., 2013).

CRISIS COUNSELING

A crisis is an event that creates havoc in a person's life to a point where his or her functioning becomes disrupted (Sandoval, Scott, & Padilla, 2009). In other words, a crisis upsets a person's whole system (system meaning body). The first step, therefore, when faced with an adolescent who is in a crisis is to begin by connecting with the adolescent (Sandoval et al., 2009). Often, the only thing needed to calm a young person down during a crisis is a provider's physical presence. The next step, as suggested by Sandoval et al. (2009), is helping adolescents feel safe, while attending to their immediate needs (e.g., water, food, and shelter). Subsequently, providers should consider the whereabouts of adolescents' social supports. Connecting adolescents to their parents, caregivers, and teachers, for example, is critical; these familiar sources can provide adolescents with quick relief. Finally, providers should provide adolescents with referrals for long-term counseling to address the aftermath of their crisis (Sandoval et al., 2009). Not all crises are the same, however. Therefore, interventions used to address a crisis need to be personalized for the person and for the crisis. A few common crises that can upset the development of adolescence are described below: death, suicide, self-harm, and natural disasters.

Death and Suicide and Crisis Counseling

Early death by violent means and self-inflicted injuries is difficult to comprehend. The reasons why adolescents kill themselves are certainly a focus of researchers; however, until suicide is completely eliminated, interventions to reduce risk factors for suicide need to continue to expand and improve. It is encouraging that researchers are discovering that addressing suicide in schools through education about suicide, providing adolescents with crisis hotlines, educating parents about removing potential weapons from their home, and accurately diagnosing psychiatric disorders in young people are all rather simple means to reducing suicide (Karaman & Durukan, 2013). This section will explain the current impact of suicide as it relates to adolescents, some of the variations observed among different cultures and races, and the counseling interventions to reduce suicide among this age-group.

It is interesting to consider the findings specific to Morin and Welsh's (1996) study; interested in urban (poor and overrepresented by black people) and suburban (wealthy and over-represented by white people) adolescents' perception of death, these researchers asked adolescents between the ages of 13 and 18 what their definition of death was. Suburban adolescents reported death as the "absence of life" (31.6%); urban adolescents agreed (27.2%) but also believed death to be an "existence in another place" (27.2%) and due to violent means (as reported by delinquent youth). Additional survey

questions included adolescents' age when they first understood the concept of death (6.6 years old for suburban vs. 8.7 years old for urban adolescents), which person in their life died first (suburban adolescents stated older relatives [70.6%]; urban adolescents reported that the person was their caregiver [25%], persons who had an accidental death [16.7%], and death through violent means [8.3%]), how often they have experienced the act of suicide in other people (47% of suburban adolescents stated that they had experienced suicide; whereas only 8% of urban adolescents had experienced it), and their idea of what constituted a negative experience related to death (suburban adolescents reported that "suffering" [31.6%] and "uncertainty" [26.3%] are areas most bothersome to think about as related to death; urban adolescents, on the other hand, reported that "loss of loved ones," "dying young," "getting shot," and "nightmares about death" were answers that reflected their fear of death (Morin & Welsh, 1996, para. 16). It is thought provoking that only urban adolescents considered violence and death to be linked (Morin & Welsh, 1996).

In 2007, there were a total of 34,598 suicides among the U.S. population for both adult and adolescent populations combined; 4,140 of these suicides accounted for adolescents between the ages of 15 and 24 (U.S. Department of Health and Human Services, 2010). In 2009, the suicide rate for adolescents ages 15 to 24 was reported. For every 100,000 adolescents living in the United States, black or African American male (10.4) and female (2.1), American Indian or Alaska Native male (28.9) and female (11.4), Asian or Pacific Islander male (8.0) and female (4.4), Hispanic or Latino male (10.7) and female (2.3), and white—not Hispanic or Latino—male (19.4) and female (4.1) committed suicide (U.S. Department of Health and Human Services, 2010). Specifically considering the number of white and black adolescents' death by suicide (12.5 vs. 23.5, respectively), one can see for themselves that white adolescents represent almost double the number of suicides as that of their black peers. The suicide attempt rate, however, is another story. For high school students in

Grades 9 to 12, Hispanic (11.3%) and black (7.6%) adolescents (female and male), as reported in 2005, are more likely to attempt suicide than white (7.3%) adolescents (U.S. Department of Health and Human Services, 2010). As for suicidal ideation, white (16.9%), Hispanic (17.9%), and black (12.2%) adolescents again deviate from one another.

Interventions designed to treat adolescents who are struggling with the death of a loved one or their own suicidal thoughts should be personalized according to the person's background (race, gender, SES). Clearly, the above research shows that to take a one-aim approach to treat all racial and gender-specific groups will undermine effective treatment. Suicide is a serious issue that needs to be dealt with, as it is the third leading cause of death for young people of ages 10 to 24, and more than 250,000 young people under the age of 25 die by suicide every year (Balis & Postolache, 2008; World Health Organization, 2013). Morin and Welsh (1996) state that interventions designed for adolescents who have experienced the death of a loved one should be simple. For instance, adolescents responded in surveys used by researchers Morin and Welsh (1996) that attentive listening and open dialogue with someone who cares (e.g., parent or provider) provide significant relief for them during the time of grief (Table 10.2). In this way, providers should strive to build rapport with their clients

through active listening. Allowing adolescents to speak openly about their concerns from their point of view can be a first-step approach for providers to open up the way for their clients to begin to trust them.

Adolescents from suburban homes are most comforted through the feelings of grief by someone telling them "Your loved one is in a better place," whereas adolescents from urban communities find it comforting to be told "live well and avoid gangs" or "be strong" (Morin & Welsh, 1996). Interventions addressing suicidal thoughts and behaviors (self-harm by cutting) are not complicated to understand or put into action. Letting adolescents know that there is help available is often a powerful and simple tool to use to reduce suicidal behavior from going to dangerous levels. For instance, providers can tell their clients from the very start of counseling that they are there to help them and they are on their side. Providers can also encourage peer support for reducing suicide ideation in young people. Signs of Suicide, for instance, is a school-based prevention program that places the power to help in the hands of the population most likely to witness the needs of at-risk adolescents: their peers (Aseltine & DeMartino, 2004). Providers, therefore, should strive to make opportunities available in the community for adolescents to join together for a common purpose. Additionally, providers may find that developing group

Table 10.2 The Therapeutic Impact of Listening

The Roles of the Provider	*Therapy Outcomes for Adolescents*
To allow adolescent clients the opportunity to lead the direction in therapy as they feel comfortable to do so	Adolescents feel a sense of empowerment and leadership, perhaps unreflective of other aspects of their lives
To listen while using nonverbal responses in order to provide adolescent clients with feedback without interrupting their dialogue	Adolescents experience their provider's nonverbal behavior as empathic and focused on their concerns for care
To be intentional with their display of empathy and concern; making it their goal to identify, through empathy, with their adolescent clients	Identification with a provider makes adolescents feel like they are not alone, creating a sense of connection
To become the therapeutic tool used to build rapport and relationship with their clients	Adolescents have a sense of partnership with their provider and a hand in their own treatment

counseling dynamics that encourage peer support is the open door for adolescents who are normally rejected by their peers in school to begin to feel supported and to make friends.

In addition to giving adolescents comfort in knowing that help is available, it is important that interventions aim to reduce their suicidal thoughts and actions by increasing their hope. To develop or increase hope in adolescents, providers should provide interventions that increase their client's self-esteem and belief in external resources (e.g., teen hotline) available to meet their personal needs and goals (Roswarski & Dunn, 2009). The use of encouragement may also prove impactful for changing a person's suicidal ideation into hope (Deeley & Love, 2013). Providers, for instance, can provide adolescent clients with evidence that life is worth living. Asking them who they love in their life or what they want to be when they grow up are ways to focus their attention on goals and things they do not want to give up, such as their relationship with their best friend. At times, adolescents do not realize the actual outcome of suicide. Their wish to "just go to sleep" is an everlasting sleep, and when you remind them of this outcome by saying that "you will never get to hang out with your best friend again," it can provide young people with insight into the permanency of the choice to commit suicide.

Interested in looking at the fears young people have about counseling, Ægisdóttir, O'Heron, Hartong, Haynes, and Linville (2011) explored ways providers can help their clients look past the stigma of seeking help through counseling services. Their research, though done with young adults (mean age was 21.69 years), is applicable also for adolescents, as research shows that adolescents, too, have fears related to their expectations and concerns about counseling (Stewart, 2014).

Two groups were formed, and both were given directions to pretend to be a person who was seeking counseling services for depression—to imagine going into an initial intake session. Then, one group was given a vignette that portrayed the intake provider they came into

contact with as neutral—this provider was nice, assessed their issue of depression, and addressed referral sources for their outpatient care; the second group was given a vignette that portrayed the intake provider as, again, nice and competent in their assessment of issues, and offered referral, but this provider also talked openly about the clients' possible fears and thoughts about counseling (i.e., openly discussing the stigma of seeking help). In other words, the difference between the two was one group talked openly about counseling and addressed potential client fears about coming into counseling and the other group did not. In the end, the group that read the vignette that addressed counseling fears and the stigma of asking for help were more inclined than the other group to state that they would continue treatment after the initial intake session (Ægisdóttir et al., 2011).

Their research has implications for the retention rate for clients; furthermore, this research suggests that providers, from the very outset of their work with new clients, whether young or old, should address the stigma in society that states that it is inappropriate to seek help, receive counseling services, or have a mental illness (Corrigan, Druss, & Perlick, 2014; Cummings, Lucas, & Druss, 2013; Girma et al., 2014; Tzouvara & Papadopoulos, 2014). For example, providers can begin by asking adolescents the following questions: What are your feelings about being here? What do you think of me? What do you think that your friends or family think of you being here, and do they know that you are here? Unfortunately, when young people do not feel able to reach out for help or when that help is unavailable (e.g., parents working late), they are more likely to display inappropriate and dangerous behaviors in an attempt to communicate their emotional turmoil (Roswarski & Dunn, 2009). Often, this form of communication is labeled in the research as "self-harm" or "cutting."

Self-Harm

Self-harm is defined in the literature as the deliberate harm of oneself without the intent to commit suicide (Flett, Goldstein, Hewitt, &

Wekerle, 2012). Others, however, define it more broadly by stating that self-harm includes acts with suicidal intent (Ougrin, 2012; Young, Sproeber, Groschwitz, Preiss, & Plener, 2014). Regardless, adolescents' choice to self-harm is a growing concern. More and more adolescents are beginning to engage in one form of self-harm or another at earlier ages (Stallard, Spears, Montgomery, Phillips, & Sayal, 2013). For adolescents between the ages of 10 and 24 years, the two most common forms of self-harm, or self-injury, are "poisoning" (45.3%) and "cutting/piercing" themselves (26.3%); Centers for Disease Control and Prevention (2014). Other methods of self-harm common among this age-group are the following: burning, rubbing their skin raw, and self-hitting (Walsh & Muehlenkamp, 2013). Research shows that the common age when self-harm begins in adolescence is at the age of 12 or 13 years (Stallard et al., 2012). In a longitudinal study that took place over the course of 4 years, a sample of 12- and 13-year-olds were asked about their self-harming behavior beginning when they were in the eighth grade. Twenty percent of adolescents who reported self-harming thoughts at Interval 1 still reported them at Interval 2 (6 months later). Additionally, 10% of them admitted to engaging in active self-harm (cutting) within those two interval periods (Stallard et al., 2012).

Adolescents, both male and female, are more likely to self-harm when they have peer-avoidant relationships, have a depressed mood, or are engaging in substance abuse (marijuana for girls and hard drug use for boys [e.g., heroin] increase their chances of self-harm by six times); in addition, boys are inclined to self-harm in response to bullying (Stallard et al., 2013). Some of the common reasons why adolescents self-harm include wanting an emotional release, to punish themselves, to "cleanse" themselves from past physical and sexual abuse, to play with death, to experience an emotional numbing from their emotional pain, to feel a sense of control over themselves, or to prevent future occurrences of abuse, again, through their perception that self-harm will somehow reduce their chances of future victimizations (Sandy, 2013).

Being in a restricted facility (e.g., psychiatric hospital) increases the risk of self-harm (Sandy, 2013). When this occurs, self-harm is depicted by nursing staff as manipulative and attention seeking. Not entirely false, adolescents seek attention because they have no other form of communication that seems to them to be appropriate to receive the care they desire to have (Sandy, 2013). Reportedly, adolescents begin cutting after confined in an environment because it is a way to communicate their feelings of isolation. Their sense of disempowerment drives them to cut in order to express their emotion and frustration about their situation (Sandy, 2013). Therefore, providers working in these settings should be cautioned to understand that an adolescent admitted into their facility with self-harming behaviors may actually be trying to express something through this behavior. Providers, then, should begin by asking adolescents why they cut, what message they are trying to send, and what triggers their cutting to begin with. Perhaps, when providers begin to understand the message behind the act, they will be in a better position to help. More interventions to address these populations are examined next.

When admittance into a community-based treatment program is recommended, discharge planning should begin the day adolescents enter into treatment. Providers should be collaborating with parents to find out what services their adolescents already have and will need once discharged. The dilemma then can become that adolescents who do not readily self-harm may begin to do so more pervasively once they are admitted into an inpatient facility (Richardson, Surmitis, & Hyldahl, 2012). This is called the "contagion effect," and it has implications for why adolescents who are not at imminent risk should be considered first for outpatient care rather than inpatient care because their likelihood of "contracting" self-harming behavior from a peer increases (You, Lin, Fu, & Leung, 2013). The idea is that adolescents entering into inpatient care who do not self-harm will learn how to do so from their peers. Obviously, this is not an ideal situation. Certain psychiatric conditions, such as borderline personality disorder (BPD), may place adolescents at greater risk for contracting self-harming behavior from peers (Drabble, Bowles, & Barker, 2014; Jarvi, Jackson, Swenson, & Crawford, 2013).

Providers and doctors alike, then, should prescreen adolescents at intake for BPD. When BPD is diagnosed, caution should be warranted. A consideration of the pros and cons for admitting an adolescent with BPD into inpatient care may be one possible intervention. Adolescents with BPD are prone to the contagion effect because of their desire to fit in (Courtney-Seidler, Klein, & Miller, 2013). Recommending inpatient versus outpatient care should be carefully examined for these patients. Especially risky is putting an adolescent who is not already self-harming but has BPD into a psychiatric locked down facility. The reason is that adolescents diagnosed with BPD are known for their attention-seeking behaviors and need for outward approval from others to fulfill their need for feelings of self-assurance and self-efficacy (Courtney-Seidler et al., 2013). Regardless, providers can reduce the chance of contagion occurring in group settings by making concerted efforts that group members do not talk about self-harm in the group. Staying away from this subject altogether may reduce the chances of others learning the behavior.

Unfortunately, to date, there is little empirical research or designed clinical study (e.g., studies that utilize random sampling and large sample groups) that is specifically designed to reduce the behavior of self-harm in adolescents or adults; in addition, research and interventions that are available seem to lack in support (Washburn et al., 2012). For example, Oldershaw et al. (2012) tested out CBT with adolescents of ages 12 to 18 years to find out if CBT-directed decision making would reduce deliberate self-harm. Despite their findings, only half of their sample returned for posttesting, which then created difficulty with using the data to generalize for all people.

However, there is one form of counseling that is showing some promising results. Dialectic behavior therapy was developed for BPD patients, but because self-harm is a symptom of BPD (Jarvi et al., 2013; Washburn et al., 2012), researchers have begun to study its use, also, with adolescents and adults who are self-harming, outside of the diagnosis of BPD (see Exercise 10.2).

Exercise 10.2

Counseling Adolescents Who Self-Harm

1. When assessing adolescents for the presence of self-destructive behaviors, what are some symptoms that might show up as evidence that an adolescent is cutting?

2. How can providers manipulate their counseling to make it unique to each adolescent client dependent on his or her engagement in self-harm, life circumstances, and embedded risk factors?

3. Considering the evidence that contagion effect is a real phenomenon, what are some ways providers can safeguard against adolescents who do not cut learning to cut from their peers in a group counseling setting?

4. Please differentiate suicidal ideation, suicidal threat, and suicidal gestures and how your intervention might be different for a client struggling with each of the noted suicidal behaviors.

Natural Disaster

Droughts, hurricanes, and tornadoes are a few examples of natural disasters. They happen throughout the world but are especially destructive when they occur in undeveloped Third World countries that lack resources (Julca, 2012). Natural disasters around the globe are dramatically increasing in numbers (350 annually vs. 69 in 1970); one reason for the increase is because of climate change (e.g., the rise and fall in temperatures are responsible for an increase in rainfalls and droughts; Julca, 2012). The rise in natural disasters means that more people are being affected by their aftermaths. Therefore, it is important for providers wanting to work in crisis settings to be prepared to work with clients experiencing trauma as a result of living through a natural disaster. Areas to assess for in these populations are the following: homelessness as a result of disaster, death of a loved one, physical disabilities, PTSD, job loss, to name a few. In response to families experiencing these outcomes, many children and adolescents are left feeling confused, distressed, helpless, and frustrated with their circumstances (Mearidy-Bell, 2013).

Providers need to be aware that when approaching adolescents who have witnessed or lived through a natural disaster, their cognitive capacity may be compromised at that very point in time; their ability to self-evaluate and participate in counseling may not be possible. For this reason, providers are encouraged not to begin counseling right away but to, instead, provide interventions to de-escalate adolescents' experience of crisis by providing immediate relief—then, once the crisis is lessened and their cognitive abilities are freed up, providers can begin to implement interventions designed for long-term counseling (e.g., CBT; Sandoval et al., 2009).

Providers should be aware of the symptoms often portrayed by victims of natural disasters. Mearidy-Bell (2013) studied the aftermath of natural disaster in 15 adolescents between the ages of 12 and 17 years. Her aim was to find out what behavior change, if any, the 15 adolescents would present with following a natural disaster (most of her sample consisted of adolescents who lived through a hurricane). Four behavior themes showed up: (1) avoidant relationships and isolating, (2) an increase in verbal altercations with family and friends, (3) withdrawal, and (4) overprotectiveness. These areas point to intervention possibilities.

Nastasi, Jayasena, Summerville, and Borja (2011) believe that communities, family, and school contexts are the areas where interventions to address children's and adolescent's crises should begin. Showing their support for research in these areas, these authors remark that to provide adolescents with interventions through the family context could mean building up their broken families, providing home relief to those who are homeless, and helping families to rebuild normalcy within their contexts so life can resume for all family members.

Providing school-based community programs is another idea. These community-based programs are beneficial when developed to address adolescents in a group setting. Healing is thought to begin as a result of the peer-group atmosphere that caters to an understanding that one is not alone in one's distress (Sandoval et al., 2009). Additional interventions to address adolescent crisis as a result of a natural disaster include school-based counseling, play and art counseling, community-based psychotherapy, bibliotherapy, and treatment specifically designed to address PTSD symptoms (e.g., eye movement desensitization and reprocessing [EMDR] and CBT) (Sandoval et al., 2009).

EMDR was created to work with a person's trauma by using hand movements that "forces" a person receiving it to move his or her eyes back and forth. Reportedly, when this eye movement occurs, people are able to uncover and process their traumatic experiences (Sandoval et al., 2009). There has been much research into EMDR's effectiveness with trauma (Rost, Hofmann, & Wheeler, 2009; Shapiro, 2012; Solomon, Solomon, & Heide, 2009). Sandoval et al. (2009) state that EMDR has been found successful with child and adolescent populations. However, some investigators report otherwise. For instance, Greyber, Dulmus, and Cristalli (2012) provide a review for studies done between 1998 and 2010 concerning EMDR's use with children and adolescents who experienced trauma (Table 10.3). They found these studies to be "unsubstantiated" because of their lack of empirical support and recommended for future research to be undertaken prior to saying that EMDR is appropriate for adolescents and children.

CBT, on the other hand, works with specific symptoms to reduce its effect on a person's overall experience of the trauma and crisis (Sandoval et al., 2009). It is effective because of its structured approach to teaching adolescents skills for living and effective problem solving. CBT, furthermore, motivates adolescents to challenge

Table 10.3   Counseling Techniques for Adolescents Who Have Lived Through a Natural Disaster

School-Based Counseling

Providers utilize adolescent clients' family members, teachers, and health care professionals to effect change in a young person's life.

Providers co-collaborate with other providers to attempt to change systems of structure (e.g., school and home environments) that invoke trauma and risk factors for adolescents' functioning (e.g., addressing the issue of death and grief; Keys, Bemak, & Lockhart, 1998).

Play and Art Counseling

Providers can utilize play and art counseling with adolescent clients who are resistant to verbal and behavioral interventions (Martinez & Lasser, 2013).

When providers use play counseling as an intervention with adolescents following a natural disaster, there are themes that show up in an adolescents' play style that guide counselors through the therapeutic journey.

Themes of control often show up first; these include behaviors that reflect fixing objects, breaking objects, and sorting objects. Following Theme one, clients will progress toward themes of nurturing and acceptance (less violent and aggressive play is noticed). Providers, therefore, become aware of when to terminate counseling based on the themes of play adolescents engage in (Dugan, 2010).

Community-Based Counseling

Providers responding to a natural disaster are likely to make contact with adolescents who are experiencing trauma as a result of living through a natural disaster.

Providers coming into contact with this dynamic need to remain calm and proactive. They should use their own stability as a model and grounding point for adolescents to replicate.

After providing quick relief, providers should connect adolescents to family, friends, and resources of referral in the community.

Bibliocounseling

Once rapport and trust are established, providers can use bibliocounseling (assigning book reading to increase interest in counseling) with adolescents who have experienced trauma due to natural disasters to help adolescents work through the trauma by addressing it through chapter topics.

Providers need to remain interactive in the process of bibliocounseling, giving reading assignments and then addressing the themes that come up frequently in the readings with their adolescent clients (Christenbury, Beale, & Patch, 1996).

their own negative thoughts and to adjust their thinking to align themselves with positive functioning. The important feature of CBT is to reduce the anxiety of the trauma so that adolescents can begin to function again at their baseline (Sandoval et al., 2009).

Whaley (2009) gives providers a step-by-step guide to addressing trauma/crisis in people following natural disasters. Adults within his sample had all experienced Hurricane Katrina. Whaley (2009) recommends that providers begin by assessing peoples' experience of the event. By simply inquiring about the people's perception of the event, finding out loss of resources, and assessing their total functioning might be helpful during this initial stage. Furthermore, he suggests that providers should not call people "victims," but instead, they should refer to them as "survivors." Helping them to change their perception around the event, then, might provide aid in their ability to do so once they are out of the proximity of the provider.

Finally, contingent on the provider's assessment, if the person is experiencing trauma that is not causing specific distress, verbal empathic response interventions may be all that is needed; however, Whaley (2009) states that when the trauma is severe in nature (e.g., symptoms resemble PTSD such as "emotional numbing" and "avoidance"), providers need to use interventions that are empirically supported to help that person. Other symptoms of PTSD that providers should watch out for are the following: nightmares, recurrent distressful thoughts, dissociation, a person's inability to remember the event or things associated with it, emotional upset about the event (e.g., anger, fear), feeling separated from other people, flat affect, hyperarousal, and/or reckless behavior (APA, 2013).

In conclusion, though Whaley (2009) reflected his research on an adult population experiencing trauma/crisis, his research is found to be applicable to adolescent populations as well. The reason is as follows: The *DSM-5* criteria for PTSD diagnosis clearly states that the symptoms contained within PTSD are for those 6 years old and older (APA, 2013). Providing therapeutic models that address trauma in adolescence *only*

would be nice to highlight, yet this is another area that seems to be understudied.

FAMILY COUNSELING

White picket fence, Labrador Retriever, two-car garage, everlasting marriage, being their own boss in a financially productive business, and two children who never fight, have no issues, and are successful throughout all of their lives is likely the picture that gleams through the minds of adolescents when they think about the perfect family and life. People, however, realize early on in life that their idea of the perfect family is far from the truth. Instead, they realize that family is not only something they are predestined into but also one family from the next is exceptionally unique. For instance, Mike, who is in the sixth grade, comes to realize that not all parents are remarried like his—something he realized as a result of spending the night at his friend Johnny's house whose parents are still married. Sara, whose mother is severely abused every night by her alcoholic father, is jealous of her friend Megan whose mom and dad display affection for each other, play video games with their children, and regularly attend Megan's school functions. Multiple children versus one child, divorce versus remarriage, stepchildren versus no children, sexual abuse versus love, emotional distance versus enmeshment, gay versus heterosexual parents, parental substance abuse versus parental religiosity, black versus white, Hispanic, multiracial, Asian, or Indian/Alaskan family culture, and the like all create the uniqueness of the family identity.

Providers would do well to remember that families are *all* different; they should use this knowledge of difference to guide their therapeutic practice with families. There are myriad family counseling interventions; for the purposes of this chapter, however, only a few will be referenced. Those cited were chosen because of their uniqueness and empirical support; also, they are new interventions that are gaining in momentum. Two interventions are (1) enhancing parent–adolescent communication and (2) home-based counseling services.

Family Communication

Parents and adolescents understand, speak, and communicate from two very different perspectives (Wehrman & Field, 2013). For this reason, communication between parents and their adolescent children is often confused. Parents want their children to somehow think, act, speak, and behave like an adult; but they cannot think, act, speak, and behave like adults because, simply, they are not yet adults (Wehrman & Field, 2013). Unfortunately, this disrupts the relationship between children and their parents. Each feels as though the other "just doesn't understand." Providers, therefore, have a mighty role in this picture. However, they can actually continue to disrupt the communication if they, too, begin to expect adolescents to think, act, speak, and behave like adults.

First of all, Wehrman and Field (2013) caution that many times providers are overwhelmed with the idea of *everyone* within the nuclear family being included in counseling. However, when providers leave family members out, such as small children or adolescents, the family structure is incomplete. With some family members absent, the question becomes "How can you fix communication between family members when they are not present?" Including all family members, therefore, is the first, and probably the most important, step to competent family counseling to address family communication problems.

From the moment a family enters into the counseling room, providers, whose attention should be on the family's verbal and nonverbal communication patterns, should note the family's dynamic. It is important to pay attention to this aspect. What chair each family member chooses to sit on and his or her personal emotional displays are important to attend to. Seating arrangement, for one, can provide the provider with insight for who holds the power of authority (Wehrman & Field, 2013).

A suggested first intervention to address family communication is to ask the family to draw

(providers helping in this process) a family genogram (Wehrman & Field, 2013). Family genograms are much like a family tree (Curtis & Berman, 2010). The purpose of them is to shed light on the family dynamics, their interactions, past divorces, current marriages, broken relationships, deaths, and number of relatives. Relationships, communication patterns, and genetic patterns are all displayed through this manageable exercise (Curtis & Berman, 2010; Wehrman & Field, 2013).

The second step is for the provider to ask each family member the reason for attending counseling. If interruptions occur, providers should use strategies to "block" family members from cutting off other family members from speaking (Wehrman & Field, 2013). Essentially, the provider is helping family members to see and understand that when interruption or arguing occurs effective communication cannot take place. In this light, providers are using their own behavior to model appropriate communication (see Exercise 10.3).

The third step is for the provider to implement a "Weekly Check-in Scale"—asking families, as a team, to pinpoint when the problem (the one that brought them into counseling) was the worst (Wehrman & Field, 2013). Then, over the course of counseling, this scale is attended to in order to help show families their progress in counseling and to determine when counseling should be terminated.

Wehrman and Field (2013) end by suggesting that providers, in the middle of their session, take a break. They advocate that taking a break gives providers time to orient themselves to what is happening (the themes), to plan what homework to give to their clients, and to receive consultation if warranted; this break also provides the opportunity for family members to adjust and think about what is taking place.

Home-Based Counseling

Providers are now, more than ever, entering into home environments because of the need for home-based family counseling services. Research

Exercise 10.3

The Importance of Parent and Adolescent Communication

1. What is important to consider before implementing interventions in order to bring about greater communication between family members?

2. Describe why from the beginning to the end of counseling, each step providers take to implement interventions must be intentional. What family dynamics should providers attend to most on first meeting their clients?

3. Think about the benefits and costs of following a step-by-step structured plan for counseling families. Can you give details of a possible setback that may spring up as a result of using a structured approach with adolescents?

shows home-based family counseling to be successful with whole families, children, and adolescents (Hammond & Czyszczon, 2014; Mattek, Jorgenson, & Fox, 2010; Sari, 2014; Scarborough, Taylor, & Tuttle, 2013; Tate, Lopez, Fox, Love, & McKinney, 2014). Often used with families experiencing poverty (Mattek et al., 2010), children with a developmental disability (Sari, 2014), and children in child protective services (Scarborough et al., 2013), this approach to counseling is a creative opportunity for providers to engage their clients in their own environments while gaining insight into each family member's point of view. For example, how the parents discipline the children

in their home, whether mom and dad are both home at night to help with homework (whether there is both mom and dad, or either, as well), whether *all* the children have their own bedrooms, and so on can paint a vivid picture of their client's contexts.

Hammond and Czyszczon (2014) contend that home-based counseling services are understudied, lacking in specialized training, and chiefly provided to families who are at risk (poverty), and is a last line of defense to intervene in a crisis—for example, in-home domestic violence—to prevent the situation from escalating to children being placed in residential facilities or foster care homes (Case Scenario 10.1).

Case Scenario 10.1

Mark

Mark, a 14-year-old freshman, is a social recluse because of his race. He is black and attending a predominantly white high school. Making the step from eighth to ninth grade was a challenge for Mark. He had two friends leaving eighth grade, but both of those friends went to other high schools. Now Mark finds himself all alone. Though he does not experience outright

(Continued)

Case Scenario 10.1 (Continued)

bullying, he is rejected for his lack of ability to fit in with the image and appearance of his peers. Every day, Mark feels more and more depressed and alone. He begins to fantasize about being dead and going to sleep without ever waking up. His love for writing brings new meaning when he begins to depict his fascinations with death onto paper. He writes about his wish to die and plans to kill himself. He gives graphic details into the many ways that would result in death. One day, Mark makes the mistake of leaving his journal on the couch in his family's living room. Coming home late from work, Mark's mother finds her son's journal and begins reading it. She is frightened by what she reads and runs upstairs to ensure Mark's safety. Finding him in his room crying, she first assures her son that everything will be okay and then leaves the room to call for help.

Responding to her call is a local crisis team (a team of individuals trained on crisis intervention and suicide risk assessment). After assessing Mark for suicidal ideation and plans for self-harm, the crisis team decides that Mark needs a higher level of care. Mark is transferred to an inpatient treatment facility that caters to adolescents dealing with suicidal ideation. After just a few hours in the treatment center, Mark meets his counseling provider Sue, who begins by introducing herself and explaining the dynamics of the facility, the stipulations regarding confidentiality, and her intentions for the initial meeting. She also begins by asking Mark to tell her about his thoughts regarding being in the hospital. In addition, she asks, "Are you suicidal right now?" "Do you have any suicidal thoughts or intents?" Then she tells Mark that she is going to do a psychosocial assessment with him; she explains the dynamics of the assessment and what Mark can expect to occur during their meeting. Finally, she tells Mark, when he feels comfortable to do so, to begin by telling her about himself and what brought him into treatment.

During the assessment, Sue listens intently to Mark's concerns. She makes it a point to listen more than to speak. She lets Mark lead by explaining his circumstances around school and his feelings of rejection and inability to make friends. When he stops speaking, she politely prompts him with questions regarding his family relationships, history of depression and suicidal thoughts, and social and environmental contexts. She is especially interested to know what type of home life Mark has. Are his parents divorced? Does he have siblings? What is his relationship like with his parents? Has he received inpatient treatment before? Knowing the risk factors for future suicide completion, Sue also asks him about his mental health history. For instance, she is interested in whether or not he has a history of suicide attempts or self-harm. She is also interested to know if there has been suicide in his family (genetic disposition), whether he knows anyone who committed suicide (contagion effect), and what other symptoms he experiences, if any, that couple with the suicidal thoughts and depression.

Sue also understands that having family involvement is important to a person's recovery. Regardless of whether or not he has a good relationship with his parents, Sue also knows that it is mandatory per state laws that she includes Mark's parents in the treatment. Unfortunately, Mark's parents are divorced. Despite this fact, however, she still must include both parents in counseling since joint custody exists. She begins by calling Mark's mom and then calls his dad. Both seem to be very concerned and willing to be involved in their son's treatment. She tells them there will be a family session prior to his discharge from the hospital. Both state that they will be present for it. Mark is also encouraged by his parent's involvement.

Every day Sue makes it a point to meet with Mark even if it is only for a few minutes. She knows how important rapport building is with her clients. As Mark talks about his depression and dissatisfaction with life, Sue tries to instill in Mark a sense of hope by saying that "you can make it through this season of your life." She also empathizes with his position of rejection and really hears him out regarding his experience of having no peer social support systems. She designs creative activities that have the opportunity to move Mark into a direction of healing. For instance, she asks him to write 10 things he is grateful for. Her goal is to challenge his thoughts and cognitions that have an impact on his depression and suicidal thoughts (Alavi, Sharifi, Ghanizadeh, & Dehbozorgi, 2013). After each short session, Mark's mood seems to improve. He is no longer experiencing suicidal thoughts and has reported his feelings of encouragement related to his ability to make friends on his unit.

Discharge is only a few days away for Mark. Sue sets up a family session where each person is encouraged to share his or her views. Sue really focuses on opening up the communication pathways between Mark and his parents, addressing the need for his parents to take the initiative to ask Mark on a daily basis what his feelings are and whether or not he is having any suicidal thoughts at that time. Sue educates his mom and dad about the precautions to take if Mark endorses suicide again. She tells them that calling a crisis team and taking Mark to the hospital are keys to getting him the help he needs. She also reminds them that suicide is serious and should be taken as such. In the end, Sue makes referrals for Mark to see a provider for individual counseling, to be in a mental health intensive outpatient program, and makes appointments for him to follow up with both a primary care doctor and a psychiatrist. After the family session, Mark is discharged into the care of his parents.

IMPLICATIONS FOR COUNSELING ADOLESCENTS

Clinical Review of Case

The case of Mark is a picture of the effect of suicidal thoughts and depression on a young person's outlook on life and inward torment as a result of social seclusion. Mark felt very alone and abandoned by people; he had no friends and felt a lack of parental support at home despite the finding that his parents cared about his health. Unfortunately, Mark did not tell his parents about his suicidal thoughts or depression; he simply wrote his feelings on paper and then wished for somebody to understand his depth of despair.

Taken very seriously throughout this case sample is the experience of suicidal thoughts. Certainly, what can be seen from beginning to end is the steps to treatment that need to take place in order to intervene in a suicidal person's life. From the crisis team stepping in to Mark being admitted into inpatient psychiatric treatment, his thoughts and intent to commit suicide are taken seriously. It is important to understand the literature that states that people who commit suicide often give hints along the way that they are thinking about doing so (Renaud et al., 2014). Obviously, then, an outward blatant indicator, such as writing the intent down, should not be ignored. Sue, the provider who works at the hospital in this case, knows these risk factors. She also takes Mark's fascination with dying very seriously.

Right from the beginning, readers should notice how Sue made it her purpose in every meeting to build rapport and trust with Mark. She allowed him to lead the direction in counseling despite her impromptu prompting when things slowed down. She practiced patience while he took his time in explaining his feelings and circumstances. She did not tell him he was wrong or cut him off when he was speaking. She also made it her goal to make sure that he felt heard and supported. She told him the stipulations of confidentiality. She educated him about the hospital dynamics and the need for this type of help for intervening in these types of situations. In addition, she involved his parents in his treatment and made time for a family session prior to discharge. She, then, made sure to make appropriate recommendations, referrals, and appointments for Mark in outpatient settings.

Application of Ethics

As reviewed in previous sections, suicide is a serious matter. It should not be taken lightly. Providers are mandated reporters. This means that when a client endorses thoughts to harm self or others, providers must make the appropriate calls to agencies. At times, this means making a call to the police or the person in danger, and at other times, this means calling a crisis team to provide a greater intervention for a suicidal person, for instance. Once a person is taken into inpatient treatment, providers within that setting are also mandated to abide by these laws.

Managed care companies and hospital standards generally require that providers provide treatment based on scientific and evidence-based research. The implication here is that providers are using therapeutic and medical interventions that have proved to be successful through rigorous research endeavors. Equal consideration of the population within the study and the population with which one wants to use the intervention is important. For instance, it is unethical to use a type of intervention or tool with a Spanish-speaking Hispanic male when that intervention or tool has been found effective only with white, English-speaking women. This is suggestive of the research by Shallcross (2012), because providers are at times unskilled or unwilling to use evidence-based research to guide their therapeutic focus; these types of intervention errors are perhaps occurring more often than one would like to think.

The implication here is that there needs to be a greater focus on the part of counselor educators to educate counseling students on how to evaluate research to meet the needs of their individual clients. Certainly disturbing is the thought that counseling providers are perhaps using research shown to work only with adults with children and adolescents. When this occurs, it likely goes unnoticed by the untrained eye. Striving to uphold high ethical standards should be the aim of all providers. The intent of managed care and the impact of their control over patient treatment, though at times spoken negatively about, are perhaps going to be the driving force for counseling providers to begin to take seriously the need to base their counseling interventions on empirically supported evidence-based research (Shallcross, 2012).

SUMMARY

This chapter was focused on the interventions currently being used in the counseling field with adolescent clients. Consider, for instance, that adolescents living in the 19th century, not too long ago, were treated like small adults (Rogers, 2008). There was zero emphasis on "children being children"; rather, children and adolescents were dressed in adult clothes, given adult jobs, and expected to help with the family income (Rogers, 2008). Today, adolescents are enabled to live within their developmental age. They are also protected more and more by state and government laws.

This chapter articulated that individual counseling is especially helpful for adolescents who are more comfortable in one-on-one sessions. Coaching and mentoring are two areas currently receiving attention in both the literature and counseling practices. Providers can use the information gathered about these two topics to inform their work with clients. For instance, creating an environment personalized to each client's needs, focusing on the here and now, and encouraging adolescents to tell their stories through narrative form are creative ways for providers to engage their clients in treatment.

Mentorship programs are designed to reduce the risk factors for at-risk youth through adult mentorship. Although research in this area is lagging behind, it is certainly a step in the right direction for offering these young people help in the midst of great hardship (e.g., homelessness, foster care). Group counseling is an open door to help more than one person at a time. It has brought new light to therapeutic practice by its ingenious way of using the group dynamics to instill personal change. Group counseling has been shown to be especially effective with adolescents who struggle with depression and shyness. It teaches these young people how to socialize and trust others; in addition, it shows them that they are not alone.

Counseling interventions for crisis situations were also addressed. The interventions to use with adolescents who have experienced trauma due to suicide, self-harm, death, and natural disasters are summarized. Family counseling was also highlighted. It was also important to discuss under this topic parent–adolescent communication and home-based counseling services.

KEYSTONES

- Counseling interventions are intentionally designed to change clients' behavior by providing them with insight into how their behaviors are affecting themselves and others in a negative way.

- Providers must be cautious of their appearance, demeanor, and nonverbal behaviors that may at any time influence their adolescent clients to discount their professionalism, trustworthiness, and desire to build rapport with them.

- Not all behavior is considered equal; at times, providers will see evidence of serious adolescent delinquency, and at other times, providers will see evidence of experimentation typical for adolescents' developmental level (e.g., smoking marijuana every day vs. smoking marijuana one time).

- Coaches focus on adolescents' academic success, behavioral changes to reach specific goals, and a one-on-one personalized rapport experience between coach and adolescent to create change.

- Mentors are adults who provide adolescents with mentorship focused on academic success and opportunities to participate in extracurricular activities.

- Providers are interested in a person's past, current turmoil, irrational beliefs, and negative cognitions that are undermining their ability to function.

- Providers provide specific interventions designed with clients in mind. Providers consider an adolescent client's SES, racial and ethnic ties, gender, sexual orientation, family context, peer relationships, school context, and psychiatric disorder(s) prior to performing counseling interventions.

- Suicide, self-harm, and natural disasters are all crises providers should expect to see when working with adolescents. Researchers are focused on uncovering the risk factors for these crises and successful interventions to reduce them.

- Family counseling interventions are designed with every family member in mind; providers believe that issues reside not in just one family member but in all members as a whole. Increasing family communication and providing in-home services are two interventions used by providers to reduce family friction.

REFERENCES

Adams, M. (2012). Problem-focused coaching in a mainstream primary school: Reflections on practice. *Coaching Psychologist, 8*(1), 27–37.

Alavi, A., Sharifi, B., Ghanizadeh, A., & Dehbozorgi, G. (2013). Effectiveness of cognitive behavioral therapy in decreasing suicidal ideation and hopelessness of the adolescents with previous suicidal attempts. *Iranian Journal of Pediatrics, 23*(4), 467–472.

American Counseling Association. (2014). *About ACA.* Retrieved from http://www.counseling.org/about-us/about-aca

American Psychiatric Association. (2013). *Diagnostic and statistical manual of mental disorders* (5th ed.). Washington, DC: Author.

Aseltine, R. H., Jr., & DeMartino, R. (2004). An outcome evaluation of the SOS suicide prevention program. *American Journal of Public Health, 94*(3), 446–451.

Balis, T., & Postolache, T. (2008). Ethnic differences in adolescent suicide in the United States. *International Journal of Child Health and Human Development, 1*(3), 281–296. Retrieved from http://www.ncbi.nlm.nih.gov/pmc/articles/PMC2845977/

Bannan, N. (2010). Group-based problem-solving therapy in self-poisoning females: A pilot study. *Counseling & Psychotherapy Research, 10*(3), 201–213.

Bartle-Haring, S., Slesnick, N., Collins, J., Erdem, G., & Buettner, C. (2012). The utility of mentoring homeless adolescents: A pilot study. *American Journal of Drug and Alcohol Abuse, 38*(4), 350–358. doi:10.3109/00952990.2011.643985

Bennett, L. R. (2012). Adolescent depression: Meeting therapeutic challenges through an integrated narrative approach. *Journal of Child and Adolescent Psychiatric Nursing, 25*(4), 184–194. doi:10.1111/jcap.12003

Bing, S., & Hongling, X. (2013). Peer group influence on urban preadolescents' attitudes toward material possessions: Social status benefits of material possessions. *Journal of Consumer Affairs, 47*(1), 46–71. doi:10.1111/j.1745-6606.2012.01246.x

Bond, C. L., Woods, K., Humphrey, N., Symes, W., & Green, L. (2013). Practitioner review: The effectiveness of solution focused brief therapy with children and families: A systematic and critical evaluation of the literature from 1990–2010. *Journal of Child Psychology and Psychiatry, 54*(7), 707–723.

Cantor, D. (2000). The role of group therapy in promoting identity development in ADHD adolescents. *Journal of Psychotherapy in Independent Practice, 1*(2), 53–62.

Cashin, A. (2008). Narrative therapy: A psychotherapeutic approach in the treatment of adolescents with Asperger's Disorder. *Journal of Child and Adolescent Psychiatric Nursing, 21*(1), 48–56. doi:10.1111/j.1744-6171.2008.00128.x

Cashin, A., Browne, G., Bradbury, J., & Mulder, A. (2013). The effectiveness of narrative therapy with young people with autism. *Journal of Child and Adolescent Psychiatric Nursing, 26*(1), 32–41. doi:10.1111/jcap.12020

Centers for Disease Control and Prevention. (2014). *National suicide statistics at a glance.* Retrieved from http://www.cdc.gov/violenceprevention/suicide/statistics/self_harm.html

Cepukiene, V., & Pakrosnis, R. (2011). The outcome of solution-focused brief therapy among foster care adolescents: The changes of behavior and perceived somatic and cognitive difficulties. *Children and Youth Services Review, 33*(6), 791–797. doi:10.1016/j.childyouth.2010.11.027

Christenbury, L., Beale, A. V., & Patch, S. S. (1996). Interactive bibliocounseling: Recent fiction and nonfiction for adolescents and their counselors. *School Counselor, 44,* 133–145.

Corrigan, P. W., Druss, B. G., & Perlick, D. A. (2014). The impact of mental illness stigma on seeking and participating in mental health care. *Psychological Science in the Public Interest, 15*(2), 37–70. doi:10.1177/1529100614531398

Costello, E. J., Copeland, W., & Angold, A. (2011). Trends in psychopathology across the adolescent years: What changes when children become adolescents, and when adolescents become adults? *Journal of Child Psychology and Psychiatry, 52*(10), 1015–1025. doi:10.1111/j.1469-7610.2011.02446.x

Courtney-Seidler, E. A., Klein, D., & Miller, A. L. (2013). Borderline personality disorder in adolescents. *Clinical Psychology: Science and Practice, 20*(4), 425–444. doi:10.1111/cpsp.12051

Culp, A. M. (1995). Adolescent depressed mood, reports of suicide attempts, and asking for help. *Adolescence, 30*(120), 827–837.

Cummings, J. R., Lucas, S. M., & Druss, B. G. (2013). Addressing public stigma and disparities among persons with mental illness: The role of federal policy. *American Journal of Public Health, 103*(5), 781–785. doi:10.2105/AJPH.2013.301224

Currie, M., & Startup, M. (2012). Doing anger differently: Two controlled trials of percussion group psychotherapy for adolescent reactive aggression. *Journal of Adolescence, 35*(4), 843–853.

Curtis, K., & Berman, D. (2010). The picture that tells a family's thousand words. *Journal of Practical Estate Planning, 12*(1), 19–46.

Dang, M. T., & Miller, E. (2013). Characteristics of natural mentoring relationships from the perspectives of homeless youth. *Journal of Child and Adolescent Psychiatric Nursing, 26*(4), 246–253. doi:10.1111/jcap.12038

Deeley, S. T., & Love, A. W. (2013). Longitudinal analysis of the emotion self-confidence model of suicidal ideation in adolescents. *Advances in Mental Health, 12*(1), 34–45. doi:10.5172/jamh.2013.12.1.34

Drabble, J., Bowles, D. P., & Barker, L. A. (2014). Investigating the role of executive attentional control to self-harm in a non-clinical cohort with borderline personality features. *Frontiers in Behavioral Neuroscience, 8*(1), 274. doi:10.3389/fnbeh.2014.00274

Du, Y.-S., Jiang, W., & Vance, A. (2010). Longer term effect of randomized, controlled group cognitive behavioural therapy for Internet addiction in adolescent students in Shanghai. *Australian & New Zealand Journal of Psychiatry, 44*(2), 129–134.

Dugan, E. R. (2010). Working with children affected by Hurricane Katrina: Two case studies in play therapy. *Child and Adolescent Mental Health, 15*(1), 52–55.

Ægisdóttir, S., O'Heron, M. P., Hartong, J. M., Haynes, S. A., & Linville, M. K. (2011). Enhancing attitudes and reducing fears about mental health counseling: An analogue study. *Journal of Mental Health Counseling, 33*(4), 327–346.

Eunsook, H., Milgram, R. M., & Rowell, L. L. (2004). Homework motivation and preference: A learner-centered homework approach. *Theory Into Practice, 43*(3), 197–204.

Falck, R. G. (2012). Surveying teens in school to assess the prevalence of problematic drug use. *Journal of School Health, 82*(5), 217–224.

Falkenström, F., Granström, F., & Holmqvist, R. (2014). Working alliance predicts psychotherapy outcome even while controlling for prior symptom improvement. *Psychotherapy Research, 24*(2), 146–159. doi:10.1080/10503307.2013.847985

Farruggia, S. P., Bullen, P., & Davidson, J. (2013). Important nonparental adults as an academic resource for youth. *Journal of Early Adolescence, 33*(4), 498–522.

Ferreira, P. H., Ferreira, M. L., Maher, C. G., Refshauge, K. M., Latimer, J., & Adams, R. D. (2013). The therapeutic alliance between clinicians and patients predicts outcome in chronic low back pain. *Physical Therapy, 93*(4), 470–478. doi:10.2522/ptj.20120137

Fletcher, J. (2013). Adolescent depression and adult labor market outcomes. *Southern Economic Journal, 80*(1), 26–49.

Flett, G., Goldstein, A., Hewitt, P., & Wekerle, C. (2012). Predictors of deliberate self-harm behavior among emerging adolescents: An initial test of a self-punitiveness model. *Current Psychology, 31*(1), 49–64. doi:10.1007/s12144-012-9130-9

Frederick, J., & Goddard, C. (2007). Exploring the relationship between poverty, childhood adversity and child abuse from the perspective of adulthood. *Child Abuse Review, 16*(5), 323–341.

Frels, R. K., Onwuegbuzie, A. J., Bustamante, R. M., Garza, Y., Leggett, E. S., Nelson, J. A., & Nichter, M. (2013). The roles, purposes, and approaches of selected mentors in school-based mentoring: A collective case study. *Psychology in the Schools, 50*, 618–633.

Gillath, O., Bahns, A. J., Ge, F., & Crandall, C. S. (2012). Shoes as a source of first impressions. *Journal of Research in Personality, 46*(4), 423–430. doi:10.1016/j.jrp.2012.04.003

Gillham, J. I., Reivich, K. J., Brunwasser, S. M., Freres, D. R., Chajon, N. D., Kash-MacDonald, V. M., . . . Seligman, M. P. (2012). Evaluation of a group cognitive-behavioral depression prevention program for young adolescents: A randomized effectiveness trial. *Journal of Clinical Child & Adolescent Psychology, 41*(5), 621–639. doi:10.1080/15374416.2012.706517

Girma, E., Möller-Leimkühler, A. M., Müller, N., Dehning, S., Froeschl, G., & Tesfaye, M. (2014). Public stigma against family members of people with mental illness: Findings from the Gilgel Gibe Field Research Center (GGFRC), Southwest Ethiopia. *BMC International Health & Human Rights, 14*(1), 1–15. doi:10.1186/1472-698X-14-2

Gogel, L., Cavaleri, M., Gardin, J., & Wisdom, J. (2011). Retention and ongoing participation in residential substance abuse treatment: Perspectives from adolescents, parents and staff on the treatment process. *Journal of Behavioral Health Services & Research, 38*(4), 488–496. doi:10.1007/s11414-010-9226-7

Goldston, D. B., Daniel, S. S., Erkanli, A., Reboussin, B. A., Mayfield, A., Frazier, P. H., & Treadway, S. L. (2009). Psychiatric diagnoses as contemporaneous risk factors for suicide attempts among adolescents and young adults: Developmental changes. *Journal of Consulting and Clinical Psychology, 77*(2), 281–290.

Goosby, B. J., Bellatorre, A., Walsemann, K. M., & Cheadle, J. E. (2013). Adolescent loneliness and health in early adulthood. *Sociological Inquiry, 83*(4), 505–536. doi:10.1111/soin.12018

Grace, M., Kivlighan, D. M., & Kunce, J. (1995). The effect of nonverbal skills training on counselor trainee nonverbal sensitivity and responsiveness and on session impact and working alliance ratings. *Journal of Counseling & Development, 73*(5), 547–552.

Granados, S., Winslade, J., De Witt, M., & Hedtke, L. (2009). Grief counseling groups for adolescents based on re-membering practices. *Journal of School Counseling, 7*(34), 1–26.

Grant, A. M. (2013). Steps to solutions: A process for putting solution-focused coaching principles into practice. *Coaching Psychologist, 9*(1), 36–44.

Greyber, L., Dulmus, C., & Cristalli, M. (2012). Eye movement desensitization reprocessing, post-traumatic stress disorder, and trauma: A review of randomized controlled trials with children and adolescents. *Child and Adolescent Social Work Journal, 29*(5), 409–425. doi:10.1007/s10560-012-0266-0

Guo, B., Aveyard, P., Fielding, A., & Sutton, S. (2009). Do the transtheoretical model processes of change, decisional balance and temptation predict stage movement? Evidence from smoking cessation in adolescents. *Addiction, 104*(5), 828–838. doi:10.1111/j.1360-0443.2009.02519.x

Gyllensten, K., Palmer, S., Nilsson, E., Regnér, A. M., & Frodi, A. (2010). Experiences of cognitive coaching: A qualitative study. *International Coaching Psychology Review, 5*(2), 98–108.

Habib, M., Labruna, V., & Newman, J. (2013). Complex histories and complex presentations: Implementation of a manually-guided group treatment for traumatized adolescents. *Journal of Family Violence, 28*(7), 717–728. doi:10.1007/s10896-013-9532-y

Hammond, C., & Czyszczon, G. (2014). Home-based family counseling: An emerging field in need of professionalization. *Family Journal, 22*(1), 56–61. doi:10.1177/1066480713505055

Hannen, E. K., & Woods, K. (2012). Narrative therapy with an adolescent who self-cuts: A case example. *Educational Psychology in Practice, 28*(2), 187–214.

Hazelden Betty Ford Foundation. (2014). *What is an intervention?* Retrieved from http://www.hazelden.org/web/public/faqintervention.page

Higham, J. E., Friedlander, M. L., Escudero, V., & Diamond, G. (2012). Engaging reluctant adolescents in family therapy: An exploratory study of in-session processes of change. *Journal of Family Therapy, 34*(1), 24–52.

Hopson, L. M., & Kim, J. S. (2004). A solution-focused approach to crisis intervention with adolescents. *Journal of Evidence-Based Social Work, 1*(2–3), 93–110.

Hughes, J. N., & Chen, Q. (2011). Reciprocal effects of student–teacher and student–peer relatedness: Effects on academic self-efficacy. *Journal of Applied Developmental Psychology, 32*(5), 278–287.

Hurd, N., & Zimmerman, M. (2010). Natural mentors, mental health, and risk behaviors: A longitudinal analysis of African American adolescents transitioning into adulthood. *American Journal of Community Psychology, 46*(1–2), 36–48. doi:10.1007/s10464-010-9325-x

Jarvi, S., Jackson, B., Swenson, L., & Crawford, H. (2013). The impact of social contagion on non-suicidal self-injury: A review of the literature. *Archives of Suicide Research, 17*(1), 1–19. doi:10.1080/13811118.2013.748404

Julca, A. (2012). Natural disasters with un-natural effects: Why? *Journal of Economic Issues, 46*(2), 499–510.

Karaman, D., & Durukan, İ. (2013). Suicide in children and adolescents. *Current Approaches in Psychiatry/Psikiyatride Guncel Yaklasimlar, 5*(1), 30–47. doi:10.5455/cap.20130503

Keys, S. G., Bemak, F., & Lockhart, E. J. (1998). Transforming school counseling to serve the mental health needs of at-risk youth. *Journal of Counseling & Development, 76,* 381–388. doi:10.1002/j.1556-6676.1998.tb02696.x

King, K. A., & Vidourek, R. A. (2011). Enhancing parent–child communication about drug use: Strategies for professionals working with parents and guardians. *Prevention Researcher, 18*(2), 12–15.

Kirby, K. (2008). Client attitudes and behaviors. In F. Leong (Ed.), *Encyclopedia of counseling* (Vol. 2, pp. 486–491). Thousand Oaks, CA: Sage. doi:10.4135/9781412963978.n155

Kramer, J., Conijn, B., Oijevaar, P., & Riper, H. (2014). Effectiveness of a web-based solution-focused brief chat treatment for depressed adolescents and young adults: Randomized controlled trial. *Journal of Medical Internet Research, 16*(5), e141. doi:10.2196/jmir.3261

Kress, V. E., & Hoffman, R. M. (2008). Empowering adolescent survivors of sexual abuse: Application of a solution-focused Ericksonian counseling group. *Journal of Humanistic Counseling, Education and Development, 47*(2), 172–186.

Kubrin, C. E., & Wadsworth, T. (2009). Explaining suicide among blacks and whites: How socioeconomic factors and gun availability affect race-specific suicide rates. *Social Science Quarterly, 90*(5), 1203–1227. doi:10.1111/j.1540-6237.2009.00654.x

Lander, L., Howsare, J., & Byrne, M. (2013). The impact of substance use disorders on families and children: From theory to practice. *Social Work in Public Health, 28*(3–4), 194–205. doi:10.1080/19371918.2013.759005

Lee, M. Y., Wong, B. P., Chow, B. W., & McBride-Chang, C. (2006). Predictors of suicide ideation and depression in Hong Kong adolescents: Perceptions of academic and family climates. *Suicide and Life-Threatening Behavior, 36*(1), 82–96.

Liem, G. D., & Martin, A. J. (2011). Peer relationships and adolescents' academic and non-academic outcomes: Same-sex and opposite-sex peer effects and the mediating role of school engagement. *British Journal of Educational Psychology, 81*(2), 183–206.

Livingston, J. A., Bay-Cheng, L. Y., Hequembourg, A. L., Testa, M., & Downs, J. S. (2013). Mixed drinks and mixed messages: Adolescent girls' perspectives on alcohol and sexuality. *Psychology of Women Quarterly, 37*(1), 38–50.

Lynch, A., Lerner, R., & Leventhal, T. (2013). Adolescent academic achievement and school engagement: An examination of the role of school-wide peer culture. *Journal of Youth and Adolescence, 42*(1), 6–19. doi:10.1007/s10964-012-9833-0

Mander, J., Wittorf, A., Klingberg, S., Teufel, M., Zipfel, S., & Sammet, I. (2014). The patient perspective on therapeutic change: The investigation of associations between stages of change and general mechanisms of change in psychotherapy research. *Journal of Psychotherapy Integration, 24*(2), 122–137. doi:10.1037/a0036976

Martinez, A., & Lasser, J. (2013). Thinking outside the box while playing the game: A creative school-based approach to working with children and adolescents. *Journal of Creativity in Mental Health, 8*(1), 81–91. doi:10.1080/15401383.2013.763688

Matson, J., & Williams, L. (2014). Depression and mood disorders among persons with autism spectrum disorders. *Research in Developmental Disabilities, 35*(9), 2003–2007. doi:10.1016/j.ridd.2014.04.020

Mattek, R. J., Jorgenson, E. T., & Fox, R. A. (2010). Home-based therapy for young children in low-income families: A student training program. *Family Journal: Counseling and Therapy for Couples and Families, 18*(2), 189–194.

Mayes, S., Calhoun, S., Murray, M., & Zahid, J. (2011). Variables associated with anxiety and depression in children with autism. *Journal of Developmental and Physical Disabilities, 23*(4), 325–337. doi:10.1007/s10882-011-9231-7

McCoy, K. M. (2012). Mental health issues of adolescents and adults with ASD: Depression and anxiety. *Counseling and Human Development, 45*(1), 1–16.

Mearidy-Bell, L. (2013). Adolescent victims of natural disasters: A phenomenological study on lived experiences and behaviors displayed after a crisis. *Journal of Human Behavior in the Social Environment, 23*(4), 536–551.

Meyer, K. C., & Bouchey, H. A. (2010). Daring to DREAM: Results from a mentoring programme for at-risk youth. *International Journal of Evidence-Based Coaching and Mentoring, 8*(1), 67–84.

Mitchell, M. L. (2013). National CARES mentoring movement. *Reclaiming Children and Youth, 22*(1), 30–34.

Moran, H., Pathak, N., & Sharma, N. (2009). The mystery of the well-attended group. A model of personal construct therapy for adolescent self-harm and depression in a community CAMHS service. *Counseling Psychology Quarterly, 22*(4), 347–359. doi:10.1080/09515070903334573

Morin, S., & Welsh, A. (1996). Adolescents' perceptions and experiences of death and grieving. *Adolescence, 31*(123), 585–595.

Nastasi, B. K., Jayasena, A., Summerville, M., & Borja, A. P. (2011). Facilitating long-term recovery from natural disasters: Psychosocial programming for tsunami-affected schools of Sri Lanka. *School Psychology International, 32*(5), 512–532.

National Institute on Alcohol Abuse and Alcoholism. (2014). *Underage drinking*. Retrieved from http://www.niaaa.nih.gov/alcohol-health/special-populations-co-occurring-disorders/underage-drinking

Nippold, M. A., Frantz-Kaspar, M. W., Cramond, P. M., Kirk, C., Hayward-Mayhew, C., & MacKinnon, M. (2014). Conversational and narrative speaking in adolescents: Examining the use of complex syntax. *Journal of Speech, Language, and Hearing Research, 57*(3), 876–886. doi:10.1044/1092-4388(2013/13-0097)

Oldershaw, A., Simic, M., Grima, E., Jollant, F., Richards, C., Taylor, L., & Schmidt, U. (2012). The effect of cognitive behavior therapy on decision making in adolescents who self-harm: A pilot study. *Suicide and Life-Threat Behavior, 42*(3), 255–265. doi:10.1111/j.1943-278X.2012.0087.x

Ormhaug, S. M., Jensen, T. K., Wentzel-Larsen, T., & Shirk, S. R. (2014). The therapeutic alliance in treatment of traumatized youths: Relation to outcome in a randomized clinical trial. *Journal of Consulting and Clinical Psychology, 82*(1), 52–64. doi:10.1037/a0033884

Ougrin, D. (2012). Commentary: Self-harm in adolescents: The best predictor of death by suicide?—Reflections on Hawton et al. (2012). *Journal of Child Psychology and Psychiatry, 53*(12), 1220–1221.

Ozdemir, Y., Kuzucu, Y., & Koruklu, N. (2013). Social problem solving and aggression: The role of depression. *Australian Journal of Guidance and Counseling, 23*(1), 72–81.

Ozono, H., Watabe, M., & Yoshikawa, S. (2012). Effects of facial expression and gaze direction on approach–avoidance behaviour. *Cognition & Emotion, 26*(5), 943–949. doi:10.1080/02699931.2011.641807

Qing, W., & Millward, I. (2014). Developing a unified psychological model of coaching and mentoring in supporting the learning and development of adolescents. *International Journal of Evidence Based Coaching and Mentoring, 12*(2), 91–108.

Quiroga, C. V., Janosz, M., Bisset, S., & Morin, A. S. (2013). Early adolescent depression symptoms and school dropout: Mediating processes involving self-reported academic competence and achievement. *Journal of Educational Psychology, 105*(2), 552–560. doi:10.1037/a0031524

Radke, S., Güths, F., André, J. A., Müller, B. W., & de Bruijn, E. A. (2014). In action or inaction? Social approach-avoidance tendencies in major depression. *Psychiatry Research, 219*(3), 513–517. doi:10.1016/j.psychres.2014.07.011

Renaud, J., Séguin, M., Lesage, A. D., Marquette, C., Choo, B., & Turecki, G. (2014). Service use and unmet needs in youth suicide: A study of trajectories. *Canadian Journal of Psychiatry, 59*(10), 523–530.

Richardson, B. S., Surmitis, K., & Hyldahl, R. (2012). Minimizing social contagion in adolescents who self-injure: Considerations for group work, residential treatment, and the Internet. *Journal of Mental Health Counseling, 34*(2), 121–132.

Rogers, J. S. (2008). Picturing the child in nineteenth-century literature. *Children & Libraries: Journal of the Association for Library Service to Children, 6*(3), 41–46.

Rost, C., Hofmann, A., & Wheeler, K. (2009). EMDR treatment of workplace trauma. *Journal of EMDR practice & research, 3*(2), 80–90. doi:10.1891/1933-3196.3.2.80

Roswarski, T. E., & Dunn, J. P. (2009). The role of help and hope in prevention and early intervention with suicidal adolescents: Implications for mental health providers. *Journal of Mental Health Counseling, 31*(1), 34–46. *Epidemiology, 47*(1), 29–42.

Salmela-Aro, K., Aunola, K., & Nurmi, J. (2008). Trajectories of depressive symptoms during emerging adulthood: Antecedents and consequences. *European Journal of Developmental Psychology, 5*(4), 439–465. doi:10.1080/17405620600867014

Sandoval, J., Scott, A. N., & Padilla, I. (2009). Crisis counseling: An overview. *Psychology in the Schools, 46*(3), 246–256.

Sandy, P. (2013). Motives for self-harm: Views of nurses in a secure unit. *International Nursing Review, 60*(3), 358–365. doi:10.1111/inr.12038

Sari, O. T. (2014). Outcomes of play-based home support for children with autism spectrum disorder. *Social Behavior and Personality: An International Journal, 42*(1), 655–805.

Scarborough, N., Taylor, B., & Tuttle, A. (2013). Collaborative home-based therapy (CHBT): A culturally responsive model for treating children and adolescents involved in child protective service systems. *Contemporary Family Therapy: An International Journal, 35*(3), 465–477. doi:10.1007/s10591-012-9223-5

Shallcross, L. (2012, September). Sidebar: Counselors weigh in on evidence-based counseling. *Counseling Today* (A publication of the American Counseling Association). Retrieved from http://ct.counseling.org/2012/09/page/7/

Shapiro, E. (2012). EMDR and early psychological intervention following trauma (Original research article). *European Review of Applied Psychology, 62*(4), 241–251. doi:10.1016/j.erap.2012.09.003

Sirmaci, N., & Ceylan, M. (2014). The effects of cognitive awareness strategies taught with cognitive coaching method on achievement, attitudes and cognitive awareness skills of students. *International Journal of Academic Research, 6*(1), 374–379. doi:10.7813/2075-4124.2014/6-1/B.50

Siu, A. Y. (2014). Effectiveness of Group Theraplay® on enhancing social skills among children with developmental disabilities. *International Journal of Play Therapy, 23*(4), 187–203. doi:10.1037/a0038158

Skovholt, T., Trotter, M., & Kao, J. (2008). Individual therapy. In F. Leong (Ed.), *Encyclopedia of counseling* (Vol. 2, pp. 644–646). Thousand Oaks, CA: Sage. doi:10.4135/9781412963978.n208

Solomon, E. P., Solomon, R. M., & Heide, K. M. (2009). EMDR: An evidence-based treatment for victims of trauma. *Victims & Offenders, 4*(4), 391–397. doi:10.1080/15564880903227495

Stallard, P., Sayal, K., Phillips, R., Taylor, J. A., Spears, M., Anderson, R., . . . Montgomery, A. A. (2012). Classroom-based cognitive behavioural therapy in reducing symptoms of depression in high risk adolescents: Pragmatic cluster randomised controlled trial. *British Medical Journal, 345,* e6058.

Stallard, P., Spears, M., Montgomery, A. A., Phillips, R., & Sayal, K. (2013). Self-harm in young adolescents (12–16 years): Onset and short-term continuation in a community sample. *BMC Psychiatry, 13*(1), 1–25. doi:10.1186/1471-244X-13-328

Stewart, P. M. (2014). What happens in therapy? Adolescents' expectations and perceptions of psychotherapy. *Journal of Child and Family Studies, 23*(1), 1–9.

Tate, K. A., Lopez, C., Fox, R., Love, J. R., & McKinney, E. (2014). In-home counseling for young children living in poverty: An exploration of counseling competencies. *Family Journal, 22*(4), 371–381. doi:10.1177/1066480714530268

Thompson, R. B., Corsello, M., McReynolds, S., & Conklin-Powers, B. (2013). A longitudinal study of family socioeconomic status (SES) variables as predictors of socio-emotional resilience among mentored youth. *Mentoring & Tutoring: Partnership in Learning, 21*(4), 378–391.

Tzouvara, V., & Papadopoulos, C. (2014). Public stigma towards mental illness in the Greek culture. *Journal of Psychiatric and Mental Health Nursing, 21*(10), 931–938. doi:10.1111/jpm.12146

Uhrlass, D. J., Schofield, C. A., Coles, M. E., & Gibb, B. E. (2009). Self-perceived competence and prospective changes in symptoms of depression and social anxiety. *Journal of Behavior Therapy and Experimental Psychiatry, 40,* 329–337. doi:10.1016/j.jbtep.2009.01.001

Umeh, C. S. (2013). Assessment and management of shyness using group cognitive behavioral therapy among selected Nigerian adolescents. *IFE Psychologia, 21*(3-S), 268–276.

U.S. Department of Health and Human Services. (2010). *Health, United States, 2010: With special features on death and dying.* Retrieved from http://www.cdc.gov/nchs/data/hus/hus10.pdf

U.S. Department of Health and Human Services. (2011). *Marijuana facts: What parents need to know* (Revised). Retrieved from http://www.drugabuse.gov/sites/default/files/parents_marijuana_brochure.pdf

Vitaro, F., Boivin, M., Brendgen, M., Girard, A., & Dionne, G. (2012). Social experiences in kindergarten and academic achievement in Grade 1: A monozygotic twin difference study. *Journal of Educational Psychology, 104*(2), 366–380.

Vogel, M. (2012). Story matters: An inquiry into the role of narrative in coaching. *International Journal of Evidence Based Coaching and Mentoring, 10*(1), 1–13.

Walker, O. L., Degnan, K. A., Fox, N. A., & Henderson, H. A. (2013). Social problem solving in early childhood: Developmental change and the influence of shyness. *Journal of Applied Developmental Psychology, 34,* 185–193. doi:10.1016/j.appdev.2013.04.001

Walsh, B., & Muehlenkamp, J. J. (2013). Managing nonsuicidal self-injury in schools: Use of a structured protocol to manage the behavior and prevent social contagion. *School Psychology Forum, 7*(4), 161–171.

Waltman, S. H., Hetrick, H., & Tasker, T. E. (2012). Designing, implementing, and evaluating a group therapy for underserved populations. *Residential Treatment for Children & Youth, 29*(4), 305–323. doi:10.1080/0886571X.2012.725374

Washburn, J. J., Richardt, S. L., Styer, D. M., Gebhardt, M., Juzwin, K. R., Yourek, A., & Aldridge, D. (2012). Psychotherapeutic approaches to nonsuicidal self-injury in adolescents. *Child & Adolescent*

Psychiatry & Mental Health, 6(1), 14–21. doi:10.1186/1753-2000-6-14

Wehrman, J. E., & Field, J. (2013). Play-based activities in family counseling. *American Journal of Family Therapy, 41*(4), 341–352.

Werblow, J., Urick, A., & Duesbery, L. (2013). On the wrong track: How tracking is associated with dropping out of high school. *Equity & Excellence in Education, 46*(2), 270–284. doi:10.1080/10665684.2013.779168

Whaley, A. L. (2009). Trauma among survivors of Hurricane Katrina: Considerations and recommendations for mental health care. *Journal of Loss & Trauma, 14*(6), 459–476. doi:10.1080/15325020902925480

Wintre, M. G., & Bowers, C. D. (2007). Predictors of persistence to graduation: Extending a model and data on the transition to university model. *Canadian Journal of Behavioural Science, 39*(3), 220–234. doi:10.1037/cjbs2007017

Wolter, J. A., DiLollo, A., & Apel, K. (2006). A narrative therapy approach to counseling: A model for working with adolescents and adults with language-literacy deficits. *Language, Speech and Hearing Services in Schools, 37*(3), 168–177.

World Health Organization. (2013). *Suicide claims more than 60,000 lives yearly in the Americas.* Retrieved from http://www.paho.org/hq/index .php?option=com_content&view=article&id=89 87:suicide-claims-more-than-60-000-lives-yearly-americas-&Itemid=1926&lang=en

You, J. Y., Lin, M. P., Fu, K., & Leung, F. (2013). The best friend and friendship group influence on adolescent nonsuicidal self-injury. *Journal of Abnormal Child Psychology, 41*(6), 993–1004. doi:10.1007/s10802-013-9734-z

Young, R., Sproeber, N., Groschwitz, R. C., Preiss, M., & Plener, P. L. (2014). Why alternative teenagers self-harm: Exploring the link between non-suicidal self-injury, attempted suicide and adolescent identity. *BMC Psychiatry, 14*(1), 1–25. doi:10.1186/1471-244X-14-137

Zgierska, A., Amaza, I. P., Brown, R. L., Mundt, M., & Fleming, M. F. (2014). Unhealthy drug use: How to screen, when to intervene. *Journal of Family Practice, 63*(9), 524–530.

Zhang, N., & Burkard, A. W. (2008). Client and counselor discussions of racial and ethnic differences in counseling: An exploratory investigation. *Journal of Multicultural Counseling and Development, 36*(2), 77–87.

Zinck, K., & Littrell, J. M. (2000). Action research shows group counseling effective with at-risk adolescent girls. *Professional School Counseling, 4*(1), 50–59.

11

SCHOOL COUNSELING
INTERVENTIONS

INTRODUCTION

Adolescents' primary domains of functioning are in their homes and schools. Many families have come to view the school as a supportive network that helps their adolescents prepare for the world of work and life in general, especially as it pertains to academic and career development. Likewise, many adolescents may find that their first experiences with counseling services may be in their school's guidance counseling office for academic scheduling needs, completing vocational interest inventories, or for issues related to challenges they are having at home or school. There are numerous sources of a student's referral to a school counselor's office. These offices are generally seen as resource centers for needs within the school/academic culture that highly values student performance and academic achievement to the student's greatest potential. There are instances in which school counselors are sought for student assistance with behavioral and mental health issues. For the range of adolescents represented in any given school or school district, school counselors are most effective when they have a pulse of their school environment, understand the student body's cultural strengths and challenges, as well as forge caring relationships with students,

especially students facing mental health, relationship, substance-related, and learning challenges.

After reading this chapter, readers will be able to do the following:

- Demonstrate knowledge of the ethical standards for school counselors

- Identify the various roles, tasks, and services provided by school counselors

- Describe distinguishing characteristics of school counseling

- Understand innovative interventions when working with adolescents in schools

- Understand the nature of self-injurious behaviors in adolescents

- Describe how school counselors interface with multiple systems of care

- Demonstrate the ability to integrate core competencies of school counseling

- Utilize a case scenario to identify student needs and appropriate response by the school counselor

THE ROLE OF THE SCHOOL COUNSELOR

Although the term *guidance counselor* was used in the past, either *professional school counselor* or *school counselor* is the appropriate term used to describe the professional employed within the school setting to provide academic, personal, social, and career development to all students within a comprehensive school counseling curriculum. School counselors recognize that adolescence is a period marked with tremendous growth and polarities. On the one hand, adolescents experience rapid physical and hormonal growth, remain dependent on parental guidance and provision, and lack fully developed decision-making skills as their brains continue to grow. On the other hand, there is a marked desire for independence, autonomy, new social relationships, and self-expression that was not likely part of their earlier childhood days. Among the expected challenges associated with such drastic changes in needs, behaviors, and relationships, there are adolescents who are not able to successfully traverse the typical developmental challenges and those who have distress that directly affects their ability to learn and their lives in general. For example, a student may arrive in the guidance office for issues related to test anxiety, social anxiety, learning assessment needs, pregnancy issues, and bullying, to name a few. In these situations, the school counselor must maintain the overarching aim to assist with removing barriers to student academic performance and mobilize their interpersonal relationship skills, assess the need for intervention, recognize the severity of the identified problem, anticipate best means of intervention, and maintain a pulse of how this issue intertwines with the individual student, his or her classmates, and the school community as a whole.

School counselors play a pivotal role within the school setting because of their mental health training, position within the school, and access to students (American School Counselor Association [ASCA], 2014). The ASCA (2014) describes the primary role of the professional school counselor as developing and delivering a comprehensive school counseling program designed to support students in their academic, personal, social, and career development. The ASCA

School Counselor Competencies (2012b), created to be consistent with the ASCA National Standards (2004) and the Council for Accreditation of Counseling and Related Educational Programs Standards (CACREP, 2009), clearly outline the "knowledge, abilities, skills and attitudes that ensure school counselors are equipped to meet the rigorous demands of the profession" (ASCA, 2012b, p. 1).

Through the clear articulation of school counseling programs, foundations, management, delivery, and accountability, the ASCA (2012b) competencies also provide a framework for school counselors and school counseling programs to meet the needs of all students through education, prevention, and intervention. As a result, a competent school counselor working within a comprehensive school counseling program will have the necessary knowledge, skills, and abilities to provide the responsive services required to address the diverse mental health needs as they present in a school setting as per both CACREP (2009) and ASCA (2012b).

School counselors must have the ability to identify and understand a crisis situation, decide the appropriate response, and then respond with a carefully designed intervention to address the need with strategies to assist during and after the situation (ASCA, 2012b). Specific examples of responsive services include interventions that provide support to an individual in response to crises (ASCA, 2012b). Depending on the type of crisis or crisis situation, school counselors support others within the school and community through leadership, communication, and collaboration when appropriate (ASCA, 2012b).

School counselors provide indirect services such as referrals, collaboration, and consultation to support students and their families dealing with mental health issues and problematic behaviors (ASCA, 2012b). School counselors provide referrals to mental health professionals in the community for students and their families to receive support. ASCA (2012b) describes collaboration as the partnership that occurs between school counselors and other stakeholders in an attempt to increase communication, thereby helping everyone work collaboratively to support students through difficult situations. Through consultation, school counselors indirectly support students by helping teachers, parents, and other stakeholders understand the nature of mental health challenges and resultant behaviors and how these interface with adolescent academic performance and development.

Consistent with the ASCA Ethical Standards for School Counselors (2010), there are very clear guidelines for school counselors to follow when concerned about a student possibly being a danger to oneself or to others. After identifying the concern and "careful deliberation and consultation with other counseling professionals" (ASCA, 2010, p. 3), school counselors must communicate the concern to parents/guardians and other necessary authorities. School counselors must articulate their assessment of the risk to the parents while ensuring that parents understand the seriousness of the concern and that the risk is understood even if the student attempts to "deceive in order to avoid further scrutiny and/or parental notification" (ASCA, 2010, p. 3). Finally, school counselors must also comply with their legal and ethical responsibilities associated with the response and release of the students to ensure that the appropriate support is in place (ASCA, 2010).

School counselors must also adhere to the American Counseling Association (ACA) Code of Ethics (2014), which asserts that counselors are responsible for encouraging and creating partnerships, creating and maintaining boundaries, and adhering to issues of confidentiality (ACA, 2014). Exceptions to confidentiality include situations in which the counselor needs to disclose information or breach confidentiality to protect the student from imminent harm (ACA, 2014), such as self-injurious thoughts and related behaviors. White-Kress, Costin, and Drouhard (2006) addressed the potential ethical dilemmas and issues school counselors face when supporting students in various areas of their lives. They suggest that school counselors should always err on the side of caution and consult the school district's legal counsel if unsure whether a breach of confidentiality is warranted (White-Kress et al., 2006). Citing the court's tendency to side with parents in terms of breaching the confidentiality of minors, White-Kress et al. (2006) recommend that school counselors carefully consider both their ethical and legal responsibilities while carefully reflecting on their own personal reaction to avoid possible transference of their own emotions onto the situation.

CASE SCENARIO

Consider the case scenario of Adrienne (Case Scenario 11.1) to better understand key elements regarding the professional responsibilities of school counselors. After reading the case scenario, complete Exercise 11.1 before proceeding to the discussion formed to illuminate underlying concerns for school counselors in working with adolescents like Adrienne.

Case Scenario 11.1

Adrienne

Adrienne is a 12-year-old Caucasian female who was referred to the school counselor by a concerned classmate named Becky. Becky rushed to the counseling office after seeing

(Continued)

Case Scenario 11.1 (Continued)

Adrienne make a cut on the inside of her wrist with an oddly shaped piece of metal while in class a few minutes prior. Becky reported that she saw Adrienne rubbing a rigid piece of metal up and down the inside of her arm before stopping at the inside of her left wrist and cutting herself so deeply that she brought blood to the surface. Becky added that Adrienne asked to go to the bathroom so she realized it was her chance to tell the teacher. At that time, Becky discreetly reported what she observed to the teacher and then asked to go to the counseling office to report the situation. Thankfully, the teacher allowed Becky to leave the class and then quickly followed up with a phone call to the counseling office to notify the school counselor, Mrs. Martin, of the urgency of the situation.

Mrs. Martin was working on paperwork when she received the phone call and saw Becky burst into the office. Before allowing Becky to begin sharing, Mrs. Martin reminded Becky of the role of the school counselor and shared about the limits of confidentiality. Becky was agreeable and shared that she understood that Mrs. Martin was there to help students, and for that reason, she felt comfortable telling her what had just happened in class. Mrs. Martin listened carefully and took notes as Becky retold the events. Mrs. Martin wrote down the date, time, location, name of the reporting student, and the exact details as reported to her. Immediately on receiving the information, Mrs. Martin called the school nurse since it involved a student who was a danger to herself, blood, and a possible medical emergency. Mrs. Martin then rushed to the lavatory where she found Adrienne hiding in a bathroom stall. Since Mrs. Martin had already established rapport with Adrienne in previous counseling sessions, it was easy for Mrs. Martin to convince the teen to share what was troubling her and quickly see light blood trickling from Adrienne's forearm.

Though the cuts were not severe and the nurse was now attending to them, Mrs. Martin knew that she needed to notify others of the incident and work cooperatively with them to ensure that Adrienne's safety remains central to the administrative processes on which they were about to embark. Mrs. Martin reminded Adrienne about the limits of confidentiality and added that since she was concerned about Adrienne's safety and well-being, she would need to consult with other professionals and Adrienne's parents. Adrienne put her head down and said, "Please, don't tell my parents! They will be so disappointed in me." Mrs. Martin acknowledged Adrienne's concern and expressed that she cared about Adrienne and her feelings. Mrs. Martin coupled her empathic response with the fact that she was obligated to ensure her safety. She recognized that as a school counselor, she had no choice but to share all safety concerns with those she identified. She added that she had to communicate with Adrienne's parents because she was a minor, and school counselors need to partner with parents to keep students safe. Mrs. Martin reassured Adrienne by sharing that she has had years of experience and knew careful ways to share difficult information with parents that would help them to listen and respond. Pulling on the richness of their already established school counselor–student relationship, Mrs. Martin reminded Adrienne of all the times she had supported Adrienne previously and asked Adrienne to trust that she would do her absolute best to support her in a positive way. Adrienne weakly smiled and told Mrs. Martin that she understood and that she trusted her even though she was afraid. Adrienne more willingly allowed the nurse to see the deeper cuts she had been hiding.

Mrs. Martin then asked Adrienne for the details about what happened. Adrienne slowly described the situation with the exact same details that Becky reported just minutes earlier.

As the nurse began cleaning the cut, Mrs. Martin asked Adrienne for the item she used to cut herself. Adrienne blushed and said that she did not know what it was or where it went. When Mrs. Martin expressed how concerned she was for Adrienne's safety and that she did not want anyone else to get hurt with the object, Adrienne nervously admitted that it was a jagged piece of metal she found in the hallway and that she swallowed it moments earlier because she did not want to get into trouble for having it in school.

Since the extent of the physical damage was unclear at that time, Mrs. Martin and the nurse asked Adrienne to stay very still and explained that they would need to get her medical attention immediately. Within seconds, the school nurse radioed the building principal to notify him of the need for an ambulance to assist and transport Adrienne to the hospital. The nurse then asked Adrienne several questions about the piece of metal such as the size and shape of the object. Adrienne's anxiety increased as she saw the increasing concern and alarm from the adults around her. Mrs. Martin reassured Adrienne that an ambulance would be there shortly and that they were properly trained to help her and get her safely to the hospital for necessary medical treatment.

Mrs. Martin fully took on the role of soother and liaison between Adrienne and the professionals now working intensely with the teen. Through the process, Mrs. Martin remained extremely concerned about Adrienne's mental health status due to the recent events. She told Adrienne that she needed to speak with someone specially trained to help adolescents dealing with self-injurious behaviors. She added that although she was professionally trained as a school counselor, she did not have the adequate training to help Adrienne to the same extent as a mental health professional who specializes in self-injurious thoughts and behaviors. Mrs. Martin told Adrienne that she strongly recommended having a mental health evaluation at the hospital so they could help immediately. Knowing that Adrienne would not easily share with someone she did not know, Mrs. Martin encouraged Adrienne to be honest during the intake and trust that they would help her and her parents to get the necessary mental health assistance she needs so she would not have to continue struggling alone with the things that were ailing her.

While waiting for the ambulance, they agreed that the school nurse should monitor Adrienne's physical well-being until the ambulance arrived and Mrs. Martin should call home to inform Adrienne's parents. Mrs. Martin immediately called home and asked to speak with one of Adrienne's parents—either Mr. or Mrs. Lee. Adrienne's mom answered the phone and shared that her husband was also at home at the time. Mrs. Martin then asked if they could both be on the phone line while she shared extremely important information. Mrs. Martin then calmly and clearly articulated the events to them and asked if they were close enough to the school to get there quickly and ride to the hospital via the ambulance or whether they would prefer to meet Adrienne at the hospital. Mr. and Mrs. Lee shared that they lived close to the school and would be there within minutes. Thankfully, they arrived just prior to the ambulance.

Despite feeling frantic and nervous about the seriousness of the situation, Mr. and Mrs. Lee expressed their sincere gratitude and appreciation for the school's quick response. While Mrs. Martin guided them toward Adrienne's location, she strongly encouraged them to ensure that Adrienne receive a complete psychological and psychiatric evaluation after receiving medical treatment for swallowing the metal and for the cut on her wrist. Mr. and Mrs. Lee agreed to the recommendation and promised to provide an update to the school once things were under control. Mrs. Lee then joined Adrienne in the ambulance while Mr. Lee followed closely behind in his car. Adrienne was immediately taken to the local hospital where she received the necessary medical treatment and a full psychological evaluation.

Exercise 11.1

Counseling Adrienne

1. Identify Adrienne's presenting problem. What are some key psychosocial concerns that Adrienne presents with?
2. Are there any ethical concerns for Mrs. Martin in this case, if so what are they?
3. In working with Adrienne, what role did Mrs. Martin undertake? Did she meet the competency requirements? How could her role as a school counselor have differed?
4. How would you have handled the case of Adrienne?

Key Psychosocial Concerns

At the time of the incident, Adrienne did not qualify for special education services or have any mental health diagnoses. However, based on Adrienne's presenting concerns and the previously established rapport with her school counselor, psychosocial concerns were immediately evident. Mrs. Martin had counseled Adrienne several times throughout middle school when Adrienne had scheduled counseling appointments to talk about social situations and family issues. Despite meeting with her several times, Adrienne's presenting concerns had never been significant enough to require a breach of confidentiality nor did they prompt Mrs. Martin to think that Adrienne was having self-injurious thoughts or behaviors. Regardless of the severity of her prior presenting concerns, Adrienne's self-injurious behaviors clearly showed her need for medical and mental health evaluations to keep her safe.

Diagnostic Issues

As previously noted, Adrienne had not presented with any concerning thoughts or behaviors prior to the incident at school nor did she qualify for special education services or have any mental health diagnoses. Regardless, Mrs. Martin took the referral about Adrienne's crisis behaviors

seriously and promptly responded in a manner consistent with the ASCA Ethical Standards for School Counselors (2010), which included consultation, communication, reporting, and supporting, as required. Mrs. Martin appropriately consulted with appropriate school personnel, contacted and informed Adrienne's parents, and reported the specific incident and the presenting concerns regarding Adrienne's danger to herself, and she also complied with her legal and ethical responsibility, which included recommending and ensuring that Adrienne receive immediate medical and mental health evaluation to ensure her safety. Her responses were also consistent with the ASCA School Counselor Competencies (2012b), which require school counselors to involve "appropriate school and community professionals as well as the family in a crisis situation" and to refer students to "community resources to meet more extensive needs such as long-term therapy or diagnoses of disorders" (p. 10).

Competent school counselors are required to have an in-depth understanding of the ethical use of assessments and assessment procedures across individual and group settings (CACREP, 2009). As a result, the role of school counselors in diagnostic issues related to self-injurious behaviors would involve assessing the situation by understanding and identifying factors associated with the negative behaviors as well as the barriers impeding the student's ability to make healthy choices. Since the counseling process often requires school counselors to utilize assessments to help students determine areas of strength, interests, abilities, or other factors, there may already be results related to the student's learning style, career interests, or personality traits, among other possible assessments. However, school counselors do not often conduct formal assessments related to self-injurious thoughts or behaviors.

White-Kress et al. (2006) recommended that school counselors informally assess the details surrounding the disclosure of the self-injurious behaviors or other issues outside of the school counselor's domain of expertise as well as the length of time since the initial behavior, frequency of the behavior, instrument(s) used, triggers, and stressors contributing toward the behaviors. After assessing the situation, and with cultural differences in mind (CACREP, 2009), school counselors may refer to a more appropriate mental health professional to conduct additional assessments (White-Kress et al., 2006). If school counselors are competent in formally assessing a certain area of mental health concern and the responsibility is within the scope of their professional role, they will select appropriate instruments and use caution with administering, interpreting, and making evaluations based on the instruments (CACREP, 2009). Regardless of whether or not they provide formal assessments for mental health issues, school counselors need to understand the concepts related to standardized and nonstandardized testing such as the reliability and validity of various measures so that they can communicate and interact with other mental health professionals regarding the results.

Other diagnostic issues related to the current situation involve Adrienne's secrecy surrounding her self-injurious thoughts and behaviors. An adolescent's desire to keep troubling areas of his or her life secret is expected, and school counselors must become adept at relationship building within their schools and keenly assessing for students who are silently struggling.

Since she had not previously shared her thoughts or behaviors with anyone prior to the incident at school, an important diagnostic issue to consider was whether Adrienne would be forthcoming during the mental health evaluation intake at the hospital. To prevent the possibility that she would be selective or secretive about what she shared, Mrs. Martin encouraged Adrienne to be open and honest during the intake, and she encouraged Mrs. Lee to share Adrienne's tendency to be secretive with the mental health professional prior to the appointment. Mrs. Martin even offered to speak with the hospital staff, but only once Adrienne's parents signed appropriate release forms for such disclosures. Adrienne admittedly agreed that she was hesitant to tell the truth, but she realized that she needed help since she could no longer control her thoughts and was now hurting herself. Adrienne successfully bridged the positive relationship she had with her school counselor to a good/cooperative relationship with hospital staff.

Critical Questions in a Crisis Situation

School counselors need to consider several questions when faced with a situation in which a student may be struggling with a quiet desire to injure self. The ASCA Ethical Standards for School Counselors (2010) provides a clear description of how to respond to a situation in which a student is a danger to herself, but it is essential to gain an understanding of the situation by doing a risk assessment and asking necessary questions to determine whether the student does pose a danger to self or to others. School counselors should be mindful of details associated with the student's potential danger to self and may consider asking questions regarding the length of time since the initial self-injurious thoughts or behaviors, frequency, instruments used, triggers, and stressors as well as other critical questions needed to assess the overall risk, depending on the situation and the student's responses. Additional questions to assess the student's risk may also help the school counselor to gather necessary information to keep the student safe. Had the student previously presented as a danger to herself or made any previous attempts to harm herself or others? Had the student previously been hospitalized or admitted to an alternative placement for mental health services? Is there a family history of mental health concerns, self-injury, suicidal ideation, or suicidal attempts? And finally, perhaps the most important question a school counselor needs to consider is, where is the student right now and how quickly can I get to her?

Counseling Responses

Regardless of the source of the referral, school counselors are often the point person in times of crisis and must prioritize responsibilities based on urgency, assess the seriousness of the event, and respond immediately to the higher priority situations. As soon as a school counselor becomes aware that a student may be a potential danger to herself or to others, the appropriate professional response is to comply with written school policies and procedures.

Depending on the additional school supports available, school counselors may also need to consult with school resource officers, social workers, or other student support service professionals employed by the school to keep students safe; respond to schoolwide emotional concerns (e.g., student death); and encourage healthy growth and social development within the context of the school's academic structure. In consultation with other professionals and by following the school district's written policy and procedures, school counselors can have a significant impact on the outcome of students in elementary, middle and junior high, and high school settings (ASCA, 2012b).

Consistent with the ASCA Ethical Standards (2010), it is necessary and appropriate to begin the conversation with a statement that expresses the school counselor's "purposes, goals, techniques, and rules of procedure" (p. 1) as well as the definition and limits of confidentiality. It is extremely important for school counselors to begin the session with this information as it helps the student understand what to expect from the interaction and it minimizes the potential for an ethical dilemma. By explaining the limits of confidentiality before a counseling session, the counselor ensures that the student can immediately feel comfortable because she is aware of what can and what cannot stay confidential within the counseling session.

First and foremost, the school counselor cannot leave the student unattended for any reason. If it is necessary to leave the room, the school counselor must request that another competent school professional such as another counselor, counseling secretary, or administrator stay with the student until the counselor returns. Again, referring to the school district's policies and procedures is of high importance as districts often have written policies or procedures to follow in situations where a student is considered a danger to herself. If the school does not have previously established policies or procedures to follow, the school counselor should immediately consult with the administration and contact a parent or guardian if there is a concern about student safety, all the while ensuring that the student is not left alone at any point.

During conversation with the parents, the school counselor should use counseling and communication skills to gently share the information. Since they may or may not be aware of their student's self-injurious behavior, parents' emotional responses vary greatly from surprise to fear, disappointment, confusion, or other conflicting emotions. School counselors can prepare parents for the conversation by first creating an atmosphere of trust and respect by reminding parents of the school counselors' role in supporting students. They should also describe the limitations of confidentiality and share that these limits were also shared with their student prior to the student disclosing about self-injurious thoughts and behaviors. By reassuring parents that the student understood the limits of confidentiality prior to sharing, parents can rest assured that their student is ready for them to be aware of their thoughts and behaviors even if the information is a total shock or surprise to them. Additionally, school counselors should articulate their commitment to ongoing communication and collaboration, as necessary, with parents to help parents feel more at ease and comfortable with the school counselors' efforts and genuine concern.

Another important consideration for school counselors is to ensure that they are making a "good-faith effort to keep both parents informed [and] maintaining focus on the student and avoiding supporting one parent over another" (ASCA, 2010, p. 4) unless the school has proof of a court order that removes a parent's rights. For the current scenario, Mr. Lee was with his wife when the school counselor called home so he was equally aware of the situation because Mrs. Lee repeated everything to him while Mrs. Martin was on the phone.

DISTINGUISHING CHARACTERISTICS OF SCHOOL COUNSELING

The profession of school counseling is based on the commitment to "create opportunities for equity in access and success in educational opportunities" (ASCA, 2010, p. 1) for all students through school counselor advocacy, leadership, collaboration, and consultation (ASCA, 2010). Additionally, school counselors are committed to several beliefs about their professional responsibility, including beliefs that every individual (a) deserves to be treated with respect and dignity and should "have access to a comprehensive school counseling program" (ASCA, 2010, p. 1), (b) should receive the adequate support to "move toward self-direction and self-development and affirmation within one's group identities" (ASCA, 2010, p. 1), (c) should have information about educational choices and an understanding of potential future outcomes based on the choices, (d) has the right to privacy particularly regarding the relationship between the school counselor and the student, and (e) has "the right

to feel safe in school environments" (ASCA, 2010, p. 1). To help school counselors achieve the goals of the profession within the tenets outlined, ASCA (2010) developed ethical standards to centralize the ethical responsibilities, thereby creating more continuity among school counselors, counselor educators, and supervisors. The standards provide clarity to the professional expectations of school counselors for the purpose of "self-appraisal and peer evaluations" (ASCA, 2010, p. 1) and for informational purposes for all stakeholders.

School counselors are appropriately trained and certified or licensed by a state to provide comprehensive and developmental services designed to address the academic, personal, social, and career development needs of all students (ASCA, 2010, 2014). Unlike other counseling or therapeutic professional roles, school counselors do not diagnose students or provide ongoing intensive therapeutic counseling services (ASCA, 2012b). ASCA School Counselor Competencies (2012b) include the referral of students for "long-term therapy or diagnoses of disorders" (p. 10) because school counselors provide services that are more consistent with brief counseling and incorporate a tremendous amount of prevention, intervention, collaboration, psycho-education, and consultation.

In conjunction with the ASCA National Model (2012a), the ASCA National Standards for Students (2004) provide the framework for school counselors to support students in acquiring the attitudes, knowledge, and skills associated with their academic, personal, social, and career development. The standards for students are intended to help school counselors prepare students for adulthood by providing them with a comprehensive school counseling program that addresses each domain. Regarding the topic of self-injurious behaviors, the personal/social development domain is the most applicable as it requires school counseling programs to help students "understand and respect self and others" (ASCA, 2004, p. 9). Within the domain, several competencies and indicators are relevant for the current topic. Indicators for students include increasing awareness of self, expressing feelings, demonstrating self-control, adjusting to personal roles, engaging in decision making, problem solving, viewing alternative options for solving problems, coping with stress, and seeking help when needed (ASCA, 2004).

The intent of the ASCA National Standards for Students (2004) is similar to the ASCA Position Statement regarding the early identification, prevention, and intervention of harmful behaviors. In summary, distinguishing characteristics of school counseling include the commitment of school counselors to support students in their academic, personal, social, and career development so that students can make healthy choices and "minimize or eliminate harmful behaviors that place [them] at risk" (ASCA, 2014, p. 35).

INNOVATIVE INTERVENTIONS

The role of the professional school counselor requires active prevention, identification, and intervention of harmful behaviors (e.g., self-injury; ASCA, 2014) as part of a comprehensive school counseling program and in collaboration with other school personnel and stakeholders. Particularly for situations such as physical threat to self or to others, school counselors need to be acutely aware of the potential for school environments and ill-informed staff to unintentionally promote or fail to address harmful behaviors (Holcomb-McCoy, as cited in ASCA, 2014, p. 35).

ASCA (2014) provides specific recommendations for identifying, preventing, and intervening when a student presents as a danger to himself or herself. These recommendations target school counselors' attention to identifying risk factors and preventing behaviors that are harmful by training staff to "identify and assist students in crisis" (p. 35), bolstering social support among peers, creating an adult mentoring or monitoring system, and offering classroom guidance lessons specifically designed to teach and promote healthy skills related to resiliency and good choices. Recommendations also include increasing the availability of responsive services, improving the school counselor's use of effective referral process to community and

other supportive agencies, and advocating for resilience training for all students and parents (ASCA, 2014). Through the use of these evidence-based practices, active leadership on schoolwide teams, and preventive initiatives, school counselors can engage in activities designed to better utilize student strengths and diminish risk factors (White & Kelly, 2010) while also increasing collaboration among school faculty and the early identification of harmful behaviors (ASCA, 2014).

While implementing evidence-based interventions, school counselors need to be keenly aware of their ethical responsibility to protect the confidentiality of adolescent consumers (ASCA, 2014). School counselors must recognize the difference between providing schoolwide or target group preventions and the interventions that require school counselors to protect the information shared within a counseling session because "a student who has a counseling relationship with a professional school counselor has the right to privacy and confidentiality" (ASCA, 2014, p. 12). Schoolwide prevention and intervention activities, such as assemblies or classroom presentations that the school counselor provides to all students, vary significantly from target group interventions in which school counselors provide specific interventions for a smaller group of students who are identified to potentially benefit from the interventions. An example of a schoolwide intervention for self-injurious behaviors could be an assembly for the entire school on the topic of suicide prevention or positive coping mechanisms, whereas an example of a target group intervention could be a small group intervention that a school counselor may facilitate for several weeks following the assembly to support a smaller group of students. The school counselor could identify specific students for the group who may benefit from interventions related to the topic of self-injurious behaviors because of their personal experience with self-injurious behaviors or their interest in preventing others from engaging in the behaviors.

Based on these recommendations, school counselors could consider a host of evidence-based and innovative interventions. Keeping in mind the culture of the school and the level of support for the school counseling program, school counselors should advocate for early identification, prevention, and intervention of behaviors that are harmful and utilize data collection methods to identify needs and measure the effectiveness of the interventions (ASCA, 2014; CACREP, 2009). A positive school climate is a school setting that is conducive to learning and that encourages tolerance and acceptance of all students regardless of their differences. "Professional school counselors collaborate with others in the school and community to promote safe schools and confront issues threatening school safety" by developing and implementing prevention and intervention opportunities to promote a positive school climate (ASCA, 2014). Some examples of opportunities to create a positive school climate include school counselors' attempts to reduce negative factors such as suicide, violence, bullying, or harassment. Attempts to increase the positive factors that contribute toward school climate include prevention and intervention activities that support positive choices such as increasing academic achievement, attendance, building positive relationships, and conflict resolution (ASCA, 2014). Reviewing the data with kindergarten through 12th-grade school counselors, administrators, faculty, staff, and other stakeholders will result in positive public relations and hopefully bolster support for the school counseling program and the implementation of the interventions.

SELF-INJURIOUS BEHAVIOR

Several professional organizations including CACREP and ASCA outline and recommend specific competencies for professional school counselors to provide the most comprehensive services for all students (ASCA, 2012b; CACREP, 2009). Essentially, ASCA (2014) recommends specific evidence-based innovative interventions for school counselors to utilize in the identification and prevention of at-risk or self-injurious behaviors. Described as "an intentional act with the objective to do harm to the body without leading to a result of death" (White-Kress et al., 2006, p. 31),

self-injurious behaviors often include cutting, hitting, burning, biting, or otherwise injuring oneself for the purpose of doing self-harm. Through "proactive leadership in identifying, preventing, and intervening with students' at-risk behaviors" (ASCA, 2014, p. 31), school counselors will be able to address the risk factors of self-injurious behaviors and greatly reduce their occurrence because of the specific interventions. Additionally, it is important to note that "the intent of the person who is engaging in self-injurious behavior is not of a suicidal nature" (Favazza, as cited in White-Kress et al., 2006, "Confidentiality and Responsibilities to Students", para. 6) despite the deliberate intent to engage in self-injurious behaviors (White-Kress et al., 2006).

School counselors need to adhere to the components of the ASCA School Counselor Competencies (2012b) that relate to self-injurious behaviors while delivering a comprehensive school counseling program with appropriate responsive services and multitiered approaches to meet the needs of all students through direct and indirect service. School counselors are to provide appropriate responsive services, including crisis response, when necessary (ASCA, 2012b). More specifically, school counselors are to "understand what defines a crisis, the appropriate response and a variety of intervention strategies to meet the needs of the individual, group or school community before, during and after crisis response" (ASCA, 2012b, p. 9).

Another example of self-injurious behavior comes from Lucas who was recently caught with prescription medication in the classroom setting. Although he initially reported that it was prescribed for him, he forgot the appropriate procedure for submitting prescriptions to the school nurse's office. The school counselor and school nurse contacted Lucas's parents and found out that they were unaware of the prescription. As it turned out, Lucas admitted that he was buying prescription pills from various friends because he needed to find a way to cope with the stress and pressure of meeting his parents' high academic expectations. Lucas's attempt to self-medicate, paired with feelings of inadequacy, resulted in his ongoing abuse of prescription medications regardless of their possible side effects or interaction effects. After consulting with Lucas about the dangers of taking medications that were not prescribed for him, Lucas said that he did not care because he was under so much pressure to succeed that he would rather feel numb from the pills. Thankfully, Lucas and his parents were agreeable to the school counselor's referral to an outside mental health facility to assist Lucas in understanding the dangers of his self-injurious behaviors.

INTERFACING WITH MULTIPLE SYSTEMS OF CARE

White-Kress et al. (2006) suggest that it is unreasonable for school counselors to be competent in all student situations or issues. As a result, an appropriate professional response is for school counselors to reflect on their level of competence prior to making decisions (White-Kress et al., 2006). Depending on the severity, frequency, and mental health concerns associated with a student's needs, the school counselors' role varies but, at a minimum level, requires them to communicate the information to parents (White-Kress et al., 2006). If the minimum of care is solely to report the situation to parents, the school counselor should also provide important information such as phone numbers for local resources, including emergency numbers and crisis hotlines, to both the student and the parent.

Within the context of school counselors' responsibilities, they may find it necessary and appropriate to refer to "counselors who are competent to work with this population" (White-Kress et al., 2006). If it is determined that a referral is appropriate and parents follow through with the recommendation, school counselors can communicate and collaborate with other mental health professionals, agencies, or systems of care after receiving a signed consent to release and receive information as required by the school district and mental health provider (White-Kress et al., 2006). After making the referral, White-Kress et al. (2006) strongly recommend that school counselors "maintain regular contact with a student's mental health professional and work closely with this person" (p. 207).

School counselors make referrals to outside mental health agencies after acknowledging that a student's needs are beyond the scope of the school counselor's role and/or that of the school setting (ASCA, 2014). For example, if the responsive services outlined in a comprehensive school counseling program do not prove to be sufficient enough to address concerning behavior such as self-injurious behaviors, school counselors are professionally trained and are required to refer. Additionally, since school counselors "do not provide long-term therapy in schools" (ASCA, 2014, p. 51), school counselors appropriately refer when they recognize that long-term therapy would be beneficial or necessary for the student.

For schools or school districts that prefer not to make recommendations to particular agencies or systems of care, school counselors should encourage parents to review the list of mental health providers covered by their insurance company. Parents can usually easily access providers covered by their insurance by logging in to their health insurance website and searching for local mental health providers who specialize in various mental health topics such as self-injurious behaviors. If online access is not available, school counselors can encourage parents to call their insurance company directly and then contact mental health providers individually. Other times, school counselors can share a local listing of all mental health professionals separated by specialty area if such a resource is available within the community. Regardless of the method, school counselors should make every effort possible to help parents identify and access competent mental health providers.

INTEGRATING CORE COMPETENCIES (SCHOOL COUNSELING)

American School Counseling Association

The ASCA National Model (2012a) provides the framework for the school counseling profession by establishing clear recommendations for designing and implementing comprehensive school counseling programs to support students in their academic, personal, social, and career developments. Key themes of the model include (a) an emphasis on providing rigorous learning opportunities to all students, (b) clear student outcomes, (c) consistent delivery system, (d) decisions based on data, and (e) support for qualified school counselors implementing the comprehensive school counseling program (ASCA, 2012a). The model "creates unity and focus toward improving student achievement" (ASCA, 2012a, p. 1) because it clearly summarizes and outlines appropriate roles and responsibilities of professional school counselors within the context of comprehensive school counseling programs including the following components: (a) foundation, (b) management, (c) delivery, and (d) accountability (ASCA, 2012a).

Foundation. The *Foundation* component of the ASCA National Model encompasses the development of a comprehensive school counseling program with a clear program focus and consistency with student competencies and professional competencies (ASCA, 2012a). A preventive, developmental, and comprehensive school counseling program based on the ASCA National Standards (2012a) is prepared to meet the challenges associated with the identification, prevention, and intervention of self-injurious behaviors. The *Foundation* of the comprehensive program requires adherence to student competencies (ASCA, 2004) and professional competencies (ASCA, 2012a), so students who attend schools with comprehensive school counseling programs as outlined per the ASCA National Standards (2012a) receive preventive and developmentally appropriate academic, personal, social, and career development that should include prevention of self-injurious behaviors. As a result, it is appropriate to assume that these students should demonstrate the competencies as outlined by the ASCA National Standards for Students (2004) and know how to make healthy choices for their academic, personal/social, and career development.

Management. The *Management* component includes the specific tools and documents needed for school counselors to document, organize,

measure, and evaluate the services provided (ASCA, 2012a). Regarding the *Management* component of the model, school counselors should use their organizational and data collection skills to determine student needs, create action plans, and utilize data to measure the effectiveness of their program, including prevention and intervention activities related to self-injurious behaviors. For example, school counselors could easily create a survey or needs assessment to collect information about self-injurious behaviors, they could use a use-of-time assessment to determine whether they are giving appropriate time for prevention and intervention activities, or they could bring the concern of self-injurious behaviors to the attention of advisory council members to discuss and determine a plan of action.

Delivery. The *Delivery* component includes all direct and indirect services provided by school counselors within the comprehensive school counseling program to support students, parents, and all stakeholders (ASCA, 2012a). For the actual *Delivery* of the model, school counselors provide developmentally appropriate school counseling curriculum and individual student planning to all students and responsive services such as individual and group counseling to further support students. Regarding self-injurious behaviors, school counselors may engage in direct services that may include initial individual counseling to students struggling with thoughts or behaviors to self-injure, they may lead a group designed to promote positive decision making, or they may respond to crisis situations. Indirect services such as communication and collaboration with parents about individual crisis situations or concerns, training school personnel to identify and report potential self-injurious behaviors, and raising awareness through school counselor involvement in committees about preventing self-injurious behaviors are all examples of indirect services that benefit students.

Accountability. The final component, *Accountability*, provides the direction and impetus for school counselors to collect and utilize data to measure the effectiveness of the school counseling program, to make appropriate decisions based on the data, and to communicate "how students are different as a result of the school counseling program" (ASCA, 2012a, p. 4). The *Accountability* component of the model provides the framework for school counselors to measure the effectiveness of school counseling prevention and intervention activities within the context of the school counseling program. For example, school counselors could review data such as the total number of self-injurious behaviors reported each year, the most common type of behaviors, the most common referral source, or other helpful patterns that could help school counselors make decisions about the most effective ways to identify, prevent, and intervene. Collecting and evaluating information from students, parents, school personnel, and other stakeholders regarding the school counseling program's effectiveness in identifying, preventing, and intervening with self-injurious behaviors could also be beneficial to improve services and further support students.

CACREP (2009) also requires school counselors to demonstrate additional proficiency and competency across the following domains through demonstrated knowledge, skills, and practices: (a) foundations; (b) counseling, prevention, and intervention; (c) diversity and advocacy; (d) assessment; (e) research and evaluation; (f) academic development; (g) collaboration and consultation; and (h) leadership.

Foundations. Regarding the *Foundations* domain, CACREP (2009) requires school counselors to acquire knowledge pertaining to the professional role, legal and ethical issues, organizations supporting the profession, models of comprehensive school counseling programs, developmental and resiliency models, and appropriate school responses related to attending to crises or other urgent situations. Within this domain, school counselors must demonstrate necessary skills and practices to demonstrate adherence to ethical and legal standards. School counselors must also competently advocate for the role of the school counselor by articulating the identity of the role and the necessity for a comprehensive program.

As required by this domain, school counselors will respond appropriately to situations in which students require mental health interventions to achieve their educational and vocational goals, contribute toward a positive school culture, and intervene in individual and schoolwide crises, all within the context of professional ethics and legal requirements.

Counseling, Prevention, and Intervention. School counselors must have knowledge and demonstrate skills and practices outlined by the *Counseling, Prevention, and Intervention* domain (CACREP, 2009). By acquiring the knowledge of specific counseling theories and the effectiveness of counseling and wellness initiatives, school counselors will then be trained to plan and implement developmentally appropriate and comprehensive school counseling programs. When a potential or actual crisis occurs, school counselors will understand and identify interventions to address the situation. When faced with a student who is engaging in or considering engaging in self-injurious behaviors, the school counselor will immediately assess and manage the situation while also recognizing personal and professional limitations related to competence. As appropriate, school counselors will consult with other school professionals, seek supervision, and refer to the appropriate community resources, depending on the situation and level of need (CACREP, 2009).

Diversity and Advocacy. The *Diversity and Advocacy* domain (CACREP, 2009) requires school counselors to understand, identify, demonstrate, and advocate to meet the needs of all students through carefully designed "school policies, programs, and services that enhance a positive school climate" (p. 42). School counselors promote a positive school climate and engage others in creating an environment conducive to the positive engagement of all students and families. School counselors need to be prepared to be equally responsive to schoolwide and individual crises as well as anticipate, prevent, and respond to them as they present in the specific populations represented within the school.

Assessment. School counselors are also required to be competent in the *Assessment* domain (CACREP, 2009), which means that they must have the knowledge, skills, and practices to understand and identify factors that may negatively influence students. Through appropriate training, curricular experience, demonstrated knowledge, and skill competence, school counselors need to understand the negative influence of factors such as undiagnosed or untreated mental health concerns, abuse, or other violent situations encountered by students (CACREP, 2009). School counselors will need to identify the signs and symptoms of substance or other forms of abuse and consider appropriate forms of assessment (CACREP, 2009). Related to self-injurious thoughts and behaviors, school counselors will conduct informal assessments to gather relevant information to inform their decisions related to assisting and supporting students and their families through referral to other mental health professionals who specialize in self-injurious thoughts and behaviors.

Research and Evaluation. The *Research and Evaluation* domain (CACREP, 2009) requires school counselors to understand and utilize data-driven research while designing comprehensive school counseling programs. School counselors will be aware of relevant strategies to evaluate outcomes of school counseling services, utilize data, demonstrate accountability, and employ best practices as articulated in relevant research literature. Through the utilization of data, school counselors will develop methods for measuring the effectiveness of "school counseling programs, activities, interventions, and experiences" while continually improving programs based on the data (CACREP, 2009, p. 42). It is essential for school counselors to collect data about the prevalence of mental health concerns as well as data about the particular strategies and interventions that prove to be the most effective in preventing

and/or reducing their prevalence with special attention to populations represented within the school system.

Academic Development. Regarding the *Academic Development* domain (CACREP, 2009), school counselors must focus on the required knowledge, skills, and practices to support all students in their academic development and achievement. By merging the efforts of the school counseling program with the school's overall mission to educate all students, school counselors will adjust the comprehensive program to meet individual student needs and ultimately progress toward closing the achievement gap (CACREP, 2009). Since engaging in self-injurious thoughts or behaviors is a barrier to learning and overall academic achievement, this competency is relevant to the school counselors' role in preventing and intervening with self-injurious behaviors as part of a comprehensive school counseling program, including responsive services.

Collaboration and Consultation. Through the *Collaboration and Consultation* domain (CACREP, 2009), school counselors are required to understand, promote, and implement prevention and intervention strategies involving other stakeholders. Essential components of this domain include increasing communication, providing resources, making referrals, and utilizing strategies that include various stakeholder groups (CACREP, 2009). Students will benefit from the partnerships that result from the expertise of school counselors who initiate and promote collaboration among all stakeholders. For situations when students or families do not have proper insurance coverage or access to necessary mental health services, the increased collaboration and consultation with stakeholders could result in easier access to resources or assistance that they otherwise would not have had access to without the partnership. For example, by increasing collaboration and consultation among the mental health professionals within a community, school counselors could help create a resource of local mental health services available to assist students struggling with self-injurious thoughts or behaviors.

Leadership. Finally, the *Leadership* domain of the CACREP Standards for School Counseling Programs (2009) requires school counselors to have the necessary knowledge, skills, and practices to effectively lead others within the school setting and community. CACREP (2009) encourages school counselors to take an active role "in the design, implementation, management, and evaluation of a comprehensive developmental school counseling program" (p. 45) in addition to the various leadership roles to benefit all students. Specific examples of the skills and practices required by the domain include a school counselor's leadership in developing a presentation about self-injurious behaviors that is then presented to teachers during a faculty meeting or to parents during a parent presentation. Through leadership opportunities, school counselors will provide necessary and timely education about self-injurious behaviors that could ultimately help teachers and parents identify early warning signs and triggers or prevent the occurrence of such behaviors.

In summary, CACREP (2009) requires professional school counselors to be appropriately trained to have the necessary knowledge, skills, and practices to support all students in their academic, personal, social, and career development through the utilization of a comprehensive school counseling program. Counselors in training need to demonstrate competence across all CACREP domains (2009) and ASCA School Counselor Competencies (2012b) prior to becoming professional school counselors who carry the tremendous privilege and responsibility of counseling adolescents competently. Without consistency across the profession and high expectations for school counselors to carefully and creatively address students' needs through education, prevention, and intervention, adolescents would neither receive the service or support they deserve nor be able to achieve their best academically.

EVIDENCE-BASED DECISION MAKING

School counselors are committed to building comprehensive school counseling programs that are "based on data-driven decision making" (ASCA, 2014, p. 9). Under the management function of their role, school counselors use assessments and tools to collect and use data to create action plans, make decisions, and continually improve services. Under the accountability function of their role, school counselors demonstrate school counseling programming's impact on student achievement, attendance, and behavior. They analyze the school counseling program assessments and assist applying the outcomes to better improve their programs toward the betterment of the student body they serve. Using data to make decisions is also an important aspect of the role of the school counselor when supporting students who are potentially a danger to themselves or to others. More specifically, school counselors use "data to develop and evaluate preventive and responsive services" (ASCA, 2014, p. 35) regarding their effectiveness in identifying, preventing, and intervening in situations.

IMPLICATIONS FOR COUNSELING ADOLESCENTS

Counseling adolescents competently in the school setting requires school counselors to be appropriately trained and committed to the school counseling profession as well as the ethical and legal responsibilities to adolescent students and their parents. School counselors must adhere to ASCA Ethical Standards (2010), ASCA National Standards for Students (ASCA, 2004), ASCA School Counselor Competencies (2012b), and the ACA Code of Ethics (2014) while promoting comprehensive programs based on the ASCA National Model (2005). Addressing the diverse and unique needs of students requires professionalism and training unique to school counseling graduate programs and the school counseling profession. For CACREP-accredited school counseling programs, school counselors in training are required to meet the requirements of the program and have the knowledge, skills, and abilities to adhere to the CACREP Standards (2009) including those standards specifically related to school counseling. Once employed in a school setting, competent school counselors can support students by encouraging their resilience and academic success (ASCA, 2014) through the delivery of a comprehensive curriculum and referrals to mental health counselors when appropriate.

Clinical Review of Case

As this chapter comes to a close, a revisiting of Adrienne's case study is warranted to round out understanding of her crisis. Adrienne's case requires counselors to reflect on their knowledge, skills, and abilities related to the professional response required when a student presents a danger to herself. Counselors working with children and adolescents must be aware of their professional, ethical, and legal responsibilities to parents. Counselors must be aware of and abide by their professional responsibilities concerning school policies and procedures in handling situations in which there is a potential danger to self. Counselors must also adhere to appropriate ethical standards and the legal requirements surrounding expectations in communicating with parents, potentially breaching the confidentiality of students, and responding appropriately to ensure student safety. For the current case, the counselor responded appropriately in terms of professional, ethical, and legal responsibilities, but it is essential to note that minor variations in the case scenario could result in differences in the response that may be more appropriate based on the presenting information. Counselors who are unsure of the appropriate response should consult with other counselors or appropriate personnel (ASCA, 2010) to determine the most appropriate response for unique situations.

Implications for Counseling

Regarding the implications for counseling and required counselor competencies, the CACREP Standards (2009) meticulously outline the importance of Helping Relationships and Assessments as two of the common core curricular areas required of all counseling students. The Helping Relationships competency (CACREP, 2009) is relevant to counseling adolescents because of the emphasis on helping and wellness through prevention and crisis intervention. School counselors are committed to creating a helping relationship that empowers and educates all students to achieve their academic, personal, social, and career development goals through a developmentally appropriate and comprehensive school counseling curriculum (ASCA, 2014). Additionally, school counselors are responsible for identifying barriers to the mental wellness of students and then designing, implementing, and evaluating the prevention or intervention strategies used to support students. If the student needs additional support to achieve mental wellness, school counselors may also refer to a mental health agency to ensure that students are receiving necessary support from another helping professional more appropriately trained for long-term therapy.

School counselors who are trained and competent in understanding the nature and models of helping relationships will have the skills to effectively support the diversity of needs within a diverse population of adolescents. For example, when school counselors need to provide crisis intervention for students struggling with self-injurious thoughts or behaviors, they will have the skills necessary to effectively and professionally utilize psychological first aid strategies to help the student receive the necessary support (CACREP, 2009).

Based on the ASCA National Model (2014), comprehensive school counseling programs are designed to address the academic, personal, social, and career development of all students by providing responsive services to help students with developmental and mental health issues.

Appropriate responsive services for supporting students with self-injurious behavior may include "internal and external referral procedures, short-term counseling or crisis intervention focused on mental health or situational concerns" (ASCA, 2014, p. 50) as appropriate methods of demonstrating the helping relationship.

Application of Ethics and Standards

School counselors must be keenly aware of relevant ethical standards to respond appropriately and professionally to situations in which they find themselves supporting children or adolescents who potentially pose a danger to themselves or to others. These situations can be peculiar to the school systems in which they work and require closer ethical attention and adjustments to situations such as school violence. Nevertheless, there are overarching ethics that extend across school settings, events, and populations. First and foremost, school counselors are to adhere to the ASCA Ethical Standards for School Counselors (2010) and attend to those that specifically address situations in which students present as a danger to themselves or to others (A.7). Additionally, school counselors need to consult with appropriate school personnel and make decisions as per school policies and procedures in an overall effort to support students' academic progress. As previously stated, school counselors also need to adhere to the ACA Code of Ethics (2005) and comply with those regarding school counselors' responsibilities regarding confidentiality.

Applying the national and professional standards while employed as a school counselor simply requires an understanding of and an adherence to the relevant standards, competencies, and ethical and legal guidelines of the profession. Professional school counselors who are competently trained to meet the demands of the role should not have a problem complying with the expectations because they would have already demonstrated the competence and skills necessary prior to completing their graduate coursework, meeting the graduation requirements of their program, and

passing state licensing or certification requirements. After completion of all requirements and when employed as a professional school counselor, it is essential for school counselors to continually seek professional development to stay current with updates to school counseling standards, competencies, and evidence-based preventions and interventions. School counselors must also comply with the written policies and procedures of their individual school district as well as with the expectations of other state or national professional organizations.

Summary

School counselors tend to be most effective when they have a pulse of the school's environment, they understand the student body's cultural strengths and deficits, and they are able to forge caring relationships with students. This chapter relays the distinguishing characteristics of school counseling; it is important for the school counselor to be aware of the roles, tasks, and services he or she may provide. As families come to view the school as a supportive network that helps their adolescents, school counselors often interface with multiple systems of care. With this comes the understanding that there are specific ethical standards for counselors in schools. Additionally, to counsel adolescents in schools competently, one must understand the innovative interventions for adolescents that are effective in this setting.

Keystones

- Most important, the primary keystone is for counselors-in-training and current school counselors to commit themselves to the level of professionalism and ethical decision making required to meet the extremely rigorous demands of the professional school counseling role. Counseling adolescents competently in the school setting requires proper training and continual compliance with various professional standards and organizations (ACA, 2005; ASCA, 2012b; CACREP, 2009). Professional organizations such as ASCA (2014) also provide resources such as position statements that clearly outline the national organization's response to various topics and the responses expected from competent and professional school counselors.

- Professional school counselors are "prepared to recognize and respond to student mental health crises and needs" (ASCA, 2014, p. 50) because of their training and position within the school. Since mental health needs are often first identified within the school setting, school counselors are often the first point of contact for students to recognize the need for mental health intervention or support (White-Kress et al., 2006) and address concerns through prevention, intervention, education, and referral to community resources (ASCA, 2014). School counselors need to ensure that they respond appropriately to crisis situations including assessment of risk (ASCA, 2014).

- Responsibilities of the school counselor include focused attention and effort in reducing the negative stigma surrounding the topic of mental health (ASCA, 2014).

- School counselors provide relevant information to students, teachers, and other stakeholders to increase the awareness of making healthy choices and engaging in positive behaviors instead of focusing solely on mental health issues.

- Through education, advocacy, and collaboration, school counselors can improve the culture of the school setting and increase the understanding, acceptance, and awareness of how to support students toward receiving mental health treatment or services when appropriate (ASCA, 2014).

- CACREP standards highlight eight core experiences and knowledge associated with professional counselor education: (1) professional orientation and ethical practice, (2) social and cultural diversity, (3) human growth and development, (4) career development, (5) helping relationships, (6) group work, (7) assessment, and (8) research and program evaluation

(CACREP, 2009). These standards have been established to ensure that community and school counseling students develop a knowledge base, ethical standards, and professional counselor identity within CACREP-accredited programs and are prepared for careers in the various areas professional counselors work (i.e., mental health and human services, educational institutions, private practice, government, business, and industrial settings; CACREP, 2009). School counselors should seek to adhere to these training standards regardless of accreditation status of his or her graduate program.

- Today's adolescents are a diverse group that present a vast array of counseling challenges that span several areas of their lives (e.g., personal, familial, community, education, addiction, and legal challenges); meeting their needs must be grounded in community and school counselor education, preparation, and intervention.

- Professional counselors are uniquely educated, ethically bound, and practically prepared to meet the needs of adolescents presenting in community mental health and school counseling settings.

REFERENCES

American Counseling Association. (2014). *ACA code of ethics*. Alexandria, VA: Author.

American School Counselor Association. (2004). *ASCA national standards for students*. Alexandria, VA: Author.

American School Counselor Association. (2005). *ASCA national model* (2nd ed.). Alexandria, VA: Author.

American School Counselor Association. (2010). *Ethical standards for school counselors*. Retrieved from http://www.schoolcounselor.org/asca/media/asca/home/EthicalStandards2010.pdf

American School Counselor Association. (2012a). *The ASCA national model: A framework for school counseling programs* (3rd ed.). Alexandria, VA: Author.

American School Counselor Association. (2012b). *School counselor competencies*. Retrieved from http://www.schoolcounselor.org/asca/media/asca/home/SCCompetencies.pdf

American School Counselor Association. (2014). *ASCA position statements*. Retrieved from http://www.schoolcounselor.org/files/PositionStatements.pdf

Council for Accreditation of Counseling and Related Educational Programs. (2009). *2009 Standards*. Alexandria, VA: Author.

White, S., & Kelly, F. (2010). The school counselor's role in school dropout prevention. *Journal of Counseling & Development, 88*(2), 227–235.

White-Kress, V. E., Costin, A., & Drouhard, N. (2006). Students who self-injure: School counselor ethical and legal considerations. *Professional School Counseling, 10*(2), 203–209.

12

RELATIONAL AND CAREER ISSUES

INTRODUCTION

While career and relational issues in adolescence may seem as though they are two separate constructs, relationships are pervasive across every stage of development and have a lasting impact on decision making, values, and self-identity that ultimately lead to the formation of career paths. Parents, siblings, and peers all have a significant impact on life choices. As adolescence marks the transition from childhood to adulthood, many life choices surround preparation for higher education and training necessary for future careers. This chapter seeks to identify significantly influential relationships, discuss normative career development, and synthesize the interactions of these elements.

The interconnectedness of these issues is widely recognized by researchers and developmental theorists. As Schultheiss (2003) notes, "What transpires in our relationships may be key to the facilitation or hindrance of our ability to progress effectively through challenging career tasks and our ability to benefit from more traditional career counseling practices" (p. 301). It is this viewpoint that summarizes the following discussions throughout the chapter. Relationships affect not only academic and career success but also decision making, interests, abilities, and nearly every other influential factor in career choice. Who we spend time with often affects how we perceive the world, the extracurricular activities we involve ourselves in, and how we spend our time. Given the numerous life transitions during adolescence, relationships are of even greater value in understanding career counseling of adolescents.

As such, this chapter will seek to discuss the factors that influence the transition of adolescents, including parents, peer groups, and schooling. Understanding relevant biological and career development is also crucial in defining influential factors; thus, this chapter will detail some of the most common and applicable theories of development specific to career and relational issues. Career-specific approaches as well as challenges to career counseling will be briefly discussed, and implications for practice including assessments and the use of career counseling in school will be reviewed. This chapter will offer readers the opportunity to gain a frame of reference in understanding career issues across settings. After reading this chapter, readers will be able to do the following:

- Understand the developmental, peer, familial, and environmental influences that affect the transition to adolescence. Additionally, readers will understand how these influences might affect counseling.

- Describe career development using Super's (1975) life span development theory. Additionally, readers will be able to identify life roles and developmental tasks during the various stages of life that affect career development.

- Identify and apply various career counseling strategies

- Understand the influence of multicultural factors in the process of career counseling

- Identify challenges to career counseling

- Differentiate normative versus problematic development

- Demonstrate basic knowledge of the assessments commonly used by career providers. Readers should also be able to identify when and with whom particular assessments would be beneficial.

- Apply knowledge gleaned from case scenarios

TRANSITION OF ADOLESCENCE

As discussed, adolescence is characterized by the transition from childhood to adulthood and is highly influenced by peer groups, parents, and siblings. Oftentimes, this transition is known to be marked by a period of "storm" and "stress" (Hollenstein & Lougheed, 2013). Hollenstein and Lougheed (2013) describe "storm" as decreases in self-control and "stress" as increases in awareness of external surroundings (i.e., a demanding world that has expectations and consequences at home, school, work, and society). The premise is that adolescents gain greater recognition of the importance of their choices while still being developmentally inept at handling the responsibilities of adulthood. This tug of war is particularly relevant to career issues. Adolescents begin to recognize the need for career preparation while still not having the self-control necessary to make decisions tailored for a single career path.

Given this, adolescents face the challenge of beginning to create a career identity that will aid them in their transition into college and/or the workplace (Vuolo, Staff, & Mortimer, 2011). The actual identification of a specific career or college major is far less important than the development of a cohesive self-concept in relation to the world (Steinberg & Morris, 2001). In a recent study of adolescent girls examining influencing factors on career decisions, researchers found that decisions were more heavily influenced by personal factors, including values such as role conflict (one's views about his or her position in various situations and that person's expectations) and self-efficacy (one's belief in being able to succeed in certain situations; Novakovic & Fouad, 2013). This personal development occurs within the context of interpersonal relationships.

Peer Influences

Research has consistently shown the importance of parent–child relationships as well as peer groups. Overwhelmingly, literature agrees that parents are one of the greatest lifelong influences (DeVore & Ginsburg, 2005); however, research has also shown that adolescents typically spend much more time with peers as opposed to parents (Steinberg & Morris, 2001). For this reason, parental influences will be discussed later in the chapter; however, the interplay of parental and peer groups is important to note as friend choices have been shown to be influenced by parenting and home life (Steinberg & Morris, 2001).

Peer groups have been shown to have direct effects on career development, particularly in adolescence. Adolescence is often the first period of interpersonal stability and consistency (Poulin & Chan, 2010). The friendships established in adolescence are often a stable influence on decision making well into early adulthood (Kiuru et al., 2012; Poulin & Chan, 2010). These friend groups have been shown to influence attitudes, behaviors, social skills, and life goals (Poulin & Chan, 2010); however, the impact of these influences can be either positive or negative (McWhirter, Valdez, & Caban, 2013; Steinberg & Morris, 2001). For example, a study examining peer influence through the transition to early adulthood found strong correlations between best friends at the age of 15 and similar career choices (Kiuru et al., 2012).

With this in mind, it is crucial for providers of adolescents to recognize the roles that parents as well as friends have in decision making, goal setting, and life choices in both direct and indirect ways. While adolescents may not spend as much time with parents, the dynamics of home life including parental involvement and style directly affect peer relationships. Furthermore, these peer relationships directly affect multiple development areas. As such, it is recommended that providers take the time to fully understand the influencing relationships in a client's life before assessing how to assist in career development, which will provide more accuracy to that assessment.

Developmental Influences

It is crucial to recognize that the rate of adolescent maturation directly affects family and peer relationships as well as the development of self-concept (Steinberg & Morris, 2001). Thus, to fully understand the complexities of career development, one must recognize and understand the developmental influences typical in an adolescent including not only physical changes but also psychological growth. In a metareview of literature pertaining to adolescent development, Steinberg and Morris (2001) note that two thirds of all literature on adolescence identifies parents, problems, and hormones as the most influential factors on development. With this assertion, there is evidence of ongoing interactions between social, physical, and psychological growth for adolescents. In fact, physical development has been shown to be influenced by environmental factors and time as well as emotional behavioral differences (Hollenstein & Lougheed, 2013).

In addition to the obvious physical changes that occur during adolescence, this period is also marked with increased emotionality (Hollenstein & Lougheed, 2013) as well as reasoning and functioning (Steinberg & Morris, 2001). These psychological changes are a direct result of physical development and changes in brain functioning. These changes are also the driving force behind the transition from child to adult. Research has

shown the positive correlations between cognitive reasoning ability and parents' willingness to increase child autonomy (Steinberg & Morris, 2001); however, this transition is not always easy to navigate, again pointing to the importance of family dynamics in adolescent development.

Familial Influences

Adolescence is often sprinkled with periods of conflict and establishing an identity outside of the family. In the process, the adolescent may become distant from family members. Families are challenged to accommodate the tension of redefining the parent–child relationship, often contributing stress and conflict to the entire family structure itself (Hollenstein & Lougheed, 2013; Steinberg & Morris, 2001). Parental conflict is a normative part of adolescent development (Steinberg & Morris, 2001) as boundaries, norms, and expectations of the relationship are redefined. This important relational change is necessary to allow the adolescent the autonomy and freedom needed for the development of self (Steinberg & Morris, 2001); however, the family dynamics occurring within this transition can have widespread effects.

Parenting style and monitoring have direct implications on behavioral problems (DeVore & Ginsburg, 2005). In a study of 11th-grade students, family functioning was found to be a greater predictor of career development than gender, socioeconomic status (SES), or educational attainment (Penick & Jepsen, 1992).

Furthermore, studies have also demonstrated direct relationships between the parent–child relationship and success in college and careers. For example, a study of children examining parental assets and involvement found significant relationships between the parent's role and the child's success in college (Kim & Sherraden, 2011). Parental involvement has also been shown to be related to perceptions of career barriers and coping efficacy (Raque-Bogdan, Klingaman, Martin, & Lucas, 2013), crucial factors in career pursuit.

Ultimately, a balance between parental involvement and adolescent independence is necessary for the adolescent's optimal growth and development. Without some degree of freedom and autonomy during this developmental stage, the adolescent may fail to develop a sense of self necessary for career success. Identity formation has been shown to decrease anxiety and self-doubt typical to this transitional life stage (Luyckx, Vansteenkiste, Goossens, & Duriez, 2009; Usinger & Smith, 2010). Adolescents need to be able to have the freedom to explore interests and understand themselves apart from the role of child in order to prepare for the role of adult. The exploration is of particular importance in developmental theories including theories of career development.

Environmental Influences

Not only are adolescents influenced to choose careers based on their parents' career positions, but their career decisions are also influenced by peers and the groups of peers they hang around with (Turner & Ziebell, 2011). For instance, SES influences career choice. Low-income, inner-city adolescents who socialize with one another report similar career outlooks and pursuits (Krumboltz, 1996). An adolescent's overall grade point average, parental home income, and his or her stated gender are also shown to be significant variables reflected in the adolescent's career choices and self-esteem (Kim, Seo, & Cho, 2012). For adolescents who are a part of diverse cultural groups, special attention must be given to identity formation and various contributors toward their positive self-esteem building. For example, Patel, Salahuddin, and O'Brien (2008) found that Asian immigrant adolescents' self-esteem was directly related to their acculturation status (e.g., their ability to speak English) and peer support. Ruggieri, Bendixen, Gabriel, and Alsaker (2013) highlight that things such as an ability to ask questions in class (English-speaking classrooms) and fit in with peers (a sense of belonging) also affected this group's esteem.

Interestingly, the research by Ruggieri et al. (2013) suggests a reason for the findings of Patel et al. (2008). Patel et al. (2008) discovered that Asian adolescents' self-esteem and career decision making were linked to their competency in speaking English by examining the sense of belonging and self-esteem levels of adolescent immigrants in schools. Common occurrences in the English-speaking schools in America, such as playing a team sport in groups and forcing Asian adolescents to choose groups, often incited feelings of isolation and rejection and an overall fall in the adolescents' sense of well-being (Ruggieri et al., 2013).

Providers working with adolescents from low SES can refer to the Integrative Contextual Model of Career Development to inform their therapeutic interventions with adolescents (Turner & Ziebell, 2011). The Integrative Contextual Model of Career Development teaches adolescents skills relative to their contexts such as interview skills, resume writing, and assertiveness training (Turner & Ziebell, 2011). Turner and Ziebell (2011) suggest that providers should focus their interventions on the populations they are predetermined to address. For instance, providers should be cautioned regarding strictly and solely utilizing career intervention models with adolescents living in inner-city neighborhoods that are not applicable to their points of reference, experiences, relatability, and living environments (e.g., access to quality schooling and neighborhood safety). This is not to say, do not inspire or encourage exploration of a vast array of career opportunities. Instead providers should ensure that such efforts are customized to the needs, skills, abilities, interests, and aspirations of diverse cultural and economic groups (Ruggieri et al., 2013). Therefore, providers need to refer to career counseling interventions that are found to work with their population of choice.

One career counseling intervention that has been recommended for various cultural groups is narrative therapy (Thomas & Gibbons, 2009). Providers using this model should allow their adolescent clients to speak from an "egocentric" (i.e., self-serving, egotistical) viewpoint as they tell the provider their stories; during this time, providers would do well to not interrupt or try to "rewrite" their client's story. Instead, they should support clients, even when they (providers) do not agree with the stories' plot or directive (Thomas & Gibbons, 2009).

Another environmental factor for adolescents is the influence of the parental structure within the home. Thomas and Gibbons (2009) reflected on the impact of divorce on adolescent career development. They focused on this subgroup as these youth oftentimes are overwhelmed by a perceived loss of control over their lives and important decisions affecting them. Under this light, providers' nonjudgmental stance becomes essential to the therapeutic process. Nonetheless, over time, providers can help adolescent clients reshape and revamp their stories to reflect a story of self-will, self-esteem, and self-directive focus (Thomas & Gibbons, 2009).

Purpose and Calling

While there are a number of external influences that are much more easily assessed and discussed, the concept of purpose and calling is particularly relevant to career counseling but much more difficult to conceptualize. Researchers currently struggle to develop a unified understanding of the concept; however, a calling is most commonly understood as a psychological construct emphasizing destiny, duty, self-fulfillment, and happiness (Duffy & Dik, 2013). It can provide a sense of direction and purpose to the individual. Furthermore, this is a concept that is often much more culturally tied, often including spiritual conviction. This conviction may stem from a personal belief in a higher power, but it may also develop from feelings of duty to family, country, or other forces (Duffy & Dik, 2013).

Unfortunately, the concept of calling in research is relatively new with the vast majority of studies including samples of college students or adults rather than adolescents; however, a review of literature indicated that those who view their job as a calling consistently reported finding more meaning in the workplace (Duffy & Dik, 2013). For this reason, it is recommended that providers engage in conversations that explore adolescents' perspectives on purpose and

calling in career explorations. As career calling is a relatively new concept, conceptualization on an empirical and theoretical level is still necessary, particularly with diverse populations and adolescents; however, providers may work to integrate this concept into the counseling realm through the use of meaning exploration and discussion of personal passions and values.

Career Development

Within career counseling ranks, Super's (1975) life span development theory and Savickas's (2005) career counseling approach are the most popular. Super's (1975) life span development theory is one of the most cited theories that encompasses childhood and adolescent development. Additionally, several theoretical offshoots such as Savickas's (2005) approach to career counseling have been formed utilizing the theoretical underpinnings of Super's (1975) approach. For this reason, these theories will be the central career developmental theory of emphasis in this chapter. In the life span theory, Super emphasizes the role of the school as well as surrounding influence on development and career-related matters. The theory is comprehensive in nature, and it addresses life stages, roles, and tasks. Each of these areas of focus is directly related to relational aspects and career tasks specific to adolescence.

Roe's Theory of Occupational Choice

While Super's (1975) approach is one of the most notable theories, Anne Roe has also made significant contributions to perspectives on career development. Specifically, Roe emphasized the importance of early childhood and familial environment in career preference (Lock, 2005). According to this perspective, career choice is influenced by need fulfillment in parent–child relationships resulting in emotional concentration (over protective and controlling parenting), avoidance (neglect and rejection), and acceptance (needs met). Individuals are then likely to select a career path that matches their household environment (Lock, 2005). For example, a child from a cold and neglectful home is more likely to choose a career in a field such as technology in which the focus is on things rather than relationships, while a child from a warm and accepting home may be more likely to choose a career in a helping profession. Roe further offered groups of organizations and occupational levels to conceptualize career categories as shown in Table 12.1. While Roe's model has not offered a great deal of empirical support, Roe was one of the first theorists to postulate that personality, upbringing, and psychological needs contribute to career choice (Lock, 2005), ultimately leading to further development of career theories such as Super's (1975) life stages and roles.

Super's Life Stages

Super's (1975) approach includes five life stages: (1) growth, (2) exploration, (3) establishment, (4) maintenance, and (5) decline. While the later stages take place in adulthood, the first two stages are directly applicable to adolescence.

Table 12.1   Roe's Occupations and Levels

Occupations	Levels
Service	Professional and managerial: 1
Business contract	Professional and managerial: 2
Organization	Semiprofessional and small business
Technology	Skilled
Outdoor	Semiskilled
Science	Unskilled
General cultural	
Arts and entertainment	

Source. From Lock. *Taking Charge of Your Career Direction,* 5E. © 2005 South-Western, a part of Cengage Learning, Inc. Reproduced by permission. www.cengage.com/permissions

The growth stage describes the interaction of the child and his or her surrounding environment. During this stage, parents and peers are influential in the development of gender roles and emotionally driven occupational choices. Typically, this stage also occurs earlier in childhood; however, it sets the foundation for choices made during adolescence.

The next stage typical is of adolescence, the exploration stage. During this stage, adolescents are said to formulate occupational choices that can usher in efforts needed to establish a career identity (Super, 1975). Adolescents explore interests, abilities, preferences, and values pertaining to a future career. It is important to note that while this exploration can be purposeful (e.g., attending a college tour, taking classes specific to career interest), it can also occur by happenstance (Super, 1975). Regardless, exploration during adolescence helps youth identify not only their preferences in career choice but also their understanding of values that contribute to understanding life roles necessary for career development.

Life Roles

While Super (1975) describes numerous roles throughout the life span, the roles that are applicable to adolescents are student and child. Super's life span rainbow incorporates role changes throughout life including the multiple roles that require balancing. Fulfillment of these roles can occur in multiple settings including home, community, and school (Super, 1975).

Adolescents must carefully balance not only the roles of child and student while preparing to transition into numerous other roles including worker and citizen. Many high school students are able to ease into this transition by gaining employment before graduation, offering them invaluable experience for future careers. Ultimately, these roles also incorporate the crucial social relationships that have been discussed earlier. Each of these roles not only holds significant social expectations, but they also influence individual identity development. For example, the role of "child" will have drastically different expectations and meaning from family to family. As such, while all adolescents will share similar roles, each experience is still unique in nature. Super's (1975) developmental tasks help solidify individual experiences and meaning making.

Developmental Tasks

Similar to both life stages and roles, Super (1975) describes developmental tasks as a progressive movement with tasks typically occurring at specific ages (Usinger & Smith, 2010). These five tasks are (1) crystallizing, (2) specifying, (3) implementing vocational presence, (4) stabilizing, and (5) consolidating in a vocation. Crystallization is the task that most typically occurs during adolescence (ages 14–18; Usinger & Smith, 2010). There are societal expectations on youth to begin to make tentative choices about future education or training that may be necessary for a desired occupation. These choices are the tasks of crystallization.

While adolescents are not expected to specify or solidify careers, they are required to make choices regarding college attendance, classes, or extracurricular activities that may be necessary for a future career, particularly in later adolescence. Given the uncertainty of the future and the likelihood that expected college majors or careers may change, the prospect of making such decisions can be stressful and overwhelming. As such, providers need to be willing to assist individuals seeking to complete the task at hand. This assistance may take place in a variety of formats that will be discussed later; however, Super (1975) offers some suggestions specific to school settings and school-age children.

Integration of Super's Life Span Development

Given the direct implications and applicability of Super's life span theory, Super (1975) offered three specific suggestions to providers working with school-aged children and adolescents— (1) guided exploration, (2) synthesis of data, and (3) individual application. Guided exploration includes providing purposeful experiences for students to engage in that allow insight into career preferences and interests. Synthesis of data includes the time spent processing individual experiences and understanding of self, and individual application includes the formation and implementation of plans as a product of the experiences and reflections (Super, 1975).

Postmodern Approaches to Career Development

While Super's (1975) theory emphasizes individual experiences, preferences, and roles, Savickas (2002) has sought to expound on the subjective nature of career development. According to this perspective, career development is reflected in each individual's career story, which is composed of both objective careers as well as subjective career meanings (Savickas, 2002). Congruent with Super's (1975) approach, Savickas (2002) emphasizes that each individual's story reflects changing roles and occupations throughout development.

Savickas's (2002) approach to career development—career construction theory— emphasizes career development as a constructivist process. As such, it is believed that reality in itself in constructed, thus indicating that career paths are also constructed (Savickas, 2002). Furthermore, career development is influenced by surrounding factors such as cultural, familial, and social contexts. Life space is conceptualized as the social roles an individual must fulfill as well as the arenas in which the roles are fulfilled (Savickas, 2002). Savickas (2002) also proposed career development stages describing career-related growth throughout the life span. During adolescence, Savickas describes the corresponding stage as "exploration." At this stage, an adolescent must work to translate his or her self-concept into a vocational identity. When considering applications of this theory to counseling, a central premise of the theory involves the creation of a career story. As such, it is recommended that providers seeking to apply career construction theory work with clients to identify life spaces and stages through client's experiences and perceptions.

CAREER COUNSELING STRATEGIES

Regardless of theoretical orientation, specific techniques used, or counseling setting, it is imperative that adolescent career counseling efforts are future oriented and goal directed, emphasize growth, and delineate actions that can ultimately lead to career success. "Career counseling has been conceptualized as a process wherein individuals are guided through the collection and integration of varied information about themselves and the world of work, followed by a rational process of decision making" (Schultheiss, 2003, p. 302). This developmental stage is crucial for future establishment of a career (Usinger & Smith, 2010) as decisions made during adolescence directly aid in the transition to college or the workplace (Vuolo et al., 2011).

This transition is affected by external factors such as cultural expectations, SES status, or family system as well as internal factors such as self-concept, occupational knowledge, or self-esteem (Hirschi, 2011). For this reason, it is imperative that counseling theories and approaches be comprehensive in nature and recognize the complexities of factors that influence career decisions. Unfortunately, there is often a gap in career counseling services during adolescence. In a 2013 study of middle school students, the majority of participants felt as though their career and social counseling needs (advice about college, interests) were not being met as compared with the personal needs of students (McCotter & Cohen, 2013). This lack of attending to these various needs may be a reflection of the changing role expectations of school providers; however, it is imperative that providers advocate for the care of career-related matters both in schools and other clinical settings.

Furthermore, given the above assertions highlighting the importance of relational career approaches, two theories have been identified as having specific and direct implications for both relational and career development during adolescence: (1) peer coaching and (2) relational career counseling. While there are numerous theories of career counseling, these outgrowths have gained increasing attention in research and practice, contributing to the evidence base for practice. Evidence-based practices can be understood as approaches that have been validated through scientific research and development of therapeutic protocols. As such, research contributing to the evidence base for each of these theories is discussed as well.

Peer Coaching

Peer coaching is a more informal approach to career counseling in which the provider takes the role of the mentor to model strong career-oriented relationships (Parker, Hall, & Kram, 2008). In doing so, the provider is able to encourage the client to continue to seek mentorship relationships in future career settings to better internalize learning and create successful career environments (Parker et al., 2008). In essence, "life-span issues of adulthood mean that career learning has moved from a one-time education credential to an ongoing lifelong process" (Parker et al., 2008, p. 487). This approach has been shown to be related to positive career outcomes and increased psychosocial support for clients (Parker et al., 2008). As such, research has sought to identify the psychological conceptualization of peer coaching in order to develop models of training for coaching within an evidence-based lens (Wang & Millward, 2014).

In this approach, there is an emphasis on the interpersonal affirmation of both identity and competency (Parker et al., 2008). Both of these facets are of particular importance in adolescence given the developmental crossroad. The approach encourages interpersonal and interactive learning (Parker et al., 2008), offering a positive influence on career choice. Most notably, this approach can be easily adapted and applied to multiple settings (Parker et al., 2008).

For example, while the providers take on a peer coach role, they are also able to help establish coaching relationships through community resources. In a school setting, they may be able to establish formal peer coaching programs to offer guidance in exploration as suggested by Super (1975). Overall, the approach allows for greater flexibility on the part of the provider to adapt learning to the specific interests and preferences of the student.

Relational Theory

"As career researchers, educators, and practitioners, we need to move from acknowledging the importance of individuals' relationships to a more fully delineated and integrated understanding of relational influences, connections, and disconnections in our clients' lives, work, and career decisions" (Motulsky, 2010, p. 1079). This quote offers incredible insight into the theoretical underpinnings of the relational approach to career counseling and fully connects with the importance of interpersonal relationships during this developmental stage. Relational theory places emphasis on the contextual and influential role of relationships in career roles, decision making, and success (Schultheiss, 2003), thereby making this theory particularly applicable to adolescent populations.

As highlighted throughout this chapter, adolescents and relationships are essential points of assessment and encouragement. In relational career counseling, providers must consider relationships, roles, and values during assessment (Schultheiss, 2003). This assessment should include both positive and negative relationships as well as how these relationships influence the individual's career development, exploration, and decision making (Schultheiss, 2003). An example of positive relationships might be seen through supportive interactions that offer a safe environment for individual growth and affirmation, while negative relationships might be seen through critical interactions that offer a controlling environment leading to self-doubt and indecision. Peer relationships and friendship can

often offer both positive and negative influences. Once this information is gathered, the therapeutic alliance and other significant relationships may be utilized as a source of intervention rather than simply a support system (Schultheiss, 2003). For example, a provider may encourage a client to seek perspectives from a positive, influential person.

In a qualitative study (one that looks at participants' self-reports rather than quantitative, numeric measures) with adult women in relational therapy, Motulsky (2010) found that adolescents' self-reported interpersonal relationships play a significant role in career movement and transition into those careers. The relational therapeutic approach recognizes the interplay between relationships and cultural and engendered ideas surrounding career roles within a social context (Motulsky, 2010). For this reason, the relational therapy can contribute to both individuals' relational development and development of self, ultimately contributing to positive career development.

MULTICULTURAL FACTORS

While multiculturalism is crucial to every area of emphasis in counseling, career counseling is uniquely influenced by cultural values such as role expectations, SES, education, and discrimination. These factors affect clients on both individual and systemic levels on career choice and decision making and affect both the context of career counseling as well as the process (Arthur & McMahon, 2005). For this reason, providers' systemic evaluation of the contributing cultural factors in career decision making and best-fitting approach to fit client's unique needs and values are essential (Arthur & McMahon, 2005). It may also be of value to consider the utilization of culture-specific career strategies (Mayes & Hines, 2014), particularly in instances of cross-cultural or intergenerational counseling situations.

Self-concept, stability, self-esteem, self-efficacy, role expectancies, career-related aspirations, and decisions all vary across gender and ethnicity (Ali & Menke, 2014; Novakovic &

Fouad, 2013; Steinberg & Morris, 2001). Culture affects career barriers such as poverty, racism, oppression, and inequality across gender, age, ethnicity, and religion (Flynn, Duncan, & Evenson, 2013; McWhirter et al., 2013; Raque-Bogdan et al., 2013; Steinberg & Morris, 2001). It is not surprising that research has shown significant differences in work values and career development across gender (Hirschi, 2010). These value differences are critical factors in career decision and are often formed during adolescence.

Adolescents are often expected to begin to form their own belief systems and cultural identities (Steinberg & Morris, 2001). In this process, it is not uncommon for cultural values to differ from the family of origin, exasperating the normative parent–child conflict. Values and traditions of any given culture may be incongruent with expected behaviors and norms of occupational culture (Brown, 1992). For this reason, it is recommended that providers work carefully with clients to develop biculture identities and the ability to code-switch as necessary for career and familial success. Clients must have a strong understanding of their own personal identity and self-concept as well as acceptance of their various cultural identities.

CHALLENGES TO CAREER COUNSELING

As mentioned earlier, cultural dynamics can pose a challenge in career counseling; however, numerous other factors can create additional trials as well. Being aware of these challenges can help the provider better aid the client in building self-efficacy and navigating the barriers presented. Challenges may be internal such as individual differences or career indecision as well as external such as disability or language. These challenges should be assessed during the initial phases of counseling.

Internal Challenges

Internal challenges encompass a wide variety of individual differences such as personality, behavioral patterns, career indecision, and interpersonal skills. For example, a recent study by Converse, Piccone, and Tocci (2014) demonstrated that adolescent self-control significantly influences career success and educational attainment. It is widely acknowledged that certain personalities are a better "fit" for certain careers. Theories of personality are the foundational underpinning of popular career assessments to be discussed later.

In addition to personality differences, career indecision is a common challenge, particularly during adolescence. Career indecision is a developmental concern that can be caused by a multiplicity of factors including a lack of structure for understanding and making career choices, external barriers that prevent or inhibit the implementation of preferred career choices, conflict between equally attractive options, and conflict with others over these choices (Osipow, Carney, & Barek, 1976, as cited in Baker, 2002; San Diego, 2010). Career indecision can be influenced by a wide array of factors including personal indecisiveness, anxiety, parental attachment, gender, self-esteem, perfectionism, and culture (Creed, Wong, & Hood, 2009; Emmanuelle, 2009; Jung, 2013; Oztemel, 2013; San Diego, 2010).

Given the prevalence of career indecision, it is imperative that career providers are equipped to work with clients who are struggling with indecision. Career-specific assessments and interventions may help reduce or prevent career indecision (Baker, 2002). When an individual is experiencing career indecision, it is recommended that providers utilize decision-making models, experiential learning, and Socratic questioning to help guide the client through the decision-making process.

Finally, while relationships may seem external in nature, the long-lasting internal characteristics that are forged in social context heavily influence career development. For example, a study of 486 students demonstrated that those with more secure attachment perceived greater social support, fewer career barriers, and had higher efficacy in academic and career domains (Wright, Perrone-McGovern, Boo, & White, 2014).

Relational challenges can be unique and multi-faceted; however, they must be assessed and understood by the provider.

External Challenges

The vast majority of external challenges are interrelated with multicultural factors such as language, finances, relationships, and discrimination (McWhirter et al., 2013). One such challenge that can be particularly relevant in school-aged children is disability. Disabilities that may affect career counseling include both physical and mental impairments. In both instances, the importance of transition services, including instruction, community services, and support to help increase career-related independence and achievement, is imperative (Doren, Lombardi, Clark, & Lindstrom, 2013).

External as well as internal factors often interact placing certain individuals in the "at-risk" category. In these instances, approaches specific for addressing career concerns of at-risk youth such as Postschool Achievement Through Higher Skills (Doren et al., 2013) should be considered. Identifying risk factors and becoming aware of overcoming the challenges can help clients have optimal success in academic, career, and social arenas.

NORMATIVE VERSUS PROBLEMATIC DEVELOPMENT

Distinguishing between normative adolescent maturation and problematic issues can be particularly challenging given the interpersonal and intrapersonal conflict that is typical of the developmental stage. Adolescence is wrought with difficulties and challenges (Steinberg & Morris, 2001); thus, differentiating between normal and abnormal must occur on a continuum. Unfortunately, identifying the specific point at which behaviors become dysfunctional and detrimental rather than simply faulty adolescent decision making is highly subjective.

Steinberg and Morris (2001) offer specific suggestions in helping to differentiate normative versus problematic development. Specifically, the authors suggest that providers consider the frequency, origin, and duration of the behavior (Steinberg & Morris, 2001). Occasional experimentation may be considered normative behavior; however, enduring patterns of high-risk behavior may be problematic to career development as well as overall development. Similarly, problems originating in early life are likely to be of greater concern than problems originating in adolescence. Finally, normal problem behaviors typically resolve during adolescence, whereas abnormal problem behaviors often carry into adulthood (Steinberg & Morris, 2001).

In addition to understanding the factors surrounding the behavior, the client's peer groups and friendships can also offer valuable insight into developmental concerns (Steinberg & Morris, 2001). A great deal of research has focused on understanding specific concerns regarding interpersonal patterns including aggression, rejection, withdrawal, and victimization (Steinberg & Morris, 2001). Each of these patterns is often typical of related psychopathology.

As such, risk factors including behaviors as well as interpersonal functioning should be examined thoroughly in differentiating between normal and abnormal adolescent development. If necessary, the provider must rule out psychopathology as a contributing factor to adolescent problem behaviors as various mental disorders often have a detrimental impact in vocational and academic arenas. Early intervention during adolescence may help alleviate these detriments and may aid in career development and success.

ASSESSMENTS

While assessments are important to the field of counseling as a whole, they are particularly relevant during adolescence for a number of reasons. Furthermore, career counseling commonly includes assessments of varying forms including aptitude and interests measures. In school settings, the vast majority of students will undergo both academic and psychological tests to aid in career decisions. For this reason, providers of adolescents must have a thorough understanding of relevant assessments including college entrance exams, alternative diploma exams, and career-related measures.

College Entrance Exams

The Scholastic Aptitude Test (SAT) and the American College Testing (ACT) are college entrance exams administered to students in the 11th and 12th grades. Both exams aid in predicting students' future academic success in college (Lane, Kalberg, Mofield, Wehby, & Parks, 2009). The SAT is the most commonly used standardized test in the United States and comprises three sections that measure the student's (1) critical reading, (2) mathematics, and (3) writing abilities (Richardson, Abraham, & Bond, 2012). The ACT exam measures students' ability to reason, infer conclusions, and analyze information (Lane et al., 2009). Although they differ in content, the SAT and ACT exams have strong statistical correlations (Richardson et al., 2012). The use of aptitude testing in college admissions is highly debated given the continuing criticism over possible socioeconomic and cultural biases inherent to these assessments.

General Educational Development

The General Educational Development (GED) test is designed to be an alternative to a high school diploma (Tuck, 2012). As high school graduation rates have declined, the popularity of the GED as an alternative degree has risen (Tuck, 2012). Unfortunately, students with GEDs have a greater risk of lower lifetime earnings and college graduation rates as well as increased health and wellness issues and incarceration rates as compared with those with high school diplomas (Tuck, 2012). Furthermore, the majority of those with GEDs will pursue employment after completion rather than pursuing higher education (Tuck, 2012).

Myers-Briggs Type Indicator

The Myers-Briggs Type Indicator (MBTI), based on Jung's theory of psychological typology, is designed to categorize personality into consistent types (McCaulley, 2000). Personality is categorized into one of 16 types based on propensity toward (a) extraversion or introversion, (b) sensing or intuition, (c) thinking or feeling, and (d) judging or perceptive function (McCaulley, 2000). The MBTI can be used to aid career planning, problem solving, and improving communication, or determining learning style. School providers often use the MBTI to aid students searching for future career paths. It is also worth noting that adolescents who are inclined to be introverted and thinking personality types tend to have greater academic success and higher IQ scores (Sak, 2004).

Holland's Hexagon

Holland's theory of vocational choice is foundational to most contemporary vocational theories and inventories (Miller, 1998). Holland theorized that all individual personalities reflect a combination of six types: (1) realistic, (2) investigative, (3) artistic, (4) social, (5) enterprising, and (6) conventional (RIASEC). Often referred to as "Holland's Hexagon," these constructs form the RIASEC structure that Holland uses to connect preferences to work choices and environments to personality (Armstrong, Day, McVay, & Rounds, 2008). The RIASEC types are used as a framework for several inventories, including Holland's Self-Directed Search, Miller's mapping procedure (Miller, 1998, pp. 2–3), and the Interest-Finder (Wall & Baker, 1997). School and career providers often use Holland's hexagon-based inventories to encourage students to follow career paths that will complement their personality types.

Strong Interest Inventory

The Strong Interest Inventory (SII) integrates Holland's Hexagon model of interest and vocational options and has become one of the most widely used vocational assessment tools. Strong published the SII in 1927 to measure respondents' interest patterns and likely occupational satisfaction (Leierer, Blackwell, Strohmer, Thompson, & Donnay, 2008). By measuring occupational propensities and interests, the SII can help predict students' college major (Bailey, Larson, Borgen, & Gasser, 2008). High school students seeking vocational direction are encouraged to use the results from the SII when planning for college and career.

Armed Services Vocational Aptitude Battery

The Armed Services Vocational Aptitude Battery (ASVAB) career exploration program began in 1968 as an assessment tool for high school providers to provide post–high school planning for students (Baker, 2002). The U.S. Department of Defense provides this program free of charge to high schools and to individuals interested in joining the military. Currently, the largest system of vocational assessment and career exploration for adolescents, "more than one-fourth of all high school seniors will have participated in the ASVAB Program during their high school years" (Baker, 2002, p. 359). The program utilizes two age-appropriate and developmentally appropriate assessments to help identify occupations of congruent interest and ability. By incorporating elements of the RIASEC model and the Interest-Finder, the ASVAB matches student interests and abilities with vocations and possible careers (Baker, 2002).

IMPLICATIONS FOR COUNSELING ADOLESCENTS

Ultimately, adolescence marks a crucial transitional stage from childhood to adulthood that is most notably reflected in normative career and relational changes. For this reason, it is imperative that providers of adolescents across all settings have a thorough understanding of the developmental implications on careers and relationships as well as how intricately these two areas relate. Given the emphasis on career-related choices in academic settings, it is particularly important for school providers to recognize specific strategies to aid adolescents in progressing through this stage without complications. Further suggestions and strategies specific to school settings can be found in Chapter 11.

Regardless of settings, it is recommended that providers familiarize themselves with developmental theories to guide providers in conceptualizing and differentiating between normative and problematic developmental career concerns. Such theoretical frameworks will also help ensure that providers offer age-appropriate diagnosis when necessary. This is particularly important given the gravity of potential lifelong, chronic diagnoses. It is recommended that providers err on the "lesser" of any diagnosis in working with adolescents, as it is often difficult to differentiate between developmental factors, environmental concerns, cultural influences, and actual pathology. For example, some urban youth in a particularly violent community with broken homes may be more aggressive in nature due to upbringing rather than potential pathology such as oppositional defiant disorder. Labeling such an individual with a disorder may only exasperate cultural expectations of violence, thus limiting career potential.

Once providers appropriately conceptualize the client and diagnosis, providers must be certain that theoretical orientations, techniques, and interventions are congruent with the client. In adolescents, this often may mean adapting theories developed for adults to reflect development and level of functioning. When possible, providers must take care to identify the evidence and research pertaining to the application of their theory of choice with adolescent populations. When working with career and relational concerns, it is important that theoretical orientations adequately address the complexities of factors including development, culture, and familial dynamics.

Clinical Review of Case

To aid in the development of client conceptualization and application, a case study has been included (Case Scenario 12.1). Additionally, questions to be considered regarding Sarah's case are provided in Exercise 12.1. The case of Sarah highlights a number of the points discussed above including the importance of developmental, relational, and multicultural factors in career counseling. For Sarah, her developmental concerns are evident. Not only must Sarah begin to navigate the transition into adulthood as marked by increased responsibilities such as care for her siblings or holding a job, but Sarah must also begin to make decisions about her future career consistent with the crystallization stage of career development (Usinger & Smith, 2010). The provider must continue to evaluate Sarah's successful progression through these developmental stages and offer assistance when needed.

Case Scenario 12.1

Sarah

Sarah is a high school junior who has sought counseling to address her plans beyond graduation. Sarah comes from a low-income family in a rural community. Sarah has sought counseling previously for concerns with her family system. Sarah currently works two jobs outside of school and has few close friends. While Sarah wants to attend college to pursue a nursing career, her family expects Sarah to work full time to support her eight younger siblings, and no one in Sarah's family has ever completed a college education. Sarah has not been in contact with her father since she was born. Sarah's mother has developed late-stage cancer with a terminal prognosis. As her mother has been undergoing treatment and been hospitalized on numerous occasions, Sarah has needed to care for her siblings and their household. Despite the added stress, Sarah has continued to earn high grades in all her classes. Sarah is hoping that you might be able to help her decide whether or not she should pursue college.

Exercise 12.1

Case Considerations

1. Consider the assessments discussed throughout the chapter. Which assessments may be helpful in working with Sarah and why?

2. What further information might you want to address multicultural considerations on Sarah's career indecision?

3. What stage of career development is Sarah in? Why?

4. What specific goals might you set while working with Sarah? What techniques might you use to address these goals?

Relational factors are also particularly important in Sarah's case as her familial relationships currently have a great influence on her career indecision. Furthermore, Sarah has minimal support outside of her family as indicated by her lack of friendships and peer groups. Addressing relational factors will be important, as Sarah must be fully aware of influential relationships. These relationships may also offer evidence pertaining to Sarah's relational values and beliefs.

These values and beliefs will be particularly important in aiding Sarah in her decision-making process. For example, it will be important to understand whether Sarah's cultural orientation is collective or individualistic in order to identify her perspectives on familial responsibility. It is also important to recognize that Sarah's family history and SES likely influence Sarah's perceptions of college as well as her family's perceptions. This may offer information regarding the likelihood of familial support if Sarah chooses to pursue higher education. Ultimately, the complexities contributing to Sarah's decision-making process are crucial for a provider working to address career indecision in adolescents.

Application of Ethics

While the vast majority of concepts throughout the American Counseling Association *Code of Ethics* (2014) are relevant to career and relational counseling, there are some ethical mandates that are of particular importance given what has been discussed thus far. First and foremost, providers must match their approach to client's developmental and cultural needs (American Counseling Association, 2014, A.1.c, A.2.c). Given the nature of career counseling, providers in this setting must be certain to recognize the developmental stages influencing career-related concerns as well as contributing cultural and familial factors in decision making.

Furthermore, it is important to consider the importance of personal values in career counseling. While every counseling relationship has the ability to be influenced by provider values and biases, the career setting is particularly vulnerable

as personal values such as individualism versus collectivism, familial norms and expectations, spiritual calling and purpose, and role expectations are intricately intertwined with career decisions. For this reason, it is crucial for providers to be aware of their values in order to avoid imposing values directly or indirectly in the counseling relationship (American Counseling Association, 2014, A.4.b).

Summary

Adolescence is a period marked with numerous life transitions and decisions that are heavily influenced by those around them including peers, family, and individual development. Providers working with adolescents must have a thorough understanding and familiarity with normative development, peer group influences, and ways in which they can contribute to future career success. To do so, it is recommended that providers familiarize themselves with both overall development as well as career-specific development. Career-specific strategies for counseling adolescents may include peer coaching or relational theoretical approaches.

It is also imperative that providers familiarize themselves with multicultural factors and career-specific challenges that may contribute to career decisions and success. In understanding these factors, providers may gain a better understanding of differentiating between normative and problematic development. Finally, assessments are a common occurrence during career counseling in adolescents to help individuals understand their personality, interests, and possible career choices. Utilization of assessments may help guide and encourage adolescents into choices that are congruent with individual values, interests, and abilities, thus potentially contributing to career success.

Keystones

- Providers should understand the developmental, peer, familial, and environmental influences that affect the adolescent life stage. Career providers must be able to differentiate problematic development from what is normative development and normative peer group influences in order to understand the ways in which these factors can be used to contribute to future career success.

- There are a variety of career counseling strategies that providers may utilize; however, the provider should become familiar with when and with whom particular strategies are commonly used. Providers must keep in mind the impact that multicultural factors may play in the process of therapy and in their decision to use certain interventions.

- Providers should be aware of the various challenges they may experience in career counseling and the ways to overcome the challenges.

- Providers should be aware of the various theories related to relational and career aspects of adolescents including Roe's theory and Super's theory.

- Providers should be aware of the various techniques including peer coaching and other similar modalities.

- There are a variety of assessment tools and techniques to be utilized to assess adolescents' career choices.

- Basic knowledge of the assessments commonly used by career providers is necessary. Career providers should know when and with whom particular assessments would be most beneficial.

REFERENCES

Ali, S. R., & Menke, K. A. (2014). Rural Latino youth career development: An application of social cognitive career theory. *Career Development Quarterly, 62,* 175–186. doi:10.1002/j.2161-0045.2014.00078.x

American Counseling Association. (2014). *ACA code of ethics.* Alexandria, VA: Author.

Armstrong, P. I., Day, S. X., McVay, J. P., & Rounds, J. (2008). Holland's RIASEC model as an integrative framework for individual differences. *Journal of Counseling Psychology, 55*(1), 1–18. doi:10.1037/0022-0167.55.1.1

Arthur, N., & McMahon, M. (2005). Multicultural career counseling: Theoretical applications of the systems theory framework. *Career Development Quarterly, 53,* 208–222.

Bailey, D., Larson, L., Borgen, F., & Gasser, C. (2008). Changing of the guard: Interpretive continuity of the 2005 Strong Interest Inventory. *Journal of Career Assessment, 16*(2), 135–155.

Baker, H. E. (2002). Reducing adolescent career indecision: The ASVAB career exploration program. *Career Development Quarterly, 50*(4), 359–370.

Brown, A. (1992). Organizational culture: the key to effective leadership and organizational development. *Leadership & Organization Development Journal, 13*(2), 3-6.

Converse, P. D., Piccone, K. A., & Tocci, M. C. (2014). Childhood self-control, adolescent behavior, and career success. *Personality and Individual Differences, 59,* 65–70.

Creed, P. A., Wong, O. Y., & Hood, M. (2009). Career decision-making, career barriers, and occupational aspiration in Chinese adolescents. *International Journal for Educational and Vocational Guidance, 9,* 189–203. doi:10.1007/s10775-009-9165-0

DeVore, E. R., & Ginsburg, K. R. (2005). The protective effects of good parenting on adolescents. *Current Opinion in Pediatrics, 17,* 460–465.

Doren, B., Lombardi, A. R., Clark, J., & Lindstrom, L. (2013). Addressing career barriers for high risk adolescent girls: The PATHS curriculum intervention. *Journal of Adolescence, 36*(6), 1083–1092.

Duffy, R. D., & Dik, B. J. (2013). Research on calling: What have we learned and where are we going? *Journal of Vocational Behavior, 83*(3), 428–436. doi:10.1016/j.jvb.2013.06.006

Emmanuelle, V. (2009). Inter-relationships among attachment to mother and father, self-esteem, and career indecision. *Journal of Vocational Behavior, 75,* 91–99. doi:10.1016/j.jvb.2009.04.007

Flynn, S. V., Duncan, K. J., & Evenson, L. L. (2013). An emergent phenomenon of American Indian secondary students' career development process. *Career Development Quarterly, 61,* 124–140. doi:10.1002/j.2161-0045.2013.00042.x

Hirschi, A. (2010). Positive adolescent career development: The role of intrinsic and extrinsic work values. *Career Development Quarterly, 58,* 276–287.

Hirschi, A. (2011). Career-choice readiness in adolescence: Developmental trajectories and individual differences. *Journal of Vocational Behavior, 79*(2), 340–348.

Hollenstein, T., & Lougheed, J. P. (2013). Beyond storm and stress: Typicality, transactions, timing, and temperament to account for adolescent change. *American Psychologist, 68*(6), 444–454.

Jung, J. Y. (2013). The cognitive processes associated with occupational/career indecision: A model for gifted adolescents. *Journal for the Education of the Gifted, 36*(4), 433–460.

Kim, S., Seo, Y., & Cho, M. (2012). Character strengths and career development of academically gifted adolescents. *Journal of Asia Pacific Counseling, 2*(2), 209–228.

Kim, Y., & Sherraden, M. (2011). Do parental assets matter for children's educational attainment? Evidence from mediation tests. *Children and Youth Services Review, 33*(6), 969–979.

Kiuru, N., Salmela-Aro, K., Nurmi, J., Zettergren, P., Andersson, H., & Bergman, L. (2012). Best friends in adolescence show similar educational careers in early adulthood. *Journal of Applied Developmental Psychology, 33*(2), 102–111.

Krumboltz, J. D. (1996). A learning theory of career counseling. In M. L. Savickas & W. B. Walsh (Eds.), *Handbook of career counseling theory and practice* (pp. 55–80). Palo Alto, CA: Davies-Black.

Lane, K. L., Kalberg, J. R., Mofield, E., Wehby, J. H., & Parks, R. J. (2009). Preparing students for college entrance exams. *Remedial and Special Education, 30*(1), 3–18. doi:10.1177/0741932507314022

Leierer, S., Blackwell, T., Strohmer, D., Thompson, R., & Donnay, D. (2008). The newly revised Strong Interest Inventory: A profile interpretation for rehabilitation providers. *Rehabilitation Counseling Bulletin, 51*(2), 76–84.

Lock, R. D. (2005). *Taking charge of your career direction: Career planning guide* (5th ed.). Belmont, CA: Brooks/Cole.

Luyckx, K., Vansteenkiste, M., Goossens, L., & Duriez, B. (2009). Basic need satisfaction and identity formation: Bridging self-determination theory and process-oriented identity research. *Journal of Counseling Psychology, 56*(2), 276–288.

Mayes, R. D., & Hines, E. M. (2014). College and career readiness for gifted African American girls: A call to school providers. *Interdisciplinary Journal of Teaching and Learning, 4*(1), 31–42.

McCaulley, M. H. (2000). Myers-Briggs Type Indicator: A bridge between counseling and consulting. *Consulting Psychology Journal: Practice and Research, 52*(2), 117–132. doi:10.1037/1061-4087.52.2.117

McCotter, S., & Cohen, S. (2013). Are middle school counseling programs meeting early adolescent needs? A survey of principals and providers. *Journal of Counselor Preparation and Supervision, 5*(1), 6–27.

McWhirter, E. H., Valdez, M., & Caban, A. R. (2013). Latina adolescents' plans, barriers, and supports: A focus study group. *Journal of Latina/o Psychology, 1*(1), 35–52. doi:10.1037/a0031304

Miller, M. (1998). Broadening the use of Holland's Hexagon with specific implications for career providers. *Journal of Employment Counseling, 35*(1), 2–6.

Motulsky, S. L. (2010). Relational processes in career transition: Extending theory, research, and practice. *Counseling Psychologist, 38*(8), 1078–1114. doi:10.1177/0011000010376415

Novakovic, A., & Fouad, N. A. (2013). Background, personal, and environmental influences on the career planning of adolescent girls. *Journal of Career Development, 40*(3), 223–244.

Oztemel, K. (2013). An investigation of career indecision level of high school students: Relationships with personal indecisiveness and anxiety. *Online Journal of Counseling and Education, 2*(3), 46–58.

Parker, P., Hall, D. T., & Kram, K. E. (2008). Peer coaching: A relational process for accelerating career learning. *Academy of Management Learning & Education, 7*(4), 487–503.

Patel, S. G., Salahuddin, N. M., & O'Brien, K. M. (2008). Career decision-making self-efficacy of Vietnamese adolescents: The role of acculturation, social support, socioeconomic status, and racism. *Journal of Career Development, 34*(3), 218–240.

Penick, N. I., & Jepsen, D. A. (1992). Family functioning and adolescent career development. *Career Development Quarterly, 40*(3), 208–223.

Poulin, F., & Chan, A. (2010). Friendship stability and change in childhood and adolescence. *Developmental Review, 30*(3), 257–272.

Raque-Bogdan, T. L., Klingaman, E. A., Martin, H. M., & Lucas, M. S. (2013). Career-related parent support and career barriers: An investigation of contextual variables. *Career Development Quarterly, 61,* 339–353. doi:10.1002/j.2162-0045.2013.00060.x

Richardson, M., Abraham, C., & Bond, R. (2012). Psychological correlates of university students' academic performance: A systematic review and meta-analysis. *Psychological Bulletin, 138*(2), 353–387.

Ruggieri, S., Bendixen, M., Gabriel, U., & Alsaker, F. (2013). Cyberball: The impact of ostracism on the well-being of early adolescents. *Swiss Journal of Psychology, 72*(2), 103–109. doi:10.1024/1421-0185/a000103

Sak, U. (2004). A synthesis of research on psychological types of gifted adolescents. *Journal of Secondary Gifted Education, 15*(2), 70–80.

San Diego, R. J. (2010). Investigating effects of anxiety and perfectionism as predictors of adolescent career indecision. *International Journal of Research and Review, 5,* 120–132.

Savickas, M. L. (2002). Career construction: A developmental theory of vocational behavior. In D. Brown & Associates (Eds.), *Career choice and development* (4th ed., pp. 149–205). San Francisco, CA: Jossey-Bass.

Savickas, M. L. (2005). The theory and practice of career construction. In S. D. Brown & R. W. Lent (Eds.), *Career development and counseling: Putting theory and research to work* (pp. 42–70). Hoboken, NJ: Wiley.

Schultheiss, D. E. (2003). A relational approach to career counseling: Theoretical integration and practical application. *Journal of Counseling & Development, 81,* 301–310.

Steinberg, L., & Morris, A. S. (2001). Adolescent development. *Annual Review of Psychology, 52,* 83–110.

Sue, D. W., Arrendondo, P., & McDavies, R. J. (1992). Multicultural counseling competencies and standards: A call to the profession. *Journal of Multicutural Counseling and Development, 20*(2), 64–88.

Super, D. E. (1975). Career education and career guidance for the life span and for life roles. *Journal of Career Education, 2*(2), 27–42.

Thomas, D. A., & Gibbons, M. M. (2009). Narrative theory: A career counseling approach for adolescents of divorce. *Professional School Counseling, 12*(3), 223–229.

Tuck, E. (2012). Repatriating the GED: Urban youth and the alternative to a high school diploma. *High School Journal, 95*(4), 4–18.

Turner, S., & Ziebell, J. C. (2011). The career beliefs of inner-city adolescents. *Professional School Counseling, 15*(1), 1–14.

Usinger, J., & Smith, M. (2010). Career development in the context of self-construction during adolescence. *Journal of Vocational Behavior, 76*(3), 580–591.

Vuolo, M., Staff, J., & Mortimer, J. T. (2011). Weathering the great recession: Psychological and behavioral trajectories in the transition from school to work. *Developmental Psychology, 48*(6), 1759–1773.

Wall, J., & Baker, H. (1997). The Interest-Finder: Evidence of validity. *Journal of Career Assessment, 5*(2), 255–273.

Wang, Q., & Millward, I. (2014). Developing a unified psychological model of coaching and mentoring in supporting the learning and development of adolescents. *International Journal of Evidence Based Coaching and Mentoring, 12*(2), 91–108.

Wright, S. L., Perrone-McGovern, K. M., Boo, J. N., & White, A. V. (2014). Influential factors in academic and career self-efficacy: Attachment, support, and career barriers. *Journal of Counseling & Development, 92,* 36–46. doi:10.1002/j.1556-6676.2014.00128.x

13

CHEMICAL AND BEHAVIORAL ADDICTIONS

INTRODUCTION

The profession of addiction counseling is a relatively new specialization area within the behavioral health profession. Throughout history, there have been "addiction counselors," including physicians, psychiatrists, psychologists, social workers, clergy, family therapists or individuals in recovery, and formally trained addiction counselors (Burrow-Sanchez, Lopez, & Slagle, 2008). Today, the profession has moved from a field that was dominated by mostly paraprofessionals and medical professionals to a field that predominantly consists of individuals with graduate degrees in the various fields of behavioral health, including those who are specifically trained and certified as addiction counselors.

The field of addiction counseling has various comprehensive and nationally recognized certification programs that enable those individuals without traditional or formal education to meet minimal requirements to work in this field. These certification programs allow many individuals the opportunity to counsel this distinct population. Examples of such certifications include Certified Substance Abuse Counselor, Certified Addiction Personnel, and Substance

Abuse Counselor. To acquire these certification credentials, individuals are required to attend a defined number of continuing education training hours of addiction counseling trainings, amass hours of direct counseling experience with clients, and work under the supervision of a licensed or certified supervisor. These credentials are widely recognized and highly recommended for individuals who want to work in the field of addiction, particularly for those who do not have specific traditional educational training (Association for Addiction Professionals, n.d.).

Historically, treatment approaches for substance use disorders (SUDs) were confrontational in efforts to obliterate defense mechanisms individuals with SUDs may have (Winters, Botzet, & Fahnhorst, 2011). Treatment programs were created for adults diagnosed with alcoholism, and drug abusers and adolescents were initially "treated" through the same programs. It was in the 1950s that hospitals and churches began to realize that adolescent substance users presented behaviors different from those of adults and thus may require a different treatment approach (Winters et al., 2011). Unfortunately, adolescents continued to be treated with adult-based programs until the 1980s (Winters et al., 2011).

Today, addictions treatment is largely grounded in evidence-based practices (Winters et al., 2011). Researchers and providers eventually gained the understanding that adolescents tend to binge substances more, they are less capable of recognizing a problem, and they tend to have more comorbid psychiatric issues than do adults (Winters et al., 2011). Additionally, both peer influence and immediate gratification concerns are factors unique to treatment with adolescents and should be addressed throughout therapy (Winters et al., 2011).

Currently, addiction counselors are educated and trained to be much less confrontational and more collaborative, while coupling the interventions and activities with comprehensive theory and research (Winters et al., 2011). The focus of counseling is on understanding the ecological, systemic, familial, and trauma history factors and their influence on adolescent addictions. As you will learn in this chapter, theoretical approaches for the treatment of addictions have expanded beyond a sole loyalty to cognitive behavioral theory, which has long been the standard theory of choice in addiction counseling (National Institute on Drug Abuse [NIDA], 2014a). As such, this is a very exciting time for those considering professions in addiction counseling and for mental health counselors and other helping professionals who will inevitably work with clients, families, and communities directly affected by substance use and/or abuse and process addictions.

What exactly do we mean by addictions? Addictions are formed by excessive use, which in turn directly activates the brain's reward system that is involved in the reinforcement of behaviors and production of memories (*Diagnostic and Statistical Manual of Mental Disorders*, fifth edition [*DSM-5*]; APA, 2013). Substances or activities one may use or abuse in excess produce such an intense activation of the reward system that normal activities may be neglected (*DSM-5*). There are two types of addictions to be examined in this chapter—(1) chemical and (2) behavioral. According to *DSM-5*, substance-related (chemical) disorders consist of 10 separate classes of drugs: (1) alcohol, (2) caffeine,

(3) cannabis, (4) hallucinogens, (5) inhalants, (6) opioids, (7) stimulants, (8) sedatives-hypnotics-anxiolytics, (9) tobacco, and (10) unknown substances. Behavioral addictions, also known as process addictions, are repetitive and excessive behavioral patterns that activate the brain reward system in a fashion similar to those activated by drugs of abuse and produce behavioral symptoms comparable to those produced by substance-related disorders (*DSM-5*). Due to established peer-review evidence, the *DSM-5* lists only gambling disorder as a behavioral or process addiction; however, Internet gaming, sex, love, exercise, shopping, and food have all been identified as possible behavioral addictions (NIDA, 2014a; *DSM-5*).

Additionally, the prevalence of behavioral and chemical addictions that adolescents are exposed to and participants in magnifies the importance that addiction counselors be formally educated, experienced, and knowledgeable of the evidence-based research, diagnosis, treatment, theories, and interventions that can aid this population in overcoming the negative relationships that adolescents have developed with substances and behaviors. Providers often experience much trepidation when engaging adolescents who exhibit chemical and/or behavioral addictions because often they have not used the drugs and they do not understand the behaviors with which their clients are engaged. Feelings of inadequacy and hopelessness can abound when considering the myriad challenges drug-affected adolescents (and their families) face. As an addiction counselor, it is critical to have a basic understanding of the potentially addictive and dangerous behaviors and substances that adolescents are involved in.

To help navigate the various needs adolescents face, a general knowledge of the chemicals and behaviors, symptoms, and treatment is necessary. One of the most comprehensive websites that all new and experienced addiction counselors should have bookmarked on their computer is the Substance Abuse and Mental Health Services Administration, commonly known as SAMHSA. SAMHSA is a governmental organization that has emerged as the leading resource for those working in the area of addictions. The organization's website (www.samhsa.gov) provides providers with the opportunity to view pictures of the various types of drugs, learn the street terminology of illegal substances, observe paraphernalia, and understand the direct effects of these drugs as well as the warning signs of use and abuse. Additionally, resources, books, posters, bookmarks, and other valuable items are available at this website. Finally, practical applications, best practices, examples of programs and interventions as well as scholarly research, grants, parent information, recent and archived publications and current data, and trends about substance abuse are available, and the vast majority of these items are freely provided.

The purpose of this chapter is to provide a survey of both chemical and behavioral addictions as it pertains to adolescents. Theories, policies, activities, and interventions that are designed to meet the needs of adolescents who are experimenting with, recreationally using, abusing, and addicted to these substances and behaviors are discussed. After reading this chapter, readers will be able to do the following:

- Be aware of the prevalence of adolescent substance use in America

- Understand screening and diagnosing adolescent chemical and behavioral addictions

- Know the difference between behavioral and chemical addictions

- Be able to discuss the types of care for adolescents with behavioral and chemical addictions

- Be able to determine the types of treatment modalities used for adolescent substance use and addictions

- Improve awareness of the theoretical framework for counseling adolescents, including behavioral, cognitive behavioral therapy (CBT), motivational interviewing (MI), motivational enhancement treatment, functional family therapy, functional behavioral therapy, and brief strategic family therapy (BSFT)

- Identify protective risk factors including peers, parents, and spiritual and religious aspects

- Understand factors that help prevent adolescents from developing addictions

ADOLESCENCE AND CHEMICAL ADDICTIONS

Statistics/Prevalence

According to SAMHSA (2013a), approximately 1.5 million adolescents meet the criteria for a substance-related disorder, and of these, only about 7% actually receive treatment for their disorder. There are several reasons why adolescents may not receive treatment: limited insurance coverage, lack of motivation, lack of treatment programs specific for adolescents in the community, and treatment program inconsistencies (Winters et al., 2011). In 2011, there were approximately 181,005 emergency department visits by adolescents aged 12 to 17 years that involved the use of alcohol, illicit drugs, or intentional misuse or abuse of pharmaceuticals (SAMHSA, 2013a). For adolescents being admitted to treatment programs for substance abuse, a predominant number are referred by the juvenile justice system, followed by self-referral or referral by other individuals, and schools or community organizations (SAMHSA, 2013b).

Drugs are ever-evolving, and there are trends in the use and abuse of chemicals. For example, beer may be laced with cocaine, and with new advancements and the legalization of marijuana in some states, the amount of THC (Tetrahydrocannabinol) in marijuana can be more easily altered and experimented by adolescents. According to the Centers for Disease Control and Prevention (CDC, 2010), 8.7% of people ages 12 and older reported illegal drug use within the previous months. Alcohol remains the leading drug involved in underage substance abuse, and underage drinkers consume 11% of all alcohol in this country (CDC, 2011). Excessive alcohol use is the third leading cause of behavior-related death in America for all ages (CDC, 2011). As for other substances, the use of marijuana and prescription pills (e.g., Ecstasy) continues to rise among American adolescents (Marsh, 2011).

Given the trends of adolescent substance use, providers should understand that "substance use is exacerbated by the fact that early initiation of drug or alcohol use is related to increased legal problems, driving under the influence, and physical, emotional, and sexual abuse" (Winters et al., 2011, p. 417). It also means that adolescents who use substances earlier are at a higher risk of developing an SUD (Winters et al., 2011). Figure 13.1 provides a view of past month drug use for 12- to 17-year-olds in the year 2012. According to the combined 2010 and 2011 data, 10.3% of adolescents between 12 and 17 years of age drank alcohol for the first time, and 6.3% of that age-group used an illicit drug (SAMHSA, 2013b). It is important to address addiction challenges because adolescents' early use of substances such as alcohol, tobacco, and illicit drugs have indicated increased likelihood of their continuing toward later substance abuse and associated concerns that can plague them throughout their adulthood (Peterson, 2010). Specifically, misusing alcohol can result in alcohol dependence, which can then adversely affect one's health, personal and social relationships, and behaviors (National Institute on Alcohol Abuse and Alcoholism (2005) and may lead to engagement in other illegal activities such as driving under the influence and committing violent and nonviolent crimes or other reckless behaviors (Isaacson, Hopper, Alford, & Parran, 2005).

The number of young people consuming both legal and illegal substances is a major issue around the world, especially in the United States, where it has turned into a major health and safety concern (Monti, Barnett, O'Leary, & Colby, 2001). The costs of adolescents using and abusing controlled substances include significant harm to the abusing individuals, their families, and communities. Additionally, it affects one's social, medical, and judicial systems (Cosden, 2001). Substance use among adolescents may be attributed to the challenges associated with their age and developmental stage, which according to Cicchetti and Rogosch (2002) include issues involving identity, sexuality, peer relationships, academic pressures, and autonomy. Society continually searches to find the cure that will change these behaviors; however, researchers continue to determine why adolescents use drugs, and to develop prevention and rehabilitation programs, in order to address communities, parents, peers, schools, churches, and other stakeholders. Although much time, resources, research, and finances have been dedicated to addressing the

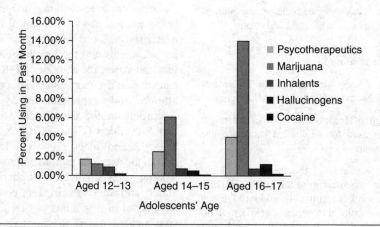

Figure 13.1   2012 Past Month Use of Illicit Drugs: 12–17 Year Olds

Source. Substance Abuse and Mental Health Services Administration (2013a).

prevalence of drug use and abuse and its prevention among American adolescents, drug use continues to be a leading health risk (Peterson, 2010). The provider's role in adolescent addictions and prevention can be numerous; however, it is first important to understand how to screen and diagnose substance-related disorders.

What Constitutes Chemical Addictions?

Adolescent substance use can be understood through a stage of use model. The first level is experimental and involves exploration of substances often in response to peer pressure, which Nowinski (1990) called the experimental stage. The second level is substance misuse and is characterized by instrumental use, which is further divided into hedonistic use and compensatory use. Hedonistic use is when the adolescent uses drugs to experience mood swings, and compensatory use is when the adolescent uses drugs to compensate for emotions of anger, sadness, and loneliness (Nowinski, 1990). The third level of substance use is called substance abuse; in this stage, the substance use becomes habitual and creates substance dependence. Schaeffer (1987) called this stage *addiction* while Nowinski (1990) called it the *compulsion stage*. After gaining an understanding of substance use, there must be a commitment to using instruments to determine where clients are on the aforementioned continuum.

Diagnosis

Although the *DSM-5* includes various addictions diagnoses, the provider needs to be well educated and practiced in diagnosing. Attention must be paid to the essential features of each diagnosis, identifying their presence prior to assigning that diagnosis. An SUD includes cognitive, behavioral, and physiological symptoms revealing the individual's continued use despite serious resulting problems (*DSM-5*). Table 13.2 provides a variety of service levels and a description of

their intensity levels. A significant characteristic of SUDs is "an underlying change in brain circuits that may persist beyond detoxification" (*DSM-5*, 2013, p. 483). SUDs consist of impaired control (e.g., persistent desire to regulate substance use, or a great deal of time spent obtaining substance), social impairment (e.g., failure to fulfill major role obligations or presence of interpersonal problems), risky use (e.g., using substances in hazardous situations, or using despite persistent/recurrent physical or psychological problems), and pharmacological criteria such as tolerance and withdrawal symptoms (*DSM-5*). Tolerance is when increasingly larger doses of a substance are consumed to achieve the desired effect or a markedly reduced effect occurs after consuming the usual dose. Withdrawal symptoms are seen when the concentration of the substance within the body decline in an individual who previously maintained prolonged heavy substance use. After developing withdrawal symptoms, people generally consume the substance again to relieve the symptoms. However, it is important to know that neither tolerance nor withdrawal is necessary to diagnose an SUD (*DSM-5*). Depending on the number of symptoms, or criteria met, the diagnosing professional should specify a severity level (e.g., mild, moderate, severe). Most of the substance-related disorders, but not all, can be diagnosed as a use, intoxication, or withdrawal disorder. Intoxication includes symptoms as a result of the recent ingestion of the substance (these symptoms will vary depending on the substance type). Adolescents may have not only a substance-related disorder but also a co-occurring disorder that interacts with the individual's use of the substance.

For example, 17-year-old Mark has been diagnosed with a cannabis use disorder; however, during the course of counseling, it is revealed that Mark has very high general anxiety and limited coping skills. He reports that he began smoking marijuana on entering high school, after the death of his mother when he experienced an increase in his anxiety symptoms. Now, smoking pot helps him manage his symptoms. The provider desires to treat both the anxiety and the cannabis use, as they are inter-related; thus, she diagnoses Mark as having generalized anxiety disorder and moderate cannabis use disorder.

Assessing for the co-occurring of mental health symptomology and underlying physical/medical concerns is pertinent to providing an accurate assessment of the substance use or behaviors. Richardson, Memetovic, Ratner, and Johnson (2011) identified that both social (e.g., peers influence, parental-familial use) and biological (e.g., cognitive processing development, impulse control) influences affect adolescents and their choices and behaviors. Other researchers have found that the high comorbidity of mental health symptomology and substance use may often lead to substance use by adolescents in an attempt to self-medicate their symptoms (Battista, Pencer, McGonnell, Durdle, & Stewart, 2013; Brunelle et al., 2013; Hurd, Michaelides, Miller, & Jutras-Aswad, 2014). For instance, a provider will need to be aware of the symptoms of impulsive disorders and differentiate those from the behavioral addictions—as well as from the disruptive behavioral disorders such as oppositional defiant disorder, conduct disorder, and so on. Is the issue that adolescents are unable to control their impulse to act on a behavior or that they are addicted to video games? Are they unable to control their shopping or do they simply not place value on money? Are they using video games to escape their stress and anxiety about socializing with others, or do they truly have an addiction to the games? These are the type of questions providers will need to explore in order to provide accurate diagnoses between the existence of a mental health disorder, an addiction, and the existence of comorbid disorders.

There are two issues a provider must consider when diagnosing: (1) comorbidity and (2) progression. Perepletchikova, Krystal, and Kaufman (2008) stated, "Comorbidity is the rule, not the exception" (p. 1131). Studies suggest a neuro-biological link between behavioral and substance addictions (Grant, Brewer, & Potenza, 2006). Adams (2009) noted that both addictive substances and addictive behaviors have similar effects on the brain; both of these activities affect the body's natural reward systems and encourage continued use in those who develop addictions. Subsequently, helping professionals must consider the possible comorbidity of behavior addictions with other chemical addictions. In terms of treatment, both tend to respond positively to the same psychosocial and pharmacological treatments (Grant, Potenza, Weinstein, & Gorelick, 2010).

Progression is another concept to consider when diagnosing. Progression depends on the frequency of use, the amount of use or time spent utilizing the behavior, and the psychological dependency that develops as the individuals become dependent on the substance or behaviors as their coping skills for dealing with their stress or problems. Providers need to be able to identify both physical and behavioral signs of addictions. Severe use is noted when there is an increased tolerance for the substance or increase in the behavior in both amount and frequency. Impairment in school, family, and peer relationships and concern expressed by others are indicative of dependency. Often, the substance or behavior is used to maintain the individuals' sense of self, either through control of their emotions or their self-definition. Providers may use screening tools to assess for the progression and comorbidity of an adolescent's substance-related presentation.

Screening

Saitz, Mulvey, Plough, and Samet (1997) found that around 45% of cases of substance use go unnoticed by primary health care providers. For adolescents specifically, the majority of adolescent substance abusers are never identified (Evans & Sullivan, 2001). It is essential for helping professionals to depend on screening tools designed for adolescents in order to determine their relationship with a substance or behavior. The lack of use of screening instruments by practitioners can have severe implications in terms of treatment in determining the stage of use. Private health settings also generally do not adequately screen for the use of drugs (McPherson & Hersch, 2000). This lack of screening for substance use in health care could be potentially harmful; early screening to identify substance users is very important for detection and prevention of protracted alcohol and drug use, as prolonged use may lead to abuse or dependency (SAMHSA, 2011). There are many adolescent substance use and behavioral screening instruments identified in the literature, which make it difficult to establish which screening instruments are the most effective and easiest to use (McPherson & Hersch, 2000). However, it is clear that the use of substance abuse screening instruments is critical in the treatment of adolescents. Some examples of screening tools are included in Table 13.1. Clearly, the addiction counselors need to keep themselves educated and up-to-date on the variety of screening instruments available and the ethics that guide their appropriate use.

Levels of Care

Screening and diagnoses of substance-related disorders all inform the type of treatment the adolescent should receive. Levels of severity and intensity of the substance use should be derived from diagnostic and screening tools. Once the adolescent's substance use habits and related factors have been professionally assessed, the individual will be referred to one of five treatment levels (Winters et al., 2011). These levels range on a continuum of service intensity from early intervention to medical intervention (see Table 13.2 for descriptions of each intervention style).

CASE SCENARIO

Review the case of Melanie (see Case Scenario 13.1). Her problems are somewhat typical of an adolescent with substance-related problems. For this exercise, get with a partner and discuss Melanie's case. Provider 2 should act as the treating provider and Provider 1 should act as the provider who conducted Melanie's intake and is now referring her to Provider 2. Considering what you've learned thus far about addictions, diagnosis, screening, and level of care, answer the questions in Exercise 13.1.

Table 13.1 Substance-Related Disorders Screening Tools

Instrument	Description
Adolescent Drinking Index (ADI)	24-item rating scale. Used for adolescent drinking problems, and assists with treatment planning.
Substance Abuse Subtle Screening Inventory Adolescent Version (SASSI-A)	100 items. For adolescents likely to have substance abuse or dependence. Contains items to help identify those unwilling or unable to admit substance abuse.
Drug Use Screening Inventory-Revised (DUSI-R)	159 items. Can be used with youth who exhibit emotional and behavioral problems. Highlights treatment needs, and can be used to monitor progress.
Teen Addiction Severity Index (T-ASI)	Mostly used in clinical settings. 154 items. For adolescents with substance abuse, psychiatric, and co-occurring disorders.
Car, Relax, Alone, Forget, Friends, Trouble (CRAFFT)	A free, brief screening tool for substance abuse in adolescents. Six items. Screens for various drugs as well as alcohol use.

Source. Arizona Department of Health Services (n.d.).

Table 13.2   Levels of Intervention and Continuum of Service Intensity

Intervention Level	Description of Services
Early intervention	Commonly consists of educational or brief intervention services
Outpatient treatment	Adolescents generally attend 6 hours or less per week for a period, depending on the progress and treatment plan
Intensive outpatient	Adolescents attend treatment during the day (up to 20 hours per week) but live at home. Length of treatment ranges from 2 months to 1 year
Residential/inpatient treatment	Programs that provide treatment services in a residential setting from 1 month to 1 year
Medically managed intensive inpatient	Most appropriate for adolescents whose substance use, biomedical problems, and/or emotional problems are so severe that they require 24-hour primary medical care for a length of time depending on their progress

Source. Winters et al. (2011).

Case Scenario 13.1

Melanie

Melanie is a 16-year-old Caucasian female. She was originally brought into the emergency department at her local hospital due to alcohol poisoning after binge drinking at a party. She lives at home with her 10-year-old brother, 18-year-old brother, and her mother. Her mother is the manager at a local bank, and although she tends to work long hours, she is usually home by 6:30 p.m. and is often home on weekends. Melanie's mother states that over the past year, Melanie's behavior and mood have been quite erratic—"Sometimes Melanie is fine, but then there are times when she is in the darkest of moods and just mean." Melanie seems to ignore her curfew, as she often does not return home until after 12:00 a.m. She has been in trouble legally for underage drinking and possession of marijuana within the past 2 years. Melanie told the hospital personnel that she usually drinks or smokes marijuana alone, approximately two to five times a week. She tends to have two to three beers or two shots of hard liquor at a time. She reports that her use of substances isn't a problem because it helps her maintain control of her emotions.

ADOLESCENCE AND BEHAVIORAL ADDICTIONS

When people hear the term *addiction*, they most often think of chemical-, or substance-, related addictions. Much less is known about the behaviors that can be destructive and addictive.

Behavioral addictions share a common and underlying psychopathological basis as is the case for substances; however, these behaviors continue to be minimized and misunderstood by society and treatment professionals alike (Kwon, Kim, Cho, & Yang, 2013; Villella et al., 2011). As mentioned in the introduction to the chapter,

Exercise 13.1

Treating Melanie

During the course of the professional conversation between Counselor 1 and Counselor 2, discuss your answers to the following questions:

1. If any, what diagnoses might you consider for Melanie? Why? Are there any diagnoses outside of substance-related disorders that should be considered?

2. At this point, what level of care do you think Melanie requires?

3. What screening tools, if any, might you use as Counselor 1? What screening tools would you find helpful as Counselor 2?

4. What factors in Melanie's case may affect Melanie's treatment? What should be considered? And how might these issues be addressed?

behavioral addictions are excessive behaviors that stimulate the individual, which in turn cause functional impairments in social situations, disturb interpersonal relationships, and disrupt major role obligations (Alavi et al., 2012). The reason why there is a lack of sufficient clinical information on behavioral addictions is due in part to the fact that many of these behavioral addictions are not illegal and members of society engage in them; thus, it is hard to imagine that these behaviors can be detrimental to either adolescents or adults. For example, the term "addiction can refer to a range of excessive behaviors, such as video gaming, binge eating, sex, media use, sports and exercise, love, pathological work, or gambling" (Alavi et al., 2012, p. 291). Unfortunately, gambling is the only behavioral addiction with a diagnostic classification in the *DSM-5* (see Diagnosing and Screening section); however, it is not the only process addiction treated by counselors.

Types of Behavioral Addictions

Behavioral addictions, like chemical addictions, refer to a range of excessive behaviors, such as gambling, shopping, television compulsion, exercise, work, sex, Internet use, gaming, and overeating (Albrecht, Kirschner, & Grüsser, 2007). These behaviors are carried out despite the knowledge that adverse consequences may occur (Grant et al., 2010). Some behaviors, such as video gaming, are a form of adolescent bonding, while other behaviors, such as Internet use, have become part of the adolescents' daily lives (King, Delfabbro, Griffiths, & Gradisar, 2012; Kurti & Dallery, 2012). The Internet is no longer a luxury; it is necessary for school and family life; like other aspects of our society, the Internet can be used inappropriately and can cause maladaptive behaviors. For example, children and adolescents can overindulge in gaming, can use the Internet to access pornography, and may use social media as the primary focus of their life, consuming their time and energy and diminishing their desire for personal interaction and relationship (King et al., 2012; Kurti & Dallery, 2012). As such, currently, children and adolescents constitute the majority of those experiencing gaming addiction; these games can begin to dominate a child or adolescent's life, replacing real-life relationships with those online, and consuming more and more time from the daily life, deviating him or her from responsibilities and social activities (Hagedorn & Young, 2011).

These behaviors are difficult to diagnose and treat because adolescents have what seems to be unlimited access to technology and spend a great amount of time engaged in these activities. As a result, excessive time spent on technology has been normalized making it difficult to identify if there is a problem. For providers, the key to determining and preventing behavioral addictions lies heavily in the monitoring of adolescents' use of technology (Alavi et al., 2012). It is important for the providers working with adolescent populations to understand the dual relationship that exists between technology and the adolescent today. It is not only a necessity in some aspects, such as their school work and family communication, but it has also become their primary means of communication with the world. Treatment needs to focus on the management of the use and encouragement of the development of positive and healthy coping skills for interacting with others as well as dealing with the underlying emotions that the technology allows the child or adolescent to avoid or escape (King et al., 2012).

It is vital that addiction professionals gain specialized education and training regarding these behaviors. Each of these behavioral addictions has its own set of symptoms and adverse effects; however, counselors can use Brown's diagnostic criteria to screen for signs that a particular behavior has become addictive (Alavi et al., 2012).

Gambling Addiction

Currently, the *DSM-5* includes gambling under its addiction diagnoses. The essential feature of gambling disorder is persistent and recurrent maladaptive gambling behavior that disrupts personal, family, and/or vocational pursuits. Individuals with this disorder should exhibit a cluster of four or more symptoms listed in the *DSM-5*. It is anticipated that in the future additional diagnostic criteria will be provided for Internet and gaming addictions. Also, providers should be aware that behavioral addictions also need to be considered in this comorbid realm, as their utilization may be a coping skill, albeit an unhealthy one, to deal with emotions, mental

health symptomology, or underlying medical issues.

Adolescents are participating in high-risk gambling behavior at an ever-increasing level. As such, it is important that helping professionals do not minimize this population's involvement in various types of betting activities. Jacobs (2005) suggests that adolescents bet on horse and dog races. They also wager on their personal skills such as pool (billiards), bowling, and basketball as well as their video gaming skills; they also gamble on the Internet. Some of the reasons why they gamble are for money, items, and influence; to relieve boredom; and/or to feel a sense of excitement, power, and importance (Jacobs, 2005).

Because there are no diagnostic criteria for behavioral addictions apart from gambling, experts such as Brown (as cited in Alavi et al., 2012) have created some diagnostic considerations providers may use in diagnosing adolescents with process addictions. Brown's diagnostic criterion may be used to help counselors screen for maladaptive behaviors.

Recent findings support the assumption that common mechanisms underlie the development and maintenance of both behavioral and substance-related addiction (Alavi et al., 2012). According to Alavi et al. (2012), individuals "suffering from behavioral addictions describe craving, excessive behavior, psychological and physical withdrawal symptoms, loss of control, and the development of tolerance" (p. 293). Providers treating adolescents with Internet or media addictions may find Young's Internet Addiction Scale, the Smartphone Addictions Scale, and the Young Diagnostic Questionnaire for Internet Addiction as useful screening tools.

EVIDENCE-BASED INTERVENTIONS IN TREATING ADOLESCENTS WITH ADDICTIONS

Though the number of adolescents involved in substance use is an ever-growing trend that could lead to addiction (Bonomo & Bowes, 2001), the truth is that most of these adolescents will not become addicts. One of the most important aspects of working with adolescents is to understand that for the vast majority of them, their use and abuse of alcohol and drugs and engaging in destructive behaviors is largely a developmental, not pathological, issue. Generally speaking, adolescents are likely to be experimenting (e.g., testing out the effects), binging (i.e., consuming large quantities of a substance or overly excessive engagement in an activity in one instance), and perhaps abusing (maladaptive pattern of substance use or activity engagement). However, adolescents are usually not yet addicted (includes tolerance, withdrawal, and dependence symptoms). Adolescent substance use and involvement in destructive behaviors are much more likely to be a function of their adolescent risk-taking tendencies as opposed to a long-term characteristic. To this point, it is very important that providers understand that adolescents are not little adults. They are still developing and changing and therefore should be treated as such. That is not to say that this is not an important issue. However, it is important that the vast majority of this population be treated from a developmental, ecological, educational, and preventive perspective to determine if the adolescent level of use or involvement in a behavior warrants additional treatment.

Theoretical Framework for Counseling Adolescents With Addictions

Using an ecological framework when working with adolescents is critical to understand the complex relationships, settings, and dynamics of an adolescent and how those factors affect their choices and behaviors. Bronfenbrenner (1979) put forth this model and argued that adolescent development is influenced not only by their proximal relationships (closer relationships and systems such as family, peers, school, and community) but also by distal relationships (seemingly not as influential or close factors such as the media and government policies). Basically, to be an effective provider, all of these factors

need to be addressed and be a part of the treatment of adolescents. In addition to addressing these relationships, providers must also utilize all of the systems (e.g., school, juvenile justice, child welfare, medical) that these individuals come into contact with for treatment. It is important for providers to understand and appreciate the need to have a multisystemic approach to working with their clients. This may include collaboration and coordination of services with the consumer's physician or psychiatrist if medical or psychiatric concerns exist, or any other services the client may require or previously be involved with. In the following section, several approaches to treating adolescents with chemical and behavioral addictions are briefly reviewed.

Behavioral Approaches

Behavioral interventions assist adolescents in actively participating in their recovery, and it enhances their ability to resist drug use (NIDA, 2014a). With behavioral approaches, providers likely provide incentives for abstinence, work toward modifying attitudes and behaviors related to the addiction, may assist in family communication, and increase coping skills to better deal with problematic environmental cues (NIDA, 2014b). Below are some behavioral treatments shown to be effective in treating adolescent chemical and behavioral disorders (NIDA, 2014b).

Cognitive Behavioral Therapy. CBT is viewed as the leading treatment approach in dealing with both substance and behavioral addictions (Du, Jiang, &Vance, 2010; King et al., 2012). This can be provided in both individual and group settings and can support the utilization of CBT to assist in the development of self-monitoring skills for identified triggers, as well as in the management of urges and cravings through healthier coping skills. Thus, CBT assists individuals in monitoring their thoughts and how these influence their behavioral choices. Treatment then aims to provide positive coping skills and interventions to assist the individual in making more positive behavioral choices, thus managing their emotions in a more productive and positive manner.

Motivational Interviewing. MI has also "become accepted as a science-based intervention that supports client engagement in substance abuse treatment" (Dickinson, Edmundson, & Tomlin, 2014). This client-centered approach attempts to influence clients to consider making changes and will be further explored in this chapter.

The behavioral health field has long held the belief that a solid therapeutic relationship is essential for any change to occur for a client. Thus, tailoring the therapeutic intervention to match the client's need is of most importance. Therapy sessions—focusing on developing an understanding—and supportive therapeutic relationship—to deal with the numerous defenses common to addictions, including denial, rationalization, and intellectualization—are useful. Identifying risk factors is also important; however, understanding the individual adolescent has been identified as important in treatment planning as well as treatment outcomes.

MI readily accepts that each client will be at a different stage of preparedness to change and acceptance of the need to change. Its intent then is to assist clients in assessing their behaviors and choices, determining what adjustments or needs are necessary, and determining the risks of maintaining these behaviors. Providers utilizing MI employ asking open-ended questions, providing affirmations, reflective listening or parroting back what the client is stating, and periodically providing summary statements to help the client conceptualize his or her choices and behaviors. Most important, MI is nonjudgmental of the client, assuming the client is inherently good, and setting the goal to assist the client in improving his or her choices, behaviors, and coping skills.

In addiction counseling specifically, MI includes assisting the client to examine the usefulness of interventions and strategies in controlling the use of substances or behaviors, allowing the adolescent to determine the benefits or consequences of his or her choices (King et al., 2012). Burke (2011) found that the usefulness of MI includes its ability to be utilized in brief sessions, fitting well into both managed care and treatment settings (outpatient and inpatient). Providers utilizing this approach help empower the client with personal assessment skills and the ability to make better choices.

Motivational Enhancement Therapy (MET). MET is a counseling approach that helps adolescents dissolve their ambivalence about engaging in treatment and quitting their substance use or maladaptive behavior (NIDA, 2014a). It is based on MI and usually incorporates an assessment of the adolescents' motivation for treatment, followed by one to three individual sessions with a counselor (the provider attempts to help the client develop the desire to engage in treatment via nonconfrontational feedback). The provider should be empathic yet directive when discussing the need for treatment, and ultimately, the provider attempts to get the adolescent to say self-motivational statements to strengthen his or her motivation. When met with resistance, the provider merely responds neutrally (NIDA, 2014b). MET is typically not used as the sole treatment for adolescents with chemical and behavioral use problems.

Adolescent Community Reinforcement Approach (A-CRA). In A-CRA interventions, influences in the adolescent's life that reinforce the substance use or behavior are replaced with healthy family, social, and educational reinforcements (NIDA, 2014a). Once the adolescent's needs and functioning levels have been assessed, the provider should choose procedures to address problem-solving, coping, and communication skills from the 17 A-CRA procedures (NIDA, 2014a). Additional procedures should be used to encourage participation in healthy social and recreational activities (NIDA, 2014a).

Contingency Management (CM). CM allows for immediate and tangible reinforcements for positive behaviors to modify problem behaviors (NIDA, 2014a). Adolescents can earn minor incentives (prizes or vouchers) in exchange for engaging in treatment, abstaining from drug use or behavior engagement, and achieving treatment goals (NIDA, 2014b). The overarching aim of CM is to reduce the influence of reinforcement from using drugs or behaviors. CM has been applied in a variety of settings, and even parents can be trained on how to use this method at home (NIDA, 2014b). This approach is commonly used in conjunction with a psychosocial or medication treatment (NIDA, 2014a). While behavioral approaches are quite effective in treating adolescents with chemical and process addictions, family-based approaches have also proved to be effective.

Family-Based Approaches

Stable family relationships, support from peers and friends, and healthy relationships were cited by Moos (2007) to increase the positive outcomes of change and recovery in individuals with addictions. Addiction counselors then will want to incorporate family support and therapy to assist the adolescent as well as the family as a whole. Providers need to be sure to assess and incorporate family system dynamics when addressing chemical use or abuse, especially in the adolescent population. Family members experience significant levels of stress in response to and coping with an individual's substance use. Family member's own degree of healthiness, or unhealthiness, can also influence the substance use of adolescents, by enabling, supporting, or challenging the behaviors. Coping and support are important not only for the user but also for the family members.

Orford, Copello, Velleman, and Templeton (2010) state, "Good quality social support, in the form of emotional support, good information and material help, is an invaluable resource of affected family members, supporting their coping efforts and contributing positively to their health" (p. 36). Shelef, Diamond, Diamond, and Liddle (2005) not only found that the alliance between the client and the therapist is important for change in adolescents but also found that the parental alliance has a significant impact on change with substance use and behavioral

change. Additionally, support groups for families are available. One such program is Drug Addiction Support (www.drug-addiction-support.org), which provides education to family members on various drug effects, treatment options, and answers to family questions on how to deal with their family member. Below are several family-based approaches to therapy.

Brief Strategic Family Therapy. BSFT is based on a family systems theory. Over 12 to 16 sessions, the therapist establishes a relationship with each family member, observes how each member interacts with another, and helps the family change negative interaction patterns (NIDA, 2014a). BSFT can be used with families for a variety of different reasons in various settings (NIDA, 2014a).

Family Behavior Therapy. Family behavior therapy combines behavioral contracting and contingency management to address substance use and other behavioral issues (NIDA, 2014a). The adolescent and at least one caregiver are involved in treatment planning and choosing interventions from a list of treatment options (NIDA, 2014b). Family members should be encouraged to utilize behavioral strategies learned in therapy within the home environment (NIDA, 2014a). Preventative goals should be set, reviewed, and rewarded at each session (NIDA, 2014a).

Functional Family Therapy. Functional family therapy "combines a family systems view of family functioning (i.e., unhealthy family interactions underlie problem behaviors) with behavioral techniques so that communication, problem-solving, conflict resolution, and parenting skills may be improved" (NIDA, 2014a). The essential treatment strategies include engaging the entire family in the treatment process while enhancing their motivation for change, and modifying family members' behavior (NIDA, 2014a).

Multidimensional Family Therapy (MDFT). MDFT is a comprehensive family- and community-based treatment frequently used for substance-abusing adolescents (NIDA, 2014a). This treatment approach aims to generate familial competency and collaboration with systems such as schools, community centers, or juvenile justice (NIDA, 2014a). Sessions are not restricted to one location and may in fact be held in a variety of settings (NIDA, 2014a). MDFT has been shown to be effective for severe substance use cases and in helping these individuals reintegrate into the community (NIDA, 2014a).

Recovery/Support Services

Adolescents recovering from chemical or process addictions may benefit from recovery support services that reinforce what was learned in treatment and improve the individual's quality of life (NIDA, 2014a). These services may include continuing care, mutual help groups (i.e., 12-step programs), or peer recovery support (NIDA, 2014a). Recovery support programs tend to provide a safe communal place to share and process mutual struggles. However, recovery and support services are not to exist in place of treatment (NIDA, 2014a). Below are several types of recovery and support services.

Assertive Continuing Care (ACC). ACC is considered a home-based continuing-care support service (NIDA, 2014a). According to NIDA (2014a), this approach is generally delivered by trained clinicians. It aims to prevent relapse and is usually employed after the adolescent completes therapy utilizing the A-CRA (NIDA, 2014a). ACC utilizes positive and negative reinforcement to shape behaviors, along with training in problem-solving and communication skills (NIDA, 2014a).

Mutual Help Groups. Mutual help groups are groups such as the 12-step programs Alcoholics Anonymous (AA) and Narcotics Anonymous. These groups are free and generally provide ongoing support for people with substance-related addictions (NIDA, 2014a). AA approaches have been found to be effective for adolescents who participate in meetings (Sussman, 2010).

Support Groups. Most support groups, especially 12-step-influenced groups, regardless of

their focus, have a similar structure. Individuals meet to discuss their current status, sharing their success and difficulties, and provide encouragement and feedback to one another regarding possible coping skills. Anonymity is the cornerstone on which these groups are based, and members provide only their first names and all abide by the rule "what's said in group, stays in group." Members may take the role of sponsor for others. Sponsors are those members with a significant period of sobriety or time without utilizing the unhealthy behavior. Sponsors meet with the individual both in meeting settings and outside of those meetings. They provide feedback and support on a more individualized basis; however, they do not take on the role of counselor. Encouraging clients to attend support groups is an integral aspect of treating this population. To this end, it would be remiss of any counselor working with adolescents to not include the use of a peer support system in their counseling.

Specific support groups for counselors to consider include the Al-Anon and Al-Ateen, which are family support groups and resources for family members, sibling, and friends of addicted individuals. Al-Ateen may be an ideal way for adolescents to understand their relationship with drugs and alcohol as well as their parents' and guardians' relationship with these behaviors (http://www.al-anon.alateen.org/). Though these groups focus on alcohol use and abuse no matter the substance, families can benefit from attending these meetings. Additionally, many of these meetings are offered electronically, which may appeal to adolescents. There are also many faith-based treatment programs, developed specifically for adolescents. One example is Teen Challenge USA (http://teenchallengeusa.com/). Additionally, there are specific support groups for teens, including Gamblers Anonymous and Sex and Love Addicts Anonymous. Additional information is available at www.projectknow.com/research/12-step-behavioral

School and After School Programming. School-based programming has been found to be a positive intervention in both prevention and treatment of adolescent addiction. School counselors, nurses, teachers, and parents are primed to identify adolescent warning signs with an understanding of the individual characteristics that may support drug use and identify appropriate interventions personalized to that adolescent (Garnefski & Okma, 1996). Treatment providers, regardless of the setting, need to have specialized training to provide interventions and education to adolescents with substance or behavioral addictions in a manner in which they will identify with and respond to, thus assisting them to improve both their coping skills and emotional state (Byrnes, Miller, Aalborg, Plasencia, & Keagy, 2010; Du et al., 2010).

IDENTIFYING AND UTILIZING PROTECTIVE AND RISK FACTORS

Research indicates that the main risk factors for adolescents are related to individual, peer, family, school, and community (Hawkins, Catalano, & Miller, 1992; Felix-Ortiz & Newcomb, 1992). Surprisingly, these risk factors are also the protective factors required to help adolescents to abstain from developing an unhealthy relationship with alcohol, drugs, and harmful behaviors. Protective factors are attributes or conditions that when present mitigate or eliminate risk and increase health and well-being. Protective factors may include help finding resources, supports, and coping strategies to adequately manage the stressors of life, circumstances, or communities.

Below, please find examples regarding four specific protective factors that are critical in affecting change in the use of drugs, alcohol, and harmful behaviors for adolescence.

Parenting

It is a myth that parents instinctively know how to care for and protect their children. Parenting is a difficult life role, and there are no instructions for helping adolescents through their various group and individual challenges, especially if this involves substance use or addictive behaviors.

Parenting becomes more difficult when either or both parents abuse drugs or alcohol or accept unhealthy behaviors in their own lives, thereby supporting or encouraging these attitudes and behaviors in their children. When considering the constellation of a family that is drug affected, many things must be considered. Though this can be discouraging to the helping professional when they find out that a parent is abusing, McCord (1998) identifies that when at least one parent can provide consistency and stability, positive outcome for the adolescent can be achieved. As such, it is critical that the helping professional work with the nonabusing parent by encouraging, strengthening, and providing the parent with the support, education, and the tools needed to continue to support their child. This is where counselors can be most helpful in assisting adolescents.

National Institute on Alcohol Abuse and Alcoholism (2005) indicates that parents' drinking behavior is positively associated with their children's patterns of drug abuse. Therefore, parents who are struggling with an adolescent who is participating in destructive behaviors or experimenting with drugs and alcohol may have to address their own use and perspective of these behaviors and substances to help establish a substance-free and positive home environment as their adolescents strive toward more healthful behaviors.

Another parental factor to address is the parent–child relationship. Parents today spend less time monitoring and have less effective ways of monitoring their children (Macaulay, Griffin, Gronewold, Williams, & Botvin, 2005). This disconnection between parents and adolescents may have a negative effect on the adolescent's ability to abstain from using drugs and alcohol at a young age. Additionally, parents not monitoring or modeling healthy engagement in activities impede the adolescent's ability to create those safeguards for himself or herself. In current society, both parents and adolescents tend to be busy, which can result in parents and adolescents not spending enough time on connecting at an emotional level. Even when the parents and adolescents are physically present, there are many distractions such as technology, television, work, and many other impediments that limit interactions of parents and children. Conversely, parents who closely monitor their children, set rules, and communicate disapproval for unhealthy behaviors and choices have children who are less likely to engage in alcohol use (O'Donnell et al., 2008). Strong families, mentors, and communities are the key to helping adolescents through this difficult developmental stage. Therefore, it benefits the adolescent and the addictions professional to include the entire family in the treatment of the abuser.

Peers

Similar to parents, peers have a strong influence on the adolescent (Nowinski, 1990; Richardson et al., 2011). Peer approval of substance use has been identified as a significant risk factor for increasing the likelihood of substance use and subsequent dependency (Elkington, Bauermeister, & Zimmerman, 2011; Taylor, Lloyd, & Warheit, 2005). This influence can be either positive or negative; these relationships affect the adolescent's view of both substances and harmful behaviors (SAMHSA, 2013a). As peer relationships are very important to adolescents, counselors should address the impact of the client's peer relationships on treatment, and how one might help the client build healthy, protective relationships with peers.

Public Policies

Under the umbrella of the public policies are the Harm Reduction programs. These programs have been a big part of our society since the 1920s. The programs are generally controversial, including, but not limited to, education and reduction of harm to the user, the family, and the community. The Harm Reduction Coalition defines harm reduction as a set of practical strategies designed to reduce the negative consequences of drug use. Some of the strategies they

support are safer use of drugs and encouragement of manageable use of drugs as opposed to abstinence. The overall goals of these programs are to manage risky behaviors (e.g., substance use) that affect not only the individual but also the family and community. These harm reduction programs are met with considerable push back from individuals and communities. Providers must take advantage of these programs and activities and get their clients involved in positive activities that support healthy decisions and living. Some examples include the National Council for Behavioral Health and their mental health first aid program (http://www.thenationalcouncil.org/about/national-mental-health-association/) and NIDA (http://www.drugabuse.gov/publications/topics-in-brief/drug-abuse-prevention).

To be effective when working with this population, it is equally important for helping professionals to be aware of the risk factors that affect this population's decision to use and abuse chemicals and potentially destructive behaviors in order to cope with life. Risk factors are then defined as any factor, behavioral, emotional, psychological, that either increases (risk) or decreases (protective) the likelihood of the addictive behavior by the individual (Feinberg, 2012).

Zucker, Donovan, Masten, Mattson, and Moss (2009) identified distinct predictors or risk factors of alcohol and other chemical use and abuse for both children and adolescents. It is important for the helping professional to know that these factors should only be used as guidelines for treatment plans and initial diagnosis. In other words, the criteria listed in the charts should be viewed as collateral information in the context of the client and the client's family and community (Table 13.3).

You will note that there are two factors, internalizing feelings and externalizing feelings, in this list that may seem incongruent. The information in the aforementioned table should be used contextually, because adolescents who internalize their feelings may be susceptible to anxiety and depression. On the other hand, adolescents who externalize their feelings may

Table 13.3   Risk Factors for Children

- Having a friend or close siblings who use alcohol or drugs
- Internalizing feelings instead of expressing them
- Externalizing feelings
- Social problems
- Poor impulse control
- Engaging in high-risk behaviors
- Poor parental supervision and/or inconsistent discipline
- Trauma (including parental divorce)
- Victimization
- Poor academic performance
- Problems controlling the child's temper outbursts
- Parental alcoholism
- Caucasian heritage

exhibit poor emotional and behavioral self-control and may be at risk of being diagnosed with a conduct disorder. It is important to seek to understand each adolescent in context and make a determination using assessments and screening as well as the criteria listed above to develop the most effective and comprehensive treatment plan for the child. Similar to the afore-mentioned risk factors outlined for children is a list of risk factors for adolescents. Again, the criteria in the table should serve as a guideline to help helping professionals determine the presence of an SUD for an adolescent. For this chart, the greater the number of criteria met by the adolescent, the more likely he or she has an SUD (Table 13.4).

SPIRITUALITY AND RELIGION

An additional protective factor that deserves special attention is spirituality and religion. Histori-cally, the term *spirituality* has been synonymous with religion (Heinz, Epstein, & Preston, 2007); though these two terms are interconnected, they represent two very different concepts. Religion is a set of beliefs, practices, and doctrines that explains creation and authority of the universe (Rabbi Moshe ben Asher, 2001). Typically, mem-bers of a specific religion worship together in a house of worship such as a church, mosque, or synagogue; they follow structured rituals and generally have a well-defined dogma (Ellwood & McGraw, 2010).

Spirituality is an individual and personal practice (Miller, 1998) that does not subscribe to traditions and is more often unstructured (Ellwood & McGraw, 2010). One of the empha-ses of spirituality involves trying to figure out fundamental questions regarding life's meaning and purpose (Carroll, 1999). Spirituality can be viewed in relation to character, virtue, and one's responsible relationship to the self, to others, and to the world (Staussner, 2004).

It behooves the helping professional to first be knowledgeable and comfortable discussing these

Table 13.4   Risk Factors for Adolescents

- Family history of SUDs
- Affective illness
- History of suicidal attempts
- Loss of loved one
- Low self-esteem
- High level of stress
- Poor social skills or maladaptive coping skills, social isolation
- Troubled relationship with parents
- Parental permissive attitude toward deviant behavior
- Overly strict parental behaviors toward deviant behaviors
- Adolescent coming from a single parent or blended family
- Feelings of alienation or running away from home
- Low commitment or low expectations for school
- Early use of cigarettes
- High levels of involvement with drug-using friends
- Antisocial behaviors (conduct behaviors)
- Poor impulse control
- Early experimental substance use
- Legal problems during adolescence
- Absence of strong religious beliefs
- Unsuccessful attempts to stop or cut back on substance use
- History of substance withdrawal
- Having experienced one or more alcohol "blackouts"
- Continued substance abuse in spite of consequences
- Use of chemical prior to or during school

two important constructs and second to be aware that more than two thirds of American adolescents report participation in religious youth groups and more than half report attending religious services 2 to 3 times per month (Smith & Denton, 2005). Additionally, 84% of adolescents believe in God, and about half of these adolescents indicate that their faith is either very important or extremely important in terms of the way they make decisions and live their lives (Smith & Denton, 2005). Additionally, adolescent's involvement in religiosity has been associated with increased ability to be self-reflective and to engage in abstract thinking, psychological adjustment, and self-regulation (Fowler, 1981; McCullough & Willoughby, 2009).

Furthermore, it is important to note that religious involvement is a significant protective factor and acts as a buffer for youth with regard to their involvement in drug use, problem behavior, overall delinquency, violence, and other unhealthy behaviors (Koenig, King, & Carson, 2012). Aiding this specific population in understanding how the rules of religion and their use of spirituality may allow them to understand and manage the ambiguities and difficulties of life (Carroll, 1999) is criteria to successfully treating adolescents. Consequently, it is vital for helping professionals to include both spiritual and religious activities and interventions in their work with this population.

Ethical and Legal Issues

In general, there is a shortage of well-prepared providers who address chemical addiction disorders (Goodman, 2001). There is even more of a shortage of qualified providers to address behavioral addictions such as sexual addictions in the United States where an estimated 17 to 37 million Americans suffer from this specific behavioral disorder (Hagedorn, 2009). To this end, education and training is one of the most important areas to address when discussing the ethical and legal issues in addiction counseling. Formal higher education training programs that are CACREP's accredited have received a mandate that requires that master's level counselors (mental health and school counselors) be educated in the prevention, intervention, and treatment of addicted clients (CACREP, 2009). This new standard illustrates the importance of addictions training. In addition to this mandate, it is also strongly encouraged that counselor educators receive additional training in addictions so they can speak to the issues of addictive disorders across the curriculum.

Additional ethical issues related to counselor competence include possessing specific training for working with children and adolescents, as well as acquiring specific instruction for working with multicultural populations.

Though it has been mentioned earlier, it must be reiterated that it is unethical to provide treatment to adolescents without having specific training in working with this population. Kaczmarek (2000) takes this ethical issue one step further; he asserts that counselors who are trained to work with adolescents are not qualified to work with children, because each of these populations have unique developmental and treatment issues (Bukstein, 2009). A similar competency issue that has received attention is the fact that little emphasis is placed on multicultural competence in the training of addiction counselors (Lassiter & Chang, 2008). Specifically, contemporary addiction models are viewed as "culturally blind" (Castro & Hernandez-Alarcon, 2002). Stated plainly, it is important for counselors to be skilled in addressing acculturation, cultural identity, spirituality, and gender as they pertain to adolescents' use of substances and engagement in behaviors that can be destructive (Rastogi & Wadha, 2006; Wong & Longshore, 2008; Zenmore, Mulia Ye, Borges, & Greenfield, 2008). These unique factors should be present in treatment plans and be instrumental in the manner in which the counselor helps the client.

An additional ethical issue that was cited at the beginning of the chapter is the fact that approximately a third of all addiction counselors are in recovery ("Field Grapples With Sobriety," 2006). These individuals are critical to the success of the profession; however, it is clear that we need to make sure that there are some standards that ensure the protection of not just the client but the recovering counselor also. Currently, AA Guidelines (2008) request that these individuals have 3 to 5 years in abstinence before they are hired as an addiction counselor; however, there is no enforcement of this suggestion. With this sizable amount of recovering individuals employed as counselors, this is a significant ethical and legal issue for the profession.

A final ethical and legal issue is the profession's steadfast commitment to implementing only evidence-based practices designed specifically for adolescents (Fahy, 2007). The empirically verified interventions mentioned in this chapter have been proven to improve client outcomes. Nevertheless, there remains a disconnection between research, practice, training, and education, and it is very troubling. Unfortunately, practitioners, counselor educators, and addiction training agencies are generally not in sync with the newest research (Crabb & Linton, 2007; Moore et al., 2004); with relapse rates between 50% and 90%, the gap between research and practice may be the most important ethical and legal issue that must be addressed immediately.

SUMMARY

Approximately 1.5 million adolescents meet the criteria for a substance-related disorder (SAMHSA, 2013b). Addiction counseling is a relatively new specialization within the behavioral health profession. There are a variety of nationally recognized and comprehensive certification programs. Examples of certifications include certified substance abuse counselor, certified addiction personnel, and substance abuse counselor. Historically, treatment of substance use was confrontational, whereas today, addictions treatment is largely informed by evidence-based practice. Adolescent's use of substances tends to differ from adult substance use, thus presenting the need for treatments oriented specially toward adolescent substance users. Addiction counselors for adolescents are provided with screening and diagnosis concerns in this chapter. This chapter explains the difference between chemical and behavioral addictions. Counselors must be able to determine types of treatment modalities used for adolescent substance use or addictions; this understanding likely stems from improved awareness of the theoretical framework for counseling adolescents (i.e., CBT, MI, BSFT). An even more integral role for counselors working with adolescents using substances is to understand factors that help prevent youth from developing addictions.

KEYSTONES

- Providers should become familiar with the prevalence of adolescent substance use in their communities, as well as with the different types of substances used and substance effects.

- There are specific tools, including Brown's Diagnostic Criteria, that counselors may use to assist with screening and diagnosing adolescent chemical and behavioral addictions.

- While behavioral and chemical addictions differ in some ways, they operate on similar neurobiological systems. It is important for counselors to understand the ways in which various substances cause the body to react.

- An ecological theoretical framework and a multisystemic approach are widely used in counselor care for adolescents with behavioral and chemical addictions.

- A variety of treatment modalities are used for adolescent substance use and addiction behaviors; providers should know when and how to use these treatments in order to practice competently.

- Providers should understand the factors that help prevent adolescents from developing addictions. The provider and the client should evaluate factors in the adolescent's life that may either impede or be advantageous in overcoming their addictions.

REFERENCES

Adams, E. H. (2009). *REMS: Experience and future directions*. Food and Drug Institute Update, FDAAA, A Year Later, January/February, 2009.

Alavi, S. S., Ferdosi, M., Jannatifard, F., Eslami, M., Alaghemandan, H., & Setare, M. (2012). Behavioral addictions versus substance addiction: Correspondence of psychiatric and psychological views. *International Journal of Preventative Medicine, 3*(4), 290–294.

Albrecht, U., Kirschner, N. E., & Grüsser, S. M. (2007). Diagnostic instruments for behavioural addiction: An overview. *GMS Psycho-Social Medicine, 4*, 1–11.

Alcoholics Anonymous. (2008). *Guidelines*. Retrieved from http://www.aa.org/assets/en_US/mg-10_foraamembers.pdf

American Psychiatric Association (2013). *Diagnostic and statistical manual of mental disorders* (5th ed.). Washington, DC: Author.

Arizona Department of Health Services. (n.d.). *Adolescent substance abuse screening instruments: Attachment A*. Retrieved from http://www.azdhs.gov/bhs/guidance/catsu_attach_a.pdf

Association for Addiction Professionals. (n.d.). *National Certification Commission for Addiction Professionals*. Retrieved from http://www.naadac.org/about-the-nccap

Battista, S. R., Pencer, A., McGonnell, M., Durdle, H., & Stewart, S. H. (2013). Relations of personality to substance use problems and mental health disorder symptoms in two clinical samples of adolescents. *International Journal of Mental Health and Addiction, 11*, 1–12. doi:10.1007/s11469-012-9395-0

Bonomo, Y. A., & Bowes, G. (2001). Putting harm reduction into an adolescent context. *Journal of Paediatrics and Child Health, 37*(1), 5–8.

Bronfenbrenner, U. (1979). Contexts of child rearing: Problems and prospects. *American Psychologist, 34*(10), 844–850.

Brunelle, N., Bertrand, K., Beaudoin, I., Ledoux, C., Gendron, A., & Arseneault, C. (2013). Drug trajectories among youth undergoing treatment: The influence of psychological problems and delinquency. *Journal of Adolescence, 36*, 705–716.

Bukstein, O. (2009). Substance use disorders and ADHD. *CNS Spectrums, 147*(7 Suppl. 6), 10–12.

Burke, B. L. (2011). What can motivational interviewing do for you? *Cognitive and Behavioral Practice, 18*, 74–81.

Burrow-Sanchez, J., Lopez, A., & Slagle, C. (2008). Perceived competence in addressing student substance abuse: A national survey of middle school counselors. *Journal of School Health, 78*, 280–286.

Byrnes, H. F., Miller, B. A., Aalborg, A. E., Plasencia, A. V., & Keagy, C. D. (2010). Implementation fidelity in adolescent family-based prevention programs: Relationship to family engagement. *Health Education Research, 25*(4), 531–541. Retrieved from http://www.ncbi.nlm.nih.gov/pmc/articles/PMC2905922/. doi:10.1093/her/cyq006

Carroll, J. J. (1999). Compatibility of Adlerian theory and practice with the philosophy and practices of Alcoholics Anonymous. *Journal of Addictions & Offender Counseling, 19*, 50–61.

Castro, F. G., & Hernandez-Alarcon, E. (2002). Integrating into drug abuse prevention and treatment with racial/ethnic minorities. *Journal of Drug Issues, 32*, 783–810.

Centers for Disease Control and Prevention. (2010). *Nutrition*. Retrieved from http://www.cdc.gov/nutrition

Cicchetti, D., & Rogosch, F. A. (2002). A developmental psychopathology perspective on adolescence. *Journal of Consulting and Clinical Psychology, 70*(1), 6–20.

Cosden, M. (2001). Risk and resilience for substance abuse among adolescents and adults with LD. *Journal of Learning Disabilities, 34*(4), 352–358.

Council for Accreditation of Counseling and Related Educational Programs. (2009). *2009 standards for accreditation*. Alexandria, VA: Author.

Crabb, A. C., & Linton, J. M. (2007). A qualitative study of recovering and nonrecovering substance abuse counselors' belief systems. *Journal of Addictions & Offender Counseling, 28*, 4–20.

Dickinson, D. M., Edmundson, E., & Tomlin, K. (2014). Implementing motivational interviewing. *Journal of Teaching in the Addictions, 5*(2), 39–57. doi:10.1300/J188v05n02_04

Du, Y., Jiang, W., & Vance, A. (2010). Longer term effect of randomized, controlled group cognitive behavioral therapy for Internet addiction in adolescent students in Shanghai. *Australian & New Zealand Journal of Psychiatry, 44*, 129–134.

Elkington, K. S., Bauermeister, J. A., & Zimmerman, M. A. (2011). Do parents and peers matter? A prospective social-ecological examination of substance use and sexual risk among African American youth. *Journal of Adolescence, 34*, 1035–1047. doi:10.1016/j.adolescence.2010.11.004

Ellwood, R. S., & McGraw, B. A. (2010). *Many peoples, many faiths*. Los Angeles, CA: Pearson.

Evans, K., & Sullivan, J. M. (2001). *Dual diagnosis* (2nd ed.). New York, NY: Guilford Press.

Fahy, A. (2007). The unbearable fatigue of compassion: Notes from a substance abuse counselor who dreams of working at Starbucks. *Clinical Social Work Journal, 35*, 199–205.

Feinberg, M. E. (2012). Community epidemiology of risk and adolescent substance use: Practical questions for enhancing prevention. *American Journal of Public Health, 12*(3), 457–468.

Felix-Ortiz, M., & Newcomb, M. D. (1992). Risk and protective factors for drug use among Latino and white adolescents. *Hispanic Journal of Behavioral Sciences, 14*(3), 291–309.

Field grapples with sobriety time for counselors in recovery. (2006, December 11). *Alcoholism & Drug Abuse Weekly, 18*(47), 3–4.

Fowler, J. W. (1981). *Stages of faith: The psychology of human development and the quest for meaning.* New York, NY: Harper & Row.

Garnefski, N., & Okma, S. (1996). Addictions-risk and aggressive/criminal behavior in adolescence: Influence of family, school, and peers. *Journal of Adolescence, 19,* 503–512.

Goodman, A. (2001). What's in a name? Terminology for designating a syndrome of driven sexual behavior. *Sexual Addiction & Compulsivity, 8,* 191–213.

Grant, J. E., Brewer, J. A., & Potenza, M. N. (2006). The neurobiology of substance and behavioral addictions. *CNS Spectrums, 11*(12), 924–930.

Grant, J. E., Potenza, M. N., Weinstein, A., & Gorelick, D. A. (2010). Introduction to behavioral addictions. *American Journal of Drug and Alcohol Abuse, 36*(5), 233–241.

Hagedorn, W. B. (2009). The call for a new *Diagnostic and Statistical Manual of Mental Disorders* diagnosis: Addictive disorders. *Journal of Addictions & Offender Counseling, 29,* 110–127.

Hagedorn, W. B., & Young, T. (2011). Identifying and intervening with students exhibiting signs of gaming addiction and other addictive behaviors: Implications for professional school counselors. *Professional School Counseling, 14*(4), 250–260.

Hawkins, J. D., Catalano, R. F., & Miller, J. Y. (1992). Risk and protective factors for alcohol and other drug problems in adolescence and early adulthood: Implications for substance abuse prevention. *Psychological Bulletin, 112*(1), 64–105.

Heinz, A., Epstein, D. H., & Preston, K. L. (2007). Spiritual/religious experiences and in-treatment outcome in an inner-city program for heroin and cocaine dependence. *Journal of Psychoactive Drugs, 39*(1), 41–49.

Hurd, Y. L., Michaelides, M., Miller, M. L., & Jutras-Aswad, D. (2014). Trajectory of adolescent cannabis use on addiction vulnerability. *Neuropharmacology, 76,* 416–424.

Isaacson, J. H., Hopper, M. J. A., Alford, M. D. P., & Parran, M. T. (2005). Prescription drug use and abuse. *Postgraduate Medicine, 118*(1), 19–26.

Jacobs, D. F. (2005). Youth gambling in North America. In *Gambling problems in youth* (pp. 1–24). New York: Springer.

Kaczmarek, P. (2000). Ethical and legal complexities inherit in professional roles with child and adolescent clients. *Counseling and Human Development, 33*(1), 1–24.

King, D. L., Delfabbro, P. H., Griffiths, M. D., & Gradisar, M. (2012). Cognitive-behavioral approaches to outpatient treatment of internet addictions in children and adolescents. *Journal of Clinical Psychology: In Session, 68*(11), 1185–1195.

Koenig, H., King, D., & Carson, V. B. (2012). *Handbook of religion and health.* New York, NY: Oxford University Press.

Kurti, A. N., & Dallery, J. (2012). Review of Heyman's addiction: A disorder of choice. *Journal of Applied Behavioral Analysis, 45*(1), 229–240.

Kwon, M., Kim, D., Cho, H., & Yang, S. (2013). The smartphone addiction scale: Development and validation of a short version for adolescents. *PLoS ONE, 8*(12), 1–7.

Lassiter, P. S., & Chang, C. Y. (2008). Perceived multicultural competency of certified substance abuse counselors. *Journal of Addiction and Offender Counseling, 26,* 73–83.

Macaulay, A. P., Griffin, K. W., Gronewold, E., Williams, C., & Botvin, G. J. (2005). Parenting practices and adolescent drug-related knowledge, attitudes, norms and behavior. *Journal of Alcohol and Drug Education, 49*(2), 67–83.

Marsh, C. N. (2011). *Help-seeking decisions among college students: The impact of mental health service affordability* (Unpublished doctoral dissertation). University of Alabama, Tuscaloosa. Retrieved from http://acumen.lib.ua.edu/u0015_0000001_0000794/document/u0015_000 0001_0000794?page=1&limit=40

McCord, J. M. (1998, January). Iron, free radicals, and oxidative injury. In Seminars in hematology (Vol. 35, No. 1, pp. 5–12).

McCullough, M., & Willoughby, B. (2009). Religion, self-regulation, and self-control: Associations, explanations, and implications. *Psychological Bulletin, 135,* 69–93.

McPherson, T. L., & Hersch, R. K. (2000). Brief substance use screening instruments for primary care settings: A review. *Journal of Substance Abuse Treatment, 18,* 193–202.

Miller, W. R. (1998). Researching the spiritual dimensions of alcohol and other drug problems. *Addiction, 93*(7), 979–990.

Monti, P. M., Barnett, N. P., O'Leary, T. A., & Colby, S. M. (2001). Motivational enhancement for alcohol-involved adolescents. In P. M. Monti, S. M. Colby, & T. A. O'Leary (Eds.), *Adolescents, alcohol, and substance abuse: Reaching teens through brief interventions* (pp. 145–182). New York, NY: Guilford Press.

Moore, K. A., Peters, R. H., Hills, H. A., LeVasseur, J. B., Rich, A. R., Hunt, W. M., . . . Valente, T. W. (2004). Characteristics of opinion leaders in substance abuse treatment agencies. *American Journal of Drug and Alcohol Abuse, 30*(1), 187–204.

Moos, R. H. (2007). Theory-based processes that promote the remission of substance use disorders. *Clinical Psychology Review, 27,* 537–551.

National Institute on Alcohol Abuse and Alcoholism. (2005). *Alcohol alert: Screening for alcohol use and alcohol related problems.* Bethesda, MD: National Institutes of Health. Retrieved from http://pubs.niaaa.nih.gov/publications/aa65/AA65.htm

National Institute on Drug Abuse. (2014a). Evidence-based approaches to treating adolescent substance use disorders. In *Principles of adolescent substance use disorder treatment: A research-based guide.* Retrieved from http://www.drugabuse.gov/publications/principles-adolescent-substance-use-disorder-treatment-research-based-guide/evidence-based-approaches-to-treating-adolescent-substance-use-disorders

National Institute on Drug Abuse. (2014b, January). *Principles of adolescent substance use disorder treatment: A research-based guide* (NIH Publication 14-7953). Retrieved from http://www.drugabuse.gov/sites/default/files/podata_1_17_14.pdf

Nowinski, J. (1990). *Substance abuse in adolescents and young adults: A guide to treatment.* New York, NY: W. W. Norton.

O'Donnell, L., Stueve, A., Duran, R., Myint-U, A., Agronick, G., San Doval, A., & Wilson-Simmons, R. (2008). Parenting practices, parents' underestimation of daughters' risks, and alcohol and sexual behaviors of urban girls. *Journal of Adolescent Health, 42*(5), 496–502.

Orford, J., Copello, A., Velleman, R., & Templeton, L. (2010). Family members affected by a close relative's addiction: The stress-strain-coping-support model. *Drugs: Education, Prevention and Policy, 17*(S1), 36–43.

Perepletchikova, F., Krystal, J. H., & Kaufman, J. (2008). Practitioner review: Adolescent alcohol use disorders: Assessment and treatment issues. *Journal of Child Psychology and Psychiatry, 49*(11), 1131–1154. doi:10.1111/j.1469-7610-2008-01934.x

Peterson, J. (2010). A qualitative comparison of parent and adolescent views regarding substance use. *Journal of School Nursing, 26*(1), 53–64. doi:10.1177/1059840509355586

Rabbi Moshe ben Asher, P. (2001, October 20). Spirituality and religion in social work practice. *Social Work Today, 1*(7), 1–5.

Rastogi, M., & Wadha, S. (2006). Substance abuse among Asian Indians in the United States: A consideration of cultural factors in etiology and treatment. *Substance Use & Misuse, 41,* 1239–1249.

Richardson, C. G., Memetovic, J., Ratner, P. A., & Johnson, J. L. (2011). Examining gender differences in emerging tobacco use using the adolescents' need for smoking scale. *Addiction, 106,* 1846–1854. doi:10.1111/j.1360-0443.2011.03496.x

Saitz, R., Mulvey, K. P., Plough, A., & Samet, J. H. (1997). Physician unawareness of serious substance abuse. *American Journal of Drug and Alcohol Abuse, 23*(3), 343–354.

Schaeffer, B. (1987). *Is it love or is it addiction: Falling into healthy love.* New York: Harper and Row.

Shelef, K., Diamond, G. M., Diamond, G. S., & Liddle, H. A. (2005). Adolescent and parent alliance and treatment outcome in multidimensional family therapy. *Journal of Consulting and Clinical Psychology, 73*(4), 689–698.

Smith, C., & Denton, M. L. (2005). *Soul-searching: The religious and spiritual lives of American teenagers.* New York, NY: Oxford University Press.

Staussner, L. (2004). *Clinical work with substance-abusing clients* (2nd ed.). New York, NY: Guilford Press.

Substance Abuse and Mental Health Services Administration. (2011). *Results from the 2010 National Survey on Drug Use and Health: Summary of national findings.* Bethesda, MD: U.S. Department of Health and Human Services.

Substance Abuse and Mental Health Services Administration. (2013a, August 29). *The CBHSQ report: A day in the life of American adolescents: Substance use facts update.* Retrieved from http://www.samhsa.gov/data/2K13/CBHSQ128/sr128-typical-day-adolescents-2013.htm

Substance Abuse and Mental Health Services Administration. (2013b, September). *Results from the 2012 national survey on drug use and health: Summary of national findings* (NSDUH Series H-46, HHS Publication No. SMA 13-4795). Rockville, MD: Author. Retrieved from http://www.samhsa.gov/data/nsduh/2012summnatfinddettables/nationalfindings/nsduhresults2012.htm

Sussman, S. (2010). A review of Alcoholics Anonymous/Narcotics Anonymous programs for teens. *Evaluation & the Health Professions, 33*(1), 26–55. doi:10.1177/0163278709356186

Taylor, J., Lloyd, D. A., & Warheit, G. J. (2005). Self-derogation, peer factors, and drug dependence among a multiethnic sample of young adults. *Journal of Child & Adolescent Substance Abuse, 15*(2), 39–51. doi:10.1300/J029v15n02_03

Villella, C., Martinotti, G., DiNicola, M., Cassano, M., LaTorre, G., Gliubizzi, M. D., . . . Conte, G. (2011). Behavioral dependences in adolescents and young adults: Results from a prevalence study. *Journal of Gambling Studies, 27,* 203–214.

Winters, K., Botzet, A., & Fahnhorst, T. (2011). Advances in adolescent substance abuse treatment. *Current Psychiatry Reports, 13*(5), 416–421. doi:10.1007/s11920-011-0214-2

Wong, E. C., & Longshore, D. (2008). Ethnic identity, spirituality, and self-efficacy influences on treatment among Hispanic American methadone maintenance clients. *Journal of Ethnicity in Substance Abuse, 7*(3), 328–340.

Zenmore, S. E., Mulia Ye, N., Borges, G., & Greenfield, T. K. (2008). Gender, acculturation, and other barriers to alcohol treatment utilization among Latinos in three national alcohol surveys. *Journal of Substance Abuse Treatment, 36,* 446–445.

Zucker, R. A., Donovan, J. E., Masten, A. S., Mattson, M. E., & Moss, H. B. (2009). Developmental processes and mechanisms: Ages 0–10. *Alcohol Research & Health, 32*(1), 16–29.

14

Divorce Impact

Introduction

Divorce in the United States is an issue. Studies repeatedly show that the divorce rate in the United States hovers around 50% and that the rate of divorce has changed from previous decades (Kennedy & Ruggles, 2014). This information reflects that multiple generations have been affected by divorce and that divorce remains a relevant treatment issue for mental health providers.

Wallerstein, Lewis, and Blakeslee (2000), in their well-known and often-cited longitudinal research on divorce, note that the impact on children and adolescents is not just felt during the time of the divorce. Since publication in 2000, divorce trends and statistics have developed, reflecting some of what Wallerstein et al. (2000) purport, including that divorce is a life-changing experience for all involved and that many times the toll on children and adolescents is correlated with psychological, emotional, educational, self-esteem, anger and aggression, substance abuse, and relational issues (VanderValk, Spruijt, de Goede, Maas, & Meeus, 2005). While most researchers agree that divorce can be detrimental, and there is often tragedy and heartache for many involved, the idea has also surfaced that the impact of divorce has overfocused on the negative and neglected to consider any hopeful results of divorce (Wallerstein, Lewis, Blakeslee, Hetherington, & Kelly, 2005).

While 50% is often accepted and cited as the number of annual divorces, the details behind the statistic reveal that divorce has drastically increased in recent years rather than leveled off or declined. Divorce rates in the United States have been recorded for close to 150 years, but numbers are irregular and inconsistent across the nation. Currently, statistics are more accurately drawn from the 2008 addition of specific questions regarding divorce, remarriage, and widowing. Numbers strongly reflect that divorce in the United States rose 40% between 1980 and 2010 (Kennedy & Ruggles, 2014).

Both the rate of divorce and the reasons behind divorce matter when reviewing the national statistics. Over the past few decades, there has been a shift in the patterns behind divorce, including cultural, gender, and age-related patterns, as well as the length of marriage and the rate of remarriage. A few such patterns include that the duration of marriage has increased, the age at which one marries has increased, and the rate of remarriage has decreased. Although divorce statistics have been gathered sporadically and inconsistently through the past 150 years, sociological changes and current divorce trends are affecting adolescents because the experience is more common and acceptable. Adolescents are no longer singled out as different or experiencing the same amount or depth of problems as data showed previously, nor are all divorces high conflict or devastating to family and individual functioning (Gatins, Kinlaw, & Dunlap, 2013; Kelly & Emery, 2003; Kennedy & Ruggles, 2014). The challenge before the provider is to digest the information regarding the impact of divorce and how statistics and commonality has changed in recent years.

The objective of this chapter is to provide readers with general knowledge of how divorce may affect adolescent clients and the counseling process. After reading this chapter, readers will be able to do the following:

- Identify three main cultural themes in divorce that should be considered when counseling adolescents and their families

- Identify how changing social trends have affected divorce rates in American society

- Describe factors in the adolescent's life that may mediate his or her experience of divorce, including cultural issues related to mediating factors

- Demonstrate research-based knowledge on how divorce can affect an adolescent relationally and emotionally

- Gain basic knowledge on what research indicates as far as how divorce affects adolescents and adults interpersonally

- Describe how separation and divorce, including parental conflict and alienation, change the dynamics of the family system and each member's role

- Increase awareness of posttraumatic stress disorder, including posttraumatic growth in adolescents

- Demonstrate how grit and protective factors interplay in adolescent counseling

- Understand cultural, individual, and adolescent elements conducive to a productive and supportive therapeutic environment

- Demonstrate application of knowledge from this chapter to a case scenario

- Understand the ethical implications in working with adolescents of parents who are in

the process of a divorce or have divorced (or separated)

- Apply knowledge gleaned from case scenarios

CULTURAL CONSIDERATIONS

There are three main cultural themes in divorce. First, the divorce rates are higher in individualistic and industrialized countries. Divorce prevalence in the United States is often understood to exist because of availability and attitudes toward divorce as an *actual* option for those involved. However, providers might consider that even with overarching individualistic or collectivistic themes, there are variations in different microcultures or networks that affect the decision to divorce or the way in which a couple/family might experience divorce. For example, an individual's social network (that exists within the larger individualistic society) might affect the decision a couple makes to stay in a deteriorating relationship or divorce. Also, divorce changes how the miniature family network relates, communicates, and survives a massive shift in its previous structure (Afifi, Davis, Denes, & Merrill, 2013; Toth & Kemmelmeier, 2009). A second theme is that divorce rates are higher in countries with educated and financially independent women. Afifi et al. (2013) note that in the United States immigrant women have more options for divorce, as they might come from cultures that limit their rights and power within the marital relationship and cultures that encourage community and family over individual wants or needs. Third, divorce rates are lower in cultures that have a religious focus. For individuals seeking divorce, religious affiliation can serve as a deterrent because of solidified social connections and ties that affect an individual's or couple's behaviors, beliefs, and decisions. The impact of social networks is important here too, where couples might feel that they have limited options because of a religious group they are affiliated with that does not encourage or support divorce or possibly the loss of support postdivorce. Other notable cultural themes include age, ethnicity and race, geographic location, and social class (Afifi et al., 2013; Mullins, Brackett, Bogie, & Pruett, 2004).

Given these cultural ideas, providers are urged to consider divorce from multiple angles, cognizant of how broader cultural attitudes affect divorce and how an adolescent's experience might be affected by the strength of his or her social networks (e.g., other friends whose parents have been through a divorce) or gaps in his or her social networks (e.g., an adolescent with few friends is more isolated). Additionally, cultural and generational issues must be factored in, as adolescents experience divorce that contradict other values they adhere to (Afifi et al., 2013; Toth & Kemmelmeier, 2009). For example, an adolescent's parents might choose to divorce even though the family's religious affiliation discourages divorce. Overall, when considering the mental health and treatment needs of adolescents encountering a divorce situation, providers must consider the variety of ways by which one individual can experience different perspectives on divorce, such that the experience might be an intricate blend of the adolescent's individual experience, gender and age, as well as "generational differences, cultural differences, power, religion and immigration patterns" (Afifi et al., 2013, p. 244).

Changing Social Trends

Current statistics reflect that divorce is more common than it was even two decades ago. The divorce rate for baby boomers is higher than for those who were born before World War II; baby boomers continue to divorce at a rapid rate as they age, and they also divorce more easily than previous generations. There are fewer legal constraints, additional social and economic choices for women, not to mention less of a social stigma (Kennedy & Ruggles, 2014; Mullins et al., 2004; Toth & Kemmelmeier, 2009). As more couples divorce, the experience is more common with a widening variety of social, cultural, and religious

circles. This means that more adolescents are experiencing turbulent family environments where parents have decided to separate, divorce, and possibly remarry. These changes allow for developing and transforming attitudes toward divorce, pushing the cultural boundaries of what is socially acceptable regarding marriage and divorce as well as developing a pattern of what is "normal" in American culture.

As divorce rates change, adolescents are entering a period of time when divorce is more common as an option, but the cultural structure of marriage has also changed. Fewer young people are choosing to marry early; it is becoming more common to marry after the age of 30, choose cohabitation over marriage, or never marry. This in and of itself would lower the national divorce rate. It is possible that if these individuals did choose to marry earlier—that is, in their 20s, the divorce rate would have stayed the same or continued to increase, as it has been with the baby boomers. Education and economic options for women broaden choices for women to select a life and relational style that they prefer, outside of what was acceptable in previous years—to marry for relational connection and financial stability. Also, because options have increased, younger people might choose more carefully who they want to marry, which is possibly someone different from who they might have married at an earlier stage in life before they finished adolescence and in the beginning years of young adulthood. Even as options increase and cultural acceptance flexes, and generational cohorts reveal trends of marital stability, relationships are still at risk of producing painful and high-conflict splits (Kennedy & Ruggles, 2014; Toth & Kemmelmeier, 2009).

Mediating Factors

As providers and researchers adjust to more sophisticated research methodologies and cultural adjustment to divorce, mediating factors are getting more attention. Mediating factors are those aspects of an adolescent's life and development that have a weighted impact on how he or she handles day-to-day life. Research supports that there are a number of equally important factors that affect an adolescent's interpersonal stability other than the divorce itself (Lansford, 2009; Sandler, Wheeler, & Braver, 2013; Simons, Simons, Landor, Bryant, & Beach, 2014). Personality, age of the adolescent at the time of divorce, predivorce adjustment, community and religious group views, parenting style, level of interparental conflict, and aspects of the legal process are some examples of mediating factors that must be considered in an adolescent's experience of the divorce process. Adolescents might also have to handle aspects specific to the divorce process such as court involvement, attorneys, court-appointed professionals, mental health professionals, mediators, visitation, and custody issues. Other mediating factors include but are not limited to the presence of relational strife with the family system, cultural background and intergenerational connections, communication issues, economic status, and quality of parenting. As reflected in the aforementioned lists, divorce presents adolescents a complicated set of factors to navigate. Table 14.1 offers a summary of characteristics and variables that mediate the link between divorce and adolescent well-being.

Cultural Issues and Mediating Factors

Mediating factors are of particular importance when a provider maintains sensitivity to cultural issues within interpersonal relationships, particularly in an industrialized and individualistic country. As our culture expands, research reflects that views on divorce are not categorical or linear, but instead, they are integrative to include personal beliefs and cultural values. To say the least, culture and the level of represented individualism in a society or group has a tremendous and complex influence on attitudes toward divorce, where specifics of the situation, principles, and consequences are considered at varying degrees (e.g., Toth & Kemmelmeier, 2009). For example, Simons et al. (2014) focused on an African American sample and mediating

Table 14.1 Mediating Variables to Consider in Divorce Research and Treatment

Adolescent characteristics
  Age at time of divorce
  Personality
  Loss and change in important parental relationships
  Mental health issues
  Predivorce adjustment
  Stage of development
Demographic characteristics
  Legal issues
    Divorce laws and policies
    Grounds for divorce
    Child custody policies
    Child support policies and enforcement
    Stress of the initial separation
Family and parenting characteristics
  Interparental conflict
  Intergenerational connections
  Parents' well-being
  Predivorce family adjustment
  Quality of parenting
  Quality of parenting postdivorce
Social and economic characteristics
  Income
  Religious beliefs
  Stigmatization of divorce
Additional issues to consider
  Remarriage, stepparents, or stepsiblings
  Genetic effects

Source. Kelly, J. B., & Emery, R. E. (2003). Children's adjustment following divorce: Risk and resilience perspectives. *Family Relations*, 52, 352–362.

variables linked to adult romantic relationships. The authors looked at quality of parenting (i.e., supportive/nurturing, hostile/aggressive) and other constructs (e.g., anger management) as important to determining how familial experience affects an adult's formulation of romantic relationships. Their findings support the idea of multiple mediating variables determining relational skills for adults, indicating that "children appear to acquire scripts or skills that are tacitly relied upon and enacted during interaction with romantic partners" (Simons et al., 2014, p. 376).

EMOTIONAL AND RELATIONAL IMPLICATIONS OF DIVORCE

Much research on the impact of divorce focuses on childhood and adolescent experience and how they fare educationally, relationally, and emotionally, as well as how divorce affects them in adulthood. Research repeatedly shows that children are heavily affected by divorce in multiple areas of functioning, although research is expanding to include changing cultural acceptance with divorce, lower social stigma, and changing statistics. Developmentally, research repeatedly indicates that adolescent response to divorce has its strongest impact "in the areas of psychological adjustment, self-concept, behavior/conduct, educational achievement, and social relations" (VanderValk et al., 2005, p. 534). Adolescents usually have more difficulty during a divorce and soon after it is final, with diminishing effects as they emerge into adulthood. Throughout adolescence, an adolescent might experience more educational performance issues, psychological and emotional problems, problem relationships, early sexual experiences and intercourse, behavioral and conduct issues, as well as lower levels of psychological well-being (Lansford, 2009; VanderValk et al., 2005).

Research presents conflicting evidence that sparks debate regarding the impact of divorce. While it is common to see divorce as an isolated, negative event, providers must consider additional factors that mediate an adolescent's well-being. In other words, what other factors might affect an adolescent's experience of parental separation and divorce. Table 14.2 provides a list

Table 14.2   Mediating Factors

Mediating factors that influence the impact of divorce on adolescent well-being
Specifics of a divorce situation
Level of violence
Level of familial discord/parental discord
Financial security and economic problems
An adolescent's developing personality
Social preferences
Social network
Existence of other stressful situations
Social, emotional, cognitive, and personality issues that impact an adolescent during or after divorce or into adulthood
Age and developmental stage
Marital conflict
Parenting time
Parenting practices
Custody arrangements
Quality of parenting

of several factors that may affect the impact of divorce on an adolescent's well-being. For instance, specifics of a divorce situation would be important to understand, including level of violence and discord, financial security and economic problems, an adolescent's developing personality, social preferences, social network, and existing stressful situations, such as academic challenges. Also, not all adolescents experience devastating effects from parental divorce. Lansford (2009) notes,

> The majority of children whose parents divorce do not have long-term adjustment problems, but the risk of externalizing behaviors, internalizing problems, poorer academic achievement, and problematic social relationships is greater for children whose parents divorce than for those whose parents stay together. Different children may manifest adjustment problems in different ways. (p. 142)

Therefore, maintaining awareness of common risk factors and the repetition of problems noted in research, providers understand that there are social, emotional, cognitive, and personality issues that can affect an adolescent both during and after a divorce, even into adulthood. Research has expanded and matured, moving beyond dichotomous categories of intact and divorced families to including factors such as age, marital conflict, parenting time and practices, custody arrangements, and quality of parenting (Amato, 2005; American Psychological Association, 2004; Gatins et al., 2013; Kelly & Emery, 2003; Lacey, Kumari, & McMunn, 2013; Sandler et al., 2013; VanderValk et al., 2005). Adolescence is well-known as a critical period for development and a particularly sensitive time when life situations can have lasting effects and influences growth stages to come (Erikson, 1994). As mentioned previously, most agree that divorce is a challenging situation that affects all involved, yet debate continues as to which factors determine why some adolescents carry psychological and relational issues into adulthood and some do not. Overall, with multiple longitudinal studies, improved research methodologies, and attention to mediating factors, the impact of divorce remains both controversial and complex.

Gender Differences

For adolescents, disruption and upset to the family system can aggravate mental health issues such as depression and anxiety, and social and relationship difficulties, compounding difficulties in the individuation process expected in adolescence. Data regarding gender-specific problems within divorce are inconclusive; however, research results repeatedly reveal that both boys and girls face challenges when their parents divorce, at the roles they might be "asked" to play, and due to the impact of the divorce. Both boys and girls can feel torn or caught in the middle as their parents proceed through a divorce process, and both boys and girls can be engaged in helping their parents solve disagreements or manage the difficulties of divorce through parentification, triangulation, or parental alienation as parents compete for leverage and stability in the process (Baker & Ben-Ami, 2011; Gatins et al., 2013; Kelly & Johnston, 2001; Perrin, Ehrenberg, & Hunter, 2013).

Family Systems and Adolescent Developmental Stage

One element of divorce as it relates to adolescent development is how the experience of divorce affects an adolescent's relational health. From a family systems perspective, divorce interrupts an adolescent's experience of clear, separate, hierarchical relationships in which he or she is able to develop appropriate relational skills (Perrin et al., 2013). Providers must remember that both adolescent boys and girls are affected by relational strain between their parents and any diffusion of boundaries between parent and child, such as the pull for emotional support or loyalty to one parent or another. With parents who are separated, divorcing, or divorced, adolescents remain sensitive to the presence and intensity of conflict and feeling "caught" between their parents. Especially during a time when an adolescent is accomplishing aspects of individuation and navigating changes within the parent–child dyad, changes in the marital dyad heighten the risk of emotional dysfunction that might be internalized or externalized (American Psychological Association, 2004; Lansford, 2009; Perrin et al., 2013).

Attachment Theory and Relational Development

Attachment theory is a long-standing theory that individuals vary in their ability to relate to others throughout life based partly on the quality of the relationships they had in early years. Supportive and unsupportive caregiving relationships can affect whether an individual is insecure or secure in relationships later in life. Such research is important when considering how divorce changes an adolescent's family and caregiving experience, as well as how the experience shapes secure or insecure relational patterns for the teen. Fraley and Heffernan (2013) progressed attachment research by looking at how an early experience, such as divorce, produces attachment styles that are not only broad and overarching but also relationally specific. Traditionally, attachment research has had a general overview. Table 14.3

offers a review of the varying attachment styles, the parenting style, and the resultant relational development of the child or adolescent. Meaning, an adolescent who experiences an insecure caregiving environment will emerge into adulthood with an insecure relational style. Research looking at specific situations such as parental divorce can help providers understand how attachment styles might translate into adulthood in different ways, leaving the possibility that an adolescent's ability to develop strong, secure relationships later in life is more nuanced and contextual than a direct, linear link between divorce and insecurity in interpersonal relationships.

These results reflect that while there are implications for an adolescent who experiences parental divorce, insecure attachments are not always the result. The insecure relationships might be more specific within the parent–child relationship, possibly in a relationship that was more fragile to begin with, and that outside of this parent–child relationship, there are more chances for secure adult attachments (Fraley & Heffernan, 2013). Ongoing life experiences change how an adolescent relates to others in both family and extrafamilial relationships.

Table 14.3   Attachment Styles

Secure	*Avoidant*	*Ambivalent*	*Disorganized*
Secure, explorative, happy	Not very explorative, emotionally distant	Anxious, insecure, angry	Depressed, angry, completely passive, nonresponsive
Aligned with the child, in tune with/ sensitive to the child's emotions	Unavailable or rejecting	Inconsistent and sometimes intrusive parent communication	Ignore, don't see child's needs, parental behavior was frightening/ traumatizing
Believes and trusts that his or her needs will be met	Subconsciously believes that his or her needs likely will not be met	Cannot trust that his or her needs will be met	Confused and unaware of how to have his or her needs met
Able to create meaningful relationships, empathic, able to set appropriate boundaries	Avoids closeness or emotional connection, distant, critical, rigid, intolerant	Anxious and insecure, controlling, blaming, erratic, unpredictable, sometimes charming	Chaotic, insensitive, explosive, abusive, untrusting but at the same time desiring security

Source. From Ainsworth, Blehar, Waters, and Wall (1978), Main, Kaplan, and Cassidy (1985), and Sigelman and Rider (2012).

While attachment styles are often understood in a linear fashion, such that secure attachments in childhood set the stage for secure attachments in adulthood (and vice versa), interpersonal experiences *throughout* different stages of development affect the shaping of an individual's ability to function emotionally in relationships, including extrafamilial relationships (Fraley, Roisman, Booth-LaForce, Owen, & Holland, 2013). Providers cannot adequately attend to an adolescent's experience of divorce, or an adult whose parents divorced, with a simplistic understanding of attachments. Ongoing relational experiences in adolescence, including extrafamilial relationships, such as friendships and therapeutic relationships, offer an adolescent chances at increasing or decreasing social and emotional competence, negotiating emotions as he or she emerge in relationships. A few examples include an adolescent navigating stages of personal growth and development, maintenance of relationships, endurance of hardship, and growth of self-awareness, all of which would affect emotional existence in intimate relationships. Providers can work to capitalize on a variety of emotional and relational experiences throughout childhood and adulthood beyond divorcing parents, including those in caregiving, social, therapeutic, and educational settings that might be important to an adolescent client.

Table 14.4   Developmental Risk Factors for Adolescents

Risk factors associated with social and emotional growth through divorce

- Ability to form and maintain close intimate relationships
- A foundational sense of self and individual psychological characteristics
- Perseverance
- Resilience
- Self-control
- Self-esteem

For providers treating adolescents enduring parental divorce, or adults whose parents divorced, treatment might focus on what scripts or skills were formulated that relate to intimate, emotional relationships and attachment styles. This is of particular importance because social support systems are a critical element in an adolescent (or adult) handling the impact of challenging life events such as divorce. If there are difficulties with trust, self-esteem, anger management issues, and recognition and expression of emotions, it is likely that these mediating factors will affect the quality of relationships an adult is able to create and maintain later in life, including his or her own romantic relationships, marriage, or extrafamilial friendships.

Developmental Risk Factors

Family of origin is understood to be the foundational influence for childhood experience of function or dysfunction, intervening in the way an adolescent views oneself and others. Divorce can affect the formation of insecurities and dysfunction in romantic relationships, although, as noted above, research is expanding to present other factors as important to understanding an adult's emotional and relational functioning. Divorce is not always a singular factor in determining whether a child experiences an array of problems based on his or her parent's divorce (American Psychological Association, 2004; Fraley & Heffernan, 2013; Lansford, 2009; Wallerstein et al., 2005).

An adolescent's social and emotional growth through divorce is related to a set of risk factors, including the ability to form and maintain close, intimate relationships; a foundational sense of self and individual psychological characteristics; and having skills such as perseverance, resilience, and self-control (see Table 14.4). With regard to self-esteem, research supports that younger children and adolescents whose parents divorce are at a higher risk for developing both emotional and behavioral issues because they may not be able to psychologically or cognitively adjust to the reality of the divorce and the reasons behind it. As a result, it is possible that they internalize the situation and blame themselves, something that might happen before they have the chance at individuation because the divorce is occurring during a sensitive developmental period (Fraley & Heffernan, 2013; Haine, Sandler, Wolchik, Tein, & Dawson-McClure, 2003; Lansford, 2009; Simons et al., 2014).

EMOTIONAL AND RELATIONAL IMPLICATIONS OF DIVORCE IN ADULTHOOD

Many research studies have looked at whether parental divorce has a lasting impact on a child or adolescent's view of and existence in intimate, romantic relationships. Experience with the strain of divorce, changes in the family system, introduction of new family members (e.g., a parent's boyfriend or girlfriend, stepparents, stepsiblings), exposure to long-term parental conflict, abuse, and domestic violence are all factors that challenge an adolescent's ability to exist in emotionally intimate relationships with strong interpersonal skills (American Psychological Association, 2004; Lansford, 2009; Simons et al., 2014). Essentially, research has been inconclusive regarding divorce being a precursor to a child or adolescent's marital quality in adulthood.

Challenges in the Research Process

A number of studies have looked at how divorce affects interpersonal issues and the challenges of measuring such results. First, the difficulty of studying parental divorce and the impact on offspring often has multiple limitations, including that recalling negative life events might sway a respondent to recall a situation more negatively. Second, longitudinal studies of both parents and their children (i.e., not just one or the other) are rare, and many times the age of the respondent at the time of the study is not always the age at the time of the divorce. Third, the normative parent–child difficulties and changes experienced during adolescence can filter

research participant answers, possibly overemphasizing the negative and underrepresenting resilience and adjustment. This highlights the negative attributes of divorcing parents as compared with parents in an intact marriage (Gatins et al., 2013). Fourth, a growing body of research reflects that the parenting quality is a highly important mediator when determining whether a child or an adolescent experiences long-term problems as a result of parental divorce. These studies again point to the importance of mediating variables in an adolescent's life and development before naming divorce as the foundational link between interpersonal problems, intergenerational transmission of divorce, interpersonal limitations or skill deficits, mental health difficulties, and emotional maturity (Amato, 2005; Amato & Booth, 2001; Gatins et al., 2013; Lansford, 2009; Simons et al., 2014).

Adult Functioning and the Sleeper Effect

This also highlights the importance for providers to remember, with an adult client, to adequately attend to the impact of divorce experienced as a child or adolescent, as there may be residual emotional or relational issues. As adolescents who experience divorce situations age, they come in contact with life situations that challenge the social and emotional maturity that divorce may have affected. For example, the negative effects or challenges of divorce for an adolescent will look different at ages 14, 21, and 35. The challenges that an adolescent encounters at any given age with regard to parental divorce might prove to be stressful in different ways at different ages.

Amato (2010) notes that within the research regarding divorce, studies are cropping up that look at the positive aspects of a marital relationship that can help sustain and stabilize a relationship, such as humor and forgiveness. Additional research can be done in these areas that might affect treatment provision for adolescents who might need additional support in learning positive interpersonal skills that clearly affect divorce rates and marital satisfaction, as well as teaching positive relational skills that would affect their emotional development and adult relationships later in life. Providing emotional care and support to adolescents experiencing divorce, especially regarding the knowledge and research available on the impact of divorce, can set adolescents up for seeking help at other times in their lives. For example, one adolescent who experienced supportive and educational counseling while her parents divorced might be more willing to seek help or might be more open to premarital education or marital therapy or she might deal with lingering distress, painful memories, or feelings of loss that need to be resolved (Kelly & Emery, 2003; Williamson, Trail, Bradbury, & Karney, 2014). Knowledge of available help acclimates adolescents or young adults to possible interventions, as well as increases their awareness of how their family history might affect their approach to marriage, commitment, and risk level for divorce.

The Sleeper Effect

Not all affecting elements of a divorce will show up before and during the occurrence. As noted earlier, the research regarding the impact of divorce is variable and controversial. Findings suggest that adolescents adjust to their family situation in a variety of ways. Maturation plays a factor in an adolescent's response, as well as intervening relationships and positive life experiences outside of familial discord. There is some evidence that delayed effects exist for children and adolescents of divorce. This theory suggests that some adolescents cope well during the divorce but see more challenges and difficulties surface later in life. This is referred to as the "sleeper effect." Research addresses this concept with longitudinal studies, finding that adolescents reach adulthood and begin to interact with their personal belief systems surrounding romance, intimacy, commitment, and marriage (Chase-Lansdale, Cherlin, & Kiernan, 1995; Kelly & Emery, 2003; VanderValk et al., 2005).

Providers aware of such theories can set the stage for an adolescent's view of help seeking,

including future issues that might arise because an adolescent client addresses issues of marital role models, commitment, and emotional interactions. Help seeking can move beyond the issues of the moment and integrate the idea that divorce is not an emotionally mutually exclusive life event but one that can compound an adolescent's problems in adult relationships and marital stability. As providers help adolescents navigate healthy responses to the emotional turmoil divorce can bring, seeing divorce as a long-term issue can be helpful. Cultural elements exist in this realm too. Risk factors that affect help seeking in marital health include, but are not limited to, social economic status, ethnicity, and level of education (Williamson et al., 2014). Without attaching a stigma, a provider can reflect to adolescent clients how current and potential problems might reveal themselves, laying the groundwork for a pathway to help seeking later in life.

FAMILY SYSTEMS, RELATIONAL BOUNDARIES, AND LEGAL ISSUES

Parentification and Triangulation

An adolescent's adjustment in a divorce situation includes challenging experiences within family dynamics, including the possibility that parents look to their children for emotional support (Kelly & Emery, 2003; Perrin et al., 2013) or to help regulate and solve family problems. Family system issues, such as triangulation, parentification, or blurred relational boundaries can emerge or be magnified during divorce. *Parentification* is a term that describes when a child or adolescent plays an adult role in the family from loosened or diffused generational boundaries. This might look like an adolescent who provides a peer relationship to a parent or helps as a caregiver to a parent who expresses a variety of needs during a divorce. *Triangulation* is commonly referred to within family systems when a child or adolescent plays a role in the marital dyad to help alter or resolve disagreements. Adolescents might be highly involved as "referees" or they might be more of messengers who relay information between parents (e.g., "You tell your dad that if he does not keep to the assigned custody schedule . . ."). Triangulation is highly problematic because it can breed competition for the adolescent's attention, support, or love, often putting the adolescent in a position to "choose" one parent over the other and then exist in the other parent's response (e.g., silent treatment, disappointment, anger, withdrawing affection, finances, or love). Both triangulation and parentification are established changes in the family system when boundaries become more diffuse. Triangulation is notably a negative experience for the child, while research has not fully established parentification as uniformly linked to negative life and relational experiences. For a provider, this means paying particular attention to the role an adolescent might be playing between his or her divorcing parents, what the challenges and emotional ramifications are, and if there are any positive elements to present parentification (e.g., increased maturity and decision making,

heightened sensitivity to others) (Perrin et al., 2013). Counseling tips for identifying and dismantling triangulation within a family system are described in Table 14.5.

Parental Conflict and Alienation

High levels of parental conflict can reach an extreme and can lead to the controversial concept of parental alienation. In some situations, one parent clearly pushes the adolescent away from the other parent, strongly criticizing the other parent's characteristics. Such focused criticism, anger, or hostility, and the environment in which it can occur (e.g., the other parent has no chance to respond or counter the information or one parent forbids mention of the other parent) influences an adolescent's experience of divorce and his or her response to the family situation and the other parent (Baker & Ben-Ami, 2011; Kelly & Emery, 2003). This type of relational environment has consequences for an adolescent's developing self-esteem; the negative messages might relay or be interpreted as the "bad"

Table 14.5   Counseling Tips to Avoid Triangulation

How to Avoid Triangulation	
Impartiality	Be impartial to each family member; create a rapport with each individual, giving equal attention to each member
Roles and boundaries	Identify roles and boundaries; pay attention to the role an adolescent may be playing between his or her divorcing parents; identify the purpose of this role; highlight the current boundaries of relationships within the family and who may be overstepping whose boundaries
Challenges and ramifications	What are the challenges for the adolescent in playing this role? What are the ramifications for the adolescent if he or she continues in this role?
Parentification	If parentification is present, identify the existence of any positive elements
Illuminate	Highlight the family's pattern of triangulation, including each member's role in the process and the ramifications for each party
Reset	Remove the adolescent from the position of mediator or intermediary between his or her parents. Reset boundaries for the adolescent and encourage both parents to agree to be mindful of those boundaries. In session, the provider may teach the family how to communicate with each member.

parent does not love him or her. Other possible ramifications include the adolescent internalizing criticism and negativity or believing that parental love depends on agreement or acceptance of the critical messages. The adolescent can also be caught in a manipulative parent–child relationship that does not let the child/adolescent form his or her own thoughts and experiences of both parents. Research by Baker and Ben-Ami (2011) indicate that self-esteem is affected by parental alienation; they propose the notion that "to turn a child against the other parent is to turn a child against himself or herself" (p. 485).

Providers must take responsibility for understanding complicated and controversial concepts such as parental alienation and applying such understanding in treatment and other roles. For example, controversy over the existence of a diagnosable syndrome, parental alienation syndrome (PAS; Gardner, 2002), has received a lot of attention and is a delicate topic when custody arrangements are being made during a divorce and the parent–child relationships are reviewed. Evaluations of PAS repeatedly note a lack of empirical research and qualities required for pathology and does not encourage distinguishing an alienated child from ways a child or adolescent might respond to changes in family, relational dynamics, or one specific parent (Kelly & Johnston, 2001; Nichols, 2014). For example, a provider would need to understand the background an adolescent has with both parents and factor in the multiple variables that affect the parent–child relationship. There are multiple ways in which an adolescent can exist in relationship with his or her parents, including having a positive relationship with both parents. Also, the adolescent might have an affinity with one parent or be allied with one parent, meaning he or she prefers one parent without completely rejecting the other parent. In an allied situation, the adolescent might express ambivalent feelings toward this parent and might resist contact with the parent. Estranged relationships can exist between a parent and child, different from an alienated child or adolescent. With

alienation, rejection of one parent is exaggerated and disproportionate, without ambivalence, and hatred or intense dislike are openly expressed. Such feelings are often confusing to others who are aware of or part of the divorce process, such as treatment providers or extended family. Importantly, both background information and intervening variables inform assessment of the parent–child relationship and to what degree alienation might exist (Kelly & Johnston, 2001).

The negative impact of how divorcing parents treat one another must be considered in both research and interventions for adolescents. Amid controversial research results, it is clear that the quality of parenting deserves paramount clinical and research attention. Parents, adolescents, attorneys, treatment providers, custody evaluators, guardian ad litems, providers, and family members can all benefit from understanding the negative implications of parental alienation, high levels of parental conflict, and other relational implications for the parent–child relationship, even when such behaviors originate with a parent who believes that his or her perspective is founded in the truth and is protective of the adolescent. Furthermore, providers must be aware of and able to distinguish healthy responses from adolescents and preteens, who have a growing capacity to acknowledge, identify, and express ownership over emotions and relational experiences, including experiences with an unreliable, manipulative, disinterested, or abusive parent. Adolescents might distance themselves from a parent to self-protect. Such self-protective behaviors can be easily misinterpreted within custody disputes that focus on alienation or can prove to be challenging with forced custody arrangements that are often easier with younger children. These examples serve to heighten the importance of providers being aware of reasonable and healthy actions the adolescent is taking to adapt to a challenging family and relational situation (Baker & Ben-Ami, 2011; Kelly & Emery, 2003; Kelly & Johnston, 2001; Lansford, 2009; Sandler et al., 2013).

PRACTICE IMPLICATIONS

Awareness of the Issue

As providers embrace work with adolescent clients who endure divorce, awareness of current issues and research is imperative. Previously mentioned research is expanding in many areas of divorce and revealing a number of different inconclusive and controversial responses on the topic. Divorce has far-reaching cultural and community links that are important to understand. For instance, a provider might need to be aware that an adolescent's parents might choose to permanently separate instead of divorce but that the marital dyad and family still has a high level of discord. Additionally, the adolescent might lose friends, family, or community relationships based on a divorce. For example, a religious organization might frown on the divorce or close family friends may no longer socially engage because they feel that they have to choose sides.

There are many aspects of divorce that research looks at and that are worthy of further attention, including issues such as race and ethnicity, gender and role issues, premarital cohabitation, early marriage, material hostility, quality parenting, paternal feelings of anger and dissatisfaction, interaction with the noncustodial parent, and parental discord (Kelly & Emery, 2003; Lansford, 2009; Sandler et al., 2013). There are also developmental and interpersonal issues that prove their importance. These include but are not limited to emotional maturity, attachment and relational issues, self-esteem, infidelity, high levels of criticism and contempt in the marital relationship, poor relationship and problem-solving skills (Amato, 2010; Baker & Ben-Ami, 2011; Fraley et al., 2013; Fraley & Heffernan, 2013; Gottman & Silver, 2000; Kelly & Emery, 2003). As providers develop a style of interaction with divorce treatment, maintenance of research is crucial; providers must work from a knowledge base that includes relevant information regarding divorce and options for treatment.

Awareness of the Impact

Research on divorce creates a diversified picture and a picture that is constantly developing. As providers absorb the information available that forms such a picture, there are multiple aspects relevant to adolescents that deserve ongoing attention. As our culture grows and expands, we are no longer in a place to see a life event such as divorce as distinctively good or bad. With multiple individuals involved, cultural and individual development, and more sophisticated research methodologies, our understanding of the impact of divorce must be broader. Providers are in a position to maintain vigilance so as to provide the best, most-informed, and effective interventions that also take an adolescent client's perspective into consideration.

Individual Differences and Quality of Parenting

Providers working with adolescent clients, parenting plans, or the divorcing parents must maintain awareness of individual differences. Not all adolescents experience their parents' divorce in the same way at the same time. Some adolescents might adjust well to the dynamics of the situation at the time but then may have other issues as they enter adulthood. Others might have an extremely difficult time with their parents' divorce while it occurs, and the negative effects may diminish over time. An adolescent might also experience personal, relational, and emotional difficulties throughout multiple stages of growth and development.

Research reveals that consistency and the quality of parenting are important regarding the impact of divorce. Adolescents might be struggling with how their parents handle finances and financial strain, as well as inconsistent rules. Such consistency might help with some of the recognized ways that adolescents experience divorce, including externalizing behaviors such as sexual activity, academic performance, and substance use and abuse (Fergusson, McLeod, & Horwood, 2014; Lansford, 2009; VanderValk et al., 2005). Consistency in households would also offer the chance for an adolescent's positive choices and progress regarding sex, academic success, and drug and alcohol use. This is one area that reflects how an adolescent can get lost within a divorce, particularly not receiving credit or recognition for positive experiences and decisions. For example, one adolescent who struggles with math makes a small but significant grade on an algebra test that raises his grade from a C to a B, but not without much work on his part. Of course, intact families overlook and miss aspects of their adolescents' lives, too. However, research does suggest that consistency in divorcing households helps close the gap between what can slip through the cracks that might not in an intact marriage (Gatins et al., 2013). This also highlights the issue of quality of parenting and the importance of post-divorce coordination between parents when possible.

Table 14.6   Divorce-Related Measures

Assessment Options in Treatment Planning

Beck Youth Inventories-Second Edition (BYI-II)

Behavior Assessment System for Children-Second Edition (BASC-2)

Caught in the Middle Scale

Children's Perception of Interparental Conflict Questionnaire (CPIC)

Family Structure Survey

Mood and Anxiety Symptom Questionnaire (MASQ)

Multigenerational Interconnectedness Scale (MIS)

Parent-Child Boundaries Scale-Third Edition (PBS-III)

Parentification Scale

Relational Assessment Questionnaire (RAQ)

Relationship Awareness Scale (RAS)

Relationship Structures Questionnaire

Thomas Killman Conflict Scale (TKI)

THE THERAPEUTIC ENVIRONMENT

Cultural and Individual Differences

Providers who allow research to inform their practice and treatment plans make space for cultural considerations and individual differences to be considered. When adolescents are given the chance to exist in a divorce and define their own experience, providers open options for individuation, personal development, and resilience. The possibility for an adolescent to assign his or her own negative experience with divorce, increases autonomy and decreases blame and assumed impact. Research reflects that the negative impact still exists but that it might be experienced in many different ways at different times across the life span. As noted previously, adolescents have multiple developmental tasks that divorce could influence. For example, enduring divorce might not be an adolescent client's main clinical concern, but his or her social relationships or educational responsibilities might be.

The details of the divorce are also important in treatment provision, attention to issues beyond family structure, and the parent-child relationship. One client might have parents who fell out of love and another client whose parents have a public, volatile divorce. Providers must then appropriate assessments and interventions based on individual differences, client goals, and specifics of the divorce. Table 14.6 lists possible assessment measures to include for adolescents or adults, ranging from personality and functioning to mental health and psychopathology issues that might arise for a client who has divorce as a presenting problem or treatment consideration. Focusing on individual differences pushes providers to balance many areas of research, including an individualized approach that recognizes broader life experiences and common developmental expectations. At this time, it seems that blending individual, cultural, familial, and developmental concerns is also an area for further research.

The Adolescent's Perspective

Providers must keep in mind to ask an adolescent about his or her experience of divorce beyond the logistics of enduring visitation, schedules, and rips in the family structure. Gatins et al. (2013) suggest that adolescents are rarely asked about the experience of divorce. Providers must limit making assumptions and instead balance academic and research information with societal and community assumptions regarding divorce and must not forget to include an adolescent's personal response of experience. Progressing without such information can cause a provider to miss important details regarding family function, an adolescent's view of his or her family of origin, and his or her perspective on current and potential issues that the divorce brings about. Interestingly, an adolescent's perspective regarding familial relationships is likely to be more informative and helpful diagnostically, because "the adolescent's unique perspective of family dysfunction appears to extend to both other members of the family system because it is associated with adolescent-parent shared realities. . . . involving both the mother and the father" (Jager, Yuen, Bornstein, Putnick, & Hendricks, 2014, p. 413). Additionally, this perspective adds details to the subsystems that exist within a family, not just the parent–child dyad. Information about the family system and existing subsystems can reflect areas that need therapeutic attention, areas that might be negatively influencing an adolescent's developmental needs and interpersonal relationships (Perrin et al., 2013). Attending regularly to the social, emotional, and relational content informing their experience allows for providers to help adolescents deal with individual or family crises and remain attentive to stress accumulation that can lead to the formation of internal and external responses. Adolescents may deal with a number of issues outside of their control during a divorce, such as continued problems between the parents, lower quality of parenting, deteriorating quality in the parent–child relationship, challenges with financial resources, or faulty assumptions about their guilt in the divorce process (Lansford, 2009; VanderValk et al., 2005). Other issues that might affect an adolescent's stress level might include issues related directly to the divorce, such as custody schedules and interaction with attorneys and other professionals.

An adolescent's personal experience could inform treatment planning and affect the clinical relationship, including encouraging a positive, intervening relationship and growing therapeutic rapport. Gatins et al. (2013) note that an adolescent, as a product of his or her family of origin, might feel he or she has fewer emotional or relational options, and clinical interventions can encourage an adolescent not to develop a self-fulfilling prophecy of isolation. Specific attention to an adolescent's individual experience is highly important in the divorce process, including adjustment postdivorce when an adolescent's personality, ability to navigate challenging situations and emotions, and changes in the parent–child and interfamilial relationships are all relevant.

If an adolescent begins to understand divorce as one factor that might affect his or her future relationships, access to social and emotional support provides him or her an experience with help seeking, as well as a chance to see his or her life as a landscape that extends beyond the immediate issues regarding the divorce. As research shows, individuals do adjust to challenging and difficult situations, and adolescent reaction to parental divorce is usually most intense at the time immediately after the divorce, a period of time that frequently requires tremendous amounts of adjustment for all involved. (Luhmann, Eid, Hofmann, & Lucas, 2012; VanderValk et al., 2005). Furthermore, an informed provider must take into account that an adolescent might be experiencing psychological pain without clearly struggling with clinical problems often seen with children and adolescents experiencing divorce (e.g., anxiety, depression) (Amato, 2010). In other words, some adolescents might *seem* fine, and providers cannot always benchmark problems with more obvious symptomatology.

TREATMENT, PREVENTION, AND GROWTH

Treatment attention must be given toward possible mending of the parental relationship so that cooperative parenting can become a part of the divorce process. Amato (2005) notes that cooperative parenting is not the norm—that interparental conflict is the main factor that raises stress and negatively affects child and adolescent experience with divorce. Chronic, unresolved conflict is one ground-level area that providers can take part in when they have access to multiple family members. Divorce is not an isolated event that has a distinct beginning and end, but it is an experience for all involved as they adjust to the change in the family, even after an extended period of time (possibly years), that might have included emotional or physical abuse, chronic conflict, parentification, and/or triangulation, among other challenging relational difficulties (American Psychological Association, 2004; VanderValk et al., 2005).

Research and Prevention Programs

Additional options for providers involve both prevention programs and support for interventions. Use of evidence-based treatment for the specific problems that divorce includes, such as parental mental distress and adolescent externalizing and internalizing, is important. However, providers and researchers alike can help close the gap between evidence-based trials that include training and supervision with what options divorcing families have in their communities. Meaning, options for interventions must move beyond experimental program efficacy research to delivery and availability. Appropriate levels of service determined by the level of needs is crucial; all families, couples, and adolescents do not have the same level of need regarding mental health and relational issues surrounding divorce. Delivery and availability also include community awareness and motivation for families to seek help, an area that needs more research attention. Many families attune to the needs of children in a divorce and seek assistance with the process. Determining risk, need, commitment, and attrition would be aspects that would help close this experimental gap. Also helpful in disseminating treatments and programs would be individuals and organizations that already deal with divorce, which might include providers, attorneys, community-based programs, and family courts that could provide a wider base of institutional support for divorcing families and teens and might also provide research numbers that could be used to reinforce treatment efficacy. Providers must be familiar with what programs and options are available and be able to tailor treatment to specific clientele, all while paying attention to how adjustments might hinder program replication and effectiveness. Finally, researched and implemented programs must fit a community's cultural needs (Haine et al., 2003; Luhmann et al., 2012). As mentioned previously, culture and ethnicity are important elements of a client's background and demographics that would determine whether, or what parts, of a treatment are a good fit or would need attention for expansion. Through education and participation in program implementation, providers can be a part of maintaining a focus on evidence-based treatments applicable for different types of divorce situations. Such a commitment expands the options for adolescents and their families and can change the experience and legacy of the impact of divorce for adolescents.

Treatment Options for Posttraumatic Stress Disorder in Adolescents

Given the widely accepted reality that family of origin provides us with a template for life and relational skills (Simons et al., 2014), providers can include treatment modalities that help adolescents name specific emotions, as well as skills for resolving conflict in a way that might contrast their experience with their parent's divorce. Many times, divorce situations might include treatment for serious mental health situations and symptomatology such as posttraumatic stress disorder, depending on the experience of the adolescent and the environment of the family both pre- and postdivorce.

> Trauma-focused treatments are predominately based on cognitive behavioral models, which aim to optimize adaptive functioning in youth. These interventions typically use a combination of the following treatment components: trauma re-exposure, violence education and cognitive restructuring, emotion expression and regulation, social problem solving, safety planning, and parent training. (Vickerman & Margolin, 2007, p. 621)

Overall, these treatment options help providers and adolescents focus on addressing the trauma and can include a focus on externalizing behaviors such as violence and aggression, or strategies for coping and prevention. Providers must attend to their ethical responsibility of competence when stepping into the treatment of more serious situations that might include experience with physical or sexual abuse or exposure to domestic or community violence.

Assessment Options

Providers can make use of assessments when individualizing treatment with adolescents who are experiencing divorce. Many research studies gauge relational and emotional functioning with assessments. At times, providers might find themselves unsure of what to assess for or which assessments are available to them. For instance, a provider might want to find out more about an adolescent's family structure or if there are issues specific to the divorce that are of concern but not voiced by the client (e.g., parental alienation).

Table 14.6 provides a list of potential sources of which providers can be aware. This list is not exhaustive, but it can serve as a starting point for ascertaining treatment options based on research. Providers also own the responsibility to be appropriately trained to use, interpret, and apply these assessments, including awareness of reliability and validity issues. For instance,

providers must choose appropriate assessments for their client's age-group or be aware of an assessment's limitations.

Clinical and Diagnostic Issues

As noted earlier, there are a number of externalizing and internalizing behaviors that are relevant to assess when treating an adolescent in a divorce situation. A number of concepts and treatments remain controversial, such as parental alienation, PAS, and diagnostics in children and adolescents. It is the responsibility of providers to practice competently under CACREP (Council for Accreditation of Counseling and Related Educational Programs), American Counseling Association (ACA), American Psychological Association or related ethical standards when working with adolescents (ACA, 2014; American Psychological Association, 2010). Vickerman and Margolin (2007) recommend a comprehensive assessment of all relevant treatment issues before beginning treatment. This might include not only the adolescents' symptoms and treatment needs but also would expand to details of the divorce, adolescent exposure to various types of abuse, evaluation of existing risk situations (e.g., Is the adolescent still in contact with a possible abuser?), situations that require emotional flexibility such as relocation and housing in domestic violence shelters, and considering the possibility of co-occurring experiences such as domestic violence and child physical abuse. Personality and subjective well-being (SWB) are also important in understanding the adolescent's current ability to withstand daily stressors and trauma treatment, including personal strengths that can be drawn on during treatment (Margolin & Vickerman, 2007; Sodermans & Matthijs, 2014; Vickerman & Margolin, 2007).

Posttrauma Growth

Amato (2005) suggests that to lower the rate of divorce is not enough to ease the impact of divorce on children and adolescents, but that research in the field of divorce, family, and marital health serves as a starting point for understanding what our culture needs in the form of social and relational support. This means that providers can take part in community programs and familial and individual interventions helping families and adolescents who are already experiencing divorce as a preventive factor for adolescents who will likely marry and face similar marital challenges, remaining mindful that our society "will become increasingly dependent on the emotional functioning, economic productivity, and leadership of a declining number of young adults" (Amato, 2005, p. 90).

As research develops its focus on factors related to but also beyond divorce, providers can also develop a focus that includes multiple elements of an adolescent's life beyond the experience with parental divorce. For example, as discussed earlier, more sophisticated research models repeatedly show the importance of mediating factors. A provider interacting with an adolescent experiencing the disruption of divorce might be mindful of a number of things, such as the predivorce adjustment, impact of parenting quality, and the possibility of parental alienation. One possibility for providers includes involving an adolescent's parents in a treatment plan. Simons et al. (2014) recommend that parenting education classes should include a focus on the future, where parents learn about how crucial supportive parenting is to a child or adolescent developing much-needed interpersonal skills. If including parents is not possible or advisable, providers can help an adolescent focus on building a support system beyond his or her immediate family. Outside an adolescent's parental relationships, other intervening social events and relationships can help fill the gap the teen is experiencing with the changes within the family (VanderValk et al., 2005).

Apology and Relational Repair

Issues of apology and forgiveness receive more attention as relevant aspects of legal processes, including heightened emotional experiences such as medical malpractice, personal injury, and criminal offense. Robbennolt (2008) notes that, in general, research reflects that apologies mark the decision-making process, influencing

claimants' perceptions, judgments, and decisions in ways that are likely to make settlement more likely—for example, altering perceptions of the dispute and the disputants, decreasing negative emotion, improving expectations about the future conduct and relationship of the parties, changing negotiation aspirations and fairness judgments, and increasing willingness to accept an offer of settlement. (p. 350)

Research on the influence of apology becomes significant when alternatives and solutions to divorce are considered. In what ways can both the counseling and legal processes of divorce include or promote emotional experiences that have a positive and reparative effect on a couple, their children, and the family? Maldonado (2013) suggests expanding options for couples beyond parenting education and mediation. In this, professionals can include a focus on facilitating reconciliation when possible, as well as exploring ideas for developing educational programs that include a forgiveness component. Such exploration and development supports the idea that as they step into adulthood, children and adolescents need to maintain connectedness with parents beyond financial support—that is, for emotional and social support as well. The possibility of parents functioning together with less animosity, or even less emotional distance, attends to the long-term impact of divorce, marital discord, and the adjustments children and adolescents are called on to make in multiple areas of their lives when their parents divorce.

Research Overview. Since the mid-1980s, issues of apology, forgiveness, reconciliation, and repentance have gained research exposure. These concepts are notably interdisciplinary, intertwining economical, philosophical, psychological, legal, spiritual, religious, biological, and emotional terms (Smith, 2013; Taft, 2013; Worthington, 2003). The healing and relational implications of repair highlight why apology and repentance are potential options in divorce negotiations and settlements. The available literature on apology addresses common cultural misunderstandings and misconceptions involving similarities between apology, forgiveness, reconciliation, and repentance. These aspects of relational and emotional repair are often thought to be one and the same, but they are actually separate and interrelated concepts that can be part of a sequential process. Literature has also reviewed the role of apology in legal settings, legislation on the protection of an apology, differing definitions of apology, the role and recommendations of legal council, and the utilization and meaning of apology in settlement processes (Robbennolt, 2008; Taft, 2006, 2013; Worthington, 2003).

Research from personal injury, medical malpractice, and personal criminal offense proceedings lead psychology and counseling to consider how apology could change the terrain of a divorce experience. Implementing the reparative process into legal matters is a sensitive issue that highlights the need for legal professionals, mediators, providers, and other professionals to be cognizant of what potential an apology holds for a client or what capacity an apology holds to change the divorce and what might be accomplished for a client, the divorce, litigation or settlement, the family's future, and the children.

Appropriate Apologies and Professional Training

Other considerations include different ways in which clients and attorneys approach apology, existing legislation on apology, and when an apology might hinder a process underway. Professionals involved with the divorce process must be attentive to when repair is appropriate and what type of apology would be welcome and helpful. Apology in abusive or high-conflict divorces may harm, strain, or exacerbate existing issues. Additionally, apology as a legal strategy can have negative implications in a settlement process, and certain types of apologies can prove

to complicate matters or derail progress (Robbennolt, 2008; Taft, 2013).

Clients and professionals alike can easily misunderstand the role or meaning of what an apology or reconciliation means. Linguistic and cultural elements of concepts like apology, forgiveness, reconciliation, remorse, and repentance must be clearly understood by all involved. Professional training, awareness, and education are paramount for those who engage apology in a legal process. Also important are personal or professional bias, which can be seen in a tendency to undervalue an apology, making assumptions about a client's desire for and perception, understanding, or experience of an apology or preemptively assigning a certain value to an apology (Robbennolt, 2008; Taft, 2013).

Potential for Research and Change. Open empirical questions remain about how a preparative process could affect adolescent experience of divorce, what types of couples would be willing to pursue this option, what role different professionals play, what education and training is needed, and in what ways parents' positive, repairing relational and emotional interactions could change the short- and long-term consequences of divorce? Psychology and counseling can reflect on strides made in available research, notably that apologizing can lead to "more favorable attributions, more positive and less negative affect, improved physiological responses, decreased need to punish, and more likely forgiveness" (Robbennolt, 2008, p. 352). Current divorce research focuses on the influence that divorce has on children and adolescents. There is a need for more empirical studies that link divorce and apology, highlighting positive elements of relationships and exploring what role repair and apology could play for couples and their children and adolescents.

Resilience and Grit

Additional research and intervention can focus on the effect that divorce has on adolescents, specifically in the area of resilience and posttrauma growth. Research on SWB, or how a person thinks and feels about his or her life and life circumstances, reveals that negative life events are harder to adapt to, including divorce. Whether addressing optimism or response to adversity, resilience research focuses on a person's positive and adaptive response to failure, challenge, or adversity. Resilience may also include additional psychological aspects that help with overcoming life challenges and SWB. Beyond resilience and overcoming adversity, grit is the "perseverance and passion for long-term goals. Grit entails working strenuously toward challenges, maintaining effort and interest over years despite failure, adversity, and plateaus in progress" (Duckworth, Peterson, Matthews, & Kelly, 2007, p. 1087), or "having consistent interests—focused passions . . . not just having resilience in the face of failure [or adversity], but also having deep commitments that you remain loyal to over many years" (Perkins-Gough, 2013, p. 16). Reviewing these definitions, it is appropriate to consider how adolescent clients could both apply and develop resilience and grit to the emotional challenges that divorce presents.

With regard to life events, a person's well-being, resilience, and grit can affect stress management and the developmental process. Interestingly, and important to divorce treatment, providers can observe that research reveals that challenging life events influence a person's affect and cognition differently. This is relevant in working with adolescents in divorce situations because affect might reveal itself in various ways and the impact depends on the details of the event and the adolescent as an individual, and therefore, it would affect chosen interventions (Kelly & Emery, 2003; Luhmann et al., 2012).

Protective Factors

As research methodologies expand and reveal a dynamic picture of divorce and divorce support, there are protective factors to reducing the risk of consequences for children and adolescents. First, quality parenting is one factor that has been shown to affect adolescent adjustment in the experience of divorce and into adulthood. Warmth, involvement, and support all affect adjustment, as do their counterparts of inattentive parenting, harsh instruction, and involvement and absence or a less supportive presence (Kelly & Emery, 2003; Sandler et al., 2013; Simons et al., 2014). Multiple sources reflect that "one of the best predictors of children's psychological functioning in the marriage and after divorce is the psychological adjustment of custodial parents (usually mothers) and the quality of parenting provided by them" (Kelly & Emery, 2003, p. 356). For providers, this means that mentally healthy parents are a major part of an adolescent's adjustment to a challenging family situation. This also means that mentally and emotionally unhealthy parents are a major part of what an adolescent must endure. Second, if an adolescent client can maintain relationships with both his or her custodial parent and the nonresident parent, strength and resilience can grow in the divorce adjustment. However, it is important to note that an adolescent might choose to self-select out of a relationship with an abusive, estranged, emotionally challenging, or inattentive parent. Visitation and aspects of visitation such as length and regularity of visits, as well as overnights with both parents, in healthy situations, is important and beneficial. Even in high-conflict divorces, positive parenting and overnights with both mother and father play a role in adolescent mental health stability. Third, limited or diminished parental conflict affects an adolescent's divorce experience. Fourth, adolescents are in a position to make choices about the type of relationship they will have with each parent, which might include a set of complex factors such as relationship history, psychological stability of the parent and the adolescent, quality of parenting, and the adolescent's feelings regarding the divorce. For providers, this might mean including parental education and conflict education as part of treatment for divorcing adults who are interested in protecting their children from a negative divorce experience (Kelly & Emery, 2003; Sandler et al., 2013).

Case Considerations

Consider the following case scenario that illustrates the experience of an adolescent male whose parents recently divorced. As you read through the case of Bennett, try to identify his developmental stage and the impact his parents' divorce may have, identify cultural and mediating factors that may play a role in counseling, and elements of this case that may indicate specific considerations in treating Bennett and/or his family. After reading through Case Scenario 14.1, use your counseling skills to complete the tasks in Exercise 14. 1 with a partner. Once you have completed the tasks, continue reading the subsequent sections for a thorough clinical review of the case and ethical implications.

Case Scenario 14.1

Bennett White

Bennett White is a 14-year-old, Indian American male whose mother brought him to a local community counseling center for individual counseling. Mrs. White reported that over the past month Bennett had been repeatedly in trouble at school for a "negative attitude and defiant behavior." At home, he is reportedly easily irritated, he often provokes his younger sister purposefully, and generally retreats to his room.

Bennett is the middle child, with an older sister (age 25) and a younger sister—Isla—who is 11. Although his older sister lives overseas, and has lived overseas for 5 years, Bennett stated that he has a good relationship with her. He and his older sister are able to speak with each other for several hours at least once a month. Bennett also admitted that he intentionally provokes his younger sister "because she's always the good one—the baby—who doesn't have to take on any new responsibilities. Which is annoying."

Mr. and Mrs. White are the biological parents of all the three children. Mr. and Mrs. White are both immigrants from India who moved to America a few months after their marriage 28 years ago. Prior to their separation 12 months ago, the Whites had been married for 27 years. Mrs. White reports that the couple divorced due to Mr. White's infidelity, while Mr. White reports that their separation was due to years of miscommunication and changes in their life goals. Approximately 3 months ago, the divorce was legally finalized.

Prior to the parental separation, both Mrs. White and Bennett describe their family as "close-knit." Bennett recalled taking family vacations and camping trips often until he was approximately 12 years old. He reported that even though he maintained a close relationship with his mom and dad at the time, family time became scarce. Bennett reported that he and his dad used to enjoy talking and building things. He reported that he and his mom used to joke a lot and watch TV together as they have a similar sense of humor. It was also reported that around this time Mr. White had lost his job, so Mrs. White returned to nursing; however, this was often a topic of contention in the family. Mrs. and Mr. White both reported a strong faith background, with beliefs consistent with conservative Christians. Mrs. White reported that the whole family was fairly active in their church community in

(Continued)

Case Scenario 14.1 (Continued)

some capacity. The White's describe the church's response to their divorce as mixed, with some supporters and some who were against their divorce. Mrs. White expressed that she was unsure of how Bennett's friends had responded to the divorce and whether or not their interactions with her son had changed.

Currently, Mrs. White is a nurse at a local hospital, and Mr. White recently moved to a new city for a position as an aviation engineer. While the White's share joint custody, Mrs. White retains primary custody, so both Isla and Bennett live with her and spend some weekends with Mr. White. Bennett described his parents as "annoying," because he feels that they are constantly arguing when they do speak with each other. Bennett reported that sometimes his parents would talk negative about each other around him and his younger sister. At times, Mr. and Mrs. White communicate with each other via Bennett. He reports that he is often left to relay messages about pick-up times and finances to either parent. During one counseling session, Bennett expressed that sometimes he is angry with his father for his infidelity and for making Bennett have to be the one to reach out if he wants to talk with his dad. He reports being angry at his mother for needing him to help her out so much around the house. Bennett expressed that he feels he needs to be more responsible now, protect his mother and sister, and mediate between his parents to keep the peace. He reported that sometimes, even though he wants to spend time with his dad or talk to him, he does not reach out to his father for fear of hurting his mother more or causing friction.

Exercise 14.1

Case Considerations

Task 1: Culture, spirituality, and society	A. Given the client's cultural background, what cultural considerations should the provider make?
	B. How might the broader American cultural attitudes affect the divorce?
	C. How might Bennett's experience be affected by the strength of his social networks or gaps in his social networks if there are any?
	D. What generational and cultural issues must be factored in if Bennett's experience of divorce contradicts other values his family adheres to?
	E. Imagine that Bennett is an adolescent male with parents who've emigrated from India, where they had an arranged marriage and are now seeking a divorce. How might these cultural factors change to affect Bennett's experience of the divorce?

Task 2: Mediating factors and attachment

A. What mediating factors exist in the case of Bennett, and how might they affect how he experiences his parents' divorce?

   a. Adolescent characteristics?

   b. Legal issues?

   c. Family/parenting characteristics?

   d. Social and economic characteristics?

B. What mediating factors exist that will likely influence the impact of the divorce on Bennett's well-being?

   a. Specifics of the divorce situation?

   b. Social, emotional, cognitive, and personality specifics?

C. Can you identify the attachment style Bennett has with his parents? How has this attachment style and parenting style mediated (or not done so) the impact of the divorce?

Task 3: The changing dynamics of the family system

A. Is parentification present in this case? Explain.

B. Does triangulation exist in Bennett's family system? Describe.

C. What boundaries are being crossed or what roles are confused in this family system? Are there any ramifications or benefits to the current set-up of the family dynamics? Explain.

Task 4: Treatment and assessment

A. Describe Bennett's perspective of his parents' divorce and the affect it has likely had on him.

B. What cultural and individual differences would be important for you as the provider to consider in counseling Bennett?

C. As a provider, would you include apology, forgiveness, or relational repair aspects as part of your intervention with Bennett? Why or why not?

D. What protective factors exist for Bennett?

Task 5: Ethical and legal considerations

A. Using your knowledge of the American Counseling Association Ethical Code, when working with adolescents of divorced or divorcing parents, why should you pay special attention to ethics regarding informed consent and confidentiality?

IMPLICATIONS FOR COUNSELING ADOLESCENTS

Clinical Case Review

The case of Bennett provides a number of issues related to the impact parental divorce (or separation) may have on an adolescent. On the surface level, it appears that Bennett is simply angry and irritated by the shift in his family dynamics and the role he's been forced to subsume. Parentification is merely alluded to in this case, as Bennett may be taking on more responsibilities at home (i.e., becoming the protector). There is clearly some triangulation occurring within the family, with Bennett playing the role of messenger and rescuer. Not only does he have to hear two people he loves speak poorly of each other, but he's also trying to keep the peace between his parents—neglecting his own emotional needs. Bennett's externalizing behaviors, such as the negative attitude, irritability, and provoking his sister, are more likely his external expression of the inner turmoil he feels. At a deeper level, Bennett likely feels hurt by the fact that his parents are not tending to his emotional needs. Parental divorce (or separation) is often experienced as a loss (and may include a period of grief or mourning) for children and adolescents. To some degree, Bennett may be feeling hurt by the loss of his relational bond with his mom and dad or the loss of how he idealized his parents' marriage or his father's character; he may even just be trying to adjust to the physical separation between him and his father. The idea of divorce being experienced as loss could be considered a cultural assumption (in America) and is likely mediated by any number of developmental, spiritual, or cultural factors.

Developmentally, Bennett is at the stage where he is developing his sense of self and trying to explore his independence. Some of the irritability and external behaviors that Mrs. White noted could be in part due to this phase in his life. This may be mediated by the features of his personality. For example, it would be of interest to note how emotional stress or strain traditionally affected Bennett prior to the familial dysfunction. Additionally, the amount of tension Bennett is holding between his conservative spiritual beliefs about marriage and fidelity and the reality of his parents' divorce is likely to also mediate how he experiences the divorce and how the divorce affects his well-being and his developing self-identity.

Bennett and his siblings seemed to have a fairly secure attachment to their parents, and the parents appeared to have been generally responsive to their children's needs. The responsiveness to Bennett's needs has clearly shifted, likely due to the dynamics of triangulation; thus, Bennett may be experiencing much confusion and emotional-cognitive discomfort. On the other hand, because he is securely attached to both his mother and father, he is probably aware at some level that both his parents care for him and that his parents are likely both just hurting. With a secure attachment to his parents and a supportive older sister and friends, Bennett is more likely to be firm in his understanding of who he has been taught to be. One would hope that the effect on his self-identity development would not be too dramatic; however, family finances and the level of contention and immaturity between his parents could have a greater impact. The divorce may have also affected him interpersonally. Bennett's mother mentioned some tension in their church community, and it's possible as a result that Bennett's and his family's support network has shrunk. Due to less people his mother is able to depend on for help, Bennett may now have to take on more responsibilities around the house, including taking care of his younger sister. A smaller support system, triangulation, and the loss of immediate contact with a significant loved one, combined with more responsibilities and spiritual and cultural tension could result in a divorce affecting an adolescent to a greater degree. As has been discussed in this chapter, however, there are a number of factors that can mitigate or mediate the impact of parental divorce on an adolescent's development and experience. Because cases such as Bennett's can be quite complex, providers might opt to also use assessment measures, family therapy, forgiveness and apology techniques, and community programs as adjuncts to whichever treatment modality they choose in counseling the adolescent client.

Application of Ethics

The ACA (2014) delineates professional expectations and ethical standards of practice for those providing counseling services. There are several ethical considerations that are pertinent to working with adolescents whose parents are divorced, separated, or in the process of either. First and foremost, providers should strive to be culturally and spiritually sensitive (ACA, 2014, A.2.c). Providers should pay special attention and be sensitive to the cultural and spiritual beliefs that a client may have about divorce. In fact, some providers may have to help adolescents navigate the beliefs they were raised to have about divorce when they compete with the reality of their parent's divorcing. On that note, clients' cultural and religious belief systems may vary from the service provider; thus, it is important that the provider be aware of this and makes efforts to avoid imposing his or her own personal values (ACA, 2014, A.4.b). For some clients, other members in their support network (i.e., extended family, godparent, or caregiver) are highly important and influential in their lives; thus, providers should not fear enlisting the help of members of the adolescent's support group to help him or her progress (ACA, 2014, A.1.d).

Although a provider may be counseling an adolescent individually, the provider must still follow the legal and ethical standards of informed consent and confidentiality with a minor. While the adolescent may be identified as the client, providers have a legal responsibility to the adolescent's legal guardian. Additionally, the provider should be aware of his or her responsibility to the adolescent and the limitations of confidentiality (ACA, 2014, B.5). Children and adolescents of divorced or divorcing parents are a special population for which much care and caution should be placed in documentation and ensuring that one has consent from the proper individual—the parent(s) with legal custody. If divorced parents share custody, informed consent is generally necessary from both parties. Providers should be aware of their legal jurisdiction's standards, definitions, and the rights of the various types of custody. At times, the provider may have family counseling sessions. It is important that the provider clarify who the client is and the nature of the relationship the counselor will have with each member at the outset of counseling (ACA, 2014, A.8). Finally, providers should be aware that they may be called on to advocate for the adolescent they are working with professionally (ACA, 2014, A.7.a, b). Considering the issues discussed in this chapter, it may be especially important for service providers counseling adolescents of divorce to advocate for the individual in order to address potential barriers or obstacles that may inhibit access of his or her growth and development (ACA, 2014, A.7.a, b).

SUMMARY

An adolescent's response to divorce involves a complex set of factors, all of which must be considered when understanding the cultural, familial, and individual response to divorce, as well as when considering treatment interventions. A provider's role involves increasing awareness of current research in all these areas, limiting therapeutic assumptions, and practicing with competency in such a delicate therapeutic arena. Statistical data reveal that divorce remains a significant issue within our culture and deserves continued attention from providers seeking to assist with the effect divorce has on all family members involved in a divorce. Mediating factors gain more attention in research and treatment, revealing that divorce is a multifaceted experience for adolescents and requires much from them as they traverse through an already challenging time in life. A number of areas remain open for research and future direction: mediating factors that influence an adolescent's divorce experience, such as predivorce adjustment; exposure to abuse or violence; subsequent development postdivorce; teasing out areas of impact in different emotional and relational domains (i.e., focusing research on specific areas of impact rather than maintaining a direct, linear view of divorce); essential treatments if therapeutic time is limited; timing of treatment and the possibility of delayed effects; extending use of evidence-based research programs and interventions to inform clinical practice; and involving positive elements of change and posttrauma growth.

KEYSTONES

- There are three main cultural themes in divorce that should be considered when counseling adolescents and their families. First, the divorce rates are higher in individualistic and industrialized countries. Second, divorce rates are higher in countries with educated and financially independent women. Third, divorce rates are lower in cultures that have a religious focus.

- Changing social trends have affected divorce rates in American society.

- Factors in the adolescent's life may mediate his or her experience of divorce, including cultural issues related to mediating factors. Providers should be able to identify aspects of an adolescent's life and development that have a weighted effect on how he or she handles day-to-day life.

- Developmentally, research repeatedly indicates that adolescent response to divorce has its strongest impact "in the areas of psychological adjustment, self-concept, behavior/conduct, educational achievement, and social relations" (VanderValk et al., 2005, p. 534). Adolescents usually have more difficulty during a divorce and soon after it is final, with diminishing effects as they emerge into adulthood.

- There are some research challenges in studying how divorce affects interpersonal issues. Results of studies indicate the importance of mediating variables in an adolescent's life and development before naming divorce as the foundational link between interpersonal problems. To perform competently, providers should have knowledge of how divorce may affect adult functioning and be aware that the impact of the divorce may not be immediately identifiable at the time of divorce.

- Separation and divorce (including parental conflict and alienation) change the dynamics of the family system and each member's role. This role change for adolescents may have grave ramifications if sustained; however, in the case of parentification, this role change may also have some positive effects.

- Providers should have knowledge of the cultural, individual, and adolescent elements conducive to a productive and supportive therapeutic environment. Providers should consider cultural and individual differences as they interact with adolescents and families in the divorce process. Divorce-related measures also exist and can be of assistance in certain cases.

- Divorce and separation also bring legal and ethical questions to the table. Providers must be aware of informed consent, confidentiality, and other areas of ethical concern when working with adolescents.

- Along with evidence-based treatments for specific adolescent problems related to divorce, providers and researchers can help close the gap with prevention and training programs and awareness of what options divorcing families have in their communities. Delivery and availability of these services should include community awareness and motivation for families to seek help.

- Providers should understand the research on concepts such as apology, forgiveness, and relational repair while counseling adolescents of divorced parents. When working with children and adolescents of divorcing/divorced parents, providers should also have some knowledge of the research on resilience, grit, and the presence of protective factors and how these may affect adolescents' stress management and their developmental process.

REFERENCES

Afifi, T. D., Davis, S., Denes, A., & Merrill, A. (2013). Analyzing divorce from cultural and network approaches. *Journal of Family Studies, 19*(3), 240–253.

Ainsworth, M. D. S., Blehar, M. C., Waters, E., & Wall, S. (1978). *Patterns of attachment: A psychological study of the strange situation.* Hillsdale, NJ: Lawrence Erlbaum.

Amato, P. R. (2005). The impact of family formation change on the cognitive, social and emotional well-being of the next generation. *Future of Children, 15*(2), 75–96. Retrieved from www.futureofchildren.org

Amato, P. R. (2010). Research on divorce: Continuing trends and new developments. *Journal of Marriage and Family, 72,* 650–666.

Amato, P. R., & Booth, A. (2001). The legacy of parents' marital discord: Consequences for children's marital quality. *Journal of Personality and Social Psychology, 81*(4), 627–638.

American Counseling Association. (2014). *2014 ACA code of ethics.* Alexandria, VA: Author. Retrieved from http://www.counseling.org/knowledge-center/ethics

American Psychological Association. (2004). *An overview of the psychological literature of the effects of divorce on children*. Washington, DC: Author. Retrieved from http://apa.org/about/gr/issues/cyf/divorce.aspx

American Psychological Association. (2010). *Ethical principles of psychologists and code of conduct*. Washington, DC: Author. Retrieved from http://www.apa.org/ethics/code/index.aspx

Baker, A. J. L., & Ben-Ami, N. (2011). To turn a child against a parent is to turn a child against himself: The direct and indirect effects of exposure to parental alienation strategies on self-esteem and well-being. *Journal of Divorce & Remarriage, 52*, 472–489.

Chase-Lansdale, P. L., Cherlin, A. J., & Kiernan, K. E. (1995). The long-term effects of parental divorce on the mental health of young adults: A developmental perspective. *Child Development, 66*, 1614–1634.

Duckworth, A. L., Peterson, C., Matthews, M. D., & Kelly, D. R. (2007). Grit: Perseverance and passion for long-term goals. *Journal of Personality and Social Psychology, 92*(6), 1087–1101.

Erikson, E. H. (1994). *Identity and the life cycle*. New York, NY: W. W. Norton.

Fergusson, D. M., McLeod, G. F. H., & Horwood, L. J. (2014). Parental separation/divorce in childhood and partnership outcomes at age 30. *Journal of Child Psychology and Psychiatry, 55*(4), 352–360.

Fraley, R. C., & Heffernan, M. E. (2013). Attachment and parental divorce: A test of the diffusion and sensitive period hypotheses. *Personality and Social Psychology Bulletin, 39*(9), 1199–1213.

Fraley, R. C., Roisman, G. I., Booth-LaForce, C., Owen, M. T., & Holland, A. S. (2013). Interpersonal and genetic origins of adult attachment styles: A longitudinal study from infancy to early adulthood. *Journal of Personality and Social Psychology, 104*, 817–838.

Gardner, R. A. (2002). Parental alienation syndrome vs. parental alienation: Which diagnosis should evaluators use in custody disputes? *American Journal of Family Therapy, 30*, 90–115.

Gatins, D., Kinlaw, C. R., & Dunlap, L. L. (2013). Do the kids think they're okay? Adolescents' views on the impact of marriage and divorce. *Journal of Divorce & Remarriage, 54*(4), 313–328.

Gottman, J. M., & Silver, N. (2000). *The seven principles for making marriage work: A practical guide from the country's foremost relationship expert*. New York, NY: Three Rivers Press.

Haine, R. A., Sandler, I. N., Wolchik, S. A., Tein, J., & Dawson-McClure, S. R. (2003). Changing the legacy of divorce: Evidence from prevention programs and future directions. *Family Relations, 52*(4), 397–405.

Jager, J., Yuen, C. X., Bornstein, M. H., Putnick, D. L., & Hendricks, C. (2014). The relations of family members' unique and shared perspectives of family dysfunction to dyad adjustment. *Journal of Family Psychology, 28*(3), 407–414.

Kelly, J. B., & Emery, R. E. (2003). Children's adjustment following divorce: Risk and resilience perspectives. *Family Relations, 52*, 352–362.

Kelly, J. B., & Johnston, J. R. (2001). The alienated child: A reformulation of parental alienation syndrome. *Family Court Review, 39*(3), 249–266. doi:10.1111/j.174-1617.2001.tb00609.x

Kennedy, S., & Ruggles, S. (2014). Breaking up is hard to count: The rise of divorce in the United States, 1980–2010. *Demography, 51*, 587–598.

Lacey, R. E., Kumari, M., & McMunn, A. (2013). Parental separation in childhood and adult inflammation: The importance of material and psychosocial pathways. *Psychoneuroendocrinology, 38*, 2476–2484.

Lansford, J. E. (2009). Parental divorce and children's adjustment. *Perspectives on Psychological Science, 4*(2), 140–152.

Luhmann, M., Eid, M., Hofmann, W., & Lucas, R. E. (2012). Subjective well-being and adaptation to life events: A meta-analysis. *Journal of Personality and Social Psychology, 102*(3), 592–615.

Main, M., Kaplan, N., & Cassidy, J. (1985). Security in infancy, childhood, and adulthood: A move to the level of representation. *Monographs of the Society for Research in Child Development, 50*(1–2), 66–104.

Maldonado, S. (2013). Facilitating forgiveness and reconciliation in "good enough" marriages. *Pepperdine Dispute Resolution Law Journal, 13*(1), 105–130.

Margolin, G., & Vickerman, K. A. (2007). Posttraumatic stress in children and adolescents exposed to family violence: I. Overview and issues. *Professional Psychology: Research and Practice, 38*(6), 613–619.

Mullins, L. C., Brackett, K. P., Bogie, D. W., & Pruett, D. (2004). The impact of religious homogeneity on the rate of divorce in the United States. *Sociological Inquiry, 74*(3), 338–354.

Nichols, A. M. (2014). Toward a child-centered approach of evaluating claims of alienation in high-conflict custody disputes. *Michigan Law Review, 112,* 663–688.

Perkins-Gough, D. (2013). The significance of grit: A conversation with Angela Lee Duckworth. *Educational Leadership, 71*(1), 14–20.

Perrin, M. B., Ehrenberg, M. F., & Hunter, M. A. (2013). Boundary diffusion, individuation, and adjustment: Comparison of young adults raised in divorced versus intact families. *Family Relations, 62,* 768–782.

Robbennolt, J. K. (2008). Attorneys, apologies and settlement negotiation. *Harvard Negotiation Law Review, 13*(2), 349–398.

Sandler, I. N., Wheeler, L. A., & Braver, S. L. (2013). Relations of parenting quality, interparental conflict and overnights with mental health problems of children in divorcing families with high legal conflict. *Journal of Family Psychology, 27*(6), 915–924.

Sigelman, C., & Rider, E. (2012). *Life-span human development* (7th ed.). Belmont, CA: Wadsworth, Cengage Learning.

Simons, L. G., Simons, R. L., Landor, A. M., Bryant, C. M., & Beach, S. R. H. (2014). Factors linking childhood experience to adult romantic relationships among African Americans. *Journal of Family Psychology, 28*(3), 368–379.

Smith, N. (2013). Just apologies: An overview of the philosophical issues. *Pepperdine Dispute Resolution Law Journal, 13*(1), 35–104.

Sodermans, A. K., & Matthijs, K. (2014). Joint physical custody and adolescents' subjective well-being: A personality × environment interaction. *Journal of Family Psychology, 28*(3), 346–356.

Taft, L. (2006). On bended knee (with fingers crossed). *DePaul Law Review, 55*(2), 601–616.

Taft, L. (2013). When more than sorry matters. *Pepperdine Dispute Resolution Law Journal, 13*(1), 181–204.

Toth, K., & Kemmelmeier, M. (2009). Divorce attitudes around the world: Distinguishing the impact of culture on evaluations and attitude structure. *Cross-Cultural Research, 43,* 280–297.

VanderValk, I., Spruijt, E., de Goede, M., Maas, C., & Meeus, W. (2005). Family structure and problem behavior of adolescents and young adults: A growth curve study. *Journal of Youth and Adolescence, 34*(6), 533–546.

Vickerman, K. A., & Margolin, G. (2007). Posttraumatic stress in children and adolescents exposed to family violence: II. Treatment. *Professional Psychology: Research and Practice, 38*(6), 620–628.

Wallerstein, J. S., Lewis, J. M., & Blakeslee, S. (2000). *The unexpected legacy of divorce: A 25 year landmark study*. New York, NY: Hyperion.

Wallerstein, J. S., Lewis, J., Blakeslee, S., Hetherington, E. M., & Kelly, J. (2005). Is divorce always detrimental to children? In R. P. Halgin (Ed.), *Taking sides: Clashing views on controversial issues in abnormal psychology* (3rd ed., pp. 298–321). Dubuque, IA: McGraw-Hill/Dushkin.

Williamson, H. C., Trail, T. E., Bradbury, T. N., & Karney, B. R. (2014). Does premarital education decrease or increase couples' later help seeking? *Journal of Family Psychology, 28*(1), 112–117.

Worthington, E. (2003). *Forgiving and reconciling: Bridges to wholeness and hope*. Downers Grove, IL: Intervarsity Press.

15

GENDER-SPECIFIC AND LGBTQ ISSUES

I am no bird; and no net ensnares me: I am a free human being with an independent will.

—Charlotte Brontë (*Jane Eyre*)

I was not ladylike, nor was I manly. I was something else altogether. There were so many different ways to be beautiful.

—Michael Cunningham (*A Home at the End of the World*)

INTRODUCTION

In today's society, the topic of gender and sexuality is ever-changing and growing. Though more open communication is happening than ever, we as a society still have quite a long way to go in even beginning to address this topic. Gender and sexuality are particularly crucial topics in counseling adolescents because adolescence is typically the time when people are exploring their own gender identity and their sexuality. There are many adolescents who struggle with issues of gender or sexuality, and many seek counseling to get help with these struggles making it essential for any counselor who works with adolescents to be well equipped to help the adolescent through these struggles. Though adolescents who struggle with lesbian, gay, bisexual, transgender, and queer (LGBTQ) issues might

also have similar health and mental health concerns compared with those who do not have the complexity of the coming-out process, societal discrimination or bullying from peers and bias against gender and sexual minorities can add additional challenges and stressors for these adolescents (Society for Adolescent Health and Medicine, 2013).

The controversy surrounding topics of sexuality and gender identity has been ongoing for centuries. Erotic sexual activity between persons of the same sex has been recorded throughout history and can be seen in writings of ancient Greece as well as of other ancient civilizations (Balswick & Balswick, 2008). In Native American culture, the Two-Spirit is a person who would wear clothes or perform tasks associated with both genders or outside of the gender binary. The Two-Spirit was often elevated to a position of honor as a warrior or shaman, and they were seen to have special powers (Girshick, 2008; Green, 2008). In 19th-century India, the British viewed the Hijras, or India's *third gender*, as vile and tried to control and eradicate them from the Indian society (Hinchy, 2014). Today, the debate over allowing homosexual couples to be legally married rages on in many states. More and more acceptance and recognition is being given to the LGBTQ community, but there is still a very long way to go in the way of acceptance and equality.

Though LGBTQ get lumped together in the acronym, it is important to understand that each letter stands for a very distinct sexual orientation or gender identity. It is also important to understand the difference between sexual orientation and gender identity and expression. Sexual orientation refers to one's romantic attachments and sexual attractions, while gender identity refers to one's inner sense of being a man or a woman, somewhere in between, or something entirely different. Transgender persons can also be lesbian, gay, straight, or bisexual persons because their gender identity is different from their sexual orientation. In the LGBTQ community, using the correct term is very important because these terms refer to their identity.

After reading this chapter, readers should be able to do the following:

- Understand the definitions of gender specific, lesbian, gay, bisexual, transgender, and queer and the varying definitions

- Become familiar with transgender identity development and related concerns

- Discuss issues pertaining to parental reactions and development

- Review ethical practices in counseling adolescents with LGBTQ concerns

- Apply case scenarios to knowledge gleaned from this chapter

Definitions of Key Terms

Before our discussion begins, it might be helpful to define some of the terms that will be used in this chapter. Gender and sexuality are ever-changing topics that are often confused with jokes and slurs from the common vernacular, so it is helpful to operationally define the terms for this chapter. These definitions are derived from the University of California at Berkeley Gender Equality Resource Center (2014).

Asexual: A person who is not sexually attracted to any gender and may refrain from sex completely.

Bisexuality: A person who is attracted to two sexes or two genders but not necessarily simultaneously or equally. It is a common misconception that bisexuality is defined as a person who is attracted to *both* genders or *both* sexes, but there are not only two sexes (see intersex and transsexual) and there are not only two genders (see transgender).

Coming out: To recognize one's sexual orientation, gender identity, or sex identity and to be open about it with oneself and with others.

Drag: The act of dressing in different-gendered clothing and adopting gendered behaviors as part of a performance. Drag queens perform femininity theatrically, and Drag kings perform masculinity theatrically. Drag may be performed as a political comment on gender, as parody, or simply as entertainment, and does not necessarily indicate sexuality or gender identity.

Gay: When a man is attracted to other men.

Gender identity: An individual's internal sense of gender, which may or may not be the same as one's gender assigned at birth. Since gender identity is internal, it isn't necessarily visible to others and should not be confused with a person's sex.

Genderqueer: A person whose gender identity is neither man nor woman, is between or beyond genders, or is some combination of genders. Some genderqueer people identify under the transgender umbrella while others do not.

Homosexuality: Sexual, emotional, and/or romantic attraction to the same sex.

In the closet: Keeping one's sexual orientation and/or gender or sex identity a secret.

Intersex: A set of medical conditions that feature congenital anomaly of the reproductive and sexual system. That is, intersex people are born with "sex chromosomes," external genitalia, or internal reproductive systems that are not considered "standard" for either male or female.

Lesbian: When a woman is attracted to other women.

LGBTIQ: Lesbian, gay, bisexual, transgender, intersex, queer.

Out (of the closet): Refers to varying degrees of being open about one's sexual orientation and/or sex identity or gender identity.

Pansexual: A person who is fluid in sexual orientation and/or gender or sex identity.

Queer:

- An umbrella term to refer to all LGBTQ people

- A political statement, as well as a sexual orientation, which advocates breaking binary thinking and seeing both sexual orientation and gender identity as potentially fluid.

- A simple label to explain a complex set of sexual behaviors and desires. For example, a person who is attracted to multiple genders may identify as queer.

- Many older LGBT people feel that the word has been hatefully used against them for too long and are reluctant to embrace it.

Sexual Orientation: The deep-seated direction of one's sexual (erotic) attraction. It is on a continuum and not a set of absolute categories. Sometimes referred to as affection, orientation, or sexuality, sexual orientation evolves through a multistage developmental process, and may change over time. Asexuality is also a sexual orientation.

Sex Reassignment Surgery/Sex Confirmation Surgery: A term used by some medical professionals to refer to a group of surgical options that alter a person's sex to match the person's sex identity.

Transgender:

- Transgender people are those whose psychological self ("gender identity") differs from the social expectations for the physical sex they were born with—for example, a female with a masculine gender identity or who identifies as a man. To understand this, one must understand the difference between biological sex, which is one's body (genitals, chromosomes, etc.), and social gender, which refers to levels of masculinity and femininity.

- An umbrella term for transsexuals, cross-dressers (transvestites), transgenderists, gender queers, and people who identify as neither female nor male and/or as neither a man nor a woman. Transgender is not a sexual orientation, so transgender people may have any sexual orientation. It is important to acknowledge that while some people may fit under this definition of transgender, they may not identify as such.

Transsexual: Transsexual refers to persons who experience a mismatch of the sex they were born as and the sex they identify with. A transsexual sometimes undergoes medical treatment to change his or her physical sex to match his or her sex identity through hormone treatments and/or surgically. Not all transsexuals can have or desire surgery.

Transvestite: Individuals who will regularly or occasionally wear the clothing socially assigned to a gender not their own, but are usually comfortable with their anatomy and do not wish to change it (i.e., they are not transsexuals). *Cross-dresser* is the preferred term for men who enjoy or prefer women's clothing and social roles. Contrary to popular belief, the overwhelming majority of male cross-dressers identify as straight and often are married. Very few women call themselves cross-dressers.

Gender Identity Development

When considering gender identity and sexuality in children and adolescents, one must have an understanding of gender identity development, and there are several different theories of gender identity development. Kohlberg (1966) first introduced a developmental stage model of gender identity. In his model, children first come to understand the basic ideas of being a "boy" and "girl" as defined by their culture or how they are being taught by those around them. As children's understanding of gender matures, they begin to develop *gender stability*, which is the idea that gender is stable for each individual. An example of gender stability would be that a girl is still a girl, even if she is dressed in what might be considered to be boy's clothes. This is also the stage where children begin to understand gender as not only being defined by observable characteristics (e.g., clothes, toy preference, hair length) but also more subtle differences (e.g., personality characteristics, occupations, and assigned tasks). Next, children develop *gender constancy*, which is the understanding that the gender of an individual is a permanent and constant attribute of that individual. Kohlberg (1966) noted that gender constancy motivates children to identify with gender norms themselves and develop rigid views about gender.

Ruble et al. (2007) attempted to identify the cognitive process of developing gender constancy by building on the work of Kohlberg (1966). They stated that children in a more immature stage of gender stability (i.e., around 5 years of age) will have the most rigid gender-based thinking. They also found that children in a more developed stage of gender constancy actually recognized more flexibility in terms of gender-based appearance, behavior, and roles for themselves and for their peers. Ruble et al. (2007) found that a mature idea of gender constancy was associated with more flexible understanding of gender.

Feminist and queer theories of gender identity development emphasize the impact of cultural conceptions of gender and external motivation to conform. Bilodeau and Renn (2005) found that children are rewarded for gender-conforming behavior such as young girls being rewarded with praise or other social cues for nurturing behavior like cradling a baby doll, whereas boys may be rewarded for action-oriented behavior like driving a toy car. Bilodeau and Renn (2005) found that this praise motivates children to develop gender-conforming behaviors. According to Bem (1983), children develop gender schemas from their cultural environment at a very young age. Their process of identity development is a cognitive process of identifying with a particular gender. According to Johnson, Sikorski, Savage, and Woitaszewski (2014), "Bem (1983) theorized gender is assigned cognitive primacy wherein children learn gender is a more important and, thus, defining attribute than, say, race or eye color (p. 58)." Bem (1983) stated that schemas based on the gender binary are potentially harmful and restrictive to children, so raising children who do not develop gender schemas will give them more flexibility and freedom in terms of their own authentic identity development.

Transgender Identity Development

The development of gender identity for transgender individuals is distinct and can be complicated by their environment. Research is scarce on the process of gender identity for transgender individuals. Much of the literature surrounding LGBT identity development has been (a) dominated by a focus on sexual orientation versus gender identity and (b) guided by research on individuals who have sought medical or mental health treatment (Bilodeau & Renn, 2005; Grossman & D'Augelli, 2006; Johnson et al., 2014). The medical model has traditionally focused on distress due to the conflict between a transgender person's biological sex and that person's gender identity. The medical model has traditionally focused on resolving the gender conflict by either working to change the person internally through gender identity therapy or helping the person change his or her appearance through dressing, hormones, or surgery. This model seems to treat the transgender identity as a pathology in need of treatment and has contributed to further stigmatization of transgender individuals. The stigmatization of transgender individuals may also create challenges and concerns for parents of children who exhibit gender nonconforming behavior, as they are led to believe that something is "wrong" with their child and they may try to "fix" it.

Carver, Yunger, and Perry (2003) conducted a study that investigated gender identity in children. This study focused on the extent to which children feel the need to conform to expected gender norms, their view of themselves as gender typical or gender atypical, and their sense of being content with their gender. These variables were then compared and contrasted with the child's peer relations and how their peers perceived them. The findings seemed to challenge the consistently held feminist view that it is harmful for children to view themselves as strongly gender conforming. Unfortunately, children who reported feeling gender atypical tended to also report negative peer relations and were perceived negatively by their peers. The authors found that the factor that was most harmful was the external pressure (termed *felt pressure*) these children felt to conform to gender norms, not the extent to which they actually do conform to the gender norms. This was shown by the fact that the children who reported feeling strongly gender atypical yet had low external pressure to conform did not have the same negative reports of peer relationships.

Egan and Perry (2001) explored the conceptions of fourth to eighth graders regarding the extent to which they are gender conforming, their contentment with their biological sex, the external pressure for gender conformity, and the degree to which they thought their gender was superior. Like Carver et al. (2003), Egan and Perry (2001) postulated that pressure for gender conformity was harmful, especially for girls. They recommended that educators and parents help promote strong gender identity development by encouraging freedom and flexibility to explore gender-typical and -atypical behaviors. They also recognized the positive effects of identifying with their gender group and feeling as though they are gender typical. They also helped debunk some of the claims made by the medical model approach by explaining the source of the distress that transgender children may feel. The pathology, according to these theories, does not lie in the child's identity conflict but in the conflict between children's individual gender identity and the external pressure they feel to be someone they feel that they are not, suggesting that the treatment should not be aimed at the child but at the child's environment.

Brill and Pepper (2008) discuss the developmental milestones of transgender children.

Gender identity tends to emerge by the age of 2 or 3 and it is influenced by biological and sociological factors such as learning the "gender" of toys or clothes from both adults and peers. In this stage, children may turn away from or chastise those who cross the gender divide; they may actively seek out same-sex models and other cues for learning how to act. This process is true for all children including those whose gender identity does not match their genitalia. They actively strive to socialize themselves according to their inner sense of gender, and by this age, many children can identify male and female based on external appearances such as hair length. Even at this very early age, some children already begin to tell their parents that they sense a keen difference between what they are told they are and what they know about their own gender identity and a transgender identity is often very clear by this age. By age 3 to 4 years, children tend to have a sense of their own gender identity and are increasingly aware of anatomical differences. Since their own basic gender identity has been established, they begin to incorporate information into gender schemes— organized sets of beliefs and expectations about male and female gender roles. Their stereotypes are based on what children have been exposed to by the media, family values, and social interactions. Many gender-variant children at age 3 or 4 years struggle with language to express their differences, and may say things such as "I feel like a boy," "I want to be a girl when I grow up," "I am a girl," "I wish I was a girl," "I wish I was a boy," "God made a mistake with me," "I am half boy and half girl," or "My heart is boy, but my body is girl."

By the age of 4 to 6 years, gender tends to be associated with specific behaviors. For example, girls wear dresses—so anyone with a dress on is a girl. Boys play with cars—so anyone playing with cars is a boy. By this age, indicators of gender variance clearly emerge in many children. Examples of gender variance may include the following: boys playing dress-up repeatedly fashioning dresses out of whatever they can find (tablecloths, towels, Mother's T-shirts) and girls starting to refuse more feminine clothing, including dresses, feminine underwear, or bathing suits. By this age, many transgender children have been consistent and persistent in their cross-gender identity for several years, and it starts to become obvious to parents or to those around them that this is not just a phase. By age 5 to 7 years, children have an understanding of gender consistency and stability meaning that they understand that one's gender is not going to change: Man is a man even if he has long hair and wears dresses. At this age, gender identity has stabilized, so the attachment to stereotypical behaviors subsides and a fuller expression of self and fuller expression of gender is possible. For example, girls (even those who are not transgender) may adamantly declare that they don't like dresses or the color pink anymore and gravitate toward athletic clothing or new colors. But gender stereotypes and roles limit their dreams and experiences at this age, and if a child enjoys doing something that is different from the norm, the child might feel embarrassed or uncomfortable because others signal to them that this is wrong. If a child is significantly gender variant or transgender and is forced to limit his or her expression, the child may develop behavioral problems and may even begin to express suicidal ideation.

Pubertal changes may begin around age 9 to 12 years, and it is common for a subset of the children who have been expressing gender variance throughout childhood to reject this form of self-expression now. Many parents say that it is during these years that their child's gender variance is no longer an issue. However, for those children who are transgender at this age, the pubertal changes begin and the underlying gender dysphoria can even more strongly emerge in some children. This may be the time when the family finally recognizes that their child is actually transgender. For a child who is transgender, these changes can be the beginning of depression, self-neglect, and self-destructive behaviors. For ages 12 to 18 years, gender identity generally becomes fully developed. This is when the hormonal and concurrent physical changes of puberty may solidify the feeling in a gender-variant teenager that he or she is going through the "wrong" puberty. Adolescents may show signs of serious social withdrawal and depression that later develop into a transgender identity.

Sexual Identity Development

Several authors throughout the years have sought to understand the stages of sexual identity development for gay and lesbian individuals. Cass's (1979) model, which is arguably the most commonly used model, consists of six stages: (1) identity confusion, (2) identity comparison, (3) identity tolerance, (4) identity acceptance, (5) identity pride, and (6) identity synthesis. According to Cass (1979), the process of gay and lesbian identity development begins with a conscious awareness of same-sex feelings. The first stage involves confusion, turmoil, and denial, and the second stage involves increased feelings of alienation and the feeling of being "different" from heterosexual peers. In the third stage, the individual tolerates same-sex feelings but does not yet accept the possibility of being gay or lesbian, making the individual feel even more isolated. Identity acceptance occurs in the fourth stage, even though most individuals will attempt to blend in or pass as heterosexual at this stage if they feel that it is needed. In the fifth stage, involvement in the lesbian or gay community, the tendency to dichotomize heterosexuals and gay or lesbian people, pride of being gay, and anger with oppression based on sexual orientation commonly occur. The public and private aspects of the self begin to merge, as the individual grows less concerned with hiding a gay or lesbian identity. The final stage involves the complete integration of one's gay or lesbian aspect of self. Feelings of anger and pride are less intense, and there is less of a need to isolate oneself from the heterosexual world.

Parental Reactions and Development

Often, LGBTQ adolescents fear the responses of their parents, and it is not uncommon for parents to react negatively or even abusively to the news that their child is homosexual or questioning their gender (Zera, 1992). It has been found that parental responses tend to be more positive than was previously thought, and Savin-Williams and Dube (1998) have been able to develop a developmental model of parental reactions (Table 15.1).

According to Savin-Williams and Dube (1998), parent's progress through stages is similar to those proposed by Kubler-Ross (1969) for people facing imminent death. Mahoney (1994) states that parents mourn

the loss of the heterosexual identity of their child and their hopes, dreams and expectations for a

traditional life for their lesbian or gay child; the lack of grandchildren and the special relationship of being in a grandparent role; their perceived lack of success as parents and as individuals; and the improbability of changing their child's orientation. (pp. 24–25)

The initial reaction of the parents may be one of shock, which Savin-Williams and Dube (1998) say is not a developmental stage, but is included (Figure 15.1). Not all parents react with shock because many have suspicions about their child prior to finding out, such as suspicions about gender-atypical behaviors or thinking that their child is different in some way (Savin-Williams & Dube, 1998).

Experience of Violence

Negative attitudes toward homosexuality and gender issues put LGBTQ adolescents at a high risk for verbally and physically violent attacks from other students (Coker, Austin, & Schuster,

Table 15.1   Developmental Model of Parental Reactions

Shock	Not a developmental stage, but a common initial reaction. Many parents react with shock and disbelief.
Denial and isolation	Parents may deny the existence of their child's revelation or may pass it off as "just a phase" or "experimentation." Parents may feel isolated like they are the only ones who have ever had to deal with this.
Anger	Parents become angry and may direct rage toward their child or others. This stage may also be characterized by placing blame on others for their child's homosexuality.
Bargaining	The parents may try to negotiate with God or with the child to strike some kind of trade (e.g., an obedient life for the child's conversion). In this stage, the parent may strive even harder to maintain secrecy and fiercely guard the family secret.
Depression	This stage is often where extreme guilt and shame plague the parents. They might isolate themselves from friends and family members. They may also feel depressed over the thought of their child living a sad and lonely life as a homosexual person.
Acceptance	Parents are able to acknowledge that they have a homosexual child. Family equilibrium is restored, and it is no longer a family secret. The child's greater good becomes more important than the parent's ideals, though very few reach a point where they are proud of their child's sexuality.

Source. Savin-Williams, R. C., & Dubé, E. M. (1998). Parental reactions to their child's disclosure of a gay/lesbian identity. *Family Relations, 47,* 7–13.

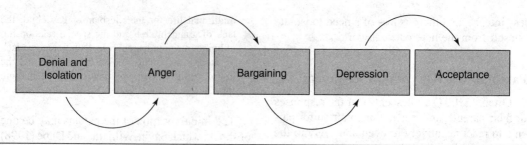

Figure 15.1   Stages of Parental Development

Source. Savin-Williams, R. C., & Dubé, E. M. (1998). Parental reactions to their child's disclosure of a gay/lesbian identity. *Family Relations, 47,* 7–13.

2010). Though many LGBTQ youth experience bullying, teasing, harassment, physical assault, and threatening behaviors from their peers or community, it is not the experience of every LGBTQ adolescent and should not be assumed. The Centers for Disease Control (2011) conducted Youth Risk Behavior Surveys from 2001 to 2009 where students from six urban school districts were surveyed. According to their data, the percentage of LGB students who had been threatened or assaulted with a weapon on school grounds ranged from 12% to 28%. According to a study done by Birkett, Espelage, and Koenig (2009) where 7,000 seventh- and eighth-grade students from a large mid-western county were surveyed, LGBQ youth were more likely than heterosexual youth to report high levels of bullying and substance use. They also found that students who were questioning their sexual orientation reported more bullying, homophobic victimization, unexcused absences from school, drug use, feelings of depression, and suicidal behaviors than either heterosexual or LGB students.

Transgender individuals also face a disturbing amount of abuse against them. The popular 1999 movie "Boys Don't Cry" was the true story of the life and eventual murder of Brandon, a young transgender man who was labeled female at birth. Teena was quietly living as a man in rural Nebraska, and no one knew that he was anatomically female. Teena did not take hormones or have any surgeries at the time of his death. He was raped and killed by two former friends who found out that he was anatomically female. Unfortunately, stories like this one are too common in the transgender world (Teich, 2012). Bullying and verbal abuse in addition to hate crimes and physical abuse are often perpetrated against transgender individuals who have chosen to live as a different gender.

The Coming-Out Process

The process of coming out or revealing one's true sexual or gender identity can be the most difficult and most important part of an LGBTQ adolescent's life. This process may be drawn out and dramatic or it could be something that is always known and understood about the individual rendering the process almost unnecessary. Coming out can be a scary, difficult, and even violent or scarring experience for an LGBTQ teen, but on the other hand, it can be a very satisfying and fulfilling experience. Many people who have come out express relief over not having to hide anymore and being able to live a life that is true to their own hopes and dreams (Teich, 2012). LGBTQ adolescents may seek counseling to work through and assist with the coming-out process. Counseling can be a source of support in the tumultuous time of the coming-out process (Exercise 15.1).

Exercise 15.1

Sophia—Knowledge Application

Pretend that you are a counselor at a local community counseling center and that Sophia is your newest referral. After reading the scenario of Sophia below, use the knowledge you've gained in the chapter so far to answer the succeeding questions.

Sophia, 17, enters therapy for anxiety and identifies ambivalence about her sexual orientation as a major factor. While Sophia says that she has always been attracted to females, she is also sometimes attracted to men and feels that she is betraying her current partner, a woman, by even considering such thoughts. She is confused about her true orientation and does not understand what is happening to her. Sophia came out at an early age and described her coming-out process as "a piece of cake." She says that she has always been a "Tom boy," so when she told her mother (a single mother of three) that she was a lesbian her mother was not surprised in the least and accepted Sophia immediately. Sophia has been dating other girls her age for several years and has been with her current girlfriend for about 9 months. Recently, Sophia has been attracted to a young male teacher in her school and has been having sexual fantasies about him. Sophia soon realizes that she has been feeling sexually attracted to a male friend as well. This has caused Sophia a great deal of anxiety because she thought that she "knew herself better than this," and she thinks that she may no longer be homosexual. Sophia says that she still loves her girlfriend and is still sexually attracted to her, but she is confused by these other feelings she has been having. Sophia also reveals with much shame that she wants to become pregnant one day, and she hates the idea that she may never get to do that in a same-sex relationship. Sophia is seeking counseling for her anxiety and to work through issues pertaining to her sexuality.

Application

1. How would you conceptualize Sophia's situation? What additional information would you want to know? Why?

2. How would you help Sophia to understand herself and her desires better?

3. What are some internal and external assets that you notice right away that could be built on?

4. What are some resiliency factors that could be built on in treatment? How would you go about this?

5. Devise a treatment plan for Sophia. How would you go about forming goals? What would you want to know in order to form short-term goals? What about long-term goals?

Ethical Practice in Counseling LGBTQ Adolescents

In counseling adolescents dealing with LGBTQ issues, it is considered unethical to discriminate against these clients. Counselors who do not feel competent to discuss these issues with the client should be forthcoming with their perceived lack of knowledge up front and give clients the option of seeking help from someone else.

Counselors should be ready with an appropriate referral if this is the case.

In counseling adolescents, there is always the question of confidentiality between the adolescent and the legal guardians. In most states, the guardians have the legal right to see the adolescent's records. The ACA (2014) *Code of Ethics* states that counselors should inform parents or legal guardians of the confidential nature of the counseling sessions and strive to establish a collaborative relationship with them that respects the parents' or guardians' responsibilities to take care of the adolescents. This can get very tricky in practice, especially when clients do not want their parent to know yet about their sexuality. It is best to be aware of the laws pertaining to this in your state, so that if a problem arises you can be prepared.

SUMMARY

Awareness on gender and sexuality in the changing and growing society is crucial for counseling adolescents, as adolescence is a stage when youth tend to explore their identity (including gender identity) and their sexuality. Adolescents struggling with LGBTQ concerns may present to a counselor with other mental health concerns with additional stressors related to societal marginalization. Counselors should understand the definitions of gender specific, lesbian, gay, bisexual, transgender, transexual, and queer to converse competently with the LGBTQ community. This chapter discusses issues related to parental reactions and development of adolescents exploring gender identity and sexuality. There are specific ethical standards that have recently changed in the field of counseling; counselors must be abreast of these standards to practice competently and ethically when working with adolescents with LGBTQ concerns.

KEYSTONES

- Counselors should understand the definitions of key terms relevant to working with the LGBTQ community, and that these definitions may vary.

- When working with adolescents with LGBTQ concerns, it is important that the counselor have a foundational understanding of adolescent development, the development and identifiers related to gender and sexuality exploration, and common parental reactions. Specifically, counselors should have an understanding of transgender identity development.

- Although society has made much advancement in the equal treatment of individuals in the LGBTQ community, many individuals are still marginalized and exposed to violence and prejudice within society and their communities. Counselors should be aware of the possible complexity of issues with adolescents presenting with concerns related to gender and sexuality.

- Counselors should have some basic knowledge regarding the coming-out process.

- According to the ACA (2014) Code of Ethics, it is considered unethical to discriminate against clients presenting with LGBTQ issues.

REFERENCES

American Counseling Association. (2014). *2014 ACA code of ethics (as approved by the ACA governing council)*. Alexandria, VA: Author.

Balswick, J. K., & Balswick, J. O. (2008). *Authentic human sexuality: An integrated approach* (2nd ed.). Downers Grove, IL: Intervarsity Press.

Bem, S. L. (1983). Gender schema theory and its implications for child development: Raising gender-aschematic children in a gender-schematic society. *Signs, 8*(4), 598–616.

Bilodeau, B. L., & Renn, K. A. (2005). Analysis of LGBT identity development models and implications for practice. *New Directions for Student Services, 111,* 25–39. doi:10.1002/ss.171

Birkett, M., Espelage, D. L., & Koenig, B. (2009). LGB and questioning students in schools: The moderating effects of homophobic bullying and school climate on negative outcomes. *Journal of Youth and Adolescence, 38,* 989–1000.

Brill, S. A., & Pepper, R. (2008). *The transgender child: A handbook for families and professionals* (Kindle ed.). San Francisco, CA: Cleis Press.

Carver, P. R., Yunger, J. L., & Perry, D. G. (2003). Gender identity and adjustment in middle childhood. *Sex Roles, 49,* 94–109. doi:10.1023/A:1024423012063

Cass, V. C. (1979). Homosexual identity formation: A theoretical model. *Journal of Homosexuality, 4,* 219–235.

Centers for Disease Control and Prevention. (2011, June 6). Sexual identity, sex of sexual contacts, and health-risk behaviors among students in grades 9–12: Youth risk behavior surveillance, selected sites, United States, 2001–2009. *Morbidity and Mortality Weekly Report, 60* (Early Release).

Coker, T. R., Austin, S. B., & Schuster, M. A. (2010). The health and health care of lesbian, gay, and bisexual adolescents. *Annual Review of Public Health, 31,* 457–477.

Egan, S. K., & Perry, D. G. (2001). Gender identity: A multidimensional analysis with implications for psychosocial adjustment. *Developmental Psychology, 37,* 451–463. doi:10.1037//0012 I649.37.4.45I

Girshick, L. B. (2008). *Transgender voices: Beyond women and men.* Hanover, NH: University Press of New England.

Green, A. I. (2008). Health and sexual status in an urban gay enclave: An application of the stress process model. *Journal of Health and Social Behaviour, 49,* 436–451.

Grossman, A. H., & D'Augelli, A. R. (2006). Transgender youth: Invisible and vulnerable. *Journal of Homosexuality, 51*(1), 111–128.

Hinchy, J. (2014). Obscenity, moral contagion and masculinity: Hijras in public space in colonial North India. *Asian Studies Review, 38*(2), 274–294.

Johnson, D., Sikorski, J., Savage, T. A., & Woitaszewski, S. A. (2014). Parents of youth who identify as transgender: An exploratory study. *School Psychology Forum: Research in Practice, 8*(1), 56–74.

Kohlberg, L. (1966). A cognitive-developmental analysis of children's sex-role concepts and attitudes. In E. E. Maccoby (Ed.), *The development of sex differences* (pp. 82–173). Stanford, CA: Stanford University Press.

Kubler-Ross, E. (1969). *On death and dying.* New York, NY: Macmillan.

Mahoney, D. (1994). *Staying connected: The coming out stories of parents with a lesbian daughter or gay son* (Master's thesis) (Vol. 33-04, p. 1154). Guelph, Ontario, Canada: University of Guelph.

Ruble, D. N., Taylor, L. J., Cyphers, L., Greulich, F. K., Lurye, L. E., & Shrout, P. E. (2007). The role of gender constancy in early gender development. *Child Development, 78*(4), 1121–1136.

Savin-Williams, R. C., & Dube, E. M. (1998). Parental reactions to their child's disclosure of a gay/lesbian identity. *Family Relations, 47,* 7–13.

Society for Adolescent Health and Medicine. (2013). Recommendations for promoting the health and well-being of lesbian, gay, bisexual, and transgender adolescents: A position paper of the society for adolescent health and medicine. *Journal of Adolescent Health, 52,* 506–510.

Teich, N. M. (2012). *Transgender 101: A simple guide to a complex issue* (Kindle ed.). New York, NY: Columbia University Press.

University of California at Berkeley Gender Equality Resource Center. (2014). *Definition of terms.* Retrieved from http://geneq.berkeley.edu/lgbt_resources_definiton_of_terms

Zera, D. (1992). Coming of age in a heterosexist world: The development of gay and lesbian adolescents. *Adolescence, 27*(108), 849–854.

16

SEXUALLY MALADAPTIVE BEHAVIORS

INTRODUCTION

Sexual development is an important aspect of adolescence and includes a wide range of thoughts, feelings, and behaviors (Vasilenko, Lefkowitz, & Welsh, 2014). While working with adolescents, it becomes important to differentiate normal sexual behavior from maladaptive behavior. Of particular interest are sexual offending behaviors, as juveniles (adolescents involved in the juvenile justice system) commit approximately 20% of rapes and anywhere from 20% to 50% of child sexual abuse cases in the United States each year (Hart-Kerkhoffs, Doreleijers, Jansen, van Wijk, & Bullens, 2009). Trends in rates of juvenile sexual offense arrests as well as recidivism over the past 10 years have shown little decline (Keogh, 2012). As the number of juvenile sex offenses continues to rise, the tangible and intangible costs to victims, communities, child welfare systems, and state correctional facilities will also grow (Geradin & Thibaut, 2004). Providers, including school counselors who work with adolescents, will need to be informed on how to treat sexually maladaptive behaviors. While reading this chapter, the following questions can guide the reader's learning:

What is sexually maladaptive behavior? What are the general characteristics of juvenile sex offenders? What are the etiological factors for sexual offending in juveniles? How are adolescent sex offenders assessed? What are the evidence-based treatments for juvenile sex offenders?

Specifically, at the end of this chapter, readers will be able to do the following:

- Describe the etiology of sex offending behaviors in adolescence

- Identify classification systems used for juvenile sex offenders

- Identify multicultural factors important in the assessment and treatment of juvenile sex offenders

- Distinguish between assessment instruments for juvenile sex offenders

- Improve understanding of the role of attachment in adolescent sex offending, particularly insecure styles of attachment

- Identify examples of evidence-based treatment protocols for juvenile sex offenders

- Use case illustrations to demonstrate understanding of keystones from the chapter

Introduction to Sexually Maladaptive Behaviors in Adolescence

Several issues in dealing with sexually maladaptive behavior in adolescence make this a critical aspect of both assessment and treatment for the mental health provider. The question of when sexual behavior becomes maladaptive continues to be debated in the literature. Overall, research has demonstrated that most adolescents make responsible choices regarding sexual behaviors (Baams, Overbeek, Dubas, & van Aken, 2014). Responsible choices include those actions by adolescents that are not hurtful, illegal, coercive, forceful, or threatening. However, there is a subset of the adolescent population that demonstrates greater impulsiveness in their decision making regarding their sexuality and participate in potentially risky behaviors. Whether heterosexual or homosexual, these risky behaviors lead to consequences such as sexually transmitted infections, HIV, and adolescent pregnancies (Szielasko, Symons, &

Price, 2013). Additionally, the use of the Internet, cellular phones, and social media also influence sexual development in adolescence, with an increasing number of adolescents reporting regular use of pornography, sexually explicit chat rooms, and "sexting" through Internet usage (Vasilenko et al., 2014). These behaviors are often considered unsafe but may or may not be maladaptive. In fact, most sexual behaviors belong on a continuum from adaptive to maladaptive. Table 16.1 presents an example of a maladaptive and a nonmaladaptive sexual behavior continuum (see Exercise 16.1).

Juvenile Sex Offending as Maladaptive Sexual Behavior

Sexual offending is considered a primary example of a maladaptive sexual behavior in adolescence. Sexual offending is defined as "nonconsensual sexual behavior involving another person and encompassing force and/or

Table 16.1 Example of a Maladaptive Versus a Nonmaladaptive Sexual Behavior Continuum in Adolescence

Clinically Nonmaladaptive	Response/Correction May Be Needed	Clinically Maladaptive—Requires Intervention
Sexual conversations with age-appropriate peers	Chronic preoccupation with pornography	Compulsive masturbation
Sexually explicit jokes or obscenities within cultural norms	Sexually aggressive conversations or jokes	Sexual conversations with younger peers/children
Handholding, kissing, hugging	Sexual preoccupation or anxiety	Child sexual abuse
Flirting, dating	Touching genitals without permission	Sexual assault
Solitary masturbation	Single occurrences of exposure/peeping with same-aged peers	Forced penetration
"Making out," fondling, petting	Drawing sexualized pictures	Sexual contact with animals
Monogamous intercourse		Genital injury to others

Exercise 16.1

Culture Activity

Cultural factors often play a large role in what behaviors are considered sexually maladaptive. Consider your own upbringing. What sexual behaviors were considered normal in adolescence for you? Which were not? Take some time to think about what variables influenced your answers (i.e., gender, ethnicity, religion). As a provider, how might your beliefs about maladaptive sexual behaviors influence your work with adolescents?

manipulation" (Keogh, 2012, p. 4). There are several different ways that juvenile sex offenders are classified in the literature, often based on either the type of crime (rape or molestation) or the type of victim (child or peer). Historically, juvenile sex offenders have been studied based on theories of adult sexual offending, despite numerous differences in presentation and treatment needs (Terry, 2013). The clinical belief that "once a sex offender, always a sex offender" from the adult literature has not been supported in juvenile offenders (Lussier, Van Den Berg, Bijleveld, & Hendriks, 2012). In fact, it appears that a large number of juvenile sex offenders do not commit additional sexual crimes in their lifetime (Caldwell & Dickinson, 2009), especially if systematic treatment is made available.

Who Are Adolescent Sex Offenders?

Juvenile sex offenders are overwhelmingly male, with only about 2% to 4% of adolescent sex offenders being female. In the United States, juvenile sex offenders are primarily Caucasian and come from two-parent homes. It is unknown if more juvenile sex offenders are Caucasian than other races or if Caucasians tend to report more frequently (Gibson & Vandiver, 2008). Although there are higher numbers of juvenile Caucasians charged with sex crimes each year, minority populations, such as African Americans, Latinos, and other youth of color represent up to two thirds of the incarcerated

population (Underwood, Phillips, von Dresner, & Knight, 2006). Juvenile sex offenders can range from approximately 10 years of age to just under 18 years, although the International Association for the Treatment of Sexual Offenders does not recommend labeling children under 12 as "sex offenders." The average age is typically 14 years for males and 13 years for females (Robertiello & Terry, 2007).

Within the judicial system, there are three types of situations that can lead to charges as a juvenile sexual offender. These include juveniles who may be engaged in consensual sexual activity but based on legal standards are unable to consent. In these cases, both partners can be charged with a sexual offense. There is also the first-time sex offender who has used force or manipulation with an identifiable victim. The victims can be much younger than the offender or they can be peers or adults. Finally, there are repeat juvenile sex offenders who have already completed treatment and have continued to offend. Among these are often those who are more aggressive or even violent in their assaults (Gibson & Vandiver, 2008).

Case Scenario

Consider the case of *Bobby* that illustrates elements of sex offender counseling, including screening for risk and needs, etiological factors, and intervention (see Case Scenario 16.1).

Case Scenario 16.1

Bobby

Bobby is a 14-year-old male who was adjudicated for a charge relating to sexual abuse of a minor. Bobby forced a 7-year-old neighbor female into engaging in sexual contact including vaginal intercourse. He was not sentenced to a secure care juvenile correctional facility but was mandated by the court to participate in intensive counseling on an outpatient basis. His judge ordered that his provider address not only underlying emotional and behavioral concerns but also issues pertaining to deviant sexual fantasies and criminal-thinking errors.

He is currently in the eighth grade at a school in a district that is between downtown and a large number of urban developments. Due to issues of confidentiality, his school officials are not aware of his sexually maladaptive behavior. Bobby lives in a poorer section of his school district that runs along the edge of an impoverished neighborhood, known for many criminal activities and gang presence. Bobby catches the bus to and from school on a daily basis. Bobby's home consists of his biological father, stepmother, a younger brother, and an older sister. Though Bobby's parents seem happily married, his sibling relationships are reportedly strained. Bobby states that he does not get along with his siblings; "My brother is crazy, he came after me with a knife, and my sister is just annoying." Bobby's younger brother denied being a victim of sexual abuse by Bobby, despite his strained relationship with his brother.

Bobby was referred for counseling in the community with an outpatient provider with the goals of decreasing deviant sexual fantasies, decreasing cognitive distortions, improving victim awareness, and implementing a relapse prevention plan. His probation officer monitors Bobby's behavior in the community and in the school, and Bobby is mandated to participate in periodic maintenance polygraph examinations. While at school, however, Bobby struggles with getting along with some of his teachers and peers. For example, after a confrontation with his teacher Bobby stated, "This school should be knocked down and blown up." This school district's policy has been a zero tolerance policy for violent language on school property (and on school buses) due to the recent school shootings. The penalty for such language and behavior is an indefinite suspension. The school's policy was written in a way that mandates the student to receive counseling to address "anger management and bullying" issues and acquire a letter from the provider indicating that he can safely be readmitted into the school building. Bobby's state laws require that during this period he be offered alternative schooling options. Hence, Bobby has been enrolled in an alternative school for students with emotional and behavioral issues.

Academically Bobby is an average student, despite the aforementioned behavioral concerns. He has no previous legal involvement prior to the sexual abuse charges. His struggle for the past 3 years has been his inconsistent behavior when at school and at home. Bobby has been known to cycle from making consistent positive decisions to making very poor choices while at school and displaying negative behavior patterns that include bullying and threatening peers and teachers. Although each part of the cycle lasts months at a time, his moods and emotions do not fluctuate, and his provider is able to rule out the possibility of a bipolar disorder (*Diagnostic and Statistical Manual of Mental Disorders, fifth edition* [DSM-5]; APA, 2014).

Due to his negative behaviors at school, Bobby has gained a reputation as a troublemaker. As a consequence for his negative behaviors, Bobby has several suspensions for verbal altercations, walking out of class, negative behavior on the bus, threatening other students, and threatening the school. Even in the midst of these consequences, he denies full responsibility and frequently blames others. His symptom presentation approximates attention-deficit/hyperactivity disorder combined type and other disruptive behavioral disorders.

Bobby also reports that he has several friends, but few are close. Bobby also regularly argues with authority figures and has stated on several occasions, "I hate most adults, but really those who want to rule over me." When asked the cause of his attitude, he said, "I should be able to make my own choices and be in charge of my own life." However, Bobby denies a history of alcohol and drug abuse.

ETIOLOGY OF JUVENILE SEX OFFENDING

Research is vast on the etiology of sexual offending in adolescence. Although a "typical" profile for a juvenile sex offender does not exist, there are etiological factors that are common in the literature that can help guide assessment and treatment (Gibson & Vandiver, 2008). These etiological factors include family factors, attachment issues, relationship challenges, neurological factors, abuse history, psychopathologies, and exposure to pornography. The following sections provide information regarding these etiological factors and what is known via published literature. Table 16.2 summarizes etiological factors of juvenile sex offenders.

Table 16.2   Etiological Factors Related to Juvenile Sex Offending

Poverty	Difficulties with peer relationships
Attachment	Neurobiological factors
Psychopathology	History of physical abuse
History of sexual abuse	Incarcerated parent
Parental substance abuse	Depression/anxiety
Conduct disorder	Male gender

FAMILY FACTORS

A higher rate of family dysfunction has been found among juvenile sex offenders. Types of dysfunction include parental rejection and/or separation, physical abuse and/or neglect, familial substance abuse, and a pattern of criminal behavior within the family (Seto & Lalumiere, 2010). Other family variables such as negative communication patterns have also been identified (Righthand & Welch, 2004). Sometimes a parent or other relative may have committed prior sexual offenses, and the child may have viewed or been exposed to sexually deviant behaviors or pornography as a result. A large majority of sexual abuse occurs within the home, which may include an adult perpetrator (Nelson, 2007). Although exact mechanisms for family variables and sexual offending in adolescence have not been identified, it is clear from the literature that family dynamics matter and require assessment and intervention throughout the adolescent's contact with the juvenile justice system (Underwood & Knight, 2006).

Attachment-Related Issues

Poor or disorganized attachment has also been identified as another possible etiological factor in the literature. In fact, several studies have linked sexual offenders and insecure attachment (Marshall, Hudson, & Hodkinson, 1993; Zaremba & Keiley, 2011). Attachment theory was first proposed by John Bowlby and has become influential in conceptualization and treatment within the counseling field. Attachment is defined as a system of behaviors aimed at seeking protection and comfort from a primary caregiver in times of stress (Priddis & Howieson, 2009). Attachment is formed largely in infancy and early childhood. The experiences an infant has in response to actions of caregivers are internalized, creating an internal working model that will shape future expectations, reactions, and relational behaviors across the life span (Hinnen, Sanderman, & Sprangers, 2009). There are four styles of attachment that form as a result of interactions with a primary *caregiver*, which is a term that generally refers to one identified primary individual who provides for an infant's primary needs (e.g., comfort, food, social interaction, and emotional needs). These initial interactions between the infant and the world become the foundation of future trust relationships, social interactions, and even cognitive development. Additionally, secure attachment (between caregiver and child) is optimal and essential for positive child development. Secure attachment develops with consistent caregiving and predicts better academic, social, and behavioral outcomes with a decreased risk of psychopathology across the life span (Merz, Schuengel, & Schulze, 2008). Contrastingly, insecure attachment styles include preoccupied/anxious (where the children have learned to be concerned and unsure of the world around them, especially caregivers), dismissing (where the children experience their needs as unimportant and may result in them fending for themselves or even taking on parental roles), and fearful attachment (in which the children tend to be hypervigilant and unsure of their physical and emotional well-being based on caregiver–child interactions). These more troubling attachment styles have lasting effects that extend into adolescent and adult challenges for the children experiencing them. In other words, all attachment styles that fall outside of what is considered a secure

attachment style (and positive caregiver bond) are associated with the child experiencing greater relational difficulties and higher levels of psychopathology (Baker, Beech, & Tyson, 2006).

Given the increased probability of early and consistent family problems in adolescent sex offending populations, insecure attachment styles are often present in juvenile sex offenders and can complicate assessment and treatment (Merz et al., 2008). Some researchers have proposed that sexual offending may be a type of disorganized attachment behavior (Zaremba & Keiley, 2011). Adolescents with an insecure attachment style might believe that they have to use coercion or manipulation to meet their relational and sexual needs, as these behaviors have been successful with their primary caregivers in the past (Priddis & Howieson, 2009). Additionally, adolescents with an insecure attachment style are more likely to have deficits in social skills. There is also a link between insecure attachment and personality disorders, specifically borderline and antisocial tendencies, which are both seen in higher levels among juvenile sex offenders, especially once they reach adulthood (Baker et al., 2006). Adolescents with insecure attachment styles are also more likely to lack a complex self-image, demonstrating an inability to view and imagine the self in different ways. This can also lead to difficulties in interpreting behavioral and verbal cues from others, especially when there is conflict (Burk & Burkhart, 2003). While additional research is needed to explore attachment and juvenile sexual offending, having an understanding of possible attachment style can provide valuable information for counseling interventions with this population.

Relationship Challenges

Adolescent sex offenders tend to struggle with peer relationships and may lack developmentally appropriate social skills. For example, within social relationships, many juvenile sex offenders have difficulty initiating conversations, engaging in conversation, decoding affective cues (e.g., other's emotional states, especially in response to one's own behavior or conversation), and other social cues during peer interactions (Underwood, Robinson, Mosholder, & Warren, 2008). Some juvenile sex offenders report feelings of loneliness, low self-esteem, and report isolating themselves from peers as a result of difficulties in peer relationships. Many of their difficulties described earlier are frequently manifestations of a preoccupation with the self and excessive self-absorption (Keogh, 2012). Alcohol and drug abuse is often observed as a result of poor social skills and social isolation—especially to blunt one's experience of social rejection. Substance use can be particularly salient to treatment issues, and some juvenile sex offenders admit to having used controlled substances when committing their offense(s). As a result, assessing the juvenile's history of use and current use (and abuses) of substances becomes an important part of treatment planning (Nelson, 2007).

Neurobiological Factors

Cognitive dysfunction is considered another important etiological factor that requires provider attention in the delivery of sex offender services for sex offending juveniles (Underwood et al., 2008). It is estimated that between one quarter and one third of juvenile sex offenders may have some type of neurological impairment (Robertiello & Terry, 2007). In numerous studies, juvenile sex offenders have demonstrated slightly lower scores on general intelligence, performance intelligence, and verbal intelligence than other juvenile offenders, although the findings have not reached statistically significant levels (Seto & Lalumiere, 2010). In fact, the average intelligence score for juvenile sex offenders is 88 (mean of 100 [$\mu = 100$] and standard deviation of 15 [$SD = 15$]), while the mean for other juvenile offender populations is approximately 90, which is within a "normal range" of intelligence (Cantor, Blanchard, Robichaud, & Christensen, 2005). Two main areas of cognitive impairment have also been identified and include deficits with executive functions (planning, abstract thinking, impulse control, and cognitive

flexibility) and deficits in expressive and receptive language (Righthand & Welch, 2004). In addition to cognitive dysfunction, juvenile sex offenders may also have lower levels of academic performance and difficulties within the school system. Juvenile sex offenders are more likely to be diagnosed with learning disabilities and to be placed in special education classes than other juvenile offenders. This is especially true for mathematics and reading classes (Keogh, 2012). Additionally, many report high instances of disruptive behaviors and truancy. Parental involvement in school may also be lower.

Abuse History

The "cycle of abuse" hypothesis is considered another important etiological factor in juvenile sexual offending. According to this hypothesis, juvenile sex offenders' abuse is a direct result of their own sexual abuse histories in which they were the victims (Robertiello & Terry, 2007). In fact, in a meta-analysis by Seto and Lalumiere (2010), juvenile sex offenders were five times more likely to have been sexually abused than their peers. Additional data suggest that anywhere between 32% and 46% of juvenile sexual offenders report being sexually abused at some point prior to committing a sexual offense (Keogh, 2012). Rates of physical abuse and neglect are also high for this population. This becomes an important factor, as individuals who have been abused tend to show less empathy, struggle more with recognizing emotions in others, and have greater difficulty thinking abstractly (Gibson & Vandiver, 2008). Cognitive distortions, discussed in detail later in the chapter, are also common among individuals who have been abused and are frequently seen in juvenile offender populations (Underwood, von Dresner, & Phillips, 2006).

Psychopathologies

Another etiological factor for juvenile sexual offending includes offender psychopathology.

There appears to be a great deal of heterogeneity (diversity of issues) among these adolescents in terms of diagnoses and personality factors. Depression and anxiety, specifically social anxiety, are frequent mental health challenges for this population (Righthand & Welch, 2004). Suicidal tendencies may also be elevated among juvenile sex offenders. There do not appear to be, however, higher incidences of psychotic or other dissociative symptoms (Gibson & Vandiver, 2008). Conduct problems are frequently seen in juvenile sex offenders, along with antisocial tendencies (Underwood, von Dresner, et al., 2006). In terms of personality characteristics, dependent, schizoid, and avoidant traits are found most often in this population (Keogh, 2012). There appears to be a great deal of other variables to consider when psychopathology is considered, such as caregiver influences, crime-ridden and impoverished neighborhoods, and the juvenile's outlook of the world are general examples (Terry, 2013). The professional provider's awareness of possible psychopathology offers much promise in treatment planning and effectiveness, as discussed later in the chapter.

Exposure to Pornography via Technology

The effects of viewing sexually explicit materials, such as pornography, have long been known to be a risk factor for sexually acting out among some youth. Accessing images that are sexually explicit can affect current as well as future sexual and emotional development (McEllrath, 2014). Although viewing pornography does not in and of itself lead to sexual offending, one concern is the adolescent's ability to access these images without much effort. With the Internet, smartphones, and other technological devices, sexual material is readily available and even marketed to adolescents (Wells, Mitchell, & Ji, 2012). In one study, male juveniles stated that they had watched explicit Internet sites out of curiosity and to seek sexual arousal (Quayle & Taylor, 2006). Deviant sexual material and images, whether seen on the Internet or sent through text messaging or e-mail,

can act as a catalyst for acting out sexually with children, peers, or adults. Additionally, the frequency and ease of access to this material may normalize and justify sexual misbehaviors for adolescents struggling with impulse control and sexually deviant fantasies. Adolescents may also engage in what seems to them as innocent sexual behaviors, such as sexting with friends, and then be charged with a sexual offense (Driemeyer, Spehr, Yoon, Richter-Appelt, & Briken, 2013). There is an urgent need for more research on the specific effects that viewing sexually explicit materials via technology may have on patterns of juvenile sex offending.

ETHNIC MINORITY JUVENILE SEX OFFENDERS

Within the juvenile sex offender population, there are minority groups who require special considerations throughout the process of assessment and treatment. One group includes female juvenile sex offenders, who are different from their male peers in several ways. Not only do they tend to be younger at the time of their first offense, but they are also five times more likely to have been sexually abused themselves (Gibson & Vandiver, 2008). Most female juvenile sex offenders almost always select a known victim, usually a relative, and often the abuse occurs when the juvenile is babysitting. A typical victim is usually much younger than the offender. Females tend to have more behavior problems and prior mental health diagnoses as well. Females are also less likely to use force and are more likely to commit an offense as part of a group (Robertiello & Terry, 2007).

Ethnic minorities, such as African American and Latino juveniles, tend to be overrepresented in incarcerated populations of juvenile sex offenders. In fact, when compared with nonminority youth, youth of color are far more likely to be arrested, adjudicated, and sentenced to long treatment programs with higher security (Stevenson, Sorenson, Smith, Sekely, & Dzwairo, 2009). Ethnic minorities are also more likely to come from family backgrounds with economic strain and likely to have been raised by a single mother. They are also more likely to have poor school attendance and weaker community supports than other sex offender populations (Underwood & Knight, 2006). These factors are important to consider during both assessment and treatment of minority group populations.

Juveniles with developmental disabilities also form a distinct group of offenders. For example, they are more likely to engage in sexually inappropriate behaviors that are nonassaultive in nature, such as public masturbation, voyeurism, or exhibitionism. They are also less discriminating in selecting a victim and are four times more likely to have been sexually abused than are other juvenile offenders. They also face difficulty in expressing their sexuality, as they are often not encouraged to date or express sexual needs because of their disabilities (Gibson & Vandiver, 2008) (see Exercise 16.2).

There are numerous ways in which juvenile sex offenders are classified within both the clinical and the juvenile justice realms (Underwood et al., 2008). There is some concern in the literature related to empirical validation and typologies of adolescent sexual offending, in that studies vary widely in their methodology, often present contradictory findings from one another, and are difficult to compare (Rasmussen, 2004). However, a typological approach is helpful for mental health providers in several ways. First, it allows for greater comprehension of important variables, including risk factors for recidivism, possible motivations for sexual behaviors, and developmental challenges. Additionally, typologies allow for differentiated treatment strategies that can improve clinical outcomes (Gamache,

Diguer, Laverdiere, & Rousseau, 2012). The most basic typologies utilized for adolescent sex offenders are dichotomous and classify either by age (preadolescent offending or adolescent offending) or victim (child or peer/adult). Although these classification systems provide a rudimentary way of separating offenders, they lack sophistication and possible clinical utility when designing treatment plans (Robertiello & Terry, 2007).

Models of Classification/Typologies

Dichotomous models have added to our understanding of etiological factors and have contributed to more sophisticated typological models (Gunby & Woodhams, 2010). For example, research on victim choice has provided several commonalities that can be utilized by mental health providers. Both peer/adult abusers (rapists) and child abusers are broadly similar in terms of family dysfunction in the literature. However, child abusers tend to be younger at age of first offense, select either male or female victims who are known to them and approximately 5 years younger, and most often commit the abuse in the victim's home (Worling, 2002). Child abusers are also more likely to have deficits in social functioning, to be more socially isolated, and to use verbal manipulation, such as threatening a child that they will "get into trouble" if he or she does not comply. Adolescents who select peer/adult victims are more likely to use violence such as a weapon, use substances, and most often choose a victim whom they do not know (Gunby & Woodhams, 2010).

One of the first sophisticated typology systems developed for adolescent sex offenders

---

Exercise 16.2

Etiology Activity

Based on the case scenario of Bobby, what etiological factors can you identify?

was O'Brien and Bera's (1986) model. This model is clinically derived, based on the experiences of the authors while working with juvenile sex offenders (Robertiello & Terry, 2007). Several dimensions were identified, including (a) motivation for behavior, (b) personality characteristics, (c) family dynamics, (d) age of victim, and (e) sexual history. Based on these dimensions, seven different types of offenders were classified. First are the naive experimenters, who are characterized as younger at the time of their first offense and lacking in sexual knowledge and social skills. Another typology is the undersocialized child exploiter group, who are more socially isolated, have no history of other types of delinquent behavior, are insecure, have poor self-esteem, and come from dysfunctional families. Sexual aggressives, on the other hand, are more likely to come from violent family backgrounds, who use aggression and even violence during their offense, abuse peers or adults, use alcohol or other substances, and have a history of delinquency. Sexual compulsives are more likely to be quiet, more anxious, engage compulsively in sexual fantasies, and demonstrate paraphilic behaviors. A pseudosocialized typology includes adolescents who are more narcissistic, are highly intelligent, lack intimacy, and have very superficial relationships with peers. The final two typologies include disturbed impulsives, who behave impulsively and often have high levels of psychopathology, and group-influenced offenders, who offend largely based on peer influence (O'Brien & Bera, 1986).

One of the first empirically based models derived mainly from meta-analysis of the literature was developed by Prentky, Harris, Frizzell, and Righthand (2000). This model is based on type of offense. They identified six different typologies: (1) child molesters, (2) rapists, (3) sexually reactives (those whose behavior was socially learned based on prior abuse history), (4) fondlers, (5) paraphiliac offenders, and (6) others (those who do not fit into a distinct profile). These typologies were utilized in developing the Juvenile Sex Offender Assessment Protocol

(J-SOAP-II), which will be discussed later in the chapter (Rasmussen, 2004). Typologies for higher risk juvenile sex offenders based on the violence associated with their offense have also been proposed. Sexually violent youth are those who use threats of death or weapons during a sexual offense. Predatory sexually violent youth are those who utilize violence and attack unknown victims who are either peers or adults. Although adolescents with these typologies are rare, they represent greater risk for communities and may benefit from more individualized treatment (Miccio-Fonseca & Rasmussen, 2009).

Research on personality variables and juvenile sex offending has also contributed to classification systems. The Minnesota Multiphasic Personality Inventory has been used to identify personality factors that may be unique to juvenile sex offenders. When compared with other juvenile offenders, adolescent sex offenders tend to score higher on the psychopathic deviate, paranoia, and schizophrenia subscales (Oxnam & Vess, 2006). In another study, adolescents who had committed anal rape scored significantly higher on the schizophrenia scale as well as on the psychopathic deviate scale than other sex offender groups, which suggests that elevations on these scales may help differentiate types of sexual offending (Oxnam & Vess, 2008). The Millon Clinical Multiaxial Inventory (MCMI) has also been utilized to develop personality profiles for juvenile sex offenders. In general, peer offenders have more narcissistic and antisocial traits, while child offenders have elevations on the schizoid, avoidant, and dependent scales. When utilizing the Millon Inventory to identify juvenile sex offenders from general juvenile offenders, the scale on the MCMI most often elevated in the sexual discomfort scale, which measures anxiety and preoccupation related to sexuality as well as sexual impulses. Additionally, the profile of child abusers is very different from peer abusers and general juvenile offenders on the MCMI, indicating a need to consider victim choice in treatment planning (Glowacz & Born, 2013).

RECIDIVISM

Typologies are also highly correlated with recidivism. Recidivism refers to a relapse in criminal behavior following incarceration or treatment for a crime (Berenson & Underwood, 2001). For juvenile sex offenders, recidivism is primarily concerned with repeat sexual offenses (Koegh, 2012; Worling, 2002). In general, studies have shown that juvenile sex offenders are more likely to reoffend nonsexually following treatment (Caldwell & Dickinson, 2009). Justice systems routinely rely on providers to evaluate the level of risk of juvenile sex offenders in making decisions regarding prosecution, detention placement, level of security needed, and release back into the community (Elkovitch, Viljoen, Scalora, & Ullman, 2008). Recidivism for sexual reoffending remains low in most published studies, usually in the range of 10% to 20% (Miner, 2002).

Risk Factors for Recidivism

There appear to be risk factors for sexual recidivism in juvenile populations. Table 16.3 summarizes known risk factors for recidivism. Both age at time of first offense and prior sexual offenses are consistent predictors of

recidivism (Hendriks & Bijleveld, 2008). Worling (2002) proposed a model that highlights "promising" risk factors, "possible" risk factors, and "unlikely" risk factors, based on the current availability of empirical support. Risk factors deemed "promising" included prior sexual offenses, age at first offense, deviant sexual interest, selecting an unknown victim, social isolation, parental rejection, and high-stress family environments. Characteristics that may be "possible" risk factors include obsessive sexual interest, impulsiveness, and an environment that supports reoffending, such as lack of supervision and access to similar victims, selection of a male child as a victim, use of weapons or violence, and aggression. Unlikely risk factors include denial of the offense, lack of empathy, history of nonsexual crimes, and a personal history of sexual abuse.

Models for Assessing Recidivism Risk

Becker (1998) proposed a three-track model of recidivism, which can be used to assign level of risk, based on risk factor assessment. The first track is considered a "dead-end," where the offender commits no further crimes. The second track includes those for whom sexual offending

Table 16.3   Recidivism Risk Factors

Promising	Possible	Unlikely
Prior sexual offenses	Obsessive sexual interests	Denial of offense
Younger age at first offense	Impulsiveness	Lack of empathy
Deviant sexual interests	Use of aggression	History of nonsexual crimes
Unknown victim	Limited parental supervision	History of sexual abuse (victimization issues)
Social isolation	Gang involvement	
Parental rejection	Male victim	
High-stress family environment	Use of weapons	
Prior legal involvement		
Deviant sexual fantasies		
Sexual preoccupation		

as a juvenile was part of a larger pattern of offending, with a large variety of crimes being committed that are not necessarily sexual in nature. The third track includes offenders who continue with abnormal sexual behaviors and reoffend sexually. Clearly, sexual recidivism is highest for those on the third track of this model. In fact, an average juvenile sex offender who falls within the parameters of Track 3 may continue to commit more than 380 sexual offenses during his or her lifetime (Nelson, 2007). Thus, correctly determining risk for recidivism becomes an important part of both the assessment and the treatment protocols for juvenile sex offenders (see Exercise 16.3).

SCREENING AND ASSESSMENT OF JUVENILE SEX OFFENDERS

Because recidivism risk and etiology (e.g., the origins of sex offending behaviors) matter in terms of treating juvenile sex offenders, assessment is usually the first step when a juvenile enters treatment (Berenson & Underwood, 2001). Once a juvenile has been accused of a sexual crime, he or she enters the juvenile justice system. There are several phases through which the juvenile will then move within the juvenile justice system. These include pretrial, presentencing, treatment, release, monitoring, and follow up. Screening and assessment by a clinician often takes place in the presentencing phase, where risk needs to be determined for placement and decisions regarding restriction and supervision are suggested (Metzner, Humphreys, & Ryan, 2009).

Levels of Care

Based on screening and assessment, the adolescent is placed in one of several different levels of treatment that reflect the risk of both recidivism as well as the needs of the juvenile (Underwood, von Dresner, et al., 2006). The highest level of care is provided by institutional (residential in nature) facilities. Types of correctional environments include intensive treatment units, which are medium to maximum security facilities for high-risk offenders. Typically, the juvenile will be incarcerated for anywhere between 18 and 24 months. Residential treatment units are generally designed for medium-risk offenders and are located in minimum security facilities. There may also be specialized facilities for offenders with developmental disabilities, and some states use private staff–secure residential facilities that coordinate with the juvenile justice system (Berenson & Underwood, 2001). Each of these institutional settings provides security for both the offender and the community.

For offenders who are deemed lower risk, there are also community-based settings that provide treatment. Juveniles may begin treatment in a transitional facility; this level of care is a structured residential setting that focuses on both treatment and life skills. Group homes provide slightly less structure and provide more access to the community through school and work programs. Therapeutic foster care continues to be an option for some juvenile offenders who are transitioning back into the community, where they live with foster families and may participate in day treatment or outpatient services. Other adolescents may be served in the

Exercise 16.3

Classification Activity

Based on the case scenario, how might Bobby be classified based on offense committed and risk of recidivism? Be sure to support your thoughts with specifics from the case.

community through outpatient centers including private practice settings and community outreach programs. Community-based programs can also be a part of transition planning for reintegration into the community (Berenson & Underwood, 2001). Ideally, in the screening and assessment phase, before formal treatment begins, transition plans will be developed so that the adolescent and his or her family are aware and other community partners can be involved long before the youth is released. This allows for optimal outcome (Underwood, Phillips, et al., 2006).

The Diagnostic Clinical Interview

During presentencing and early treatment, a semistructured interview is typically recommended as part of a comprehensive assessment (Caldwell & Dickinson, 2009). This is an opportunity for the provider to build rapport with the adolescent and family, which is critical for optimal outcome (Underwood & Knight, 2006). Before beginning the screening and assessment process, the provider will need to explain the limits of confidentiality and obtain informed consent from both the adolescent and the parent/ guardian (Underwood et al., 2008). The clinical interview has several important components. First, a mental status exam should be administered as an initial screening for psychopathology as well as to identify stressors that may contribute to deviant sexual behaviors. Additionally, a sexual aggression history should also be obtained. A sexual-aggression history includes information about sexual development, knowledge, and experiences (Fletcher & Shaw, 2000). During this part of the interview, it is also helpful for the provider to address the adolescent's beliefs about gender roles, his or her sexual arousal patterns, sexual attitudes, and sexual orientation (Underwood et al., 2008). Information related to the use of pornography, "sexting," or other similar behaviors should also be noted (Quayle & Taylor, 2006).

It is also imperative to obtain as complete a psychosocial history as possible. Factors related to family, community, ethnicity, and cultural values become a crucial part of the treatment process. Additionally, information related to education and learning, family stressors, and alcohol and substance use is also critical. A full developmental history, if available, is also prudent. Examining individual developmental milestones will help identify possible concerns, such as the ability to form appropriate peer or family relationships. A medical and psychiatric history should also be obtained as part of the clinical interview. Recent research has pointed to high percentages of juvenile sex offenders with co-occurring mental health and substance use disorders, which can complicate treatment. Some of the complications include similarly used forms of denial and minimization seen in substance users and sexual abusers. Additionally, the presence of a mental health disorder may suggest other etiological factors that must be considered in the appraisal and treatment of adolescents with sexually maladaptive behavior (Underwood, Warren, Talbott, Jackson, & Dailey, 2014).

Co-Occurring Mental Health Disorders

During the interview, it is also helpful to conceptualize possible diagnoses related to sexual offending utilizing the *DSM-5*. Co-occurring disorders generally refer to a sexually aggressive charge, a mental health disorder, and substance use issues. Paraphilic disorders may be considered, including voyeuristic disorder, exhibitionistic disorder, frotteuristic disorder, sexual masochism, sexual sadism, or pedophilic disorder. However, the *DSM-5* cautions against diagnosing adolescents with these disorders before the age of 18 due to developmental factors (American Psychiatric Association, 2014).

Nevertheless, traits may be present and should be noted as part of a comprehensive assessment plan, as they can influence treatment outcome and risk assessment. For example, juvenile sex offenders often report higher levels of atypical sexual fantasies, interests, and behaviors, although these experiences are not often accounted for in treatment programs (Hempel, Buck, Cima, & van Marle, 2013).

Juvenile sex offenders are also likely to have other co-occurring mental health disorders. Common disorders in the juvenile sex offender population include anxiety disorders, depressive disorders, psychosis, attention-deficit/hyperactivity disorder, behavior disorders such as conduct disorder, and substance abuse disorders (Hempel et al., 2013; Underwood et al., 2014). Estimates for male juvenile sex offenders in treatment with a mental health diagnosis range from 20% to 60%, while for females in care, it can be as high as 70% (Teplin, Abram, McClelland, Dulcan, & Mericle, 2002). Youth with high levels of reported mental health symptoms often receive longer sentences and frequently will not qualify for community-based programs, resulting in more time in residential settings and/or incarceration (Underwood et al., 2014). It is,

therefore, critical to have a full understanding of possible mental health needs during the course of sex offender treatment. It is important to keep in mind, however, that with adolescents, psychiatric diagnoses are far less stable than they are for adults and, therefore, a diagnosis should not necessarily dictate treatment (Underwood et al., 2008).

To assist in organizing and treating mental health symptoms, Berenson and Underwood (2001) designed a categorical system for use with juvenile sex offenders. They proposed utilizing the following clusters: affective based, anxiety based, psychotic based, co-occurring mental health with a substance abuse disorder, personality based, disruptive behavior based, and neurologically based. Examples for each of these categories are summarized in Table 16.4.

Table 16.4   Examples of Organization of Co-Occurring Mental Health Symptoms

Symptom Cluster	Examples	Common DSM-5 Disorders
Affective	Feelings of sadness, hopelessness, worthlessness, agitation, lethargy, sleep disturbances, and lack of motivation	Major depression, dysthymia/pervasive depression, and bipolar disorders
Anxiety	Experiences persistent nervousness, tension, apprehension, and fear; may include panic attacks, extreme worry, and hypervigilance	Posttraumatic stress disorder, obsessive compulsive disorder, generalized anxiety disorder and panic or phobia disorders
Psychotic	Inability to distinguish external reality from internal reality, hallucinations, delusions, paranoia, social withdrawal, and ideas of reference	Schizophrenia, schizoaffective, schizophreniform, and substance-induced disorders
Substance use and mental health disorders	Presence of a substance use disorder that is independent from a mental health disorder	Various substance use disorders
Personality	Pervasive patterns of functioning that affect cognition, perception, mood, and behavior that are rigid and maladaptive	Personality disorders
Disruptive behavior	Marked impulsivity, destruction of property, deceitfulness, and aggressive acts	Oppositional defiant disorder, conduct disorder, and intermittent explosive disorder
Neurological	Disorders that limit intellectual functioning; most common is attention-deficit/hyperactivity disorder	Attention-deficit/hyperactivity disorder and attention deficit disorder, learning disorders, motor disorders, and pervasive developmental disorders

Source. From Berenson and Underwood (2001).

Note. DSM-5, Diagnostic and Statistical Manual of Mental Disorders, fifth edition.

Many treatment programs are not equipped to handle youth with severe mental health symptoms, yet specialized services are not always available (Miccio-Fonseca & Rasmussen, 2009). Juveniles who have chronic and persistent mental health concerns may require special housing or even a specialized mental health facility where sex offender treatment is also available and the focus of therapy is on reducing negative mental health symptoms and increasing prosocial behaviors (Grisso & Underwood, 2005). During assessment, the clinician has the opportunity to evaluate the need for mental health treatment and to help make decisions about treatment needs (see Exercise 16.4).

Clinical Assessment Instruments for Juvenile Sex Offenders

In determining possible co-occurring mental health concerns, providers will often use empirically supported clinical assessment instruments. Assessment instruments can also be employed throughout the treatment process, both to evaluate progress and to assist with client self-exploration (Watkins & Campbell, 2000). Many of these instruments can also be utilized in evaluating problematic behaviors and risk of recidivism (Underwood et al., 2008).

Assessing Mental Health

Although there are numerous options for assessing the mental health of youth, several instruments tend to be relied on more heavily in the literature. Both the Child Behavioral Checklist and the Youth Self-Report (Achenbach, 1991) are frequently used to assess behavioral and emotional problems in youth. The Child and Adolescent Functional Assessment Scale (Hodges, 1995) assesses functioning in eight domains: (1) school/work, (2) home, (3) community, (4) behaviors, (5) moods/emotions, (6) self-harm, (7) substance abuse, and (8) cognition. The Child Severity of Psychiatric Illness (Lyons, Libman-Mintzer, Kisiel, & Shallcross, 1998) is a measure of high-risk behaviors, overall functioning, and psychiatric symptomology.

The Behavior Assessment System for Children-Revised (Reynolds & Kamphaus, 1998) includes an adolescent as well as a parent form that examines internalizing and externalizing problems as well as adaptive skills. The Phallometric Assessment (Marshall & Fernandez, 2000) assesses the degree of sexual deviance in adolescents who are at greater risk for recidivism due to age or use of violence in committing their offense. Additionally, utilizing substance abuse screenings such as the Adolescent Drug Involvement Scale (Moberg & Hahn, 1991) can help determine the degree to which an adolescent may struggle with substances for treatment planning.

Assessing Risk and Recidivism

Risk assessments with juvenile sex offenders specifically examine the risk of recidivism based on empirically supported factors related to reoffending. Several widely used risk instruments are discussed within this section. One of the most commonly used measures is the J-SOAP-II

Exercise 16.4

Risk Activity

In the case of Jessica presented in Chapter 1, what factors might be important from her history? What might her risk be for recidivism based on this chapter's content?

Answer the same questions for the case of Bobby.

(Prentky & Righthand, 2003). The J-SOAP-II is an evidence-based assessment of risk factors that have been linked to both sexual and violent offending in juveniles. The measure is designed for use with males 12 to 18 years of age. No cutoff scores have been provided for risk level, and the J-SOAP-II is recommended as part of a more comprehensive assessment and not in isolation (Hempel et al., 2013). The J-SOAP-II has four scales that include measures of (1) sexual drive/preoccupation, (2) impulsive/antisocial behavior, (3) intervention variables such as treatment motivation, and (4) community stability/adjustment. Studies involving the J-SOAP-II indicate moderate to high interrater reliability ranging from .75 to .91, as well as internal consistency alphas from .68 to .85 (Prentky & Righthand, 2003). Risk prediction studies have indicated that the scale for sexual deviance and/or sexual preoccupation is the better predictor of sexual recidivism than other scales, including the impulsive/antisocial behavior scale (Powers-Sawyer & Miner, 2009).

Another frequently used risk assessment with juvenile sex offenders is the Juvenile Sexual Offense Recidivism Risk Assessment Tool-II (Epperson, Ralston, Fowers, DeWitt, & Gore, 2006). This assessment is based on a review of the juvenile's criminal record related to the charged offense. It shows high rates of reliability between raters ($r = .89$ or higher; Hempel et al., 2013).

The Estimate of Risk of Adolescent Sexual Offense Recidivism (ERASOR; Worling & Curwen, 2001) is another tool that can be used to assess youth between the ages of 12 and 18 years. The ERASOR provides a risk estimate based on short-term factors and cannot predict risk for more than 1 year. The ERASOR examines sexual interests, attitudes, and behaviors; past sexual assaults; psychosocial functioning; and family functioning. Parts of the ERASOR can also be used to assess treatment progress and assess other clinical needs (Hempel et al., 2013). Reliability and internal consistency are in the range of excellent (Viljoen, Elkovitch, Scalora, & Ullman, 2009; Worling, 2002).

The Juvenile Risk Assessment Scale (JRAS; Hiscox, Witt, & Haran, 2007) is also used to differentiate low-, moderate-, or high-risk juveniles based on nine static factors and five dynamic factors. In addition to similar historical and psychosexual elements, the JRAS also examines victim selection variables including age, gender, and degree of force.

Two additional assessments are often used for risk determination despite not being specifically for juvenile sex offending populations. The Structured Assessment of Violence Risk for Youth (Borum, Bartel, & Forth, 2003) is designed to assess violence risk in juvenile populations. In addition to examining historical, social, and individual dynamics related to offending behaviors, the Structured Assessment of Violence Risk for Youth also highlights possible protective factors, such as prosocial involvement, social supports, and commitment to school (Hempel et al., 2013). The Hare Psychopathy Checklist: Youth Version (Forth, Kosson, & Hare, 2003) is based on research that supports psychopathy as a risk factor for reoffending. The Hare Psychopathy Checklist: Youth Version utilizes a semistructured interview as well as police reports and other justice documents to determine risk level across interpersonal, affective, antisocial, and behavioral domains.

Assessment is the first step in developing a comprehensive treatment plan that takes into account individual factors and needs. It is imperative that the adolescent and caregiver be involved in the assessment process. In fact, the American Counseling Association's Code of Ethics (2014) specifically indicates this requirement. Evidence-based practice calls for continual reassessment and evaluation of treatment throughout the offender's time in managed care (Underwood, Phillips, et al., 2006) throughout all points of an adolescent's stay in juvenile justice services (e.g., during intake, treatment, reintegration into community, probation, etc.).

TREATMENT OF JUVENILE SEX OFFENDERS

The primary task when treating juvenile sex offenders is protection of the community (Shaw, 2001). Juvenile sex offenders are often more treatable than adult offenders for several reasons. For instance, an adolescent's sexual behavior is less deeply ingrained, and adolescents are still exploring pathways to sexual gratification (Poortinga, Newman, Negendank, & Benedek, 2009). As discussed previously, there is a low level of recidivism among juvenile sex offenders who complete sex offender treatment programs. It is, therefore, important that treatment be structured and, above all, evidence based (Worling & Curwen, 2001). Within the juvenile justice system, evidence-based treatments are defined as "a body of knowledge, also obtained through the scientific method, on the impact of specific practices on targeted outcomes for youth and their families" (Underwood, von Dresner, et al., 2006, p. 287). According to the National Institute of Mental Health, evidence-based practices include the following:

1. A minimum of two control group studies or a large series of single-case studies

2. At least two researchers

3. Treatment manual utilization

4. Training for therapists with written protocols

5. Adequate clinical samples

6. Significant results from outcome tests

7. Clinical reviews of program functioning and symptom outcomes

8. Reports on long-term outcomes following treatment completion

9. Two or more studies that demonstrate treatment superiority over medication, placebo, or other established treatment protocols (Underwood et al., 2008)

In working with juvenile sex offenders, evidence-based treatments utilize several outcome principles. These principles include assessment of risks and needs, enhancing intrinsic motivation for change, providing objective interventions that are structured, skills training, using positive reinforcements, utilizing community resources for support, and providing measurable feedback through assessment of practices and processes (Underwood, von Dresner, et al., 2006). For juvenile sex offenders, there are important treatment

goals, which are considered universal, based on the work of the National Task Force on Juvenile Sex Offending (Underwood & Knight, 2006).

It is important to note that most evidence-based programs will have these goals integrated into their treatment protocol to ensure optimum outcome (Berenson & Underwood, 2001).

There are several limitations of these and other evidence-based models with juvenile sex offenders. Among these limitations are considerations regarding the lack of randomization trials and low sampling of minority juveniles. Additionally, there is a lack of representation of females, individuals with intellectual disabilities, and those with severe and persistent mental illness. Costs associated with executing such studies (e.g., staffing needs, statistical analysis, interpretation, and writing and distributing the results) can also be a factor in conducting research for community programs that rely on limited budgets. These limitations increase the risk of recidivism as well as continued mental health problems for juvenile sex offenders, making this yet another area for future research on evidence-based treatments and juvenile sex offenders (Underwood & Knight, 2006).

Components of Evidence-Based Treatment Programs

There are several elements that appear to be core aspects of juvenile sex offender treatment and are often seen across evidence-based protocols. The most common modalities for treatment include group and family interventions. Individual work is often not recommended as a sole modality for juvenile sex offending, but it can be utilized to address other concerns, including psychopathology (Poortinga et al., 2009).

Psycho-Education

Most treatments include a psycho-educational component, given the developmental level and needs of juvenile populations. These are often delivered in a group or didactic format and are meant to enhance individual work. Treatment protocols include a variety of content and most often consist of the following:

Victim awareness

Arousal reconditioning

Healthy masculinity

Thinking errors

Relapse prevention

Sex education/positive sexuality

Anger management

Social skills training

Substance abuse

Cognitive restructuring

Assertiveness training

The sexual assault cycle

Use of sexual history and maintenance polygraphs (Berenson & Underwood, 2001)

Relapse Prevention

Relapse prevention is a common element in juvenile sex offender treatment. Originally designed for work with substance abuse, relapse prevention has excellent clinical utility with maladaptive behaviors (Metzner et al., 2009). For juvenile sex offenders, relapse prevention stresses that their sexual behaviors are not impulsive but part of a pattern of action with warning signs based on the individual offender's personality. For example, a rapist may demonstrate an escalation in anger, or a child molester may exhibit symptoms of anxiety or depression (Underwood, von Dresner, et al., 2006). Relapse prevention stresses that the risks of reoffending are always present, and the offender must learn to not only recognize precursors but also acquire and utilize new skills to cope with times of high risk for relapse. In light of relapse prevention's primary interventions being intensely focused on self-awareness, identifying one's erroneous thinking, and precursors of illegal behaviors, a choice to reoffend following treatment is seen as deliberate and does not occur by chance (Berenson & Underwood, 2001).

A relapse prevention is imperative for communities and individuals supporting the offender, such as family members, probation or parole agents, child welfare workers, or other service providers. Relapse prevention planning essentially begins at the start of a juvenile's sex offender treatment and should increase as the center of focus as the juvenile progresses through the sex offender program. As the juvenile gets close to community release, increased communication with the offender about his or her relapse cycle becomes stridently important in identifying high-risk situations (Poortinga et al., 2009).

Cognitive Behavioral Interventions

Sex offender treatment programs should contain cognitive behavioral therapy (CBT) techniques as part of the protocol as well. This population's propensity toward defensiveness and rampant refusal to face their misbehaviors often leads to most juvenile sex offenders not initially believing that they require treatment and are often identified as highly resistant to that treatment (Underwood, von Dresner, et al., 2006). It is also common for these youth to exhibit externalizing behaviors such as blame of the victim, disproportionate anger, fighting, and resistance to authority figures. Issues related to minimization, denial, and lack of victim empathy are common maladaptive patterns of thinking, which influence behavior (Metzner et al., 2009). There are several specific targets for CBT interventions with juvenile sex offenders, including deviant sexual arousal, thinking errors, belief systems, and self-regulation (Poortinga et al., 2009). CBT elements are often a fundamental part of group work with adolescent offenders and will focus on improving interpersonal relationship skills. Additionally, a CBT approach within group therapies offers the offender additional chances to take responsibility for his or her behaviors among his or her peers, learn to identify, and restructure cognitive distortions (Terry, 2013). Victim empathy can also be addressed through group CBT techniques (Underwood et al., 2008).

Pharmacotherapy

Pharmacotherapy refers to the use of chemicals (i.e., medications, hormone therapy) as a complement to therapeutic interventions. It is often combined with juvenile sex offender treatment for a variety of reasons. Not only do a high percentage of offenders have co-morbid disorders that may need medication management, but some pharmacological agents can also be used to treat sexual hyperarousal (Metzner et al., 2009). Research has highlighted the role of monoamine neurotransmitters, such as dopamine, serotonin, and norepinephrine, in the regulation of human sexual behaviors. These have also been connected with impulsivity and aggression. Selective serotonin reuptake inhibitor (SSRI) medications are utilized in the treatment of paraphilias and compulsive sexual behaviors. SSRI medications have also been clinically shown to reduce arousal, drive, and preoccupations with sexual behaviors. The most commonly used SSRI is fluoxetine, which is one of only a few SSRIs approved for use in children. Hormonal modulating agents can also be utilized with juvenile sex offenders, although their use is limited and remains controversial. In studies with adult males, antiandrogens have been utilized to successfully reduce testosterone levels. More research is needed, however, on the use of these medications with juveniles (Poortinga et al., 2009). However, in developing a comprehensive treatment plan, pharmacotherapy, such as utilizing SSRI medications, may be an important component depending on individual needs.

Evidence-Based Treatment Models

There are several evidence-based treatment protocols that can be used to treat juvenile sex offenders in both institutional and community settings. Although a comprehensive review of all possible treatment protocols is beyond the scope of this chapter, those that are presented herein meet evidence-based criteria and continue to show positive outcomes in the literature (Worling & Curwen, 2001). Many programs being utilized

with juvenile sex offenders were not necessarily designed for this population or were adapted from programs utilized with adult sex offenders (Terry, 2013). Clinicians working with juvenile sex offenders are encouraged to research programs and receive additional training as indicated (Underwood & Knight, 2006). The following programs are utilized primarily in institutional or correctional facilities. Table 16.5 summarizes the current evidence-based protocols for treating adolescent sex offenders.

Family Integrative Transition (FIT). The primary focus of FIT is on juveniles with co-occurring disorders, such as substance abuse or mental health diagnoses. The FIT model combines several other treatment approaches, including multisystemic therapy, motivational enhancement therapy, relapse prevention, and dialectical behavior therapy. The program begins approximately 2 months before the release date of the offender and continues for 4 to 6 months while the juvenile is readjusting to the community. Several specialized therapists work with the offender and his or her family, strengthening family and community supports. The FIT model has demonstrated a significant decrease in recidivism for those youth who participate and complete (Aos, 2004).

Mode Deactivation Therapy (MDT). MDT combines CBT approaches, dialectical behavior therapy, and mindfulness to treat youth who have high levels of co-occurring disorders and are considered treatment resistant or have failed treatment in the past. MDT is useful in treating youth with posttraumatic stress disorder, conduct disorder, and personality-disordered traits. MDT is also useful for reducing both aggression and suicidal ideation in juvenile sex offenders (Apsche & Ward, 2002).

Dialectical Behavior Therapy (DBT). Developed primarily for the treatment of individuals with borderline personality disorder, DBT can also be used with adolescent sex offenders. Youth participate in both a group and an individual session each week. Groups focus on interpersonal

Table 16.5 Evidence-Based Treatment Approaches for Sexually Maladaptive Behaviors

Treatment	Level of Care	Special Clinical Focus	Notable Outcomes
Family integrative transition	Community	Co-occurring disorders	Decrease in recidivism
Mode deactivation therapy	Secure facilities	"Treatment resistant" co-occurring disorders	Reduces aggression and suicidal ideation
Dialectical behavior therapy	Secure residential community	Personality disorders	Reduces suicidal ideation
Aggression replacement training	Secure facilities	Violent offenders	Reduces violent recidivism
Thinking errors approach	Residential community	Thinking patterns	Increase in positive thinking patterns
Thinking for a change	Secure residential community	Designed as a group intervention	Cognitive restructuring
Motivational enhancement therapy	Secure residential community	Utilizes stages of change model	Develops intrinsic motivation
Multisystemic therapy	Community	Family/in-home interventions	Reduces recidivism and out-of-home placements
Functional family therapy	Community	Family/in-home interventions	Strong multicultural component
Multidimensional treatment foster care	Community	Family/in-home interventions	Reduces recidivism
Milwaukee	Community	Connects to resources	Reduces psychosocial impairment
Intensive aftercare program	Community	Transition from secure care to community	Strong multicultural component
Integrated sex offender treatment intervention	Secure residential community	Numerous elements for an integrated approach	Numerous outcomes

skills, distress tolerance, and emotion regulation. Individual sessions focus more on what has happened throughout the week and how conflict is resolved. These dimensions are particularly important in adolescence, and research has shown that adolescents who receive DBT have lower levels of suicidal ideation as well as fewer crisis situations (Linehan, 1993).

Aggression Replacement Training (ART). ART is one of the most extensively used treatment protocols in juvenile corrections and was designed for youth who have offended violently against people or property. The three major components

of ART include (1) structured learning to target behaviors, (2) training in anger management to target the emotional component, and (3) moral education to target the cognitive aspect of offending (Glick & Goldstein, 1995).

Thinking Errors Approach. Thinking errors approach focuses on specific criminal thinking patterns that can lead to criminal offending. Some examples of criminal thinking errors include victim stance, an "I can't" attitude, failure to put self in place of others, exaggerated pride, power thrusting, and irresponsible decision making. The premise is that youth who have offended think very differently from others and need to learn to challenge and eliminate distorted thoughts (Yochelson & Samenow, 1976).

Thinking for a Change (TFAC). TFAC is a cognitive approach that focuses on restructuring juvenile offender's thinking along with teaching prosocial problem-solving skills. The restructuring occurs as the adolescent learns to consciously examine his or her thoughts and connect them with his or her offenses. TFAC is designed to be implemented in a group setting (Bush, Glick, & Taymans, 2002).

Motivational Enhancement Therapy (MET). MET is based on Prochaska and DiClemente's (1992) stages of change model first developed for addiction. The stages of change include (a) precontemplation, (b) contemplation, (c) preparation, (d) action, and (e) maintenance. MET attempts to help youth discover their own intrinsic motivation for change and formulate their own personal plan for change. Goals are largely client driven in this approach, although with juvenile populations some guidance may be needed. MET is typically utilized short term, but it can be very effective in helping the adolescent find the motivation for change (Underwood & Knight, 2006).

The following programs are primarily community-based treatment programs. These can be utilized as aftercare for juveniles who have been released from institutional settings or may be utilized as primary treatment for low-risk offenders (Underwood & Knight, 2006).

Multisystemic Therapy (MST). MST is an intensive community and home-based program for adolescents with antisocial behaviors. They are considered "at risk" of needing more secure placements, such as incarceration or residential centers. Therapy occurs in the home and community, and the family is an active part of the process. The primary focus is on the environment and how this influences the adolescent. MST has been shown to reduce recidivism as well as out-of-home placements for juvenile sex offenders (Randall, Henggeler, Pickrel, & Brondino, 1999).

Functional Family Therapy (FFT). Also a family-based intervention, FFT focuses on improving family communication, parenting, and problem-solving skills. There are four treatment phases: (1) impression, (2) motivation, (3) behavior change, and (4) generalization. FFT is particularly helpful in addressing co-occurring behavior disorders, such as conduct disorder, oppositional defiant disorder, and disruptive behavior disorder. FFT also includes extensive integration of multicultural components, such as ethnic or religious values (Alexander, Pugh, Parsons, & Sexton, 2000).

Multidimensional Treatment Foster Care. Multidimensional Treatment Foster Care is an intense intervention that includes extensive training for parent or guardians on working with juvenile sex offenders when they return home. Services for the adolescent also occur for several months and focus on reducing criminal behavior, establishing positive peer relationships, improving family relationships, and improving school attendance. Parents continue training for up to 12 months after the juvenile has completed his or her services with a focus on learning to manage behavior (Chamberlain & Mihalic, 1998).

Wraparound Milwaukee. Wraparound Milwaukee connects the adolescents and their families with resources at school and in the community to help meet individual needs. The program's main focus is to reduce out-of-home placements. The program also contributes to improved social functioning in youth. The program has shown promise in reducing psychosocial impairment for both youth and their families (Burns & Goldman, 1999).

Intensive Aftercare Program (IAP). IAP was designed to assist with the transition from secure placement back into the community. There are five main principles to this approach: (1) preparation for increased freedom and responsibility, (2) facilitating interactions with the community, (3) assisting the adolescent and community supports, (4) learning to develop new resources and supports, and (5) monitoring the amount of collaboration between the offenders, their families, and the community. The IAP model has also shown promise not only with Caucasian but also with African American offenders (Altschuler & Armstrong, 1998).

Integrated Sex Offender Treatment Intervention (ISOTP). There are also models of treatment for juvenile sex offenders that show promise and are undergoing rigorous empirical research. One such model is the ISOTP (Rehfuss et al., 2013; Underwood, Dailey, Merino, & Crump, in press; Gerhard-Burnham, Underwood, Speck, Williams, Crump, in press). Underwood, von Dresner, et al. (2006) report that among treatment groups at moderate risk, adolescents receiving this approach to treatment "significantly increased their ability to accept responsibility for offenses, develop internal motivation for change, understand risk factors and apply risk management strategies, empathize, show remorse and guilt, analyze cognitive distortions, and maintain quality of peer relationships" (p. 6). ISOTP is an integrated approach employing CBT, which promises further reductions in recidivism and interpersonal changes, resulting in a healthier attitude and perspective toward sexual behavior (Underwood & Knight, 2006).

IMPLICATIONS FOR COUNSELING ADOLESCENTS

Because sex offending behaviors among adolescents are not projected to decline, providers must be aware of the numerous facets of working with this population (Keogh, 2012). The Council for Accreditation of Counseling and Related Educational Programs standards are met across several different areas when providers develop competence with this specialized population of adolescents. There are several important ethical points to be aware of as well when working with juvenile sex offenders. As previously discussed, informed consent and confidentiality when working with adolescents are unique and require extra attention from the provider. Additionally, issues of professional competence when working with an adolescent population, administering batteries of screening assessment tools, as well as implementing evidence-based treatment must also be attended to and are specifically mentioned in many professional codes (Underwood et al., 2014). Although rewarding, working with youth who sexually abuse can be stressful, and issues of self-care become important for ethical practice (see Exercise 16.5).

Clinical Review of Case

While the results of a standardized risk assessment (i.e., J-SOAP-II or ERASOR) for sexual risk recidivism may be in the low to moderate range, Bobby is more than likely a moderate to high risk recidivate sexually from a clinical perspective. His lack of juvenile justice contact, involved family, and lack of substance abuse serve as prosocial factors. However, the intensity of his sexual behavior, preoccupation with deviant sexual fantasies, school problems, and anger

Exercise 16.5

Treatment Activity

Based on the case of Bobby, what treatment level is needed (incarceration vs. community based) and why? Which type of treatment approach might be recommended based on this chapter's content?

management problems are concerning risk factors. This case illustrates the need for the provider to integrate both the actuarial and the clinical risk factors in the treatment planning process. In these cases, the provider may have to implement clinical overrides to endure public safety of client care in the advent that the actuarial risk scores are lower.

Though Bobby committed a serious sexual crime by violating the neighbor child, he was not adjudicated to a secure care juvenile correctional facility. Being placed in a secure care correctional facility, residential treatment program, or outpatient clinic is often not reliably done by the judicial system. Multiple factors including the discretion of the judge, sentencing guidelines, and having a private lawyer may serve as mitigating factors as it relates to classification and assignment to care. This case illustrates the need for the provider to fully examine the details of the sexual crime rather than the charge or placing agency itself. That is, the charge or placement might not be consistent with the risk for recidivism.

Bobby's behavior is significant, and he presents as a risk to the community, yet the school may not be afforded opportunities to realize the dynamics of his sexual risk. Part of the school's ignorance regarding the case dynamics is related to issues of confidentiality and privacy. Even though Bobby is a significant risk to the community, his civil rights to confidentiality and privacy must be maintained. To work through the issues of confidentiality and privacy, Bobby's probation officer will need to work closely with his therapists and parents in securing proper releases of information to share treatment concerns.

Bobby's anger is pervasive in that he displays poorly modulated behavior at home with his family members and sibling, school officials, and peers. While his explosive anger may not be directly related to sexual crimes, his provider will need to address these anger issues. This case illustrates the need for the provider to understand that anger often serves as the psychological construct that feeds the sexualized aggression.

It may be assumed that the aggressive behavior serves as a form of sexualized behavior and if provided certain opportunities, the offender might engage in sexualized behavior.

SUMMARY

Juvenile sex offenders represent a segment of the adolescent population in need of clinical services from competent providers. Because adolescent sexual offending results in costs to victims, communities, child welfare systems, and state correctional facilities, providers need to understand who juvenile offenders are, how they are classified and treated within the juvenile justice system, how to properly assess them for treatment planning, and what evidence-based programs are available. Multicultural factors related to this population are also important in assessment and treatment. Working competently with this population, as well as advocating for evidence-based protocols and innovative community and family-based approaches, will improve outcomes for these adolescents as well as provide additional safety for the communities in which they live.

KEYSTONES

- In adolescence, sexual behaviors change. For some, they become maladaptive. Sexually offending is one form of maladaptive behavior.

- Juvenile sex offenders are a heterogeneous population who need specialized and targeted treatment for optimal outcome.

- The etiology of sex offending varies widely. Some common etiological factors include family dynamics, attachment, social relationships, neurobiology, abuse history, psychopathology, and exposure to pornography via technology.

- When working with juvenile sex offenders, the provider should be aware of multicultural factors. Youth of color, females, and youth with developmental disabilities have unique needs.

- There are several different ways by which juvenile sex offenders are classified. Often, this is based on victim type or type of offense. There are also more sophisticated models including O'Brien and Bera's (1986) as well as a model on which the J-SOAP-II is based.

- Personality variables, as measured by instruments such as the Minnesota Multiphasic Personality Inventory and Millon Adolescent Personality Inventory can also be used for classification.

- Recidivism is moderately low with juvenile sex offenders. There are several risk factors for recidivism, including Worling's model and Becker's three-track model.

- Screening and assessment provides for correct placement of the juvenile and aids in creating an individualized treatment plan.

- There are different levels of supervision for juvenile sex offenders. These include incarceration settings as well as community settings.

- During the assessment, rapport should be established and a thorough clinical interview should be conducted. Things to include in the interview are the mental status exam, a sexual aggression history, a psychosocial history, as well as a developmental history.

- It is also important to assess for co-occurring mental health disorders as part of the clinical interview. Formal assessment instruments such as the Child Behavioral Checklist, Youth Self-Report, Child and Adolescent Functional Assessment Scale, and Behavior Assessment System for Children-Revised can be utilized as well.

- Assessing for alcohol and substance abuse is also necessary for adolescent sex offenders. Again, formal instruments such as the Adolescent Drinking Index or the Adolescent Drug Involvement Scale can be utilized.

- There are several instruments with which the provider can assess recidivism risk. These include the J-SOAP-II, Juvenile Sexual Offense Recidivism Risk Assessment Tool-II, ERASOR, and the JRAS.

- When treating adolescent sex offenders, the provider needs to utilize evidence-based treatment protocols to ensure optimal outcome. Components

of evidence-based therapy programs for this population include psycho-education, relapse prevention, CBT techniques, and pharmacotherapy.

- There are several evidence-based models discussed in the chapter that show good outcomes. Providers should consider these and other appropriate models when working with this population.

REFERENCES

Achenbach, T. M. (1991). *Integrative guide for the 1991 CBCL/4-18, YSR, and TRF profiles.* Burlington: University of Vermont, Department of Psychiatry.

Alexander, J., Pugh, C., Parsons, B., & Sexton, T. (2000). Functional family therapy. In D. S. Elliot (Series Ed.), *Blueprints for violence prevention* (Vol. 3). Boulder, CO: Venture.

Altschuler, D. M., & Armstrong, T. L., (1998). Recent developments in juvenile aftercare: Assessment, findings, and promising programs. In A. R. Roberts (Eds.), *Juvenile justice: Policies, programs, and services* (2nd ed., pp. 448–472). Chicago, IL: Nelson-Hall.

American Counseling Association (2014). ACA Code of Ethics. Alexandria, VA: Author.

American Psychiatric Association. (2014). *Diagnostic and statistical manual of mental disorders* (5th ed.). Washington, DC: Author.

Aos, S. (2004). *Washington State's family integrated transitions program for juvenile offenders: Outcome evaluation and cost-benefit analysis.* Olympia, WA: Washington State Institute for Public Policy.

Apsche, J. A., & Ward, S. R. (2002). Mode deactivation therapy and cognitive behavior therapy: A description of treatment results for adolescents with personality beliefs, sexual offending and aggressive behaviors. *The Behavior Analyst Today, 3*(4), 460–470.

Baams, L., Overbeek, G., Dubas, J. S., & Van Aken, M. A. (2014). On early starters and late bloomers: The development of sexual behavior in adolescence across personality types. *Journal of Sex Research, 51*(7), 754–764.

Baker, E., Beech, A., & Tyson, M. (2006). Attachment disorganization and its relevance to sexual offending. *Journal of Family Violence, 21*(3), 221–229. doi:10.1007/s10896-0026-9017-3

Becker, J. (1998). What we know about the characteristics and treatment of adolescents who have committed sexual offenses. *Child Maltreatment, 3*, 317–329.

Berenson, D., & Underwood, L. A. (2001). *A resource guide: Sex offender programming in youth correction and detention centers.* Washington, DC: Council for Juvenile Correctional Administrators and The Federal Office of Juvenile Justice Delinquency Prevention.

Borum, R., Bartel, P., & Forth, A. (2003). *Manual for the structured risk assessment of violence in youth* (Version 1.1). Tampa: University of South Florida.

Burk, L. R., & Burkhart, B. R. (2003). Disorganized attachment as a diathesis for sexual deviance: Developmental experience and the motivation for sexual offending. *Aggression and Violent Behavior, 8*, 487–511. doi:10.1016/S1359-1789(02)00076-9

Burns, B. J., & Goldman, S. K. (1999). *Systems of care: Promising practices in children's mental health 1998 series: Vol. 4. Promising practices in wraparound for children with serious emotional disturbance and their families.* Washington, DC: Center for Effective Collaboration and Practice, American Institutes for Research.

Bush, J., Glick, B., & Taymans, J. (2002). *Thinking for a change: Integrated cognitive behavior change program.* Washington, DC: National Institute of Corrections.

Caldwell, M. F., & Dickinson, C. (2009). Sex offender registration and recidivism risk in juvenile sexual offenders. *Behavioral Sciences & the Law, 27*, 841–956. doi:10.1002/bsl.907

Cantor, J., Blanchard, R., Robichaud, L., & Christensen, B. (2005). Quantitative reanalysis of aggregate data on IQ in sexual offenders. *Psychological Bulletin, 131*, 555–568.

Chamberlain, P., & Mihalic, S. (1998). *Blueprints for violence prevention, book eight: Multidimensional treatment foster care.* Boulder, CO: Center for the Study and Prevention of Violence.

Driemeyer, W., Spehr, A., Yoon, D., Richter-Appelt, H., & Briken, P. (2013). Comparing sexuality, aggressiveness, and antisocial behavior of alleged juvenile sexual and violent offenders. *Journal of Forensic Sciences, 58*(3), 711–718. doi:10.1111/1556-4029.12086

Elkovitch, N., Viljoen, J. L., Scalora, M. J., & Ullman, D. (2008). Assessing risk of reoffending in adolescents who have committed a sexual offense: The accuracy of clinical judgments after completion of risk assessment instruments. *Behavioral Sciences & the Law, 26*, 511–528. doi:10.1002/bsl.832

Epperson, D. L., Ralston, C. A., Fowers, D., DeWitt, J., & Gore, K. S. (2006). Actuarial risk assessment with juveniles who offend sexually: Development of the Juvenile Sexual Offense Recidivism Risk Assessment Tool–II (J-SORRAT-II). In D. Prescott (Ed.), *Risk assessment: Theory, controversy, and emerging strategies of youth who have sexually abused* (pp. 118–169). Oklahoma City, OK: Wood & Barnes.

Fletcher, A. C., & Shaw, R. A. (2000). Sex differences in associations between parental behaviors and characteristics and adolescent social integration. *Social Development, 9*, 133–148.

Forth, A. E., Kosson, D. S., & Hare, R. D. (2003). *The psychopathy checklist: Youth version.* Toronto, Ontario, Canada: MultiHealth Systems.

Gamache, D., Diguer, L., Laverdiere, O., & Rousseau, J. (2012). Development of an object relation–based typology of adolescent sex offenders. *Bulletin of the Meninger Clinic, 76*(4), 329–364.

Geradin, P., & Thibaut, F. (2004). Epidemiology and treatment of juvenile sexual offending. *Pediatric Drugs, 6*(2), 79–91.

Gerhard-Burnham, B., Underwood, L. A., Speck, K., Williams, C. Crump, Y. (in press). The lived experience of the adolescent sex offender: A phenomenological case study. *Journal of Child Sexual Abuse.*

Gibson, C., & Vandiver, D. M. (2008). *Juvenile sex offenders: What the public needs to know.* Westport, CT: Praeger.

Glick, B., & Goldstein, A. P. (Eds.). (1995). *Managing delinquency programs that work.* Lanham, MD: American Correctional Association.

Glowacz, F., & Born, M. (2013). Do adolescent child abusers, peer abusers, and non-sex offenders have different personality profiles? *European Child & Adolescent Psychology, 22*, 117–125. doi:10.1007/s00787-012-0333-2

Grisso, T., & Underwood, L. A. (2005). *Screening and assessing co-occurring disorders in the juvenile justice system.* Washington, DC: The Federal Office of Juvenile Justice Delinquency Prevention (OJJDP) and The National GAINS Center for People with Co-Occurring Disorders in the Justice System.

Gunby, C., & Woodhams, J. (2010). Sexually deviant juveniles: Comparisons between the offender and offence characteristics of child abusers and peer abusers. *Psychology: Crime & Law, 16*(1–2), 47–64. doi:10.1080/10683160802621966

Hart-Kerkhoffs, L., Doreleijers, T., Jansen, L., van Wijk, A., & Bullens, R. (2009). Offense related characteristics and psychosexual development of juvenile sex offenders. *Child and Adolescent Psychiatry and Mental Health, 3,* 19. doi:10.1186/1753-2000-3-19

Hempel, I., Buck, N., Cima, M., & van Marle, H. (2013). Review of risk assessment instruments for juvenile sex offenders: What is next? *International Journal of Offender Therapy and Comparative Criminology, 57*(2), 208–228. doi:10.1177/0306624X11428315

Hendriks, J., & Bijleveld, C. (2008). Recidivism among juvenile sex offenders after residential treatment. *Journal of Sexual Aggression, 14*(1), 19–32. doi:10.1080/13552600802133852

Hinnen, C., Sanderman, R., & Sprangers, M. (2009). Adult attachment as mediator between recollections of childhood and satisfaction with life. *Clinical Psychology & Psychotherapy, 16,* 10–21.

Hiscox, S. P., Witt, P. H., & Haran, S. J. (2007). Juvenile Risk Assessment Scale (JRAS): A predictive validity study. *Journal of Psychiatry & Law, 35,* 503–539.

Hodges, K. (1995, March). *Psychometric study of a telephone interview for the CAFAS using an expanded version of the scale.* Paper presented at the Eighth Annual Research Conference on A System of Care for Children' Mental Health: Expanding the Research Base, Tampa, FL.

Keogh, T. (2012). *The internal world of the juvenile sex offender: Through a glass darkly then face to face.* London, England: Karnac Books.

Linehan, M. (1993). *Cognitive-behavioral treatment of borderline personality disorder.* New York, NY: Guilford Press.

Lussier, P., Van Den Berg, C., Bijleveld, C., & Hendriks, J. (2012). A developmental taxonomy of juvenile sex offenders for theory, research, and prevention: The adolescent-limited and the high-rate slow desister. *Criminal Justice and Behavior, 39,* 1559–1581. doi:10.1177/0093854812455739

Lyons, J. S., Libman-Mintzer, L. N., Kisiel, C. L., & Shallcross, H. (1998). Understanding the mental health needs of children and adolescents in residential treatment. *Professional Psychology: Research and Practice, 29*(6), 582–587.

Marshall, W. L., & Fernandez, Y. M. (2000). Phallometric testing with sexual offenders: Limits to its value. *Clinical Psychology Review, 20*(7), 807–822.

Marshall, W. L., Hudson, S., & Hodkinson, S. (1993). The importance of attachment bonds on the development of juvenile sex offending. In H. E. Barabee, W. L. Marshall, & S. M. Hudson (Eds.), *The juvenile sex offender* (pp. 164–181). New York, NY: Springer.

McEllrath, R. (2014). Keeping up with technology: Why a flexible juvenile sexting statute is needed to prevent overly severe punishment in Washington State. *Washington Law Review, 89*(3), 1009–1034.

Merz, E., Schuengel, C., & Schulze, H. (2008). Intergenerational relationships at different ages: An attachment perspective. *Aging & Society, 28,* 717–736.

Metzner, J. L., Humphreys, S., & Ryan, G. (2009). Juveniles who sexually offend: Psychosocial intervention and treatment. In F. M. Saleh (Ed.), *Sex offenders: Identification, risk assessment, treatment, and legal issues* (pp. 241–261). London, England: Oxford University Press.

Miccio-Fonseca, L. C., & Rasmussen, L. A. (2009). New nomenclature for sexually abusive youth: Naming and assessing sexually violent and predatory offenders. *Journal of Aggression, Maltreatment, & Trauma, 18,* 106–128. doi:10.1080/1092 6770802616431

Miner, M. H. (2002). Factors associated with recidivism in juveniles: An analysis of serious juvenile sex offenders. *Journal of Research in Crime & Delinquency, 39*(4), 421–436. doi:10.1177/00224 2702237287

Moberg, D. P., & Hahn, L. (1991). The adolescent drug involvement scale. *Journal of Child & Adolescent Substance Abuse, 2*(1), 75–88.

Nelson, M. (2007). Characteristics, treatment, and practitioner's perceptions of juvenile sex offenders. *Journal for Juvenile Justice Services, 21*(1–2), 7–16.

O'Brien, M., & Bera, W. (1986). Adolescent sexual offenders: A descriptive typology. *Newsletter of the National Family Life Education Network, 1,* 1–5.

Oxnam, P., & Vess, J. (2006). A personality-based typology of adolescent sex offenders using the Millon Adolescent Clinical Inventory. *New Zealand Journal of Psychology, 35*(1), 36–44.

Oxnam, P., & Vess, J. (2008). A typology of adolescent sexual offenders: Millon Adolescent Clinical Inventory profiles, developmental factors, and offence characteristics. *Journal of Forensic*

Psychiatry & Psychology, 19(2), 228–242. doi:10.1080/14789940701694452

Poortinga, E., Newman, S. S., Negendank, C. E., & Benedek, E. P. (2009). Juvenile sex offenders: Epidemiology, risk assessment, and treatment. In F. M. Saleh (Ed.), *Sex offenders: Identification, risk assessment, treatment, and legal issues* (pp. 241–261). London, England: Oxford University Press.

Powers-Sawyer, A. B., & Miner, M. H. (2009). Actuarial prediction of juvenile recidivism: The static variables of the Juvenile Sex Offender Assessment Protocol-II (J-SOAP-II). *Sexual Offender Treatment, 4*(2), 1–13.

Prentky, R., Harris, B., Frizzell, K., & Righthand, S. (2000). An actuarial procedure for assessing risk with juvenile sex offenders. *Sexual Abuse: A Journal of Research and Treatment, 12*(2), 71–93.

Prentky, R., & Righthand, S. (2003). *Juvenile Sex Offender Assessment Protocol-II (J-SOAP-II) manual*. Washington, DC: U.S. Department of Justice, Office of Justice Programs, Office of Juvenile Justice and Delinquency Prevention.

Priddis, L., & Howieson, N. (2009). The vicissitudes of mother-infant relationships between birth and six years. *Early Child Development and Care, 179*(1), 43–53.

Prochaska, J. O., & DiClemente, C. C. (1992). In search of how people change. *American Psychologist, 47*(9), 1102–1114.

Quayle, E., & Taylor, M. (2006). Young people who sexually abuse: The role of new technologies. In M. Erooga & H. C. Masson (Eds.), *Children and young people who sexually abuse others: Current developments and practice responses* (pp. 115–127). New York, NY: Routledge.

Randall, J., Henggeler, S., Pickrel, S., & Brondino, M. (1999). Psychiatric comorbidity and the 16-month trajectory of substance-abusing and substance-dependent juvenile offenders. *Journal of the American Academy of Child and Adolescent Psychiatry, 38*(9), 1118–1124.

Rasmussen, L. A. (2004). Differentiating youth who sexually abuse: Applying a multidimensional framework when assessing and treating subtypes. *Journal of Child Sexual Abuse, 13*(3–4), 57–82. doi:10.1300/J070v13n03_04

Rehfuss, M. C., Underwood, L. A., Enright, M., Hill, S., Marshall, R., Tipton, P., & Warren, K. (2013). Treatment impact of an integrated sex offender program as measured by J-SOAP-II.

Journal of Correctional Health Care, 19(2), 113–123. doi:1078345812474641

Reynolds, C. R., & Kamphaus, R. W. (1998). *BASC: Behavior assessment system for children: Manual.* Circle Pines, MN: American Guidance Service.

Righthand, S., & Welch, C. (2004). Characteristics of youth who sexually offend. *Journal of Child Sexual Abuse, 13*(3–4), 15–32. doi:10.1300/J070v13n03_02

Robertiello, G., & Terry, K. (2007). Can we profile sex offenders? A review of sex offender typologies. *Aggression and Violent Behavior, 12,* 508–518. doi:10.1016/j.avb.2007. 02.010

Seto, M. C., & Lalumiere, M. L. (2010). What is so special about male adolescent sex offending? A review and test of explanations through meta-analysis. *Psychological Bulletin, 136*(4), 526–575. doi:10.1037/a0019700

Shaw, R. (2001). Why use interpretative phenomenological analysis in health psychology? *Health Psychology Update, 10,* 48–52.

Stevenson, M. C., Sorenson, K. M., Smith, A. C., Sekely, A., & Dzwairo, R. A. (2009). Effects of defendant and victim race on perceptions of juvenile sex offenders. *Behavioral Sciences & the Law, 27*(6), 957–979. doi:10.1002/bsl.910

Szielasko, A. L., Symons, D. K., & Price, E. L. (2013). Development of an attachment-informed measure of sexual behavior in late adolescence. *Journal of adolescence, 36*(2), 361–370.

Teplin, L. A., Abram, K. M., McClelland, G. M., Dulcan, M. K., & Mericle, A. A. (2002). Psychiatric disorders in youth in juvenile detention. *Archives of General Psychiatry, 59*(12), 1133–1143.

Terry, K. J. (2013). *Sexual offenses and offenders: Theory, practice and policy* (2nd ed.). Belmont, CA: Wadsworth.

Underwood, L. A., & Knight, P. (2006). Treatment and postrelease rehabilitative programs for juvenile offenders. *Child and Adolescent Psychiatric Clinics of North America, 15*(2), 539–556.

Underwood, L. A., Phillips, A., von Dresner, K., & Knight, P. D. (2006). Critical factors in mental health programming for juveniles in corrections facilities. *International Journal of Behavioral and Consultation Therapy, 2*(1), 108–141.

Underwood, L. A., Robinson, S. B., Mosholder, E., & Warren, K. M. (2008). Sex offender care for adolescents in secure care: Critical factors and counseling strategies. *Clinical Psychology Review, 28,* 917–932. doi:10.1016/j.cpr.2008.01.004

Underwood, L. A., von Dresner, K. S., & Phillips, A. L. (2006). Community treatment programs for juveniles: A best-evidence summary. *International Journal of Behavioral and Consultation Therapy, 2*(2), 286–304.

Underwood, L. A., Warren, K. M., Talbott, L., Jackson, L., & Dailey, F. L. (2014). Mental health treatment in juvenile justice secure care facilities: Practice and policy recommendations. *Journal of Forensic Psychology Practice, 14,* 55–85. doi: 10.1080/15228932.2014.865398

Underwood, L. A., Dailey, F. L., Merino, C., & Crump, Y. (in press). Results from a multimodal program evaluation of a four year statewide juvenile sex offender treatment program. *Journal of Prison Re-entry & Education.*

Vasilenko, S. A., Lefkowitz, E. S., & Welsh, D. P. (2014). Is sexual behavior healthy for adolescents? A conceptual framework for research on adolescent sexual behavior and physical, mental, and social health. *New Directions for Child and Adolescent Development, 2014*(144), 3–19.

Viljoen, J. L., Elkovitch, N., Scalora, J., & Ullman, D. (2009). Assessment of reoffense risk in adolescents who have committed sexual offenses: Predictive validity of the ERASOR, PCL:YV, YLS/CMI and Static-99. *Criminal Justice and Behavior, 36*(10), 981–1000.

Watkins, C. E., & Campbell, V. L. (2000). *Testing and assessment in counseling practice.* Mahwah, NJ: Erlbaum.

Wells, M., Mitchell, K. J., & Ji, K. (2012). Exploring the role of the Internet in juvenile prostitution cases coming to the attention of law enforcement. *Journal of Child Sexual Abuse, 21*(3), 327–342. doi:10.1080/10538712.2012.669823

Worling, J. (2002). Assessing risk of sexual assault recidivism with adolescent sexual offenders. In M. C. Calder (Ed.), *Young people who sexually abuse: Building the evidence base for your practice* (pp. 365–375). Lyme Regis, England: Russell House.

Worling, J. R., & Curwen, T. (2001). *The "ERASOR": Estimate of risk of adolescent sexual offense recidivism* (Version 2.0). Toronto, Ontario, Canada: Safe-T Program, Thistletown Regional Centre.

Yochelson, S., & Samenow, S. (1976). *The criminal mind.* New York, NY: Aronson.

Zaremba, L. A., & Keiley, M. K. (2011). The mediational effect of affect regulation on the relationship between attachment and internalizing/externalizing behaviors in adolescent males who have sexually offended. *Children and Youth Services Review, 33,* 1599–1607. doi:10.1016/j.childyouth.2011.04.011

17

WHO IS THE CLIENT? KEY ETHICAL AND LEGAL ISSUES

INTRODUCTION

The welfare of clients is a major concern within society and it seems that joining together over their well-being is something we can all agree on. A legal counseling practice should be something providers aspire to embody and not simply do. According to Parrott (2003), the foundation of legal counseling is "virtuous." It was further stated that virtue should be defined as a trait or a part of one's character, rather than a principle (Parrott, 2003). This pathway to virtue in a legal practice should start with a legal competence, including knowledge of laws and civil rights (Parrott, 2003). The aforementioned establishes that providers have a responsibility to clients to provide a quality of professional services. Furrow (1980) stated,

> Legally, the provider must possess the degree of learning, skill, and ability that others similarly situated ordinarily possess; exercise reasonable care and diligence in the application of knowledge and skill to the patient's [client's] needs; and use their best judgment in the treatment and care of patients. (p. 23)

When working with adolescents, there are unique ethical challenges and dilemmas of which

providers need to be cognizant. Oftentimes, legal and ethical obligations conflict when considering the rights of minors. Defining who the client is can aid in addressing these conflicts; however, further understanding of the intricacies of ethics specific to minors allows the provider to better meet the needs of the client. Koocher (2003) cautions professional providers to consider the key stakeholders (e.g., parents, adolescents, case managers, court officials), whose legal and ethical responsibility is of concern, and what issues must be addressed and by whom for counseling services with minors to be done in the most impacting and ethical manner.

This concern for ethics is evident in research findings corresponding to the behavioral health care of minors, and adolescents in particular. Common dilemmas found within research include issues related to provider competency, client's rights, confidentiality, consent to treatment, treatment modality, and direction of the therapeutic process (Bodenhorn, 2010; Hermann, 2002; Koocher, 2003; Lawrence & Robinson-Kurpius, 2000). In school settings, most prevalent issues have been shown to include evaluating suicidality, reporting suspected child abuse, determining harm to oneself or others, maintaining confidentiality of student records, having dual relationships with teachers and staff, and concerns related to educational laws, educational malpractice, and parental rights (Bodenhorn, 2010; Hermann, 2002). While less common, school providers have also had to navigate harassment of students by other students, statutory rape, and minors' abortion rights (Hermann, 2002). Across settings, developmental level of the client influenced the types of ethical challenges faced by the provider (Bodenhorn, 2010).

With consideration of the existing wealth of research, this chapter seeks to address the most common and pervasive ethical challenges encountered in counseling adolescents. Some of these issues have been conceptualized to mirror applicable codes of ethics to better aid in considerations of best practices. As such, future chapters discuss topics related to the ethical and legal concerns providers face in identifying their clients. Key ethical and legal issues further delineate the following topics:

- Defining the client
- Confidentiality
- Collaborative care
- Consent to treatment
- Dual relationships
- Clinical competence

Throughout this chapter (and the textbook, in general), it is important to note that the term *parent* will be used to describe those in the legal role of caregiver. This may be a biological parent(s); however, it may also include legal guardians. At the onset of professional services and within direct inquiry, providers should confirm the individual who is legally responsible for the adolescents. This is especially important when working with parents who are divorced or in the process of divorce (Bodenhorn, 2010). Confirming who has been given custodial rights to consent to treatment is crucial to provide clarity on parental consent for the adolescent's mental health services involvement.

This chapter aims to assist the reader in identifying who the client is when working with adolescents. To do so, this chapter reviews the legal challenges and ethical considerations pertinent to a therapeutic relationship with adolescents. By the end of this chapter, readers will be able to do the following:

- Determine who the client is
- Decipher when informed consent and adolescent assent is applicable
- Understand how to determine the parameters of confidentiality
- Become aware of exceptions to the rules of consent and confidentiality when treating minors
- Understand how to apply the concepts of confidentiality and informed consent to cases
- Demonstrate knowledge of issues related to collaborative care, dual relationships, and gaining clinical competence

WHO IS THE CLIENT?

Treating adolescents in counseling presents a number of unique ethical challenges (Koocher, 2003). The legal issues and challenges that behavioral health professionals are faced with when treating adults are similar to those when treating adolescents. How these legal issues and challenges are dealt with, however, takes on a different process due to two factors that make counseling relationships with adolescents unique. The first distinguishing factor purports that the "adolescent has limited (if any) legal capacity" (Sankaran & Macbeth, 2010, chap. 9, p. 110). Sankaran and Macbeth (2010, chap. 9) suggest that "the second factor is that the mutual relationship between provider and [adolescent] must bend to accommodate a third party or third and fourth parties)—the parent(s) [guardians]" (p. 110).

In working with adolescents in a counseling relationship, case and statutory law reflect a tension that reveals a strain and a balance between two schools of thought of case and statutory law and counseling ethics. First, the law presumes that parents have the right to decide how to raise their children, control their children's legal rights, have their children's best interests, and have a level of discernment, maturity, and experience to lead by example (Sankaran & Macbeth, 2010, chap. 9). However, and second, both legal and ethical standards support the recognition that adolescents have some level of independence that undermines their parent's personal wishes (Sankaran & Macbeth, 2010, chap. 9). For instance, adolescents should be given the right to make decisions regarding their own mental health treatment. Of course, on the one hand, parents obviously have the right to make decisions they deem fit for their adolescent son or daughter; nonetheless, adolescents, as persons with maturing cognitive complexity, should have a say in their treatment especially since research shows the importance of provider–client rapport building and trust (refer to Chapter 9).

The inherent dilemma is anchored on the fact that the provider will be treating the adolescent (especially in individual counseling sessions) and the strength of the provider–client bond can be compromised if one of the two is stifled in their respective roles. In other words, the provider is ethically charged to extend respect, hold the confidences, engender trust, and adhere to issues of autonomy (e.g., self-determination), and the general beneficence of the adolescent client within counseling services. The role of the adolescent is to share freely, take risks within the provider–client relationship to be truly known (successes, failures, secrets, and confidences), make efforts to try new things, as well as play an active role in identifying goals jointly (shared between himself or herself and the provider). These two roles can be inherently challenged by adding others into the dynamic with varying levels of "power" and influence regarding the counseling services as is often indicated when a parental figure exerts their legal right to join the two-way relationship between the provider and the client.

This challenge, more often than not, has implications regarding the therapeutic change that can take place for adolescents, who by their very developmental process are suspended between the dependency of childhood and the independence of adulthood. Furthermore, adolescent development is full of incidences and expressions of autonomy, differentiating from parents, and finding one's identity. Expressions of these developmental tasks are often seen in counseling sessions and therapeutic themes therein. Adolescents who are anxious, are suspicious, or have direct knowledge of parents being aware of and directing counseling work are less likely to share their experiences, concerns, and challenges in an open manner. The balancing act of the tensions between parental rights, the minor's cognitive competency, and the goals of therapy is further complicated by the changing dynamics of the family structure itself.

At present, the nuclear family is no longer the standard that all families experience or aspire for. For example, it is no longer unusual for adolescents to have separated or divorced parents who may or may not agree about decisions regarding the mental health care of their adolescent. Additionally, providers, depending on the setting in which they work, may work with adolescents who live primarily with an extended family member or a foster parent who may only be in the adolescent's life for an undetermined amount of time and who has limited legal decision-making rights for the adolescents. In such situations, it is imperative that professional providers understand that the tension between parental rights and adolescent rights with regard to the bounds of therapeutic treatment has been undergoing rapid changes for several years, and is governed primarily by state-specific statutes. Furthermore, it is imperative that providers become familiar with the legal standards regarding this issue in the state in which they work. These standards include giving adolescents more independence regarding their individual treatment–related decisions (Sankaran & Macbeth, 2010, chap. 9) and offer that professional providers learn to navigate the intrinsic tension between parents and adolescent clients with open discussion of challenges, the professional's legal limitations (e.g., self-harm or other-harm behaviors), and how the parent and the child plan to discuss concerns regarding confidentiality issues within their therapeutic relationships.

Why must providers know and understand this information? Knowledge and understanding of this tension, the legal implications, parental rights, and adolescent confidentiality needs are all required because the individual with decision-making authority is not the client but a third party—an adult—who has the legal authority to make decisions with the client—the adolescent (Sankaran & Macbeth, 2010, chap. 9). Any behavioral health professional who counsels an adolescent without getting legally sufficient consent risks being sued for "potential tort or malpractice liability" (Sankaran & Macbeth, 2010, chap. 9, p. 110). Regardless of whether the services provided were "appropriate and satisfied all applicable standards of care," the provider is still responsible for any repercussions of the unauthorized care (Sankaran & Macbeth, 2010, chap. 9, p. 110). Establishing who has the authority to consent to treatment for the adolescent can be a murky yet important endeavor and can have implications for success or challenge within the therapeutic relationship.

The Adolescent Client

By virtue of their developmental state, adolescents have a greater need for trust, and they value providers who honor and maintain a sense of integrity about the client's privacy (Blunt, 2006). For adolescents in particular, this relational agreement with the provider is essential for the minor's participation in the treatment process (Blunt, 2006). From a legal standpoint, adolescents have reduced autonomy and are not developmentally mature enough to protect their own interests fully (Hathaway, 2013). On that note, it is vital for providers to ensure the integrity of adolescents' rights (Hathaway, 2013). The circumstances surrounding the embarkation of a counseling relationship with an adolescent should always be thoroughly examined. Some issues that providers should consider include "to whom providers owe the ethical obligation of confidentiality, parental consent and legal rights, informed consent [and assent] and the competency level of the minor" (Ledyard, 1998, p. 171). So the question for the provider becomes, "Who exactly is my client when working with adolescents?" Consider the hypothetical case of Elsie (Case Scenario 17.1) as the basis for framing this chapter's discussion on minors' rights.

COUNSELING ADOLESCENTS: KEY ETHICAL CONSIDERATIONS

Codes of Ethics

The behavioral health profession has widely recognized the need for defining ethical

---

Case Scenario 17.1

Elsie

Elsie is a 15-year-old girl who is brought to a community mental health clinic by her mother. On intake, Elsie's mother described herself as a single parent, as she and Elsie's father divorced 2 years ago. He is currently serving in the military and is on tour for 1 year in Iraq. Initially, Elsie presents with concerns regarding anxiety, appetite and sleep schedule changes, and a depressed mood. During the course of treatment, the client reveals that she is pregnant and unsure what to do regarding her choices. She reports that she has the support of her 16-year-old boyfriend Aaron. Elsie is insisting that she is unwilling to tell her mother about her pregnancy.

standards for care. As such, codes of ethics have been implemented for nearly every area of specialty within the field of counseling. For example, the American Counseling Association (ACA, 2014) and the American School Counselor Association (ASCA, 2010) both offer important considerations for professional providers and providers in training. There are many other relevant codes of ethics from other professional organizations along with state and national credentialing bodies; however, it is essential that counseling students, educators, and practitioners working with adolescents are acclimated to these codes in particular and the codes' specific application toward this diverse population. Unfortunately, while many practitioners have had training on ethics, only 8% reported they referred to the codes frequently (Bodenhorn, 2010). Given the importance of referring to relevant standards in many ethical decision-making models, this is particularly concerning.

Consent to Treatment

As emphasized throughout this chapter thus far, a parent has the legal rights over his or her adolescent's records. While there are certain exceptions within the school counseling setting regarding consent and records (Keim & Cobia, 2010), a parent (or other legally appointed guardian) is the only one who is able to consent to his or her adolescent's treatment unless there are special legal limitations concerning the adolescent and such care (e.g., foster care placement, child welfare, juvenile justice involvement). In the professional counseling field, informed consent is "the formal permission given by a client that signals the beginning of the legal, contractual agreement that allows treatment to be initiated" (Lawrence & Robinson-Kurpius, 2000, p. 133). Though informed consent through appropriate documentation (verbal or written per state and professional stipulations) serves as a legal contract for treatment, an adolescent does not have the legal right to enter into counseling without his or her parent's consent.

Parental Consent

With this in mind, it is absolutely crucial for the provider to determine who the "parent" is or who has custodial and legal rights for the adolescent's medical treatment. Particularly in situations with noncustodial, separated, or divorced parents, releasing information to a noncustodial parent can put the provider at risk for legal proceedings (Lawrence & Robinson-Kurpius, 2000; Remley & Herlihy, 2010). When a provider works with adolescents in the midst of divorce proceedings, it is important for the providers not to take sides with one parent over another, to differentiate between the role of the provider and the child custody evaluator, and to remain current on any changes made to custodial rights (Remley & Herlihy, 2010). When counseling adolescents, obtaining parental consent for the minor to receive services can be murky waters considering various family structures in society currently. Providers should exercise caution considering issues of consent for adolescents of divorced or separated parents—or in situations in which the client is brought to seek services by a nonbiological guardian (Sankaran & Macbeth, 2010, chap. 9). In such instances, the provider should take steps within reason to clarify who has legal custody of the adolescent and whether the parent who consents to treatment has legal custody (Sankaran & Macbeth, 2010, chap. 9). For example, in the case of Elsie, the provider should clarify whether Elsie's mother has sole custody of Elsie and whether Elsie's father is an absent parent, or otherwise has no custodial rights to Elsie. If both Elsie's mother and father share legal custody, consent for treatment should be sought from both parents and in some cases may be required.

Extenuating circumstances, such as distance living or hostile parental interactions with each other, may restrict the likelihood of receiving both parents' signatures on such consent forms. This difficulty can be further aggravated when and if the provider finds that involving a noncustodial parent would be therapeutically beneficial; it might be difficult for the provider to receive such consent from the custodial parent (Sankaran & Macbeth, 2010, chap. 9). In the event that parents who share legal custody do not agree about counseling services, it may be necessary for the court to intervene and decide whether the services would be of benefit to the minor (Sankaran & Macbeth, 2010, chap. 9). This additional legal involvement may prolong the adolescent's access to counseling services and may incite tension between the parent and the provider. This scenario gets even more complicated when an adolescent client's parents divorce during the course of counseling. In such a situation, a provider may continue providing services to the minor; however, he or she must desist services if one of the parents requests so. This dilemma presents the provider with an opportunity to reclarify and reconfirm who has the authority to provide consent to services of the adolescent (Sankaran & Macbeth, 2010, chap. 9). Furthermore, it is incumbent on the provider to obtain associated divorce decrees to ensure accuracy of information.

Another challenge for providers to consider is to be aware that, while the adolescent may have a parent–child relationship with the individual that brings him or her to treatment, the "parent" may not actually have the legal right to make decisions regarding the adolescent's provision of services. In fact, many states do not provide stepparents or relatives (i.e., grandparents or extended family members who informally serve as parental figures) the power to consent to services (Sankaran & Macbeth, 2010, chap. 9). A note of distinction is warranted here as an "investigation" of parental rights must be undertaken by the provider; however, the professional provider's understanding that only a parent with legal custody has authority to consent to a minor's treatment is essential. With that in mind, if nobody raises questions about whether or not a particular parent has the authority to consent, then providers are not obligated to enquire about parental custody (Sankaran & Macbeth, 2010, chap. 9). Once questions of legal authority arise, however, the provider does have an ethical duty to clarify the situation (Sankaran & Macbeth, 2010, chap. 9). While consent from the parents is needed in the majority of treatment of minors, there are some exceptions to this rule. Professional providers must stay abreast of changes in state laws and professional ethical requirements throughout their professional lives. What follows is additional information regarding the informed consent process and further articulation of issues related to assent.

Informed Consent

Once traversing the minefield of who has the legal authority to make decisions for the adolescent's counseling, professional providers are encouraged to involve parent(s) and the adolescents in informed consent processes. These processes are best executed when consent documentations are directed toward the adolescent's developmental level, to assist both the adolescent and the parent to fully understand the document's content and purpose (Glosoff & Pate, 2002; Vitiello, 2008). Though there are many times when adolescents are not legally able to provide such consent, the provider who is seeking to attain the adolescent client's assent or "active affirmation or willingness to volunteer" (Vitiello, 2008, p. 183) can be a positive element within the burgeoning provider–client relationship. It should be noted that although assent is not a legal concept, it is certainly an ethical ideal opportunity to strengthen therapeutic efforts.

Process of Informed Consent. The initiating activity of counseling is the retrieval of informed consent. Informed consent is the basic right of the client to choose whether or not to enter into or remain in a counseling relationship (ACA, 2014). To make this decision, all parties—adolescent or adult—must be provided with adequate information regarding the counseling process and the provider (ACA, 2014). The ACA Code of Ethics (2014) advises that providers are obligated to review the rights of the client and the provider both in writing and verbally (ACA, 2014, p. 6). Many practitioners and ethicists would provide that the informed consent process is ongoing throughout treatment; thus, the provider should appropriately document all discussions of informed consent (ACA, 2014, A.2.a) and practice-based practices to maintain such records according to state and ethical mandates.

Assent. According to the ACA Code of Ethics (2014), assent to services by an adolescent must be sought by the provider. Unfortunately, assent is not required for the treatment of minors. Minors currently have no legal rights to deny inpatient care, and parents can commit children unwillingly (Koocher, 2003; Lawrence & Robinson-Kurpius, 2000). In instances where a parent seeks inpatient or hospitalized care for his or her child, providers should serve as advocates for the children to seek the least restrictive treatment setting that is still safe for the client (Koocher, 2003).

Including the Adolescent in Decision Making. Additionally, the adolescent is to be included in the decision-making process (ACA, 2014). Oftentimes, providers are working not only with adolescents but also with their caregivers, parents, siblings, or other family members. This requires the provider to balance the client's ethical rights to choose, his or her ability to provide consent or assent for services, and the legal responsibilities and rights of the parent (or family) to protect and make decisions for the adolescent (ACA, 2014). Because the provider may be working with multiple clients (in a family setting), the ACA suggests that providers explicitly identify which person(s) is the client(s) and provide a description of the provider's relationship with each involved person at the outset of services (ACA, 2014, A.8). For example, in the case of Elsie, during the first session, the provider should identify Elsie as the client with both Elsie and her mother present. Additionally, the provider should outline the boundaries of the relationship he or she will have with Elsie and her mother. At that time, one might also detail the importance of the adolescent's privacy/confidentiality of specific information in relationship to building rapport with the provider.

Now consider adolescents who have been mandated, or required by law, to receive one's services as a provider. Is the client then the guardian (which may be the state) or the mandated adolescent attending each session? If the client is not the adolescent, then what does this mean with regard to confidentiality? The ACA requires that providers discuss the limitations to confidentiality at the outset of services when working with adolescents mandated for counseling (ACA, 2014, A.2.e). What this means is that the provider has the obligation to explain the types of information that will be shared with others, and the provider must additionally identify with whom this information will be shared (ACA, 2014). Of course, the reason would have one wonder whether or not this standard would actually result in the willing participation of the adolescent in treatment. In fact, an adolescent who does not wish to receive services may deny assent, but this does not necessitate the cessation of treatment. The ACA code of ethics advises providers to relay to the client the "potential consequences of refusing counseling services to the best of his/her ability" (ACA, 2014, A.2.e, p. 6). In working with adolescents, it is important for providers to differentiate parental consent from minor assent, in obtaining informed consent from one's clients.

Exceptions to the Rule: Competency of the Minor

There are several exceptions to the provision of services to adolescents without parental consent; however, these exceptions vary by state and jurisdiction (Lawrence & Robinson-Kurpius, 2000; Ledyard, 1998; Sankaran & Macbeth, 2010, chap. 9; Welfel, 2002). Even consent procedures for school providers vary from other settings (Keim & Cobia, 2010). One of the exceptions is the provision of counseling services in emergency situations (Ledyard, 1998; Sankaran & Macbeth, 2010, chap. 9). Informed consent is generally an accepted policy in most counseling service situations with adolescents; however, Keshavarz (2005) illuminated that it "is not always possible to adequately explain and discuss the full range of possibilities in an emergency setting" (p. 233). In most jurisdictions, emergency situations do not require consent, purportedly to reflect the notion that if enough time was allotted to consult, a parent would more than likely consent to the provision of services to the adolescent in distress (Sankaran & Macbeth, 2010, chap. 9).

Other exceptions may include emancipated minors, mature minors, or minors with certain medical conditions (Koocher, 2003; Lawrence & Robinson-Kurpius, 2000; Remley & Herlihy, 2010). Emancipated minors are determined by the court and may include individuals who have been married, are enlisted in the military, or have gained financial independence and live apart from parents (Koocher, 2003; Lawrence & Robinson-Kurpius, 2000; Remley & Herlihy, 2010). For emancipated minors—adolescents who are no longer legally under the control of their parents—parental consent for the provision of treatment is unnecessary (Lawrence & Robinson-Kurpius, 2000; Ledyard, 1998; Sankaran & Macbeth, 2010, chap. 9). According to Gustafson and McNamara (1987), adolescents older than 14 years are generally considered to have similar capabilities as adults in making the decision to agree to receive counseling services.

The notion of the mature minor operates as another exception to the confines of informed consent, allowing that under certain circumstances the adolescent may be considered mature enough to seek out services without the involvement of a parent or guardian in a few states (Sankaran & Macbeth, 2010, chap. 9). Definitions of mature minors vary from state to state. As such, it is important for providers to be aware of their state legislation that is relevant to consent to treatment for minors (Glosoff & Pate, 2002). In many states, minors with medical conditions such as pregnancy or sexually transmitted diseases may also be able to seek treatment without consent of their parents (Koocher, 2003; Lawrence & Robinson-Kurpius, 2000). Additionally, many jurisdictions allow minors to seek therapy for sexual and substance abuse and seek advice regarding sexual activity (transmitted diseases, contraception, pregnancy, and birth control options), and/or mental health issues related to HIV without parental consent (Blunt, 2006; Corey, Corey, & Callanan, 1998; Keshavarz, 2005; North, 1990; Sankaran &

Macbeth, 2010, chap. 9; Welfel, 2002). With the concept of the mature minor, adolescents can generally consent—depending on jurisdiction—to their own treatment for conditions that are of relatively minimal risk in nature (Lawrence & Robinson-Kurpius, 2010; Ledyard, 1998; Sankaran & Macbeth, 2010, chap. 9).

In the case of Elsie, she revealed to her provider that she was pregnant and was weighing her options regarding pregnancy. Elsie sought treatment at the request of her mother's concern about Elsie's drastic mood change and anxiety symptoms. In short, Elsie did not seek treatment regarding her pregnancy. Her sharing her pregnant state within the counseling relationship is one of confidentiality (privacy regarding topics shared with others), as opposed to one of informed consent. In the scenario, it is clear that Elsie and her mother have already agreed to the terms of counseling services; during the course of treatment, it was discovered that Elsie was pregnant and wanting advice on her options. Depending on the specifications of the provider's informed consent form, he or she may be obligated to relay the pregnancy to Elsie's mom regardless of desires to keep it private. If this is indeed the case, the provider would fare well to discuss this obligation with Elsie and include language in their sessions about the information that will be shared, provide ample opportunities for Elsie to share the information, and discuss the costs and benefits (for example) of such a revelation and its delivery. If the consent does not require such sharing, the provider may continue providing services to Elsie's presenting problems; need to obtain Elsie's consent to discuss, plan, and problem solve regarding the pregnancy; and even consider how various supports (including her mother, possibly) within Elsie's life might assist her during this difficult time of life that she can choose from which to mature.

For the mature adolescent to make his or her own decisions regarding services requires his or her understanding of the risks and benefits to various treatment possibilities (Keshavarz, 2005). Regardless, consenting rights are generally provided for adolescents who are "self-supporting, married, pregnant, or have a child of their own, are enlisted in the military, or have been declared emancipated by the court" (Keshavarz, 2005, p. 233).

Privileged Communication and Confidentiality

Privacy is held in high regard here in the United States. It refers to the people's right to not have their personal lives intruded on beyond their desires. Although not specifically found in the U.S. Constitution, privacy established its significance in the Harvard Law Review in 1890 (Warren & Brandeis, 1890). The Harvard Law Review maintains that every person has an imminent right to privacy that the law must safeguard. This argument was expanded in the 1914 *Schloendorff v. The Society of New York Hospital*. The landmark case of *Schloendorff v. The Society of New York Hospital* (1914) established that a person has the right to control his or her own body. Within the case, Mary Schloendorff was admitted to New York Hospital. While admitted, Schloendorff gave consent to examine and determine if a fibroid tumor was malignant; however, she withheld consent to remove the tumor. The physician found that the tumor was malignant and then removed the tumor against Schloendorff's wishes. The court ruled that removing the tumor without Schloendorff's consent established medical battery. As previously stated, this landmark case recognized the right to have control of one's own body (*Schloendorff v. The Society of New York Hospital*, 1914). Other cases, following *Schloendorff v. The Society of New York Hospital* (1914), further expanded on defining privacy as a right.

Confidentiality is perhaps one of the greatest ethical conflicts when counseling children and adolescents. Confidentiality has been defined as a "professional's promise or contract to respect clients' privacy by not disclosing anything revealed during counseling except under agreed upon conditions" (Glosoff & Pate, 2002, p. 22). This contract seeks to protect the counseling relationship and strength of its alliance (Isaacs & Stone, 2001).

A lack of confidentiality may limit client disclosure or affect a provider's ability to form a trusting, therapeutic alliance (Isaacs & Stone, 2001; Koocher, 2003; Lawrence & Robinson-Kurpius, 2000). As such, a provider's ability to maintain confidentiality with the client is directly related to the success of the counseling process.

Unfortunately, responsibilities of confidentiality are confounded between law and ethics in work with minors. Federal and state laws, written policies, and applicable ethical standards necessitate that providers have a responsibility to protect the confidentiality of information received, via any medium, when they are working with adolescents (ACA, 2014). Providers' legal obligations are in direct conflict with ethical obligations (Lazovsky, 2008; Ledyard, 1998; Mitchell, Disque, & Robertson, 2002; Remley & Herlihy, 2010). Of course, providers also have a responsibility to the parents and legal guardians of a minor—usually defined as an individual under the age of 18. This responsibility includes "informing parents/legal guardians about the provider's role and the confidential nature of the provider–client relationship, which must be consistent with current legal and custodial arrangements" (ACA, 2014, p. 7). The legal obligation is to the parent despite the ethical obligation to the child as the client (Glosoff & Pate, 2002; Koocher, 2003). The rights of a minor are legally determined, and the ethical principle of client autonomy is contradictory to legal rights given to parents (Mitchell et al., 2002; Remley & Herlihy, 2010).

Given this incongruity, it is recommended that a provider consider a number of factors in discussing confidentiality with both the child and the parent. The adolescent's developmental age, competency, and counseling setting should help guide the provider in determining confidentiality practices (Glosoff & Pate, 2002; Isaacs & Stone, 2001; Mitchell et al., 2002). Furthermore, an adolescent's development may affect his or her desires for confidentiality and privacy. A young client may have little need for confidentiality; however, older adolescents may desire elevated levels of privacy in that they may be more protective of their private lives.

This increase in confidentiality reflects normal adolescent struggles with autonomy and authority (Koocher, 2003; Remley & Herlihy, 2010). The provider should not assume whether the adolescent does or does not want to keep information private from parents (Remley & Herlihy, 2010). These expectations should be addressed during the informed consent procedure at the onset of counseling (Isaacs & Stone, 2001; Lawrence & Robinson-Kurpius, 2000; McCurdy & Murray, 2003).

Regardless of confidentiality procedures established, there are certain limitations to confidentiality both legally and ethically. Most commonly, these exceptions include suspected abuse or neglect of a child (or adolescent), harm or danger to others, or harm or danger to self (Koocher, 2003). In spite of the commonality of these exceptions, there is a general lack of consensus among professionals in knowing when to breach confidentiality. Specifically, understanding legislation about child abuse or neglect as well as defining *harm* can be difficult.

When considering breaching confidentiality due to suspected abuse or neglect of a child, it is important to fully understand the factors affected by legislation such as who must make the report, when the report must be made, whether to make an oral or a written report, what information is required, whether past or current abuse must be reported, and which perpetrators must be reported (Remley & Herlihy, 2010). These factors may affect a provider's good faith protection in reporting. Additionally, state legislation also may affect what is constituted to be abuse. For example, consensual sexual activity of minors may be considered sexual abuse in some states and, thus, needs to be reported (Koocher, 2003; Moyer, Sullivan, & Growcock, 2012). Age and onset of adolescence can also affect what constitutes abuse (Koocher, 2003). Given this, it is imperative that providers familiarize themselves with applicable state legislation regarding mandated reporting laws.

Unfortunately, risk, harm, and danger are not universally defined within the realm of counseling either (Craigen & Cole, 2012), and there is little consensus about when providers must breach confidentiality for suspected harm (Duncan, Williams, & Knowles, 2013; Moyer et al., 2012; Rae, Sullivan, Razo, & de Alba, 2009; Remley & Herlihy, 2010). As risky behaviors occur on a continuum (Craigen & Cole, 2012; McCurdy & Murray, 2003), it is difficult to determine at what point breaching confidentiality is necessary. For this reason, researchers suggest that the following factors be considered: frequency, intensity, duration, severity, type of behavior, provider values and background, state legislation, cultural implications, setting, developmental level, and chronological age (Glosoff & Pate, 2002; Isaacs & Stone, 2001; Kress, Drouhard, & Costin, 2006; Rae et al., 2009). In evaluating the potential risk of the behaviors, it is recommended that providers evaluate suicidality in addressing self-harm as well (Kress et al., 2006). As there are no legal or professional guidelines for determining the severity of risk, professional judgment must be used in breaching confidentiality (Isaacs & Stone, 2001; McCurdy & Murray, 2003). When unclear, both clinical and legal consultation is recommended before breaching confidentiality to protect provider liability (Kress et al., 2006; Lawrence & Robinson-Kurpius, 2000; Ledyard, 1998). It is important to remember that providers are protected for good faith reporting but are not protected for harm or injury to the client if they fail to report suspected harm (Remley & Herlihy, 2010). Breaches may also need to be made in various legal proceedings or due to school policy.

One of the most important and common questions a provider for adolescents will ask himself or herself is, "When should I break confidentiality?" (Sullivan, Ramirez, Rae, Peña Razo, & George, 2002). Confidentiality is generally broken to inform parents of risk-taking adolescents or to relay the harm (or potential harm) that the adolescent's behavior could result in (Sullivan et al., 2002). At the same time, providers are tasked with trying to encourage open communication and trust during counseling. For example, if Elsie had been engaging in risky sexual behavior (promiscuity without protection), then the provider may have a legitimate reason to break confidentiality.

Pregnant adolescents present another legal conundrum, which will be elaborated on later in this section. But in Elsie's case, there is currently no evidence of risk taking or potential harm as she is still trying to wade through her decision process. One way for providers to avoid or manage situations such as this is to explicitly outline in the informed consent with both the parent and the adolescent during the initial session what circumstances, or issues, the provider will break confidentiality for. According to Weiner (2001), the focal point of the client–provider relationship is trust, which is further evidenced by the fact that confidentiality issues have moved away from the notion that the provider knows what's best for his or her client toward the idea that the client knows what's best for himself or herself. Nevertheless, it is important that the provider be aware that ethical dilemmas require the provider to break confidentiality and have an awareness that confidentiality "test[s] the provider's boundaries such that not taking action in protecting the client may allow the [adolescent] to suffer, hurt themselves, or others" (Blunt, 2006, p. 3). Examining the factors of frequency, intensity, duration, severity, type of behavior, provider values and background, state legislation, cultural implications, setting, developmental level, and chronological age in Elsie's case will help inform a provider's decision to inform her parent(s) or not.

Research has shown that a number of factors may affect a provider's willingness to breach confidentiality. For example, providers were shown to be most likely to breach confidentiality in instances in which behaviors were directly observed versus reported, occurred on school grounds during school hours, or were clearly detailed in facility or school policy (Moyer et al., 2012) and were less likely to breach confidentiality for unlawful activity or parental/family matters (Lazovsky, 2008). In each instance, decisions to break confidentiality were influenced by ethical, legal, procedural, and professional–personal reasons (Lazovsky, 2008). The procedural and professional–personal influences should be clearly detailed to the client at the onset

of counseling (Koocher, 2003), and breaches should be logged and documented as per agency, ethical, and legal directives.

When breaches in confidentiality are necessary, it is crucial that the provider inform the adolescent of the need to breach confidentiality, seek his or her permission, and disclose only the minimum details necessary (Glosoff & Pate, 2002). In such instances, the provider should relay this breach in a manner comprehensible to the adolescent; however, the providers should seek to be as least obtrusive as possible (ACA, 2014; Craigen & Cole, 2012) as confidentiality breaches can engender disruption and distrust within the therapeutic relationship. Working to build a strong alliance that can sustain such an impact is necessary with adolescents.

Additional Legal Considerations

Maintaining confidentiality helps providers earn their client's trust and preserve the ongoing therapeutic relationship. Confidentiality is an ethical standard rather than a legal statute. According to Parrott (2003), privileged communication is known as the legal concept of confidentiality. Privileged communication indicates a legal rather than an ethical view. It specifies the legal circumstances for breaking confidentiality with a client. The aforementioned establishes that confidentiality is not an absolute right, especially among minors. Goldstein (2007) stated that "Privilege is a right that exists by statute that protects patients from having their confidences revealed as testimony during a legal proceeding in court or in a legislative or administrative hearing" (p. 176). However, there are exceptions to the rule. For example, a court-ordered disclosure will permit a disclosure about an adolescent that would otherwise not be allowed. The following two landmark cases will expound on the other exceptions to privacy.

Exceptions to Privacy

Many behavioral health professionals will encounter the issue of reporting a client's threat to harm another person. There is an ethical, professional, and/or moral duty that professionals must uphold to prevent potential harm when they are in a position to do so. If an adolescent treatment provider feels that the adolescent presents a risk of violence to another, the two subsequent landmark cases will provide professionals with a foundation to draw from. In the case law of *Tarasoff v. Regents of University of California*, the Supreme Court of California ruled that mental health professionals have a duty to protect individuals who are being threatened with bodily harm by a client. In the case of *Tarasoff v. Regents of University of California* (1976), Tarasoff's parents stated that the psychiatrists had a duty to warn them and/or their daughter of the threats made by their patient Poddar to kill Tarasoff. The ruling of this case resulted in the commonly known "duty to warn." For most providers, the "duty to warn" can be troubling. According to Brooks (1999, chap. 8), if a provider believes that an adolescent poses a threat to someone, there are two questions that have to be answered: (1) Is there a legal statute or landmark decision that imposes the "duty to warn" in the situation and (2) If there is no legal requirement, does the provider feel a moral obligation to warn someone? The first question speaks of a legal view. Although *Tarasoff v. Regents of University of California* (1976) applies in California, other states have adopted the Tarasoff decision by holding providers responsible when failing to warn of an impending violent threat by a client (Brooks, 1999, chap. 8). The answer to the second question is a matter of an ethical view.

The landmark case of *Jablonski by Pahls v. United States* (1983) expanded on the "duty to protect and warn" established by *Tarasoff v. Regents of University of California* (1976). In *Jablonski by Pahls v. United States* (1983), Jablonski was dating Ms. Kimbell and threatened to kill her and her mother. A risk assessment was conducted at the VA Hospital he was taken to. The provider failed to review Jablonski's prior records (which detailed a violent history) and deemed him not to be a risk and released him

from the facility. The doctor warned Ms. Kimbell to leave Jablonski, but made no mention of his potential violence. Once Jablonski was released, he killed Ms. Kimbell. *Jablonski by Pahls v. United States* (1983) placed emphasis on doctors reviewing previous records in the formulation of risk assessments. This expanded on the duty to protect by allowing the involuntary hospitalization of a dangerous person. According to Brooks (1999, chap. 8), when an adolescent threatens to harm another person or self, the mental health professional having conflicting legal and ethical obligations can proceed in the following ways: (1) the behavioral health professional can go to court and request a court order authorizing the disclosure; (2) the behavioral health professional can make a disclosure that does not identify the adolescent who has threatened to harm another as a client; (3) if the adolescent has been mandated into treatment by the juvenile justice system, the behavioral health professional can make a report to the justice system to allow this sort of information to be disclosed; (4) the behavioral health professional can make a report to medical personnel if the threat presents a medical emergency that poses an immediate threat, and/or (5) the behavioral health professional can obtain the client's consent.

One of the commonly known exceptions to the privacy rule is reporting child abuse and neglect. There are many types of child abuse, but the fundamental component that spans the different types of child abuse is the emotional effect on the child. Child abuse transcends bruises and scars. All states have statutes requiring reporting when there is reasonable belief and/or suspicion that there is child abuse or neglect. While every state has a legal statute in reporting child abuse or neglect, each differs on specifics. Brooks (1999, chap. 8) stated that often training will be needed to review a state's laws to explain child abuse and neglect, because each person's definition of what child abuse or neglect is may differ vastly from the legal definition. When reporting, it is protocol to inform the family, unless doing so would place the child in danger. The program should continue to work with the family while

Child Protective Services or facsimile therein investigates the complaint throughout the process. As shown above, privileged communication among adolescents can be complicated. As shown throughout this chapter, providers walk a very fine line in providing treatment for adolescents, particularly those involved within the legal system.

Collaborative Care

Collaboration with the adolescent client often starts with collaboration with their parents (Glosoff & Pate, 2002) as the provider carefully navigates the aforementioned tensions. The careful and successful navigation of this process can provide a rich foundation for the burgeoning therapeutic relationship and much utilization of counseling microskills such as reflections, summaries, identifying feelings, and effective body language. Ideally, providers are able to work with the adolescent and parent collaboratively to define boundaries of confidentiality, goals for treatment, and overall direction of the therapeutic process. In each of these arenas, providers should seek to protect the child through discretion and professional judgment (Mitchell et al., 2002).

In healthy, collaborative therapeutic relationships, a provider is able to offer the parent overall general feedback regarding treatment direction (in broad strokes) rather than specific details and information about the content and process of each session (Mitchell et al., 2002). Inevitably, the provider will experience the reluctant, reticent adolescent who seeks intense privacy and possibly overbearing parents who insist on counseling details. Following professional ethical codes, legal mandates, and informed consent, documentation can then be wielded along with effective counseling skills, provider personality, provider creativity, consultation and supervision helps, and patience in an overall effort to provide the best, sensitive, and competent services for both the adolescent and the concerned parent.

Toward this end, ensuring that the parent feels heard and the concerns are validated (Mitchell et al., 2002) becomes the focus of parental

interactions. Furthermore, it may be necessary for the provider to explain the role of confidentiality in the counseling relationship and the provider's professional and legal duty to breach confidentiality if any concerns to safety arise (Mitchell et al., 2002; Remley & Herlihy, 2010). This interaction may include a general explanation of the conflict between ethical and legal obligations and further validation of the parent's concerns. If the parent continues demanding information, the provider can look for opportunities to encourage parent-to-adolescent disclosures in the context of a joint session when appropriate (Mitchell et al., 2002; Remley & Herlihy, 2010). Initial discomfort of the adolescent requires additional conservations (depending on any time limits that exist), and the adolescent may be amenable to disclosing information or desire provider assistance in the message's delivery. Throughout the process, the provider is keen to highlight positive aspects that exist within the parent–child relationship (e.g., love and care, concern, dedication, permitting and paying for counseling), allow opportunity for practicing the conversation through role play or empty chair techniques, and discuss possible costs and benefits of such disclosures. In reality, providers may decline to provide information, especially in instances where the adolescent's request is valid and issues of safety may be involved (e.g., abuse and neglect experiences). With this declination of information sharing, legal and ethical ramifications may result from the provider's staunch desire to protect the confidentiality of the adolescent client. Specifically, the provider may face legal consequences if the parent desires to assert their legal rights to information. For this reason, clinical and legal consultation is recommended for providers determining whether to withhold information from the parent (Mitchell et al., 2002; Remley & Herlihy, 2010).

Collaborative Therapeutic Goals

Beyond issues surrounding confidentiality, a collaborative relationship is also crucial in establishing therapeutic goals. In an ideal counseling situation, the adolescent's and the parent's goals and interests are congruent. Unfortunately, this is often not the case and the adolescent's interests may or may not be held in high regard by the parents (Koocher, 2003). It is important for the provider to consider both cultural values and parenting approaches when assessing a parent's wishes for his or her adolescent's rights. The provider's communications must be sensitive to the family's cultural values as well as the parent's desires for the adolescent while still working for the client, the adolescent.

Providing treatment for adolescents presents providers with unique challenges, particularly critical legal issues. Legal matters are generally strictly defined for individuals over the age of 18. However, these matters can be complicated with individuals under the age of 18, particularly when each state has the ability to enact its own laws and regulations. For example, some states allow adolescents to consent to their own treatment, whereas other states do not. This section will focus on critical legal issues that providers may face when treating adolescents like privileged information and consent to treatment and disclosure among other professionals, in addition to addressing relevant landmark cases—some of which are highlighted throughout this chapter.

When seeking to understand both adolescent and parental goals for the counseling process, it is important that the provider does not presume either congruence or incongruence of goals for either party (Koocher, 2003). The provider must take the time to fully evaluate the goals of both parties to be able to successfully collaborate with both the adolescent and the parent. Doing so often entails the provider's use of mediation skills and ability to recognize discrepancies to balance both parties' interests (Koocher, 2003). As such, the provider may take on the role of adviser, expert, advocate, mediator, rescuer, and service coordinator in soliciting a positive and collaborative parent–adolescent–provider relationship (Koocher, 2003; Remley & Herlihy, 2010).

Despite the provider's best attempts, there may be instances in which collaboration cannot be achieved. This may be due to drastic differences between the adolescent's and the parent's wishes or due to inability to balance cultural values and personal belief systems; however, it also may be cause for greater concern. If parents refuse to work collaboratively with their adolescent's provider, it is the provider's role to be concerned for the adolescent's well-being (Capuzzi, 2002). Even greater, there is a possibility that the adolescent's safety may be at risk, and the parent may be trying to prevent any disclosures concerning abuse, for example. Regardless of the parent's refusal for treatment, liability for the minor's safety is of paramount concern to the professional provider (Capuzzi, 2002). In these cases, providers must be willing to seek legal and clinical consultation to determine whether a report to a protective agency needs to be made (Capuzzi, 2002).

Dual Relationships/Multiple Relationships

There are aspects of the behavioral health provider's role that require special attention regarding maintaining one's primary role, responsibilities, and tasks as a behavioral health provider rather than other roles (e.g., friend, family member, supervisor, administrator, clergy, etc.). Having dual relationships (also known as multiple relationships) is an ethical dilemma that pervades work and may be especially difficult for the adolescent client. The provider's relationship with the adolescent's parent is also affected by this difficulty. Behavioral health professionals are often required to fulfill multiple roles such as lunchroom supervisor, chaperone, course scheduler, substitute teacher, or coach (Remley & Herlihy, 2010). For this reason, it is particularly important for the various contexts in which providers find themselves working along with the benefit or detriment to the client for such multiple relationships, as well as the nature of the dual relationship (Gonyea, Wright, & Earl-Kulkosky, 2014).

To best manage dual relationships, it is recommended that behavioral health providers clarify roles at the onset of counseling (Koocher, 2003) by evaluating his or her ability to manage the dual relationship without causing harm or detriment to the client or crossing ethical or legal boundaries, as indicated by professional ethical codes. To assist in best managing multiple relationships, consultation and/or supervision may be sought to assist in navigating the relationships, as well as provide professional guidance on the situation (Gonyea et al., 2014). Of utmost importance in all of the navigating, negotiating, and clarification is the adolescent client's needs and best interests; all other roles are deemed secondary to the client's needs (ACA, 2014). If the relationship cannot be managed, the provider may need to provide the client with a referral (Gonyea et al., 2014) and only with much consideration, care, and attention to ethical requirements (ACA, 2014) and demonstrating clinically competent decision making.

Clinical Competence

Clinical competence is a term that generally means performing within legal and ethical parameters that are considered standard for a profession. This term applies to all aspects of behavioral health practice and extends to all clients served. Clinical competence with adults, however, does not necessarily translate to clinical competence with minors (Lawrence & Robinson-Kurpius, 2000) in that developmental, educational, minority status, and consent issues are ongoing factors affecting the counseling relationship, interventions, and techniques. For this reason, counseling adolescents require appropriate training and experience including behavioral health professionals remaining abreast of state-of-the-art developmental psychology, theories, and techniques as well as obtaining proficient knowledge in adolescent psychopathology (Lawrence & Robinson-Kurpius, 2000), and engaging adolescents in a diverse, multiculturally competent manner (Koocher, 2003). The competent behavioral health provider working with adolescents will also be skilled in working from a family system's perspective as understanding familial influence and developing collaborative relationships with families will both directly affect the adolescent engaged in individual counseling (Remley & Herlihy, 2010). Exercise 17.1 provides several questions regarding the ethical and competent treatment for the case of Elsie. Consider the information provided thus far in the chapter and attempt to answer the questions in Exercise 17.1 before proceeding.

Exercise 17.1

Counseling Elsie

Consider your state legislation and ethical requirements. How do these requirements influence any concerns pertaining to mandated reporting? How does Elsie's pregnancy change her rights to confidentiality?

What are Elsie's rights as a minor?

Who is the client ethically? Who is the client legally?

How might you balance Elsie's ethical rights and her parent's legal rights?

What role might Elsie's father have in consent and treatment?

IMPLICATIONS FOR COUNSELING ADOLESCENTS

Clinical Review of Case

The case of Elsie, presented at the beginning of this chapter, provides a number of issues regarding informed consent and confidentiality for the behavioral health provider to consider. First, the provider must confer with Elsie and her mother through an initial meeting in which the provider outlines roles and boundaries within the counseling relationship. The provider's initial identification of what information is shared with the parent and corresponding legal, ethical, and professional challenges is essential to help establish trust and openness within the therapeutic relationship. As Elsie's parents are divorced, it is important for the provider to identify whether or not Elsie's mother is the custodial parent by reviewing the divorce decree and custody documents. In this case, Elsie's parents share custody, which requires the provider to obtain in writing or document verbal consent to treatment from both of Elsie's parents.

Next, issues of confidentiality require careful articulation and navigation. While adolescents do have rights to privacy and for their information to be kept confidential, a provider must use clinical discretion as to whether a breach to confidentiality would be in the best interest of the adolescent, within legal bounds and ethical standards. In Elsie's case, legal statutes guide whether or not an adolescent can seek services themselves for advising/counseling regarding issues related to sexual activity. The provider must also review his or her state laws, professional ethics, and informed consent agreement (verbal and written) to decipher whether or not the provider is obligated to inform Elsie's mother of the pregnancy. Additionally, the provider should answer the following questions: Is there currently a substantial risk to Elsie or another, if confidentiality is kept at this time? What options does the provider have, and what are those options contingent on?

In this case, the provider is faced with how to avoid undermining the concept of confidentiality and privileged communication and still be able to give appropriate information to others who share concern and responsibility for the minor's welfare, as well as help maintain the client's best interest (Ledyard, 1998). The Number 1 question to consider throughout this chapter regarding Elsie is "Who is the client?" In this case, Elsie is the client, but her mother is her legal guardian and has rights to know what her daughter's care entails and the results of or changes in the course of therapy. How the discussion of what, when, how, and if Elsie's mother is told about the pregnancy, or anything regarding Elsie's treatment, is dependent on a document known as informed consent. Informed consent is a document, as well as an ongoing process, that delineates the terms of treatment. This includes location, privacy, payment, and when and under what circumstances the parents of a minor would become more involved in treatment. In essence, the form should detail when and for what an adolescent's parents may be told specific information throughout treatment.

Application of Ethics

Research has shown that providers who have received recent training on ethical and legal matters felt most prepared to deal with issues; however, less than half of the study's participants had received recent training (Hermann, 2002). The study also revealed that providers who had taken a course in legal or ethical issues, gained professional licensure, and obtained National Board for Certified Providers certification felt better prepared to address ethical issues (Hermann, 2002). With this in mind, it is crucial that counseling students, educators, and practitioners understand the importance of preparation and training on ethical and legal considerations as preparation has been shown to be directly related to a provider's confidence in ethics as well as his or her likeliness to adhere to standards (Glosoff & Pate, 2002).

When training in ethics, it is important to ensure active and experiential learning in order to facilitate students' ability to demonstrate, apply, and adhere to ethical standards (Glosoff &

Pate, 2002). To do so, Bodenhorn (2010) recommends the use of case studies and role play in ethical decision making. Ultimately, counseling students, educators, and practitioners must take personal responsibility in continuing necessary training and education.

Implications for Practice

In consideration of ethical practices with children and adolescents, the use of ethical decision-making models is both a recommendation for best practice and an ethical mandate (ACA, 2014, I.1; ASCA, 2010, G.3; Ledyard, 1998). In choosing an ethical decision-making model, Cottone and Claus (2000) offer a detailed summary of models that have been created specifically for addressing ethical issues. The ASCA (2010, G.3) also recommends the use of the STEPS model in their code of ethics. Ultimately, a provider's ability to demonstrate the use of a decision-making model and adherence to necessary steps protect the provider in cases of legal concerns.

Furthermore, there are specific, practical applications for providers to protect themselves in working with minors (Lawrence & Robinson-Kurpius, 2000). Throughout the field, providers must continue to adhere to the role of advocacy, particularly in work with children and adolescents, a vulnerable population. This may include advocacy to parents, teachers, and school administrators (Glosoff & Pate, 2002). The following are recommended best practices for providers of children and adolescents (Glosoff & Pate, 2002; Koocher, 2003; Lawrence & Robinson-Kurpius, 2000):

- Practice within limits of competency
- Gain training and experiences necessary to fully develop competency
- Know applicable state legislation
- Clarify expectations regarding confidentiality during informed consent at onset of counseling
- Seek a collaborative relationship between the client and the parents

- Keep accurate and objective records of all interactions and counseling sessions
- Maintain adequate liability coverage
- Confer and consult with qualified clinical and legal colleagues
- Give preference to least restrictive treatment possible
- Be aware of personal value systems and potential contradictions with client value systems

School-Specific Implications for Practice

Given that schools have different legal requirements for practice per the Family Educational Rights and Privacy Act, it is also important to recognize specific ethical implications in schools. Most predominantly, researchers suggest the implementation of school policies to guide providers in ethical practice (Capuzzi, 2002; Glosoff & Pate, 2002; Kress et al., 2006; Moyer et al., 2012). The policies should encompass issues such as confidentiality, referrals, and parental consent.

In establishing a school policy, providers should seek to establish collaborative relationships with school administrators (Capuzzi, 2002; O'Connell, 2012). School administrators have been shown to be generally supportive of the provider's roles within the school as well as the students' needs for confidentiality; however, when confidentiality breaches are necessary due to safety concerns, many administrators desire to be notified (O'Connell, 2012). For this reason, policies regarding when and how to notify administrators for such breaches should be in place.

If schools do not have the capacity to offer counseling services necessary for the student, the school is responsible for making the necessary referrals (Capuzzi, 2002). As such, a formal referral policy including both contact information providers and other mental health professionals with expertise in counseling children and adolescents as well as financial information and resources should be made. Schools must clarify who have the financial responsibility in instances of referral.

Finally, it is important to note that parental consent is not legally required for school providers; however, many schools have implemented policies to best develop collaborative relationships with parents. Such policies vary, but Glosoff and Pate (2002) have offered potential suggestions such as requiring parental consent before beginning counseling, written parental refusal for counseling services, or parental consent only if providers see a client for a certain number of sessions or more. Ultimately, school providers must be aware of current policies in place. If there are no guidelines, providers should seek to work collaboratively with administrators to implement such policies.

SUMMARY

While no text can be comprehensive, this chapter seeks to serve as an introductory summary of ethical considerations specific to working with adolescents. With consideration of research and applicable ethical codes, some of the central issues related to counseling minors include defining the client, maintaining confidentiality, offering collaborative care, gaining consent for treatment, managing dual relationships, and developing clinical competence. These issues are prevalent throughout applicable codes of ethics from regulatory bodies in the field of counseling.

Furthermore, research has shown that a provider's likelihood to practice ethically is directly related to his or her training and education on ethical and legal matters (Hermann, 2002). For this reason, the implications for education are addressed. The use of ethical decision-making models within counseling is an ethical mandate and should be applied to work with children and adolescents as well. Best practices should seek to address common ethical issues as well as encompass consideration and care to both the minor and the provider. Finally, specific implications for practice in both school and nonschool settings are discussed.

KEYSTONES

- While the adolescent is the identified client, he or she represents a special population in which a third party—a parent or guardian—must be involved in the treatment process.

- The level of parental or guardian involvement in counseling services is dependent on many factors. For treatment to even commence, an informed consent form is required. There are many exceptions to this rule. Assent for treatment by the adolescent is an ethical standard but not a legal necessity for treatment.

- The parameters of confidentiality are murky, particularly for providers working with adolescents; however, there are specific factors a treating provider should consider when contemplating a breach of confidentiality.

- Become aware of exceptions to the rules of consent and confidentiality when treating minors.

- Due to the ethical and legal standards that confound the adolescent–provider relationship, it is important to use a collaborative approach to treatment.

- Additionally, providers should be aware of how to manage dual relationships, as they are more prominent in clinical work with adolescents.

- Providers should always strive to gain more knowledge and experience in working with adolescents in a variety of settings in order to perform their duties responsibly and competently.

- Providers should be aware of landmark cases such as *Tarasoff* and *Schloendorff* that inform their abilities to practice legally and ethically.

REFERENCES

American Counseling Association. (2014). *2014 ACA code of ethics.* Alexandria, VA: Author.

American School Counselor Association. (2010). *Ethical standards for school counselors.* Alexandria, VA: Author.

Blunt, D. R. (2006). *Confidentiality, informed consent, and ethical considerations in reviewing the client's psychotherapy records* (ERIC Document Reproduction Service No. ED490794). Retrieved from http://www.counseling.org/resources/library/Selected%20Topics/Ethics/Confidentiality.pdf

Bodenhorn, N. (2010). Exploratory study of common and challenging ethical dilemmas experienced by professional school providers. *Professional School Counseling, 10*(2), 195–202.

Brooks, M. (1999). *Legal and ethical issues.* Bethesda, MD: National Center for Biotechnology Information. Retrieved from http://www.ncbi.nlm.nih.gov/books/NBK64357/

Capuzzi, D. (2002). Legal and ethical challenges in counseling suicidal students. *Professional School Counseling, 6*(1), 36–46.

Corey, G., Corey, M. S., & Callanan, P. (1998). *Issues and ethics in the helping professions* (5th ed.). Pacific Grove, CA: Brooks/Cole.

Cottone, R. R., & Claus, R. E. (2000). Ethical decision-making models: A review of the literature. *Journal of Counseling & Development, 78*(3), 275–283 . doi:10.1002/j.1556-6676.2000.tb01908.x

Craigen, L., & Cole, R. (2012). Self-injury and eating disorders in minors: When should the human service profession break confidentiality? *Journal of Human Services, 31*(1), 56–71.

Duncan, R. E., Williams, B. J., & Knowles, A. (2013). Adolescents, risk behavior, and confidentiality: When would Australian psychologists breach confidentiality to disclose information to parents? *Australian Psychologist, 48,* 408–419. doi:10.1111/ap.12002

Furrow, B. (1980). *Malpractice in psychotherapy.* Lexington, MA: Lexington Books.

Glosoff, H. L., & Pate, R. H., Jr. (2002). Privacy and confidentiality in school counseling. *Professional School Counseling, 6*(1), 20–28.

Goldstein, A. (2007). *Forensic psychology emerging topics and expanding roles.* Hoboken, NJ: Wiley.

Gonyea, J. L., Wright, D. W., & Earl-Kulkosky, T. (2014). Navigating dual relationships in rural communities. *Journal of Marital and Family Therapy, 40*(1), 125–136. doi:10.1111/j.1752-0606.2012.00335.x

Gustafson, K. E., & McNamara, J. R. (1987). Confidentiality with minor clients: Issues and guidelines for therapists. *Professional Psychology: Research and Practice, 18,* 503–508.

Hathaway, W. (2013). Ethics, religious issues, and clinical child psychology. In D. F. Walker & W. L. Hathaway (Eds.), *Spiritual interventions in child and adolescent psychotherapy* (pp. 17–39).

Washington, DC: American Psychological Association. doi:10.1037/13947-002

Hermann, M. A. (2002). A study of legal issues encountered by school providers and perceptions of their preparedness to respond to legal challenges. *Professional School Counseling, 6*(1), 12–20.

Isaacs, M. L., & Stone, C. (2001). Confidentiality with minors: Mental health providers' attitudes toward breaching or preserving confidentiality. *Journal of Mental Health Counseling, 23*(4), 342–356.

Jablonski by Pahls v. United States, 712 F.2d 391 (9th Cir. 1983).

Keim, M. A., & Cobia, D. (2010). Legal and ethical implications of working with minors in Alabama: Consent and confidentiality. *Alabama Counseling Association Journal, 35*(2), 28–34.

Keshavarz, R. (2005). Adolescents, informed consent, and confidentiality: A case study. *Mount Sinai Journal of Medicine, 72*(4), 232–235.

Koocher, G. P. (2003). Ethical issues in psychotherapy with adolescents. *Journal of Clinical Psychology, 59*(11), 1247–1256. doi:10.1002/jclp.10215

Kress, V. E., Drouhard, N., & Costin, A. (2006). Students who self-injure: School provider ethical and legal considerations. *Professional School Counseling, 10*(2), 203–209.

Lawrence, G., & Robinson-Kurpius, S. E. (2000). Legal and ethical issues involved when counseling minors in nonschool settings. *Journal of Counseling & Development, 78*(2), 130–136.

Lazovsky, R. (2008). Maintaining confidentiality with minors: Dilemmas of school providers. *Professional School Counseling, 11*(5), 335–346.

Ledyard, P. (1998). Counseling minors: Ethical and legal issues. *Counseling and Values, 42*(3), 171–177. doi:10.1002/j.2161-007X.1998.tb00423.x

McCurdy, K. G., & Murray, K. C. (2003). Confidentiality issues when minor children disclose family secrets in family counseling. *Family Journal, 11*(4), 393–398. doi:10.1177/1066480703255468

Mitchell, C. W., Disque, J. G., & Robertson, P. (2002). When parents want to know: Responding to parental demands for confidential information. *Professional School Counseling, 6*(2), 156–161.

Moyer, M. S., Sullivan, J. R., & Growcock, D. (2012). When is it ethical to inform administrators about student risk-taking behaviors? Perceptions of school providers. *Professional School Counseling, 15*(3), 98–109.

North, R. L. (1990). Legal authority for HIV testing of adolescents. *Journal of Adolescent Health Care, 11,* 176–187.

O'Connell, W. P. (2012). Secondary school adminis-trators' attitudes toward confidentiality in school counseling. *NASSP Bulletin, 96*(4), 350–363. doi:10.1177/0192636512466936

Parrott, L., III. (2003). *Counseling and psychotherapy* (2nd ed.). Pacific Grove, CA: Brooks/Cole/ Thomson Learning.

Rae, W. A., Sullivan, J. R., Razo, N. P., & de Alba, R. G. (2009). Breaking confidentiality to report adolescent risk-taking behavior by school psychologists. *Ethics & Behavior, 19*(6), 449–460. doi:10.1080/10508420903274930

Remley, T. P., Jr., & Herlihy, B. (2010). *Ethical, legal, and professional issues.* Upper Saddle River, NJ: Pearson Education.

Sankaran, V., & Macbeth, J. (2010). Legal issues in the treatment of minors. In E. Benedek, P. Ash, & C. Scott (Eds.), *Principles and practice of child and adolescent forensic mental health* (pp. 109–130). Arlington, VA: American Psychiatric.

Schloendorff v. The Society of New York Hospital, 211 N.Y. 125, 105 N.E. 92 (1914).

Sullivan, J. R., Ramirez, E., Rae, W. A., Peña Razo, N., & George, C. A. (2002). Factors contributing to breaking confidentiality with adolescent clients: A survey of pediatric psychologists. *Professional Psychology: Research and Practice, 33*(4), 396–401.

Tarasoff v. Regents of University of California, 17 Cal. 3d 425 (1976).

Vitiello, B. (2008). Effectively obtaining informed consent for child and adolescent participation in mental health research. *Ethics & Behavior, 18*(2–3), 182–198. doi:10.1080/10508420802064234

Warren, S., & Brandeis, L. (1890). The right to privacy. *Harvard Law Review, 4*, 193–220.

Weiner, J. (2001). Confidentiality and paradox: The location of ethical space. *Journal of Analytical Psychology, 46*(3), 431–442.

Welfel, E. R. (2002). *Ethics in counseling and psychotherapy.* Pacific Grove, CA: Brooks/Cole.

18

SUPERVISION AND CONSULTATION

INTRODUCTION

Training for behavioral health providers requires supervision from licensed providers to ensure the safety of clients by novice providers and to provide guidance and direction for the emerging provider as they develop their skills and learn the minutia involved in the therapeutic process. The supervision process affords the providers a unique opportunity to glean valuable experience and insight from a seasoned professional while discovering their personal strengths and weaknesses that will affect their functioning in the therapeutic process. While the supervision process postulates a rich resource for personal and professional growth, many providers graduate to licensure with nominal understanding of the supervision process and are often placed in positions of leadership which require them to supervise other emerging providers in the initial stages of their career. This often leaves the provider feeling inadequately equipped to fulfill the role of supervisor that often requires focused development on their part to bridge the gap in their learning. In this situation, many providers refer to their own experience of supervision and proceed to emulate the supervision style their supervisor used regardless of its efficacy or appropriateness.

To ensure competency in supervision, CACREP (Council for Accreditation of Counseling and Related Educational Programs) and other professional standards provide an outline for developing skills in this domain of functioning. These standards,

which will be addressed in more detail later in the chapter, cover basic fundamentals such as the purpose of clinical supervision and diverse frameworks and models of clinical supervision. These standards for supervision provide foundational scaffolding for the trainee to build on as the trainee matures in his or her professional development (Welch, 2003).

Another domain of functioning closely associated with supervision is consultation. Like supervision, providers may function in the role of a consultant in diverse venues and need the requisite knowledge and skills to exercise this role effectively. Consultation, just like supervision, involves specific competencies that must be learned to function effectively. Providers are often invited to share their knowledge and skills with individuals, organizations, and communities to improve their performance and function more effectively. This offers the provider an opportunity to function in the role of a consultant, which differs from the role of a therapist or a supervisor. While multiple skill sets are used interchangeably among these various roles, the purpose and function of consultation is fundamentally different from the other modalities of service.

After reading this chapter, readers should be able to do the following:

- Understand the definitions of supervision and consultation and how these roles vary in their functioning

- Become familiar with the supervisory relationship and the multidimensional aspects of supervision

- Understand models of consultation and its relationship with the supervision process

- Discuss critical characteristics of effective consultation

- Become familiar with the theories, skills, and processes involved within supervision and consultation

- Understand how competencies in supervision and consultation prepare the provider to effectively influence his or her community

SUPERVISION DEFINED: HISTORICAL AND CONTEMPORARY TRENDS IN CLASSIFICATION

The earliest concept of supervision may be closely identified with the notion of mentoring. Mentoring can be loosely traced back in history to Homer's epic poem *The Odyssey*. In this classic work, the character Mentor is a friend and an advisor to Odysseus, King of Ithaca. Odysseus goes off to fight in the Trojan War and entrusts Mentor with the care of his son Telemachus. More specifically, Mentor was left in charge of the royal household, which involved fulfilling various roles such as a father figure, role model, provider, teacher, encourager, and challenger (Carruthers, 1993). The idea of mentoring is extrapolated from this caricature and is associated with implementing the various roles of advisor, father figure, provider, and so on. While some authors have voiced concerns regarding the accuracy of this association with the character Mentor (Roberts, 1999), this is generally the accepted origin of the concept of mentoring.

Definition of Supervision

Supervision incorporates many of the characteristics of mentoring; however, it differs with regard to the level of power differential and authority exerted in the supervision relationship. While there is no one conclusive definition of supervision, various models have been put forth. One widely accepted definition of supervision derives from the seminal work of Bernard and Goodyear (2013). They describe supervision as follows:

> Supervision is an intervention provided by a more senior member of a profession to a more junior member or members of that same profession. The relationship is evaluative and hierarchical, extends over time, and has the simultaneous purposes of enhancing the professional functioning of the more junior person(s), monitoring the quality of professional services offered to the clients that she, he, or they see, and serving as a gatekeeper for those who are to enter the particular profession. (p. 7)

Falender and Shafranske (2004) offer another widely accepted definition of supervision:

> A distinct professional activity in which education and training, aimed at developing science-informed practice, are facilitated through a collaborative interpersonal process. It involves observation, evaluation, feedback, and facilitation of supervisee self-assessment, and the acquisition of knowledge and skills by instruction, modeling, and mutual problem solving. In addition, by building on the recognition of the strengths and talents of the supervisee, supervision encourages self-efficacy . . . [and] is conducted in a competent manner in which ethical standards, legal prescriptions, and professional practices are used to promote and protect the welfare of the client, the profession, and society at large. (p. 3)

Both of these definitions provide comprehensive descriptions of clinical supervision. Bernard and Goodyear's (2013) definition might be described as enumerating the specific structures of supervision, while Falender and Shafranske's (2004) definition may focus more on the functions of supervision, detailing the specifics such as observation, evaluation, and feedback. While these two definitions may differ in their scope of emphasis, both highlight the critical functions involved in supervision.

One common characteristic found in these definitions is the description of a senior member in the profession providing guidance to a developing junior member in the profession. This characteristic mirrors a mentoring relationship where an individual more knowledgeable in a specific area of expertise shares wisdom with a learner. However, a mentoring relationship differs from supervision's evaluative nature and level of authority and power exerted by the supervisor over the supervisee. Supervision is provided in a formal relationship while mentoring may be provided in an informal relationship.

The second notable characteristic of these two definitions is the observation, evaluation, and development of the supervisee's clinical skills. Many observers would characterize the evaluation and development of the supervisee's skills as the primary purpose of supervision. However, other authors have noted that this goal is secondary to the protection of the general public (Falender & Shafranske, 2004). Bernard and Goodyear's definition emphasizes the role of the supervisor as the gatekeeper to the profession that monitors the therapeutic services offered to the client. These points underscore the importance of protecting the public from malpractice. Falender and Shafranske further reinforce this idea by emphasizing the protection of the welfare of the client through ethical standards and legal prescriptions. While supervisees are not expected to function without errors, the supervisor has the responsibility of providing clinical oversight to minimize risk for the client.

Finally, another principle exhibited in these definitions of supervision is the development of the supervisee as a professional in the field. The process of supervision provides an opportunity for the trainee to become acculturated to the profession with an established member of the field who assists the trainee in their logical progression toward becoming colleagues. Falender and Shafranske (2004) note that supervision focuses on developing the strengths and talents of the supervisee as a means for increasing the trainee's level of self-efficacy. The validity for emphasizing the development of the trainee's strengths was initially introduced and discussed in previous chapters describing the recent impact of positive psychology on the field of mental health and its emphasis on nurturing human strengths (Seligman & Csikszentmihalyi, 2000). Further corroborating evidence for emphasizing and nurturing supervisee's strengths may be found in popularized business management science literature. In their book *Strengths Based Leadership*, Tom Rath and Barry Conchie (2009) discussed a study on employee engagement performed by the Gallup Organization in 2005. In this study, employees who were ignored by their managers were found to have a 40% chance of becoming disengaged on their job. Employees whose managers focused on their weaknesses had a 22% chance of becoming disengaged on the job. Employees whose managers focused on their strengths had a 1% chance of becoming disengaged on their job. The same logic can be utilized with supervision. Supervisors who emphasize developing their supervisee's strengths are more likely to have their supervisees engaged in the supervision process that further enhances the supervisory alliance, which is found to be a necessary condition for successful supervision (Falender & Shafranske, 2004).

These three principles embedded within the definitions of supervision (supervision by a senior member in the field, development of the supervisee's clinical skills, and professional development of the supervisee) provide a structural framework for discussing and exploring the details and competencies involved in clinical supervision (Exercise 18.1).

Exercise 18.1

What Is Supervision?

Now that you have reviewed the definition of supervision, please describe in your own words what supervision is, how it might differ from a mentoring relationship, and to whom this relationship applies.

The Supervisory Relationship: A Foundational Principle for Effective Supervision

As previously stated, supervision is a process formulated around the relationship between a senior member in the profession guiding and evaluating an emerging junior member of the profession. The relationship is multidimensional with the supervisor exercising diverse roles such as an evaluator, encourager, teacher, mentor, and model. All of these roles, however, are dependent on developing a strong alliance between the supervisor and the supervisee.

Research investigating treatment outcomes for psychotherapy have found the therapeutic alliance between the patient and the therapist to be a significant predictor of treatment success (Horvath, 2001). This evidence supports a commonsense appeal that would naturally assume that the quality of the therapeutic relationship between the therapist and the client would affect the treatment outcome. The supervisory alliance is not exempt from this maxim.

Theodore Roosevelt once said that people do not care how much you know, until they know how much you care. That statement resonates with the concept of supervision and bears truth to the importance of the supervisory alliance. While the supervisor may have significant knowledge and clinical expertise to impart to the supervisees, if the supervisees do not feel that the supervisor has their best interest in mind, they may be resistant to accepting any constructive advice the supervisor may have, or worse, become antagonistic with the supervisor. Just as the therapeutic relationship in psychotherapy is based on trust and confidentiality, the supervisory relationship is also based on these same premises.

Falender and Shafranske (2004) discuss the development of the supervisory alliance by initially describing how the therapeutic alliance between a therapist and a client originates. The therapeutic alliance is initially forged with the provider and the client working together on change goals. As a result of working together toward a mutual goal, a bond develops. Bordin (1994) describes this bond as a feeling of mutual respect, understanding, and trust. Bordin continues to describe how the supervisory alliance is similarly developed. It begins with the supervisor and trainee developing reciprocally developed goals for the supervisee (e.g., improving conceptualization skills). A bond further develops between the supervisor and the trainee as a result of the mutual goals. Furthermore, Bordin goes on to describe a list of personal characteristics of supervisors that trainees have endorsed as highly rated supervisor qualities. These include characteristics such as an attitude of acceptance, empathy, validation, encouragement, warmth, and understanding.

The supervisor characteristics may be thought of as necessary conditions of rapport building within the supervisory relationship (Exercise 18.2). When a supervisor is intentional about displaying these qualities, the likelihood of developing a strong supervisory alliance is improved.

Alliance Ruptures

In any relationship that occurs, conflict can often arise and cause division, rifts, and ruptures. Within the supervisory alliance, ruptures that

---

Exercise 18.2

Supervisory Alliance

Please describe the importance of the supervisory alliance and its overall impact on the supervision process. Provide any examples of past supervisory relationships.

occur threaten the possibility of further progress in supervision and possibly compromise the supervisor's capability to monitor and safeguard the client (Falender & Shafranske, 2004). To resolve the rupture in the supervisory alliance, the supervisor may utilize the same process employed to repair the therapeutic relationship such as the clinical model developed by Safran and Muran (2000).

Safran and Muran's first step is to identify the cause of the rupture in the alliance that is identified as the rupture marker. Several causes that have often been identified include feelings of shame, parallel process, and boundary violations (Falender & Shafranske, 2004). The second step of the resolution process is for the supervisor to encourage the trainee to explore the block of affective expression. The block is creating the impasse, which cannot be crossed. The third step involves having the trainee explore and assert their experience of the rupture (Safran & Muran, 2000). Through this process, a resolution can occur and transform the rupture back to a working alliance. These three steps are listed in Table 18.1.

SUPERVISION COMPETENCIES: DEVELOPMENT OF SUPERVISEE'S CLINICAL SKILLS

Developing the supervisee's clinical skills is the chief goal of the supervision process. To accomplish this task, identifiable goals or competencies are developed to ensure that a minimal standard has been reached. Falender and Shafranske (2008) developed a competency approach to supervision, which provides benchmarks for supervisee development. Their model is based on three pillars, which include the supervisory relationship (previously discussed), inquiry, and educational praxis. Inquiry is the process for facilitating the understanding of the therapeutic process while educational praxis is developing learning strategies for the supervisee to develop knowledge and skills. These pillars are listed in Table 18.2.

Several skills have been identified for the supervisor as well as for the developing supervisee (Falender & Shafranske, 2004). These skills are considered to be competencies to be developed. They are divided into several groups such as knowledge, skills, values, social context overarching issues, training of supervision competencies, and assessment of supervision competencies. The first group knowledge would include competencies such as having knowledge of models, theories, and modalities of supervision as well as knowledge of ethics and legal issues. Skills would include behaviors such as developing the ability to build a supervisory alliance, providing effective formative and summative evaluations, and ability to set boundaries. The

Table 18.1   Safran and Muran's (2000) Three Steps to Resolving Ruptures in Supervisory Alliance

Step 1	Identify the rupture marker
Step 2	Supervisor encourages exploration of block to affective expression
Step 3	Trainee explores and asserts experience of the rupture

Source. Safran, J. D., & Muran, J. C. (2000c). Resolving therapeutic alliance ruptures: Diversity and integration. *Journal of Clinical Psychology/In Session: Psychotherapy in Practice,* 56(2), 233–243.

Table 18.2   Falender and Shafranske's (2008) Three Pillars of Supervision Competency

Pillar 1	Supervisory relationship
Pillar 2	Inquiry
Pillar 3	Educational praxis

values competency includes being respectful, having sensitivity toward diversity, and commitment to lifelong learning. The competency of social context and overarching issues includes competencies such as diversity issues, ethical and legal issues, and awareness of the sociopolitical context within which supervision is conducted. Training and supervision competencies include completing coursework in supervision, and receiving supervision with some type of observation such as videotape or audiotape feedback (Falender & Shafranske, 2004).

These competencies are used as benchmarks for the supervisor to evaluate within each supervisee. How these skills are developed within each supervisee is also determined by the supervisor's approach to supervision (Exercise 18.3).

Supervisory Styles

There are many different types of approaches to supervision just as there are many different kinds of supervisors. These approaches function as a model for supervision and may be classified as either an extension of psychotherapy-based theory or developed specifically for supervision (Goodyear & Bernard, 1998). Those approaches that are developed specifically for supervision are often referred to as process-based approaches.

Psychotherapy-based approaches to supervision have been developed from each of the major theoretical orientations such as psychodynamic, cognitive behavioral, client-centered, existential-humanistic, as well as family-systems theories. Each of these theory-driven approaches appears to provide consistency and

reinforcement of the therapeutic process as it is reflected in the supervisory experience. While supervision might be conceptualized as a microcosm of psychotherapy due to its similar nuances and parallel patterns, Falender and Shafranske (2008) have noted that the aims of supervision differ from therapy and often require broader approaches and learning strategies that are personalized with the goals of supervision. Therefore, psychotherapy-based approaches may not fulfill all of these parameters.

To provide an example of a psychotherapy-based supervision approach, the following cognitive therapy approach will be explored. To begin, a supervisor utilizing the cognitive therapy approach would commence by assessing the client's problems, cognitions, and behaviors (Beck, Sarnat, & Barenstein, 2008). Next the supervisor would determine the specific skills the supervisee should employ with the client for effective treatment. Finally the supervisor would assist the supervisee in conceptualizing any difficulties in the process and develop a plan for remediation as needed. To further reinforce the development of the cognitive approach, the supervision session is structured to mirror a typical therapy session with a client. For example, the supervision session begins with a check-in with the supervisee to determine how he or she is doing. In a typical therapy session, the therapist begins every session with a mood check to assess the client's level of well-being. Next in the supervision session, the agenda for the session is explored. Setting the agenda is also the second step in a typical therapy session. This is followed by prioritizing the agenda,

Exercise 18.3

Natural Skills and Competencies

List your natural skills and competencies you believe would assist you as a supervisor. Compare your strengths with those competencies identified by Falender and Shafranske (2004) and discuss your similarities with those identified competencies as well as critical growth areas.

discussing the problems, assigning homework, providing a summary, and giving feedback. All of these steps in supervision are a replication of the steps followed in cognitive therapy, which are consistently followed, in sequential order (Beck et al., 2008).

Process-based approaches to supervision, as previously mentioned, are specifically developed with the goals of supervision in mind. Their purpose is to articulate the component roles, tasks, and processes within supervision (Falender & Shafranske, 2004). One example of this approach is Bernard's (1997) Discrimination Model. This model has three specific areas of focus: process skills, conceptualization skills, and personalization skills. The second part of this model displays three general roles of the supervisor: (1) the teacher role, (2) the provider role, and (3) the consultant role. The purpose of this model is to provide a simplified map so that supervisees can conceptualize their interventions (Falender & Shafranske, 2004).

Both psychotherapy-based approaches and process-based approaches to supervision meet specific needs of the supervision process. Supervisees need to be knowledgeable of various approaches to supervision to provide them an opportunity to explore which approach may suit them. While these approaches are not an exhaustive list of different methods and styles, they provide a basic framework for describing fundamental differences in areas of focus.

CONSULTATION: DEFINITION AND MODELS OF IMPLEMENTATION

Consultation, as previously mentioned, is another mode of functioning that a supervisee should become familiar with in his or her clinical training. Consultation, unfortunately, often receives even less attention in clinical training than supervision. As a result, graduates from counseling programs are often unprepared to function in this role on entering the field and may even result in avoidance. To begin, the concept of consultation will be defined and its utilization and functioning will be explained.

Definition of Consultation

There have been many different definitions of consultation put forth over the years; however, there is still no general consensus on one definition. Knoff (1988) describes it as "a collaborative process involving two peer or collegial professionals in a *non-hierarchical* relationship" (p. 245) and a relationship in which the consultant may have more knowledge, experience, and specifies a problem-solving process. This definition is remarkable because it notes that consultation can be provided by anyone who has expertise in a certain field. A consultant is not limited by their status. While there has not been a consensus on one definition, there have been some agreed-on aspects of consultation. These include the idea that the goal of consultation is to solve problems; consultants help consultee's view the problem as part of a larger system to understand how it developed; it involves a tripartite nature of consultant, consultee, and client system; and that the goal of consultation is to improve the client system and the consultee (Dougherty, 2005).

Consultation differs from supervision with regard to authority and power that are inherent in the supervisory relationship. In a consultation relationship, the consultee has the option to accept or ignore the advice given (Exercise 18.4). In a supervisory relationship, if the supervisee ignores the directions given by the supervisor, there may be specific consequences applied to that action. Another difference between consultation and supervision is that the consultant does not assume legal or clinical responsibility for the actions of the consultee.

Caplan (1970) developed an initial system for understanding consultation, which has continued to serve as a model for many years. He described consultation as a process of providing expertise to a consultee to assist the consultee in providing better service. Providing better service is a broad

Exercise 18.4

What Is Consultation?

Now that you have reviewed the definition of consultation, describe in your own words what consultation is and how you might apply it in your practice.

term and can apply to many different avenues of expertise. In his model, Caplan described three categories of consultation: (1) client centered, (2) consultee centered, and (3) program centered. Client-centered case consultation involved a consultee seeking information regarding how to deal with a specific client. The consultant then assesses the problem and makes a recommendation regarding the solution. Consultee-centered case consultation focuses on helping the consultee with problems regarding a particular group of similar clients. In this approach, the focus is on improving the consultee's functioning (Scileppi, Teed, & Torres, 2000). The third category is the program-centered consultation. The focus of this style is on program planning, evaluation, and administration. Caplan's model articulates the direction of the relationships involved in consultation and provides a solid foundation to build on. Caplan's three categories can be found in Table 18.3.

The Consultative Process

In 1992, Lachenmeyer outlined stages that often take place during the consultative process. The stages are as follows: (1) gaining entry, (2) negotiating the contract, (3) building the relationship, (4) defining the problem, (5) presenting and choosing alternative solutions, (6) implementing the intervention, and (7) evaluating and terminating the consultation. The stages outlined in this process are often utilized by industrial organizational psychologists and have proved to be fairly consistent.

In the first stage, the consultant gains entry into the consultative relationship. This can be formal or informal depending on the nature of the consultation. From the beginning, the program head or primary contact of the organization needs to be supportive of the consultant. On entry, the consultant becomes aware of the organizational culture recognizing formal and informal structures within the organization.

The second stage of the process involves negotiating the contract or outlining the expectations of the relationship. Again, this process may be formal or informal depending on the nature of the consultation. During this process, the consultant will discuss expectations and time lines with relevant stakeholders and establish terms of the agreement.

The third stage involves building relationships within the organization. During this

Table 18.3   Caplan's (1970) Three Categories of Consultation

Item	Category	Description
Category 1	Client centered	Consultee seeks information on how to deal with a specific client
Category 2	Consultee centered	Consultee seeks help to deal with a group of specific clients
Category 3	Program centered	Consultation focuses on program development and evaluation

Source. Caplan, G. (1970). *The theory and practice of mental health consultation*. New York: Basic Books.

phase, the consultant will establish rapport with the staff. This may involve spending time in places where the staff congregates such as employee lounges, cafeterias, or conference rooms. The physical presence of the consultant over time reduces fears and breeds familiarity with the staff. This builds trust in the relationship, which is a key factor for the staff to consider the consultant's recommendations.

The fourth stage in the consultative process involves defining the problem. This has been described as the most significant step in the consultation process. Lachenmeyer (1992) suggests starting at the highest accessible level in the system (e.g., consultee centered vs. client centered). Care should be taken to identify the problem correctly because of the impact it will have on the intervention process.

The fifth stage involves presenting and choosing alternative solutions to the identified problem. The consultant should begin this process by considering what may have been previously tried and why it failed. Then other alternatives with their advantages and disadvantages should be considered. The consultee is involved in this process because ultimately he or she decides which plan the agency will commit to.

The sixth stage is implementing the intervention stage. During this stage, the consultant monitors the intervention to ensure that it is executed properly. Errors are corrected if they occur, and the consultant continues to work to ensure the validity of the intervention.

Finally, the last stage involves evaluating and terminating the consultation. A summative evaluation is initiated to determine the effects of the intervention. Then the consultant writes a report documenting the consultation process, including the consultant's activity, interventions used, and relative outcomes. This report is given to the stakeholders for their review. At this point the consultant would exit the agency.

The consultative process as articulated by Lachenmeyer (1992) is often used in formal consultations. However, the steps in the process can be modified to provide personalized consultation when consulting with just one person. Steps are scaled down to meet the needs of the individual (Exercise 18.5).

Characteristics of Effective Consultants

Just as supervision requires specific competencies to perform adequately, consultation also requires several skills that are necessary for effective service. Dougherty (2005) describes many of these skills such as interpersonal and communication attitudes. The premise for interpersonal and communication attitudes is based on Carl Roger's (1967) building blocks of person-centered therapy. These include having unconditional positive regard or acceptance toward the consultee, developing empathy or understanding of the consultee's experience, and displaying genuineness.

Developing robust interpersonal communication skills is a critical factor for effective consultation. This skill incorporates the ability to create, maintain, and terminate relationships in a professional manner. This skill may be evidenced by putting the consultee at ease, creating an environment that is conducive to collaboration, creating an appropriate image from the perspective of the consultee, exuding confidence, and being

---

Exercise 18.5

Clinical Skills and Competencies

List what clinical skills and competencies you could use to assist you in the third stage of the consultative process, which involves building relationships within the organization.

able to use humor appropriately. Another closely associated skill is the ability to communicate effectively. Consultants need to be able to utilize a broad repertoire of communication skills to effectively transfer their message to the consultee. This may be displayed through nonverbal attending (e.g., open body posture); actively listening to the consultee's intended meaning; clarifying, paraphrasing, and summarizing specific points of a discussion; and using plain language that the consultee can understand (Dougherty, 2005).

The ability to effectively problem solve is another critical competency for the consultant. This skill is paramount because the main purpose of the consultation relationship is to identify a problem that needs to be solved and provide recommendations for its solution. The consultant can demonstrate effective problem-solving skills by (a) defining consultation as a problem-solving activity, (b) defining the problem the consultee needs fixed, (c) examining the surrounding conditions of the problem, (d) analyzing and interpreting relevant data, (e) designing interventions for specific situations, and (f) evaluating problem-solving attempts.

Another relevant skill is the ability to work with organizations. While this may appear to be an easy task, organizational forces can have a negative impact on the consultation experience and thwart progress. Consultants should be able to become accepted by members of the organization where the consultation will occur, use organizational analysis, provide feedback, utilize surveys to determine attitudes of organizational members, develop organization-wide interventions, determine the climate of the organization, and determine the culture of the organization (Dougherty, 2005).

Effective consultants should be able to work with a variety of groups. Group work is quite common in the consultation arena and a necessary skill for the consultant to develop. The ability to work with groups effectively can be described as gently reminding the group when they get off task, managing conflict within the group context, managing agendas of meetings, and facilitating concrete communication among group members.

Due to the diversity in our society, an effective consultant is one who can also address problems and situations within its cultural context. Multicultural competence includes the ability to understand the impact of one's culture on professional practice, valuing and understanding the impact of other cultures, adapting a culturally responsive consultation style, and possessing specific knowledge about the minority group served in the consultation process (Dougherty, 2005).

Finally, displaying ethical and professional conduct in the consultation process is also a hallmark of a successful consultant. Providing sound ethical judgment in conflict situations is a timely skill that is truly needed. Some vital abilities that assist consultants in acting in a professional manner are the ability to maintain integrity and confidentiality, adherence to the ethics code, engaging in consultation only within professional limits of competency, and maintaining personal and professional growth.

Consultant Roles

During the consultation process, consultants may exercise multiple roles to meet the challenges presented and effectively resolve problems. One classification of consultation roles was developed by Lippit and Lippit (1986), which described roles on a continuum ranging from directive to nondirective. Directive roles provide opportunities for the consultant to function as a technical expert, while nondirective roles allow the consultant to facilitate the consultee's expertise. Directive roles that a consultant may utilize are an advocate, expert, and trainer/educator. Several nondirective roles that are often employed include a collaborator, fact finder, and process specialist (Dougherty, 2005).

When a consultant is operating as an advocate, this is the most directive role that he or she can operate in. When advocating, a consultant may attempt to persuade the consultee to do something the consultant views is in the consultee's best interest based on his or her superior knowledge. Another way that a consultant might advocate for the consultee is to fight for the rights of the consultee when the consultee is unable to do so.

The role of an expert is another common role that consultants take on when consultees need knowledge or advice. Consultants are taking on the role of an expert when they are diagnosing problems in the organization and when they offer recommendations for previously identified problems. One caveat to be aware of is the possibility for the consultee to develop dependence on the consultant to solve his or her problems and never fully engage in the development of their own problem-solving capabilities (Dougherty, 2005).

Consultants often utilize the other directive role of trainer/educator both formally and informally. Organizations often ask the consultant to function in this role by developing workshops and seminars for employees to facilitate the transfer of knowledge. An advantage of this role is the ability to assist the consultee in professional development by providing the skills and knowledge necessary for optimum functioning (Dougherty, 2005).

Nondirective roles include the functioning as a collaborator. In this role, the consultant works with the consultee on a task. The consultant does not perform tasks that the consultee can perform but assists with expertise that the consultee needs. Another nondirective role is the fact finder. When functioning in this capacity, the consultant obtains information, analyzes it, and provides the interpretation to the consultee. This may include reading records, interviewing, and surveying methods. It may be very simple and finished quickly, or it may be very complex and take extended amounts of time depending on the topic of interest (Dougherty, 2005).

Another nondirective role that consultants may function as is a process specialist. In this role, the consultant focuses on the problem-solving process and how the steps are accomplished. The purpose is for the consultee to understand the chain of events that affect normal behavior (Exercise 18.6). An example of a process specialist role would be a consultant who assists a school administrator in organizing more effective meetings by using agendas (Dougherty, 2005).

IMPLICATIONS FOR COUNSELING ADOLESCENTS

This chapter has provided an overview describing two distinct processes of supervision and consultation. Knowledge and exposure to both of these processes is essential for the development of a competent provider. Supervision provides the opportunity for a provider to impart his or her knowledge and wisdom to the next generation of counselors, while consultation provides opportunities for the provider to function as an expert and assist organizations in their process of development. Many practitioners in the field who work with adolescents and agencies that involve adolescents are often functioning in these roles without adequate knowledge and training. It is the responsibility of educators, trainers, and counselors to ensure appropriate exposure and training in these areas, so that those who counsel others will practice competently and professionally.

Exercise 18.6

Skills and Abilities

How do the skills and abilities used in the consultative process differ and relate to the skills used in providing therapy and supervision?

CACREP Implications and Ethical Considerations

To ensure competency within the counseling profession and safety to the general population, CACREP (2009) has developed standards that address the roles of supervision and consultation in provider education and training. Supervision is initially discussed in Section G of the common core curricular standards under the Professional Orientation and Ethical Practice subsection as a requirement involving the understanding of provider supervision models, practices, and processes. It is further discussed as an applied Practicum and Internship requirement in Section III—Professional Practice. This states that trainees shall receive a minimum of 1 hour per week of individual supervision and a minimum of 1.5 hours per week of group supervision. In the Career Counseling section, under subsection L—Skills and Practices, counselors are to be able to demonstrate the ability to provide effective supervision to career development facilitators. The School Counselor section, under subsection D—Skills and Practices, notes that counselors should be able to demonstrate their ability to recognize their limitations as a school provider and to seek supervision or refer clients when appropriate. It is also discussed in the Doctoral Standards Counselor Education and Supervision section under the Professional Identity, Knowledge subsection that notes learning experiences beyond the entry level are needed in the theories and practices of provider supervision. Finally, under Section IV of Doctoral Learning Outcomes, there is an entire section dedicated to supervision and divided into Knowledge and Skill/Practices sections. The Knowledge section notes that counselors understand the purposes of clinical supervision, understand theoretical frameworks and models of clinical supervision, understand the roles and relationships related to clinical supervision, and understand the legal, ethical, and multicultural issues associated with clinical supervision. The Skills/Practice subsection notes that counselors should demonstrate the application of theory and skills of clinical supervision and develop and demonstrate a personal style of supervision (CACREP, 2009).

Consultation is also discussed in several sections of the 2009 CACREP standards. It is first mentioned in the Helping Relations subsection of the Professional Identity Section and mentioned as a required understanding of a general framework for understanding and practicing consultation. It is further described in the Career Counseling section as needing understanding of models of consultation relevant to career development. It further notes that one should be able to demonstrate the ability to establish and maintain a consulting relationship with people that can influence a client's career. In the School Counseling section, there is a complete subsection titled Collaboration and Consultation. In this subsection, counselors are directed to develop knowledge of systems, theories, models, and processes of consultation in school system settings (CACREP, 2009).

Application of Ethics

As described above, the CACREP standards emphasize the importance of developing knowledge and competence in the areas of supervision and consultation. Ethically, the absence of such training in provider programs would be considered unethical. Developing competencies in these two areas ensures public safety and assists the developing provider in acquiring future resources that will facilitate personal and professional growth.

Providers who develop the specific competencies outlined in the supervision and consultation sections will be able to provide services to supervisees and organizations in a proficient and ethical manner. Ethical violations will likely be reduced because providers will know how to manage conflicts effectively and provide equitable solutions for all parties involved as they function in the roles of supervisor and consultant. Supervisee and organizational satisfaction scores will further increase as a result of increased performance. These outcomes will strengthen the counseling profession and provide a model of ethical practice for future generations of counselors.

Summary

Supervision and consultation are professional roles that enable the provider to function effectively when given substantial consideration. Each one has established competencies that set the standard for exemplary performance. Training programs that emphasize these competencies provide their trainees an opportunity to develop a greater understanding of the therapeutic process and increase their level of confidence in their ability to function as a proficient provider. With the imminent modifications in the landscape of health care, counselors who develop their skills and proficiencies in areas such as supervision and consultation will better prepare themselves to adapt during this season of change.

Keystones

- Supervision is defined as an intervention provided by a more senior member of a profession to a more junior member or members of that same profession. The relationship is evaluative and hierarchical, extends over time, and has the simultaneous purposes of enhancing the professional functioning of the more junior person(s), monitoring the quality of professional services offered to the clients that she, he, or they see, and serving as a gatekeeper for those who are to enter the particular profession.

- The supervisory alliance is a foundational principle for the effectiveness of supervision. Supervisor characteristics that strengthen this alliance include an attitude of acceptance, empathy, validation, encouragement, warmth, and understanding.

- Developing the supervisee's clinical skills is the chief goal of the supervision process.

- There are many different types of approaches to supervision just as there are many different kinds of supervisors. These approaches function as a model for supervision and may be classified as either an extension of psychotherapy-based theory or developed specifically for supervision (Goodyear & Bernard, 1998). Those approaches that are developed specifically for supervision are often referred to as process-based approaches.

- Consultation is defined as a service provided by a senior mental health professional or by any individual who possesses the particular expertise needed by a consultee, regardless of the parties' relative status or profession.

- Characteristics of effective consultants include strong interpersonal skills, communication skills, problem-solving skills, skills in working with organizations, group skills, skills in dealing with cultural diversity, and ethical and professional behavior skills.

- During the consultation process, consultants may exercise multiple roles to meet the challenges presented and effectively resolve problems. These roles may include being an advocate, expert, trainer/educator, collaborator, fact finder, and process specialist.

- Supervision provides the opportunity for a provider to impart his or her knowledge and wisdom to the next generation of counselors, while consultation provides opportunities for the provider to function as an expert and assist organizations in their process of development.

References

Beck, J. S., Sarnat, J. E., & Barenstein, V. (2008). Psychotherapy-based approaches to supervision. In C. A. Falender & E. P. Shafranske (Eds.), *Casebook for clinical supervision: A competency-based approach* (pp. 57–96). Washington, DC: American Psychological Association.

Bernard, J. M. (1997). The discrimination model. In C. E. Watkins Jr. (Ed.), *Handbook of psychotherapy supervision* (pp. 310–327). New York, NY: Wiley.

Bernard, J. M., & Goodyear, R. K. (2013). *Fundamentals of clinical supervision* (5th ed.). New York, NY: Pearson.

Bordin, E. S. (1994). Theory and research in the thera-peutic working alliance: New directions. In C. A. Falender & E. P. Shafranske (Eds.), *Clinical supervision: A competency based approach* (p. 96). Washington, DC: American Psychological Association.

Caplan, G. (1970). *The theory and practice of mental health consultation.* New York, NY: Basic Books.

Carruthers, J. (1993). The principles and practices of mentoring. In B. J. Caldwell & E. M. A. Carter (Eds.), *The return of the mentor: Strategies for workplace learning* (pp. 9–23). London, England: Falmer Press.

Council for Accreditation of Counseling and Related Educational Programs. (2009). *2009 standards.* Retrieved from http://www.cacrep.org/wp-content/uploads/2013/12/2009-Standards.pdf

Dougherty, A. M. (2005). *Psychological consultation and collaboration in school and community settings.* Belmont, CA: Brooks/Cole, Cengage Learning.

Falender, C. A., & Shafranske, E. P. (2004). *Clinical supervision: A competency-based approach.* Washington, DC: American Psychological Association.

Falender, C. A., & Shafranske, E. P. (2008). *Casebook for clinical supervision: A competency-based approach.* Washington, DC: American Psychological Association.

Goodyear, R. K., & Bernard, J. M. (1998). Clinical supervision: Lessons from the literature. *Counselor Education and Supervision, 38*(1), 6–22.

Horvath, A. O. (2001). The alliance. *Psychotherapy, 38,* 365–372.

Knoff, H. M. (1988). Clinical supervision, consultation, and counseling: A comparative analysis for supervisors and other educational leaders. *Journal of Curriculum and Supervision, 3*(3), 240–252.

Lachenmeyer, J. R. (1992). *Consultation.* In J. A. Scileppi, E. L. Teed, & R. D. Torres, *Community psychology: A common sense approach to mental health* (pp. 129–133). Upper Saddle River, NJ: Prentice Hall.

Lippit, G., & Lippit, R. (1986). *The consulting process in action* (2nd ed.). La Jolla, CA: University Associates.

Rath, T., & Conchie, B. (2009). *Strengths based leadership.* Washington, DC: Gallop.

Roberts, A. (1999). Homer's Mentor: Duties fulfilled or misconstrued. *History of Education Journal.* Retrieved from http://www.nickols.us/homers_mentor.pdf

Rogers, C. R. (1967). *On becoming a person: A therapist's view of psychotherapy.* (2nd ed.). London: Constable.

Safran, J. D., & Muran, J. C. (2000). Resolving therapeutic alliance ruptures: Diversity and integration. *Journal of Clinical Psychology, 56*(2), 233–243.

Scileppi, J. A., Teed, E. L., & Torres, R. D. (2000). *Community psychology: A common sense approach to mental health.* Upper Saddle River, NJ: Prentice Hall.

Seligman, M. E. P., & Csikszentmihalyi, M. (2000). Positive psychology: An introduction. *American Psychologist, 55*(1), 5–14.

Welch, B. L. (2003). Supervising with liability in mind. *Insight: Safeguarding Psychologists Against Liability Risks, 1,* 1–6.

19

USE OF TECHNOLOGY WITH ADOLESCENTS

Telemental Health Treatment

INTRODUCTION

Technology has affected every element of contemporary human life, including the service provision in all types of helping and medical professions. The past, present, and future of the field of counseling and other related behavioral health fields is intricately affected by these changes and includes both benefits and risks. Along with counseling, other fields of study are focusing on how to integrate technological advances into ethical practice and service delivery. An abundance of new ideas and products exist for integration into many areas of counseling, including but not limited to education and online learning, consumer and practitioner communication, record keeping, and ethical and legal considerations. The field of counseling has responded, as many other professions have, by pushing to remain contemporary. Awareness of technological advances and options for integration encourages research that promotes the importance of impact on service providers and their consumers, including children and adolescents (Slone, Reese, & McClellan, 2012). Advancing technologically

in health care fields is a priority not only for individual practitioners and educators but also for federal and state agencies, as well as for professional governing boards (Harris & Younggren, 2011; U.S. Department of Health and Human Services, 2014).

Specifically, at the end of this chapter, you will be able to do the following:

- Discuss the advantages and disadvantages of media affecting the lives of adolescents

- Articulate the psychological effects of "always being on" for adolescents and how it evidences in symptom manifestation

- Understand cyberbullying, cyber stalking, and cyber harassment and how technology overlaps with social interactions of adolescents

- Articulate the various ways in which adolescents communicate online with one another

- Discuss the risks, benefits, and uses of telemental health (TMH) and common ways to engage the TMH process

- Discuss the differences between digital natives versus digital immigrants and its impact on the mental health of adolescents

- Understand the cultural and developmental nuances of individual adolescent group's engagement with technology

- Integrate technology in assigned case studies and respond to exercises

TECHNOLOGY IN MENTAL HEALTH WITH ADOLESCENTS

While providers work to adjust to technology being a part of service provision, it is difficult for providers to remain up to date given the rapid pace of technological advancements. This provides a challenging environment for providers to balance ethics and service delivery. Particularly for those who treat adolescents, there is an expectation to remain current, which can contribute to professional frustration. When one element of technology is accepted, researched, and adapted, even greater options for communication and interaction appear on the market for consumers. Needless to say, it is a challenge for providers to maintain professional awareness and interaction with technological advancements, all while pushing forward to provide up-to-date and relevant treatment for today's adolescents.

Digital Natives

The current generation of adolescents are considered to be *digital natives*. This is a widely used term that describes a generation that is growing up with technology instead of having it introduced to them at a later stage in life (*digital immigrants*). A digital native is brought up surrounded by computers and technological options, so he or she is familiar with how technology touches all parts of his or her life (Kolmes, 2012).

The reality of technology integration in their lives reflects how different this generation is from its predecessors, and this is reflected in a national survey of approximately 800 adolescents (Madden, Lenhart, Duggan, Cortesi, & Gasser, 2013). Nearly 78% of adolescents have a cell phone, and about 74% of adolescents access the Internet on cell phones, tablets, and other mobile devices. Similarly, one in four adolescents is a "cell mostly" user, a distinctly different comparison with the 15% of adults who are "cell mostly" users. Furthermore, among the adolescents who own a smartphone, half are "cell mostly" users. This means that a large majority of adolescents own a cell phone or smartphone, and they prefer using these devices over desktop or laptop computers. Numbers reflect that 93% of adolescents have access to a computer, and more than 20% of them have a tablet computer; 71% of adolescents who use a computer share one with family members.

As digital natives, adolescents today lead the way in mobile connectivity. Meaning, even though most adolescents were online in some way in 2006, today, mobile connectivity is "always on" and fully mobile. Just as adults are no longer limited to stationary connections through a laptop or desktop, adolescents take their lives, their education, their relationships, and their questions to the Internet; their cell phone is their point of connection. As technological advancements continue, adolescents have the familiarity and the expectation to stay connected in multiple ways.

Interestingly, socioeconomic status and parental income do not neatly divide which adolescents have access to technology and which do not. Both higher income and lower income families have adolescents with cell phones. Some differences lie in older adolescents being more likely to have a cell phone, which is likely to be a smartphone, than younger adolescents. Urban and suburban adolescents are more likely to have a smartphone than adolescents living in rural areas. While adolescents from a lower income bracket might be less likely to use the Internet, there is an equal or greater possibility that these adolescents will have their cell phone as their primary point of connectivity.

These statistics reflect the reality that our world has changed. This generation of adolescents lives online, unlike any generation before them. Knowledge and awareness of what this means for providers is paramount to understanding ethical treatment and best practices, but the reality is that counseling must keep pace with advancements and life online to provide the best care and expand treatment options (Maheu, McMenamin, Pulier, & Posen, 2012).

New Age of Telehealth

Historically, traditional counseling is understood to be "face to face" (F2F), where a provider and his or her consumer(s) are physically in the same room. Transition to including technology into counseling practice not only expands the availability of services and consumer choice but also demands regulation in practice and licensure. Generally, the approach to mental health counseling is changing. There is a new vernacular that is now common within technology, including words such as *telehealth*, or "the use of electronic information and telecommunications

technologies to support long-distance clinical health care, patient and professional health-related education, public health and health administration" (U.S. Department of Health and Human Services, 2014). Other important terms used in telehealth are described in Table 19.1.

The term *telemental health* describes this transition to providing mental health services technologically, which can include counseling sessions, assessments, and diagnostic interviews. Movement out of traditional F2F counseling facilities presents treatment providers, educators, students, and trainees alike with the responsibility of respecting this growth and responding with best practices, venturing into new spaces to maintain provision of care for those in need. Since telehealth presents this undeniable situation, providers are obligated to respond to the demand. There are both benefits and risks to progressive technological changes, each of which deserve attention.

Table 19.1   Common Abbreviations and Vocabulary Used in Telehealth

Word	Abbreviation	Description
Telepsychiatry		Psychiatric services delivered online
Telepsychology		Psychological services delivered online
Telemental health	TMH	Mental health services provided online
Face to face	F2F	The more traditional format of counseling services; the consumer and the provider are physically in the same location
Electronic health record	EHR	Electronic format of a consumer's record, contact information, important documents, and forms
Patient-centered medical home	PCMH	Coordination of multiple disciplines in a consumer or patient's health treatment; providers may be a part of an interdisciplinary medical team treating a consumer
Cyberbullying/digital bullying		Aggression toward or willful repeated harm to an individual using computers, cell phones through avenues such as social media forums, and public or private messages
Video teleconferencing	VTC	Use of video forums to meet with another person who is in a different physical location
Personal computer	PC	A personal laptop or desktop computer; other technological options are tablets and smartphones
Information and communication technology	ICT	Technological avenues for input, retrieval, and organization of information and communication

BENEFITS AND RISKS OF TMH PRACTICE

Benefits of TMH

Availability. One of the main positive elements of telehealth is availability of services. It is undeniable that reaching those who might not otherwise have access to services is a positive aspect of advancement. Within the research, one main aspect of availability that continues to challenge is the availability of treatment for the individuals in rural communities. Based on the Council for Accreditation of Counseling and Related Educational Programs and other standards, this is important because counseling programs, educators, and students have a commitment to consider culturally relevant issues related to the provision of counseling services.

Adolescents in rural communities simply do not have access to multiple options when seeking counseling services. Telehealth no doubt broadens opportunities for treatment and offers the counseling field ample opportunity to research avenues for provision and treatment effectiveness. For example, Myers, Valentine, and Melzer (2007) looked specifically at telepsychiatric options for children and adolescents and focused on feasibility, acceptability, and sustainability. In this, when availability of services is assessed, it is important that the counseling field not stop at recognizing telehealth treatment options but focus on if the options are good ones. One question that might be applicable in both rural and urban areas when there is a need for counseling and mental health help is whether consumers are accessing the help *and* whether they are satisfied with the help?

Positive Impact. Beyond researching and provision in rural areas, telehealth can provide care to others who might not be interested in traditional F2F services or not have ready access to treatments needed. Current research repeatedly shows that telehealth is a feasible option for a variety of mental health issues, consumer populations, and practice areas, including geriatrics, military veterans, forensics, inpatient settings, and neuropsychological evaluations. Positive repetition of results reflects that telehealth can reach important areas in mental health and help guide professional and ethical practice to integrate telehealth in often discouraging situations. In essence, telehealth is providing an answer for unmet needs, albeit creating new challenges as we adopt and organize best practices (Luxton, Pruitt, & Osenbach, 2014; Nelson, Bui, & Velasquez, 2011; Slone et al., 2012; Turkle, 2011). As the health care industry continues to welcome ideas regarding interdisciplinary care, telehealth practitioners are a means to providing mental health and counseling referral sources. Instead of a provider rendering more exclusive services, facilities like a patient-centered medical home (PCMH) and electronic health records (EHR) are providing ways for professionals to interact and collaborate in ways that were previously extremely challenging (Maheu et al., 2012; Myers et al., 2007). At its core, a PCMH coordinates a number of service providers, such as a primary care physician, a nurse, a mental health professional, a dietician, an occupational therapist, and emergency or urgent care providers, among others. Such coordination has proved to be cost-effective and streamlined. One of the goals of the PCMH is to provide a wide range of high-quality personalized services care for a patient or client in one electronic (and possibly physical) location, which might include both medical and mental health issues. This goal represents a more organized and integrated way in which health providers can treat acute or comorbid issues. Providers might play a role in the care of a client's mental health through education, encouraging client interaction in their care, presenting treatment protocols, monitoring activity and progress, and sharing these with other providers. If a provider is part of a PCMH, it is likely that he or she would be coordinating with primary care treatment providers and coordinating both physical and mental health. The provider is one part of a focused system that seeks to quickly communicate and provide services that might otherwise be fragmented or stalled due to referrals that base from a primary care physician.

The PCMH is progress from the more traditional system, where, for example, a client would address issues related to obesity with his or her health care provider and from that care provider receive referrals and recommendations to see a provider and dietician. With a PCMH, this client has a hub for multifaceted needs, while otherwise he or she might have had to wait to see the provider and sign multiple release forms so that all the concerned professionals can coordinate and maintain awareness regarding treatment plans, results, and pertinent issues related to a diagnosis. As PCMHs progress and grow, they are using more technologies to provide services electronically, such as prescription refills, electronic visits with providers, patient group interaction, and the coordination of a patient's EHR (Dickinson & Miller, 2010; Hunter & Goodie, 2010; Strange et al., 2010).

Both in and out of PCMHs, providers are beginning to use EHRs to maintain client documents and information; however, not without difficulty. Like other issues related to TMH, there are both benefits and risks to working online with client data, such as in the use of EHRs, where a client's information is kept in electronic form. Benefits of EHRs are consolidation of client information, reduced human error, and rapid availability of content, but EHRs can be subject to security breaches and must be handled with care and knowledge (Devereaux & Gottlieb, 2012).

As the health care industry continues to welcome ideas regarding interdisciplinary care, telehealth practitioners are a means to providing mental health and counseling referral sources. Instead of a provider providing more exclusive services, facilities like a PCMH and an EHR are providing ways for professionals to interact and collaborate in ways that were previously extremely challenging (Maheu et al., 2012; Myers et al., 2007).

Additionally, positive elements and applicability of telehealth are seen in different practice areas. Many mental health–related assessments are available to take and can be scored online, making physical presence not necessary for test completion (Luxton et al., 2014). Researchers are looking at the applicability of telehealth for people of all ages, including children and adolescents (Nelson et al., 2011), and as research accumulates, studies already show that adolescents benefit from TMH interventions for specific problems or disorders such as obesity, depression, anxiety, eating disorders, stress management, smoking cessation, and drug use and abuse (Slone et al., 2012). For example, a provider might set up a smoking cessation group that includes 12 weekly virtual chat room meetings, where group participants might meet to talk and review challenges and progress. The provider could present psycho-educational concepts related to addiction, substance abuse, and cessation and allow participants to self-monitor their progress and share with the group. Another provider might choose to focus on a client's anxiety through strategies to take courageous steps through distressing situations. Adolescents can share journal art projects, the client and the therapist could listen to music together, or practice virtual high fives (Savin, Glueck, Chardavoyne, Yager, & Novins, 2011). Ultimately, providers could choose to implement a number of interventions attempted by others for specific problems or disorders in order to expand TMH repertoire for individuals and groups (Slone et al., 2012), such as video teleconferencing (VTC) to implement interventions and build therapeutic rapport.

Interventions specific to Internet interactions such as blogging (compared with private journaling) reflect therapeutic value in what adolescents can accomplish and benefit from when working online (Boniel-Nissim & Barak, 2013). Finally, research also reflects value in the way in which technology expands communication between the consumer and the provider, including text message reminders that assist with attendance, attrition rates, and premature termination (Branson, Clemmey, & Mukherjee, 2013).

Cost-Effective. Preliminary research reflects that TMH treatments are cost-effective in multiple ways. Consumers might save on lost work time or taking time off, travel costs, and child care. Time saved in traveling and waiting is important for many consumers, especially adolescents who might be missing school for appointments. For treatment providers, there is a cost-effective element to telehealth, but they must also consider the costs of proper technology, technology support, security measures, and how to respond to crises that are shared via technology (e.g., with self-harm concerns).

Consumer Choice and Specialty Services. Along with the positive element of access to treatment in rural areas, technology also allows an exponential change in the consumer's choice of service providers. Today, most of modern society exists daily in this way—communicates with others who do not live near, utilizes telecommuting as an option for work, and maintains rather elaborate relationships with those who might live across the world. Therapeutically, a consumer is no longer obligated to find a provider in their area. Research continues to reflect that Internet options for treatment provide consumers with satisfactory results, comparable with the success that consumers find with more traditional F2F meetings. When considering the positive elements of telehealth options, this point is critical to consider, as mental health needs often require frequent appointments. Additionally, specialists often cluster in urban areas, limiting access to their services if a traditional F2F model is upheld (Nelson et al., 2011).

TMH services provide opportunities for access to counseling that might not normally be available. Consumer and provider comfort levels are connected with successful telehealth treatments and must acknowledge cultural considerations, and language used must be a part of the professional's treatment considerations. For example, symptoms, treatment, and assessment might be available to a non-English-speaking consumer, meaning, a non-English-speaking client could be referred to a treatment provider who speaks his or her language, instead of only having the option to proceed in therapy with English

as a second language or not being able to proceed with therapy at all. Furthermore, consumers have the chance to meet with someone who specializes in working with specific populations or languages such as geriatrics, military personnel, LGBT (lesbian, gay, bisexual, and transgender), immigrants, or the hearing impaired (Luxton et al., 2014).

Growth as a Profession. Not only are providers warming to telehealth as a treatment option, but researchers are also continually looking at evidence-based treatments that fit within a telehealth model. Additionally, insurers and third-party payers are covering telehealth treatments. Even with tentative feelings about changes, providers are welcoming the changes through education, making suggestions for such practice, drawing ideas from other professions, and working to provide ethical guidelines for providers who have either decided to practice using technology or are interested in doing so. In general, although there is recognition of the issues at hand, educators, practitioners, and lawmakers are involving themselves in the change.

Technology offers much currently, but what will come in the future will continue to change the face of mental health services. Virtual reality has already hit TMH and will continue to grow and expand options for treatment. This includes the creation of virtual environments such as programs that appear real but are digitized, virtual intelligence agents such as a computer program that is designed to socially interact with a client, and robots such as AIBO the robot dog. This digital pet grows from puppy to mature dog depending on how it is treated. The pet can learn new tricks, has moods, and can return to a charging station when low on battery (Luxton et al., 2014; Maheu et al., 2012; Turkle, 2011). Additionally, integrating TMH as a prominent form of practice reflects an awareness of how technology is rapidly changing basic elements of the counseling profession because of how easily an individual can communicate, learn, and connect with others. This lessens the stronger boundaries that have surrounded the consumer and the provider for a long while within more traditional F2F interactions that were commonly limited to appointments in a specific location. Practitioners are now in a place that can utilize the Internet for their practice and integrate available resources for consumers, meeting the challenges that technology provides (Maheu et al., 2012).

Treatment and Rapport. With telehealth, some of the limitations of a traditional therapeutic relationship may not apply. An obvious example is that communication with a provider can be done without telephone calls, such as within a consumer portal or through a provider's website. Additionally, there are some overlapping benefits when considering telehealth practices. As mentioned previously, if consumers have more options available to them and these are more cost-effective, this in turn can positively affect treatment satisfaction and adherence. Furthermore, sessions can include others. In one study addressing the feasibility, acceptability, and sustainability of telepsychiatric services, psychiatrists were able to include parents, teachers, and therapists, diversifying and deepening a child's treatment (Myers et al., 2007). Furthermore, sessions can include other options, such as setting up virtual support groups (e.g., antibullying and addiction groups) and/or outside supports (e.g., family, teachers, mentors).

Another positive element of telehealth is the benefit of decreasing stigma. The stigma of needing and receiving mental health services has long been a focus of research for counseling and psychology. Issues such as treatment adherence, dropping out of counseling services, attrition rates, and consumer satisfaction are areas for exploration. Telehealth offers an option outside of traditional F2F treatment that might increase treatment adherence and consumer satisfaction and decrease attrition, dropout rates, and stigma. This can occur in a provider's ability to provide faster and more diversified services as a consumer's mental health issues receive needed

attention and hopefully experience a change in symptoms.

Challenging Thinking

One challenge the counseling profession faces is seeing technological advancement as positive in a piecemeal fashion. For example, do we see TMH as a good thing because it makes treatments available to individuals who might not have access to professional treatment because of where they live (e.g., rural location), because of a specific issue they need a referral for (e.g., LGBT), or because there is a language barrier (e.g., a non-English-speaking U.S. resident)? As a profession, can we move forward noting both the benefits and the risks of TMH because of how TMH changes mental health options for everyone? For instance, if an adolescent living in an urban community prefers to work with his or her provider online, is that just as positive and beneficial as an adolescent living in a rural area who seeks mental health assistance?

Risks in TMH

The counseling practice benefits from the telehealth movement by its prudence to concerns and potential problems. It is also important to maintain a focus on whether telehealth meetings and communications are an appropriate option for all consumers. Although most adolescents have a cell phone or smartphone and access to the Internet, professionals need to consider cultural issues that might impede treatment effectiveness, such as cultural groups that rely more heavily on interpersonal connection and nonverbal interactions (Savin et al., 2011).

Current Research. Telehealth is a relatively new option for treatment, as there is still limited amount of research covering relevant topics of feasibility and sustainability. This is especially true of treatments and interventions for adolescents. As a result, authors seeking to find what works for ado-lescent treatment often reference adult research and corresponding literature (Nelson et al., 2011; Slone et al., 2012) and make applications to adolescents.

Privacy and Security Issues. There are consider-able issues when looking at privacy, security, and TMH. Currently, there is an imbalance in the num-ber of providers who are moving forward using TMH as part of the treatment services and a lag in the ethical codes and guidelines to both guide these professionals and protect the public. Although a national licensure in professional counseling is a possibility in the future, providers must work with current suggestions for best practices and guide-lines to provide optimal services that uphold cur-rent counseling and psychological ethical codes and guidelines (Maheu et al., 2012). Reflected in the statistics previously described, the use of cell phones and smartphones as communication hubs highlights how adolescents expect to interact with others, including their treatment providers.

Providers are encouraged to maintain aware-ness of their role in maintaining best practices to ensure privacy, security, and confidentiality. This responsibility includes awareness and knowl-edge of how the Health Insurance Portability and Accountability Act (HIPAA) and the Health Information Technology for Economic and Clin-ical Health Act apply to their work in TMH. Furthermore, state laws are different nationwide, and providers are responsible for applicable stan-dards and guidelines (Luxton et al., 2014; Maheu et al., 2012).

To maintain privacy, practitioners have to consider the challenges TMH presents. Beyond awareness and integration of national- and state-level guidelines, providers must consider the logistical cost of practicing TMH while uphold-ing privacy and security. This might include legal counsel, administrative training, technological support, network infrastructures, data storage costs, necessary equipment, adequate security measures, encryption software, and ongoing training regarding technological developments. While it is tempting to use the latest, greatest,

easiest, or most popular applications, providers are encouraged to be aware of the privacy state-ments and the structural set up of the platforms they use (Devereaux & Gottlieb, 2012; Maheu & McMenamin, 2013; Schwartz & Lonborg, 2011).

Dealing With Emergencies

Before assuming the role of providing TMH, providers need to review their level of compe-tence for both technical and clinical work, in addition to reviewing recommended protocol for suicide prevention and response. Additionally, professionals need to understand that their con-sumer might live in a location where emergency hospitalization, involuntary admittance, and duty-to-warn laws might be different from their own. Even though jurisdiction is a controversial issue and is handled on a case-by-case basis, when it comes to TMH practice, multiple sources note that the prevailing jurisdiction is where *the consumer resides* (American Telemedicine Asso-ciation, 2013; Harris & Younggren, 2011).

Handling emergencies is an essential part of a provider's willingness to work with TMH. Based on current research and the development of prac-tice guidelines in both psychology and other disciplines, a few manageable suggestions are provided here. First, all consumers should pro-vide emergency contact information in their informed consent. This requires that the provider review related issues of confidentiality since an emergency contact is not always provided in more traditional settings. Second, providers need to acquire contact information for local emer-gency resources. As part of a consumer begin-ning treatment, a practitioner can enlist the help of the consumer to gather reasonable options. Third, as something that might be overlooked or seem burdensome, providers need to determine if there are any changes to the consumer's loca-tion, personal support system, or emergency contact on a regular basis (American Telemedi-cine Association, 2013).

Forming a Safety Plan. Beyond awareness and adherence to state and professional organizational regulatory guidelines, providers must take certain precautions when working with adolescent consumers through the Internet. Once a provider feels comfortable moving into the informed consent phase and beginning treatment, there are a few recommended practices for forming a safety plan. First, the provider needs to have details of a consumer's physical location and contact information. At the start of every session, a provider needs to find out the physical location of the consumer, in case the consumer is talking from a different place than the physical address noted in the consumer's contact information. Consumer location is also important so that a provider can research licensure requirements. Second, providers need to gather contact information for local medical and psychiatric providers. Third, an additional mode of contact for the consumer is important to obtain in case the consumer cannot be reached or communication is broken during session (Luxton, O'Brien, McCann, & Mishkind, 2012).

A fourth step for providers is to obtain an emergency contact or a "local collaborator" who might be a family member or friend of the consumer. This individual, with the consumer's permission, can provide information regarding the consumer and can be contacted to assist in the event of an emergency. Providers are advised to check in with the consumer regarding the status of the consumer's relationship with the local contact, as relationships can change or be affected during the course of therapeutic treatment (e.g., an adolescent consumer's parents begin a contentious divorce and custody issues are at hand). As in more traditional treatment relationships, providers are advised to be aware of how disclosures made to others during an emergency situation can affect treatment and must be attended to if and when treatment resumes. Providers must take care to clearly define the role that an emergency contact has in the consumer's treatment and emergency plan (American Telemedicine Association, 2013; Luxton et al., 2012).

Fifth, as a matter of professional support in the time of an emergency, providers can locate and maintain a relationship with a colleague who would be able to help in the event of an emergency.

For example, if the provider is unable to maintain telephone or Internet contact with the consumer in an emergency, a colleague can connect with a local emergency dispatch. Finally, provider awareness of local treatment options might be necessary for an appropriate referral to help with continuity of care and help focus on the welfare of the consumer as he or she moves through the trauma of an emergency (Luxton et al., 2012).

An emergency response plan can be outlined during the informed consent process, but it also needs to be revisited and updated throughout treatment. Providers must make sure that the information in the safety plan is up-to-date so that the provider can respond appropriately and quickly if the need arises. Special attention must be given to an adolescent's age and maintaining contact with the consumer's parent or guardian, if needed.

Using an Emergency Contact or Support Person. Although treatment may never include an emergency, providers and consumers both need to have an explicit and written understanding of how emergencies will be handled. An informed consent and safety plan need to include a contact person. When gathering this information, providers can include questions about whether this contact person is aware of the consumer needing or entering therapy and what his or her relationship is to the consumer. However, providers must remember that a consumer may not be cooperative in managing a challenging situation; it is also possible that the emergency contact or support person would not be available or cooperative. Therefore, professionals need to be prepared with contact information for local emergency care and resources for their consumers (American Telemedicine Association, 2013).

Challenge to Traditional Mental Health Services

One change in the provision of telehealth services is the impact that technology has on traditional human interaction. The social implications of technological advances have been researched extensively, highlighting concerns and benefits that technology provides in human relationships. With regard to therapeutic interaction, which has long been based on relational trust, building rapport, and the importance of nonverbal communication cues, technology has forced a huge shift in how a consumer and a provider connect. Research comparing F2F and TMH treatments consistently reflect consumer satisfaction, and most studies highlight the demand that telehealth interactions make on the relationship between the two interacting parties. While research reveals that many clients are willing and able to interact online with a provider, it is necessary to maintain consideration on client comfort level (even if there is willingness), particularly because TMH facilities might involve emotional content, just as they would in a more traditional setting.

There are a growing number of ways to interact through technology, including social content, status updates, texting, emoticons, tweeting, avatars in virtual worlds, and file, video, and picture sharing. All of these are avenues that close gaps in time and space between people as has never been experienced before. This highlights the human ability to adapt and enjoy such interactions, but the need for human interaction cannot be overlooked even when considering the positive elements of telehealth (Turkle, 2011).

Providers must be mindful to consistently evaluate consumer comfort level with the use of telehealth interactions, even after a thorough informed consent that notes differences and risks compared with traditional options (Luxton et al., 2014). Some ethical, professional, and relational considerations include consumer comfort level and experience with technological interactions, contraindications for telehealth treatment, personal preferences, history of difficulty in treatment, safety concerns, and treatment adherence and progress. Additionally, practitioners have to be attentive to working with consumers without being able to view and integrate nonverbal information such as eye contact, physical movement, body posture, facial expressions, or pausing for thought. Practitioners and consumers alike will

not have this information if they interact over the phone, as well as other missed relational and emotional cues such as emotional moments of sadness, tearing or crying, anger, frustration, and others (Luxton et al., 2012; Luxton et al., 2014). Table 19.2 outlines some of the technological and individual components that a provider can consider in TMH treatment provision.

Technical Issues. Another risk to working technologically is the complications that can occur and affect treatment provision. Luxton et al. (2014) offer some insight into why technical issues affect TMH interactions. Even if providers seek to remain professional and practice ethically, there are often technical issues that cannot be avoided that affect treatment provision. Providers can take precautions to address potential issues and interruptions with clients and describe a plan of action for a dropped call, poor audio, or network connections. These examples are everyday normal technical issues, but in a TMH situation when personal issues might be addressed, the impact can impede therapeutic progress. While research repeatedly shows a balanced satisfaction between TMH treatment and traditional F2F treatment, one issue that can stand out is client frustration with interruptions. Providers are advised to attend to client frustrations regarding technical issues, as well as adjust treatment plans and session content, and include a chance for clients to offer feedback regarding their experience when such problems arise. For example, after three separate attempts to connect on a regularly scheduled VTC call, a client and provider decide to stop attempting to connect and reschedule their appointment. Prior to this occurring, the provider needs to have a plan for such an occurrence that both the client and the provider can revert to, such as connecting by phone to reschedule if they are unable to secure an unbroken connection to complete a session. The provider can address the client's frustration by having a scheduled time off of work to meet and talk about a challenging issue, but technological issues prevent the session from occurring.

Positive repetition of results reflects that telehealth can reach important areas in mental health

Table 19.2   Recommended Considerations in Telehealth Treatment

Technical Components

Camera positioning	Camera positioning can affect eye contact and change perception of attentiveness, understanding, and listening.
Changes in personal interactions (e.g., eye contact)	Consumers and providers must be attentive to how video or phone contact changes the chance to view nonverbal interactions.
Network connection	A poor network connection can cause problems with having an uninterrupted session. Images can freeze, audio can be lost, or the call can drop. Providers are encouraged to have a contingency plan for handling poor Internet connections that affect a session.
Adequate audio and volume for both parties	At the beginning of each session, consumers and providers can check in to see that both audio and video are functioning well enough to continue in the session. This is particularly important if one person is working in a noisy environment or if there are special considerations (e.g., use of a hearing aid).
Technological anomalies, unexplained difficulties, or malfunctions	Consumers and providers might be using an application that has difficulties preventing a smooth appointment, or there can be device issues with either person's device (e.g., a computer crashing or crackling phone connection after the device is dropped in water).

Individual Components

Other individuals present or near	Providers need to check in each session about who is present, if the consumer is alone, or if there might be a parent, guardian, sibling, or friend in the vicinity "listening through the door."
Differences in technological fluency	Consumers and providers need to be adequately fluent in using chosen applications and be aware that each has available technological support so that once treatment is started, it can continue.
Either party multitasking while in session	Consumers and providers must discuss the commitment to be physically and mentally present during the session. It is easy to be on a video session and use the computer for other activities (e.g., scroll through pictures, check Facebook, or send e-mails).
Physical fatigue (e.g., staring at a computer screen)	Depending on each person's daily activities, it is important to consider how both consumers and providers might experience physical fatigue (e.g., working all day at a desk looking at a computer).
Availability of a local contact	As part of a telemental health informed consent, providers are encouraged to obtain contact information for a local/emergency individual who can provide support during treatment.

and help guide professional and ethical practice to integrate telehealth in often discouraging situations. A few such examples might be clients with debilitating depression or social anxiety or individuals and families who have a difficult time leaving home due to chronic illnesses or disabilities.

Clinical Presentation and Diagnostics. One element of removing the benefits of F2F interactions that is often forgotten is the impact on a consumer's clinical presentation. With certain diagnoses, a provider might notice certain symptoms because they are displayed physically. For instance, when working with a highly anxious person, the provider might be able to see nervous habits such as clenched fists, hand wringing, or sweating. Other diagnostic considerations that could be missed are the signs of alcohol or substance use and personal hygiene. Without physical presence, there are clear limits to the range of information available regarding a consumer's psychomotor symptoms that are important in a number of *DSM-5* diagnoses, as well as clinical judgment used to inquire further in an interview or assessment situation (Luxton et al., 2014).

Other diagnostic symptoms might be subdued because the situation allows for consumers to avoid more difficult or uncomfortable situations. For instance, if a consumer is being evaluated for symptoms of posttraumatic stress disorder or another diagnosis in the anxiety spectrum, symptoms might not be as clear because the consumer is not having to interact in anxiety-provoking situations such as a public waiting room, traveling to and from a scheduled appointment, or interacting with strangers in an office setting (Luxton et al., 2014).

Evidence-Based Outgrowths

As previously noted, technology has changed the face of mental health practice, particularly for adolescents who are considered digital natives. These changes continue to compound, and practitioners are looking for ways to ethically integrate practice with the right consumers in ethical formats. Two main areas this chapter has already addressed with regard to how technology affects counseling practice are working with consumers who are good candidates for TMH treatment and ethical and professional issues regarding telehealth services. Providers are also affected on other professional and personal levels when they choose the centralization of applications on one device as this is thought to increase client compliance with therapeutic assignments (diaries, worksheets, self-ratings, etc.; Eonta et al., 2011).

Integrating Technology and Cognitive Behavioral Therapies

Technology and smartphones now tend to be considered a common part of everyday life. The increasing availability of electronic tools generates the opportunity for service providers to efficiently and conscientiously integrate these tools in treatment (Eonta et al., 2011). Eonta et al. (2011) demonstrated that digital technology could be used to individualize and enhance evidence-based treatments that providers commonly use. For example, Eonta et al. describe the use of digital pictures to track treatment progress for an individual with obsessive-compulsive disorder and hoarding symptoms. Smartphones can also be used to record relaxation files, so that clients will likely have the recording with them at all times (Eonta et al., 2011). During cognitive behavioral therapy, a client could easily use applications to log information for thought records or rate their subjective levels of distress at any moment. In another case, a smartphone was used to photograph and send pictures of in-session work to a client with generalized anxiety and trichotillomania (Eonta et al., 2011). Some studies have shown that cell phones are useful in increasing physical activity due to specific apps created to help with exercise (Eonta et al., 2011). Additionally, electronic devices like smartphones, ipods, and ipads are so unobtrusive that they can be used without stigma (Eonta et al., 2011). Finally, technology and its ease of access has profoundly affected the ways in which humans communicate and interact (Turkle, 2011), and these changes have changed therapeutic relationship in a number of ways. Physical proximity is often considered the most important element of how technology changes treatment. Common elements of physical proximity and closeness that are important when addressing the differences between telehealth and traditional F2F therapy depend on a provider's and adolescent consumer's ability to notice or address physical responses such as lack of eye contact, slumped shoulders or a change in body posture, perspiration, and odors (e.g., alcohol)—also, physical reactions that might reflect emotional responses such as changing in breathing, clenched fists, hiding one's face in one's hands, and tears or facial expressions of someone getting "choked up."

Digital Relationships

Technology brings an ease to communication and relationships that is new and different—providers' lives can overlap with the consumers' in many unexpected ways. Kolmes (2012) discusses "digital transparency" and the reality that a consumer and a provider can occupy the same digital space. This affects therapy when either discovers information about the other based on what is available through social, professional, or personal websites. While this might be accidental (e.g., a provider searches for a physical trainer and discovers that her or his consumer has a second job as a personal trainer and yoga instructor), there is also the chance that online contact is not accidental. An interesting element that seems to divide digital natives and immigrants is an acceptance of information discovery that affects treatment. Providers must consider that a consumer's information online may not be accurate and may be crafted for specific situations or relationships. Therefore, if a provider researches the consumer, there is no guarantee that this information is accurate or that online searches inform the therapeutic process and therapeutic relationship in a positive way (Kolmes, 2012; Kolmes & Taube, 2014).

Open Communication and Evaluation

One assumption that necessitates mentioning is the fact that adolescent consumers are likely to be curious and will search out electronically available information about their service providers, including their providers. Providers can address Internet searches and information discovery, bringing the information into treatment to help maintain consumer consent and autonomy, as well as ensuring that both parties provide accurate information in the therapeutic process. Doing so gives the provider and the consumer an open avenue to discuss and normalize a consumer's curiosity about the provider and encourage open communication about secrecy and withholding information in treatment, as well as build therapeutic rapport (Kolmes, 2012; Kolmes & Taube, 2014). Beginning therapy with open communication regarding digital communication and information, providers set the stage for consumers to be open about their perceptions of the provider, therapeutic interventions, and progress.

While much research focuses on progress made with technological elements, providers can also draw from previous research regarding the importance of the therapeutic relationship, such as the social influence a provider has on therapeutic alliance. This concept is applicable to telehealth practice, too, and can be integrated into a provider's development of a strong informed consent and continual pursuit of therapeutic rapport (Reese, Conoley, & Brossart, 2002).

When consumers and providers discuss information searches and review a thorough informed consent, communication and digital boundaries are another aspect that must be considered. Technology allows for a flow of regular communication and information. There are multiple ways to contact an individual, including phone calls, voicemails, texting, blog comments, message apps (e.g., WhatsApp, Cyber Dust, SnapChat), and social and professional sites (e.g., Facebook, LinkedIn). TMH practice allows consumers and providers to interact regardless of physical location. The rapid pace at which individuals can receive communication and respond to it can increase the expectation for response and availability, but providers must still carefully choose when and how to communicate with consumers.

Particularly in treatment with adolescents, who prefer communicating online via social media and texting, providers must attend to setting boundaries and expectations for communication. For example, a provider might be willing to communicate over e-mail and text regarding treatment scheduling and appointments but might not be comfortable with e-mails and texts that contain relevant clinical information. Informing an adolescent consumer of this communication structure allows consumers and providers to settle on a way to contact and communicate with one another throughout treatment. Also, because technology provides so many ways to rapidly connect with an individual, a provider might set forth that even though texting, she or he may not always be readily available to respond or interact but can be expected to respond within an amount of time that is deemed to be professionally acceptable (e.g., within 24–48 hours), not including emergency situations.

Social Media

Social media blends what used to be clear boundaries between a consumer and a provider. Some of the issues do not have clear answers or ethical directions, and a provider is left to decide how to implement ethical codes and guidelines, as well as best practices, in the digital age. Providers and students alike are part of the cultural norm of social networking memberships and research reflects age as an interesting divider between psychology professionals and students, reflecting the differences between digital natives and digital immigrants having different approaches to social media (Harris & Robinson-Kurpius, 2014).

One way to address ethical and best practices is to provide consumers with social media policy as part of the informed consent process. In a social media policy, providers need to address the following: interaction on social media sites that includes "friending," "fanning," and "following" as well as social media policy regarding interacting on social sites, business and professional sites, rating professional performance, e-mail communication, and search engines to locate information about the consumer or the provider (Kolmes, 2010). Providers are encouraged to review current social media policies of their constituents and create their own policy and

informed consent that fits their practice and the devices, communication, and applications they use for interaction with consumers.

CULTURAL CONSIDERATIONS, ADOLESCENTS, AND TREATMENT

Multicultural Considerations With Digital Natives

Shapka and Law (2013) found that regression analyses revealed that East Asian adolescents were less likely than European-descent adolescents to engage in cyberbullying. Additionally, greater levels of parental control and less parental solicitation were closely associated with lower levels of aggression for East Asian adolescents compared with their European peers (Shapka & Law, 2013). In direct contrast to European-descent peers, East Asian adolescents were more likely to be motivated to be cyber aggressive for proactive versus reactive reasons (Shapka & Law, 2013).

Blakeney (2012) studied cyberbullying and victimization in middle schools overseas. The results of the study suggest that cyberbullying and victimization exist in schools in countries outside of the United States (Blakeney, 2012). A study completed with 3,004 teenagers in Ireland found that one in five students was a cyberbully, a cyber victim, or both (O'Moore, 2012). The international experience of cyberbullying implies that cyberbullying is a prevalent issue for adolescents, parents, and providers that require attention.

Jackson and Wang (2013) compared the use of social networking sites in a collectivist culture (China) with an individualistic culture (United States). According to the study, the U.S. participants used social network sites more, felt that these sites were more important, and had more friends on social networks than did the Chinese participants (Jackson & Wang, 2013). Personal characteristics more effectively predicted social network use in the United States than in China (Jackson & Wang, 2013). Less social network site use may be related to the emphasis that collectivist cultures place on family, friends, and one's group (Jackson & Wang, 2013). In contrast, individualistic cultures tend to emphasize the self and having more but distant relationships (Jackson & Wang, 2013). Results of this study suggest that there are cultural differences in the usage of social network sites. Providers would benefit from evaluating clients' cultural ideology when considering the use and/or the impact of social network sites in the clients' lifestyle.

Hoffman (2013) demonstrated that the use of a culture-infused counseling approach when working with adolescents who use social media is vital. Most adolescents in modern society frequently use social networking sites and smartphones, while at the same time navigating the developmental tasks of adolescence. Because adolescents—digital natives—have grown up in a vastly different environment than previous generations, Hoffman (2013) suggests that they be regarded as a distinct cultural group. A culture-infused approach to therapy should include three cultural competencies—awareness, knowledge, and skill (Hoffman, 2013). For providers working with adolescents, a culture-infused approach will help with understanding the systemic and contextual factors that influence clients' presenting problems. Additionally, it is also important that providers evaluate each individual adolescent's cultural background, as differences in individualistic versus collectivistic experiences may be present for any particular case.

Cultural Issues in Treatment Provision

There is a growing body of literature that addresses TMH treatment efficacy with a number of different counseling and psychological issues with adolescents (Slone et al., 2012). Evaluating a consumer's readiness and fit for TMH is an ethical and informed consent issue that is important to beginning and maintaining good communication and treatment between the consumer and the provider. Additionally, attentiveness to cultural issues is paramount to discovering impediments to proper telehealth

care and rapport between the consumer and the provider. There are aspects of our rapidly diversifying culture that affect adolescents, even if they are digital natives and their age and familiarity with technology would make them *seem* like excellent candidates for TMH treatment. For example, if an adolescent client is dealing with suicidality but is willing to work with a provider using VTC, it is necessary that this provider make a decision regarding whether, even with a safety plan, this adolescent would be better served with traditional counseling. This also might apply to relational or social difficulties that might be better addressed in person. Furthermore, language barriers and client experience with technology are other examples of what a provider might assess for when considering candidacy.

Just as culture is important to treating adolescents in more traditional F2F settings, cultural issues are a critical element to ensuring protection and welfare for TMH consumers.

The benefits and feasibility of telehealth services are repeatedly represented in literature, and cultural issues are often noted as one way by which a provider can attend to consumer fit for services. Specific studies regarding adolescent cultural issues are still lacking, but attention to this topic is highlighting its importance. Providers can learn from other disciplines that are embracing similar important issues and principles, such as telepsychiatry or telemedicine. One such issue is the importance of cultural differences in diagnosis and treatment. Bridging cultures between providers and consumers is foundational to the provision and path of treatment, and providers own the responsibility to inquire and learn about important elements of an adolescent's culture that would affect the therapeutic relationship, treatment, and diagnosis, keeping in mind that it is not only the consumers culture that is important but the providers as well. Especially with regard to adolescents, cultural awareness is critical because the therapeutic relationship might include family members (Savin et al., 2011).

Cultural aspects of TMH practice can be addressed at the beginning and throughout treatment. As providers attend to how a consumer's culture might affect diagnosis and treatment, they might choose to learn about the day-to-day life of a consumer and his or her local surroundings and neighborhood, spiritual beliefs or religious affiliation, and comfort with technology. Other specific issues to consider are parenting practices and what is considered normal in a given culture with regard to adolescent behavior and the cause and treatment of mental health issues. Finally, providers can attend to what the cultural norms are for family structure, interpersonal verbal and nonverbal communication, and individuality.

Pursuit of Cultural Knowledge

Providers can be proactive in pursuing knowledge about a consumer's culture, and a provider might consider bringing these options into open discussion with the consumer (Kolmes & Taube, 2014). One idea is to research where the consumer lives and keeping up with local news, as well as researching the background of the named culture or ethnic group. Doing so might help inform the provider of the population size of a town or city and important elements of a consumer's life situation that can be part of session content. Providers can also choose to consult with other practitioners who serve specific populations. If travel is not a part of the treatment, as might be the case if providers serve a remote population and plan visits to the area only occasionally, researching map and travel distances might increase a provider's awareness of how remote a consumer's location might be. Furthermore, depending on the consumer's cultural background, providers can consider (and address) that a minority consumer might hold certain stereotypes or beliefs about the provider—as a treatment provider—being part of a majority or minority group, for example. Such beliefs, if not addressed, can undermine the development of the therapeutic relationship and breed distrust of the provider, leading the provider to view a consumer's hesitancy to seek treatment (out of distrust, for

example) as treatment resistance (Luxton et al., 2014; Savin et al., 2011).

Rural or remote locations, as well as other aspects of an individual's cultural characteristics, such as spiritual beliefs or sexual orientation, are often a reason for a consumer to pursue TMH options, as discussed earlier. Providers do not necessarily have to refer clients due to a lack of experience with certain individuals, populations, or mental health problems. TMH providers can utilize and build consulting relationships with other professionals for support, training, and assistance. This might occur with a professional's interest in working with a certain cultural group, disorder, or population where he or she lacks clinical training, supervision, and experience. Optimizing consultation and education are options for professionals to continue expanding their professional skills and competency without having to limit their professional experience. Providers can pursue consulting support, continuing education, supervision, or credentialing as they enhance their competence and skills (Barnett, Younggren, Doll, & Rubin, 2007). As a provider shows interest in a consumer's cultural background and experiences, this might open up avenues of connection that would otherwise remain closed, possibly impeding therapeutic rapport (Savin et al., 2011).

Avenues of Delivery and Research Support. Three current avenues common for delivery of telehealth services are phone calls, the Internet, and videoconferencing. Slone et al. (2012) reviewed literature on research with adolescents using these video and Internet realms. Studies using videoconferencing reflect both their promising and possible superiority over F2F treatments. These authors note that the research is preliminary and has limitations with sample sizes and cultural and ethnic diversity, but these are common limitations to studies and set the stage for other researchers in the future. Internet research includes interventions with a variety of issues and also reflects promising results for substance use and other psychological issues.

Research also supports the feasible and effective way to provide therapy, although this is an area that could be included in future research with adolescent participants. A study by Reese et al. (2002) reflect that adult consumers are able to form a relational bond with their provider while working over the phone and are satisfied with the treatment they received. Providers need to consider factors such as the treatment length and consumer candidacy for telehealth treatment. Consumers who are entering treatment with more serious mental health, relational issues (e.g., personality issues), or safety issues (e.g., suicidality) may not be a good fit for treatment and can be referred out to a provider who could provide traditional or specified treatment.

Maheu et al. (2012) encourages providers to maintain a focus on research applications and progression in the field of counseling. This awareness allows providers to review and implement evidence-based practices treatment. As research continues and reveals the progression of telehealth treatments, providers can more confidently expand their practice options. While providers are often tempted to use new applications, treatment, and communication options, they must maintain awareness of what current research reflects (Schwartz & Lonborg, 2011). Staying up to date helps them keep an eye out for what avenues prove to be the most usable and important in telehealth practice, including virtual worlds, avatars, videoconferencing, gaming, cloud computing, and mobile devices, as well as privacy and security issues that relate to all these ideas or devices.

CASE CONSIDERATIONS

Read the case of David, a provider working toward competence in telehealth while counseling Alec and his mother (see Case Scenario 19.1). Focus on the advantages and disadvantages of TMH with this client. Afterward, answer the questions regarding the case in Exercise 19.1. Once you have finished both tasks, continue reading the subsequent sections for a thorough review of the case and applicable ethical standards related to TMH treatment.

Case Scenario 19.1

David—A Case of Technical and Ethical Competency

David, a recent graduate of a counseling program and a newly licensed provider in Ohio, decides that he wants to provide therapy online so that he can expand his private practice. While in school, David's ethics class spent an afternoon discussing ethically practicing online. He feels that he can pursue this ethically with his knowledge of the ACA's (American Counseling Association) *Ethical Codes and Guidelines*. David's first consumer is Alec, an adolescent male (age 16), whose mother would like David to counsel her son regarding his recently developed fear of being outside the house, especially around crowds. Alec's mother is fairly limited in her knowledge and use of technology. She feels that Alec's problems stem from being on the Internet all the time but is willing to try something that might engage her son in getting help.

(Continued)

Case Scenario 19.1   (Continued)

While Alec has generally always had difficulties in socializing with others, he recently expressed feelings of sadness, restlessness, a decrease in appetite, hypersomnia, and feeling bored with things he used to enjoy. Alec and his mother live in New York and got David's name from a family friend. Alec's mother is glad to find someone who will work online because she could not convince Alec to physically attend counseling sessions consistently. David, Alec, and Alec's mother agree to meet initially over Skype so that David can go through the informed consent and they can make a plan for treatment for Alec's presenting problem. In his haste, David forgot to ask about Alec's previous experience with his symptoms, diagnosis, and counseling. After four sessions, David realizes that his consumer might have more serious issues than he anticipated.

Exercise 19.1

Considerations—David's Case Scenario

1. As David, the provider, what diagnoses might you be considering for the case of Alec? What diagnostic criteria support your decision?

2. In one paragraph, discuss your support for or against Alec's appropriateness for online counseling, given his diagnoses. How might your decision change if it came to light that Alec had been bullied (in cyberspace and traditionally)?

3. Alec's mom seems somewhat technologically inept, yet Alec is a digital native. What cultural considerations might David need to assess for? How might cultural differences affect his approach to Alec's treatment? What are some interventions that might be used in this case? Finally, how might David discuss these cultural differences with Alec's mom?

4. Is David counseling competently? Why or why not? What issues should David address in his informed consent? Additionally, when discussing confidentiality with Alec and his mother, what should be included in that conversation?

IMPLICATIONS FOR COUNSELING
ADOLESCENTS

Clinical Review of Case

As the provider, David cannot afford to continue counseling without going back to his informed consent. It is important for him to take action in multiple ways. First, David must attend to Alec's depression, assess for suicidality, and his candidacy for counseling online. It is possible that Alec's depressive symptoms are a result of his further isolation; thus, having the online outlet would likely diminish some of his negative symptoms. Alec's appropriateness for online counseling is an interesting conundrum. Online services

Chapter 19: Use of Technology With Adolescents • 425

may be a great first step to get Alec hooked into treatment. Given his agoraphobia and social difficulties, this may be a great fit. David, however, should discuss this process as an initial step when outlining treatment with Alec and Alec's mother. It will likely become essential for Alec to engage in F2F treatment if he is unable to master F2F contact with others via the online services. Second, David must prioritize his decision to work with this consumer on the Internet without enough details of his history. During the first session, it would be ideal for David to get a thorough background history of Alec and his family. He should ask questions to both parties regarding the intensity and pervasiveness of Alec's depression. At this point, David lacks a plan for responding to an emergency, and the only person David and his consumer have in common is the client's mother. For an adolescent with a depressed mood, it is important that an emergency plan be set in place and that David also address how Alec should proceed were he unable to reach David when needed. Third, David needs to assess his readiness to provide therapy online without a thorough awareness of current research, laws, and statutes regarding telehealth in New York and Ohio and privacy and security issues. While David can still work as a TMH provider, there are a few steps he needs to take to have a strong, well-developed informed consent as well as possibly a mentoring relationship with a colleague that might help him structure this part of his practice. Continue reading the subsequent section for a more thorough understanding of how ethical standards apply to telehealth counseling.

Application of Ethics

By far, two of the most considered topics when addressing telehealth are legal and ethical concerns. These are not new concerns for fields that use telehealth, including but not limited to medicine, nursing, and psychology. Technological expansions provide all disciplines with a challenge to learn and implement, particularly in the areas of the consumer–provider relationship, treatment, interventions, legal issues, and ethical practice laws and guidelines. These issues are applicable to all disciplines and provide an opportunity for providers to interact and learn how other disciplines are handling challenges, encouraging forward movement, and keeping in tandem with consumer demand and technological developments. Reed, McLaughlin, and Milholland (2000) note how vital it is for health care professions to be active and vocal in the development of policies and delivery systems so that treatment options are applicable to those who use them too rather than solely by those who regulate the practice.

What is available from regulatory organizations indicates that the principles by which providers use telehealth for services are based on ethical codes and guidelines that have been formulated by psychology and counseling national associations. Both the ACA and the American Psychological Association (APA) address telehealth in their most recent sets of codes and guidelines. The APA has also passed a set of guidelines for telepsychology practice (ACA, 2005; APA, 2010, 2013a). These resources, in addition to others such as the American Telemedicine Association's (2013) practice guidelines and the Ohio Psychological Association's (2008) telepsychology guidelines, offer a chance for providers to educate themselves about how to go about TMH practice. These associations are pursuing education and ethical practice in recognition of the fact that technology has changed the face of mental health services. Table 19.3 outlines a set of easily accessible websites that offer resources that assist in provider awareness, training, and education, all of which are foundational to the ethical practice of TMH.

Regulation Issues

Providers are licensed by individual states, and there is no current option that blankets state requirements for TMH practice. The current regulatory system was designed before TMH was a treatment option. Technology has broken physical barriers between consumers and treatment providers, who are now up against antiquated legislation. Current regulations limit

Table 19.3   Recommendations for Ethical Codes, Guidelines, Principles, and Telemental Health Resources

www.ctel.org	Information and resources regarding legal and regulatory barriers to telehealth practice
www.americantelemed.org	Information, resources, and educational opportunities
http://www.ucdmc.ucdavis.edu/cht/research/index.html	Research articles on health informatics and tele-health and educational opportunities
www.telementalhealth.com	*Continuing education* units, training, and resources for telehealth practice
http://www.counseling.org/knowledge-center/ethics	American Counseling Association codes and guidelines, resources for competencies, and licensure requirements
http://kspope.com/telepsychology.php	Suggested articles and resources regarding telemental health

consumers and professionals alike and are less applicable to our technologically focused way of life (Harris & Younggren, 2011; Maheu et al., 2012). These regulations include concerns about licensure across states lines as well as how liability concerns are handled.

Professional Codes and Guidelines. Some states are offering their own specific guidelines, such as the OPA (2008); others push inquiries to certain codes and guidelines (APA, 2013b). Professional groups are putting forth codes and guidelines that are helpful, and professionals have increasingly more to work with. Even while there are gaps in literature and the clear, applicable policy to employ in TMH, practitioners maintain the responsibility to uphold their civil commitments (e.g., duty to protect/warn) and professional ethical codes and guidelines. Moreover, the burden of knowledge and competency does not rest with the consumer alone, but practitioners must decide on their own legal and ethical review of their responsibilities as well as that of their consumers (Younggren, Fisher, Foote, & Hjelt, 2011).

Risk Management

Privacy and Security. Privacy and security, along with competency and informed consent, are

hallmark elements of practicing TMH. With each client, the provider should consider communication differences in electronic media and educate clients on how to address potential misunderstandings (ACA, 2014). Electronic records must be kept in accordance with relevant laws and statutes (ACA, 2014). Clients should be made aware of their rights and how to protect their rights or address ethical concerns (ACA, 2014, H.5.b). Multicultural and disability concerns should be considered when providing information on websites (ACA, 2014, H.5.d). With regard to social media sites, providers should maintain separate professional and personal web pages (ACA, 2014, H.6). Informed consent should also set boundaries with regard to the use of social media (ACA, 2014). Finally, providers should respect the privacy of clients' presence on social media and take precautions to not disclose confidential information on public web domains (ACA, 2014, H.6). Technology allows a number of ways for professionals to create and store clinical notes, assessments, and data. Critical to understanding how to minimize security risk and maintain privacy is in understanding the technology behind Internet security, choosing the best way to maintain and delete records, and keeping open communication with consumers regarding privacy and security. Two important concepts in risk management are privacy and security. Privacy refers to a client's right to his or her information and the uses and disclosure of his or her health information to other sources. Security refers to the protection of electronic health information (Devereaux & Gottlieb, 2012; Schwartz & Lonborg, 2011).

Practitioners must attend to physical safeguards of data (e.g., locked office), administrative safeguards (e.g., training, policy, procedures, and access), and technological safeguards (e.g., entrance into the device that holds the data and password protection). Practitioners are also encouraged to remind consumers that they are working together to provide security for the consumers data; consumers can attend to keeping communication and therapeutic information (e.g., homework, journaling) concerning themselves secure by providing their own safeguards (Schwartz & Lonborg, 2011).

The move to EHR has already occurred, and many professionals no longer keep paper records. EHR provides a number of benefits to both the consumer and the practitioner, including ease of improved service options, delivery, access, usage, and communication. However, there are both privacy and security issues when using technology in communication and record keeping, including but not limited to data breaches and technical difficulties. For instance, if a provider pays for and uses a certain EHR software system that has technical difficulties, consumer data and contact information may not be available until the problems are resolved. Additionally, if the technical issues continue to occur, the provider might choose to terminate use of the software and transition to a new company, and there could be issues retrieving consumer data in a quick and orderly fashion (Devereaux & Gottlieb, 2012).

As providers move into practicing telehealth, it is easy to underestimate the risk associated with security of patient data and how complex the threats are to the consumer's private data stored online. Risks include human error, such as a stolen laptop. Research indicates that the likelihood of having a laptop stolen is 5% to 10% but that more than 50% of business travelers carry a laptop with confidential information on a device and that more than 60% of those travelers state that they have no plan to protect sensitive or confidential data. Another study of health care providers indicates that 18% use only a password for device protection, and of that 18%, only 23% report using stronger security measures like encryption (Schwartz & Lonborg, 2011). In the case of a TMH practitioner, could this mean that setting a laptop down at a coffee shop to return to the car for a forgotten item breaches professional and legal expectations for keeping data protected and secure?

Practical Steps in Privacy and Security. Practical considerations for securing data and maintaining privacy are available and include steps that providers can take to maintain duty, professionalism, and competency. A well-developed informed consent document that reviews practical elements of consumer treatment, records, and communication is an essential first step. Second, providers should carry out a thorough risk assessment and apply security protection to noted vulnerabilities. Providers should also take steps to verify the client's identity when interacting at a distance or with digital media (ACA, 2014, H.3). The use of technology in treatment also necessitates that providers inform clients of the benefits and limitations of using technology applications and pay special care to maintain professional boundaries (ACA, 2014). For example, providers can use encryption software on all devices that hold sensitive or confidential information, including websites, EHRs, and e-mail communications and educate the clients on their chosen security process. Encryption software is constantly improving as all kinds of businesses, not just health providers, are moving data online. Also, practitioners can easily password protect their computers and mobile devices, as well as extend security to physical offices where devices and sensitive information are kept. Third, providers can provide consumers with an organized contingency plan if devices or data are lost or stolen. Fourth, especially with regard to treating adolescents and minor consumers, providers must pay attention to ensuring the identity of the consumer, which might include connection and agreement with identified guardians who would provide treatment consent. Finally, providers can organize data so that consumer files are located in only one place that is strongly secured and maintain communications such as e-mail or text communications elsewhere (Devereaux & Gottlieb, 2012; Luxton et al., 2014; Schwartz & Lonborg, 2011).

Providers are expected to keep records and protect patient privacy under the HIPAA. To do so while providing TMH services, providers must be aware of their responsibilities to protect consumer data and inform consumers of any data breach. HIPAA compliance is a distinct challenge overall, and while its construction was written to allow for technological advancements, there are no distinct instructions for providers regarding how records should be stored and secured, leaving a very difficult situation for providers who are moving to EHRs and cloud computing (Devereaux & Gottlieb, 2012).

Competency. According to the *ACA Code of Ethics* (ACA, 2014), providers should actively try to understand the evolving nature of the profession as it relates to technology, distance counseling, and social media. Those who choose to engage in the use of distance counseling, technology, and/or social media must acquire knowledge and develop skills about related technical, ethical, and legal considerations (ACA, 2014, H.1.a). Based on current research and written commentaries on telehealth, one of the most important parts about practicing TMH is professional competency. Barnett et al. (2007) propose ideas that describe what competence is, a concept that is often hard to understand. These authors note that licensure sets a minimal standard for competence and that competence is neither fixed nor final. With regard to TMH, providers can integrate these ideas of competence as they educate themselves and practice TMH. If competence is viewed on a continuum and is not polarized, practitioners can embrace knowledge and understanding of how to implement different aspects

of TMH. Competence is a viable professional characteristic and practitioners must attend to a wide range of topics and abilities, as competence is not singular or static. This means that practitioners must pursue education and training and demonstrate ability for the services they provide, including TMH services (Harris & Younggren, 2011; Maheu et al., 2012).

Providers have the burden of maintaining ethical practice within the rapid evolution of what is available for use in TMH, and often the codes, guidelines, and regulations are hard pressed to keep up with what time policies and legislation require. Telehealth provides ample opportunity for providers to expand their practice and the populations they reach, but it is important to understand that telehealth is not a different practice of counseling but an avenue to provide services a provider is trained to provide (Luxton et al., 2012). In this, providers are responsible to the state licensing board.

TMH practice has multiple layers when it comes to competency. Kolmes (2012) describes how important it is for practitioners to be knowledgeable about technology both on and off duty. Providers must understand that their actions online might be viewed by consumers, potential consumers, or students, whether through a status update, comment, or message. Personal profiles on both professional and social websites are not always restricted, and providers' actions online reflect on their professional work. In other words, providers who choose to practice TMH are constantly discoverable. Two examples include a practitioner who comments on other mental health blogs and might mentally organize these interactions as professional activities without realizing that the comments are searchable and readable by almost anyone. A second example is a practitioner who might consult over or refer a case online and not "scrub" the identifying information enough, allowing a consumer who keeps up with the adolescent's practitioner to discover that he or she is closely described with personal details (e.g., addiction or sexual issues, age, length of treatment, and/or reason for referral).

Technological Competence. Technological know-how is a critical part of practicing TMH. This often means that practitioners are required to educate themselves beyond their current knowledge base with respect to counseling topics. Devereaux and Gottlieb (2012) suggest that practitioners have a "sophisticated understanding" of technological issues regarding privacy and security, data breaches, the potential issues that might arise related to record keeping, deletion of records, and the permanence of online content.

Technological competence ranges from the small to the imperative. For example, it is important that a provider be able to work with a computer or smartphone so as to have a smooth technological and an interpersonal connection with consumers online. This might include understanding how to download an application, secure a password, and read and understand the applications security policy. Another example would be of a provider who has a plan to handle technological difficulties that occur during a session and can implement a plan that has been discussed in the informed consent (e.g., a dropped call or poor Internet connection that freezes a video session). A final example reflects a practitioner's ability to handle an emergency based on his or her knowledge of current state regulations regarding duty to warn and involuntary hospitalization (Devereaux & Gottlieb, 2012; Luxton et al., 2012; Luxton et al., 2014). These examples reflect a few possible situations that can occur within a TMH session and require a range of competencies for a provider to respond quickly and ethically. Such knowledge and competency comes from maintaining constant connection with continued ethics and technological training. Maheu et al. (2012) propose three elements that support awareness: (1) recognition, (2) anticipation, and (3) preparation. Here, providers must first recognize how technology has changed the provision of counseling services, including the advantages and risks associated with TMH services. Second, practitioners must anticipate how technology has and will transform mental health services. Finally, providers must prepare both the opportunities and the challenges that technology ushers into practice implementation.

Appropriate Candidacy. When using technology-assisted services, providers should establish that their client is intellectually, emotionally, physically, linguistically, and functionally able to use the application (ACA, 2014). Providers can consider including the following when working with a telehealth consumer. First, cultural and individual factors must be considered before treatment begins. Not all individuals are a good fit for TMH treatment. A thorough description of a provider's approach to necessary termination and referral is appropriate and can be included in the informed consent process, even if it is uncomfortable to begin therapy with the discussion of it ending (Younggren et al., 2011); however, providers are responsible to uphold the foundational ethical principle "beneficence and nonmaleficence" and terminate therapy when treatment is no longer effective or posing a risk of harm to the consumer. To evaluate whether a consumer is appropriate for treatment, a provider can gather information regarding a consumer's presenting problem(s), his or her availability and comfort level using technology, his or her language or individual barriers that would impede efficacious treatment, and consumer willingness to participate in what TMH entails (e.g., safety plan, primary contact person, etc.) (Harris & Younggren, 2011; Luxton et al., 2014).

Informed Consent. Informed consent is a process familiar to most providers, mainly because it is a foundational element of ethical practice. Providers must ensure that their clients are aware of pertinent legal rights and limitations related to distance counseling (ACA, 2014, H.1.b). Providers engaging in distance counseling or using technology and/or social media must address several items in the informed consent process. Informed consent should include distance counseling credentials, physical practice location, and contact information (ACA, 2014, H.2.a). Additional topics to be covered include risks and benefits of use of technology, possibility of technological failure and alternate methods, response time, emergency procedures, cultural and/or language differences that affect delivery, possible denial of insurance, and social media policy (ACA, 2014, H.2.a). With the use of technology and electronic transmissions, providers should acknowledge the limitations to maintaining clients' confidentiality and use encryption standards for security measures (ACA, 2014, H.2.b–d). Gray areas begin to develop when the required content of an informed consent is discussed. With regard to TMH, informed consent provides a space for a provider to begin a relationship of openness with a consumer. Informed consent documents are often unique to the practitioner, given what he or she feels is pertinent for a consumer to review and understand on beginning treatment. Much that needs to be addressed between the consumer and the provider can get lost in a longer informed consent, so providers must take care to address important issues at the beginning of treatment as well as when any changes to its content are relevant as treatment continues.

A well-developed informed consent for TMH treatment might include state and regulatory information about location of services, personal contact information, emergency contact information, local hospital and law enforcement information in case of emergency, appropriate disclosure of the benefits and risks of TMH treatment, contingency plans for technical and security issues, record-keeping practices and an explanation of security measures currently in place, and digital communication expectations between the consumer and the provider (Devereaux & Gottlieb, 2012; Luxton et al., 2012; Maheu et al., 2012; Schwartz & Lonborg, 2011). Table 19.4 describes suggested elements to be included in a TMH informed consent form.

FUTURE RESEARCH CONSIDERATIONS

An additional consideration is the psychological and relational elements of how technology affects the relationship between a consumer and a provider. Because adolescents are more adept at living and communicating through technological means, previously accepted concepts such as attachment, nonverbal behaviors, and attunement will be prime areas for research (Kolmes, 2012). This overlaps with the research that continues to show acceptance and feasibility of telehealth, most of which offers providers ideas and guidance about relational elements to consider, best practices, and peer-reviewed research supporting evidence-based treatments via the Internet.

Table 19.4 Considerations for Telemental Health Informed Consent Forms

Provider contact information

Consumer contact information

Emergency contingency plan

    Information and role of a local contact/support person

    Local law enforcement, hospital, and emergency treatment options

Outline of communication structure

Risks and benefits of telemental health treatment

Social media policy

Security measures in place

State and regulatory information and contact information

Technical difficulties contingency plan

Termination and referral

Professional relationships are and will maintain a front seat in the consideration of how people are adapting to different ways of interacting, including how providers interact with their consumers and vice versa, including the use of technology to communicate. Additionally, research considering telehealth treatment should reflect on the feasibility of practice. For example, for adolescents using smartphones who might choose to videoconference with a treatment provider, how does the size of the device affect treatment. For instance, how does a videoconference on a device similar in size to a playing card compare with a videoconference on a larger tablet or computer monitor?

Another example is the idea behind "yelling" in texts and e-mails. It is widely understood that when capital letters are used in an e-mail or text communication the person is emphasizing what he or she is saying, and possibly "yelling." E-mail etiquette is an aspect of societal and technological norms that can be reviewed with an eye toward its presence and use in therapeutic communication. For instance, if a consumer sends a text or e-mail to a professional in all capital letters stating, "I need to talk to you immediately!" it could easily be misconstrued as a potential emergency by the mental health professional. While this can be handled with a phone call to evaluate the situation, consumer and provider understanding of professional e-mail etiquette is an aspect for both research and informed consent.

Summary

Even with a mix of benefits and risks, telehealth undeniably offers practitioners and consumers alike a new flexibility that expands the more traditional model of F2F therapy. In accepting the technological movement, educators and providers must maintain the same respect for ethical practice in this unchartered territory. Essentially, at the forefront of telehealth treatment with adolescents, provider competency, informed consent, consumer and practitioner comfort, and practitioner awareness are key issues that must be considered. Clear descriptions of risks with regard to privacy, electronic data, and working therapeutically through the Internet are of utmost importance. Ethical TMH practice must be tailored to the comfort level and needs of the adolescent consumer, provided by a provider who is familiar with the importance of technology in an adolescent's world and the resources available for effective treatment (Luxton et al., 2012; Luxton et al., 2014).

Keystones

On reading this chapter, providers and providers in training should be able to do the following:

- Gain an awareness of the current uses of technology in counseling, including education and online learning, consumer and practitioner communication, record keeping, and ethical and legal considerations

- Maintain awareness of technological advancements and implications for clinical practice, particularly for those who work with adolescents given that they are "digital natives" (Kolmes, 2012)

- Understand relevant terminology in the field of technology, which includes telemental health (TMH) describing the transition to providing mental health services

- Recognize the implications of technology on multiculturalism, access to treatment, provider competence, and consumer candidacy

- Understand both the benefits and the risks of technology in counseling adolescents. Potential benefits include improved access, collaboration, cost-effectiveness, electronic services, and electronic records. Potential risks include security breaches and concerns, added challenges in the therapeutic relationship, technology issues, and difficulties in diagnosis

- Continue to maintain awareness of current research and to develop research on various aspects of TMH, including interventions, best practices, competence, training, and regulation

- Recognize multicultural implications of increased technology such as increased access to providers who speak native languages or specialize in specific populations

- Consider the potential for reducing stigma toward mental health through the use of technology and TMH

- Adherence to ethical responsibilities and best practices as established by Health Insurance Portability and Accountability Act, Health Information Technology for Economic and Clinical Health Act, American Counseling Association, and other regulatory bodies as well as continue an awareness of regulatory issues

- Recognize the unique challenges in emergency situations and develop specific safety plans to be discussed in informed consent procedures

REFERENCES

American Counseling Association. (2005). *Code of ethics*. Alexandria, VA: Author.

American Counseling Association. (2014). *ACA code of ethics*. Alexandria, VA: Author.

American Psychological Association. (2010). *American Psychological Association ethical principles of psychologists and code of conduct*. Washington, DC: Author.

American Psychological Association. (2013a). *Guidelines for the practice of telepsychology*. Washington, DC: Author.

American Psychological Association. (2013b). *Telepsychology 50-state review*. Washington, DC: Author.

American Telemedicine Association. (2013). *American Telemedicine Association practice guidelines for video-based online mental health services*. Retrieved from http://www.americantelemed.org/resources/telemedicine-practice-guidelines/telemedicine-practice-guidelines

Barnett, J. E., Younggren, J. N., Doll, B., & Rubin, N. J. (2007). Clinical competence for practicing psychologists: Clearly a work in progress. *Professional Psychology: Research and Practice, 38*(5), 510–517.

Blakeney, K. (2012). An instrument to measure traditional and cyber bullying in overseas schools. *International Schools Journal, 32*(1), 45–54.

Boniel-Nissim, M., & Barak, A. (2013). The therapeutic value of adolescents' blogging about social-emotional difficulties. *Psychological Services, 10*(3), 333–341.

Branson, C. E., Clemmey, P., & Mukherjee, P. (2013). Text message reminders to improve outpatient therapy attendance among adolescents: A pilot study. *Psychological Services, 10*(3), 298–303.

Devereaux, R. L., & Gottlieb, M. C. (2012). Record keeping in the cloud: Ethical considerations. *Professional Psychology: Research and Practice, 43*(6), 627–632.

Dickinson, W. P., & Miller, B. F. (2010). Comprehensiveness and continuity of care and the inseparability of mental and behavioral health from the patient-centered medical home. *Families, Systems, & Health, 28*(4), 348–355.

Eonta, A., Christon, L., Hourigan, S., Ravindran, N., Vrana, S., & Southam-Gerow, M. (2011). Using everyday technology to enhance evidence-based treatments. *Professional Psychology: Research and Practice, 42*(6), 513–520.

Harris, E., & Younggren, J. N. (2011). Risk management in the digital world. *Professional Psychology: Research and Practice, 42*(6), 412–418.

Harris, S. E., & Robinson-Kurpius, S. E. (2014). Social networking and professional ethics: Consumer searches, informed consent, and disclosure. *Professional Psychology: Research and Practice, 45*(1), 11–19.

Hoffman, A. (2013). Bridging the divide: Using culture-infused counseling to enhance therapeutic work with digital youth. *Journal of Infant, Child, and Adolescent Psychotherapy, 12*(2), 118–133. doi:10.1080/15289168.2013.791195

Hunter, C. L., & Goodie, J. L. (2010). Operational and clinical components for integrated-collaborative behavioral healthcare in the patient-centered medical home. *Families, Systems, & Health, 28*(4), 308–321.

Jackson, L. A., & Wang, J. (2013). Cultural differences in social networking site use: A comparative study of China and the United States. *Computers in Human Behavior, 29,* 910–921. doi:10.1016/j.chb.2012.11.024

Kolmes, K. (2010). *Social media policy*. Retrieved from http://drkkolmes.com/social-media-policy/

Kolmes, K. (2012). Social media in the future of professional psychology. *Professional Psychology: Research and Practice, 43*(6), 606–612.

Kolmes, K., & Taube, D. O. (2014). Seeking and finding our consumers on the Internet: Boundary considerations in cyberspace. *Professional Psychology: Research and Practice, 45*(1), 3–10.

Luxton, D. D., O'Brien, K., McCann, R. A., & Mishkind, M. C. (2012). Home-based telemental healthcare safety planning: What you need to know. *Telemedicine and e-Health, 18*(8), 629–633.

Luxton, D. D., Pruitt, L. D., & Osenbach, J. E. (2014). Best practices for remote psychological assessment via telehealth technologies. *Professional Psychology: Research and Practice, 45*(1), 27–35.

Madden, M., Lenhart, A., Duggan, M., Cortesi, S., & Gasser, U. (2013). *Teens and technology 2013*. Retrieved from http://www.pewinternet.org/files/old-media/Files/Reports/2013/PIP_Teensand Technology2013.pdf

Maheu, M. M., & McMenamin, J. P. (2013, March 28). Telepsychiatry: The perils of using Skype. *Psychiatric Times*. Retrieved from http://www.psychiatrictimes.com/blog/telepsychiatry-perils-using-skype

Maheu, M. M., McMenamin, J. P., Pulier, M. L., & Posen, L. (2012). The future of telepsychology, telehealth, and various technologies in psychological research and practice. *Professional Psychology: Research and Practice, 43*(6), 613–621.

Myers, M. M., Valentine, J. M., & Melzer, S. M. (2007). Feasibility, acceptability, and sustainability of telepsychiatry for children and adolescents. *Psychiatric Services, 58*, 1493–1496.

Nelson, E., Bui, T. N., & Velasquez, S. E. (2011). Telepsychology: Research and practice overview. *Child and Adolescent Psychiatric Clinics of North America, 20*(1), 67–79.

Ohio Psychological Association. (2008). *Telepsychology guidelines*. Retrieved from http://www.ohpsych.org/psychologists/files/2011/06/OPATelepsychologyGuidelines41710.pdf

O'Moore, M. M. (2012). Cyber-bullying: The situation in Ireland. *Pastoral Care in Education, 30*(3), 209–223. doi:10.1080/02643944.2012.688065

Reed, G. M., McLaughlin, C. J., & Milholland, K. (2000). Ten interdisciplinary principles for professional practice in telehealth: Implications for psychology. *Professional Psychology: Research and Practice, 31*(2), 170–178.

Reese, R. J., Conoley, C. W., & Brossart, D. F. (2002). Effectiveness of telephone counseling: A field-based investigation. *Journal of Counseling Psychology, 49*(2), 233–242.

Savin, D., Glueck, D. A., Chardavoyne, J., Yager, J., & Novins, D. K. (2011). Bridging cultures: Child psychiatry via videoconferencing. *Child and Adolescent Psychiatric Clinics of North America, 20*, 125–134.

Schwartz, T. J., & Lonborg, S. D. (2011). Security management in telepsychology. *Professional Psychology: Research and Practice, 42*(6), 419–425.

Shapka, J. D., & Law, D. M. (2013). Does one size fit all? Ethnic differences in parenting behaviors and motivations for adolescent engagement in cyberbullying. *Journal of Youth and Adolescence, 42*, 723–738.

Slone, N. C., Reese, R. J., & McClellan, M. J. (2012). Telepsychology outcome research with children and adolescents: A review of the literature. *Psychological Services, 9*(3), 272–292.

Strange, K. C., Nutting, P. A., Miller, W. L., Jaen, C. R., Crabtree, B. F., Flocke, S. A., & Gill, J. M. (2010). Defining and measuring the patient-centered medical home. Retrieved from http://www.ncbi.nlm.nih.gov/pmc/articles/PMC2869425/#__ffn_sectitle

Turkle, S. (2011). *Alone together: Why we expect more from technology and less from each other*. New York, NY: Basic Books.

U.S. Department of Health and Human Services. (2014). *Telehealth*. Retrieved from www.http://hsra.gov/healthit/toolbox/ruralhealthittoolbox/telehealth/

Younggren, J. N., Fisher, M. A., Foote, W. E., & Hjelt, S. E. (2011). A legal and ethical review of patient responsibilities and psychotherapist duties. *Professional Psychology: Research and Practice, 42*(2), 160–168.

20

Conclusion and Future Direction

Through this book, we provided practical information for students, educators, supervisors, and administrators seeking to understand today's adolescents and best practices counseling interventions. As highlighted throughout this work, integrating traditional and newer outgrowths of evidence-based approaches with adolescents is the preferred stance. We hope that we have ignited the therapeutic fuse for continued exploration and integration of relevant findings from the literature with the varied experiences of adolescents along with specific strategies to apply knowledge gleaned from this book, including information from the case scenarios, exercises, and keystones.

In essence, we see ourselves in the role of the point guard, the member of a five-person basketball team, which brings the basketball down the court looking for teammates who are open and willing to get the basketball to further position the team for the best shot, yelling out potential plays, and organizing the team to score. The anticipated crew of students, providers, supervisors, researchers, and administrators established a significant body of clinical impressionistic, practice-based best practices, and evidence-based literature regarding the care of adolescents in need of counseling. It is our intent to offer encouragement and

direction to the process of addressing the needs of adolescents, particularly processes conducted through the identified theoretical approaches and intervention models. We understand that many of these adolescents have complicated lives and require culturally specific interventions that consider their developmental needs and unique perspectives. Our understanding is based on those in the profession who have preceded us, established landmark counseling procedures, and come out with a commitment to influence the generation of providers who render care to adolescents.

We have offered our thoughts on counseling adolescents competently and strategies to work with them in the hope that the information provided would integrate with other known counseling strategies regarding the care and treatment of these adolescents. Our views in the textbook include a perspective on adolescents solely, rather than a focus on combining issues pertaining to children and adolescents as seen in most textbooks. This sole perspective on adolescents supports the literature on the needs of adolescents, their views regarding their issues, their problem statements, and their expectations of counseling. We have been the recipients of other's research, theoretical frameworks, and best practices interventions and application, and we believe that our perspective on adolescents is a fresh review of critical issues and emerging trends. Our desire was to go one step further and build on the successes of our predecessors by offering *our* perspective on the changing needs of adolescents. Our perspective is a natural outgrowth offering culturally diverse anecdotes and case scenarios and varied ways of approaching adolescents. We hope that this work will be a positive influence to adolescents and their families and to providers.

This book offers key exercises, practical hints, and keystones for readers to fully embrace the foundational concerns of adolescents. The book adds to the literature of real-world clinical scenarios, symptom presentation, and use of screening and assessment and diagnostic considerations in the analyses of cases. It better informs readers in providing culturally sensitive interventions for treating the needs of adolescents involved in clinical settings, including outpatient clinics, schools, residential group homes, juvenile justice facilities, child welfare, and social services. We reported developmental considerations and social and cultural factors that interface with adolescents in need of counseling, and ways to ensure foundational truths are captured through all aspects of this book. We believe that this book can be used in conjunction with other texts, especially those scholarly works targeting culturally appropriate, professional, and ethical implementation of screening, assessing, diagnosing, and intervening processes for adolescents with specialized and nonspecialized needs. This book can be used by students, clinically trained providers, educators, clinical supervisors, and administrators overseeing services directed toward adolescents. It is the hope offered by these professionals that yields the most impact in the lives of adolescents.

In Section I of the book, we provided key information pertaining to foundational issues related to counseling adolescents. We discussed how this book functions as a foundational approach to knowing adolescents from a developmental, social, and cultural stance. In this section, we introduced the readers to the prevalence and characteristics of adolescents and showed the heterogeneous needs of adolescents across various socioeconomic and cultural domains. We argued

that providers are in need of experiential training to adequately integrate theory and clinical practice when working with adolescents from diverse backgrounds. This lack of experiential training sometimes results in adolescents not receiving culturally specific intervention services to remediate behaviors and developmental challenges and to improve cognitive maturation. We then discussed how this book distinguishes various adolescent developmental theories from developmental pathways. In this distinction, this book utilized qualitative research application and experiential learning approaches to facilitate clinical understanding of adolescents presented through case scenarios, exercises, and keystones integrated throughout most of the chapters. The use of these learning approaches has assisted us by forgoing the social rationales to focus on the adolescents' behaviors as manifested—for it is truly how they think and express their emotions that precipitates and perpetuates their ongoing misinterpretation and mismanagement of their emotions.

In Section I, we accounted for developmental disruptions, social class, and issues pertaining to acculturation with adolescents. We developed the foundational dimension for provider critique and engagement, developmental pathways, cognitive perspectives, and adolescent worldview. We argued that these dimensions are an extension of consideration developed within the adolescents' view of the world and their response to it. When any one of these dimensions (provider critique and engagement, developmental pathways, cognitive perspectives, and worldviews) is operating incorrectly, the adolescent may be forced to overcompensate in his or her attempts to establish balance. For example, when an adolescent believes that the world is an unsafe place based on his or her current and past experiences, he or she might strike first out of a defensive posture and emotional retaliation. Over time, his or her reaction to perceived threat becomes almost automatic. He or she structures future interpersonal encounters to support his or her thinking processes and may become excessively rigid in his or her appraisal of future events. The adolescent then acts out emotionally and without balance, with very little provocation, and believes that he or she is doing the right thing to defend against an unsafe world. It is through this intricate interplay of cognitive and emotional processes that the provider must systematically unveil the truth from fiction and previous emotional hurts.

We have asserted throughout this book that the area most affected in adolescents' development is the cognitions and the consequential emotional mismanagement that they develop and rely on for interpreting surrounding events. We argued that many adolescents rely on underdeveloped and emotionally immature cognitive and emotional processes to solve their problems, creating an underuse of other developmental processes. These adolescents have spent their early developmental years interpreting surrounding events. When providers try to change this way of thinking, the adolescent may resist initial attempts by providers. As we asserted throughout this book, it is the ability of the provider to understand the uniqueness of adolescents that assists the counseling process. Though we believe that there are several locks that must be opened to facilitate the counseling process, we hold that developmental disruptions are the first deadbolt to be unlocked in liberating new thinking and behaviors.

In Section II of the book, we wanted the reader to know about the key theoretical perspectives while working with adolescents. While the theories reviewed do not represent an exhaustive list, they nonetheless speak to some of the common perspectives. In this section, we review cognitive behavioral therapy (CBT), client-centered therapy, trauma-focused care, multicultural family systems, juvenile justice models, strength and resilience perspectives, and play therapy.

For example, with the CBT perspective, we spend considerable amounts of time on the techniques and strategies employed during the counseling session. As an example, when adolescents interface with counseling services, they may present with few words, speak in broad, often vague, generalities, and have a mistrust of mental health providers. This mistrust can result in adolescents being questionable of providers probing

into their lives. They may not take full advantage of the counseling process, mostly due to their sense of privacy that may be affected by socioeconomic challenges, religious ethics, educational disparities, rules of social interaction, and strong beliefs about self-disclosure. Many times, these adolescents adopt language and cognitive schemes that rely heavily on nonverbal communication or that are codified when interacting with outsiders. Some examples include the use of "my cousin" to refer to people whom they feel connected with and loyal to but who are not necessarily a blood relative. "We just hang out," meaning "I do not have loyalties to this person though I may interact with him or her as a devoted boyfriend or girlfriend would." "We are kicking it," meaning "I may have a sexualized relationship with my partner, yet not a committed relationship." "Stay out of trouble" may seem as if the adolescent is asserting a change of heart in his or her behavior, but in fact, it likely means that he or she is looking to be more vigilant about covering and thoughtfully communicating his or her concerns about crimes without being judged. These cognitive schemas, when recognized by the provider, allow for more focused interventions to address the underlying issues.

We also expressed how CBT starts as thoughts, progresses to feelings, and, if not corrected, morphs into a pattern of nonresponsible behavior that is described as unpredictable and disproportionate. We hold that adolescent providers need to understand the dynamics of CBT by learning all the key tenets to CBT in order to establish meaningful connections with adolescents and their families. The dilemma is that some themes of these adolescents' thoughts are firmly based in the reality of their lives in addition to emerging values and beliefs that they hold. For example, an adolescent who carries a knife to school may identify the knife as necessary to protect himself or herself from gang fights or other harassment on his or her walk to school. To simply include in the treatment plan not to carry a knife without understanding the psychology and cognitive frame of reference for carrying the knife in the first place is not only an anathema to the adolescent but also an approach in which identified interventions can make life worse for him or her. In this case, a provider's interpretation of this adolescent's frame of reference, social challenges, values, and goals are imperative to create meaningful intervention.

With the client-centered approach, we focused on the nature of the counseling relationship with the provider, and through active listening skills, unconditional positive regard, and acceptance, clients could be afforded opportunities to openly share their concerns. We wanted the reader to recognize that to approach the adolescents' presenting problems with an open mind, free of biases and assumptions that are not culturally informed is facilitative to the therapeutic alliance. We provided examples of motivational interviewing, motivational enhancement, stages of change, and other evidence-based approaches that create an inclusive therapeutic environment. Our goal was for the reader to understand that when adolescents are forced by parents into counseling, they may continue their attempts to manipulate and control the session. Without a supportive environment that is client centered, the adolescents may hide their feelings and motives. They hide their true emotions to a specific event until they choose to divulge on their terms. The use of client-centered approaches assist the adolescent in feeling more comfortable in sharing his or her underlying feelings, thoughts, and behavior.

In Section II, we argued that an understanding of the needs of the adolescent from his or her perspective is essential to helping them through managing their needs. Further in the work, we discussed how providers must assist adolescents in sharing the emotional pain of their lives. Through time, employing patience, humility, and the use of active listening skills, the provider may earn enough of the adolescents' trust for the adolescents to illuminate their issues. On the first glimpses into the stories of adolescents, providers can begin to explore rationales, motivations, and other thinking processes in a nonjudgmental manner. An attitude of positive regard and a partnership with the adolescent, which allows the

issues to be examined, must prevail at this point. The provider can be assured that this initially nonconfrontational manner espoused by Carl Rogers (1959) and William Miller and Stephen Rollnick (2002) increases the likelihood that positive rapport will give way to greater unveiling of the true underlying issues. In essence, providers must learn to wait for the truth to emerge slowly with a keen awareness that trust and rapport are the ingredients that must be achieved in the counseling process. Ultimately, the provider must aim to make the adolescent's private thoughts known to both the adolescent and the provider for further exploration, development of new ways of thinking and behaving, identification of emotional triggers, and skill building regarding other behavioral options.

With strengths-based and resilience perspectives, we challenged the reader to conceptualize the adolescent's strengths and resiliencies in addition to his or her deficits. The provider's keen attention to the client's assets and interests related to the implemented interventions and continued use of listening and utilizing empathy skills are essential to better understanding of adolescents' emotional pain. Various intervention activities such as academic interests, use of leisure time, extracurricular activities, mentoring, religious group affiliation, family involvement, and learning social skills are part of the information gathering and treatment processes that can move more precisely toward making meaningful and lasting change in these adolescents' lives. Rather than solely focus on parental concerns, the provider balances his or her data collection activities with normalizing the adolescent's experiences.

We argued that as providers begin to understand the adolescent, the therapeutic relationship serves as the basis from which the treatment plan will be developed. For example, the adolescent confronted for bringing a knife to school has a story he or she will want to share with the school counselor; "I have the knife because I need it." However, understanding the cultural factors at play in the adolescent's life, the school counselor continues the counseling process by consulting his or her own subjective personal experience (if he or she grew up in the same neighborhood and had similar challenges as the adolescent), professional experience (with other similar knife carrying students), supervisory input (certainly for reporting purposes, ethical obligations but also for therapeutic processing), or advice from other professionals skilled with working with similar adolescents. The adolescent may want to convince the provider that such illegal behavior is justified.

Through one or all of these means of reflection, the provider may become aware of other concerns of the adolescent. First, the adolescent's walk to the bus stop in the morning requires him or her to walk in front of a neighborhood drug house and gang hangout; therefore, he is threatened or afraid of other adolescents. Second, the adolescent has instigated several quarrels with other students and now anticipates their retaliation, so he or she arms himself or herself for the inevitable fight awaiting him or her. Third, the adolescent has been diagnosed with oppositional defiant disorder and attention-deficit/hyperactivity disorder and has poor impulse control and coping strategies and believes that the only way to protect himself or herself is to carry a knife. The provider's accurate assessment of the underlying issues are not needed to continue the counseling relationship, but it allows her to put forth client-specific options that the adolescent may view as applicable to his or her specific life, rather than defend choices and validate their rationale. Though we as providers ethically look to intervene and prevent such acts of aggression and violence, we are also keenly aware that we, in our own power, are not able to make decisions for our clients. We can, however, provide them viable options beyond what they have identified. For example, we could provide the adolescent with CBT techniques that would assist in changing his or her thoughts about possibly becoming a victim or perpetrator. From a strength-based standpoint, we could provide the adolescent with additional options including walking down another street or leaving earlier.

Any reasonable person would ascertain that the knife seems a logical and rational solution based on this adolescent's real circumstances. However, we highlight that it is incumbent on the provider to continue the counseling journey with the adolescent in expanding his or her emotional repertoire and reactions to his or her environment. While the provider understands why the adolescent may carry a knife to school, the provider should never condone such dangerous behavior as carrying the knife.

Section III of this book took the foundational elements and theoretical components and applied them to clinical situations using evidence-based interventions. This section addressed specific concerns that often face providers when working with adolescents such as diagnosing and treatment planning to working with difficult populations including those with addictions and sexually maladaptive behaviors. Although not exhaustive, we offered a fair representation of some of the critical areas that are the most challenging in treatment with adolescents. In this section, we wanted to extend the work of others by first presenting these topics in sequence from the outset of a professional relationship. We provided information on the screening and assessment process. From diagnostic intakes to formally using psychological tools and instruments, we presented ways to collect, interpret, and summarize critical findings related to the treatment planning process. We argued that the use of behavioral and personality inventories are no longer the sole province of psychologists, but that professional counselors, social workers, marriage and family therapists, substance abuse counselors, and psychiatrists should utilize objective measures in the treatment planning process. In this section, we discussed information pertaining to how best to utilize and incorporate diagnostic criteria in arriving at a *DSM-5* diagnosis. Incorporating the Cultural Formulation Interview, Cross-Cutting Symptom Measures, and the World Health Organization Disability Assessment Schedule (Version 2.0), providers can take full advantage of what the *DSM-5* offers by way of case conceptualizing the needs of adolescents. We provided steps to ensure that providers base their diagnoses on symptom presentation while considering the cultural nuances of adolescents and their families. In this section, we discussed treatment planning issues as well. We reviewed elements of an effective treatment plan including problem statements, goals, objectives, and outcome markers. We also focused on ways to ensure proper documentation of progress notes, treatment plans, and termination summaries. We introduced various styles of documenting that are professional and adhere to ethical obligations. In this section, we also spent considerable time reviewing actual counseling interventions. From assessment to individual therapy, we presented information on the most commonly used counseling interventions. We reviewed case management, group counseling, crisis counseling, and family therapy interventions and techniques as ways to accomplish treatment goals.

Second, in this section, we shifted from structural concerns of counseling (assessment, diagnosing, and treatment planning) to managing difficult clients in various settings. We discussed how the provider might think about the issues of culture, trauma, delinquency, cognitive frames of reference, and engagement in relationship when reflecting on specific concerns and scenarios. We saw these chapters as opportunities to expose the reader to the thoughts of the broader field with respect to managing these areas. We also saw these chapters as opportunities to shed light for the reader on the types of presenting problems of adolescents and suggested interventions. These chapters presented critical questions for the providers to explore in light of their assumptions and information suggested by alternative assumptions. In this section, we reviewed the impact of divorce on adolescents and how through their adjustment experiences, they often try on different identities to manage their various life challenges such as parental divorce. We provided helpful hints for providers to effectively engage adolescents whose families have agreed to divorce and the ways in which families might decrease the negative outcomes of divorce. In managing the emotional pain from divorce, we provided

information on chemical and behavioral addiction. This section reviewed the commonly abused substances, motivation behind abusing substances, and engagement strategies to assist adolescents in escaping alternative ways to manage emotional pain. We reviewed evidence-based treatment interventions that support decreased use of substances and promote a lifestyle of recovery. We also discussed those clients who struggle with poor sexual boundaries and sexually maladaptive behaviors including molestation and rape. We provided information on the characteristics and typologies of adolescent sex offenders and the advanced training that providers need to effectively engage this population of adolescents. We also reviewed concerns that are seen in school and the role of the school counselor in addressing these concerns. Issues such as bullying, self-injurious behavior, and peer relationships were reviewed with helpful strategies to eliminate the negative symptoms of such behavior. Where appropriate, we provided case scenarios and exercises on how best to manage the clinical dynamics of the aforementioned specialized populations. We challenged the assumptions of providers by providing evidence-based interventions on how best to manage the needs of adolescents. We wanted this section of the book to focus on the adolescents' stories and the potency of their language to not be lost to scholarly conceptualizations.

Ongoing Dialogue Needed

An ongoing dialogue exists between students, educators, clinical supervisors, administrators, and researchers regarding the care of adolescents. Though it is common to recognize the developmental, social, and cultural needs of adolescents, it is as important to be equipped with the best strategies and interventions that have proved to be useful. Many of these adolescents come from cultural backgrounds, neighborhoods, and social interactions that further complicate their case dynamics. Though the media is illuminating in some aspects, many dynamics of adolescents are lost to the provider's interpretation and a silent, but strong, push back from those not familiar with the adolescents' developmental, societal, educational, and social challenges. For those of us moved by compassion and inclination to work with adolescents, the training we receive rarely prepares us adequately to interact with adolescents without imposing a linear and pedantic rationale in our approaches. Ultimately, we may be ill equipped to address the needs of adolescents, and such a reflection is the starting point of the dialogue—that is, "Are you equipped to work with adolescents?" "Do you understand the unique challenges of adolescents?" "Do you appreciate their differences from adults?" "What role does development disruptions play in the lives of adolescents?" "How are these different from the developmental disruptions of adults?"

This book's rigorous analysis of adolescents' case scenarios is rare and is designed to stimulate ongoing dialogue about the true needs of adolescents. While it may be difficult for these adolescents to share their presenting problems in a way that allows the provider to fully grasp their emotional pain, their aims to control, their frustrations, their reactions, and their schemes, it is the hope that this book has begun a journey in searching the depths of the pain of these adolescents.

Books utilizing similar perspectives by focusing solely on adolescents are difficult to find. There is a need for more qualitative works that illuminate the adolescents' stories in their own words. Works that present the *clients* as the central focus, rather than the clients' symptoms, are even more difficult to find. However, the dynamics of adolescents are critical to understanding their perspective, deciphering their social interactions, gaining insight into their way of thinking and behaving, as well as being key to appropriate planning for their services and goal setting.

PROFESSIONAL COMMITMENT TO ADOLESCENT CARE

By definition, providers endeavor to conform to the standards and skills espoused by specific disciplines and presenting issues of their clients. Providers adhere to the disciplines and ethics with the populations they serve. Providers come from different educational backgrounds that prepare them to work in various fields ranging from paraprofessionals to professional staff members. The educational diversity represented in our ranks is needed in our communities and should be utilized to best benefit those we serve. However, the socioeconomic diversity within our ranks often represents a contrast to those we serve in diverse America. The diversity of our clients and the various ways of surviving challenges are not only remarkable but also awe inspiring for those providers not accustomed to such creativity, determination, and stamina exhibited by many adolescents. Most of our educational and training programs do not prepare us for these vast shifts in worldviews, interaction styles, and strong nonverbal communication that these adolescents use. Often, providers facing the realities of adolescents need time to adjust to the ongoing and pervasive emotional and behavioral issues facing adolescents. A commitment from providers is needed in the provision of treatment for adolescents.

For a number of these adolescents in need of counseling, their behaviors land them in out-of-home placements and in systems of care. A large body of research identifies that those adolescents requiring out-of-home placements are overrepresented and underserved when they are detained from their families and with the system (Trupin, Turner, Stewart, & Wood, 2004). Additionally, they tend to stay in these systems longer and are labeled more harshly than their counterparts. Trupin and Richards (2003) and Stanton and Samenow (2004) assert that these adolescents are grossly misunderstood in their initial entry into these systems, through their assessment process, in their level of care assignments, and in their treatment delivery. Thus, it is critical that a more accurate understanding of adolescents and a commitment to their needs is embraced by providers. Toward this end, Grisso (2011) identified professional training as insufficient to accurately assess adolescents involved with various systems of care, especially juvenile justice and child welfare. Consequently, the provider's aim to make a true and lasting difference with this population is often stilted and limited to restrictive living environments. This can leave providers feeling inadequate when faced with the multidimensional challenges these adolescents present. We offer that compassion and theoretical frameworks are starting grounds of intervention, but these are not enough to meet the needs of these adolescents. Additionally, knowledge of the key components of ethnic minority, urban issues, and multicultural counseling topics falls short of these adolescents' needs. In fact, interventions are only effective when they are coupled with culturally competent methodologies used by providers with knowledge and understanding of the developmental, social, and cultural needs of adolescents. We hold that only through active listening to adolescents and the application of proven interventions can providers embark on a meaningful journey with these adolescents to address their behaviors.

CULTURAL COMPETENCY

In many colleges and universities across the nation, thousands of students are eager to learn how to reach these adolescents. They often cite characteristics such as compassion, desire to make a difference, and ease in building relationships with adolescents as reasons for their interest in working with adolescents. Certainly, these attributes are viable and beneficial in working with adolescents. However, it is also incumbent on providers to move beyond providing compassion and judgment and go beyond a cursory knowledge of understanding and compassion and develop their knowledge base in a focused way that considers the knowledge and experiences of many of these adolescents. Providers must know these culturally competent facts and translate them into real-time intervention for these adolescents. We can no longer marvel at the harsh realities of the neighborhoods and life experiences of some adolescents and believe that our surface knowledge of

culturally competent methodologies coupled with compassion will make a difference for these adolescents. These adolescents require a genuineness and congruence in their providers and seldom allow the opportunity for partnership until an outsider proves himself or herself.

Ultimately, our understanding must be more comprehensive and move beyond cognitive knowledge that articulates that people are the same. Groups have differences that they would like to maintain as integral to their identity. Ethnic and racial minority groups have different rates of direct eye contact. Ethnic and racial minority groups experience institutionalized racism and other forms of poverty and racism that cannot be ignored. Though these facts are critical to the work we do as providers, they should never be the end of our knowledge and practice. Extension of our knowledge and practice must include more thoughtful understanding and adjustments for idiosyncratic differences within the group. For example, some adolescents are not encouraged by their social network to engage in introspective self-analysis and do not view these types of activities as worthwhile. To expect adolescents to drop their way of handling the world and take on a different way of interacting requires providing them with rationales, direct correlations to their underlying goals, encouragement to redirect their efforts, and coaching that is sensitive to the fact their lives and development do not occur within a vacuum, nor are they static.

STEPS TO TAKE

There are several steps to be undertaken by providers working with adolescents. The first step is to allow the adolescent to share his or her complete presenting problem and associated issues without provider bias. With this step, we believe that providers are ready to hear, can suspend judgmental labeling, and can allow for critical thinking processes to continue beyond detrimental labels and schemata.

The next step is for providers to push their critical thinking processes and skills beyond the foundations laid in their formal trainings and education. This push must be an ongoing effort to rethink and challenge one's viewpoint, enlightened by the fact that adolescents are developing a trajectory that tends to lead to a life of emotional dysregulation. The provider must recognize when emotional dysregulation is happening. They must also maintain firm boundaries, not succumbing to the adolescent's demands and threats or even subtle social exchanges that can be later used against providers.

The authors charge providers to embrace the research and knowledge about these adolescents and make meaningful and impactful adjustments to approaching them. This work holds a meaningful step in giving these adolescents a chance to tell their stories in totality, unscripted, and unfettered by the professional's judgment. Such storytelling provides a window for the provider to exercise both humility and a critical eye into developing the case plan. We must recognize that the adolescents not only have survived their neighborhood and family ailments but are also navigating the world with the same rules they learned in their neighborhoods. These rules, once rechanneled, will serve as a strength to catapult the adolescents into infrastructures otherwise unknown. Immediate results for our interaction styles with clients, our conceptualization of what ails adolescents, and our plan of action are developed.

Throughout this book, providers have been encouraged to think in themes, apply evidence-based practices, and look for consistency across several sessions rather than to judge adolescents on single events occurring in their lives. Furthermore, to set the stage for a positive rapport, the provider's role, boundaries, and ethical obligations should be briefly presented after direct introductions.

CONCLUSION

The realms of treatment providers and researchers seem like oil and water in many different aspects. Provider stipulations identify practical steps to improve social awareness and change expectations. The clinical question is, "Did the adolescent make meaningful progress in treatment?" The thinking of providers is often linear and requires providers to present the best trail of evidentiary practice and solutions for his or her stance. While psychology and sociology hold that there are antecedents to behaviors, no one person is an island but influences and is influenced by the world around him or her and, thus, must be analyzed through theories and hunches as to how to manage delinquent behaviors. The research question asks the following: Is the treatment intervention effective? The thinking of researchers is likewise linear and requires researchers to rely on proven assessment and treatment interventions, with appropriate research methods including statistical analyses.

If the answer to the clinical question is affirmative, a provider is charged to deliver a systematic treatment approach to ameliorate negative psychological symptoms of adolescents. The need for a sequential treatment program is apparent to responsibly apply all interventions logically and sequentially. Adherence to the fidelity of treatment programs is equally important in the provision of care. Treatment providers readily identify this type of adherence, structure, and accountability as essential components for treatment and reductions in negative symptoms. Likewise, the adolescent also recognize the need for structure within his or her home and when the provider echoes such structure, the adolescent may be afforded maximal opportunities to succeed in counseling. The issue is that while many of these adolescents are embarking on independence, they still need to abide by the rules within their families and or within the legal guardianship structure. Regardless of their past experiences that have informed their values, many adolescents may believe that the rules of their families do not apply to them. Many of them struggle with accepting responsibility for their reckless thoughts and behaviors. However, the provider must build bridges between the adolescent and his or her parent to repair damaged relationships.

Our extension of the conversation regarding counseling adolescents competently is our effort to join with other researchers in the quest to inform providers in the ways of engaging adolescents and their family members of the world around them. Our traditional training has prepared us to understand fundamentals of some human behavior and also provides a great foundation from which to launch into the special thinking of adolescents. Our partnership is based on their theoretical foundations and keen application to change delinquent thinking into opportunities for adolescents in conflict to learn morality.

REFERENCES

Grisso, T. (2011). *Forensic evaluation of juveniles*. Sarasota, FL: Publisher Resource Exchange.

Miller, W. R., & Rollnick, S. (2002). *Motivational interviewing: Preparing people for change*. New York: NY: Guilford Press.

Rogers, C. (1959). A theory of therapy, personality, and interpersonal relationships as developed in the client-centered framework. In S. Koch (Ed.), *Psychology: The study of a science: Vol. 3. Formulation of the person and the social contexts* (pp. 184–256). New York, NY: McGraw-Hill.

Stanton, E., & Samenow, S. E. (2004). *Inside the criminal mind*. San Francisco, CA: Crown Point Press.

Trupin, E., & Richards, H. (2003). Seattle's mental health courts: Early indicators of effectiveness. *International Journal of Law and Psychiatry, 26*(1), 33–53.

Trupin, E., Turner, A., Stewart, D., & Wood, P. (2004). Transition planting and recidivism among mentally ill juvenile offenders. *Behavioral Sciences and the Law, 22*, 599–610.

INDEX

ABOUT THE AUTHORS

Lee A. Underwood, PsyD, is a licensed clinical psychologist in several states, a certified sex offender treatment provider, and is affiliated with Regent University School of Psychology and Counseling and Youth Development Institute (YDI). He has 30 years of experience counseling adolescents and has published over 50 professional articles in refereed journals, 20 scholarly activities including monographs, technical reports and training manuals and has authored a supplemental text book on *Adolescents in Conflict*. His written work has focused on juvenile sex offending, adolescent mental health and substance use, trauma needs of females, forensic and cultural needs of persons involved in the juvenile justice and mental health systems, as means of distributing the findings of his research. Dr. Underwood is a renowned specialist in the area of juvenile sex offender formation. As Director of the Center for Addictions and Offender Research operated by Regent University, he and his research team are responsible for some of the cutting edge research taking place. Dr. Underwood has been recognized by the Office of Juvenile Justice and Delinquency Prevention (OJJDP), American Institutes for Research (AIR) and the Substance Abuse & Mental Health Services Administration (SAMSHA) as one of the leading program innovators for juvenile justice and community treatment programs.

He consults with the Federal Department of Justice's civil rights division regarding fair and equitable treatment for adolescents in systems of care. Dr. Underwood has provided support to the forensic psychology program at Argosy University, served as an affiliate faculty for Louisiana State University Health Science Center and visiting lecturer with Rutgers University Criminal Justice program. Dr. Underwood serves on the editorial board of The *Juvenile Mental Health Report* and *The International Journal of Behavioral Consultation and Therapy*. His research interests are geared toward questions of clinical significance for professionals in Counseling. Out of these interests, he writes this book.

Frances L. L. Dailey, PhD, is affiliated with Regent University School of Psychology and Counseling and Argosy University College of Counseling, Psychology and Social Sciences. Dr. Dailey has 15 years' experience counseling families, couples, and individuals with a wide spectrum of mental health, substance use, relationship, and career challenges. She is a consultant and Research Director to a national mental health and juvenile justice consulting firm. She has authored a supplemental text book on Adolescents in Conflict. Her written work has focused on juvenile sex offending, adolescent and mental health, trauma related issues, forensic and cultural needs of persons involved with the juvenile justice and mental health systems, as means of distributing findings of her research. The American

Counseling Association identified her as an "Emerging Leader" within the Counseling field. Dr. Dailey's research and scholarly activities include multiple refereed journal articles. Dr. Dailey was recognized by Routledge Behavioral Sciences journals for the published article titled "Mental Health Treatment in Juvenile Justice Secure Care Facilities: Practice and Policy Recommendations", published in the Journal of Forensic Psychology Practice. This was featured among the most downloaded articles published in Routledge Behavioral Sciences journals in 2014.